The Red Paper
On Scotland

Published by EUSPB

Published by EUSPB, 1 Buccleuch Place, Edinburgh EH8 9LW.
Printed by the Russell Press, 45 Gamble Street, Nottingham.

First published 1975.
All original articles copyright ©

Design and Layout by Keith Duncan and Jennifer Page.
Typeset in Times Roman by EUSPB

ERRATA
p.22 C.M. Grieve's **Albyn or Scotland and the Future** was published in **1927**.

Front cover photograph: 1971 UCS demonstration
Back cover photograph: 1913 Leith dockers' strike.
Both courtesy of Scotsman Publications Ltd.

Thanks especially to: Steve Kendrick, and Doreen Frasca, Allan Drummond, Bob Cuddihy,
Katriana Hazell, Bev Ninnes, Liz Wright, Andrew Brown, John Brown, John Forsyth and
Christine Rankine.

Contents

INTRODUCTION: THE SOCIALIST CHALLENGE   7
Gordon Brown

OLD NATIONALISM AND NEW NATIONALISM   22
Tom Nairn

DEVOLUTION AND DEMOCRACY   58
David Gow

WHAT SORT OF OVERGOVERNMENT?   69
Ronald Young

COMMUNITY DEMOCRACY   85
Colin Kirkwood

INDUSTRIAL DEMOCRACY AND WORKERS CONTROL   98
Alex Ferry

SOCIALISTS AND THE SNP   108
Ray Burnett

THE LEFT, THE SNP AND OIL   125
Bob Tait

SCOTLAND: UP AGAINST IT   134
John McGrath

CAPITALISM AND THE SCOTTISH NATION   141
John Foster

EXTERNAL CONTROL AND REGIONAL POLICY   153
John Firn

FINANCE CAPITAL AND THE SCOTTISH UPPER CLASS   170
John Scott and Michael Hughes

THE POLITICAL ECONOMY OF NORTH SEA OIL   187
Peter Smith

REGIONAL POLICY AND THE SCOTTISH ASSEMBLY   214
Bill Niven

THE SCOTTISH DEVELOPMENT AGENCY   223
Frank Stephen

GLASGOW: AREA OF NEED   232
Vincent Cable

A SOCIALIST STRATEGY FOR THE HIGHLANDS   247
Ian Carter

LAND OWNERSHIP AND LAND NATIONALISATION   254
Jim Sillars

HIGHLAND LANDLORDISM   262
John McEwen

THE SOCIAL IMPACT OF OIL   270
David Taylor

THE RISE OF SCOTTISH SOCIALISM   282
James Young

THE RADICAL LITERARY TRADITION   289
David Craig

SCOTLAND: LESSONS FROM IRELAND   304
Owen Dudley Edwards

POVERTY IN SCOTLAND   317
Ian Levitt

SCOTLAND'S HOUSING   334
Robin Cook

SOCIAL WORK: NEW DEPARTMENTS AND OLD PROBLEMS   344
Richard Bryant

PUBLIC HEALTH IN SCOTLAND   352
Donald Cameron

SCOTTISH EDUCATION: A SOCIALIST PLAN   357
Nigel Grant

Contributors

TOM NAIRN is author of 'Left Against Europe?' and of a forthcoming study, 'The Modern Janus: Nationalism and Uneven Development'. He is currently working with the Transnational Institute in Amsterdam.

DAVID GOW is a journalist, formerly with 'The Scotsman' and now with London Weekend Television's 'Weekend World.'

RON YOUNG is Chairman of the Strathclyde Region's General Purposes Committee, head of the Local Government Research Unit at Paisley College, and has published a number of papers on local government.

COLIN KIRKWOOD is editor of 'The Scottish Tenant' and has been involved in community action in Glasgow, particularly in his home area of Castlemilk.

ALEX FERRY is Glasgow District Secretary of the Amalgamated Union of Engineering Workers.

RAY BURNETT is editor of the new Scottish Political Quarterly, 'Calgacus', and was until recently a schoolteacher in Dornie.

BOB TAIT was editor of 'Scottish International' from 1969 to 1973. He is now a lecturer in Aberdeen.

JOHN McGRATH is a playwright and director of the 7:84 Theatre Company. His plays include 'The Cheviot, the Stag and the Black Black Oil', 'The Games A Bogey' and 'Boom'.

JOHN FOSTER is lecturer in politics at Strathclyde University, and author of 'The Class Struggle and the Industrial Revolution.'

JOHN FIRN is lecturer in the Institute of Economic and Social Research, Glasgow University. His book on external control and the Scottish economy is to be published this year.

JOHN SCOTT and MIKE HUGHES are lecturers in sociology at Strathclyde University, and are engaged on a comprehensive study of the Scottish Upper Class.

PETER SMITH is lecturer in economics at Glasgow College of Technology and is working on a history of the Scottish Labour Movement since 1945.

BILL NIVEN is a divisional organiser for the Amalgamated Union of Engineering Workers (T.A.S.S. Section) and a member of the General Council of the Scottish Trades Union Congress.

FRANK STEPHEN is lecturer in economics at Strathclyde University and formerly head of research for the Scottish Trades Union Congress. He has written widely on the Scottish and British economy.

VINCENT CABLE was until last year lecturer in Political Economy at Glasgow University and a city councillor. He is now working in the Foreign Office.

IAN CARTER is lecturer in sociology at Aberdeen University and has recently completed a comprehensive study of Highland underdevelopment. He is now engaged on a study of farm workers in the North East.

JIM SILLARS is Labour Member of Parliament for South Ayrshire and has written widely on land and other Scottish social and economic problems.

JOHN McEWEN is a retired forestry consultant living in Blairgowrie, who has been engaged for several years on a study of Highland land ownership.

DAVID TAYLOR is a member of the Architectural Association's On-shore Study and Advisory Group on oil and edited a recent issue of the 'Architect's Journal' on the impact of oil.

JAMES YOUNG is lecturer in history at Stirling University. He has completed a study of the decline of Liberalism in Scotland and is now studying Scottish working class culture.

DAVID CRAIG is lecturer in literature at the University of Lancaster and is author of 'Scottish Literature and the Scottish People' and a number of other books and articles.

OWEN DUDLEY EDWARDS is lecturer in history in the University of Edinburgh, co-author of 'Celtic Nationalism', and author of a number of books and articles on Irish, American and British politics.

IAN LEVITT is a researcher in sociology at the University of Edinburgh and is presently completing his thesis on the Scottish Poor Law.

ROBIN COOK is Member of Parliament for Edinburgh Central and was until 1974 Chairman of the Edinburgh Corporation Housing Committee and East of Scotland tutor/organiser for the Workers Educational Association.

RICHARD BRYANT is a community worker on the Gorbals Project in Glasgow.

Dr. DONALD CAMERON is senior lecturer in community medicine at Edinburgh University.

NIGEL GRANT is author of 'A Mythology of British Education' and 'Soviet Education' and is reader in the Department of Educational Studies at Edinburgh University.

GORDON BROWN is Rector of Edinburgh University.

Introduction: The Socialist Challenge

Gordon Brown

The irresistible march of recent events places Scotland today at a turning point—not of our own choosing but where a choice must sooner or later be made. A resurgent nationalism which forces on to the agenda the most significant constitutional decisions since the Act of Union is one aspect of what even the 'Financial Times' has described as "a revolt of rising expectations." But the proliferation of industrial unrest and the less publicised mushrooming of community action also bears witness to the sheer enormity of the gap now growing between people's conditions of living and their legitimate aspirations.

Yet the great debate on Scotland's future ushered in by the Kilbrandon report and precipitated by North Sea oil and Britain's economic crisis has hardly been a debate at all. Dominated by electoral calculations, nationalist and anti-nationalist passions and crude bribery, it has engendered a barren, myopic. almost suffocating consensus which has tended to ignore Scotland's real problems—our unstable economy and unacceptable level of unemployment, chronic inequalities of wealth and power and inadequate social services. And while Kilbrandon identified "a diffuse feeling of dissatisfaction... a feeling of powerlessness at the we/they relationship", the basic questions which face the Scotland of the nineteen-eighties remain unasked as well as unanswered: who shall exercise power and control the lives of our people? How can we harness our material resources and social energies to meet the needs of five million people and more? What social structure can guarantee to people the maximum control and self management over the decisions which affect their lives, allowing the planned co-ordination of the use and distribution of resources, in a co-operative community of equals?

Scotland's social condition and political predicament cries out for a new commitment to socialist ideals, policies and action emerging from a far reaching analysis of economy and society; a bringing together of the many positive insights, responses, and analyses to break through the deliberate separation of issues and the consequent fragmentation of people's consciousness; and a searching for a new social vision for Scotland which begins from people's potentials, is sensitive to cultural needs, and is humane, democratic and revolutionary. What this Red Paper(1)—a contribution of many socialist views to such a debate—seeks to do is to transcend that false and sterile antithesis which has been manufactured between the nationalism of the SNP and the anti-nationalism of the Unionist parties, by concentrating on the fundamental realities of inequality and irresponsible social control, of private power and an inadequate democracy. For when the question of freedom for Scotland is raised, we must ask: freedom for whom? From what? For what?

Two themes are integral and complementary in the essays which follow. The first is that the social and economic problems confronting Scotland arise not from national suppression nor from London mismanagement (although we have had our share of both) but from the uneven and uncontrolled development of capitalism and the failure of successive governments to challenge and transform it. Thus we cannot hope to resolve such problems merely by recovering a lost independence or through inserting another tier of government: what is required is planned control of our economy and a transformation of democracy at all levels. The second theme is more basic than that. We suggest that the real resources of Scotland are not the reserves of oil beneath the sea (nor the ingenuity of native entrepreneurs) but the collective energies and potential of our people whose abilities and capacities have been stultified by a social system which has for centuries sacrificed social aspirations to private ambitions. It is argued that what appear to be contradictory features of Scottish life today—militancy and apathy, cynicism and a thirst for change—can best be understood as working people's frustration with and refusal to accept powerlessness and lack of control over blind social forces which determine their lives. It is a disenchantment which underlines an untapped potential for co-operative action upon which we must build.

The vision of the early socialists was of a society which had abolished for ever the dichotomy—the split personality caused by people's unequal control over their social development—between man's personal and collective existence, by substituting communal co-operation for the divisive forces of competition. Today the logic of present economic development, in inflation and stagnation, and at the same time the demand for the fullest use of material resources, makes it increasingly impossible to manage the economy both for private profit and the needs of society as a whole. Yet the long standing paradox of Scottish politics has been the surging forward of working class industrial and political pressure (and in particular the loyal support given to Labour) and its containment through the accumulative failures of successive Labour Governments. More than fifty years ago socialism was a qualitative concept, an urgently felt moral imperative, about social control (and not merely state control or more or less equality). Today for many it means little more than a scheme for compensating the least fortunate in an unequal society. We suggest that the rise of modern Scottish nationalism is less an assertion of Scotland's permanence as a nation than a response to Scotland's uneven development—in particular to the gap between people's experiences as part of an increasingly demoralised Great Britain and their (oil-fired) expectations at a Scottish level. Thus, the discontent is a measure of the failure of both Scottish and British socialists to advance far and fast enough in shifting the balance of wealth and power to working people and in raising people's awareness—especially outside the central belt of Scotland in areas where inequalities are greater—about the co-operative possibilities for modern society.

Clearly it is easy to overestimate the potential for radical social change in Scotland today—but it is dangerous to underestimate the demand for it. For the first time since the Union, oil and the political response to it has swung the balance of influence within Great Britain in favour of Scotland, giving the Scottish Labour Movement in particular a new bargaining power. Labour has two choices: to deflect the present discontent, resisting the pressure for change until it becomes inevitable, at the risk of the success of an SNP which presumes the familiar priorities of wealth and power set over people, or to harness the wide ranging dissatisfaction in a socialist strategy which not only forces the pace of the advance towards socialism in Britain as a whole but seeks to revitalise the grass roots of Scottish society. This means drawing new links between political action and the various positive movements for control in community and industrial life, to forge a new kind of social and economic democracy. Such a strategy implies that Scottish socialists can not support a strategy for independence which postpones the question of meeting urgent social and economic needs until the day after independence—but nor can they give

8

unconditional support to maintaining the integrity of the United Kingdom—and all that that entails-without any guarantee of radical social change; the question is not one of structures nor of territorial influence, but of democracy—how working people in Scotland can increase the control they have over the decisions which shape their lives and the wealth they alone produce—and in doing so aid the struggle for a shift of power to working people elsewhere.

Social Needs

Any study of Scotland today must start from where people are, the realities of day-to-day living, extremes of wealth and poverty, unequal opportunities at work, in housing, health, education and community living generally. The gross inequalities which disfigure Scottish social life (and British society as a whole) have been obscured by a debate which merely poses the choice between separatism and unionism. For there are rich Scots, very rich Scots—and very poor Scots. The Sample Census of 1966 confirms that Scotland has a small owning and managing elite, a small but increasingly important professional and supervisory class, and a very large working class embracing over 80 per cent of Scottish people, with the balance shifting from skilled manual to service workers (2). In drawing attention to the fact that average holdings of equities were twice as high in Scotland than England and that Scotland had 11 per cent of British people with assets above £40,000, "The Economist" recently suggested that extremes of wealth were more pronounced in Scotland than in Britain as a whole (and by implication in Western Europe and America)(3). In 1971-72 there were 664 estates above £50,000 and 182 above £100,000 (with an average of two wills above £1m for each of the previous ten years)(4). In this collection, Ian Levitt draws attention to the marked inequalities in income which do not arise from differing skills, contributions to community life or needs. The top two percent earn seven per cent of total income (more than half of that coming from unearned income in investments and profits), the top five per cent earn fifteen per cent of income and the top twelve per cent of Scottish people earn as much as the bottom fifty per cent. Another dimension of inequality is explored (in this collection) by John McEwen who provides new and important evidence of the concentration of land ownership in the Highlands and Islands where 340 individuals (or companies) own sixty-four per cent (over six million acres) of the land. Four individuals own one-sixteenth, ten own one eighth, and forty own one-third and one hundred and fifty own one-half of the Highlands.

There are three distinguishing marks of the new structure of inequality in Scotland—the failure of taxation to erode the power of private property (those earning below £2000 in 1971 paid half income tax)(5), the dramatic growth of private occupational and pensions schemes to create a new structure of privilege within our social security system, and the sheer extent of poverty itself. Levitt, below, estimates that 23 per cent of Scottish people are living at or just above the poverty line set by the Supplementary Benefits Commission—one and a quarter million people concentrated in four large groups, old people, low paid workers, and their families, the unemployed and single parent families. Supplementary benefits payments have trebled since 1947 and doubled over the last decade. In showing how the poverty trap effects localities as it does individuals, Vincent Cable draws attention to the extent of multiple deprivation in areas of Glasgow. While Clydeside is the heart of the problem, the recent Bowhouse study which showed 90 per cent of families in poverty, 40 per cent of active males unemployed, and 90 per cent of child school-leavers without 'O' or 'H' levels in one area of Clackmannanshire, emphasises that community deprivation is nation-wide(6). Richard Bryant demonstrates that it would take an extra expenditure of more than 41p per person yearly to raise Scottish social services merely to the average provision of England and Wales, but the root of the problem, which cannot be solved by better or more casework, or even community action linked to corporate planning, is, he suggests, "the structural nature of poverty within an unequal society which rewards its members according to the principles of a market economy and not on the basis of human need." For, the inequalities which distort Scottish life are generated from the work-place outwards: low pay, placing at least 100,000 male workers and their families on the poverty line, insufficient provision for retirement and for families deprived of their breadwinner, and the threat and actuality of redundancy. With Scotland's unemployment figures remaining up to three times as high as the South East of England even in periods of boom, about one third of our unemployed have become long term

9

out-of-work and only 36 per cent of all unemployed receive insurance benefits.

Our other contributors show that although public expenditure in Scotland is 17 per cent higher per person than in Britain as a whole(7), existing social service provision tends to mirror rather than redress existing inequalities. While there have been nationalist appeals to Scotland's inherent capacity for democracy and equality, and our passion for social justice, it cannot be said that the controls exercised in Scotland over local authorities and social institutions—education, law and religion—have led to a searching for different concepts of welfare or standards of need. Today's poor remain stigmatised by poverty not simply because social service provision is inadequate but because there is no dominant concept of reciprocity in our social services. The failure of the Dundee Educational Priority experiment is symptomatic of how little enthusiasm there has been from local administrators and politicians for projects providing greater resources to areas of need.(8) Robin Cook points to the inadequacies of existing housing policies. One in ten houses in Scotland are substandard, "most of them if not all", concluded the Scottish Development Department, "could have been closed as unfit fifty years ago"—and despite a massive inflow of public funds into the private sector (over 40 per cent of Scottish homes are now owner occupied compared with 25 per cent in 1964), only 15 per cent of working class families are owner-occupiers (most of them living in houses built before 1919)Fewer are now able to buy their own home.(9) Donald Cameron draws attention to the prevalence of higher rates of infant mortality in Scotland—the most sensitive index of public health—with mortality among infants, as it was twenty years ago, twice as high among social classes 4 and 5 as it is among classes 1 and 2. While Richard Bryant and Colin Kirkwood draw attention to the paltry provision of social service and community facilities, Nigel Grant emphasises that the substantially greater resources devoted to education—ten times those allocated to social work—have not been the force for social equality presumed in our traditional assumptions about Scottish education or envisaged in the British reforms of the sixties. Only one in twelve of 3-5 year olds enjoy nursery provision (half the rate for Britain as a whole), 55 per cent of children leave school without 'O' or 'H' levels, 22 per cent of school leavers enjoy the day or block release rights legislated in 1944; and the proportion of the sons and daughters of working class parents among students in Scottish universities—again a most sensitive index of inequality—has been declining rather than increasing, probably to a level below that of the nineteen twenties(10). Those who argue that Scotland's democratic traditions in education can be a powerful lever for redressing inequality and regenerating Scottish society are left with the sole alternative of supporting policies for mobilising social and economic as well as educational resources in an overall strategy for ending inequality.

Community Democracy

Scotland desperately needs a widely articulated and sufficiently popular concept of welfare and need grounded in equality and reciprocity in framing social policies and social priorities. Bryant, Cameron, Grant, Cook and Levitt all point to what is urgently required merely to meet people's elemental needs—a massive expansion in housing and community amenities, a regeneration of the public sector, an improvement of public health facilities especially in the community and industrial health fields, greater concentration of educational resources among those with the least opportunities, and a phasing out of means tested benefits by adequate provision by right for the old, the single parent family, the unemployed, the disabled, and the low paid. But from community action groups—tenants associations, organisations of the unemployed, the old, the homeless, and the sick, movements to fight oil-related developments, anti-social planning decisions and so on—to the activities of specialised pressure groups and professional social workers, teachers and health workers themselves, the demand is increasingly that society be organised in a manner to cater for people's needs, that community goals be set to meet people's requirements as they express them. If the prospects for the least fortunate are to be as great as they can be, then they must have the final say—and that requires a massive and irreversible shift of power to working people, a framework of free universal welfare services controlled by the people who use them. This potential for community action in harnessing local planning to community initiatives is emphasised by Ronald Young in his study of the inadequacies of local government. But he also shows that the challenge to the Scottish Labour Movement is to stimulate and

10

co-ordinate movements towards linking what are at present sectional movements so that they involve all the poor, all the badly housed and all the deprived, and towards making more explicit social priorities and social needs from the community outwards. A first step could be compiling on a nation-wide basis an inventory of social needs, "a social audit"(11) prepared by community groups themselves. But socialism will have to be won also at the point of production—the production of needs, ideas and particularly of goods and services. And that demands ending the power of a minority through ownership and control to direct the energies of all other members of our society.

Economic Prospects

Three facts stand out from a study of the present Scottish economy: the failure to create much needed jobs and so to eliminate the disparities between Scottish and UK rates of unemployment; the inability to develop a new economic base for sustained economic growth; and the increased level of external control over the Scottish economy. That over a quarter of a million new jobs are still required over the next decade is a measure of the failure of existing economic strategies. Today the clear industrial divide is between the giants of finance and industry on an international scale (including British multinationals, second only to the Americans) and the small firms on the national market. In presenting new and important evidence, John Firn shows the extent to which the main productive sector of the Scottish economy, manufacturing industry, employing one third of Scottish workers, is both externally and monopolistically controlled.

Fifty nine per cent of manufacturing workers are employed by companies based outside Scotland and the larger the enterprise and the faster growing it is, the more likely is external control. Moreover, one hundred and ten enterprises account for nearly half of manufacturing employment, three quarters of firms with more than 5,000 employees being externally controlled and the top twenty British multinationals alone employing one in twelve of manufacturing workers in Scotland. Twice as much per capita is invested in Scotland by American capital than in Britain as a whole, Scotland being the largest area per head of population for American intervention after Canada. It is, Firn concludes, "a situation which would make it impossible for an independent Scotland to run an independent economic policy." Scotland has in fact three times as much non Scottish capital invested in her industry than even the mild Steuer report considered commensurate to maintaining some possibility of local economic control, finance capital on an international scale now playing the dominant role in integrating the international economy.(12) In drawing attention to how far Scottish finance capital is tied in a dependent way to the international capital market, John Scott and Michael Hughes, however, point to the allocative power of a small highly interconnected elite of sixty whose multiple industrial and financial directorships (and considerable political influence especially through the Scottish Council for Development of Industry) give them substantial control over economic decision-making in Scotland but whose freedom of action is constrained by the requirements of international capital as a whole. Thus, most of Scottish finance capital is invested outside Scotland, one-third of it in America. Scott and Hughes conclude that "since the purely Scottish elements of the economy are dominated by internationalised capital which recognises no mere political or territorial lines drawn on the map, the success of a socialist strategy for Scotland depends upon its being able to counter the economic power of the upper class in Scotland and its links with international capital."

John Foster traces the historical development of the dependency of the economy—and the far-reaching implications of the economic decline of the last fifty years. Today Scotland has neither the highly industrialised structure of Europe's industrialised regions nor the same concentration of services as the metropolitan areas. Agriculture has been run down to the extent that 42,000 agricultural workers are on the 95 per cent of the land which is non-industrial. Employment in the primary—agricultural and mining—sector was halved in the sixties and the manufacturing sector decreased by 6 per cent with losses most severe in textiles, shipbuilding, chemicals and metal manufacture. The assumption of the sixties was that a drastic alteration in the structure of our economy was required to fit in with market demands, through attracting highly capitalised technologically-based industries to replace apparently declining industries, but

11

today, as Bill Niven writes, drawing attention to the spread of recent closures, "the problem of redundancy covers the whole spectrum of the economy, including the so-called growth sectors." Neither Ravenscraig, electronics, the motor industry, nor Hunterston have provided the basis for a new Scottish economic revival. Indeed, it is ironic that the major growth points of the sixties were the relatively small manufacturing or service industries—food and drink, cars, clothing, insurance, banking and finance, tourism and local authority administration. Neither will oil provide a structural shift for Scottish economic progress, unless government policies are radically altered. Peter Smith, below, draws attention to the close correlation between expected income from selling oil—£5850m. p.a. by 1980—and Britain's rapidly escalating overseas debts and the projected Balance of Payments deficits—and he emphasises the consequent failure of government to stimulate British oil-related industries, citing the lost opportunities for British Steel and for the design, manufacture and installation of oil equipment generally—and the inadequacy of existing oil spin-off industries, particularly in petrochemicals. The result is a comparative dearth of available jobs, with only 30,000 workers—equivalent only to the average yearly loss in primary and manufacturing industries—likely to be directly employed in oil-related industries at the peak of expansion and only 250 more jobs projected for Clydeside. There will be little appreciable improvement in our standard of living(13) and indeed the pull of oil investment, requiring more capital yearly than all other manufacturing industry combined, has its own dangers—a shift of investment from other less profitable manufacturing to oil production. At the same time through their recent strike of capital the massive oil multinationals are, as one American finance journal put it recently, "standing in the forefront of the fight against socialism in Britain." In 1974 the labour government decided not to nationalise oil: in 1975 they offered the oil companies tax concessions worth up to £1000m a year by the 1980s.

The trend of developments in Scotland is fairly clear. In suggesting that a dual economy between east and west Scotland was emerging, the 'Economist' recently contended that Scottish industry must follow where growth beckons, while the West is forced to alter its distribution of industry. This would involve "a planned movement of labour away from the West"(14) A modified view of this picture was drawn by the SCDI in their report "A Future for Scotland"(15), proposing that the main axis of Scotland's development should be twisted from the old east-west Edinburgh-Glasgow line of their Oceanspan proposals to a new axis running from the north east, from Aberdeen to Edinburgh, to the south west, between Glasgow and Ayr. But the net effect of such policies, even if there were to be a 2 per cent unemployment rate, is that one quarter of a million new jobs will have to be found by the mid eighties, in addition to jobs to replace the probable loss of another 100,000 by 1980. Existing manufacturing industry would continue to decline, while the service sector would increase by 100,000 jobs (and by ¼m. jobs by the year 2000). But apart from tourism and possible administrative decentralisation, the study emphasises that "most growth in services cannot be seen as a generator of growth but as the result of growth generated in the basic manufacturing industries."(16) What appears therefore to be likely is, as John Firn has shown for the sixties, a continued expansion of female and semi-skilled labour, to the detriment of existing skilled trades, and the creation of opportunities in industries and services whose growth prospects are dependent on the success of mainly the multinationals in stimulating the Scottish economy as a whole. The service sector already has a concentration of low paid jobs, with 20 per cent of male local government workers, 40 per cent of retail trade workers and over 20 per cent of Government clerical workers paid at the supplementary benefits level. One group of economists has put it this way, that "we should recognise that a solution to Scotland's economic difficulties will require significant geographical shifts in employment and production... swimming with the tide is a lot easier than swimming against it."(17)

Government policy since Toothill has rested on stimulating the growth of new, mainly science based, industries through incentives and negative controls and on increased productivity in new and old. But both Frank Stephen and Bill Niven show that regional policy has in no way regenerated the Scottish economy. The performance of Scotland's economy has been best when the British economy as a whole has boomed. Only one third of the jobs required yearly in the sixties were actually created, at considerable public expense, in subsidies to private firms; development areas with labour surpluses have tended to attract capital intensive industry while labour intensive industry has moved to areas of labour shortage; three-quarters of the employment created has come from the establishment of new factories owned and operated from other regions or countries(18); and while Scottish exports have outpaced the growth of British exports as a whole, expansion would appear to have been concentrated in areas of external control—one factor contributing with higher public expenditure to what has been calculated as a higher Scottish balance of payments deficit per head than in Britain.(19) Productivity agreements have themselves led to little expansion in jobs, one trade union leader recently telling a conference of industrialists that he "did not know of any factory in Scotland where as a result of a productivity agreement a number of jobs were created."(20) While public expenditure is nearly 60 per cent of the Scottish Gross domestic product, and while public investment has run at up to £750m yearly, the effectiveness of government intervention has been limited by their desire to maintain the existing market economy. Subsidies to private industry have formed 16 per cent of UK subsidies as a whole, while subsidies to public companies have formed 11 per cent of UK expenditure in that direction. There has been little use of state purchasing policy as an instrument of regional economic policy and little publicly sponsored and publicly controlled industry developed in Scotland, especially in the manufacturing sector,—despite the fact that a number of areas—the chemical industry, man-made fibres, electrical goods, pharmaceutical and plastic goods, aircraft, the industrial plant and mechanical handling sectors of engineering—have great potential for development in Scotland if publicly directed. The Scottish Development Agency which was announced in January is "to have the responsibility and resources to play a strong entrepreneurial role in identifying and promoting industrial modernisation, growth and development", but Stephen shows how much further the government should have gone in its proposals, particularly through a co-ordination of the presently anarchic allocation of public investment in Scotland(21) and the framing of an overall Scottish structure plan, in consultation with the trade unions, and with sensitivity towards the difficulties of Clydeside. Like the National Enterprise Board, the projected resources for the agency (£200m) will be insufficient.

Thus with American and British multinationals increasingly dominant in Scotland, and with the aims of public policy being to respond rather than lead, the Scottish economy is perhaps more subject to the influence of multinationals than any other similar industrial country. Consequently the economy is not only as Niven shows an unstable one, one of the first to suffer and the last to recover in times of depression but also dependently subordinate to the international market, with an increasingly distorted and artificial division of labour, compounded by the massive export of capital. Firn highlights one aspect of this—the shortage of research and development work—but even "The Business Scotland" was moved to write, recently,

> "Scotland in calling for jobs at any price for the past ten years has been engaged in turning its economy into one akin to that of a colony, i.e. one with a high level of external control, absentee-decisionmakers and subsidiary technology."(22)

Explanations tied to a vicious circle of low productivity, bad labour relations, low investment and poor entrepreneurship abound yet it is precisely the familiar tried formulas of wider incentives, tax reliefs, assured labour markets, growth areas and native entrepreneurs which are proposed. Thus public intervention will only be as effective as the efficiency of the private sector permits. The Scottish Council's policies for administrative decentralization and their research Institute's advocacy of devolved economic management (and reduced taxation) as a means of stimulating indigenous private industry(23) ignore the extent to which regional policy sprang from the failure of existing Scottish industry to compete and, as long as Scottish financiers maintain their dependent relationship to international capital, these policies may in the event not only increase the Scottish economy's powerlessness over world market trends but increase the relative underdevelopment of our economy. In a Scottish supplement the "Investors Chronicle" put it another way:

> "If Scotland is able to achieve some degree of executive control over its own development, then what the Scottish Nationalists now call the "exploited province" could become the last frontier for the private developer."(24)

For neither the promotion of smaller scale private industry, not indeed the creation of a tax haven bears much relation to Scotland's own regional economic needs. Firstly, as Dr Stuart Holland has emphasised elsewhere, such policies might require massive, up to 75 per cent, subsidies in labour costs to remove the differential between Scottish and third world labour costs, or alternatively would require lower wages.(25) Secondly, these would lead to concentrating industrial expansion in growth areas, to the particular detriment of Clydeside. Scotland's economic difficulties are themselves **regional**. As the STUC have realistically pointed out, the loss of steel will by itself leave West Central Scotland, whose problems are as severe as any region of Europe, "emasculated beyond all recognition."(26) In his study of Glasgow, Cable shows that strategies must go further than the West Central Plan's proposed remit for a Strathclyde Economic Development Corporation, and involve publicly controlled industry. For the experience of the sixties shows that the market can no longer be seen as the efficient allocator of resources and indeed that the productive forces within our economy have outstripped the capacity of the market.

A Planned Economy

Niven argues that the public sector which employs 30 per cent of Scottish workers can be expanded in a manner which would dominate rather than respond to market requirements. Clearly the logic of present economic developments point in this direction. It is not just the demand of working people for a fuller share of the social product of their labour (and their collective power to resist the old formulas of unemployment and low wages in recession)—but also the cleft stick of labour displacing technology. The more automation there is, the greater is the need to deal with the social consequences by increased public expenditure; yet the more the government raises in taxation, the more urgent is the need for more automation. Thus, increasingly, the private control of industry has become a hindrance to the further unfolding of the social forces of production. Consequently, Michael Barratt Brown has convincingly argued that increased state intervention in social and economic affairs implies that it is no longer realistic to envisage a socialist commodity exchange market in a transition from capitalism to socialism, and as a corollary, that an ever advancing technologically-based economy is not the only way forward for underdeveloped regions or countries.(27) Whether through investment in state owned industry in the central belt or through the application of intermediate technology, as Carter proposes, to the rural areas of Scotland, it is the erosion of the power of the market—and of the multinationals who now manipulate the market—to determine social priorities that is the forging ground for socialist progress.

The question of what socialist policies are required to meet the demands, skills and needs of Scottish working people raises the question of how the Scottish Labour Movement can force the pace of the advance towards socialism in Britain. Certain definite points of advance are obvious at a British level, although this does not rule out socialists pressing for an economic control co-extensive with economic devolution under a Scottish Assembly: the public control of industries essential to the provision of social needs and services, the priorities being building and construction, food and food processing, insurance and pensions; the industries essential to the planning of services vital to the economy—the priorities being energy as a whole, land, banking and foreign trade; industries whose monopolistic position threatens the ability of society to plan its own future—the priorities being the taking over of the assets of the major British and American multinationals in Scotland; and industries essential to regional development—in Scotland's case shipbuilding and textiles being obvious cases.

Smith details what is required for the planned control of energy—the nationalisation of all offshore oil and gas industry, the private sector of BP, the British sector of Shell and the Burmah-Castrol Group, to become part of a National Hydrocarbons Authority, and of GEC to form the basis of a national nuclear corporation. But he also shows that if the benefits from oil are to be such that long term economic growth is possible then ICI should be taken over to form a public chemical corporation. The proceeds from oil could themselves be transferred into a regional development fund. A second basic area is land, vital to the future of Scotland, in providing food, timber and other services. Jim Sillars suggests a concrete plan for taking land into public ownership, John McEwen and Ian Carter in particular show what a socialist land strategy could involve and how industry suitable to the skills and needs of the local population and available resources could allow substantial local control over Highland development. Ray Burnett suggests that one obvious step could be an elected Highlands and Islands Development

Board. A third area, investigated by Scott and Hughes is the necessity for social control of the institutional investors who wield enormous financial power both in fostering privilege in our social security system and in controlling the economy. Two recent Labour Party pamphlets, "Capital and Equality" and "Banking and Insurance" propose how public control of banks, insurances and pensions companies, could have a two-sided effect: creating greater social justice in the social services and providing substantial resources for industrial investment.(28) Such a policy could be enacted without compensation and would in itself constitute a major erosion of the power of the British upper class. Public control to end the manipulative stranglehold of the monopolies would require a strategy to end the power of the British, American and European multinationals over the Scottish and British economies and in the event would require controls over foreign investment and trade, accepting a disengagement from a committment to the free movement of capital in Europe. It would as recent studies have indicated require the forging of a new international economic framework based on long-term bilateral trading agreements for exchanges of goods and services and in the long run a payments union, possibly under the United Nations organisation, for clearing and extending such trade exchanges between nations, in particular providing credit to underdeveloped countries.(29) Clearly such a strategy is far more possible in Britain as a whole, given the substantial (and often underrated) industrial and financial assets of private companies. Britain has 140 of Europe's top 400 companies and the private sector has twice as much invested abroad as foreign companies and financiers hold in Britain.(30)

Workers' Power

But the demand for the economy to be directed according to people's needs requires that the need for meaningful work be prioritised. That involves a new and creative relationship between work, education and leisure which breaks down the existing division of mental and manual labour and the extension of self management at the work place. What has often been cited as an irresoluble clash in socialist theory between regulating material production according to human needs and the principle of eliminating the exploitative domination of man over man(31) can only be met through producers controlling the organisation of the production process. Thus it is precisely the surging forwards of demands by trade unionists for real control over the decisions affecting their livelihood that will be the point of departure for socialists. In his study of industrial democracy, Alex Ferry shows that the greater the influence workers have over their working lives locally, the greater will be the demand to reduce managerial prerogatives. Workers control is impossible he suggests in a society which is not socialist—but controls developed in our present society which deny the logic of the market are the embryo of a future society. Clearly the proposals for workers shareholdings (which would, at 1 per cent in all of shares yearly, take at least fifty years to mean anything) and for workers directorships, are inadequate. But the most outspoken proponent of workers' control in Britain, Ken Coates, has seen the recent TUC proposals for industrial democracy—a supervisory board with 50 per cent workers representation having the final say in major investment decisions, closures, redeployment , location of plant and so on—as "a cautious step in the right direction."(32) The Labour M.P. for Motherwell has suggested that much more could be achieved if "these representatives could by law be able to call for a ballot of employees as to whether they wish a scheme to be prepared for the conversion of the enterprise to workers' control."(33)

Co-ordination is clearly required of workers' activity in different industries and unions. The trade unions themselves, as Ferry suggests, must take increased steps to link the demand for better conditions of work and pay with the pressure for increased control. If they do not, they will be left behind by rank and file action, such as we saw in Scotland in the last three months of 1974. Co-ordination, to be effective, must clearly be coherent around certain demands which allow a systematic advance in industry and society. The proposals of the Institute of Workers Control at the time of the UCS occupations have more relevance than ever in today's recession.(34) A first condition set by trade unions in face of threatened unemployment would be that if the existing market is inadequate to support continuous production of ships, steel, textiles and so on, then the government should be bound to investigate the possibility of raising the whole level of

15

international trade through state-guaranteed or negotiated trade exchanges. A second condition would be that if redundancies are inevitable, then government, locally or nationally, should organise alternative production to meet social needs—such as housing and community facilities—which private enterprise is failing to produce. An overriding condition would be that workers in such situations have the right to elect for control over their enterprises. Workers' control on an international scale is clearly an alternative to nationalism.

Political Options

In his recent investigation of the implications of increasing American control over the manufacturing industries of the regions of Europe, Poulantzas has suggested that the internationalisation of capital and the concentration of growth in the central axis of Europe will lead less to the much hoped for political integration of Europe but to the revival of nationalism in the peripheral regions. But the national financial and industrial elites who have increasing local political influence will remain so tied to international capital and to the international division of labour, he argues, that they are without the power to lead working people of the regions towards socialism. Scott and Hughes have suggested that such a description has relevance for Scotland and Tom Nairn shows how the combination of uneven development and oil places Scotland in the vanguard of this revolt of peripheral regions. While nineteenth century European nationalism was "a response to enforced dilemmas of underdevelopment",new nationalism is "a political response to the uneven development of capitalism which arises in areas on the fringe of metropolitan growth zones which suffer from relative deprivation and are increasingly drawn to action against this". But Scots people have never lacked a sense of nationhood or identity—and he shows how fatal it would be for socialists to dismiss nationalism as relevant only to early industrialisation or the escape from naked colonialism, to reject it "as a disease which in Europe carried off millions but in Scotland affects only the mind" in the hope that it will go away—or to suggest that recent Scottish nationalism is the peculiar affliction of a nation "where the noblest of our ancestors died manfully for a dead cause—that of the ideas of the century before".(35) A nationalism which has divided international communism—and now threatens to fragment modern Europe from the periphery inwards—is no mere bourgeois survival. But in asking what it means to be Scots today—and in investigating a Scottish culture which is organised and lived, Nairn shows the manner in which Scottish social practises and expectations were moulded in an accommodated response to the development of the British market economy and Scotland's incorporation within the Greater Britain. The speed and timing of Scottish industrialisation in the nineteenth century, he demonstrates, precluded the characteristic European-wide response to modernisation in political nationalism. Rather the aspirations which nationalism satisfied elsewhere were met by the opportunities and success of the First Industrial Revolution and the British Empire and through a subculture which exhibited a marked dissociation from political action. Thus Sir Walter Scott, tartanry, the Kailyard, militarism, and the Sunday Post—all distinctive features of Scottish identity—were all part of one cultural impasse. This anomalous mode of economic and social development emphasises that there is self-defeating fantasy in a romantic nationalism (36) which poses the issue of Scots and non-Scots as value judgements. A successful British capitalism was the kernel out of which our ways of thinking and feeling were created. Accordingly, it has been the decline of British self confidence particularly since 1945 that has created the conditions in which Scottish nationalism could become politicisable and it is precisely our critical ability to "rise above a weak national inheritance in a manner at once intellectual and universal in its aim" which could lead Scotland towards influencing a Europe "which has crawled out of the abyss of the age of nationalism—or perhaps more precisely has been dragged out of it forcibly by its own disasters and the combined powers of America and Russia."

While drawing attention to the discontinuities of Scottish cultural development, both Tom Nairn and David Craig make us aware of the importance of examining the attempts of people to rise above the here and now which failed, the tendencies which were defeated and the aspirations which were crushed. Craig concentrates on the extent to which the best Scottish writers, "who seeing to the roots of the human condition, worked with whatever forces in society bid fair to win

16

forwards to a better society", remain a radicalising and inspirational influence MacDiarmid whose love/hate relationship with the national geist has torn him between nationalism and communism is properly described as existentialist: it is a vision of a fulfilled man in a fulfilled society, a Scotland purged of second-handedness, the cultural equal of the rest of Europe Like MacDiarmid, Gibbon saw it was imperative to transform the economic and social forces which bred deprivation and alienation in industrial and rural communities. But writing at the time that he did, he was unable to reconcile a socialist ideology which presumed ever-advancing industrialization with the continuance of a rural community incapable of mounting the organised and active resistance necessary. Only the industrial working class in the towns and cities were commensurate to the demands of history.(37) In studying the birth of the Scottish Labour Movement, James Young emphasises the variety of humanist, Marxist and libertarian strands in early socialist thinking but pinpoints the importance which early socialists appreciated of forging links between socialism and industrial workers.This was a dialogue which succeeded—only to go sour in the hollowness of Labour's socialism in the late twenties. I argue elsewhere about the period which followed the First World War that where the issue of socialism against anti-socialism was fiercely contested—primarily in Scotland's central belt—there remains a definite committment to social change which the Labour Movement must further harness, and that where, in the least industrialised areas of Scotland, the issue was little posed, and socialism made little headway, the challenge still remains for socialists not only to develop, as Carter and McEwen do in this collection, a socialist strategy which relates the use of land to the social conditions and needs of these areas but also to develop an organisation and momentum.(38) We would be wrong to underestimate the experience and the education which has led particularly the industrial workers of Scotland to reject implicitly if not explicitly the values of a capitalist society.

Socialism and Nationalism

Nairn's prediction that nationalism may now be unstoppable arises from greater pessimism—the failures of socialism and the successful adaptation of international capitalism. But the question of committment is of course a matter of agency and choice—where men and women can and will make their own decisions in a situation where neutrality is increasingly impossible. In terms of imperatives, the debate about attitudes to nationalism and the SNP in particular is made possible by the inclusion of articles from Burnett, Tait, McGrath and Edwards. Bob Tait argues that a breakaway Scotland would be one important lever against multinational capitalism and that there is a radical base within the SNP which would be enhanced through its fusion with socialists. Owen Dudley Edwards sees possibilities in Scotland today for a more open society—multicultural democratic and less corrupt—where a freedom which is permanently extended can allow an avoidance of the tragedies of events in Ireland. But both Ray Burnett and John McGrath suggest that the policies of the SNP are tied to the existing consensus, that their rise to power in an independent Scotland would lead to a Scottish corporate state little different in substance from the present British state and that a socialist strategy must begin with a direct and conscious attack on international capital. The SNP, they conclude, is no place for a socialist to be.

Clearly, from what I have already said, my own view is that the SNP's "new politics" which "reject class warfare" presumes the familiar priorities of wealth and power over people. Their incoherence over the impact of multinationals on the Scottish economy, their rejection of the public ownership of land, oil and basic industries and their corresponding faith in incentives, and local entrepreneurship is a familiar blend of the old well worn formulas, which assumes the subservience of Scottish workers to private international controls.(39) Their programme for a redistributive "Scottish social justice"—which includes an inadequate £25 minimum wage, 4 per cent mortgages, a rates holiday, and strengthened occupational and pensions schemes—not only wrongly assumes that economic growth within a mixed economy will satisfy the divergent claims of all classes for a share in that growth but, as one study pointed out, will not substantially extend social services provision.(40) The SNP's divorce from the Renaissance Movement, reflecting what Nairn terms the Scots "cultural schizophrenia", has led MacDiarmid to criticise the party for having "no concern with things of fundamental importance, with the great spiritual issues underlying the mere statistics of trade and industry", and corresponds with the findings of one

17

study of local SNP officials which recorded that "feelings of Scottish identity do not exist within the context of a flourishing Scottish culture"(41). This is of course partly a reflection of the SNP's leadership which has brought the professional and commercial middle class back into politics en bloc for the first time since the Liberal decline; there were only two working class SNP candidates at the October election while there were ten managers.(42) Recent studies of the existing membership of the SNP emphasise that their support comes mainly from those groups least likely to be influenced by the collective experiences and loyalties of the workplace and working class communities.(43) This does not mean that disaffection with Labour will not lead to what one writer has called 'avarice in the absence of a clear and effective solution to long standing economic difficulties'(44). But the challenge is how at one and the same time the Scottish Labour Movement can reach to the roots of people's experiences and aspirations and lead the demand for change.

The Way Forward

There are as many Scottish roads to Socialism as there are predictions of Britain's economic doom—but most of them demand three things: a coherent plan for an extension of democracy and control in society and industry which sees every reform as a means to creating a socialist society; a harnessing of the forces for industrial and community self-management within a political movement; and a massive programme of education by the Labour Movement as a whole. Gramsci's relevance to Scotland today is in his emphasis that in a society which is both mature and complex, where the total social and economic processes are geared to maintaining the production of goods and services (and the reproduction of the conditions of production), then the transition to socialism must be made by the majority of people themselves and a socialist society must be created within the womb of existing society and prefigured in the movements for democracy at the grass roots.(45) Socialists must neither place their faith in an Armageddon of capitalist collapse nor in nationalisation alone. For if the Jacobin notion of a vanguard making revolution on behalf of working people relates to a backward society (and prefigures an authoritarian and bureaucratic state), then the complexity of modern society requires a far reaching movement of people and ideas, acting as a stimulus for people to see beyond the immediacy and fragmentation of their existing conditions and as a co-ordinator for the assertion of social priorities by people at a community level and control by producers at an industrial level. In such a way political power will become a synthesis of—not a substitute for—community and industrial life. This requires from the Labour Movement in Scotland today a positive committment to creating a socialist society, a coherent strategy with rhythm and modality to each reform to cancel the logic of capitalism and a programme of immediate aims which leads out of one social order into another. Such a social reorganization—a phased extension of public control under workers' self-management and the prioritising of social needs set by the communities themselves—if sustained and enlarged, would in E.P. Thompson's words lead to "a crisis not of despair and disintegration but a crisis in which the necessity for a peaceful revolutionary transition to an alternative socialist logic became daily more evident."(46)

But the dynamic must come from the existing layer of thousands of committed socialists in Scotland today, firstly through a more obviously democratic and accessible Labour Movement co-ordinating its work with the trade unions (beginning with factory branches) and with street committees, and secondly, through a concerted programme of political education. The early Scottish socialists believed that the bridge between their utopian ideals and the practical politics under which people suffered must be built in a massive programme of education and propaganda. Today in Scotland we have no daily or weekly specifically Scottish political newspapers, no socialist book club, no socialist labour college, no workers' university, and only a handful of socialist magazines and pamphlets.(47) We need all of these now.

It is only within such a reinvigorated socialist strategy that we can appreciate the possibilities of existing and proposed structures of government. Devolution has been all things to all people—the half way house between Westminster rule and a Scottish independence that will take us from rigs to riches; the insertion of a sixth tier of government which threatens to make us the most overgoverned country in Europe; and a fundamental extension of democracy whose every detail is of prime concern and importance. David Gow shows below that devolution was intended as none of these. In proposing "the grafting on" of a devolved Assembly to "a constitution which in its essentials has served us well for some hundreds of years", Kilbrandon's main concern was to improve checks and balances against the centralisation of governmental powers, so to secure "a restoration of public confidence" in government. Kilbrandon neither investigated the influence of private power over the political system (and how the state had assumed greater social and economic powers as a response to the failings of a market economy) nor did he examine how "the demand for more control over our affairs" might lead to greater participation.(48) Sitting at the time of UCS and heightened industrial militancy in Scotland, his limited research made him unaware, as one M.P. has put it, that "much of the feeling in Scotland was closer to the demands for workers' control than to the classic nationalism of the nineteenth century"(49). At the best Kilbrandon assumed that the continual interaction and competition of pressure groups in the political area will sustain a progressive enlargement of the possibilities of their goals being fulfilled; at the worst all will be compromised and none satisfied, with such diffuse groups as the unemployed, the elderly, the low paid with little power to wield, losing out. Consequently more than 40 per cent of those questioned in a recent ORC poll believed an Assembly in Edinburgh would be as unreachable as government in Westminster, and did not regard it as a priority.

The question is not how men and women can be fitted to the needs of the system—but how the system can be fitted to the needs of men and women. Labour must respond to "the demand for more control over our affairs" not by asking how "minimalist" or "maximalist" Assembly powers can avoid separatism nor by becoming masters of the last ditch—resisting change until it becomes inevitable—but by deploying every available level of government to increase the control working people have over their lives. For while politics should never be reduced to "Assemblyism", they will not readily be separated from it. Ronald Young shows that it is how socialists approach their responsibilities as elected representatives that is the crucial question, local government reorganisation offering the opportunity for a more integrated and politicised approach to meeting needs generated by local communities and a more viable framework for relating local to national issues. The Assembly, too, can not only enable regions and districts to make radical innovations but also be a focus for and a co-ordinating point for formulating Scotland's priorities. It offers a political control over the Scottish Office, leading both to an accountability and to a freer flow of information. It allows the framing of distinctly Scottish policies to meet social needs and requirements. It gives Scottish people a focus for bargaining with Westminster and Brussels— and gives Scottish socialists the chance to lead and influence other regions and other countries. Finally, it is clear that there is nothing inherently anti-socialist about economic devolution as long as Scottish Labour insists on genuine economic control in devolved areas nor is there anything remiss about taxation powers in relation to democratically decided levels of public service provision. But the real opportunity which present events offer is of course something more. It is the challenge to force the pace towards socialism in Britain as a whole and to reinvigorate the labour movement in Scotland from the work place and community outwards. Scotland's socialist pioneers, Hardie, Smillie, Maxton, Maclean, Gallacher, Wheatley and others, knew that socialism would not be won until people were convinced of the necessity for social control. The Scottish Labour movement is uniquely placed today to convert the present discontent into a demand for socialism: we will fail only if we ignore the challenge.

1. The Red Paper on Scotland is the second Red Paper, intended as a forum for the left to express their views on immediate issues. The first was **The Red Paper on Education,** (ed. Bob Cuddihy), Edinburgh 1970.
References in this introduction to articles or writers which are not footnoted relate to contributions to this collection.
2. **Sample Census of Great Britain, 1966,** Economic Activity Part 3 (HMSO, 1969), Table 30, pp.421-422.

3. **The Economist,** September 29th, 1973, Scottish Supplement p.5. For a discussion of wealth inequalities in Britain, see A. Atkinson, **Wealth and Inequality in Britain** (1973). For Scotland, see also L. Wright in J. Wolfe (ed), **Government and Nationalism in Scotland** (1969), pp.140-152.

4. Board of Inland Revenue, **Inland Revenue Statistics, (1973),** p.105 (HMSO, 1973).

5. Board of Inland Revenue, **Survey of Personal Incomes 1970-71** (HMSO, 1973), pp.102-3.

6. Scottish Development Department, **Bowhouse, Alloa,** Bowhouse is an area comprising 4 per cent of the population of Clackmannan County. The study was reported in the **Guardian** in October, 1974.

7. Public Expenditure in Scotland in **Investing in Scotland's Future,** p.177 (Scottish Council (Development and Industry), 1974).

8. Educational Priority: **A Scottish Study** (HMSO, 1974) esp. p. 184-5

9. See in particular R. Furbey in **Social and Economic Administration** Vol.8, No.3 (1974) pp.192-221

10. **Public Expenditure in Scotland,** op.cit., pp.160-164. I am grateful to Andrew McPherson for information on university entrants.

11. This was proposed at the time of the UCS work-in by M. Barratt Brown in **UCS: The Social Audit** (Institute for Workers Control, Pamphlet No.26, 1971).

12. M. Stuer, **The Impact of Foreign Investment,** cited in Firn.

13. See, for example, the **National Institute Economic Review** (NIESR, Aug.1974).

14. **The Economist,** op.cit., esp. pp.27-35 and p.47.

15. **A Future for Scotland,** Report by the Scottish Council (Development and Industry) (1973).

16. **ibid.,** p.109.

17. D. McKay and A. McKay in **The Scotsman,** February 5th, 1975, p.10.

18. The most recent study is Moore and Rhodes, Regional Policy and the Scottish Economy in **Scottish Journal of Political Economy,** Vol.xx1, No.3 (Nov. '74), p.233.

19. SCRI, **Scottish Manufactured Exports** (Nov.1974), Begg et al "Scotland's Balance of Trade" (1975), pointing to substantial trade deficits, quoted in **The Scotsman,** February 6, 1975.

20. Ray MacDonald in **Scotland's Goals** (1974), p.54.

21. Alexander has recently shown that only 15 per cent of total public investment is "decided primarily by Government itself", **Investing in Scotland's Future,** p.58. See also the more radical proposals of the Labour Party (Scottish Council) in **Scotland and the N.E.B.** (1973) The STUC have rightly not accepted that "the role of the SDA should be to help private enterprise to help itself." Instead they urge that the SDA be given compulsory purchase powers to take equity in Scottish companies, and have one nationalised bank under it. **Scotsman,** February 28th, 1975.

22. **Business Scotland,** February, 1975, p.48.

23. Scottish Council, **Memorandum** submitted to Lord Crowther Hunt (1974). It is discussed by David Gow below. For a variation of the theme, see **The Guardian,** Devolution Supplement (1975) and **The Financial Times** Scottish Supplement, Nov.11th, 1974. Scottish Council Research Institute, **Economic Development and Devolution** (1974), which favours wide ranging economic powers under an Assembly. See also, **The Scotsman,** Annual Financial Review, May 21st, 1974, "Need for Scots to invest in Scotland."

24. Scottish Finance and Investment, p.15, Supplement to **Investors Chronicle,** Oct.25, 1974.

25. Evidence to House of Commons **Expenditure Committee,** Vol.42, No.18.

26. **Business Scotland,** February 1975, p.45.

27. M. Barratt Brown, **From Labourism to Socialism** (1972); see also P. Mattick, **Marx and Keynes: The Limits of the Mixed Economy** (1969).

28. Labour Party, **Capital and Equality** (1972) **Banking and Insurance** (1973).

29. M. Barratt Brown, **Europe: Time to Leave and How to Do It.** (1974). See also Labour Research Department, **The Menance of the Multinationals** (1974), p.310.

30. B. Rowthorn, Britain and the World Economy: Breaking the Chains in **Marxism Today** (Aug. 1974), p.231-2. See also **Tribune,** January 24th, 1975.

31. L. Kolakowski in The Socialist Idea: A Reappraisal (1974) pp.pp. 18-35. For a reply, see E. Thompson, in **Socialist Register, 1973** pp.1-100.

32. **Tribune,** 31st January, 1975. p.3.

33. Dr. J. Bray, **Towards a Workers Managed Economy** (Fabian Tract 430, 1974), also G. Radice **Working Power** (Fabian Tract 431, 1974) and K. Coates, **Essays on Industrial Democracy** (1971)

and others.

34. M. Barratt Brown, **op.cit.,**; see also R. Murray, **UCS: The Anatomy of Bankruptcy**(1972)

35. P. Geddes, quoted in H. Hanham, **Scottish Nationalism** (1969). Also N. Poulantzas, The Internationalisation of Capital and the Nation State in **Economy and Society Vol.3, No.1 1974)** pp.145-179.

36. For an extreme view of Tom Nairn's observations, see A. Jackson The Knitted Claymore in **Lines Review** No.3 (1971), "For what could be done to restore Scots as a full living language... expel the (million) English... all paparers and media in Scots... all education in Scots... the colloquial/literary split has more of a class basis than the national one" (p.21-23).

37. See in particular L. Gibbon on Land and Glasgow in **A Scots Hairst** (ed. Munro), (1967), and H. MacDiarmid in **Whither Scotland** (ed. Glen) p.239-240.

38. G. Brown, **Socialism and Scottish Political Change,** unpublished paper (1974) see also M. Dyer on Highland voting behaviour in **The Scotsman,** November 1974, where he describes the substantial working class vote as "the silent voice of Scottish politics."

39. SNP's Four Point Economic Plan, September 1974 which acknowledges continued support for multinationals in Scotland. See also SNP Manifestoes, Feb and Oct. 1974, and articles by D. Crawford in **Scots Independent.**

40. I. Levitt, **The War on Poverty,** unpublished paper, (September, 1974).

41. H. MacDiarmid, **A Political Speech** (1972) p.9 and J. Schwartz in **World Politics** (1970) p.496.

42. **L.R.D.** Fact Service, 5 Oct. 1974. Of sixty-one candidates for which background information was found, 20 were teachers or lecturers, 10 were managerial staff (inc. one "industrial therapy manager"), 8 were solicitors, 5 were professional engineers, 4 were journalists, 4 were professional workers, 5 were company directors, and 3 were farmers. There was one joiner and one Post Office engineer.

43. Drieux, Univ. of Sorbonne, Thesis on S.N.P. (1974). See also I. McLean and J. Blochel and D. Denver in **Political Studies** (1970) and J. Cornford and J. Brand in Wolfe, **op.cit.**

44. McKay and McKay, **The Scotsman,** 7th February, 1975.

45. Gramsci, **Prison Notebooks** (1971); see also L. Magri. Problems of the Marxist Theory of the Revolutionary Party in **New Left Review,** 1970, pp.97-128 and also P. Friere, **Pedagogy of the Oppressed** (1972) and **Cultural Action for Freedom** (1972).

46. E. Thompson in **Socialist Register 1973** p.52 which is an updating of his brilliant articles, Agency and Choice in **New Reasoner,** 1958.

47. The various left parties recent pamphlets on Scotland's problems are: Labour Party (Scottish Council), **Scottish Manifesto** (1974) and **Planning for Prosperity** (1975); the Communist Party, **For a Scottish Parliament** (1974) and the periodical **Scottish Marxist;** International Socialists, **Socialism or Nationalism** (1974); International Marxist Group, **Scotland, Labour and Workers Power** (1974); and **Scottish Vanguard,** periodical of the Workers Party of Scotland.

48. Royal Commission on the Constitution (1973) esp. Paras 311, and 396. J.P. Mackintosh summed up Kilbrandon well, "The Commissioners did not search for alternative remedies in their questions; they asked almost exclusively about devolution", **Political Quarterly,** (Jan.1974) p.117. See also J. Stanyer in **Social and Economic Administration** (1974) who concluded that "The Commissioners... are not stemming the tide but swimming even faster with it." p.147

49. Norman Buchan in **Whither Scotland** (1971) p.89.

Old Nationalism And New Nationalism

Tom Nairn

'Scotland is unique among European nations in its failure to develop a nationalist sentiment strong enough to be a vital factor in its affairs... The reason probably lies in the fact that no comprehensive-enough agency has emerged; and the commonsense of our people has rejected one-sided expedients incapable of addressing the organic complexity of our national life. For it must be recognized that the absence of nationalism is, paradoxically, a form of Scottish self-determination. If that self-determination, which...has reduced Scottish arts and affairs to a lamentable pass is to be induced to take different forms and express itself in a diametrically opposite direction to that which it has taken for the past two hundred and twenty years, the persuading programme must embody considerations of superior power to those which have so long ensured the opposite process. Scottish opinion is anachronism-proof in matters of this kind...'

   C.M. Grieve (Hugh MacDiarmid), **Albyn or Scotland and the Future** (1927).

   These 'considerations of superior power' were a long time coming to Scotland. However, they have finally arrived. And as they have come—half a century later than MacDiarmid imagined—that hard-headed, 'anachronism-proof' commonsense has indeed begun to shift its ground. The nostalgic literary nationalism he led from the 20s onwards was not a 'comprehensive-enough agency' to do this. Neither were the political movements that accompanied it. The persuading programme which made the difference was the petroleum business: the largest, richest, most aggressive, and most international form of capitalism in the world.
   The result is an astonishing situation. Although (as argued below) the new Scottish separatism of the 70s is in some ways comparable to trends in Brittany, Catalonia, Wales, and other regions

22

of Western Europe, in certain respects it remains unique. Nowhere else has the transformation been so abrupt, or so extensive. Nowhere else have the essential forces at work displayed their nature so nakedly. Nowhere else—therefore—is the resultant conflict and political dilemma quite so clearly defined.

It is a substantially new dilemma. On the face of it what is happening may look like an episode of resurrection unequalled since Lazarus. But in fact, this is not only a chapter in the old book of European nationalism. Still less is it something comparable to contemporary national-liberation struggles in the Third World. Romantic interpretations along these lines are not lacking, of course. This is not surprising, because the conceptual language we have available is predominantly 'nationalist' in just this sense: it looks backwards, or out to those parts of the world still engaged in a life-or-death fight against backwardness. New movements cannot help wearing old clothes.

To Scotland's remarkable and novel dilemma there corresponds a new political movement. Like the dilemma itself, it is in a number of ways analogous to historical or mainstream nationalism. But a more careful consideration shows its different place in history, and its different character and potential. As argued below, it deserves to be called 'neo-nationalism' rather than nationalism. For there is a new character which serves to distinguish this separatism from (e.g.) Czech, Polish, South Slav and other nationalisms of the 19th centuries, or from such contemporary national struggles as those in Kurdistan, Eritrea, Bangla Desh, and the Portuguese colonies.

Let me try to summarize the difference, in a preliminary and quite incomplete fashion. 'Nationalism', in that sense which has dominated historical development since early in the 19th century, was in essence the forced reaction of one area after another to the spread of capitalism. This process has been awarded other titles too: 'westernization', 'modernization', or simply 'development'. What matters here is that this complex, long-term movement arose chiefly in areas of what one may call absolute deprivation. They were overwhelmingly feudal, or pre-feudal, in social character. They were marked, that is, by illiteracy, landlord-rule, feeble urban development, primary poverty, and absence of the socio-economic infrastructures which modernization demands. This is of course why they became (and soon felt themselves to be) 'backward', or 'under-developed'. It is why, equally, they were bound to fall victim to some variety of domination or 'imperialism'—to which the only effective response was in most cases locally-based, popular struggle: nationalism.

Neo-nationalism arises at a different, much later point in the same general process. It remains comparable to elemental nationalism in being a forced by-product of the grotesquely uneven nature of capitalist development. As the latter's blind, lurching progress impinges upon this or that region, it still poses a threat (or more exactly, a combined promise and threat) of modernization, 'imperialistic' disruption of old ways, and so on. But this now occurs at a far more advanced stage of general development, in areas which long ago emerged from the absolute 'backwardness' just referred to. Located on the fringe of the new metropolitan growth zones, they suffer from a relative deprivation and are increasingly drawn to political action against this. This action is analogous to old-style nationalism, above all in its ideology. But, precisely because it starts from a higher level and belongs to a more advanced stage of capitalist evolution—to the age of multinationals and the effective internationalisation of capital—its real historical function will be different. The impact of the oil industry on Scotland and of the U.S. multinational on the French Midi is provoking a new Scottish and Occitanian separatism; but, to a greater extent than is realised, this is a **sui generis** phenomenon which should not be assimilated to classical European or Third World 'nationalism' at all.

It is the devastating rapidity and scale of the impact of these new conditions that has made Scotland into the examplar of 'neo-nationalism' in this sense. One need only compare the oil industry's arrival to the previous, gradual (and more generally characteristic) infiltration of international corporations into the Scottish industrial belt during the 1950s and 60s, to grasp this. Yet this is only one aspect of the situation.

For the dramatic developments of the past few years are busy transforming a deeper historical situation which was, itself, quite unique. MacDiarmid was not quite accurate in saying that Scotland was alone in failing 'to develop a nationalist sentiment strong enough to be a vital factor in its affairs', in the 19th century. In fact, Western Europe is a graveyard of historical nationalities which were suppressed or submerged by the rise of what became the 18th and 19th century 'great powers'. Scotland's real peculiarity lies elsewhere. It lies in the lateness with which such absorption occurred: at the beginning of the 18th century, rather than in the later Middle Ages. It lies in the manner of the fusion: there are many stateless nationalities in history, but only one Act of Union—a peculiarly patrician bargain between two ruling classes, which would have been unthinkable earlier, under absolute monarchy, and impossible later, when the age of democratic nationalism had arrived. And it lies in the results of the bargain: a nationality which resigned statehood but preserved an extraordinary amount of the institutional and psychological baggage normally associated with independence—a decapitated national state, as it were, rather than an ordinary 'assimilated' nationality.

For two centuries after the Jacobite Rebellion of 1745-6, this freak by-product of European history posed no particular problem. The reason was simple: on the whole, the Union bargain worked as it had been intended to. Indeed it far surpassed the hopes placed in it. During the prolonged era of Anglo-Scots imperialist expansion, the Scottish ruling order found that it had given up statehood for a hugely profitable junior partnership in the New Rome. The oddity of the Union has always posed grave cultural and psychological problems in Scotland—problems recognizable, as I shall go on to argue, through a characteristic series of sub-national deformations or 'neuroses'. But it posed no real **political** problem for most of this time.

The political problem returned only with the post-World-War-II decline of the United Kingdom. This has been a slow process. The strength and stability of this old multi-national system, founded on its imperialist successes, has proved resistant to the collapse. None the less, as both great U.K. parties failed to do more than tamper with the underlying crisis, the slow foundering has begun to turn into a rout. In the early 1970s paralysis and incapacity have become undeniable, electorally as well as in terms of party strategies.

It is at this point that conditions have precipitated the neo-nationalist movement in Scotland. The oil industry has collided with the country at a moment of extreme and growing debility in the traditional political apparatus—in that conservative Unionism which a majority of Scots have supported, with little dissension, for two centuries. The consequence is perhaps the most startling aspect of the whole situation. The novel conflict in Scotland has cut into the palsied corpus of Unionism like a knife. More than any other factor, more even than the miners' strikes of 1972 and 1974, it has exposed the senility of the old consensus and its two-party system.

Pious, somewhat sleekit debates about 'Home Rule' for Scotland and Wales have appeared and reappeared in imperial politics since the 1880s. It would have dumbfounded these earlier generations of Home Rulers to see the Greater Britain caving in before new nationalist demands. They sought a modest degree of self-government in order to strengthen the Union, and Great-British nationalism. Nobody thought that one day U.K. parties would fall over one another in a competition to cede wider and wider powers, or that The Thunderer would declare defeat in advance, in a mood of world-weary resignation: 'The Scots are all assembly men now. So the practical question is what kind of assembly. No stability could be expected from setting up a Scottish Assembly in a grudging spirit with the minimum powers that a reluctant government in London felt it had to concede. It is better to devolve the widest powers...It could be that once the Scottish people have taken one step along that road they will not be satisfied with any stopping place short of full independence. If so, it would be neither possible nor desirable to keep them within the United Kingdom...'(1)

Under these conditions, unforseeable even a few years ago, the somewhat eccentric inheritance of Scottish sub-nationalism has assumed new meaning. Until the later 1960s it was, in wider European terms, an unclassifiable marginal aberration: an ex-nation turned province, neither one thing nor another—a relic from before the Flood of Europe's mainstream nationalism, as it were, more suitable for jokes than serious political analysis. MacFinnegan had slumbered comfortably through the age of national revivals, with no more than a twitch or two. It could not be imagined, then, that a drop or two of petroleum spirit would bring him staggering to his feet, demanding the restitution of of his lost political kingdom. Still less that English governments would have no alternative but to weakly placate him.

Given this turn of events, neo-nationalism has made such rapid, apparently irresistible strides because it has this old basis to stand on. Headless aberration or not, the Scottish sub-culture is far more than Europe's other submerged ethnic groups have to start from. Cramped, stagnant, backward-looking, parochial—all these and others are the epithets traditionally and rightly ascribed to modern Scottishness. But deformed as they are, these constitute none the less a strong, institutionally guaranteed identity. It is true that political castration was the main ingredient in this rather pathological complex (such was the point of the Union), and that intellectuals have been unable to contemplate it for a long time without inexpressible pain. Still, there it was: the one thing which the Scots can never be said to have lacked is identity. Once the material circumstances for a new sort of political mobilization had formed, the thistle-patch proved very useful. It gave the S.N.P., in a sense, much more to go on that comparable separatist movements in Wales, Brittany, Corsica, or the other regions.

Thus there seem to be three main ingredients in the situation. The most critical, and the newest, is the incursion of the oil business with its apocalyptic bundle of promises and menaces: this is busy creating a new material basis for political life in Scotland. The second is the decline of the all-British political system, which had already half-formed a vacuum into which new and alternative forces could rush: there is no sign of this disintegration being arrested, either in Scotland, in Ulster, or in England itself. The third is the curious quasi-national legacy of North Britain, which is being reanimated by the new kind of separatism that has made such progress in the last few years.

I do not propose to try and deal here with the first two. In any case, searching examinations of the oil companies and desperate broodings on the fate of Westminster are not lacking from the scene. I would like only to consider the third, under three headings. First, its origins, as what MacDiarmid called a 'paradoxical form of self-determination' which arose instead of nationalism. Secondly, its character in a broad political-cultural sense: the cultural sub-nationalism of tartanry. Third, its likely significance within the wider perspectives of European neo-nationalism and the Common Market.

I

'To begin with, while we have a homogeneous British State it must be noted that the organisations and institutions in civil society which comprise its bulwarks and defences have an azoic complexity the most significant feature of which for us is that civil society in Scotland is fundamentally different from that in England. What is more, much of our shared "British" ideology as it manifests itself in Scotland, draws its vigour and strength from a specifically Scottish heritage of myths, prejudices and illusions... If the left is even to begin a serious critique of our society then these differences must be taken account of'.
Ray Burnett, 'Scotland and Antonio Gramsci', **Scottish International** (No.9, Nov. 1972).

The theoretical problem posed by these remarks of Ray Burnett's could be put as follows. To understand any society as a whole, one must always distinguish between its 'State' or political and administrative structure, and its 'civil society'. The latter comprises, for example, its most characteristic non-political organizations, its religious and other beliefs, its 'customs' or way of life, its typical jokes, and so on. It is not easy to sum up all that is denoted by this Gramscian category, and there are things which will not fit neatly under either heading. But this is relatively unimportant. What matters is that they are distinguishable, and that the singular identity of a modern society depends upon the relationship between them.

Amidst these abstractions, it is important to be as specific as possible. What we are considering is the problem of understanding **modern** societies; and within that, the question of what it is that makes any **one** such society structurally distinct, 'peculiar' in relation to others resembling it in so many ways. Needless to say the question can be answered quite empirically (and it usually is): thousands of particular events always make any one place different from others. Yet this is an evasion of the real problem, which derives from the fact that societies 'hang together' in some way, as some sort of whole. And **modern** (19th and 20th century) societies hang together especially closely, and in a special way.

Gramsci describes the problem as follows. Within the last two centuries—roughly from the French Revolution to the present—there has arisen a relationship between State and society generally characteristic of modern social formations: 'The revolution which the bourgeois class has brought into the conception of law, and hence into the function of the State, consists especially in the will to conform (hence ethicity of the law and of the State). The previous ruling classes were essentially conservative in the sense that they did not tend to construct an organic passage from the other classes into their own, i.e. to enlarge their class sphere "technically" and ideologically: their conception was that of a closed caste. The Bourgeois class poses itself as an organism in continuous movement, capable of absorbing the entire society, assimilating it to its own cultural and economic level. The entire function of the State has been transformed; the State has become an "educator", etc... The main point about this modern State-society relationship—quite distinct from that of Antiquity or Feudalism—is that through it the whole people become part of society, really for the first time.

Previous State-systems and ruling castes had presided over society. By contrast (Gramsci goes on): 'In my opinion, the most reasonable and concrete thing that can be said about the ethical State, the cultural State, is this: every State is ethical in as much as one of its most important functions is to raise the great mass of the population to a particular cultural and moral level, a level (or type) which corresponds to the needs of the productive forces for development, and hence to the interests of the ruling classes. The school as a positive educative function, and the courts... are the most important State activities in this sense: but in reality a multitude of other so-called private initiatives and activities tend to the same end—initiatives and activities which form the apparatus of the political and cultural hegemony of the ruling classes'. (2)

One farther remark is indispensable here. This 'revolution which the bourgeois class has brought' necessarily affected the different social formations caught up in it at different times, and in quite different ways. Such deep diversity was inseparable from the process. The huge complexity and variety of pre-existing social evolution meant that each society had a different starting point, and was struck and transformed by the spreading wave of "modernization in different ways. Modernization and all its concomitants (industrialization, political democracy, general literacy, etc., etc.) notoriously tend towards uniformity and the standardization of many aspects of existence. But they have done so, historically, only through prolonged struggle against (and forced compromise with) this social diversity.

This is of course why **nationalism** has been a central, inescapable feature of the development of 'modern society'. There could only be modern societies, in the plural, and they could not help being very distinct from one another—even those at a similar general stage of development, as in present-day Western Europe. The State-society knot Gramsci is talking about was, so to speak, tied in remarkably different fashions in these different places. So, the normal historiographical and sociological model for it is naturally that of **one** society-cum-State. It is this modern and contemporary 'nation-State' that 'has become an educator', has 'raised the great mass of the population to a particular cultural level', generated a particular 'apparatus of political and cultural hegemony', and so forth. And we know only too well that once it has done so, in the way corresponding to its particular historical situation, the resultant particular identity is very resistant indeed to change and attack.(3)

If the general problem is posed in this way, then how does the particular problem of modern Scotland appear? As we observed already, it represents a historical oddity—but one which posed no special or anguishing problem to its own ruling class or to its neighbours in Europe, simply because this freak nature was accompanied by prolonged political quiescence. There was, almost until the present day, no urgent practical reason to decipher the enigma. Romantic superstition did well enough. Indeed (as we all know) it became in the 19th century one of those 'bulwarks and defences' of our civil society, a kind of surrogate nationalism.

While strong practical motives were absent, all the new models of nationalist history-writing pointed in another direction: towards what had become the standard European (and later world) pattern of one political State and **its** society, or one distinguishable ethnic society and **its** own State. A world where the civil societies and the States mainly fitted each other, as it were, through the normal developmental struggles of last century and this. By comparision, Scotland was a

26

hippogriff: a manifest bastard, in the world of nationalist wedlock. Incomprehensibly, this composite formation had failed to grow like the others. Although clearly an historic nation, and one which had preserved much of its inheritance after 1707—thus escaping the **Gleichshaltung** to which so many other old ethnic groups were subjected, as they were 'absorbed' into provinces of greater European powers—Scotland had failed to turn nationalist and create its own political State. It had failed to do the normal thing, at the proper time. It had disobeyed the 'logic of history'—which was of course also the logic of the way people had come to think about modern history, and analyse modern societies.

'Most Scots would, quite rightly, have laughed at the idea that the Scottish nation came to an end in 1707... it was the end of an auld sang, perhaps, but it was not yet the end of an auld people', T.C. Smout has written.(4) Only in retrospect, from the point of view of the age of nationalism, did the loss of statehood seem to overshadow the country's history so completely, condemning it to eccentricity and oblivion. Scottish society apart from the State, 'civil society', was guaranteed in its independent existence by the Union. The church, the law, the aristocracy, the bourgeoisie of the Royal Burghs: all these institutions and the dominant social classes linked to them were confirmed in what they had demanded of separate identity. So was the distinct social culture they represented.

The Scots pattern so strikingly counterposed to the usual models is therefore that of a distinct civil society not married to 'its' State. It is one of heterogeneity, not that relative homogeneity which became the standard of nationalist development. A foreign, much stronger State and political system was imposed on Scotland by the Union. Through it the country was 'managed', as Rosalind Mitchison has written, 'by a set of monarchs chosen by English politicians for English political purposes'. Except at moments of crisis, this State was 'ignorant of and indifferent to the problems of Scotland...' so that on the whole the country's government was 'ramshackle and confused in structure, improvised and halting in execution'.(5) One should add of course that this fate was chosen by the indigenous ruling class. Alien and corrupt it may have been. Still, it was so much better than what Scotland had known that they could hardly believe their luck. A later contributor to the same volume quotes a letter from one of the great Scots 'managers', Duncan Forbes of Culloden, expressing his relief at the discontinuance of the Ministerial post of Scottish Secretary. Ultimate power was best left in English hands completely: '...for some time at least we shall not be troubled by that nuisance...a Scots Secretary, either at full length or in miniature; if any one Scotsman has absolute power, we are in the same slavery as ever, whether that person be a fair man or a black man, a peer or a commoner, 6 foot or 5 foot high, and the dependence of the country will be on that man, and not on those that made him.'(6)

It is above all the class character of this composite policy which concerns us here. Naturally, it was only the most restricted 'upper crust' that had embraced Union in this way, and now looked back with horror upon the old pre-1707 chaos and tyranny. It was indeed a perfect specimen of the conceptions of one of those 'closed castes' Gramsci refers to: an 'essentially conservative' class, still largely aristocratic in nature, which emphatically did not tend to 'enlarge its class spheres' ideologically and exert a 'political and cultural hegemony' in the modern sense. The hegemony it represented was an older one. It was simply that of aristocratic or patrician 'direction' of a hierarchical social order, from above—one might almost say (emphasising the contrast with nationalism) from outside.(7) The Enlightened spirits of the Scottish ruling elite became vigorous and effective 'Improvers' during the century following Union. To this extent they were of course 'modernizing' and progressive. But none of them had the slightest doubt that this was what Progress consisted in: diffusion of light **de haut en bas,** from the educated few above to the vast, passive—if not bigoted and refractory—mass below.

There was nothing unusual about this class character, or the world-view associated with it. It prevailed over most of Europe until 1789. Still less was there anything strange about an old society being politically mismanaged by a distant, alien State: this remained standard procedure over large areas of Europe until 1918 (at least). What was originally unusual about Scotland was something different. And with the passage of time this difference became a situation that was to be quite unique.

The distant State that dominated the Scots was not the standard European Absolutism. England was the first really successful post-Absolutist State; after its revolutions of the previous century it was moving towards the even greater socio-economic transformation which, between the later 18th century and the middle of the 19th would carry it to industrial and political supremacy. This change went far beyond the bounds of the most Enlightened Despotism, the most Improving of Landowning classes. It was, as a matter of fact, the very prototype of the modern development Gramsci indicates: that 'revolution of the bourgeois class' which involved the progressive 'absorbing of the entire society' into the new State-society relationship emblemized in nationalism.

What really counts here is not only that the Scots rulers were lucky enough to have been taken over by a dynamic bourgeois culture instead of a stagnant late-feudal one. It is that this was the **first** such 'bourgeois revolution' proceeding on a sufficient territorial basis. Just because it was first, it developed gradually, and in a highly 'empirical' and de-centralized fashion. All those societies which developed later, in its wake, could not help doing so far more competitively, through a much more intense political and State organization. After the first huge strides forward England had made, after her Agrarian and Industrial Revolutions and her colonial and commercial triumphs over France, other lands were forced to be in some sense 'late-comers'—forced, therefore, to compensate for their backwardness by a more conscious, a more State-contrived and militant type of development.

Industrialisation and Civil Society

Free from these pressures—which were to be the normal tensions of uneven development in modern times—the post-1707 multi-national State permitted a more spontaneous and localized evolution of civil society. By comparision with later arrivals, the British Industrial Revolution was remarkably 'provincial' and self-sustaining in character. This was precisely the situation which the Scots inhertied, and were able to exploit. The historical situation was by nature unique, unrepeatable—so in turn was the use which the Scottish bourgeoisie made of it. No other province, no other submerged nationality of Europe, was ever to be in the same conjuncture again. Everywhere else, the rising tide of the bourgeois revolution, the forward drive of capitalist development, confronted marginal or 'backward' peoples with a far starker dilemma: uncompromising 'assimilation' or independent (nationalist) development by means of their own State and army.

Given the priority, and the structural character, of their development, the English ruling class was able to tolerate a high degree of North-British autonomy. Hence the lack of what were to become the standard practices of discrimination, ethnic oppression and **Kulturkampf.** These were not due to the milk of English Benevolence, as so many apologists of the Union have proclaimed. Benevolence, did not flow so noticeably in Ireland, or for that matter in Scotland itself beyond the Highland Line: these were 'incompatible' social formations which could not be brought into bourgeois partnership so easily. They were not to escape the normal dilemma of 'development', and its cruel consequences. The Lowland Scots did escape it, just. Through the peculiar circumstances of the Union and their own astonishing self-development in the later 18th century, they were able to establish a singular, subordinate position inside the still relatively 'open' and expanding system of English capitalism.

'In sum', writes William Ferguson, 'the economic development of Scotland in the18th. century is best regarded as constituting the so-called "take-off" phase, making possible the emergence of an industrialised society. The actual achievement of industrialisation ...was the work mainly of the 19th century'.(8) Thus, Scottish civil society advanced much farther than had been imagined possible under its foreign monarchy and State. Its dominant class had sacrificed statehood for participation in the English and colonial 'common market' of the day, trusting that this would aid the diffusion of Polite Society in their tenebrous land. In fact, society 'took off' beneath their feet, towards a revolutionary condition of industrialisation. Within the larger economic area they had entered, they had created an autonomous sub-system—in effect, an epicentre now borne along upon the grander tide of English imperial expansion. They had entered its flow at a moment when, still in formation, it could tolerate the existence of such a sub-system. Hence they were neither crushed by it, nor compelled into nationalist reaction against it—the standard fates which, one can be certain, they would not have escaped if Union had been delayed until the end of the 18th century.

28

As a part of this advance, there occurred a significant florescence of Scottish national culture. In comparison with the theocratic gloom of the 17th century, this appeared strange even to some of its protagonists. In a very celebrated letter, David Hume asked: 'Is it not strange that, at a time when we have lost our Princes, our Parliaments, our independent Government, even the Presence of our chief Nobility, are unhappy, in our Accent & Pronounciation, speak a very corrupt Dialect of the Tongue which we make use of; is it not strange, I say, that, in these Circumstances, we shou'd really be the People most distinguished for Literature in Europe?'(9) The question has been posed and re-posed ever since. It has deeply vexed nationalists, in particular, that the most illustrious phase of our cultural history should have been so strikingly non-nationalist—so detached from the People, so intellectual and universalizing in its assumptions, so Olympian in its attitudes. This vexation is understandable, yet misplaced. The Edinburgh philosophes were neither traitors to their country—as that country then was, and as they perceived it—nor cosmopolitan poseurs. They simply belonged to a unique, pre-nationalist stage of socio-economic expansion. Concentrated in such a small area and time, in a land transported so incredibly quickly out of Barbarity into Civility, they were the chief exemplars of the European Enlightenment's vision of Progress. That is, of a vision of development which was everywhere discredited and made impossible, after 1800.

At this point, one can see how important the temporal dimension is for any model of Scottish society. For, in the extraordinarily favourable conditions of the Union, the rapid progress of Scotland's new, bourgeois civil society cannot help appearing 'premature'. This is of course mainly a comparative classification. Few, even among perfervid nationalists, would regret that the country escaped so smartly from the age of witch-burning and feudal futility. But in relation to virtually every other region of Europe, Scottish advance was precocious.(10) In a number of decisive respects, the Scots had crossed the great divide of basic 'development' before the real nature of the problem had even presented itself—in most of what are now Italy and Germany, for instance, in most of Ireland and Scandinavia, and in all of Eastern Europe.

This precocity was bound to be far-reaching in its consequences. For it was Europe, Europe as a whole, which cast the general mould of 'development' and the world-view linked to it. We know what that mould inevitably consisted in: nationalism. Nationalism was the forced mode of socio-economic and political, evolution. It was to be through this that the majority of European 'backward' lands tried to achieve that break-through which history had already granted the Scots (in all essentials) by the 1820s. It was to take most of them several generations of struggle to do it. Some did not begin to succeed until after 1918; others, not until after 1945. As they fought in this direction, the original 'advanced' States, the leaders of development, were compelled into a more imperialistic and aggressive nationalism of their own. Nobody could evade the new climate, the ferocious and exacting conditions of this new epoch, in which culture was pressed—in a way that would have seemed lunatic to David Hume and the other Edinburgh Augustans—into the service of the nationality-state.

The most significant consequence, from our point of view, lies in the quite different stamp left by these two forms of social development. Normal, nationalist development depended upon the deliberate fostering and mobilization of ethnic, linguistic and other differentiae. Through it, the typical backward region or ex-province has levered itself forward into modern times with the help of its own past—in effect, by a curious sort of regression. It is of course this 'regression' which marks a good deal of what anyone will recognize as the psychology of nationalism: the mythicization of the past, evocations of the Volksgeist, and so on. Reculer pour mieux sauter: the dilemma of nationalist movements is that they have to gaze backwards, and summon up what energy they can from the particular 'inheritance' they are stuck with, in order to leap forward. Otherwise (or so it looks to them) they are bound to be trampled on by the greater powers outside. In the course of the process, all this inherited impedimenta—the substance of whatever civil society they have—assumes new meaning. It is transfigured, in a way that would have astonished the previous generations who actually lived the 'national experience' (transfigured, that is, where it is not simply invented).

This complex of events, feelings and ideas makes up nationalism: a modern, developmental phenomenon quite distinct from straightforward national and cultural differences, of the kind there have always been and always will be. In Scotland, it has never happened. The innumerable institutional and popular differentiae of Scots life have persisted. Some may have dwindled, in the

29

face of those 'assimilationist' pressures which nationalist paranoia makes so much of; but far more have remained, and certain central bastions were in any case (as we saw) guaranteed by the Union. What counts is that the Scottish middle classes were never compelled to turn to this substantial inheritance and harness it **en bloc**, to mobilize it and the social classes beneath them in a developmental struggle. The usual 'raw material' of nationalism remained, in Scotland, latent and unexploited.

The characteristic stamp left on Scotland by its initial development was very different. In an apt passage describing the history of the Kirk in the 18th century, Ian Clark writes: 'The Moderates can perhaps be compared to typical 18th century "Improvers", who canalized the stagnant stream of the Kirk to form an attractive ornamental water, spanned by elegant balustraded bridges and flanked by well-planted policies and the classical country seats of gentlemen who (of course with a Moderate as tutor) had made the Grand Tour in their youth.'(11) So, under these influences, even the Kirk—that incorrigible core of Scottishry, that veritable rib-cage of our civil society—was inducted into Civilization. At least in the case of its elite of luminaries, among whom (the same author says): 'The driving force... was a mood of cultural liberation and optimism which made the Moderate clergy aspire to play not merely a national but a European role'.

This patrician culture was not adaptable to the new, typically modern conditions created by Scotland's industrial revoltuion. 'Before the century was out', continues Clark, 'Nature began to reassert herself, and landscaping in the Moderate manner passed out of fashion'. New social earthquakes overthrew the balustrades and Polite terraces, a new landscape of social class rendered the Classical achievements incongruous and anachronistic. It had, after all, been in certain respects a superficial landscape. And its profoundly non-democratic and anti-populist character made it largely useless as an instrument of hegemony in the new conditions. Under the latter—say from the 1780s to the 1830s—Ferguson points out how 'every aspect of Scottish life was being subjected to change—sometimes slow, sometimes rapid, but seemingly inexorable. Furthermore, it was revolutionary change, not a mere shift of emphasis within the same system. It affected material conditions, these in turn brought social change, and contingent upon this... there arose new beliefs and values'. An emphatically modern society was coming into being in Scotland, an urbanized and industrial society with a rapidly-growing proletariat. It was through this formation that 'the full implications of the changes wrought in 18th century Scotland still remained to be worked out'.(12)

The normal implication of such changes was nationalism. It was in forced reaction to (or anticipation of) such revolutionary material conditions and changes that the new, nationalist beliefs and values imposed themselves across Europe. It was in this transformed milieu that it became indispensable to 'raise the great mass of the population to a particular cultural and moral level' (in Gramsci's words), 'a level... corresponding to the needs of the productive forces for development, and hence to the interests of the ruling classes.' This could only be done by means of a new, more accessible culture, one located on a far more particularistic and popular basis. It had to be far closer to the people, to their real ethnic and historical character, their language or modes of expression, and so on. It could only be Romantic in form, not Classical. Only this way could nationality be elevated into 'nationalism' and an effective mobilization of popular class forces be obtained; equally one may say that, wherever the harnessing of such forces had become less important, this was the only way they could be **contained.**

The **emergence** of modern Scotland was marked by constant social and radical agitation. This proceeded parallel with that in England but, as E.P. Thompson notes in the preface to **The Making of the English Working Class,** it was 'significantly different': 'Calvinism was not the same thing as Methodism, although it is difficult to say which, in the early 19th century, was worse... And the popular culture was very different'.(13) It also poses a significantly different question. This is of course why, under these quite different conditions, it did not result in agitation for **separatism.** In his discussion of England's popular radicalism, Thompson shows how its more revolutionary tendencies were betrayed by lack of support from above: whatever their dissatisfaction with the **ancien regime,** the new bourgeoisie feared the forces beneath them too much to take this path. Not being compelled along it—because they had already achieved adequate economic emancipation as a class—they blocked it, in an ever-closer alliance with the older landed Establishment. One may say something similar about Scotland. But the important difference is that here they were **also** obstructing and diverting the separatist or nationalist trends which were still implicit in the persistence of such a distinct civil society.

Social Heterogeneity

It still may not be grasped quite what an anomaly this presents. People look back nowadays with puzzlement at the country's 19th century lack of nationhood, its near-total absence from the great and varied stage of European nationalism. With resentment or relief (depending on their politics) they wonder: what **was** missing? In every **superficial** respect one—language—Scotland was quite exceptionally well equipped for the usual nationalist struggles. Unless one accepts a naive language-theory of nationalism, therefore, it is necessary to look a lot deeper. On the surface, around 1820-30, only one other place looked more like a nation-to-be than Scotland: that other recently deceased State, the epitome and inspirer of so much of the romantic nationality struggle of the century, Poland. Nationalism involves the reanimation of one's history. And there was nowhere else more—to coin a phrase, the needed contrary of 'history-less people'—'history-ful' than the Scotland of Sir Walter Scott.(14)

The cultural 'raw material' for nationalism—old traditions, folk-heroes, anti-Englishry, etc., etc—was not only abundant. One can observe it being fashioned in the usual way in (to take the most obvious example) the radical Robert Burns. This was the Burns who 'knelt at the tomb of Sir John the Graham, the gallant friend of the immortal Wallace' and 'said a fervent prayer for old Caledonia over the hole in a blue whinstone, where Robert de Bruce fixed his royal standard on the banks of Bannockburn...'(15) But this historical nostalgia was associated with his sympathy for the American and French Revolutions. 'For Burns in 1793'—the year in which he composed **Scots wha hae**—'Bannockburn is directly associated with the French Revolution', notes Janet Adam Smith, in the sense that 'Scotland's fight for independence could be the channel of expression, the "objective correlative", for feelings of independence that were not confined to Scotland... The swords and staves of Bruce's army must become the carronades sent... by Burns to the French Convention'. This was exactly the sort of utilization of historical materials which generally marked the formative, ascendant phases of nationalism in Europe. After Burns, hundreds of kindred spirits were to respond to the revolutionary impact with a similar new mythology, a similar vindication of their own special inheritance and its (real or supposed) universal meaning.

In Scotland however, this promising 'raw material', this newly-rediscovered historical character, could not possibly be developed in the usual way. Here, such ethnic and historical **differentiae** could not be mobilized and made part of a new national, romantic culture. Scottish civil society had advanced too far, too quickly. The new bourgeois social classes inherited a socio-economic position in history vastly more favourable than that of any other fringe or backward nationality. They were neither being ground down into industrial modernity, nor excluded from it. Hence they did not perceive it as alien, as a foreign threat or a withheld promise. Consequently they were not forced to turn to nationalism, to redress the situation. They reacted to the inexorable and revolutionary changes of the crucial period even more fiercely than their English partners—with a conservatism amplified, perhaps, by the uneasy sensation of how much more there was to repress and divert in Scotland.

Scots differentness could not be harnessed in the way that the young Burns and other radicals imagined. But it did not disappear, for that reason. It simply became a problem. This problem was a new one, specific to 19th and 20th century conditions; and I shall go on to argue that in certain respects it was **culturally** insoluble (and led therefore to a persistent alienation of the intelligentsia) although it was **practically** solved by the crude external instrument of imperialism. It was culturally insoluble because the vital transitional period, from the 1790s to the 1830s, had ushered in a new age of more organic communities—of the modern societies in which, to employ Gramsci's terms again, ruling classes had to 'construct an organic passage from other classes into their own', by means of a new, more effective 'apparatus of political and cultural hegemony'. Scotland could not become an 'organic' national community in this sense, with its own distinctive union of civil society and State. But it could not remain in the 18th century either. The problem of its bourgeoisie therefore became—put in the starkest terms—one of **neutralizing** or repressing the country's more distinctive and proto-national features.

It was only after this that the model of Scottish development indicated above—heterogeneity as between society and State—poses dramatic questions. Earlier on, it is only by a sort of romantic retrospection that the Scottish ruling class and intelligentsia can be depicted as 'betraying' their particular ethnic-national inheritance. If they spurned Scotticisms and 'uncouth manners', it was because, like similar classes from Norrland to Andalusia and from Flanders to Ruthenia, they believed in a Universal and Enlightened civilization of which—sooner or later—everybody educated would be members. There was nothing reprehensible about being a 'province' in an expanding world like this. But the world did not continue to develop in the same way: it broke down into the separate, national, mass societies of the following century—creating quite new general conditions for culture. And under these conditions Scotland was (so to speak) 'stranded'. It was in an odd, limbo-like state, betwixt and between, where it has remained ever since. It was too much of a nation, had too different a civil society, to become a mere province of the U.K.; yet it could not develop its own nation-state on this basis either, via nationalism.

Coping with this anomalous situation accounts for a good deal of the Jekyll-and-Hyde physiognomy of modern Scottishness. Before going on to consider the phenomenon, however, one very important additional modification is required. In the schema traced out so far it is the precocious progress of Scottish civil society in the later 18th and early 19th century that plays the main role. But of course, the reference here is entirely to Lowland Scotland, the geographical area of the Enlightenment and the Scottish Industrial Revolution alike (as earlier, it had been that of the Scottish Reformation).

This zone's vigorous bourgeois advance was counterpointed, in the era we have been looking at, by the wholly different fate of the Highlands. Different as English-speaking Scotland was from its southern neighbour, it actually contained a much greater internal differentiation within its own historical frontiers. The 'problem' described above enclosed another, much acuter problem inside itself. Across the Highland Line there lay a social formation distinct in language and customs, and at a completely different stage of social evolution. Gaelic-speaking Scotland had remained predominantly pre-feudal, while the Lowlands had evolved into a bourgeois society. In the 1830s, observes A.J. Youngson, 'there were still obviously two worlds in Scotland, a poor highland world and a comparatively prosperous lowland world'. Far from the former showing any signs of catching up with the latter, to form one homogeneous civil society, 'The idea of building up the highland economy was over, and was not to be revived for more than a hundred years' (until after 1945).(16)

In developmental terms the contrast is elementary: Lowland society's modern 'problem' was constituted by its fulminating, almost over-rapid advance unaccompanied by what were to be the typical (national) superstructures of State and cultural hegemony; Highland society was incapable of 'advancing' at all, in this sense. It started from too far back (having been left relatively untouched by the weak authority of the Scottish monarchy, during the period of absolutism) and was then exposed too abruptly, and too brutally, to the very dynamic capitalist societies in proximity to it. Ordinarily—as a typical piece of 'backward' Europe, like a part of the Balkans situated in the West—it should have reacted to the dilemma by generating its own nationalism, upon the basis of its own marked socio-cultural differentiae. Such a separatism would of course have been directed as much against the Scottish Lowlanders as against the English. This would have taken a long time, and many hard and complicated struggles—in some parts of Eastern Europe, it was to take well over a hundred years. But in fact the process was unable even to get started in Celtic Scotland, for the simple reason that it was stopped in its tracks by the overwhelmingly powerful reaction to the 1745 rebellion.

In this one, exceptional case, the juxtaposition of 'backward' land and 'advanced' (bourgeois) culture was so violently unequal, so hugely disproportionate, that the former had literally no chance—not even the common, difficult, fighting chance of so many nationalist movements. In 1745 an army from these backwoods had struck to within 120 miles of London, bearing with it the menace of restored absolute monarchy. This incredible near-reverse of fortunes decided the outcome. The Gaeltacht was to be allowed no farther opportunity of disrupting civilized progress. In the subsequent English and Lowland invasion its old social structure and culture were pulverized too completely for any later nationalist response to be possible. This would not have been so easy (as other examples show) if there had been a Gaelic middle class and some Gaelic towns—if social conditions had developed even to this later-feudal stage. As things were, these elementary springs of collective resistance—of national as distinct from merely individual or small-community revolt—were lacking, and the near-liquidation of a nationality was possible.

'Scotland', in the sense of Lowland civil society, was a partner with England in this process. It represented one of the strongest common interests of the Scottish and English bourgeoisies. However, the catastrophe of Celtic Scotland had a curious effect upon the Lowlanders. It has haunted them in a remarkable way from the early 19th century to the present day.

II

'We had better remain in union with England, even at the risk of becoming a subordinate species of Northumberland, as far as national consequence is concerned, than remedy ourselves by even hinting the possibility of a rupture...'
Sir Walter Scott, 'Letter...on the Proposed Change of Currency' (1826).

'So his tendency was always to the whole, to the totality, to the general balance of things. Indeed it was his chiefest difficulty (and an ever-increasing one that made him fear at times cancellation to nonentity) to exclude, to condemn, to say No. Here, probably, was the secret of the way in which he used to plunge into the full current of the most inconsistent movements, seeking, always in vain, until he was utterly exhausted...to find ground upon which he might stand foursquare... He was always fighting for the absent, eager for forlorn hopes, a champion of the defeated cause, for those portions of truth which seemed to him neglected...'
C.M. Grieve (Hugh MacDiarmid), **Annals of the Five Senses** (1923).

To a surprising extent, we are still living in the Scotland of Sir Walter Scott. He said nothing about 'modern' Scotland, in the sense of industrial or working-class Scotland. But he did show us what to do with our past. And in the context of 19th and early 20th century social development in Europe, this was a most important thing to do. One might say: he showed us, both sentimentally and politically, how **not** to be nationalists during an age of ascendant political nationalism.

The Scots bourgeois class to which he belonged had had the developmental good luck to 'take off' in the tow of England. Now, in the first half of the 19th century, their entrepreneurial capacity was granted splendid and growing opportunities. The English capitalist class did not interfere with them, to hinder or suppress accumulation or investment in Scotland. The English governing class did not close its ranks to them. In the Empire, there was room for them both.

But at the same time, the Scots middle class could not help living in a society still historically distinct from England—and one which was, as we noticed, positively replete with all the 'raw materials' of nationalism. As the cultural climate altered, as Enlightenment gave way to Romanticism, as a new sense of history spread in Europe, they were bound to acquire a keener consciousness of this. Their civil society had grown more akin to that of England, economically speaking. Yet in this deeper historico-cultural sense—a sense that was to become more and more politically important—they had also to cope with a quasi-national inheritance. The latter's proper place had been safely defined in the Augustan age: the museums and drawing-rooms of Polite Society. It could not be so safely dealt with in the new age of democracy and nationalism.

The new romantic **consciousness** of the past was, in itself, irresistable. As a matter of fact, from Ossian to Sir Walter himself, Scotland played a large part in generating and diffusing it for the rest of Europe. What mattered in Scotland itself, however, was to render this awareness **politically** null—to make certain that it would not be felt that contemporary Scotland should be the independent continuation of the auld sang. The whole emotional point of nationalism was to feel just that: our future development must spring out of this, **our** inheritance from past generations, with its special values, etc. Hence, what the new British-Scots middle class had to do was separate the inevitable new popular-national consciousness from action. One might say, very approximately: separate its heart from its head.

One has to employ such terms with trepidation. They are part of a whole language or romanticism closely intertwined with the history of nationalism; in even uttering them one feels a quicksand clutching at the ankles. It threatens to suck the victim down into the land of the 'Caledonian antisyzygy'.(17) That is, into the realm of an anguished examination of conscience and consciousness, a troubled subjective posturing, to which—for reasons I hope will be partly explained here—Scots intellectuals have been especially prone.

Taken only as metaphors, what is implied is that the complex of realities and ideas most associated with 'nationality', in that sense which had become so historically significant, had to be kept separate from 'practical', or effective politics. Those things which were most evocative, most imaginatively suggestive, had to be relegated all the more strenuously in this way. Yet, in the nature of things, such suppression could only be achieved at a certain cost. It was bound to leave characteristic marks, on both sides of the separation.

On the side of nationality—all those aspects of civil society and its past which might be seen as peculiarly Scottish—this meant a curious sort of over-emphasis on history. A new, more deeply felt historical awareness had become universal. But in Scottish conditions it was to become positively obsessional. It is this emotional displacement which lent such furious energy to Scott's great, exemplary panoramas of the country's past. This gives them that intense, elegiac character at once so seductive and so frustrating. He evoked the past (especially a relatively recent past) more powerfully than anyone else; but part of this magic is the implication that it is a past we have, in certain vital ways, irreparably lost. It is gone for good. This is why we have to be so emotional about it, and also why we have to try so hard to 'preserve', husband, patch up, and generally savour all those relics and ruins it has left behind.

On the other side—the side of the State, the manful realities of our present life, and so on—it meant an equally curious over-emphasis. Here, the stress is upon an unsentimental endorsement of the **status quo.** What is implied is sternly 'realistic' acceptance of the Union, the Great-British political hegemony, as a sort of present without history—that is, without **our** history. The private tears must never run upon this public face. It follows of course that such endorsement can never be thorough enough: nothing but the most supine, cringing, and absolute prostration will do. Hence, what accompanies the various Scottish bourgeois cults of the past is an equally constant over-adaptation to the State.

Sir Walter was the great model for this, as for so many other things. Each absurd, antipathetic detail of the **ancien regime's** Constitution was sacred to him. The same man who sobbed on The Mound at the very throught of reforming Scots Law and fulminated against the loss of the Scots Banknote, could not bear the loss of one Rotten Borough or aristocratic privilege in England. Reform and the ascent of the Whigs killed him, James Hogg maintained: 'Yes, I say and aver, it was that which broke his heart, deranged his whole constitution, and murdered him... a dread of revolution had long preyed on his mind; he withstood it to the last; he fled from it, but it affected his brain, and killed him. From the moment he perceived the veto of democracy prevailing, he lost all hope of the prosperity and ascendancy of the British Empire'.(18) The suggestion of any conflict between these two objects of devotion induced a total Tory reflex: the absolute loss of those precious 'peculiarities' of our civil society is preferable to 'even hinting the possibility of a rupture' from the United Kingdom State.

Scott was a Tory in the party sense. But this must not mislead us. For the all-British conservatism referred to here could, and did, attach itself to other British parties with equal force. Just as there was no Old Tory like a Scotch Old Tory, so there would be no Gladstonian Liberal like a Scotch one, no Imperialist like the North British variety, and no Labourite like the Glasgow Faithfuls. The Labour Party, indeed, has become the ultimate repository of this dour devotion. No speeches conjure up the old Unionist **Geist** nowadays more relentlessly than those of William Ross.

Most of the time, the conflict does not threaten in practice. It is submerged in a routine way. Scott was still struggling to define this routine, at the beginning of the century, but later on it became settled enough. The complex of Scottish 'patriotism' was subordinated in a habitual and characteristic fashion to the larger political reality of Empire. If we look ahead to that other typical Scottish intellectual, John Buchan, for example, it is to find him too bleating about the country's 'losing its historic individuality', so that '...It seems to many that we are in danger very soon of reaching the point when Scotland will have nothing distinctive to show to the world.' It was urgent, **for the sake of Britain and the Empire,** he went on, '...to intensify that consciousness of individuality and idiom, which is what is meant by national spirit... I believe that every Scotsman should be a Scottish Nationalist.'(19) Even if it meant a dose of Home Rule, he concluded.

It was not unusual for Empires to try and exploit the more picturesque and **Volkisch** sides of their provinces, to pander to petty local vanities and precious traditions (particularly military ones). The Hapsburgs and Romanovs used the technique for centuries, and Bismarck raised it to a new pitch of perfection in Germany. What is remarkable in the Scottish case is its success and solidity, and the degree to which it was self-administered. Gramsci used a story, 'The Fable of the Beaver', to illustrate the acquiescence of the Italian bourgeoisie in fascism: 'The beaver, pursued by trappers who want his testicles from which medicinal drugs can be extracted, to save his life tears off his own testicles... Why was there no defence? Because the parties had little sense of human or political dignity? But such factors are not natural phenomena, deficiencies inherent in a people as permanent characteristics. They are "historical facts", whose explanation is to be found in past history and in the social conditions of the present...'(20)

Adapting the fable to our argument one might say: in the 19th century the Scottish bourgeoisie could hardly help becoming conscious of its inherited **cojones** to some extent, its capacity for nationalism; but since this consciousness conflicted with its real, economic interests in an ususual fashion, it was forced to—at least—repress or 'sublimate' the impulse itself. The emasculation was not enforced by gendarmes and Regius Professors from London (this kind of treatment was reserved for Gaels). It was a kind of self-imposed, very successful **Kulturkampf,** one which naturally appears as 'neurosis' in relation to standard models of development. Because of its success the elements of 'pathology' inherent in it have become embedded as modern 'national traits'; but these are not really the natural phenomena, dating back to some Caledonian Original Sin, which people feel them to be. As 'historical facts', their **main** explanation is certainly to be located in the modern era itself—that is, in the last century or so, up to the present.

Cultural Sub-Nationalism

Let us consider some of the historical facts most relevant to the phenomenon. During the age of nationalism it has come to be taken for granted that the distinctively modern consciousness of nationality is 'natural': people are naturally, instinctively, nationalists (and not merely aware of being different from other folk). But in reality nationalism was a historical construct, associated with certain social strata, at a certain characteristic period of their development. Amongst these, none was more important than the intelligentsia. The new commercial and industrial middle class was indisputably the dominant force in the process; yet the way this dominance was exerted—the form of their class hegemony—owed its character to new intellectuals. It was the latter who formulated the new ideologies that were needed, and manned the first new societies, parties and other organizations. It was they who, initially, enabled the bourgeoisie to 'enlarge its class sphere technically and ideologically', and so 'pose itself as an organism... capable of absorbing the entire society', etc. By accomplishing this task, the intellectuals also won for themselves a new and greater social significance: no longer the servants of a closed aristocratic elite, they became vital elements in the cohesion of society as a whole.

Nationalism was the most important and effective of such new ideologies. Normally it developed through a recognizable number of phases, over several generations, in all those territories where new middle classes felt that tolerable 'development' for their people was impossible without rapid mobilization of their own resources and rejection of 'alien rule'.(21) Normally, too, this process was a revolutionary one—whether or not it ever resulted in a successful **coup d'etat**—in the sense that it meant trying to get rid of a non-adaptable landlord **ancien regime,** its 'reactionary' intellectual caste, corrupt and non-populist 'traditions', and so on. One may say that during this long period, over most of Europe, the standard function of an intellectual class was in this task. This is of course not to maintain that all intellectuals were xenophobes or flag-wavers. But the centre of gravity of their role as a class, their collective definition within modern social conditions, lay in the way they educated one folk or another.

In Scotland, the intelligentsia was deprived of this typical 'nationalist' role. Its new intellectual strata were to be, in a sense, unemployed on their home terrain. There was no call for the usual services. Here, the old regime and its intellectuals had crumbled away without firing a shot: they were overwhelmed by the burgeoning growth of the Scottish Industrial Revolution and the new entrepreneurial bourgeoisie linked to it. No prolonged cultural subversion was required to pull down its bastions. William Ferguson notes 'The decline of the specifically Scottish intellectualism which throughout the 18th century had without conscious effort sustained the concept of a Scottish nation'.(22) This decline was not to be counterpointed by the rise of a new 'specifically Scottish' culture, less intellectualist and more romantic, advancing the new concept of nationality appropriate to the age.

Clearly, the country did not cease to produce individual intellectuals from its own separate and quite advanced educational system. The point is simply that they could not constitute any longer a coherent, national 'class', in a sense which is quite hard to define but easy to recognise. The fact was emphasised, rather than disproved, by the well-known prominence of so many Victorian Scots in fields like medicine, engineering, and the natural sciences. As Ferguson comments again:- 'The reputation won by Scotsmen in science... did little to enhance the culture of their country. This is far from being a singular case, for science stands independent of national contexts... For good or ill, therefore, science cannot nurture the irrational bonds that make nations'. Irrational bonds: this overstates the case, and concedes too much to German-romantic theories of nationalism. The bonds are non-rational and non-intellectual, rather than those of unreason. But the underlying point is valid: a 'national culture', in that sense which had become newly important, entailed an intellectual class able to express the particular realities of a country, in a romantic manner accessible to growing numbers of the reading public—a class operating actively in the zone of general and literary culture (rather than the specializations Scots became celebrated for).

The relationship between civil society and State in Scotland precluded a fully national culture in this sense. Instead, what it led to was a strange sort of sub-national culture. An anomalous historical situation could not engender a 'normal' culture: Scotland could simply not be adapted to the new, basically nationalist, rules of cultural evolution. But since the country could not help being affected by this evolution, it produced something like a stunted, caricatural version of it. The best title for this is perhaps 'cultural sub-nationalism'.(23) It was cultural, because of course it could not be political; on the other hand this culture could not be straightforwardly nationalist either—a direct substitute for political action, like (e.g.) so much Polish literature of the 19th century. It could only be 'sub-nationalist',, in the sense of venting its national content in various crooked ways—neurotically, so to speak, rather than directly.

Among the numerous strands in the neurosis, two are especially prominent: cultural emigration, and the Kailyard School. As we shall see, the two phenomena are in fact (and contrary to appearances) closely connected. And they are connected in a way which permits one to focus much more clearly upon the significant popular-cultural reality underlying both of them: vulgar tartanry.

In the most authoritative study of the Scottish 19th century cultural scene, David Craig remarks: 'The historian is left calling Victorian culture in Scotland "strangely rootless"... We have to recognise that there did not emerge along with modern Scotland a mature, "all-round" literature...' Later, he ascribes this surprising 'void' in culture to intellectual emigration: 'During the 19th century the country was emptied of the **majority** of its notable literary talents—men who, if they had stayed, might have thought to mediate their wisdom through the rendering of specifically Scottish experience. Of the leading British "sages" of the time an astonishingly high proportion were of Scottish extraction——the Mills, Macaulay, Carlyle, Ruskin, Gladstone.'(24) Unemployable in their own country, these and many later emigres quite naturally found themselves a function in the development of English culture. For England was a milieu **par excellence** of just that 'mature, all-round' and literary thought-world Craig refers to. It was an organic or 'rooted' national-romantic culture, in which literature—from Coleridge and Carlyle up to F.R. Leavis and E.P. Thompson—has consistently played a major role.

The rootless vacuum, the great 'absence', the 'cultural schizophrenia' William Ferguson mentions in a similar context: these are metaphors, which in turn invite decipherment. What was the actual presence they denote, in Scotland—the books they wrote and read, the thoughts they had, and so on? They did not ponder mightily and movingly upon the reality of 19th century

Scotland—on the great Glasgow bourgeoisie of mid-century and onwards, the new class conflicts, the continuing tragedy of the Highlands. So what was there, instead of those missing Zolas and George Eliots, those absent Thomas Manns and Vergas? What there was increasingly from the 1820s onwards, until it became a vast tide washing into the present day, was the Scots 'Kailyard' tradition.

This was, in effect, the cabbage-patch, the home 'backyard' left behind by the emigration of so much high-culture talent. Craig traces its origins to the time of John Galt's **Annals of the Parish** (1813) and **Blackwood's Magazine,** but its major triumphs were later. The opposite of mature all-roundness is presumably infantile partiality, or fragmentariness. This label certainly fits the Kailyard industry. In his **Literary History of Scotland** J. H. Millar notes that in the 1880s two books by J.M. Barrie (**Auld Licht Idylls** and **A Window in Thrums**) '... for some mysterious reason caught the fancy of the English public to which the greater part of the dialogue must have been wholly unintelligible... The vogue of Mr Barrie's weaver-bodies and elders of the Original Secession was not long in bringing into the field a host of rivals; and the "Kailyard" School of Literature as it has been called, presently burst into existence. The circulating libraries became charged to overflowing with a crowd of ministers, precentors, and beadles notable for their dry and "pithy" wit... while the land was plangent with the sobs of grown men, vainly endeavouring to stifle their emotion by an elaborate affectation of "peching" and "hoasting"...'(25) Barrie remained the master of the **genre,** but he acquired important rivals like 'Ian Maclaren' (in reality John Watson, 'an established divine of middle age'), whose **Besides the Bonnie Briar Bush** quickly sold a quarter of a million in Britain and half a million in the USA, and S.R. Crockett (**Bloom of the Heather,** etc).

Kailyardism was the definition of Scotland as consisting wholly of small towns full of small-town 'characters' given to bucolic intrigue and wise sayings. At first the central figures were usually Ministers of the Kirk (as were most of the authors) but later on schoolteachers and doctors got into the act. Their housekeepers always have a shrewd insight into human nature. Offspring who leave for the big city frequently come to grief, and are glad to get home again (peching and hoasting to hide their feelings). In their different ways, village cretins and ne'er-do-wells reinforce the essentially healthy **Weltanschauung** of the place.

There is surely no need to go on. Everyone in Scotland knows only too well what is being referred to. The Penguin **Companion to Literature** defines the school as 'exploiting the sentimental aspects of Lowland life during the period 1880-1914', mainly through minor writers who 'pursued Scottish country quaintness into whimsical middens.' In fact it arose before 1880 and it prospers at the present day. Naturally, it has been transferred to the TV screen. **Dr Finlay's Casebook** is temporarily absent, but at the time of writing **Para Handy** and **Sutherland's Law** carry the standard on alternate evenings (in London). It is not so long since what one might call the supreme **chef d'oeuvre** of sub-cultural Scotchery flitted across the screen, 'holding up our fellow-countrymen (as J.H. Millar put it) to the ridicule and contempt of all sane and judicious human beings': **Scotch on the Rocks.** In Dundee our own cabbage-patch publishing Mafia, the D.C. Thomson gang, still thrives as George Blake observed it doing forty years ago, through 'the careful cultivation of the Kailyard strain'.(26)

Neurosis

What is the significance of this remarkably powerful and persistent sub-culture? In one sense, it may seem just another example of a widespread European trend, whereby in the 19th century provincial manners and characters were often made into **Kitsch** images for the new, mass reading public of the cities. Yet the very appeal and longevity of the phenomenon, as well as its huge popularity in Scotland itself, suggest more than this. George Blake (himself a skilled practitioner of the school) made national 'infantilism' the key to his diagnosis. What has modern literature to say about modern society in Scotland, he asks?: 'The answer is—nothing... This almost suggests a sort of national infantilism.' It is as if there were a 'conspiracy of silence' about the modern nation. All one can find is this sub-romanticism of villages peopled by morons. One is forced to admit therefore that '... what we call, loosely enough, the Kailyard strain, is persistent in Scottish writing, however much the moderns may deplore the fact, and however gallantly they seek to shock their contemporaries out of their chronic addiction to gossip around the parish pump. We always return to the point that the Scots... remain inveterately backwards in literary culture—bewildered and sentimental children bleating for the old securities of the parochial life.'(27)

There is a notable psychologism about this censorious judgement. It implies that the literary intellectuals ought to have tried harder: if only they **had** decided to write about modern bourgeois life and Social Problems, all would have been well, or at any rate better. David Craig occasionally suggests something similar: the famous emigres 'might have thought to' write in Scottish terms, if they had stayed at home. If Thomas Carlyle had chosen 'a final achieved integration with a native way of life' instead of sermonizing in London, then he and Scotland might have been better off.(28) William Ferguson comments upon the 'element of cultural schizophrenia' in 19th century Scotland: 'Loss of confidence led to a virtual collapse of Scottish culture: literature degenerated into mawkish "kailyard" parochialism and painting into "ben and glen" romanticism...'(29)

These verdicts miss an important point. The overall structure of this modern culture in fact corresponds exactly to the dilemma of Scotland's social structure since the Industrial Revolution. Emigration and Kailyardery are not merely individual, subjective responses to the situation, and it is therefore unjust to view them as treachery or loss of nerve. The cultural sub-nationalism they conspired to foster was, in its way, as much of a historical 'necessity' as the major national cultures produced in England, Germany, and the rest.

This may become clearer when one reflects on the extent to which the two main factors in the neurosis are connected. 'Thrums', 'Drumtochty' and 'Tannochbrae' were all creations of emigres. They and their unspeakable progeny were produced, also, very largely for a foreign reading public (i.e. to pander to hankerings not themselves especially Scottish in origin). The main vehicles of the school's diffusion in Great Britian were the London magazines **British Weekly** and **The Woman at Home.** These were both run, incidentally, by another classical emigre figure called William Robertson Nicoll. He is the archetypal lad o' pairts pilloried (along with Barrie and many others) in T.W.H. Crosland's **The Unspeakable Scot** (1902).(30) 'It is a singular thing', wrote Robert Louis Stevenson to J.M. Barrie, 'that I should live here in the South Seas under conditions so new and so striking, and yet my imagination so continually inhabit that cold old huddle of grey hills from which we come.' Stevenson wrote well above the Kailyard plane as a rule, yet often touched the same register in a revealing way: 'And I have come so far; and the sights and thoughts of my youth pursue me; and I see like a vision the youth of my father, and of his father, and the whole stream of lives flowing down there, far in the north, with the sound of laughter and tears, to cast me out in the end, as by a sudden freshet, on these ultimate islands. And I admire and bow my head before the romance of destiny...'(31)

Whether as the pawky simplicities of village life, or as swaggering through the heather claymore in hand, 'Scotland' in the sub-romantic sense was largely defined by emigres. The Kailyard was—and still is—very much the reverse of the coin of emigration. Its lack of 'human and political dignity' does not express some collective fault in the Scots psyche, but the 'historical fact' of the relationship between the intelligentsia and the people. This relationship was determined by the fact that the Scottish bourgeoisie did not face the need to form **its own** 'national community', through the mediation of a more rooted intellectual class and a more complex and sophisticated national culture (i.e. more 'mature, all-round', and so on). This is why it is vain to censure the writers and other intellectuals retrospectively for their failure to come up to European norms. They could not deal with modern experience in Scotland because in the relevant sense there **was no** 'modern experience': such experience was the product of culture, not its pre-existing social basis. And this culture arose in certain characteristic social and historical conditions which were, inevitably, lacking here.

Rendered jobless in these circumstances—without a middle class sufficiently exercised over the usual national problems, without a national capital-city of the kind which had become indispensable—what could the intelligentsia do? Its natural posture became to seek work outside, but at the same time (aware of its distinct origins and history) to look constantly backwards and inwards, in a typical vein of deforming nostalgia—constantly confirming a false, 'infantile' image of the country quite divorced from its 'real problems'. The real problem, of course, did not lie in the fact of factories, new cities, bourgeois family dramas, class conflicts, etc.—it lay, for the intellectuals (and therefore for the national culture) in the fact that these phenomena **did not pose** a cultural problem that had to be solved in specifically Scottish terms. We noticed the sort of 'split' in Sir Walter Scott's world-view, and how that corresponded to the Scottish bourgeoisie's peculiar position in history. Surely the later history of the intelligentsia can be seen as the continuation, the farther manifestation, of that same split? That is, of the figurative 'schizophrenia' imposed upon an intellectual stratum which, although strongly national, was in its material conditions of existence quite unable to be nationalist—unable to secrete a complete national-popular culture like its English or French peers?

Perhaps the most revealing comment of all upon the truth of the situation was provided by those emigres like 'George Douglas Brown' **(The House with the Green Shutters,** London, 1901) and 'Lewis Grassic Gibbon' (**A Scots Quair,** Welwyn Garden City, 1932-34) who became aware of the trap and tried to escape it by formulating an 'anti-Kailyard' stance of dour realism. By common critical consent, they found it extremely hard to do so, and produced work still marked by the dilemma.(32) It is almost as difficult for a Scots intellectual to get out of the Kailyard as to live without an alias (33)

The dilemma is not 'merely' an intellectuals' one. Just as the two horns of it are in fact intimately connected, so the whole thing is related to the much larger field of popular culture. For Kailyard is popular in Scotland. It is recognisably intertwined with that prodigious array of **Kitsch** symbols. slogans, ornaments, banners, war-cries, knick-knacks, music-hall heros, icons, conventional sayings and sentiments (not a few of them 'pithy') which have for so long resolutely defended the name of 'Scotland' to the world. Annie Swan and Cronin provided no more than the relatively decent outer garb for this vast tartan monster. In their work the thing trots along doucely enough, on a lead. But it is something else to be with it (e.g. in a London pub on International night, or in the crowd at the annual Military Tatoo in front of Edinburgh Castle. How intolerably vulgar! What unbearable, crass, mindless philistinism! One knows that **Kitsch** is a large constituent of mass popular culture in every land: but this is ridiculous!

Ridiculous or not, it is obviously extremely strong. In this sense, as the main body of cultural sub-nationalism, it appears to represent a national-popular tradition which has persisted more or less in the way one would expect. Precisely because it has been unconnected with a 'higher' or normal, nationalist-style culture during the formative era of modern society, it has evolved blindly. The popular consciousness of separate identity, uncultivated by 'national' experience or culture in the usual sense, has become curiously fixed or fossilized on the level of the **image d'Epinal** and Auld Lang Syne, of the Scott Monument, Andy Stewart and the **Sunday Post**—to the point of forming a hugh, virtually self-contained universe of **Kitsch.**

Pursuing the metaphor of neurosis farther, if the emigre-Kailyard dilemma can be taken to represent the plight of the nation's Ego, here surely is the Id which the intelligentsia has always had to wrestle with. On the higher plane, the level of literature and political self-consciousness, the problem appears from the time of Scott onwards as that of 'exorcising' potential nationalism in a historical situation which had become impossible for it—through (e.g.) over-adaptation to the United Kingdom or Empire, emigration, displacement of sentiment to the past, and so on. However, much of the reality in question could not be conjured away: it simply persisted in the 'repressed' state, correspondingly deformed, as an especially 'mindless' popular culture revolving in timeless circles. As we know, one principal trait of this Id-culture is an extraordinarily blatant super-patriotism—in effect, a kind of dream-nationalism which is almost the contrary of that dour, sensible, waist-coated-and-watch-chained Unionism prevalent on the country's Official Occasions. Like drink, this kind of raving ultra-chauvinism was quite harmless: as long, that is, as the 'British' ego-system remained strong enough to confine it.

There is not space here to pursue farther an analysis of what Ray Burnett calls our 'specifically Scottish heritage of myths, prejudices and illusions.' All I have tried to do is indicate in some general ways how that heritage is accessible to discussion in the Gramscian terms which he proposed. How—that is—we can relate it meaningfully to the underlying characters of our civil society, and to the latter's unusual relationship to the State which controls it. Obviously many subjects could be considered in this way, and there is a huge leeway to make up. Robert McLaughlan noted that 'Among what may be termed the Anglophobic nationalisms—Scottish, Irish, French Canadian, Afrikaaner—the first is unique in having no substantial nationalist historiography... the general weakness of Scots historical studies, which persisted until very recently, probably prevented the emergence of such a school.'(34) To take only the most obvious example: in any serious critique along these lines one is quickly brought to confront the question of the Kirk and its weight within the complex of cultural sub-nationalism. The Disruption of 1843 can still appear to many historians as 'the most momentous single event of the 19th century for Scotland, whose repercussions were felt not only in most departments of Scottish life but overseas as well.'(35) This momentous event is largely incomprehensible today; so is the real function of the national religion in 19th and 20th century development—at different moments in nationalist discussion, one finds that it is either ignored altogether as an anachronism, or else every imaginable sin and shortcoming of the national ethos is attributed to it (including of course these various 'splits' and sub-cultural faults mentioned here). So the Kirk tradition is both irrelevant to SNP Scotland **and** responsible for every one of the country's numberless unacceptable faces!

Although this and kindred discussions cannot be developed here, one or two farther points need to be made since they relate so closely to the present situation.

Over-concentration upon cultural factors (especially literature) can lead easily to an over-subjective or idealist diagnosis of the country's modern situation. This is regularly found in the annals of nationalism. It must not be forgotten that Scotland's anomalous split personality was rendered possible by—and in sense justified by—its place in a larger framework. This is what that 'paradoxical form of Scottish self-determination' Grieve-MacDiarmid referred to was really about. Ever on the scent of betrayal, nationalists have been inclined to argue that the treacheries of the Enlightenment were followed by those of the intelligentsia and the bourgeoisie in Victorian times: the mess of pottage never ceases. Yet as a way of evading historical truth, this is almost as effective as strait-laced Unionist piety. Scotland does appear as a sort of lunatic or deviant, in relation to normal development during the period in question. But one must never overlook the fact that it had found a comfortable—indeed extremely rewarding—asylum to live in, and consequently chosen to stay there. Loss of figurative 'sanity' was a heavy price, admittedly; but it was richly compensated for, at least until 1914, and every social class in Scotland shared quite consciously in that return. Imperialism was **not** imposed upon a reluctant Scots **Volk** pining for its own political identity.

Scottish non-nationalist development worked. It was because it worked, and worked for everyone except the Gaels, that a consequent form of politico-cultural nationalism did not arrive until so recently. It did not even dawn until the 1920s, after all-British imperialism had received its first severe shocks and begun to enter upon its long decline. And when it began to arrive, it could not help being plagued by the uneasy sensation that all this **ought never to have happened;** the very existence of such a bastard policy offends any nationalist's sense of human and political dignity. The easiest way out has always been to evade the issues by looking for scapegoats (the trouble being that, as MacDiarmid's many moments of mad logic make clear, nearly everyone who has lived in the country for the past two and a half centuries **can** be found guilty and retrospectively executed). Given that those most interested in the nation have so often yielded to temptation, it is really not surprising that 'no substantial nationalist historiography' has come into being. For the left—and above all for those nationalists who incline towards the left—the primary necessity is perhaps simply to look things in the face.

I have mentioned the tartan monster. Most intellectuals—and nationalists chief amongst them—have flinched away from him, dismissing the beast over-easily as mere proof of the debased condition of a nation without a State of its own. It is far more important, surely, to study this insanely sturdy sub-culture. Tartanry will not wither away, if only because it possesses the force of its own vulgarity—immunity from doubt and higher culture. Whatever form of self-rule Scotland acquires, this is a substantial part of the real inheritance bequeathed to it. Prayers to the country's 'essentially socialist' or democratic **Geist** will not make it turn a hair.

Tartanry

In considering the rapport between civil society and State, it is vital to bear in mind that these are never watertight compartments. Were one ever inclined to do so, Scottish cultural sub-nationalism would pull one up with a jerk. For among the most manifest of its characters is something which directly reflects the impress of the old British imperialist State, and reminds us sharply that it was no mere victim of history but a co-conspirator—part of the 'apparatus of political and cultural hegemony', in its own way. Popular militarism is part of that culture—a militarism far more strident than anything found in comparable levels of culture in England. This barbarism was not simply imposed from without: it represented also the 'spontaneous' contribution of Scottish society to the State, and one which deeply affected the masses.

Discussing origins of the penomenon, Ferguson points out that 'Until the end of the 18th century Scots did not share the ingrained anti-militarism of the English. They continued to take a pride in their martial traditions and one welcome aspect of the Union of 1707 was the way it consolidated the new prospects for Scots soldiers...'(36) The prospects got better and better, as imperialism prospered. They helped reconcile Highlands and Lowlands in an important sense, for after the '45 Gaelic divisions joined the British Army. 'By 1800 all the Scottish regiments, Lowland and Highland, were established, and by the end of the Napoleonic Wars each had an established reputation and a jealously guarded tradition. Quite apart from their exploits in the field these military units played a large part in Scottish life... They contributed to the maintenance of national sentiment, and the use by the Highland regiments of "the garb of old Gaul" actually gave a new and unexpected impetus to that sentiment. The Gaels, from being viewed as barbarous nuisances, became regarded as in some ways the very embodiment of Scotland. The kilt and the bagpipes acquired popularity where hitherto they had enjoyed none. The new cult was mawkish and often at variance with the facts of Scottish life...' But, in spite of these Kailyardish aspects, militarism struck deep local roots and had 'effects on the populace (which) as a whole are incalculable.' Thus—'A host of incidents could stir the blood and titillate national pride... and exotic names like Ticonderoga or Seringapatam opened up new dimensions to minds hitherto confined to neighbouring parishes and the place-names of the Bible.'

The inhabitants of Ticonderoga and Seringapatam must be pardoned for taking a different view of events. These numerous 'lands we harriet' (in Hamish Henderson's phrase) could not know they were bringing Gael and Anglophone together or broadening the horizons of Drumtochty and Barbie. However, they would be less than surprised by the deep disfigurement which really resulted from the process.

In one of his many attempts to reinvent Scottish culture single-handed, MacDiarmid comments that: 'Where Scott is strong is in the way in which his work reveals that for a subject nation the firm literary bulwark against the encroaching Imperialism is concentration on the national language and reinterpretation of the national history. Scott's work has real value where a stand is being made against Imperialism...'(37) The interest of this is not its misinterpretation of Scott, but its assumptions about Empire. By its precocious development, of course, Scotland had in Scott's own time left the category of 'subject nations' for good and joined the ranks of the 'Imperialists'. It did so in an unusual way, since it did not form its own imperialism like other small countries—Belgium and Holland, for instance. However, its role in European colonial depradation may not be inferior to theirs, and today the Cain-marks left by the adventure are deeper here.

The Scottish masses were not socialized into a unitary national culture. Inevitably they were forced to compose for themselves a bastard product that was part 'indigenous'—expressing the still quite different life and social ethic of the country—and part Great-British, or imperialist. Thus, the ultra-patriotism of tartanry is accompanied by a tradition of sentimentalized savagery which reflects Scotland's participation in two centuries of Great-British exploits, in the subjugation of many genuine 'subject nations'. All who know it from the inside appreciate that this crude Weltanschauung is also the attempt to say something unsayable, yet important, and not wholly to be dismissed for its vulgarity. But then, they must also know that obscurely-sanctioned ferocity which inhabits it, and which is never far away from the mawkish Kailyard bonhomie of 'Wha's like us?' Damned few, and all dead. Well, yes, actually we killed most of them off in our North-British uniforms.

The Jekyll-and-Hyde fragmentation of modern Scottish culture is related in an interesting way to the other great split in our history—that is, to the fact that Scotland is in a sense two nations not one, and that from the 18th century onwards the weaker of the two was systematically destroyed. Because the Anglophone reduction of Celtic society was so successful, the latter proved unable to form its own nationalist-type resistance (the reasons are entirely different from those which apply to the Lowlands). Because of this failure, many of its differentiae were appropriated by the English-speakers in the ensuing period. The latter plundered the Gaelic raw materials of nationality for their own use, so to speak. It had become safe to do so. Tribal barbarities became 'colourful' traditions.

There is in itself nothing unusual in this sort of cultural borrowing. All over Europe new nationalist movements invented or purloined histories and symbols, with small regard for historical logic or decency. However, in Scotland this borrowing—from which the very name, and so many of the icons of 'tartanry' are derived—was done not in the name of 'nationalism' but in order to enrich a sub-nationalist culture. The latter's characteristic thirst for harmless sentiments and sub-romantic imagery found perfect objects in the debris of a ruined, alien society. On a higher plane, from **Waverley** onwards the emphatic, undeniably 'historic' quality of a deceased culture provided writers with a perfect avenue for that kind of retrospective, once-upon-a-time national feeling which had become mandatory. Once the Stuarts were back in Italy for good, the **45** could become everyone's favourite tale: Prince **Tearlach's** ultimate dynastic inheritance was that boundless realm of shortcake-tins, plaid socks, kilted statuettes and whisky-labels that stretches from Tannochbrae to Tokyo.

The remarkable assemblage of heterogeneous elements, neurotic double-binds, falsely honoured shades, and brainless vulgarity which make up 'national culture' here have naturally troubled intellectuals. It is hardly too much to say that they have been unable to look at it. David Craig speaks of 'the uncertain foothold for a national literature in Scotland', and of the characteristic 'feeling that the ground in their country is shifting under their feet.'(38) When, from the 1920s forward, intellectuals began to try and look at what had happened in a more nationalist fashion, panic was the natural response. This is something of the spirit of the remarks from **Annals of the Five Senses** quoted above (as it is of **A Drunk Man looks at the Thistle,** that great national poem on the impossibility of nationalism): there is no 'ground upon which one may stand foursquare', one **is** forced to exclude, to condemn, to say No to practically everything. The only terrain available is the Kailyard, from which of course flight is obligatory—if not into emigration, then into symbolic emigration, the Cosmic Universalism MacDiarmid has made into a second home. One is driven towards 'the totality, the general balance of things' because the particular balance of things on one's country is so intolerable, because its schizophrenia threatens cancellation to nonentity.' One must fight for the absent because the present is what it is for forlorn hopes because the real hopes are so small.

There is a truth at once autobiographical and national in this, as in so many of Grieve's earlier sayings. They contrast markedly with the bloodshot lurchings and geyseric splurgings to which he increasingly gave himself, as one 'inconsistent movement' followed another. It is the lucidity of Grieve we need, rather than the dementia of MacDiarmid (not to speak of the minor bards who have lurched in his footsteps). The former reminds us that it was the situation of the intelligentsia that was hopeless, not that of the country. The problems of intellectuals in a nationalism-less nation are one thing; the real problems and 'faults' of development which produced this cultural situation are another. It is the second range of questions which really matter to the Scottish left. For the most part, left-wing intellectuals here either embraced 'nationalism' in the more or less oniric sense, or fell back more 'realistically' upon Unionism (occasionally disguised as class or other 'internationalism'). In this fashion, they were really reproducing the classical 'split personality' of the intelligentsia in their own terms.

In the new, quite altered situation it is rapidly becoming fatal to cling to these neuroses. To the extent to which a national movement really develops, a different national intellectual class must willy-nilly be constituted, one whose basis is not like that which prevailed between the ages of Scott and MacDiarmid. Are socialists to contribute to its formation? How can they, unless they have their own conception of the country's history and character, worked out through a non-romantic marxist debate in their own ranks?

III

'Le Temps tourne sur ses gonds comme une porte: et lentement, les peuples etonnes passent d'une situation a l'autre sans innocents ni coupables: ils sont la, ils n'ont pas change de place, mais un jour nouveau les eclaire. Et nous qui dependons de cette formidable mouvance, ne pouvons l'aider qu'en poursuivant notre reflexion sur nous-memes , approfondissant loyalement ce que nous fumes, ce que nous sommes.'

Morvan Lebesque, **Comment peut-on etre Breton?** (1971)

Comment peut-on etre Ecossais? I have suggested that in trying to answer this question we must take into consideration certain aspects of Scottish history since the Union. The peculiar position of Scottish civil society—too developed and too distinct to be assimilated, yet no longer requiring to make a State-form of its own—led to an interrelated series of developmental oddities. It is easiest to think of these as 'malformations' (comparing them to nationalist norms elsewhere) provided it is recognised that this kind of faulted development **worked** well enough, in an economic and external sense, under the wider conditions furnished by All-British imperialism. There may even be a case to be made out that for the industrial and commercial bourgeoisie this was a supremely, if temporarily, successful mode of development: after all, it allowed them to devote themselves to their narrower or material class ends almost entirely, with few worries about culture, nationality, or hegemony. Is this not why, among the multiple caricatures haunting Scots society, we still find that peculiarly gritty and grinding middle-class 'materialism'—a sort of test-tube bourgeois who does, indeed, think everything but business to be nonsense?

But although successful in these terms, and sufficiently popular with the masses to function as a substitute for nationalism, the system has proved temporary. Its external supports have gradually slackened and broken, until with the current economic crisis they look like disappearing. It has moved from being master of the world to being 'the sick man of Europe'. In the essay quoted above Grieve himself attributed the first stirrings of real nationalism in Scotland to the effects of the 1st World War: 'The inception of the Scottish Renaissance synchronized with the end of the War, and in retrospect it will be seen to have had a genesis in kin with other post-war phenomena of recrudescent nationalism all over Europe... It took the full force of the War to jolt an adequate majority of the Scottish people out of their old mental, moral and material ruts; and the full force of post-war reaction is bringing them to an effective realization of their changed conditions...'(39) This jolt was soon followed by that of the Depression, under which Scotland began to suffer relatively greater deprivation than many other areas of the United Kingdom. The latter's unity was reforged in certain ways by the 2nd World War and the post-war boom. Then the rot began again, this time apparently more chronically and more irreparably.

Throughout this long epoch—from the Enlightenment, by way of being the 'workshop of the world', to the long disintegration of the last half-century—Scotland conserved a remarkable amount of autonomy. In a recent resume of the country's independent traits, James Kellas writes: 'While possessing neither a government nor a parliament of its own, it has a strong constitutional identity and a large number of political and social institutions. The Act of Union... laid down that Scotland would retain for all time certain key institutions such as the Scottish legal system, and the "Royal Burghs" (local authorities). These became the transmitters of Scottish national identity from one generation to the next...'(40)

However, this 'identity' has never been entirely institutional in nature. It involves much wider questions of society and culture. George Elder Davie observes in his history of the Scottish Universities during the 19th century that it is necessary—'To discredit briefly... notions of total assimilation in favour of the rival formula of **unification in politics, separation in ethics'**, in order to grasp Scottish development. During the 18th century: 'Submergence in the political-economic system of England was combined with a flourishing, distinctive life in what Marxists conveniently, if not perhaps aptly, call the social superstructure, and a Scotland, which was still national, though no longer nationalist, continued to preserve its European influence as a spiritual force, more than a century after its political identity had disappeared. Throughout the 19th century too, in spite of increasing assimilation... the Scots stuck to this policy of apartness in social ethics.'(41) Such apartness continued to rest upon what he calls 'the distinctive life of the country... in the mutual interaction of religion, law and education.'

But this is still not wide enough. The 'identity' which it is vital for us to understand goes beyond these institutions, even in their mutual interaction; it concerns 'civil society' as a whole, and the diverse ways in which this separate character was articulated through both intellectual culture and popular or mass culture. This made us what we are. It is not a matter of the semi-autonomy of certain institutions, nor of a straightforward contest between a Scottish 'social ethic' and assimilationist influences pressuring it from without. It is a question, rather, of the profound, lacerating **contradictions** forced upon Scottish society by its anomalous mode of development.

'Identity' tends of course to be a term of approval. In the psychologistic terms which inform so much discussion of nationalism, 'identity' is what frustrated nationalities want and nation-states possess. What this myth refers to is presumably the standard type of developmental social structure associated with national-based states (which one may conveniently, if not perhaps aptly, call the normal structure-superstructure relation). In this sense, Scotland appears as a highly-developed society (as distinct from simply being a part of a larger developed area, the United Kingdom) which, nevertheless, does not possess all the standard fitments of development. It is hard to avoid metaphor in describing the situation—'decapitation', 'neurosis' or even 'schizophrenia', and so on. What these mean is that a semi-autonomous, Stateless form of development gave rise to a series of characteristic contradictions between civil society and the (non-national) State, expressed through the social culture at different levels. Expressed, therefore, in Scottish 'national consciousness', in ways which have been too little analyzed.(42)

In a more realistic, less mythical, sense one can of course say that modern Scotland has its own unmistakeable 'identity'. Is it right to refuse 'identity' to a hopeless neurotic, because he is different from others, and unhappy about the fact?

> 'Drums in the Walligate, pipes in the air,
> The Wallopin' thistle is ill to bear.'(43)

The modern Scots can complain about what they are, in the sense of not liking it; but it is mildly absurd of them to complain about lacking identity, in the sense of not being different enough from everybody else. However ill to bear, the thistle can hardly be seen as deficient in character.

I suggested earlier that this relatively well-preserved identity was one of the factors which has enabled the SNP to forge ahead so startlingly, once it had managed to break through the initial barrier. Once our 'cultural sub-nationalism' **had** become politicizable, the process of reconversion was to prove less arduous than in many comparable regions of Europe. This raises another problem, upon which it is important to say at least a word or two here. What was the 'barrier' in question, and why did it take so long for the belated modern movements of Scottish nationalism to cross it—i.e. from the 1920s to the 1970s?

The barrier appears here as another way of denoting that national 'split personality' described above. What it meant was that, in an apparent paradox, 'nationalism' was both very strong in Scotland **and** almost unbelievably feeble. This paradox arises from the different real senses being ascribed to the same word. 'Nationalism' in the sense of cultural sub-nationalism—let us say, the repressed complex of Scottishness—remained strong throughout the modern era. As Kellas says, this bears no direct connection at all with the rises and falls of SNP-type politics: 'Such consciousness is greater than the number of votes won by that party at elections. It is not necessarily concerned, as is the SNP, with "national self-determination", or with political devolution. It is rather an assertion of Scottishness on the part of an amorphous group of interests and individuals, whose identity is caught up with that of Scotland...'(44) Among such interests football is more prominent than politics, while even in more political issues '... there is rarely an overt attack on Scottish institutions from England. Instead, there is a "Scottish" and an "English" division of opinion among the Scots themselves.'

On the other hand, 'nationalism' in the fuller historical sense remained very weak—so weak that until the later 1960s it was almost wholly resistant to even the modest organization of the SNP. In the present situation typically nationalist myths about the continuous and inevitable 'rise' of the latter are bound to be invented.(45) For nationalism time is unimportant. In its nature-mythology the soul is always there anyway, slumbering in the people, and it is of no especial importance that McFinnegan opened his eyes one hundred and fifty years after everyone else. He had to get up **some** time, and what matters is the grandeur of the Wake. In reality, this politicized nationalism remained uncertain and vacillating, a matter of much-debated 'waves' of electoral support that looked anything but permanent to most observers. It could still be said in 1972 that '... The SNP has not yet established itself as a permanent force of importance in Scottish politics. Nor has it captured the full extent of national consciousness of Scotland to its own advantage.'(46)

This contradiction between a strong basis and weak political manifestation is a real one, but explicable historically. It corresponded, surely, to the main lineaments of that society-State relationship referred to previously. According to these, the specific character of that basis lay precisely in its marked dissociation from political consciousness—so that its obvious 'strength' (informing as it did most of civil society) was accompanied by 'amorphous', fragmented, parochial and other traits. Its maximal political manifestation was perhaps what Kellas calls 'The empty affirmative of most Scots to the standard survey question: "Do you think Scotland should have more control over its own affairs?"'. The dissociation signified that such 'Scottishness' was almost incapable of being mobilized in a national-political direction: its principle was a refusal of that direction. And of course, it was complemented by what one may define as 'over-Britishness' upon the place of actual, day-to-day political awareness and organization. It was this over-adaptation that turned all Scots sections of United Kingdom parties into indescribable caricatures of their English selves.

Politicised Nationalism

Looked at in this light, the puzzle is less why the SNP took half a century to break through, than why it broke through at all. There is no room here to say much about the earlier history of revived political nationalism. It is worth observing though that its dominant oddity, when compared to other forms of nationalism, is what one would expect: its whole career from the '20s to the '60s reproduces the 'split-personality' phenomenon **within the nationalist movement itself.** This took the shape, commented upon by every single observer of the SNP, of the chronic division between 'political' and 'cultural' wings of the movement—a division far deeper and more irreconcilable, one should add at once, that the customary quarrels between idealists and 'practical men' which dog all national parties.(47)

The historical 'barrier' to politicized nationalism began to be overcome when, for the first time, something like the classical 'development gap' was thrust upon Scotland. I argued above that in the country's unusual 19th century situation the middle class did not have to confront normal developmental problems: these had been solved for it by the economic revolution which had followed the Union. There was no 'nationalism-producing' dilemma, and hence no serious nationalist movement or culture. British decline alone did not create such a dilemma for the Scots. It led to uncertain stirrings, no more, and never looked likely to end in a sufficiently painful gap between English and Scottish conditions. But the impact of a new capitalism, from a fresh direction, was a different matter altogether.

Perhaps the most essential single ingredient in this dilemma has always been threat from outside. The 'under-developed' region sees development going on under foreign control, and apprehends it as a process which—if not contested and harnessed quite differently—will simply roll ove the country and exploit it. It may of course spread a little local 'development' in its wake, and distribute a few crumbs to the native middle class. The imperialists who are in charge invariably speak of 'progress' in this sense. But this sense is nothing (or so the nationalist feels) compared to what his people would get if they control the process themselves, and put it into 'their own terms'. Only in this way therefore, by a populist mobilization of the country, can the promise of development and modernization be made to outweigh its threat.

Understood in this way, the petroleum industry's incursion into Scotland is quite clearly analogous to the 'classical' historical situation associated with nationalism. It is at least a simulacrum of the dilemma that almost invariably gave rise to nationalist development. Here of course the threat from outside is not from one power, politically speaking: 'imperialism' can be identified most clearly with the United States, in the sense that most of the multinationals involved are US-based, but this indirect relationship has a logic different from the traditional one. None the less, it has given rise to a version of separate or nationalist-type development. There is a vital discontinuity in the situation—a qualitative leap, as it were—which is hidden from view by the innate structure of that nationalist ideology which has profited so largely from the change. This ideology invariably emphasizes continuity and natural 'inevitability', to the exclusion of

45

'accidents' and influences from outside. In reality, one may suspect that the process of reconversion of sub-nationalism into an effective separatism which is now going on so rapidly—by which, in Kellas's words, the SNP **is** at last 'capturing the full extent of national consciousness... to its own advantage'—would never have occurred without the shock of North Sea oil development.

To compare this situation to the historical one of mainstream nationalism is also to become aware of an important difference. The characteristic socio-economic state of 'under-development' which gave rise to the successive waves of nationalist reaction, from the era of Napoleon to that of 'de-colonization' after the Second World War, normally involved conditions considerably more backward than any in modern Scotland (with the partial exception of the Highlands). Nationalism over most of the world was, and still is, the dominant cultural form of industrialization, or 'modernization'. It is under its banner, and through its peculiar machinery, that feudal and pre-feudal societies have struggled towards literacy, economic development and mass political life, the formation of cities, and so on. Nationalism is in this sense the means by which 'modern society' is built up, in terms tolerable to the inhabitants of what would (otherwise) have been repressed and exploited backwaters, 'historyless' regions. For this reason nationalism informs most modern societies, and one may say that industrialization is (in the widest terms) what nationalism is about.

It needs little reflection to see that in Scotland and comparable regions nationalism can no longer absolve these functions. Such societies have become 'modernized' (and in certain cases, like Scotland, Catalonia, etc., become highly industrialized) without benefit of nationalism. One may not like the 'pathological' manifestations of this atypical development mentioned previously; nonetheless, it happened, and it cannot now be undone. In general, the development of capitalism required nationalism; but in particular marginal cases the system could quite well encompass such deviations, 'mongrel' developments combining features from dominant and subordinate nationalities. The complex of **real** problems facing a belated nationalism which returns to a zone of this kind is necessarily distinct from that characterizing older nationalisms. This must be a good deal of the difference between nationalism and 'neo-nationalism' (as hinted above).

This may become plainer, if one reflects more closely upon the wider field of neo-nationalism. It is a phenomenon which now affects a definite area of Western Europe, most notably the Spanish French and British States, and the Low Countries. The position in Italy and Germany is significantly different, for reasons associated with the more recent (and prototypically nationalist) development of these countries, with their defeat in the Second World War, and with the relatively advanced forms of regional government both have adopted since 1945. The other, older States were all constituted in certain key respects **before the age of nationalism proper.** They are, as a matter of fact, the 'original' nation-states which fostered modern capitalism, and whose impact upon the rest of the world precipitated the process of general 'development' (imperialism and counter-imperialism) with which nationalism became inextricably linked. For this very reason, as many scholars have indicated, they belong in a rather special category. They themselves evolved prior to the general conditions of uneven development which they foisted on the world They are not really so much 'nation-States' as 'State-nations', in which the factors of nationality had played a role quite distinct from that they would assume in nationalism proper. Put at its most simple: they were in fact multi-ethnic assemblages in which, through lengthy processes of conquest and absorption, one or another nationality had established ascendancy 'normally in late-feudal times, through the machinery of absolute monarchy). Then, when these entities were exposed to the new circumstances of the nationalist age (19th-early 20th century) they normally reacted by the maximization of this ascendancy, by reinforcement of French (Langue d'Oil), Spanish (Castilian), British (English), or Belgian (Wallon) patriotism, most often in a new imperialist framework.

This new situation enabled the historically 'composite' nature of such States to be buried politically for a time (though of course the interment was never as total as it seemed from the vantage-points of London, Paris, etc). Now, however, with the farther prolonged era of capitalist expansion since 1950 and the formation of the European Common Market, the external conditions which did so much to consolidate the old State-nations have largely gone. Their empires have disappeared, with a few insignificant exceptions. They have dwindled in status to mediocre, second-rate powers whose pretentions far outrange their capabilities. Apart from their function as the incubators of capitalism (now long in the past), they have State and military apparatuses whose main role was to terrorize each other and the 'backward' lands they had interests in. But nowadays no-one is afraid of them, and their attitudes towards one another are marked by Ruritanian envy and parish-pump bile rather than real aggression. In absurdity, the universal aspirations which still mark the speeches of President Giscard d'Estaing and Mr Wilson are on a level with the uniforms of their Palace Guards.

Once, the intellectual circles of their capitals could despise 'provincial' separatisms and parochial ways because their States stood in the van of development. They did represent civilization and a more universal culture—albeit a civilization which was imperialist in character, and transitory. But nowadays, such contempt rests on nothing but size. Madrid, London, Brussels stand for the brute facts of existence, not for what that existence means: they control larger areas and wield larger powers. Yet these areas are not large enough, in relation to the operations of modern multinational capitalism and the dominant States of our time, and their powers are feeble and antiquated by the same token. Their 'metropolitan' culture draws every day closer to that ageless joke: the idiot convinced, in spite of all the evidence, that he still has a thing or two to teach the world. As far as the United Kingdom is concerned, the Scots have at least some consciousness of their 'Kailyard' as a problem; the English are still largely unaware of having arrived there. In Edinburgh people are at least ashamed of **The Sunday Post** and STV: in London the **New Statesman** and the **Times Literary Supplement** are still taken seriously.

Thus, the bourgeois modes of domination which held such polities together have wilted. There is a most important corollary to this, which must not be overlooked. The decline of bourgeois hegemony has not been accompanied by the rise of an alternative—that is, by the emergence of an effective socialist power at the level of the old States. Had the class struggle accelerated politically at the same time, it is doubtful if Scottish and other neo-nationalist movements would have made much headway. As regards general diagnosis at least, it is hard to quarrel with 'Lutte Occitane': it has become clear since 1968 that '... Toutes les forces de renouveau ne peuvent trouver de debouches au niveau de l'Etat-Nation francais, qui apparait de plus en plus comme une "societe bloquee". S'il devait en rester ainsi, il pourrait se reproduire une situation de developpement catastrophique de l'histoire qui "pourrirait sur place au lieu de connaitre une issue positive. Seul le passage au socialisme permettrait de resoudre la crise: mais tous les recents developpements de la vie politique hexagonale ces dernieres annees montrent que ni la bourgeoisie ni les forces qui pretendent encore s'identifier aux interets historiques du proletariat ne peuvent resoudre ce qui demeure la contradiction fondamentale du mode de production capitaliste dans la phase historique contemporaine, a savoir: la contradiction existant entre une internationalisation de fait des forces productives et le maintien d'un decoupage en Etats-Nations qui sont d'ores et deja perimes...'(48) The United Kingdom's contribution to the chronicles of **la societe bloquee** needs no emphasis here: two elections in one year have returned the men who turned in hopeless circles between 1964 and 1970. In France the 'forces of renewal' led to **gauchisme** and separatism; in Great Britain they have rekindled the buried nationalist conflicts in Ireland and (now) the more deeply interred nationalities of the mainland.

Failure of Socialism

I suggested originally that two factors in combination had created the conditions for nationalist resurgence: the multinational petroleum business, and the degeneration of United Kingdom politics. But the failure of socialism is surely another way of regarding the second of these. It is the failure of the Left to advance far enough, fast enough, on the older State-nation platforms which history had provided, it is the inability of great-nation socialism to tackle advanced contradictions properly, that has made this 'second round' of bourgeois nationalisms inevitable.

To what extent is history destined to repeat itself here? The original socialist movements of the 19th and early 20th century were on the whole outflanked and contained by those contemporaneous national movements which proved stronger. When revolution came to the world of advanced capitalism, it came as fascism, the ultra-nationalist reaction to the threat of socialist and communist advance (a threat that was in fact remote). It may be worth quoting one recent historical verdict upon the conclusion of that first wave of European nationalism after World War I: 'In contrast with (the older nation states)... which enlarged the economic area and operated in the direction of expansion and progress, the newly created nation states of the 20th century became a fetter on efficiency and progress, and lent their power to the turning back of the wheels of history. Similarly, while the former... seemed to be fulfilling the destiny of a long and uninterrupted historical evolution, the latter entered upon their heritage in a psychological atmosphere of insecurity, rancour, uncertain frontiers and dissatisfied national minorities, and in consequence their search for autarky tended to be unusually aggressive and uncompromising... In a dozen different ways the peace treaties and their political consequences thwarted, hampered and obstructed the economy of Europe in a manner which had not been seen since the Industrial and the French Revolutions. At the same time, in the complex symbiosis in which the economic and the political affect each other, the capitalist economy itself appeared to have lost its capacity for expansion and adaptation... whether because of its own inner laws or because of the political responses it had stimulated.'(49)

Neonationalism need not repeat these disasters of nationalism: the world may have altered in ways that render its negative potential less great. Still, it must remain perfectly legitimate to ask whether the 'second round', the formation of still other nation states, could not lead to at least partially similar effects? It is no use at all looking to the intentions of the SNP or any other separatist movement for answers to questions like these. However new nationalism may differ from old, it has inherited much of its ideology; and it is a standard law of such ideology that '**our** nationalism will be different', not aggressive, not narrow or 'inward 'inward-looking' but progressive and 'outward-looking', not turning back the historical wheels but urging them forward (and so on). As far as Scotland is concerned, this blankness is aggravated by the intense Britishness of the nationalist movement so far ; it does show small consciousness of the huge potential for non-constitutional and non-pacific conflicts which are inherent in the situation. Westminster, which enjoyed a first moment of (entirely characteristic) metropolitan contempt for the very concept of devolution, when the Kilbrandon Report appeared a year ago, is now tumbling over itself to propitiate separatism.

But it would be absurd to confuse these antics with the reality of the English nation. It is in the logic of the whole situation that the formerly dominant nationalities will themselves be compelled by reaction to rediscover their nationalism—for that nationalism too is, in a quite different sense, 'buried' or concealed by the past equivocations of imperialism and the multi-ethnic State. They will have to 'define themselves anew' against the separtism of their former minorities (in Powell's phrase). In England's case, the prospect is sharpened by the likelihood of a phase of reaction against the prolonged economic crises which have accompanied loss of empire—a reaction which is unlikely to assume any but a nationalist form. It has already been unduly delayed, by the strength of the old political system and the fact that it has been exposed to slow wasting rather than dramatic challenges (like those which ended the IVth Republic, and ushered in Gaullism). Would we then be so far from 'a psychological atmosphere of insecurity, rancour, uncertain frontiers and dissatisfied national minorities', aggravated by bitter disputes over North Sea oil?

The contradictions and possibilities of neo-nationalism require far more study. The phenomenon is much too new to allow ready predictions as to its future course. All one can be reasonably sure of is that it will embody contradictions analogous to those of ancestral nationalism: on the one hand, the perspective of liberation to a more genuine democracy or self-rule, accompanied by emergence from debilitating provinciality and cultural estrangement; on the other hand, the tendency of the very same movement (a tendency inherent in it) towards nationaal narrowness, subjective illusion and conceit, political and economic regression, and romantic nonsense. At different times or in different conditions, one side or another may appear more prominent, or in control. But in reality both belong inextricably to the historical structure of nationalism as a mode of development—and presumably to that of neo-nationalism also. Given that the latter belongs to a new phase of development—to a far more advanced stage of capitalism and bourgeois society—it is still to be seen how the objective circumstances of these times will make its contradictions display themselves.

Reappraisal

In the existing situation, it would be invidious of anyone writing on the subject not to express as clearly as possible his own personal view of events, however tentatively. History has not yet shown what it has in store for us; but then, it never does, and ideal political positions can only be formulated retrospectively.

My main past mistake lay in assuming that the question of effective Scottish self-government would never be posed on this side of socialism. As in most errors of this kind, two different misjudgements were actually involved: overestimate of socialist potential, and underestimate of capitalism's ability to mutate further. I did not believe that the United Kingdom would take so long to free itself from the direct economic and political inheritance of imperialism, an inheritance of which the Labour Party has become a main pillar in the post-war era. Who believed, in 1964 for instance, that what the Occitan document quoted above calls a situation of 'pourrissement sur place' would persist so long? Who imagined that these stagnant equivocations would endure so unchanged, through so many external pressures and strenuous class struggles at home? Who thought in the light of later events like 1968 that political development towards socialism would continue to be so feeble, that the 'blockage' would remain so obstinate? .

On the other hand, I assumed that capitalism too was more or less committed to the existing State forms in Europe. If there was change, it lay in the direction of Western European integration—a movement outwards, seemingly opposed to separatist revivals in the old regions of the Common Market. In reality, the new and more internationalized economy has begun to provoke impulses on exactly this level, contemporaneously with the current uncertain advance towards European Union. In wholly unwitting conjunction these two forces—the decline of the old State centres, and the multinationals—have engendered a strong new reaction, a neonate separatism which has equipped itself speedily with the New Left populist and environmentalist ideologies of the 1960s (it is of no importance that they were invented with other ends in view). Mixed up with elements from traditional nationalism and 'Third Worldism', these movements are acquiring a momentum unimaginable a few years ago.

No conspiracy led to this denouement. But it goes almost without saying that contemporary capitalism can adapt itself perfectly comfortably to the creature (and even derive some advantages out ot it). Self-government has re-written itself into the agenda of the bourgeois epoch, albeit in a new form. It really makes no difference that many of the new nationalist movements think they are 'revolutionary', or that it is some kind of Communist **Geist** we see unfolding from Corsica to Cape Wrath. All nationalist trends have attracted such ideas to themselves at certain stages of their development: they need the intelligentsia, and many intellectuals are always likely to hold beliefs like these. The problem of what they mean, or can be made to mean, in the concrete historical situation of the land in question, is different altogether.

Earlier in history too, socialists were surprised by what they apprehended as the 'irrational' persistence and strength of nationality as a social force. In the time of the IInd International as well as now, it became evident that the Left had pinned far too much faith on the rationality of working-class based social struggle (understood as a potentially international force), and far too little upon the non-rational strengths of nationalism. Having made an analogous mistake (a mistake which is in reality a failure to understand the nature of capitalist development fully enough) we have to make an analogous compromise. Like it or lump it, 'logically' or no, it is necessary to accept what that development thrusts upon us. An earlier generation was compelled to swallow 'National Self-Determination' as an unavoidable phase of social evolution; we must do the same with this novel version of the same thing—this sub- or neo-national self-determination. In my view it has become totally inadmissible to oppose such tendencies in the name of an abstract internationalism, a universal socialist or class struggle that exists only in aspiration.

The question is really not at all whether new nationalism, has, or has not, a 'positive' side to it. No intellectual from a repressed or destroyed nationality has doubts about this, if he is honest with himself. Return from oblivion, the reassertion of identity, adult control of one's own affairs—it does not matter what terminology is used, the value of national liberation is plain enough. It has been plain enough to most of the world in this century, and cannot fail to be so to Bretons, Basques of Scotsmen. The question concerns the conditions under which this process occurs.

Like many others, I envisaged it waiting until circumstances would be such that it would be straightforward. Socialist conditions would actively favour it, as a collective right which would be (for the first time, in a genuine sense) natural. There would be no risk in such an environment that national self-definition would imply chauvinism—that 'national liberation' would turn itself into a new national narrowness, that nationality would again become the nationalism of an alienating State ideology.

Under capitalist conditions, as the slightest knowledge of recent history lets one know, these risks are inherent in all forms of national struggle. 'National liberation' in the essentially antagonistic universe of capitalism, with its blind, competitive, and wildly uneven development, bears a contradiction within itself. It simply cannot help lapsing into nationalism in the most deleterious sense because it is a form of adaptation to this universe. President Wilson's world of National Self-Determination (which too many socialists have translated into their own terms) was one of equal, self and other-respecting entities who—'satisfied' with their own identities, as the saying goes—could turn to wider horizons of inter-national collaboration. This bears as little relationship to the jungle realities of 1974 as it did to those of 1919.

Because of this I—again like many others—opposed the earlier bourgeois nationalism of the SNP, which seemed to amount to a carefully-cultivated thirst for this kind of doom. Intellectuals on the Left have spent much time trying to categorize forms of nationalism into the clean and the dirty, the 'progressive' and the 'reactionary' (or imperialist), and so on. And it is of course true that nationalisms differ according to where their nations stand in the general development process, those on top being more likely to be oppressive and unliberating in content. However, this sort of classification often conceals the fact that **all** national ideologies are in reality 'clean' **and** 'dirty', contain progressive and highly regressive elements. Were this not so, nationalism could not possibly have had the central historical function which it has enjoyed. As far as Scotland and the old literary and political nationalism was concerned, it looked like a version in which—both virtue of its professed content, and of the circumstances surrounding it—these regressive factors were obviously dominant.

Now that some of the bigger jungle animals have turned on the country, and shaken it into **actual** nationalism (as distinct from the largely notional dream-world of yesterday), the question is evidently different. The theoretical issue of the contradictoriness of nationalism becomes the practical problem of how, in this case, its benefits can be secured and its dangers guarded against and minimized. There are no examples of nationalist mass movements which have receded, once a certain threshold has been attained: nationalism is irreversible. Although it is still not quite clear that this threshold has been crossed by the SNP, it would be safest to assume that it will be, and that in this respect new movements will be like the old.

Socialists who accept this likelihood usually pose the practical problem in this light: nationalism here will be different, because the Left will be stronger—**we** shall prevail, and prevent it from becoming vulgar xenophobia (there are many variants of the idea, ranging from William Wallace to John Maclean, but these emphases are irrelevant to the argument). In my opinion this is a mistaken and idealist perspective, in the sense that—while one hopes it is true—the mythological guarantees which it offers are false. On the face of it, it would be unlikely that a conception so closely linked with every nationalist movement over the past century and a half was **not** a myth. In Scotland all one can be really sure of is that, given the country's modern history of 'split-personality' (or 'non-organic community'), **both** the Left and the Right are bound to be a good deal more vociferous and militant than English norms have accustomed us to. It is very unlikely that class conflicts in Scotland would assume the decorous political forms associated with the Westminster Constitution. Who would win them is another matter altogether, and one on which speculative discussion is fairly useless, as well as difficult.

The real practical problem is different. It concerns not the (real or imaginary) inner potential of a self-governing Scotland, but its external relations. These are far more likely to determine how its nationalism develops than internecine disputes, above all in the period following independence. This has always been true in the past, and it is hard to see why it should cease being true for us. Again, one suspects that awareness of this is to some extent concealed by a certain all-British complacency which still shrouds nationalist mentality: it could not happen here. But 'it' (in the sense of the worst) is too normal in the history of national-independence movements for this to be very plausible. To put it somewhat schematically: the standard situation is for a 'new nation' to be surrounded by enemies and competitors in the development jungle, whose combined pressures force it in upon itself and demand constant reinforcement of exactly that nationalism which is so distinct from the expansiveness of 'national liberation' (even if much of the content of the two things is the same).

Scotland and Europe

Consequently, one must ask what are the external relations which might (at least) minimize the risk? My view is that there exists at least an embryo of such a system of external relations, in the shape of the European Communities; and that a self-governing Scotland should try at all costs not only to stay in Europe but to help the Common Market grow into a federal or confederal system of States. This opinion coincides with one quite widely held in other regionalist and neo-nationalist movements of the Continent. There, such movements have been in the EEC from the beginning, and they belong in any case to a part of the world where it is (for obvious historical reasons) much easier to grasp the real double-sidedness and perils of political nationalism. A Breton socialist, for example: because Brittany (and even France) is too small an area to conceive of a valid socialist system arising in it, he argues that—'c'est dans le cadre de l'Europe elargie qu'il convient d'etudier les perspectives d'avenir de chaque region, perspectives s'inserant dans un programme d'ensemble d'amenagement de l'espace europeen. Mais il est clair que cette Europe ne peut etre l'Europe liberale, l'Europe des affaires. Pour construire cette Europe qui serait celle des peuples et des regions, l'election d'un Parlement europeen au suffrage universel constitue une condition fondamentale. A la faveur de l'elan populaire provoque par cette premiere consultation electorale, de l'Ecosse au Mezzogiorno, les citoyens Europeens prendraient alors conscience que l'union politique ne suffirait pas a rendre l'Europe maitresse de son destin...que notre vieux continent peut et doit concevoir son propre modele de civilisation. Une civilisation qui ne saurait etre basee sur la seule recherche de l'accroissement des biens de consommation, du profit individuel, mais sur la qualite de la vie... (qualite) liee aussi a l'epanouissement de cultures diverses, originales, plongeant leur racines dans un lointain passe'. This is, he notes, what must distinguish Europe from America: in the former—'l'uniformisation des techniques sera corrigee par l'epanouissement de cultures originales'.(50)

This consideration is reinforced by another one. If there is one really manifest difference between the circumstances of old-style nationalism and neo-nationalism it lies in the fact that the latter emerges into a world which is economically much more closely-laced and interdependent. The old ideal of economic self-sufficiency which so often accompanied ancestral nationalism has become anachronistic—and this is reflected well enough in the propaganda of the SNP and parties like it. It is no longer possible to think of 'going it alone' in quite this fundamental sense (even if it were desirable). What are the political implications? The main one is, arguably, that external relations have changed from being of primary importance to being of absolute, all-embracing importance. Because the world has shrunk and capitalism has grown more effectively international in character, it has become that much more difficult to be 'independent' in any meaningful sense. The foreign affairs of the United Kingdom and France over the last decade constitute an eloquent commentary on this fact.

Because it is so much more difficult, it is correspondingly more important. This paradox is surely plain the the Scottish case, for here what is supposed to be the main 'internal' resource and support of an independent Scotland, North Sea oil, is from the outset also a question of 'external relations'. Everyone knows that the international oil corporations are related to a complex of potentially hostile foreign powers, chief among them the United States and England. It is only the power to bargain with these that will convey any degree of reality to independence (at least, as the term is interpreted in a nationalist perspective). From the beginning, in regions like Scotland, self-government appears as either a harmless mode of local government—which is of course what Westminster hopes to achieve, with the forthcoming elected assembly—or else the **real direction** of one's own affairs, which entails control of external relations.

Acute dilemmas of this kind are inseparable from such belated nationalist development.

Admittedly, the sense of the argument is that if Scotland does achieve some measure of this real independence, it has to give it away again: the psychological problems of this for nationalism need no underlining. Yet the paradox is only apparent, for the Europe which Scotland should join need not and will not resemble the oppressive great powers of yesterday—those dominant nationalities whose exclusive cultures and State power created the situation from which we are escaping. I have no space here to discuss the European question in the way it deserves, or to combat the fashionable myths of capitalist conspiracy and bureaucratic domination that inform too many socialist attitudes towards it. In a previous book, **The Left Against Europe?** (1973), I argued that it was a mistake for the British Left to oppose entering the EEC, and it seems to me that this will apply far more forcibly and urgently for any new Scottish organized Left which emereges from the present situation.

Our future lies with those countries and peoples that are at a comparable stage of development, and which have endured a past similar to our own. They have embarked with us on the attempt to escape from this inheritance of estrangement and subordination, and they face the same perplexing problems, the same dangers, and much much the same opposing powers. I do not intend to exaggerate these common features. As always, European circumstances reflect marked diversity of development—for example, most of the continental provinces still have a peasant base which vanished from the Scottish Lowlands long ago, while political and cultural conditions vary extremely as between Alsace and Wales, or between Ulster and the Italian South. Nevertheless, I think they belong to a common family whose basic developmental dilemma has become the same.

When set in this perspective, Scotland acquires some genuine international political significance for the first time since the 18th century. For it is here, amongst other members of this family of claimants, that what she does will have the profoundest repercussions. Those relative advantages the country has retained may now enable her to advance more quickly than them to some kind of restored nationhood—in which case, it is beyond doubt that she will become the dominant example of neo-nationalist success in Western Europe. That success—whatever it amounts to in realty—is bound to be interpreted and misinterpreted, studied and misunderstood, envied and imitated by every other active separatist movement. Whether there are eventually two or five governments in the British Isles will make no difference to Scandinavia; it will be of some real importance in France. For this reason also Scottish attitudes to Europe are critical. Perhaps nobody yet knows just what ' independence' can or will signify in today's European conditions; but I have the uneasy feeling that it will not mean much, if based upon a wish to retreat from Europe altogether.

As I suggested above, it is part of the new drama of regional Europe that those capitals which once so confidently represented universal light and culture (as opposed to rural-provincial kailyardery in its many forms) have in fact lost much of their function. They have lost their real nerve, though not yet the smug and impudent pretence of it. It does not follow from this that renascent provinces and resurrected nationalities can somehow take over their old functions and themselves turn into centres of a greater more enlightened culture. It does not follow that Rennes should become a smaller Paris, or Edinburgh a replacement for London. This notion (which is a natural by-product of nationalism) ignores the sense in which these great-nation metropolises were themselves the nationalist usurpers of European culture—the usurpers and destroyers of that grander, more rational, and more cosmopolitan civilization which went before.

Here again, it seems to me that the **real** problem which is posed by separatism only makes sense in European terms. Culturally, as well as politically and economically, the reality of such belated 'independence' in the European context is bound to be quite different from what nationalist ideologies imagine. Culturally speaking, it is ludicrous to think of small nationalities doing **by themselves** what the greater ones are failing to do; but it is not at all absurd to think that in concert, in a larger framework more satisfactory to their needs and aspirations, they could contribute meaningfully to something much greater. Politically speaking, the risks of 'Balkanization' are obvious; I think it is wrong to believe they could be countered by incredibly crafty foreign policies designed to steer such tiny ships of State neatly between Standard Oil and the Kremlin, or between the Holy Loch monsters and neutrality. Economically, those very forces which have set such remarkable political trends in motion **also** demand to be approached, and mastered, on a different scale altogether.

For marxists, this kind of problem is not wholly unprecedented in their history. During the latter days of the Hapsburg Empire, they were confronted by dilemmas in certain respects similar. There was the question was whether the mixed Slav and German peoples of the huge monarchy could be spared the ordeals of an entirely separate and nationalist evolution, with the inevitable human sacrifice and travail this involved, as well as the fragmentation of the Empire's larger economic space into relatively unviable entities. Was it not possible to preserve some of the advantages of the larger development area—above all economically—and yet concede to the competing nationalities what they needed, above all culturally and in the fields of language and education? It was in its wrestle with this acute problem that the marxism of Austro-Hungarian Social Democracy rose to its greatest heights. From its efforts there arose in turn the major debate on the National Question that went on uninterruptedly until the First World War. It is often forgotten that the positions now associated with the names of Lenin and Rosa Luxemburg were originally no more than critique of the theses of Austro-Marxism, as presented in once celebrated works like Otto Bauer's **Die Nationalitatenfrage und die Sozialdemokratie** (1907) and Karl Renner's **Staat und Nation** (1899). History was to make the rejoinders much better known that these original propositions.(51)

This is principally because it proved impossible to resolve Austria-Hungary's contradictions as they had hoped. Their ideas were carried away with the Empire which foundered in 1918, as National Self-Determination triumphed all over Central and Eastern Europe in the wake of the Allied victory. Marxism's problem in that era had been to come to terms with nationalism, in a still feudal monarchial State—to realize what was best and minimize what was worst about it. **before** the great primary wave of European nationality-struggle was even half spent, and in most backward political conditions. Today, its new problem is coming to terms with a belated 'second round' of such struggles, **after** the mainstream of European nationalism has become fixed in its channels, and while a new supranational polity is still less than half achieved. Making allowances for the obvious contrasts, it remains true that marxist socialism confronts questions strikingly analogous to those of Bauer and Renner.

Need our dilemmas prove as irresolvable, and as disastrous in their consequences, as those of Hapsburg Social-Democracy? I am well aware that these too may prove fights for the absent, forlorn hopes founded upon portions of the truth which seem to me neglected. However, the general balance of things they represent is at least derived from more than the rhetoric of empty, pious internationalism, and an opportunistic exploitation of the idea of national liberation. The one thing which would be truly intolerable would be to approach these novel problems of nationality and self-government, having learned nothing from the old ones (except how to register ignorance with the wrong slogan).

At least of one thing we may be sure, and confident: these absent, universal hopes and neglected truths coincide with all that is genuinely great and memorable in our country's history. George Elder Davie observed in 1969 (a propos a seminar on nationalism at Edinburgh University), that 'On the broad view of a last two hundred and fifty years, it seems clear that one of the chief ways in which this National aspiration found a certain due outlet and satisfaction... was the signal contribution of the severer disciplines of the scientific and philosophical kind... It is here, in the international intellectual field, that Scotland in the last two centuries has made its impact.' Lamenting the lack of a paper on the subject, he went on that this more than anything else '... might have brought home to the participants that they are dealing with a nation which has made a distinctive and fundamental contribution to the civilization of our own times. Indeed, in order to understand   the national motif in Scotland it must be borne in mind that... right down to the third and fourth decades at least of the present century, the intellectual genius of Scotland was still very much alive in its distinctive themes.' So, the real question of the moment must be '... the continuing impulse to keep alive the tradition of distinctive universalism in research, in an atmosphere where sympathy with it is too often imperfect and where sometimes an apparently alien set of values complacently attempt to overlook it.'(52)

That 'distinctive and fundamental contribution' was made by the Scotland of the Enlightenment, and its 'universalism' was that of a nation which, knowing itself to be such yet innocent of nationalism, formed part of a wider, expanding European civilization whose fertile variety never precluded common ground—on the contrary, it was taken for granted that such common ground would grow more important. Nationalists are fond of grandeur. But it is here that own grand national motif resides—one as great as history has recorded of any small country, yet utterly distinct from those of romantic nationalism. If we do not believe it unimportant (as nationalists have always done) then it can be perceived as something that inclines us in the directions I have tried to outline: towards a new interdependence where our nationhood will count, rather than towards mere isolation; towards Europe, as well as towards self-rule; towards that new, more democratic and socialist Englightenment which marxism prefigured, but will never realize until nationality ceases to be nationalism and becomes a more direct contribution to the universal.

I would like to acknowledge help from comrades of "New Left Review" in working on this essay, as well as the support of the Transnational Institute in Amsterdam.

(1) **Times,** editorial of August 19, 1974, 'All Assembly Men Now.'

(2) Antonio Gramsci, **Selections from the Prison Notebooks,** trans. and edited by Q. Hoare & G Nowell Smith (1971), pp.258-60. There is some language barrier for the English-language reader due to Gramsci's formation as a Crocean Idealist. But for an argument substantially similar on the subject of nationalism and written in contemporary sociological language, see Ernest Gellner, 'Nationalism', in the volume **Thought and Change** (1964).

(3) I have tried to deal with the more theoretical questions of nationalism's sociological character and place in history, in a book to be published shortly called **The Modern Janus: nationalism and uneven development** (NLB).

(4) T.C. Smout, 'Union of the Parliaments', in **The Scottish Nation: a history of the Scots from independence to Union,** ed. G. Menzies (1972), pp.158-9.

(5) Rosalind Mitchison, 'The Government and the Highlands 1707-1745', in **Scotland in the Age of Improvement: Essays in Scottish History in the 18th Century,** edit. N.Phillipson & R. Mitchison (1970), pp.24-5.

(6) J.M. Simpson, 'Who Steered the Gravy Train, 1707-1766?' in **ibid.,** p.49. For the background to the letter see **The Life and Letters of Duncan Forbes of Culloden,** by G. Menary (1936), Ch.IV, 'The Glasgow Malt Riots of 1725.'

(7) The patriotism found in some circles of the old ruling class had little in common with nationalism (which in the modern sense always has a populist connotation). For example Andrew Fletcher of Saltoun, that doyen of modern nationalists, proposed in the second of his **Two Discourses on the Affairs of Scotland** (1698) that the harmless unemployed should be returned to a form of slavery. 'Back to servitude' was the cry, notes his biographer: 'He risked his reputation as a lover of liberty by proposing what was difficult to distinguish from a system of domestic slavery.' The 'dangerous unemployed' were to be sold to the plantations or deported to Eastern Europe to fight the Turks, at the same time. W.C. Mackenzie, **Andrew Fletcher of Saltoun: His Life and Times** (1935), Ch.VIII, 'On Unemployment.'

(8) William Ferguson, **Scotland: 1689 to the Present** (vol. IV of the 'Edinburgh History of Scotland', 1968), p.197. See also T.C. Smout, **A History of the Scottish People 1560-1830** (1969), especially Ch.X, 'The Transformation of the Economy.'

(9) David Hume, letter to Gilbert Elliot, 1757, in **Letters,** edit. Greig (1932), vol.1, p.255. For the background to the letter, see E.C. Mossner's **The Life of David Hume** (1954), Ch.27, 'Scotland's Augustans'. Mossner maintains that Hume was 'certainly overstating the case for Scottish Literature', **ibid.,** p.389, but is there any overstatement in saying that no other region of Europe comparable in population, size, and previous history was more 'distinguishe'd for Literature' at this period? A contemporary list of the 'many Men of Genius this Country produces' is given in Smout's **History**: 'Hume, Smith, Burns, Black, Watt, Telford, Robert Adam and Hutton in the first rank, Ferguson, Miller, Reid, Robertson, Allan Ramsay junior, Raeburn, William Adam, Rennie, Boswell and Hogg in the second, and a third rank crowded with talent...'(p.470).

(10) In an article in **New Left Review No.83** (Jan-Feb.1974) I tried to explore this basic aspect of Scottish development farther.

(11) I.D.L. Clark, 'From Protest to Reaction: the Moderate Regime in the Church of Scotland, 1752-1805', in **Scotland in the Age of Improvement,** op.cit., p.223.

(12) W. Ferguson, **Scotland,** op.cit., p.233.

(13) E.P. Thompson, **The Making of the English Working Class** (1963) 'Preface', p.13.

(14) Here again I must refer the reader back to the **New Left Review** article referred to above (note 10), for a longer disucssion of the point, and of Scott's function as the symbolic voice of anti-nationalist national consciousness. The term 'historyless people' was used by Marx and Engels (amongst others) to denote those so backward and ill-equipped for national struggle they had no hope of making it. The implication was usually that they were unjustified in trying, and should have resigned themselves to assimilation by the 'historical nations'. The best discussion of this mistake is in Roman Rosdolsky, **Friedrich Engels und das Problem des geschichstlosen Volker** (1964).

(15) Burns, **Letters** (1931), as quoted in Janet Adam Smith, 'Some 18th Century Ideas of Scotland', **Scotland in the Age of Improvement,** op.cit., pp.118-23.

(16) A.J. Youngson, **After the Forty-Five: the Economic Impact on the Scottish Highlands** (1973), pp.189-90.

(17) The 'Caledonian Antisyzygy' is one of the interesting minor examples of myth made out of affliction. Although the cultural reality of split personality to which it refers was of course much in evidence in the 19th century (**Dr Jekyll** the **Justified Sinner,** etc.), the formulation itself seems to come from G. Gregory Smith's **Scottish Literature: Character & Influence** (1919). Here the disease is diagnosed as racial propensity to alternate between dour matter-of-fact 'realism' (pp.5-6) and unrestrained fantasy ('confusion of the senses, the fun of things thrown topsy-turvy, the horns of elfland...' pp.19-20); 'It goes better with our knowledge of Scottish character and history to accept the antagonism as real and necessary', Smith concludes. The idea proved only too popular with the **literati,** and reappears in e.g. Edwin Muir's **Scott and Scotland** (1936) and in C.M. Grieve, on those many occasions when 'MacDiarmid' got the better of him: 'The Caledonian Antisyzygy... may be awaiting the exhaustion of the whole civilization of which English literature is a typical product in order to achieve its effective synthesis in a succeeding and very different civilization.' **Albyn** (1972), p.34.

(18) James Hogg, **The Domestic Manners and Private Life of Sir Walter Scott** (1882 edit.) pp.95-6.

(19) Sir Reginal Coupland, **Welsh and Scottish Nationalism: A Study** (1945), pp.403-4, quoting Buchan's parliamentary speech of 1932 from **Hansard.** This is the debate which led on to what Coupland calls '... the appeasement of Scottish nationalism (by) the setting up of St Andrew's House in Edinburgh'.

(20) Antonio Gramsci, **Prison Notebooks,** op.cit., pp.223-4.

(21) By far the most useful study of the actual social and class structure of typical nationalist development is that by Miroslav Hroch, **Die Vorkampfer der nationalen Bewegung bei den kleinen Volkern Europas** (Acta Universitatis Carolinae, Monographia XXIV, 1968), which deals with seven different minor nationalist movements. It is remarkable how closely the recent development of the SNP has repeated the older models he describes. See also Eric Hobsbawn, 'Nationalism', in **Imagination and Precision in the Social Sciences: Essays in Honour of Peter Nettl** (1973).

(22) William Ferguson, **Scotland,** op.cit., p.319.

(23) The term is derived from V.A. Olorunsola, **The Politics of Cultural Sub-Nationalism in Africa** (1972), a study concerned with ethnic problems in new African States. 'The phrase "one State-many nationalisms"... is particularly appropriate in describing the new States', says the author, since in many of these 'the country's nationaism can be jeopardized by its cultural sub-nationalisms'. In spite of this, 'some countries have been able to achieve a level of integration which seems surprisingly quite out of proportion to the degree of their cultural homogeneity', while in others (e.g. Eastern Nigeria) cultural sub-nationalism developed into nationalism proper, Introduction, pp.xiv-xv.

(24) David Craig, **Scottish Literature and the Scottish People, 1680-1830** (1961), pp.13-14, p.273. See especially Ch.IX, 'Emigration'.

(25) J.H. Millar, **A Literary History of Scotland** (1903), pp.656-8. Singling out S.R. Crockett's **The Lilac Sunbonnet** (1894) for assault — 'a perfect triumph of succulent vulgarity' — he adds, in words ringing true down to the present, 'though... how nauseous it is, how skilfully it makes its appeal to some of the worst traits in the national character, no-one who is not a Scot can really know.'

(26) George Blake, **Barrie and the Kailyard School** (1951), p.85. In one of the few attempts to penetrate the shroud of secrecy around the Thomson empire, it was pointed out recently that **The Sunday Post** is 'arguably the most successful newspaper in the world... the newspaper which achieves the closest to saturation. In 1971 its total estimated readership of 2,947,000 represented more than 79 per cent of the entire population of Scotland aged 15 or over...' **The Sunday Times,** July 29, 1973, 'The Private Life of Lord Snooty', by George Rosie.

(27) George Blake, op.cit. pp.80-81.

(28) David Craig, **Scottish Literature,** op.cit., p.276, pp.285-6.

(29) William Ferguson, **Scotland,** op.cit., p.317.

(30) T.W.H. Crosland, **The Unspeakable Scot** (1902). The author ended his indictment of the Scots in England with a series of rules 'for the general guidance of young Scotchmen who ...do not desire to add further opprobrium to the Scotch character.' These include: 'I. Remember that outside Scotland you are a good deal of a foreigner... X. IF WITHOUT SERIOUS INCONVENIENCE TO YOURSELF YOU CAN MANAGE TO REMAIN AT HOME PLEASE DO...'

(31) From the dedication to **Catriona,** as quoted in David Daiches, **Robert Louis Stevenson and his World** (1973), p.100.

(32) **The** best recent example of the strain is Gordon M. Williams's **From Scenes Like These,** although Alan Sharp's **A Green Tree in Gedde** (1965) is also interesting in this regard. In the case of these authors flight from the Kailyard ('The task of self-realization is like a journey', as Sharp puts it) led in the direction of the American cinema. See also P. Gregory, 'Scottish Village Life 1973: a reassessment', Scottish International, vol.7, no.1 (Feb.1974).

(33) See Hamish Henderson's 'Alias MacAlias', in **Scottish International** No.6 (April 1969). 'We are here on the edge of grey debatable land, and must walk warily', the author cautions.

(34) R. McLaughlan, 'Aspects of Nationalism', in **The Scottish Debate: Essays in Scottish Nationalism** (1970), edit. N. MacCormick, p.24.

(35) William Ferguson, Scotland, op.cit., p.313.

(36) Ibid., pp.263-5.

(37) C.M. Grieve, **Lucky Poet** (1943), pp.202-3.

(38) David Craig, **Scottish Literature,** op.cit., p.293. Craig's own general recommendation was that the intellectuals should give up the unequal struggle 'to **have** a national vantage-point', since it was self-defeating. So... 'one comes to think that a freer spirit, facing up more openly to experience at large whatever its origins, might better enable the Scottish writer to cope with the problems of living in this place at this time.' A similar spirit can be detected in a previous, less than successful, effort of my own to wrestle with the monster, 'The Three Dreams of Scottish Nationalism', **New Left Review** No.49 (May-June 1968), reprinted in altered form in **Memoirs of a Modern Scotland** (1970), an emigre anthology edited by Karl Miller. It appears in retrospect as a characteristic expression of the 'Red', outward-bound strain in the intelligentsia, as opposed to the 'Black', stay-at-home one closer to nationalism. I am indebted to Christopher Harvie for this distinction.

(39) C.M. Grieve, **Albyn,** op.cit., pp.1-12. 'MacDiarmid' then goes on to predict that the main hope for the Renaissance is Irish immigration and Catholicism, leading a re-Catholicized nation back to 'before the Reformation'.

(40) J.G. Kellas, **The Scottish Political System** (1973), p.2.

(41) George Elder Davie, **The Democratic Intellect: Scotland and her Universities in the 19th Century** (1961), 'Introductory Essay', p.xv.

(42) Perhaps the most brilliant and useful recent analysis on these lines is that of N.T. Phillipson, whose 'Nationalism and Ideology' (in **Government and Nationalism in Scotland,** edit. J.N. Wolfe, 1969) examines the 'ideology of noisy inaction' inspired by Scott, and the exact way in which the latter 'taught Scotsmen to see themselves as men... in whose confusion lies their national character.'

(43) C.M. Grieve **A Drunk Man Looks at the Thistle** (1962), p.18.

(44) J.G. Kellas, op.cit., p.129.

(45) A good example of this is provided by articles in the **Irish Times** earlier this year, by Owen Dudley Edwards, who depicts the SNP's rise as analogous to 'a great flood steadily coming in' over the years. I am grateful to the author for showing me the articles prior to publication.

(46) J.G. Kellas, op.cit., pp.136-7, and following pages.

(47) The main source remains of course H.J. Hanham's **Scottish Nationalism** (1969), with its often-quoted diagnoses of the 'small man, small town' character of the old SNP, its anti-intellectualism, etc. Among other oddities are the movement's failure to produce a leader-figure; its extremely pacific and constitutional approach; and of couse the clearly wayward nature of so much nationalist culture itself (which made it difficult for a political movement to do anything but shun it). In effect this was a split between a political movement that found it difficult to break-away from over-adaptation to 'British' norms; and a culture which was wholly adrift from them, and engaged upon something close to the fantasy recreation of the whole of modern Scottish history and social reality.

(48) **Les Temps Modernes,** vol.29, nos.324-6 (aout-septembre 1973), special issue on 'Les Minorities nationales en France'; 'texte d'orientation' presented to the General Assembly of the 'Lutte Occitane' movement, May 1973.

(49) S.Pollard, **European Economic Integration 1815-1970** (1974), pp.132-6.

(50) Michael Philoponneau, 'La Bretagne: perspectives de developpement socialiste non-centralise', in **Les Temps Modernes** op.cit., pp.389-90.

(51) A most valuable recent discussion of Austro-Marxist theory on nationality (a propos the Occitan movement) can be found in Yvon Bourdet, 'Proletariat universel et cultures nationales', **Revue francaise de sociologie,** vol.XIII (1972).

(52) George Elder Davie, from a discussion appended to **Government and Nationalism in Scotland,** op.cit., p.205.

Devolution and Democracy

David Gow

In his "personal record" of the 1964-1970 Labour Government, Harold Wilson does not even refer to the setting up in April, 1969, of the Royal Commission on the Constitution by his own Cabinet. Scotland itself does not rate a mention in the index to the 800-page book and the five separate references to Scottish nationalists simply record the fact that they won the Hamilton by-election of 1967 and took a lot of votes from Labour in other by-elections. Clearly, even by the middle of 1971, when the book was pretty well complete, the Commission could simply be ignored in case the Scottish nationalist bubble burst or left to work as a sop to the continuing debate in Scotland itself about home rule.

The whole problem, then as now, was seen in a short-term perspective of tactics and getting votes, rather than of principle. And, of course, this should neither surprise nor shock us when the author of the book in question sees his role—other than self-justification of the most small-minded kind—as both "chairman and managing director" of Great Britain, Inc., a shoe-string concern run by shoe-string policies and politicians. The main impetus of Mr Wilson and his colleagues was to ensure continued dominance in Scotland by the perfection of regional economic instruments like the REP, HIDB and planning councils as part also of Labour's attempt to modernise the whole UK economy and of its basic belief in the regional benefits that would flow from such centrally conceived policies.

The Commission (now headed by Lord Kilbrandon) duly reported in October 1973, by which time the debate about nationalism/devolution had assumee far greater meaning in Scotland with the ever-increasing number of oil-strikes (and the first rise in the price of OPEC oil)—but the SNP had not yet visibly begun to threaten Labour's electoral base north of the border. Mr Edward Heath, then Prime Minister, was even being given stick by his own Scottish party for actually daring to confirm his attachment to the Douglas-Home proposals of 1970 for a Scottish Convention. So little was perceived or foreseen of the changing circumstances in Scotland that a

(Scottish) Professor of Politics and Labour MP could write in the January 1974 issue of "Political Quarterly": "It (the Kilbrandon report) is unlikely to lead to any rapid action or to be a major. issue for politicians other than those whose constituencies or entire parties are located in Scotland and Wales."

Well, just over a month later, Mr Mackintosh lost his own seat to a Tory Earl, largely as a result of SNP intervention—and political commentators and others in London woke up on the last day of February to the (for them and, I suspect, many of us) astonishing breakthrough of the SNP. It added six seats to the one already won in 1970 and almost doubled its share of the vote to 21.9 per cent. The academic soothsayer went back to his electoral charts—and Mr Wilson, back in power, performed his usual balancing act by both proceeding to take the Kilbrandon report seriously and appointing one of the authors of the Memorandum of Dissent, Lord Crowther-Hunt, as his constitutional adviser. Willie Ross stayed at Bute House, but Terry Pitt, former head of Labour's research, moved from Transport House to the Cabinet Office to head the Kilbrandon study unit. Devolution/nationalism, now the whole issue had shifted electorally and economically, was a major concern of British policy-makers as a whole, no matter where their constituencies.

During the whole of the last year, from publication of the Kilbrandon report, the mainspring of events on the devolution front has, at the formally political level for the most part, been the SNP. Their February breakthrough forced all British parties, particularly Labour whose overall election to power depends on the Scottish votes and a disproportionate number of Scottish seats, to discuss and act upon these formal questions with a greater sense of urgency and seriousness than at any time this century. It is less true that the SNP's specific policies on oil, the EEC, land, poverty, say, did play a major role in forcing UK parties to reconsider their own economic policies. " 'It's Scotland's Oil", was an argument to be answered or ignored or smeared, but the quadrupling of the price of oil in the wake of the Arab-Israeli war last October, the miners' strike, and the threat of world recession had already forced the Labour Government and would have forced any British Government radically to re-think their economic policies, specifically energy policies and the country's control over huge proven reserves of oil off its shores. (The report of the Public Accounts Committee made this absolutely inevitable).

Labour, for instance, would have introduced its own policies for the National Enterprise Board or oil taxation/participation whatever the fortunes of the SNP. Though, it is true to say that the present priority for a Scottish Development Agency and the siting of oil-related Government offices north of the border might well **not** have emerged so swiftly. Regional economic instruments did have to be further refined as a means of ensuring that some spin-off from the oil bounty was felt in Scotland, but the main priority was still the need to react to the SNP breakthrough and overcome it and thus keep power in both Scotland and, above all, Westminster.

And what an extraordinary mess this short-sighted insistence on purely tactical questions got both the main parties into, with the results we have just seen in the October general election. In October the SNP: a) gained four more seats, making a total of 11, and increased its share of the vote to 30.4 per cent; b) replaced the Tories as the second largest Scottish party in terms of votes, if not of seats; c) came second in 42 seats, 36 of which are Labour and quite a few of which are now marginal. Though it still kept 16 seats, the Conservative Party above all looked like a relic in Scotland and traditional Labour loyalty only just kept the party in overall command. Plus the fact that the party had after much anguish achieved a measure of common commitment to devolution.

If it had not been for that volte-face, accomplished in the summer of 1974 on the most impure of motives, it is open to question whether traditional loyalty and a wary belief in the socio-economic measures implemented by the short Wilson government, would have been sufficient to get the Labour vote out. In July, as the responses to the Crowther-Hunt Green Paper were being made public and the debate was taken much further, the NEC of the Labour Party made known (not through a leak by Renee Short, as the SNP believe) that 13 Labour seats in Scotland were in danger. Earlier, in June, the Scottish executive had recommended the rejection of all the proposals (seven schemes) in the Green Paper. And, in August, a special conference voted overwhelmingly in favour of devolution in the form of a directly-elected assembly responsible for legislating on current Scottish Office functions. The special Scottish Labour manifesto even referred to a "parliament" rather than an "assembly" a month later, though this was due to the haste of compiling the document and the cleverness of its author.

The Labour Government, its national executive and its Scottish executive, had been forced to take the devolution debate within its own ranks much further than originally intended because of the overwhelming fear that they would lose power through SNP gains. (Harold Wilson did not believe he was in power until he saw the Scottish results early on October 11). The (British) NEC published its own proposals in September, followed soon after by a Government White Paper on September 17 called "Democracy and Devolution". Willie Ross said cynically: "I conceive this as a contribution towards more effective, better and closer government and I am determined that it is going to be not only acceptable but something that will last." A week later, Peter Shore said in Edinburgh: "I give an absolute assurance on behalf of all of us that whatever the result of the election in Scotland, if we are returned, the process will go on and basic decisions in the White Paper will stand." He said there could be a fully operational assembly within four or five years.

New, and critical elements had crept or been forced into the devolution debate by then but the oft-forgotten Kilbrandon report of a year before was more or less the committed policy of every political party and could not quietly be forgotten. As matters now stand, the Government have set up a special unit to work on their devolution plans under Edward Short and proven, electorally successful Labour devolutionists like Harry Ewing have been given ministerial posts. The special unit, situated in the Cabinet Office, is 20-strong and comprises top civil servants. The devolution debate is no longer about whether there should be a Scottish assembly along the lines recommended by Kilbrandon: it is now about how soon such an assembly can be set up and what powers it should have. The initial argument has been won.

I shall later tackle the wider implications of the whole and present debate about devolution. But, as a socialist and a Labour supporter, I should insist that the preceding report makes clear that I consider the debate to have been undertaken overwhelmingly in self-interested, narrow, cosmetic terms that mask the heart of the matter: who shall control the lives of the people, who shall exercise power, and who shall run the economy? There has been little or no attempt, even within the Labour Party, far less within other parties of a non-socialist nature like the SNP, to discuss this crucial issue in terms of socialist perspective and principle. The whole sorry mess bears witness to the appalling lack of political philosophy in Great Britain as a whole, when the issue is one of the most fundamental of our day.

Stagflation

In any honest appraisal of the issue, one must start from the fact of world-wide inflation and recession ("stagflation") that threatens to bring down the whole capitalist edifice in a particularly vicious trade war led by the United States against its Western European and Japanese allies and within all that grouping. The "recurring crisis of capitalism" may be a convenient cliche, but there can be little doubt that the crisis is deep, deeper certainly than the apologists of the present system admit in their usual obfuscating manner. Even the White House has now admitted that there is an American recession.

The quadrupling of the price of oil last autumn and winter has exposed the relative strengths and weaknesses of the individual capitalist nations and the soft underbelly of rapacious imperialism at the same time. The Arab and Gulf states have given notice that they want to become members of the rich man's club and the 80 billion dollars surplus enjoyed by these states has given birth to a new source of finance capital of investment at home and abroad or in the purchase of goods and services. The oil-producing states of the Middle East now to an ever-increasing extent control some of the major purse-strings of international capital and can bring Western economies, particularly weak ones like those of Britain (or Italy), to ruin simply by moving their huge reserves around.

The situation is exacerbated by the fact that the population in these states is so poor and under-developed generally that this huge surplus cannot be recycled yet sufficiently to absorb the (inflationary) goods and services available in the metropolitan capitalist countries. The events of the last year may have seen the emergence of a new, nascent Arab/Iranian capitalist class, but there is not yet sufficient evidence to suggest that they will merge their interests with the Western ruling classes or that ruthless trade war can be avoided. Behind this new ruling class lie a mass of underfed and underdeveoped people and behind them all lie the newly independent countries of the Third World who "possess" on their territory—but do not own—the other scarce raw materials upon which metropolitan capitalist countries depend to fuel their own rocketingly inflationary economies and are run by a predominantly petit-bourgeois indigenous elite.

Possibilities do, therefore, exist in reality for apocalyptic events in the world before the 20th century is out. Last year, when the oil embargo was in force against the United States (and Holland) and production was cut by the OPEC countries, rumours circulated in the Press that President Nixon's military advisers were seriously considering the options of invading Arab countries and James Schlesinger, Defence Secretary, has muttered similar warnings. Despite its defeat in Vietnam, American imperialism will not necessarily be deterred from further incursions, beyond the present covert ones as in Chile, if Third World countries possessing increasingly scarce raw materials go on from half-way national revolutions that leave them in a neo-colonial state of genuine socialist revolutions and take over the means of production in their territory. The US. could not sit idly by as its markets—already restricted, despite those new outlets in the Middle East and Iran as well as Russia—began to close up more and more.

In this perspective, it does seem as if the Western imperialists could sow their economic and financial anarchy throughout the world and bring the lot down in pestilence and war in a bid to rescue their own exploitative way of life. Seen quite coolly and unemotionally, one cannot imagine that our Western way of life—built-in obsolescence, huge needs for scarce resources, vast energy consumption, over-production and over-consumption of useless goods, garbage-piling, waste-creating—can survive for very long at its present level of growth. The way of life could collapse either from forces within itself or outside itself, either by internal social breakdown/political revolution or by external revolutions.

One may, of course, be hopelessly wrong. Another perspective is the emergence of an overtly fascist ruling class in the Western countires ready to do business with anybody abroad. Or, the recycling of Arab/Iranian surpluses prove easier with a buoyant result for the Western economies. Or, even, President Ford to persuade Mr Brezhnev and the whole Politburo in the Soviet Union and indeed in China to go the whole capitalist road (and not just settle for Pepsi), thereby creating a world capitalist government. It does seem a wee bit unlikely.

There are, seriously, forces in the world working against economic collapse and social disorder on a global scale. One has noted since the Second World War the tendency of big corporations to exorcise competition and control the market in a "planned" way. Governments in the Western world, viz. the last Conservative Government in Britain under Heath and even the new Wilson administration, mirror this trend in working towards a corporate form of state in which, ultimately—without necessarily becoming Nazi—the economy is planned and managed by central government with business and trade unions junior partners in a national coalition (or enterprise board!) stamping out internal clashes of interest. There are also obvious signs already that such a corporate state would rest on a strong-arm political and military basis, with civil liberties minimal and dissent a heinous crime.

Dr Henry Kissinger, in his original proposals of April 23, 1973, for a new Atlantic Charter wanted nothing less than a similar (but different) monolithic control over the capitalist West as the Soviet Union exercised over its sphere of influence in Eastern Europe. (This was inachievable because of the growing trade war). The European Economic Community, despite innumerable setbacks, still theoretically at least pledged itself to full economic and monetary union, followed by political union, by 1980. At one point in December 1973, King Hassan of Morocco virtually offered Euro-Arab union. 1974 has seen world conferences, largely unsuccessful, on raw materials, population and now food. Other instances of "global inter-dependence" abound.

Throughout the Western hemisphere indeed, the dominating trend of fierce competition, beggar-thy-neighbour deals, trade war, and so on has been partially offset by increasing concentration and centralisation of economic and political power in multi-national organisations like the EEC and giant corporations like ITT. The scale of the problem of supplying sufficient goods and services to the people has become so enormous that central planning and co-ordination has been seen as the only possible operative response at international as well as national and regional levels. Political institutions have not, however, so far been able to achieve the same degree of corporate efficiency as the multi-national companies, but their aim is similar: co-ordinate efforts to ensure the maintenance of the capitalist system and simultaneously destroy internal dissension. At its highest stage of development, capitalism would then be totally monolithic on a global scale, with a terrifying concentration of power in a few hands. The trend, most notably in the United States even with the disappearance of Nixon, is already there.

Kilbrandon and Corporatism

Very little indeed appears about the foregoing in any of the major documents so far issued on the issue of devolution to Scotland, though it is true to say that the most recent debate has begun to get down to the nitty gritty of economic relations as well as purely institutional cosmetics. In the first place the Government documents result from very narrow terms of reference, generally taking for granted the bourgeois form of state, and the party documents, including those of the Labour Party, don't include any rigorous economic analysis from a socialist perspective. If this whole series of articles serves any purpose, it will be precisely to begin a new kind of debate about the future of Scotland and of British socialism.

On the question of corporatism, the majority Kilbrandon contents itself with the nice liberal thought that the "vast increase in scope, scale and complexity of government business, and in manpower and other resources devoted to it, has had a cumulative effect on people's lives, and is an underlying factor in complaints about the working of the present system." There is no hope, they say, of putting the brake on, far less reversing, this trend, and list some of the ways in which (bourgeois) democracy has been weakened—on much the same grounds as the Memorandum of Dissent which similarly refers to the rubber-stamp role of backbench MPs, the party system, the growth of ad hoc bodies, secrecy of government, and even the undermining of civil liberties.

Having stated some of the regional causes of complaint, the majority commissioners conclude lamely: "... while the people of Great Britain as a whole cannot be said to be seriously dissatisfied with their system of government, they have less attachment to it than in the past, and there are some substantial and persistent causes of discontent which may contain the seeds of more serious dissatisfaction." Lord Crowther-Hunt and Professor Alan Peacock say more boldly: "Quite simply, the fact has to be faced that if we really believe that democracy means that the people and their representatives should have a real share in political power, our institutions do not make adequate provision for this today. And this at a time when a more educated citizenry has a greater capacity for playing a fuller part in the country's decision making processes than ever before in our history."

Such sentiments, noble and ineffectual as they are, would not disgrace a liberal manifesto and indeed might well have been taken from them. They scarcely begin to tackle the essential problem of power, where it lies and who holds it, in a modern bourgeois state and get the necessarily diffuse answers one might expect to a question posed at the purely institutional level. Mackintosh in that same "Political Quarterly" piece makes some play of this and then adds that throughout the responses to a special Commission questionnaire there are hints that "what has really led to dissatisfaction is disappointment over the product of government, over the level of wages and pensions, over housing and prices and the sense of generalised failure as one set of politicians after another promises certain things and then fails to provide them."

This idea, subsequently expanded in a recent piece by the same author in the "New Statesman", begins to get to the heart of the matter. It seems to me beyond doubt, despite what I said earlier about the effects of the nationalists' economic policies on the Government, that the SNP have built up a solid base, a more solid base even than they would have had on the purely institutional issue of self-government, by their policies for wealth-sharing, higher pensions, better social security, more jobs, the gradual elimination of endemic poverty through oil revenues. And this could well be built upon if the present Labour Government pursues a pro-City and pro-CBI strategy with consequent wage freezes and the whole sorry panoply of the 1964-70 pusillanimity. West Central Scotland, where the Labour base lies, could seriously continue in the SNPs favour if stagflation/unemployment get worst—as seems likely.

The plain fact of the matter is that the various schemes put forward, and in this I include the SNP idea of a sovereign Scottish (bourgeois) Parliament, would not do anything other than reflect at a local Scottish level the brutal incompetence of bourgeois institutions, their calculated hostility to the interests of the working class, and their overall control by large-scale indigenous and foreign capitalist interests. Even Kilbrandon is a bit sceptical about the value of a devolved system of government. The majority report says devolution **may** provide a greater element of political accountability and greater opportunity for participation in government, and it **may** lighten the load at the centre. It adds: "Devolution could do much to reduce discontent with the system of government. It would counter over-centralisation, and, to a lesser extent, strengthen democracy; in Scotland and Wales it would be a response to national feeling."

As if that were not lukewarm enough, it adds again: "There is no inherent reason why regional government should be more democratic or more sensitive to public opinion than central government. But devolution, depending on those operating it, could do a great deal to meet complaints which are essentially regional in character." Leaving aside the last phrase, which is patently wide of the mark, the parenthetical remark (in my italics) gives the game away. On the present basis of local/regional government, with its authoritarian, corrupt often, grossly secretive, strangledly bureaucratic mode of operating, the "Scottish Parliament" would be as effective and democratic and participatory as Edinburgh Toon Cooncil—possibly with a few Highland lairds, even Sir Alec, thrown in to into keep the working class in their place.

It is NOT a question of simply juggling around the institutional jigsaw of Britain or Scotland NOR of giving the various elected representatives more formal power to shape policy, but of creating new economic relations and a new kind of state on socialist lines if the real source of power, capital, and its agents in our institutions, are to be overcome for the benefit of all the people. It is a question of dealing in Scotland and Britain as a whole with a ruling class that deliberately manufactures inflation and calls on the working class to pay for it, that shifts its own investment around to serve its own interests, that is prepared to use the combined power of the police and armed forces to bolster its own exploitative, corrupt way of life.

Even on a formal level, the various schemes proposed leave little other than the creation of a flossy superstructure without any real power. Most of these schemes, whether for legislative or executive devolution, simply give any elected assembly or/and executive control over the traditional functions of the Scottish Office and thereby create even greater confusion. Crowther-Hunt/Peacock therefore propose an "interlocking principle" whereby the representatives and officials at one level of government are able directly to participate in the decision making of the immediately superior level. This is formally a nice idea, but in practice the proposed regional councils (which are to go ahead) and new legislative assembly would simply duplicate the administrative blockages now so obvious. In virtually every field, be it housing, education, planning, social services, these three or four levels of government would undercut and undermine each other in a bureaucratic strangle. The proposed assembly, no more really than a sort of super regional council, would either have to impose its decisions by covert operations or be made impotent, a laughing stock, by other bodies below it. (Cynics suggest that this is why Labour is now proceeding with the idea, so the SNP can reap the opprobrium of the Scottish people and the whole idea be dropped. Nice one Harold).

The real question then, as the present debate is beginning to make clear, is what economic powers the proposed assembly will have, and how far these will be separate from those of Whitehall and Westminster. When the Commission reported in October 1973, the majority view was that certain political restraints limited the scope for financial devolution. "Parliament must retain legal and effective sovereignty in all matters; the United Kingdom Government must have the control over expenditure and taxation necessary to stabilise the economy and to foster its development; a reasonable degree of equality in public services must be responsible for minimising regional disparities in general economic conditions." What the Commissioners thus proposed was an independent exchequer board, with a Scottish assembly deciding on the actual carve-up of the block grant from Westminster for the services entrusted to their responsibility. They then laughably suggest that the proposed assembly might have power of purse over vehicle excise duty and petrol duty etc. They particularly insisted that the scope for devolution in the trade, industry and employment fields would be severely limited by the obligations assumed in international agreement and by the requirements of economic management policy and that any UK Government was bound to play the leading role in minimising regional disparities in general economic conditions.

Similarly, the Memorandum of Dissent simply offered some independent revenue raising powers and sufficient financial "independence" (their quotes) of central government "while still leaving central government with the tools it needs for the overall management of the economy."

But, once the argument in favour of a formal assembly was more or less settled in theory, the Government was forced to pay attention in far greater detail to these important, crucial even, questions of the power of purse and economic management. Again, the capital the SNP could make out of the manifest failure of successive regional policies and of the transforming effect of oil discoveries played a major role. If Scotland were independent, their argument ran, the revenue from the oil would suffice to transform the employment, housing, and social services situation in Scotland. It may not have been more or much more than a "Scotsman on the make policy" and it may not have affected Labour's fundamental economic decisions with regard to economic management, but there is no doubt the SNP argument raised the devolution debate several notches further.

On September 17, 1974, on publication of the Government White Paper referred to earlier, Willie Ross suggested the powers of the assembly could be strengthened in the field of trade and industry well in advance of the Assembly being created—and then went on to say, in character, that an extension of his own responsibilities as Secretary of State might solve some of these problems "without prejudicing the economic unity of the UK." Like the Commissioners, he insisted on the "maintenance of a general uniformity of approach in the UK to the allocation of resources, to taxation arrangements and to the overall management of the economy." Peter Shore, a week later, repeated this view. "We are proposing a Scottish Development Agency to give Scotland considerable powers over the economy. But the central management of the economy, and whatever effect this has, must remain at Westminster. I am sure, however, that a great deal can still be devolved to Scotland even in this field (of trade and industry)".

This was partly in response to SNP demands for the immediate transfer to a Scottish government and parliament of activities carried on by the Departments of Trade, Industry, Energy, Employment, Environment and Social Security, as well as proposals on oil production/taxation. The Labour Party NEC, however, had previously argued that "substantial powers" in these fields would be transferred from Westminster in order to allow an assembly to make its own decisions on promoting employment and industrial regeneration. While they see the assembly presumably controlling the Scottish Development Agency, the Government and Willie Ross, obviously, so far see the SDA as an added responsibility of the inscrutable Scottish Office. So, great confusion reigns not only over how far the Government are prepared to go in this field but also on how far they will allow such powers to be exercised under "democratic" control.

An Independent Capitalism

But, perhaps, the most significant response to the Government Green Paper was given by the Scottish Council in a series of papers on this whole question that call for virtually an indigenous Scottish capitalist class, with its own financial and economic power and nascent philosophy. Their own emphasis on industrial devolution was backed by the Scottish CBI, who did, however, reject quite forcibly the idea of a Scottish assembly or the relevance of institutional changes to the deep-seated economic problems facing the UK and Scotland. The crucial fact remains, however, that both oil potential for investment and growing concentration of such investment power in Scotland's capital have made the Scottish financiers and industrialists more confident as a class in their own right and not as an adjunct of the British ruling class.

Like the various representatives of the Labour movement in Scotland, the Scottish Council argue that "the fundamental need of the Scottish economy is a substantial acceleration in rate of economic growth." But they then go on to say most significantly: "On the basis of past performance and future prospects it must be considered highly unlikely that the required acceleration can be provided by central UK Government economic control either through an improved UK growth rate, or through the application of regional policies. We suggest that the only real chance of success will be through the establishment of a devolved Scottish Government with real economic and financial powers, and that the overriding importance of more rapid economic development should be reflected in the institutional and organisational form of that Government." In this, whatever their subjective sense of difference might be, the SNP and the Scottish Council do not greatly differ: indeed, it will be interesting to see how far their aims merge and industrialists other than Sir Hugh Fraser begin to act in an overtly political manner.

The Scottish Council argue cogently enough, on the lines of the Commissioners, that—quite apart from central government ignoring or over-riding Scottish interests on a wide range of policy issues—Scottish MPs are decreasingly important in terms of modifying, initiating or reversing policy. They add that even the most inscrutable, unaccountable of offices, the Scottish Office, has lost or is losing its power to influence central government policy because of the increasing scale and complexity of the work of government departments like... Trade and Industry, Environment, Energy... A deep sense of grievance emerges, on the lines suggested by Mackintosh more generally, about the failure of central government and the poor Scottish Office to deliver the goods to Scotland in the form of increased prosperity.

"If the present economic circumstances demand specific Scottish policies and overwhelmingly they do—then there is no alternative but to place the power to implement those policies which relates directly to a Scottish political base. There should be a Scottish Government reporting directly to a Scottish Assembly, which would have complete powers over many areas of economic policy and a share in the remaining areas. It should have the ultimate ability, in subjects of policy debate with the central UK Government, to go its own way—or to take countervailing action in a related area. This implies an end to persuasion, and the start of negotiations." (And trade war). Like the SNP, the Scottish Council then rightly argue that the Scottish Office "cannot control the execution of any economic strategy that it may devise" because of the greater executive control of the DTI. And: "A body without control of these economic functions, such as that proposed in the majority Kilbrandon Report, would be little better equipped to evolve and implement a development strategy than the present institutions." They say that the Scottish view should prevail if a Scottish Government disagree with Westminster on the need, e.g., for a steel plant at Hunterston (a pet project).

The Council even go so far, in their desire to create a new Scottish ruling class endowed with the traditional panoply of bourgeois democracy, as to suggest that a Scottish Assembly could deviate from the UK legislation even in items of major importance such as prices and incomes or industrial relations "without the ultimate power of the UK Parliament being called into question"! Shorn of their their fine words, at a time when capitalism is at its most rampant and rapacious in Scotland, the ideas mean total control of any political institution by capital and an even more vicious form of appropriation of Labour's surplus value (high industrial incentives, exemption from the proposed property development tax, lower corporation tax, full Scottish budget).

In its specific response to the Green Paper, the Council argue that the critical issue for Scotland today "is its ability to generate and to originate new enterprises, and to keep and develop indigenous companies". It adds: "Industrial devolution is concerned with the location of the creative policy-making, decision-taking individuals in industry." This is a part of a basic argument that it is centrally-conceived and executed regional policies that have made Scotland into a branch plant economy on the detailed lines given by John Finn in his excellent series of articles in "The Scotsman". The argument then is that by having important government offices centrally located in Edinburgh/Glasgow, proximity will enable local capitalists to develop their ideas, expand, make profits etc. and others to site their head offices in Scotland. As they do NOT go the whole independence road, the Scottish Council simply argue in favour of "the complete translation of a number of major British agencies to Scotland, formultating and administering total British policies from Scotland."

But the sense of the creation of an independent Scottish capitalist class, whose political expression would be through domination of a SNP-type Scottish government/legislature, is still paramount. The devolution debate thus shifts in this perspective from a purely cosmetic touch to British institutions to ensure the continuing domination through new mediating factors of the British ruling class, to a distinct form of national Scottish oppression by indigenous capital allied with foreign multi-national interests. This begs a lot of questions, but the main thrust is there as it is, at a different level and in different conditions, with the **actual** emergence of a new Arab/Iranian ruling class I described earlier.

There is a great deal of force in the SCDI's arguments, particularly about the declining influence of the Scottish Office in the face of the overpowering decision making responsibilities of the DTI and Department of Energy. This has not been lessened by Willie Ross's refusal on the Drumbuie site, when the Department of Energy reportedly backed the applicants

65

enthusiastically. When it comes to the compulsory acquisition of platform construction sites, the decision on which sites will be taken over will rest with the London department, especially when the UK's over-riding need will be as swift as possible a flow of oil from the North Sea in the face of another, more widespread oil embargo imposed by OPEC in the near future. But, it is doubtful whether control by a Scottish government over not only the traditional functions of the Scottish Office but also nationalised industries, trade, industry and employment would make it any more accountable than it is now when the real power would remain largely in the hands of foreign capital and governments.

I can see the force of the argument that greater proximity of the governed to the governors through an Edinburgh-based assembly and government would give more formal accountability, particularly when a large number of elected representatives would face constant recalls at elections. But this has scarcely been borne out either at the level of local Scottish government so far or in the dealings of the Scottish Office in Edinburgh and London. Genuine control over resources and civil service would not necessarily mean a reduction in the general level of public services, as apologists of central economic management argue on the basis of present public expenditure per head, but bureaucratic uniformity and incompetence might still be unavoidable. At a time of world hyper-inflation and recession, a small Scottish economy, still controlled by outside forces, would not be able to escape the dreadful consequences—even with all the oil flowing (into the profits of the oil majors).

In a world in which the EEC is fitfully albeit but committedly working towards economic and monetary union; in which multi-national corporations control the livelihood not only of individual workers but often of whole areas and even countries; in which the condominium between the United States and the Soviet Union imposes the interests of the superpowers on the rest of the world, more or less; in which financial control rests in the hands of central bankers and large reserve-owners; in which capitalist ruling classes work together (and against each other) to promote their own falling rate of profit and to disarm the economic and political strength of the people;—in such a huge, agglomerated world of intersecting state, international and corporate interests, the only meaningful "devolution" to Scotland (or any other country) is full financial and economic control vested in the people and managed for them by their representatives.

None of the proposed models of a reformed system of Scottish government, based as they all are on liberal capitalism, corporatism, bourgeois democracy, would significantly alter the facts of gross disparity of wealth, concentrated (often foreign) ownership of capital, unplanned, anarchical areas of widespread poverty and social disorder in the country, particularly in West Central Scotland, economic, social and personal distress, exploitation, corruption and the whole sorry legacy of British imperialism in which many of Scotland's ruling class gleefully took and take part. Simply exchanging one set of capitalist rulers for another, more local set would not alter these basic facts. Only in a planned, socialist economy controlled by the people could such excesses be eliminated according to the needs of the people themselves.

A Socialist Democracy

Briefly, does the foregoing suggest a Leninist seizure of state power and socialist development? Is the only answer a strictly disciplined, tightly-knit Communist Party imposing the dictatorship of the proletariat? Is such a revolutionary perspective possible, moreover, in a purely Scottish perspective or indeed British perspective? Would not such a proposed struggle be unthinkable without a transformation of the complete British system and from then on the European system and international capital itself? I confess I don't really know. All I know is that a genuine socialist Scotland would not survive long in the face of the awesome economic and military strength of capitalist Britain, let alone of international imperialism, as the Chilean experiment showed in its specific way. The "contagion" effect would be the major hope in a decaying world order, but historical precedent suggests this effect is severly limited.

Such a perspective could only be feasible in the context of the complete emasculation of the ruling class and the joint, concerted efforts of socialists throughout the capitalist West to seize the power and instore a world-wide socialist system. In the present context of global disaster, a planned, socialist world government is not a totally idle fantasy but the only possible solution to the feasible exhaustion and destruction of the world's resources, physical and human. One is here juggling with enormous forces as yet incapable of being identified perhaps, let alone subdued. Any Scottish road to socialism must take its starting point from a rigorous analysis of these international conditions as well as of purely local conditions. Without such an understanding, any Scottish socialist experiment would be nipped in the bloody bud.

There are several reasons, moreover, for believing that the Leninist model of socialism/communism is not relevant to the present circumstances. By that I do not mean that the corruption of Leninism in the Soviet Union into Stalinism, with its attendant destructive, murderous inability to meet the needs of the Soviet people, its terrorist isolation of the rulers from the ruled, its bureaucratic stranglehold on personal and communal freedom, will always be an inevitable by-product of Bolshevik-style revolutions. What I do suggest is that the idea of a small party acting on behalf of the working class—as an entity, not as a concrete reality of materially rich individuals and groups suffering the same class fate at the hands of the ruling class—prefigures a substitutist take-over of state power by planners of uniformity ultimately unaccountable and undemocratic.

The problem, as ever, is one of size. The size and under-development of the Soviet Union are such that it is possible that only a strictly authoritarian, centralised government could and can deal with the problems of molding an efficient economic system even approximating to the actual human needs of the Soviet people. It is worthy of doubt whether even a system of decision-making soviets at factory, local and regional level would have been a democratic counter-weight to the need for central, authoritarian planning in an era of physical and economic invasion. The fact, however, that "encirclement" no longer exists does now provide the virtual framework for the democratisation of Soviet society.

The problems of Scotland cannot be measured in the same huge terms of land mass and population, nor indeed of under-development. But the fact remains that this country's problems are both comparatively minute compared with those facing the bulk of mankind and can only be grasped and dealt with in the context of global problems. What I am saying is that the fantasy of a predominantly rural, unaggressive, post-industrial Scotland will remain a fantasy until the present imperialist structures of international capital and indeed of Soviet communism are broken down and the whole basis of industrial man's relationship to his environment, physical and human, transformed. The political and cultural renewal that is so essential in Scotland can only work hand in hand with similar human renaissances throughout the rich parts of the world.

In the meantime, Scottish socialists have a unique chance of forging new models of theoretical development and beginning to try these out in practice. The essential problem is to reconcile the dictates of a centrally planned economy with democratic, local control. Theoretically, at least, this must be done on the model of soviets, recallable, accountable elected representatives in factories, communities, carrying out the specific plans and projects laid down centrally by the rotating "leaders". Absolutely direct democracy is impossible, but real political power can and must be centred in workers' control of their immediate environment, whether working or social. (Some of the more active tenants' associations, with new self-managing powers, provide the nucleus of the basic social organisation).

In a properly planned economy, with balanced management of resources, disparities in wealth and services between regions of a country like Scotland could be eliminated and the total wealth of the country spread equitably over the whole society. This need not necessarily make for uniformity or "levelling-down" as capitalist apologists insist, but for all kinds of local diversity and richness once the present system of political irresponsibility and alienation from the real centres of decision-making were replaced by one in which people felt real dignity and responsibility in co-operative organisations. The way we are going at present we will have a surplus of powerless administrators and politicians getting in the way both of strategic plans for the whole country and effective local democracy by the people themselves.

The whole enterprise must be based from the start on the principles of socialist democracy, whereby the most important element in the social system to be formed is not rubber-stamping approval of plans designated and imposed from the central authority but the right of individuals and groups to determine their own future on a co-operative basis. There will be clashes of interest between different factions or groups, or between different levels of self-management, but not in the same way or to the same extent as within the present competitive, paternalistic system.

I admit that this leaves aside some of my earliest remarks about the international scale of the problem and the inter-dependence of national economies of a world scale at this period of human history. Personally, I see no objection in principle to the concept, say, of a United Socialist States of Europe provided such a multi-national series of institutions were based on the same over-riding principles of socialist democracy, with ultimate power resting at the bottom and not being imposed from the top as the present capitalist and communist systems do. In this context Scotland is not a concept of a bourgeois capitalist nation-state but an autonomous country within a wider grouping of countries and regions. The two must be seen as inseparable as the present rise of nationalism and regionalism throughout Western Europe could easily, under capitalist bourgeois rule, simply add to the warring ruling classes and not lead to a more equitable socio-economic system working according to actual human needs.

There will no doubt be howls of protest and objections, often serious or valid, to much of the forgoing and I admit that much of what I have said is extremely tentative. The problem in Scotland is that our own bourgoisie, stripped for more than 200 years of its own political philosophy and assimilated to the ideas and practice of British imperialism can only see in autonomy its continued, reformed right to dominate and exploit and curtail freedom of the many on a smaller, more localised scale. The various labour and socialist organisations, from the trade unions passing through the Labour and Communist Parties to the Trotskyists and other fringe groupuscules, see their own political activity in terms of central authority, state capitalism, state socialism controlled from afar. They too have not formulated their demands and programmes on a sufficient level of local democracy or indeed of international solutions. They are or tend to be uniformist and centralised in their thinking.

The practical problem for a Scottish socialist is that he must continue to work within the existing organisations in the absence of a present specifically Scottish socialist party or organisation and seek to alter through tendencies the political theory and practice of these. The national road to socialism, decried by many Marxists as bourgeois idealism, if not fascism, is no such thing if it is entirely internationalist in outlook and democratic in principle and practice. The size and scale of the problems facing mankind and the fact of international communication and mutual economic dependence will remain, but the concentration of the power to deal with those issues must be seized from the hands of the imperialists and given to the people in their rich local, regional, and national variety.

What Sort Of Overgovernment?

Ronald Young

What the reorganisation of local government and the establishment of a Scottish Parliament mean for one another and for the man in the street—let alone the Socialist—is an immense and complex topic to which the constraints of a short article will not permit justice to be done: particularly when one is deeply unhappy about the terms of the debate in which these issues have been conducted, the choice is either to miss out completely critical areas of argument or to talk in cryptic or simplified short-hand. I will start by making some assertions which I hope will give a rough indication of the views which I shall attempt to justify in the body of the article. I hope that the extensive references will help anyone curious enough to pursue the allusions. Those who are looking for tactical hints on how the Scottish Labour Party extracts itself from the mess its essential conservatism has produced in relation to Devolution will, I am afraid, be disappointed. This paper is concerned to reassert a different and more basic form of devolution, of power transfer, which for too long the Scottish people and Labour party have ignored.

My argument will be that we have in the post-war period been too ready—in our dissatisfaction with the results of the various endeavours and policies of both local and central government—to rush to explanations of resource or organisational inadequacies. Hence crash programmes of expenditure and massive structural upheavals. This has tended to ignore the radical changes which could be enacted **within** existing resource and organisational constraints—if only we had the political insight, will and organisation, if only we appreciated and tried to alter the ideological drift of (a) local government administrative structures and processes and (b) professionalism and its influence on the development of the social skills of the ordinary person. The nationalist debate has been a serious distraction.

Judgements on the contribution of the new structure of local government to a development of democracy depends on one's definition of 'power' and one's view on how it can and should be shared. The current definition which seems implicit in our actions ignores, in its concentration on the 'formal' and the 'economic', three crucial aspects of the dimensions of power:-

(1) power as influence (e.g. who creates the agenda? the roles of officers and pressure groups);
(2) the self-fulfilling nature of power;
(3) the fact that concentration of administrative power (in relation to economic programmes of, for example, 'positive discrimination', tightly controlled from the centre) can, in fact, **intensify** the very problems to which the programmes are supposed to be a solution. The further distribution, in local government, of **political** power needs to be seen not just as a democratic right but as part of a political solution to social problem-solving.

We need a more optimistic view of the capacities and potential of people whether officers, members or community groups. The paternalism (of particularly the labour party) which concentrates decision-making in local authorities is dangerous in two senses: **one** in that it conceals the fact that local authorities have **never** had the capacity to supply the level or extent of service they would wish, and **secondly** that the expectation that they should and would saps initiative and can lead to a state of dependency.

Local Government and Devolution: A Confused Debate

One of the difficulties about writing on politics and government in Scotland is that ongoing discussions of political structures and processes seem even more stereotyped and facile here than elsewhere. Whether from deep cultural factors or from peculiarities of our current political and mass media systems, any signs of conceptualising in political discussion are quickly discouraged in Scotland. The country's size and history clearly make her 'establishment' a very coherent one, the value-system more uniform. Labour may be in formal control in the majority of local authorities but there is little doubt that the values to which which deference is paid owe more to Knox than to Marx.(1) We are not very good in Scottish Labour circles at asking to whose tune our government machine is dancing we tend to define 'power' (if at all) in a rather limited way as possessed by those who imprint their seal on (or are influential in) the formal decisions of government rather than by those who set up the agenda in the first place around which the skirmishing of politicians and pressure groups occurs.(2)

Specifically there tends to be an unholy ideological alliance between Scottish 'labourism' and our local government administrators and professionals which brands as academic any probing of the purposes served by our existing governmental structures and policies.

The Wheatley Commission was in this bland tradition, in effect giving those who ran local government a clean bill of health—it was the statutory framework within which they worked which was at fault, not political or administrative behaviour or assumptions. This blandness in our establishment has as its natural foil a latent populism which expresses its antagonism to 'the powers that be' in deeply emotional but generally ineffective terms. It knows what it is opposed to and supports, with fervour, the present—that is when it is about to disappear! Thus local government reorganisation is seen as creating a 'monstrous bureaucracy'—as if we were currently living with benign, responsive and effective local authorities, or as if those who malign so confidently and expectantly the new system had ever had a good word for the old!

John Mackintosh notwithstanding(3) nowhere did we see critical analysis of the Commission's analyses and assumptions of the quality of Ioan Bowen Rees' sadly neglected book on the English and Welsh recommendations.(4) This is not, however, to deny the essential validity of or need for the Wheatley **recommendations**—which I have elsewhere supported.(5) It is merely to indicate that the analysis of the nature of local government which preceded and the debate which followed those recommendations left a lot to be desired. The pious expressions of objectives and tired discussion of functions, scale and structures simply fail to relate to the simple question of how (local) government impacts on the ordinary person and the extent to which continuing social problems and feelings of powerlessness or alienation are functions of (a) inadequate local government boundaries and powers, (b) policy inadequacies, (c) resource inadequacies, (d) political inadequacies, (e) managerial incompetence, or (f) ideological confusion. One wonders whether any members of the Wheatley Commission had ever lived in or represented one of our tenemental inter-war council estates.

Indeed the 'debate' on local government reorganisation has tended to have the same unreal aspects as did the 'Great (non) Debate' on British entry to the Common Market, the antagonists making greater claims to jingoism than to intellectual acumen and the protagonists having apparently so given up hope in the capacity of internal reform as to be blindly pinning their faith on the benefits of the 'cold winds of external change.'

For all the play with such words as 'democracy' and 'power' there was, in fact, little or no discussion of the respect in which the proposed changes in structure would, in fact, make local government more 'democratic'—either in terms of the ordinary person playing a greater role in decision-making or in terms of central government relinquishing areas of administrative or financial control. Nor was this surprising—given the Commission's failure to investigate the democratic inadequacies of the contemporary local government scene.(6)

As a consequence we are now having a very confused debate in Scotland on our form of government. There are, in fact, four separate issues whose themes are intermingled—
a) the inherent merits of the 1973 Local Government Act;
b) the consequences of a Scottish Assembly for the new local government system;
c) the process of establishment of the new authorities (with various controversial decisions on staffing and structures);(7)
d) the financial problems of existing local government.

Deliberately, or otherwise, confusion between these various themes is causing bewilderment and naïve demands for neat, 'final' solutions. What is particularly sad is the way in which a series of challenges facing local government—particularly corporate planning, community action and the first two in the list above—are being debated separately, in different compartments, their essential relationships being missed. The 'debate' on the reorganisation of government structures in Scotland which we have had in the past seven years has been politically debilitating in the way it has distracted attention from questions about(a) the content and relevance of local and central government social policies, and (b) the nature and adequacy of the social assumptions of the various groups who control particularly local government.

It is now commonplace to say that the 1973 Local Government (Scotland) act was, at one and the same time, both too soon and too late:(8) that is that it reflects the needs of the 1950's and 1960's but is out of tune with a society which is now more realistic about the 'benefits' of scale and which finds itself with an 'intermediate' level of government. I find the present concern for the scale of the new local authorities suspect for the following reasons:

> 1. the people who wanted local government reorganisation halted for this reason had, to a man, nothing to say about the serious defects (on both managerial and democratic criteria) of current local authority structures and processes: or if they did, it was put down to inadequate individuals or political parties. The frustrations I meet in housing schemes of less than 10,000 population within the area of responsibility of the most progressive and sensitive local authorities of less than 100,000 population clearly indicate defects which have more to do with limited theories of management, democracy and information flow than with size! It is sad that neither the protagonists of, nor antagonists to, Wheatley gave this the attention it deserved. Fears about the 'distance' of the new local authorities are rather ironic since that is an epithet which fits most of our old authorities whose operations tend to mystify and frustrate and which have, as a whole, little or no capacity to represent or meet the real needs of the working class people. (See argument in section on 'structural weaknesses' below).
> 2. the fashionable appeal to 'smallness', to the 'community', is ambiguous. It draws on a variety of inspirations which are difficult to reconcile with one another: from Schumacher(9) to a totalitarian (Calvinist?) concern for total self-sufficiency, from anarchism to Samuel Smiles' bourgeois 'self-help' ethic. A 'self-concerning community'(10) does not sound a pleasant or caring one to me!
> 3. an exclusive concern for the small-scale fails to appreciate that problems cannot be solved at a neighbourhood (or even Scottish) level on their own. The tragedy has been

that the centralistic myth (that they **can** be solved at a national level) has gripped us for so long that the attractive option seems, to so many, to swing to the opposite extreme. It is significant that a variety of community projects—while continuing to assert the need for neighbourhood involvement and control—have emphasised the importance of linking that to action at a British level for socio-economic change.(11) It needs to be recognised that administrative and certain political needs in local government pull in apparently opposite directions: the delivery of service to consumers needing to be decentralised (and consumer influence strengthened) at the same time as policy review and resource allocation decisions are centralised. But these opposite tendencies can and must be harmonised within the operations of our government apparatus.

If the Scottish Assembly is able (a) to legislate and (b) to exercise control over the vast power Scottish Office civil servants have, it will have its hands full. These are completely different functions from the administrative ones of the Districts and Regions. Those who argue an inconsistency between Regions and the Scottish Assembly are clearly in the business of centralising power still further!

Far from there being an inconsistency between local government reorganisation and a Scottish Assembly, they permit a **start** to be made to the creation of a more relevant government structure. Our government institutions to date have failed to reflect the needs of various levels of 'community'—from the neighbourhoods upwards. However accidentally, our new structure does give us this perspective. I suspect that those who use pejoratively the term 'overgovernment' are really fearful that there is going to be too much democracy about! It is time that certain people faced up to reality and recognised that there is a neighbourhood interest, a District interest, a West of Scotland interest, for example(12)—as well as a Scottish and British one. Our current government structures frustrate this. Democracy cannot function unless the different levels which people operate can be linked together. The problem to date has been the inability of groups of people at one level to relate **their** problems to the reality of the level of government immediately above them.

What relationship **is** there in the present local government system between the individual problem and the local authority policy. Or between local government problems and central government policies? It is the absence of the effective translation of problems at one level of government on to the agenda of the next that accounts for the present frustrations with our government processes. The nationalist concern simply to alter geographical areas of control totally misses the real point about the nature of government and the consequences of a particular model of central-local government relations which has its grip on us. I think it fair to say, for example, that the vast majority of us immersed in local government find it difficult to accept that a Scottish level of government will of itself do anything about the problems in the existing relationships we have with Scottish Office: the present debate is simply passing this by!! We all have our particular hobby-horses, our particular tales.

Let me instance merely three issues. How, first, can local government be expected to conduct its affairs 'corporately' when Scottish Office is still organised vertically and finds it virtually impossible to respond to a corporate approval from **one** authority, let alone all? Have the nationalists any understanding of that sort of very real practical issue?

What, secondly, local authorities increasingly need and are coming to to demand of central government is **advice**: in too few cases can they obtain it. The Scottish Office tradition is a controlling one rather than an **advisory** or **enabling** one. Scottish Office has done little, if anything, to allow those local authorities about to embark on new programmes to learn about the attempts, successes or failures of authorities who have been there before them(13): some circulars distilling some ideas of the more 'progressive' authorities may be distributed (e.g. housing policy). But what about the follow-up? Even on major innovations by local authorities the attitude is generally unhelpful **both** in the sense of being unable or unwilling to pass on relevant information or perspectives, **and** in the sense of not helping financially innovatory projects. I have seen civil service memos which indicate quite clearly that civil servants do not understand the political reality of local government which, precisely because it is local, makes innovations and risk-taking difficult and hence sometimes requires such innovations to receive at least some financial support from central government (I am thinking of an experimental scheme for intermediate treatment and of analytical resources for a scheme of positive discrimination). Centrally the current 'model' of relations operated by central government whereby it benignly chooses a 'needy' area to give money to—rather than responding to innovation is inadequate.

Related to this is my third issue—that of research. The real understanding—potential and actual—of the nature of the problems on the local government plate are **within** local government.

True it has not yet developed processes to exploit this understanding but the importance of policy review in local government seems at least now to be receiving lip-service. Unfortunately, the central government interest is to centralise research in units in Edinburgh and London, peripheral generally to the power structure. There are good arguments indeed that the Units, far from increasing learning, are a device to **prevent** local and central government learning! These are real issues about central-local relationships which we ignore at our peril. (See notes 21 and 42).

What is wrong with our local authorities?

It seems to me the discussions of the last decade have run away from a simple question—what precisely is wrong with our local authorities that they are experienced by people—whether the' public or such field officers as social workers—as irrelevant, inhumane and unresponsive? Why the feeling of a system which is out of control or in which the 'powers that be' don't care?

Many people, it needs to be said, would deny that there is, in fact, anything wrong with the current relationship between local government and the community. "If there were, the existing councillors would soon be out on their ear"—is both the pragmatic and the democratic theorist's reply. The critique would, however, point to the extent of electoral indifference and to the many more specific indices of extreme dissatisfaction (as evidenced at Tenant Association meetings or political 'surgeries').

Caution is needed when talking about civic 'satisfaction' with local government. Satisfaction obviously stems from the relationship between expectations and perceived outcomes. Each of these is subjective and varies from group to group. The middle class person expects more and is more articulate. Do we give the same 'weight' to **his** index of dissatisfaction as that of someone who is so deferential and cowed as to accept a low standard of services? The 'democratic' measure of performance (the ballot box) ignores the vicious process whereby the dominant values of a few affect working class expectations.

That many perimeter council schemes have been sadly neglected by council authorities, have been stigmatised and used as 'dumping grounds' for 'problem families' is a clear indication of certain indefensible 'necessities' of our political system. Whom do we wish to satisfy? 'The electorate' may be a good labour answer—but hardly a socialist one!! I hasten to say that I am **not** preaching violent revolution and an end to ballot box democracy when I say this: I am rather trying to suggest that justifying government action by exclusive reference to the ballot box is dishonest and specious. Governments have considerable scope for freedom of action: the 'mandate' theory of government will simply not hold water.(14) It is a refuge of scoundrels, liars and cowards. This is appreciated—although seldom admitted—at national level: the myth unfortunately still has a grip on even the private beliefs of local politicians!

One thing above all the Labour party needs to discuss more explicitly amongst itself; that is the meaning of the ballot box. Does it **really** give the member the legitimacy he claims? What assumptions are made about electoral beliefs? Is it really true that the electorate cannot take uncomfortable truths(15), that prevarication is tactically sound? Was it **ever** true that the burning concern of the electorate was to minimise rate burdens? Or is it not that at one time these were useful rationalisations of socialists who were unable to get their way in the administration and had their consciences to appease? It is time the party decided whether their function in local government is to govern smoothly with the minimum of public fuss—the easy life—or whether it is to improve life chances.

The problem with local government is a combination of the nature of (a) its organisational structures, and (b) the beliefs which motivate elected members and officers about each other's role and the community, supporting and supported by those structures.

Structural Weaknesses

On the structural side there are two fundamental weaknesses in present local government which castrates the political process(16)—namely that neither at the political nor administrative level has there been (a) a 'neighbourhood' perspective, or (b) an overall corporate focus on the needs of the area of the authority as a whole, separate from the needs of the constituent services which made up the local authority.

The absence of the latter entails the separate development of services, with their own (limited and conflicting) perception of how people ticked and what they needed.(17) The agenda, in short, has been in the hands of the professionals (I discuss the failure of the political machine in the last section). It has been put most succinctly by Peter Marris and Martin Rein in a book 'Dilemmas of Social Reform' which should be on every Labour councillor's bedside in preference to the Paterson Report on Management Structures.

> 'The behaviour of institutions is determined by the information on which they act. If the information they attend to is biased and faulty, their actions will be neither an impartial interpretation of the common cause nor the most rational means to achieve it. The structure of communication in a complex democracy is articulated in such a way as to inhibit the exchange of some crucial information. Administration becomes separated into functional and geographically segregated bureaucracies, co-ordinated by an increasingly centralised political authority, or not co-ordinated at all when power at the centre is stultified by its divisions. There is then little communication between bureaucracies, although the interdependence of society makes the actions of each highly relevant to many others. The central political authority is left with the task of interpreting the implications of this interdependence, and devising a coherent policy for each of its bureaucratic arms. The complexity and amount of information it must assimilate is only manageable, so long as it can be reduced to mechanical systems of analysis, and this places an unforeseen power in the hands of those who devise the framework of analysis. It becomes more and more difficult to feed into this process, in any meaningful way, the needs of the ordinary citizen as he perceives them: he cannot challenge the expertise of policy analysis, nor govern the functioning of institutions. Yet the needs he expresses are ultimately the only legitimate source of political authority. Thus democracy drowns in the flood of information it is trying to master.'(18)

It is unfortunate that precisely at a time when the need for corporate planning **within** local authorities is being appreciated(19) powers have been split between Districts, Regions and undemocratic Health Boards.(20) This emphasises the need to go beyond 'corporate' to 'inter-organisational' planning(21) which was the essential argument at at the end of the previous section. What we must remember in all the managerial talk about objectives and their maximisation is that 'my' objectives are someone else's constraints! It is not much use a District maximising **its** objectives if the effect on a Region or Health Board is negative.

As far as the neighbourhood focus is concerned the failings are twofold: in the first instance the member is not given any **structural** support for his representative role in understanding and articulating the **total** needs of the geographical area which has elected him. Appointed only to committees which have a burgh or city-wide focus, he is unable to monitor the cumulative effects of council policies and their delivery on the area he represents. His whole representative role indeed is treated as illegitimate. However good a grassroots worker he may be he is reduced to the status of a medicine man who spends his time sorting out **individual** problems **and,** by incantations and blustering, gives the impression that he is pursuing collective ends. The reality is different. He is trapped in the structures and assumptions of a different world. It is here that community councils should be seen by the member as an opportunity to strengthen his representative role. On the administrative side, secondly, the way we organise our field-staff in local government as a whole does not permit the development of co-ordination and insights at grassroots level into the problems and needs of neighbourhoods—nor the administrative decentralisation to ensure delivery of service at the most effective level. I have argued elsewhere(22) that 'having understood the need to break down separatism **between** departments, the challenge is now the separatism which exists **within** departments—between H.Q. and the field staff.' Exhortations for changes in behaviour on its own is of no avail: new structures are needed if these failings are to be repaired—equally a political insistence that Chief Officers give their staff more autonomy.

One proposal which brings all these various threads together is that of the Area Committee System currently in operation in Stockport and areas of Liverpool and being edged towards in other areas.(23) I was delighted that the volume of the West Central Scotland Plan on "Social Problems" (whose introductory section is a must for Labour members) came out in favour of such a structure as an essential focus for local government to ensure that relevant, community-based information and insights are flowing into our local authorities and effecting their thinking.

The response of a lot of people is to say—where on earth are we going? Is it possible for human beings to cope with this plethora of structures and innovations? On top of reorganisation and such new processes as policy planning, on top of the complex structure of community councils, Districts, Regions and Scottish Assembly (each with their liaison processes) we are also expected to look at such devices as Area Committees? It is a fair comment, which has to be answered.

Two points need to be made: one, that there needs to be more clarity about the stages of decision-making (from problem-definition through isolation and assessment of alternatives to the actual authoritative decision and its implementation).(24) Advice and influence is a neglected aspect of power: it falls short of actual decision-making but is a crucial part of the process. People may care to dismiss it as mere 'talking' but the process is essentially a self-fulfilling one—if the analysis and advice is seen to be capable of persuading decision-makers then people will persevere and achieve results. If a fatalistic approval is adopted then nothing will be achieved and and one's fatalism proved right! At the very least the aim of the new consultative and advisory processes should be to ensure that rigorous explanations are given by the decision-makers of any difficulties in implementing the submissions of the advisory groups.(25) The second point is that we are presently in Britain undergoing nothing short of a revolution in our attitude to government institutions: in Scotland the dissatisfaction is stuck at a rather immature and naive stage which believes that all that is needed is a change in scale from government over 50 million to government over 5 million.

Changes in scale are obviously needed—but more so are changes in purpose, in the nature of the relationship between government and governed and that between different levels of government. What we are seeing just now is the uneasy co-existence of elements of two worlds. The closest parallel is the change to a preventive strategy in social work—moving away from a 'fire-engine' approach to one concerned to act on root causes. One cannot stop curative work to engage on preventive activities: while engaged on fire prevention education you don't refuse to put out fires! The adoption of preventive activities involves a double financial and administrative burden.(26)

'Life in local government is now more complicated simply because the variety of perceived conflicting pressures and values is greater than ever before: the problems of reconciling them is increasingly difficult: trying to wish this complexity away by concentrating on the efficient organisation of one's own little patch just won't do any more.'(27)

Ideological Weaknesses

The last five years have seen in England a challenge to many aspects of administration and professionalism in local government: corporate management(28) and community action(29) have, in their different ways, subjected local government professional behaviour, assumptions and ideology to a serious critique. This challenge forces a re-examination of the basis of professionalism but has not been so evident in Scotland(30) partly, no douht, because of the greater deference our culture still pays to those values, partly because of the distractions of the debate on an intermediate level of government. One of the functions of local government is supposed to be the control of the administration(31) and I would suggest that a considerable lessuii remains to be learned for those in local government. I would go further and suggest that the resistence to local government reform owes not a little to the reluctance to dispense with practices which should have been rejected many years earlier.

The planning profession was one of the first to develop a coherent ideology which soon threatened to pre-empt the political process in local government.(32) Its pre-emption takes the form of an attempt to abolish 'politics' by an assertion of the essential harmony of social life: as means, it uses a concentration on long term objectives of such a bland vagueness that no-one can disagree. In England—but not in Scotland—the younger element have been more prepared to concede the 'consensus' assumptions implicit in planning methodology, and to admit that certain groups benefit from local authority decisions and others suffer. Corporate planning at its best is concerned to break the blandness and to concentrate not on vague objectives but on the precise nature of an authority's policies, their shortcomings and the nature of the obstacles which prevent a movement from the present to an improved state of affairs. True radicalism makes its starting point not the future but the present: it asks simple but probing questions about the present which incredibly are not asked within present Scottish local authorities: e.g.

- what are the local authority's existing policies?
- whom do they benefit?
- what do they achieve?
- how far short do they fall of what we would like to achieve?
- how, in precise terms, do we go about bridging that shortfall?

It is what the corporate jargon calls 'position statements'. From these(33) it is argued that new Policy committees should be able to understand more clearly the nature of the problems in the community and to ensure that the energies, analyses and resources of the authority are being bent towards problems which have deliberately been picked out by the members as deserving attention and on which some analytical effort has been expended. I would suggest that this simply will not happen with the conventional administrative processes and structures: the superimposition of a Policy committee, a top management team of officers and a Policy Planning Unit, however necessary of themselves, are not sufficient.

The Challenge of Corporate Planning

Corporate management is the smokescreen behind which a variety of activities now shelter: it occasionally marks the unchanged processes of bureaucracy. It is, again, used to describe new (and overdue) procedures for establishing inter-departmental dialogues. Or again to indicate an assertion of autocratic control by a Chief Officer Group. "You pays your money and takes your choice." Its essence is an attack of the way our understanding of reality has been blinkered and compartmentalised by professional perceptions: it is an attempt to reassert the totality of social existence, to deny the possibility of tackling 'educational' problems, for example, in isolation of such wider issues as housing policy. Unfortunately, its philosophical message tends to get lost amongst its organisational imperatives! Even in England, where various corporate innovations preceded reorganisation and hence gave people a chance to learn, there are few signs of the essentially socialist message of the concept being practised: In Scotland the conservatism of local government is such that only about three authorities made any attempt prior to reorganisation to experiment. The chances of avoiding its bureaucratisation must accordingly be slimmer.

Corporate management **should** be about the translation of what is essentially a socialist principle into management and planning processes: in its technocratic form, however, it freezes a sociological insight into an elitist technique. It breaks down **some** artificial barriers (within the local authority) only to reinforce others (between the authority and the community). The inadequacies of some practitioners, however, should not make us throw the baby out with the bathwater.

Corporate planning principles would suggest there are untapped areas of power within even the present statutory framework of local authorities (if only the services would work with rather than against each other). Certainly in my experience the real insights and skills in relation to many problems which central government finds baffling (and sets up centralised research units or prgrammes to deal with) lie within the local authority field of operations. What, however, is certainly true is that:

1. local government has not **until now** made any attempt to establish the capacity to marshall these insights systematically and feed them to the relevant decision-makers, within or beyond local government;(34)

2. its assumptions are too paternalistic; jealous of its 'power' and reluctant to play the role of 'enabler' rather than 'provider' it carries within itself both the answer to many of the community's problems and the seeds of its own destruction.

On the first point: the real and neglected question is on **whose** terms the new system of corporate planning will be carried out? Will there be a new breed of planners who establish their own limited terms of reference, establish an image in their own likeness—fitting problems to the Procrustean Bed of their methodological requirements.(35) Or, at the other extreme, will the community councils (with community work input) establish the agenda? Will, again, the political groups be able to make the machine dance, for once, to a political tune? The options are not necessarily mutually exclusive—the real challenge is to encourage political, community and administrative developments and to establish a dialogue whereby the insights of each can educate the others.(36)

In terms of some previous comments there is one thing we should be clear about. Decision-making which is not based on the perceptions of 'life as it is' at the grass-roots is most inadequate. It is critical that, for example, regional policy planning is plugged directly or indirectly into the neighbourhood perspective. It is hoped that the new Districts will take a leaf out of the Stockport book(23) and also see the community councils not as a threat but as a necessary means of re-establishing the political purposes of local government. It now seems that there is an important role which could be played by the Region-District liaison committee which is to be established in each District—if properly serviced by the administration this could supply a missing corporate perspective of District needs.

Paternalism

On the second point about paternalism in local government it needs to be said that our representative system of government has two major defects: it may appear—on the surface of things—to be a necessary and sufficient means of keeping a check on what bureaucracy **does**. It is, however, unable to control the **size** of that bureaucracy. Indeed the inherent logic of the political process in a representative system (with a rather crude view of the electorate) seems to lead to a continual increase in the size of the bureaucracy to satisfy imagined demands as defined by professionals and politicians. Like Alice in Wonderland, the political element in local government has, as a consequence, to run harder and harder in a vain attempt to stay in the same place—as far as the appearance of control is concerned.

The other insidious factor in a representative system is the self-fulfilling, concentrating nature of political power: starved of the practice of decision-making for himself, of the feelings of satisfaction and creative achievement which flow from involvement in personal or civic design on his own terms, the ordinary citizen tends to live **down** to the lowly expectations those in authority above them tend to have of him(37), thus intensifying the extent of the bureaucratic task.

The result is an odd combination—a state of dependency in the public on the one hand but one which produces alienation and a pathological search for scapegoats. The incredible scapegoat hunting which is a feature of relations between our present levels of government—each blaming the agency immediately above for all its problems—should alert us to the fact that too much control is exercised by agencies over those immediately beneath them. While we need different levels of government, each must have more autonomy—both administrative and financial—than at present.(38)

The individuals in local government—particularly the elected member—work immensely hard (complaints, committee and political work) and sacrifice a lot. They can be forgiven for equating effort and sacrifice with achievement. Equally their anger at those who in effect challenge their legitimacy or attack the effects of the authority policies and who show no signs of wanting to make allowance for the impossible odds under which the system is working is understandable. But so, too, is that unwillingness to make allowances! It is an unhelpful 'dialogue'. Let us all agree that local government is expected to do too much: that the resources never have nor will be available to realise those expectations of local government—indeed that this very expectation that they will or should is a large measure of the 'problem'. Once this is granted we can then have a realistic and healthy discussion about social problems. Until then dialogue between local government and communities will consist largely of mutual vituperation.

For too long local and central government (and Labour Party) have given the impression that problems were capable of solution by (a) direct government action from above , (b) action defined in terms of cash—'the more cash, the more effective the programme.'

The conjunction of the community action critique and financial constraints now give us, paradoxically, a great opportunity for making a breakthrough as far as the neglected political role of local government is concerned. Local government can respond to its financial crisis in one of two ways: the first is to state simply that certain goals are simply not going to be achieved. The other way is for it to act as the catalyst for **community** action—trying to indicate clearly in public documents(39) the size and nature of any particular problems and, in conjunction with the community, agreeing then on what needs to be and can be done by local government and what by voluntary activity.(40) Only in this way, for example, will consultative processes be meaningful. (At the moment when local authorities view them as necessary, public relations exercises to **announce** decisions and the expectations of people are then dashed or their lack of experience and control over professional vocabulary makes them behave angrily, the exercises merely confirm the prejudices each side has of the other!) More to the point, only this framework will permit political control of the bureaucracy and permit the real skills and energies of ordinary people to be realised.(37)

Labour Groups

It is impossible to generalise about the activities of Labour groups in Scottish local authorities: negligible research or even writing has been carried out on this crucial subject.(41) One is, therefore, forced back on one's own biased insights, on participant observation.

One's starting point must be the basic one that a fortuitous combination of circumstances, motives and processes have propelled individual councillors, to serve voluntarily—and generally at considerable sacrifice—in council chambers. Any analysis which misses this will be totally inadequate. When one adds to this (a) a party machine which at both local and central(42) level offers no serious comment on or help towards the ongoing activities of the local authority, (b) the absence within the local authority of a whole range of political resources (ranging from the basic clerical ones to a capacity for research) and (c) a democratic ideology which emphasises the importance of meeting the most vociferous pressures, one should not be surprised that the behaviour of Labour groups tends to have little in common with socialism.

By what criteria does one judge the performance of labour groups? Electoral success (as I tried to suggest above) is really not good enough. The current fashion for measures of output might suggest to the average councillor such indices as numbers of council houses built or modernised, low rent levels and more recently perhaps the expenditure on various forms of charity to the elderly. I would suggest that these are all equally dangerous, that they confuse expenditure on physical output with achievement—particularly as far as an increase in life-chances for the ordinary person is concerned. I would suggest a simpler measure of the extent to which labour groups are likely to be playing their proper role: that is the extent of critical discussion of the nature of the problems facing the community and of the relevance of ongoing policies which **precedes** rather than slavishly reflects the officers' recommendations, the extent to which labour groups build bridges to and learn from community activists in working class areas rather than treating them as 'dangerous wreckers'.

There is nothing so sad as to see a movement supposedly representing the working class act as a means of bureaucratic oppression, turning a blind eye (or encouraging) housing policies which draw their philosophy from Poor Law assumptions, blaming the poor(43) for their state, or conducting witch hunts against those who try to represent the interests of the poor.

In Scotland—as numerous reports have indicated(44)—our urban areas have shocking concentrations of poverty and deprivation. What exactly are the views of labour groups about the causes of this—or the means to ameliorate it? Various explanations have been advanced in the literature: Bob Holman offers the neatest classification. He divides explanation into three sorts(45).

> (a) **explanations which focus on families or individuals** and regard the crucial element as inadequate child rearing or socialisation practices of a minority of parents. This leads to an emphasis on immediate programmes of intensive family casework, pre-school playgroups, nursery schools etc. **On its own** this is Sir Keith Joseph's 'cycle of deprivation' thesis
>
> (b) **explanations focussing on institutions:** this believes that the basic framework and philosophy of the social services are sound but that faults within the workings of the agencies mean that those in need are not fully reached. This leads to an emphasis on co-ordination between departments, more relevant information for the consumer etc. Holman's comment is;
>
> 'Despite the obvious scope for institutional reform it is open to the criticism that the changes it achieves are only marginal to the lot of the poor. Welfare rights activities have been attacked for giving implied support to a means-tested philosophy and level of benefits which themselves perpetuate stigma and poverty. Several community projects have discovered that service inadequacies stemmed more from a basic lack of resources than from a lack of co-ordination, poor communication or other institutional deficiencies. The conclusion is not that institutional reforms are not required but that even successes here will not mean an end to poverty.'
>
> (c) **Structural Explanations** whose basic assumption is 'that society consists of identifiable groupings whose interests are in conflict. In order to maintain a stratified society, social mechanisms of two types are required. Firstly, mechanisms which recruit to the minority positions persons who will uphold the values and assumptions of that minority and, secondly, mechanisms which demonstrate that the poor are to blame for their poverty.'

If there were some signs of labour groups discussing these issues one would have reasons for hope. But the essential feature of labour groups has, in the past, been a blinkered attitude to such problems: parochialism has blinkered them to the ideas and experiments in other areas. Legalism has blinkered them from doing anything outwith their statutory jurisdiction—hence the reluctance to liaise with voluntary groups on the problems of their area or to represent upwards to central government any rigorous statements of central government policy inadequacies. Labour groups are now showing a healthy realisation of certain institutional deficiencies: until, however, they are aware of the third explanation, their policies, for example, in relation to 'positive discrimination'(46) of concentrating **economic** resources will be counter-productive.

If working relations have been difficult to achieve **between** groups(47) and between local authorities and other agencies they have, it must be said, been equally difficult **within** groups. Only a political strategy can unite a group and enable it to pursue a political purpose: the absence of any conception of what their political task was (how many labour groups have bothered to issue real manifestoes?) has ensured two things

> (a) any innovations have been due to forceful officers or individual politicians; by stealth rather than enthusiastic group consensus;(48)
>
> (b) group activity has been essentially a negative thing—its purpose more to do with holding recalcitrant people in line than with implementing clearly thought-out political strategies. These are harsh words. I believe, however, that these inadequacies can be altered and are slight compared with the blustering superficialities of the nationalists.

With the variety of new institutions and processes, with the reduction in the frequency of elections(49), there is now a real chance that Labour groups and local parties can come into their own as places where ideas for properly using local government are critically discussed and processed. Three things, however, are required for this exploitation of the political exploitation of local government.

First is an understanding of the various realities of ideology I have been referring to: second is a strengthening of party organisation at the interfaces of the District and the Region and of local and central government where so many fantasies will continue to be indulged in its absence. The third requirement is, I suspect, the really difficult one: it is a cessation by labour members and 'radical' community activists of their internecine warfare or diplomatic ignoring of each other's existence. Each needs the other and must respect the essentially different—but complementary—role the other is playing.

Radical community work is needed (a) to develop the frustrated skills of large sections of the urban poor, and (b) to act as an independent monitor of the relevance of government policies. But the community activists cannot continue to ignore, bypass or undermine(50) the political element in local government—for all its current weaknesses. This, of course, relates to the perennial issue within the socialist debate of reform and revolution which community action has revitalised and brought within the scope of local government.(51) It is, not surprisingly, my view that preaching revolution is an easy option—a self-fulfilling one.

Conclusion

This may seem a devastating, certainly pessimistic, paper. It is not meant to be. I have never understood how causes could be advanced without a critical analysis of the nature of the obstacles which stood in their path. It is that which the labour movement in Scotland has been short on—fervour and ideals have rusted as a consequence. I have tried, however cryptically(52), to indicate some of the institutional, resource and ideological reasons for inadequate political achievements in local government. Running through the analysis has been a belief in the self-fulfilling nature of our expectations: when little is expected of individuals and the resources (of whatever kind) they are consequently given are inadequate, their performance will accord with the nature of the original expectations. In applying this analysis to excuse the political system in local government in the past—and equally now to expect it to change—we must in return now expect the elected member to do the same in relation to the ordinary person and administrative and political perceptions of his social and political inadequacy.

I have deliberately **not** talked about the mechanics of such issues as the Scottish Assembly or community councils since without facing up to deeper processes of power and government and to the need for internal structural and attitudinal changes within local government and Labour groups, such innovations will fail to realise the hope radicals have of them. They will become merely additions to a conservative and controlling bureaucracy.

We have learned a lot in the last few years about our government processes and their effect on people: the tragedy is that this learning has not come from the devolution 'debate': nor has it affected the political process in local government. It has come from the insights and frustrations of the new social work departments(53) and from the activities of those who work outside and, in many cases, in opposition to local authorities. Our present local government structures frustrate learning. Our task is surely to create, of our government structures, 'learning organisations' and then to act on those lessons!

Regardless of where we think the Scottish Assembly may take us, of fears that we may be on the slippery path to independence, our task as socialists is surely to challenge the conventional wisdom, to expose the naivety of the present debate and its neglect of simple issues of Who Benefits?

1. For one of the best discussions see Tom Nairn's two articles—**"Scotland—The Three Dreams"** and **"Scotland—Anomaly in Europe"** in **New Left Review** Nos.49 and 83.

2. The literature on 'power'—its definition and nature is legion:for the consequences of the 'labourite' view of power Ralph Miliband's books on **Parliamentary Socialism** and **The State in Capitalist Society** make stimulating reading.

3. Who did his best to keep discussion on local government re-organisation at the level he established in his succinct book **The Devolution of Power.**

4. **Government by Community.**

5. See the Local Government Unit's First Working Paper—**Notes on Strathclyde.** I have always been one of the 'desperate' supporters of local government re-organisation: I have supported it for three reasons: (a) because I saw it as the only means by which local government might be broken away from its cosy conservatism to exploit its true political role, (b) because it seemed to me that the task of harmonising the existing policies of the various constituent elements of the new authorities would surely—in breaking the old parochialisms—force a basic questioning of the basis and relevance of a whole range of policies and finally (c) because the greater scale of the new system makes patently impossible the continuation of processes mythologised as 'democratic' which were, in fact, deeply autocratic as well as ineffective. Naturally if it is one's view that local democracy is inversely related to geographical distance and requires the approval of every minor administrative activity by a committee of politicians, then the new local government system is an impossibility, a bureaucratic nightmare. The nonsense, however, is in the assumptions of the committee system as we know it (in the sense of their artificial terms of reference on the one hand and their attempt to concentrate both administrative and community power on the other).

6. Severe criticisms of the superficiality of the Radcliffe-Maud Report on English Reform were made—see Jeff Stanyer's article in **English Local Government 1958-1969** ed. J. Wiseman. The more rigorous and logical discussion which the Scottish people should have got from Wheatley is to be found in the minority Kilbrandon Report by Lord Crowther-Hunt and Professor Peacock which places the issue of devolution firmly in the area of the distribution of powers and **not** nationalist sentiment. Even the minority document did not go far enough: for a discussion of the real issues see references at note 29.

7. In which, one must say, local authorities have been indefensibly constrained (in terms of 'opening up' top jobs for which local authorities currently possess little expertise) by the curious operations of the Local Government Staff Commission.

8. Most recently by Barry Cullingworth in a paper to a Planning Conference in Glasgow, 20th November, 1974.

9. **Small is Beautiful**

10. As preached by a prominent SNP campaigner—Malcolm Slessor—whose concern at a recent B.A.S.W. Conference on **Born to Fail** was incredibly that Pitlochry's indigenous fiddler was now over the hill in another settlement! This is 'proof' of the decline of community life! His lack of interest in the small but significant assertions of tenant power in certain Scottish working class housing schemes was vivid proof of the petty bourgeois essence of Scottish nationalism!

11. See particularly the Shelter Neighbourhood Action Project (SNAP) on Liverpool and the various documents by John Benington on the Coventry Community Development Project (inspired by R.H.S. Crossman). Also the **Inter-Project Review** of the C.D.P.'s.

12. Since the end of the second world war a variety of ad hoc measures (culminating in the West Central Scotland Plan Team) have attempted to grapple with the unique—and deteriorating—situation of this area, constantly stymied by the parochial jealousies of its constituent parts.

13. This is a complex area made all the more difficult by the 'secretive', illicit nature of a great deal of central-local government relations at the **official** level. Against the critical comments, I must concede the powerful 'progressive' role which a variety of individual Scottish Office Civil Servants play in relation to cautious local authority professionals! I still worry, however, about the technocratic, apolitical nature of the official dialogue. An example is the Comprehensive Community Planning Scheme (C.C.P.)

14. See pp.25-26 of the author's paper on **The Politics of Change in Local Government** (Local Government Unit—Paisley).

15. I would suggest that far from frank assessments by elected members (indeed chairmen) of the shortcomings of their policies or departments causing a transfer of votes to opposition candidates

(as the mythology assumes) it is the opposite that happens. It is the impression of complacency which the present apologist, public relations role so easily and naturally accepted by members, which engender frustration, cynicism and low polls in local government.

16. As I argue in **Politics of Change in Local Government** (Local Government Unit).

17. For a fairly neutral but useful statement of this see particularly the opening sections of **The Sunderland Report** (HMSO).

18. For a more succinct version see Marris' article in Fabian Tract 419, **Toward Participation in Local Services.**

19. See, for example, the 1972 Bains Report (England) and the 1973 Paterson Report (Scotland).

20. See **Co-ordinating the Work of the New Authorities** (Local Government Unit).

21. Set out particularly within **Public Planning—the Inter Corporate Dimension** by Friend, Power and Yewlett.

22. **Co-ordinating the work of the New Authorities** (Local Government Unit) (also in **Politics of Change**) (ibid).

23. pp.25-28 of **Co-ordinating the Work of the New Authorities.**

24. It was good to see the interim report from the Marris Committee on **Housing and Social Work—A Joint Approach** make this point at p.13.

25. This requires procedures for mutual exchange of information between local authorities and community groups. Local government has been bad enough at seeking the views of relevant groups and in releasing relevant information at the right term in comprehensible form. It is even worse at explaining why—in relation to a range of options—it chose an unpopular one.

26. The argument is oversimplified, of course, in its assumption that preventive measures will ever in the social field make curative measures superfluous!

27. p.15 of **Co-ordinating the Work of the New Authorities.**

28. The more insightful books on this are J.D. Stewart's **Management of Local Government** and **The Responsive Local Authority**, Tony Eddision's **Local Government: Management and Corporate Planning** and **The Sunderland Report** (HMSO). None of these, however, show the problems of the relationship between corporate planning and the real live political and administrative process: parts of my own **Politics of Change in Local Government** try to cover this. See also **Current Issues in Corporate Planning for Local Government** ed. S. Merrington (INLOGOV).

29. Access to the mysteries of this field has been made easier by the recent publication of **Community Work—One** ed. by Jones and Mayo and **Current Issues in Community Work** (Gulbenkian). See also the article by Anderson and Smith on this subject in the excellent book **Participation in Politics** (ed. Parry), the journal **Community Action** (P.O. Box 665, London SW1 8D2) and the collected papers of the 1973 Scottish Directors of Social Work Conference on **Promoting Social Welfare.**

30. Scotland has been able to boast only one C.D.P. project (last of the 12 in Britain to start—in 1973), one Educational Priority Area (the last to publish—vol.5 of the EPA series (HMSO)) and a scatter of privately funded community projects with reasonably radical leanings (YVF, ASSIST, Craigmillar Festival Society (now supported by Edinburgh Corporation), Rowntree etc). That this is a reflection of our innate conservatism is clear from the failure of the Child Poverty Action Group to attract members in the West of Scotland—clearly the area of greatest need!

31. This again is an issue Wheatley seemed rather ambivalent about. For a more open discussion see the article by Owen Hartley in **Local Government Studies** February 1973 on "The Functions of Local Government": also the Sunderland Report and one of the author's own earlier papers **From Corporate Planning to Community Action?—The Repoliticisation of British Local Government** (Local Government Unit)) particularly pp.10-22. A recent book by D. Hill on **Democratic Theory and Local Government** is also valuable.

32. For a development of this theme, the following are useful:

J. Simmie: **Citizens in Conflict**

J. Davies: **The Evangelist Bureaucrat**

N. Dennis: **People and Planning, Public Participation and Planner's Blight**

D. Eversley: **The Planner and Society**

J. Raynor and J. Harden (eds) **Cities, Communities and the Young,** Vol.1

33. Stockport Metropolitan Council and Lambeth are just two authorities amongst many in England who have been working on and have published such voluminous position statements in the past two years.

34. As far as central government is concerned, the potential role of local authority associations has in the past been frustrated by typically divided voices of three separate associations.

35. For a critique of various biases in such system approaches to decsion-making as P.P.B.S. see **Systems Analysis in Public Policy** by I. Hoos.

36. See some of the documents in relation to the Strone/Maukinhill exercise in Greenock (Local Government Unit): this exercise, leaning on the experience in the same town of the first real corporate approach in Scotland to the total rehabilitation of a council estate, attempts to ensure that the 'agenda' of the exercise is set by local tenants (whose definition of the problem involved the authority's policies), that members and tenants establish a working relationship at this stage and that professional skills are the servant, not the master, of the process!

37. This is most eloquently and strongly expressed in the writings of Ivan Illich and, in Britain, Colin Ward. For a more academic discussion see article "Professionalisation, Community Action and Social Service Bureaucracies" in Keele Sociological Monograph 20.

38. Both local authorities and the Scottish Assembly will only cast aside this 'scapegoat syndrome if they are given freedom—within their overall budgetary limits—of allocating 'central' grants and expenditure in the light of their **own** priorities. Put another way—the present frustrations which have to do with the resource constraints of sub-central government can be ameloriated in one of two ways: **either** by granting or extending powers of independent revenue raising **or** by liberating the terms on which central subsidies are allocated.

39. See, as one Scottish example, the process described in the paper **An Experiment in Social Policy Formulation in Greenock and Port Glasgow** (Local Government Units). Strathclyde Region's forthcoming discussion paper on **Information Services** is another which reflects explicitly the philosophy of this paper.

40. For a socialist conversion to the dangers of 'etatism' and the role of the vulunteer. R.H.S. Crossman's **The Role of the Volunteer in the Social Services** (Cambridge University Press pamphlet) is worth study.

41. In general terms, Barry Hindess's work on the **Decline of the Working Class** is obviously relevant. Specifically within the field of local government. Reports such as the Bains and Paterson Reports on the management structures of the new authorities read—as do most consultants' documents—like Hamlet without the prince. Token gesture is made to the existence of parties but otherwise their existence, aims and activities are incredibly ignored. One of the few books which, for the national level, shows real insight into the dynamics of the inter-relationship between politicians and officials—particularly in relation to policy analysis and attempts to improve it—is Heclo and Wildavsky's **The Private Government of Public Money.** A valuable book which relates the theory and practice of local government is John Dearlove's **The Politics of Policy in Local Government.** At a different level M. Hill's **The Sociology of Public Administration** is indispensable.

42. It is significant that the **first** Scottish Labour Party local government Conference ever is being held held this year. As far as the role of local parties is concerned socialists should read C. Greene's article on "Politics, Local Government and the Community" in **Local Government Studies** (June, 1974).

43. See Ryan's **Blaming the Victim** and Bill Jordan's **Poor Parents—Social Policy and the Cycle of Deprivation.** For a brief, critical comment on housing policies see Peter Norman's paper on **The Impact of Local Authority Decisions on Local Communities in Glasgow** delivered to the November 1974 R.T.P.I. Conference in Glasgow. Also the 1973 Shelter Report on Glasgow. For a wider comment Colin Ward's **Tenants Take Over** must not be missed.. Useful case studies are found in an A.C.W. booklet edited by G. Craig (obtainable from 117 Fairholm Road, Bonwell, Newcastle).

44. Glasgow's **Areas of Need** studies: West Central Scotland Plan Vol.4: **Born to Fail.**

45. In the collection **In Cash or in Kind.** For a more extended version see the most recent edition of his **Socially Deprived Families in Britain.**

46. See Fabian Research Series 314 **Positive Discrimination and Inequalities** and Vol.4 of West

Central Scotland Plan.

47. It is interesting to note that local government reorganisation is now at long last forcing the new groups who exist within a Region to recognise that their officebearers should be meeting on a quarterly basis!

48. I am currently writing up some examples of this, particularly in relation to programmes of 'positive discrimination' in 'areas of need'.

49. Originally the idea was that elections would be held every two years: the arrival of a Scottish Assembly probably means that the frequency and intensity of electoral activity for Labour members will **not** now diminish.

50. These are three responses which it is possible to see in the activities of a lot of community activists. It is important that the implications and validity of each be openly explored!

51. See the comment in Midwinter's book **"Priority Education"** that when asked for reading references on community action, he refers to Vol.1 of E.H. Carr's series on The Bolshevik Revolution!

52. This article was commissioned, written and completed in twenty days!

53. Having had a chance to look at Richard Bryant's article in this collection—with whose message I profoundly agree—I must say that I think he seems to underestimate the contribution which the mere existence of social work departments since 1969, in creating tensions with other departments, in exposing problems too long shoved under the carpet, has made to local government. True it may now be in danger of pulling its punches in Scotland. I have just come across a very useful book **"Social Issues and The Social Services"** (ed. M. Brown) which touches on many of the neglected issues of the **political** role of Social Work in a capitalist society. The contribution by Sinfield on **"Poverty and the Social Services Department"** is particularly challenging.

Community Democracy

Colin Kirkwood

I am keen to anchor this article firmly in the reality it presumes to interpret. So the first and largest section of it will consist of a series of thumbnail sketches of Glasgow tenants associations, community newspapers, action groups, and so on. (1).

It will not be a comprehensive survey, rather a selection aiming to show the range and variety of what is happening. The reasons for confining it to Glasgow are: my own Scottish experience lies there; the role of the local authority can be well documented; the city's crop of local action is rich; and time has been very short. No greater-Glasgow chauvinism is intended.

Yoker and District Tenants Association meets monthly in the Corporation's Spiers Hall. Between 20 and 30 attend, mostly women. Tenants' complaints about repairs applied for but not done are taken by the Secretary to the local Housing Manager. Unlike the previous factor, he listens to the tenants' views, for example, they can veto house allocations.

Secretary, Mrs. McCulloch, feels strongly about "anti-social people getting put in by the Welfare. These people have to be helped, but they're not just dumping them in here. We've got a bit here ... that's the area they plump them in ... we feel we're getting more than our share." But she approves of the factor "allowing people to get their children in when they get married ... their parents are able to supervise them, we're building up a community."

Interlocking with the T.A. is the Yoker Youth Movement. Councillor Perry, the clergy, and the Police Community Involvement Dept. have been involved. Weekly activities include a youth club, disco, swimming lessons, and a dancing class. There is an intense conflict between the local activists and the paid leaders. Originally 6 local people were running the club on their own, with badminton, table tennis, billiards and lego. They accepted an offer of help from the F.E. Department, and got nine part-time youth leaders.

Mrs. McCulloch says "they just more or less go round watching kids playing ... running about wild." The local women "canny get daein' any bloody thing." She doesn't think there should be free expression with that number of kids. She's the driving force, she agrees - but insists she doesn't dominate. For example, T.A. members heard the Social Work Department were going to take over Spiers Hall. They didn't want that - the Hall is right in the middle of their street, and many of them are on social security. "Why should we walk through the street - everybody would know our business." They insisted she get up a petition against it.

The View from Gorbals and Govanhill is Glasgow's oldest community newspaper, founded in 1968 by the Gorbals Group (an interdenominational group of Christian ministers and voluntary workers). It tended then to be written by group members, the M.P., and other experts. (From early on, though, Hutchesontown T.A. was contributing its own regular article). The aim was to focus on housing conditions, and give people information about redevelopment. The paper came out monthly, and was sold in pubs, shops, and by teams of children.

In 1971, after editing The View for a year, Bill Williams suggested that it should be reorganised on the basis of local organisations contributing articles, and agreeing to sell a quota of copies. A meeting of Hutchesontown T.A., schools, churches, the ward committee, and the adventure playground, endorsed this suggestion. Now, articles are handed in on the third Monday of the month for typing, and representatives of each organisation come along on the Wednesday evening to do their own layout. Each group folds its own papers. At present, around 1500 are sold each month, more than half of them through organisations.

Last year the Corporation Social Work Department bought a reconditioned varityper for use by The View and other community papers in Glasgow. This improves the appearance, but the typing has to be paid for, so most papers are not yet using it. Another application has been made, for the Corporation to pay the typist. Recently there has been an increased flow of Corporation advertising to The View and other papers, which helps to increase the size, and cover the production costs.

Hutchesontown Tenants Association, started in 1968, covers the new Gorbals, including both SSHA and Corporation tenants. Around 50 attend the monthly meeting in a school. It tends to be mainly older women, though there is a mixture of other age groups, and some men. There has been an influx of younger folk recently - young folk only come to meetings when they've a problem, says Chairman, Roddy Kerr. The Committee of 16 members meets weekly, with an average attendance of between 8 and 12. This is the hub of the T.A., Roddy says. If you haven't got a big committee, you heap a terrific amount of work on a few officials. In H.T.A., different people are prominent in different activities. At the monthly meeting, a councillor answers questions about Corporation matters. Complaints about repairs are sent to the factor - and if they're still not done, to a councillor.

There's an annual sports day, weekly swimming club for kids, a monthly dance, lots of ladies' nights and bus runs. The T.A. has achieved a lot: toilets in the arcade, a community centre, local post offices, telephone kiosks - mostly by hard pressure on councillors. In the case of traffic risk to children in the old Rutherglen Road, the usual channels failed. The tenants went out and demonstrated in the street. A compromise was fixed up. After 9 months, they demonstrated again, and the road was permanently closed to through traffic, in spite of opposition from police and fire brigade.

Two issues currently preoccupy T.A. member, Jimmy Forsyth. One is that Corporation tenants in the scheme are now getting their T.V. aerials rent-free, while SSHA tenants like him still have to pay. The other is the smoke and smell from the nearby distillery.

Govanhill and District Residents Association meets monthly in Dixon Halls, with an average attendance of 20 - mostly council tenants, with a few private tenants and owner occupiers. They are predominantly older women, with a recent influx of some younger people. Complaints are taken and passed on to the appropriate department. Councillors and officials are not usually invited to meetings. G.R.A. sends a delegation to see them when necessary. Delegations report back at the next meeting.

Parts of Govanhill, like Robson Street, have now got local T.A.s, and don't come to G.R.A. meetings. President, Bill Towill, blames the community workers for this. He does not agree that having smaller T.A.s helps to involve more people. "It gets them into their own wee narrow question - divorces them from issues affecting everybody else ... If the issue gets settled, that's them quiet again ... whereas if you get them into one body, you give them a permanent interest in coming."

G.R.A. doesn't work by direct action. You go to one level, and if you get no satisfaction, you go to the next level up. Bill says he tends to dominate G.R.A. meetings, because of his wide involvement in the tenants and trade union movements. "The folk on the floor of the meeting don't know how local government works, they're looking for advice." He thinks T.A.s are inclined to be parochial. Politics should be brought in. But T.A.s shouldn't be the same as trade unions. They're different organisations, because there are everyday issues arising that affect women. "Women'll come if you advertise on problems. But trade union branch life is dead."

Govanhill Action Group started in May 1973 in protest against proposals to demolish 1200 tenement houses to make room for an expressway. Corporation officials said most of the houses were 'done' anyway - only 85 of them could be considered 'long-life' - and arranged a public exhibition of the proposals.

Delegates from local organisations, and interested individuals formed the action group after demonstrating outside the exhibition. The committee of about 12 meets once a month. They are now dealing also with housing problems - members have helped to set up local T.A.s (Calder Square, Annandale Square), also the Govanhill Housing Association, which will buy houses, improve them, and let them out.

The group's counter-proposal on the line of the expressway would route it not through the houses but through land owned by Templeton's Carpet Factory. Templeton's have threatened to close their factory (emloying 1500) if this is done. This alternative had not been put before the public at the exhibition because of private representations from Templeton's. The Action Group has the people of Govanhill behind it, says Davy McCracken, the Chairman. They get a turnout of 100s when they hold a meeting. Half the committee are women. There's a good age-mix - several in their 30s, one 25 year-old.

Closely associated with the Action Group is **The Working Party,** consisting of one delegate from every local organisation, plus officials from Corporation Departments. It discusses the problems of Govanhill. The local delegates say what they would like to see happening. The Working Party has decided to look for premises in the area, to be rented by the Corporation for them - something like a biggish shop, to be an information centre, a meeting place for local organisations, a place to meet officials from the house improvement section, to get free legal advice, etc. The View would be based there, so would the community workers. Davy McCracken feels it's a good idea to have lots of different, independent organisations - but then get them all to come together in the Action Group and be represented on the Working Party. "A Community Council would be a follow-on from what we're doing."

Gairbraid Treatment Area Group formed in 1971 in 2 blocks of tenements in Maryhill, earmarked for demolition. At a meeting the residents elected a committee of 10, which over the next year took action on issues like burst pipes and vandalism, and organised a playgroup, bingo, and nights out at the Maryhill T.U.C. Club.

The rehousing policies of the Housing Management Department became the main focus. Some of the houses offered to families were in a terrible state, and far from Maryhill. So whenever a family got an offer, someone from the committee went to see it with them. Several older tenants were threatened by officials at the house letting section at Clive House, if they refused an offer. So it was decided that pensioners would be accompanied there by committee members.

The BBC made a film publicising their campaign. The result was that the next set of offers were all new houses, in Maryhill. Whenever the offers started to get worse, the group organised a new demo - culminating in April 1972 when they occupied the stairway and house-letting section at Clive House with mothers, prams and kids. The Housing Management tried to disembowel the action group by rehousing most of the key activists early on. But they overcame this move by coming back regularly to continue to play their part.

Eileen Thompson is suspicious of Community Councils and of the Corporation's current overtures to the tenants. Participation doesn't go far enough. There should be an obligation on local authority not only to note people's views but to **act** on them. Local people should control local planning.

Possilpark Tenants Association meets monthly in Hawthorn Primary School. It covers an area of poor quality prewar council houses. Normal meetings attract 160 people, mostly women, but a good lot of men. About a fifth are pensioners, the rest mostly middle-aged. Tea and a cake is served at the meeting. The committee is very active and consists of 2 young men, 2 young women, and 3 older folk. The President takes repairs complaints to the factor. The Association helps those who get into rent arrears - but not 'anti-social' tenants - and help people get rent and rates rebates. They organise bus runs and a big Xmas party.

The main thing just now is the Environmental Improvement Project. The houses have been sandblasted. The old palings, ashpits and drying greens are being removed, and the backcourts are being landscaped with new drying greens, chutes for children, kickabouts for toddlers, and bricked-in refuse containers. The backs are to be lit up by searchlights. A new park has been created, with football pitches, changing rooms, sports facilities, rows of trees. The T.A. complained about the siting of the new bins and got them moved. The one backcourt completed so far is really beautiful. The committee wonder—is this just a showpiece?

There is a problem with one contractor, whose men are breaking and stealing materials and blaming it on "the vandals". President, John Mullen, says there are only a few vandals - its the contractor and his men who are doing most of the damage. However, they decided to read out the names of several vandals at a recent T.A. meeting. John has been told to "leave community councils to the councillors".

Garthamlock Tenants Association has been going since the scheme was built, 18 years ago. Average attendance at this year's monthly meetings was 60. The 13-strong committee meets weekly and is extended to include anyone becoming active in the community. Each member covers 1 or 2 streets for membership.

The environmental sub-committee was active in Facelift Garthamlock (1972) - they ran anti-litter campaigns, worked on restoring the Old Proval Hall, and planted trees in gardens. For the first time, Corporation Departments were drawn into closer contact with the community, and were forced to co-operate with each other.

The Association helps problem families. They're not hostile to them, except when the Housing Management bring in too many.

A Community Survey is being put out, with questions on transfers, repairs, facilities wanted, part-time education, unemployment, buses, etc. "We hope ... (it) ... will give us an accurate picture ... use the answers given to press the authorities for support in our fight to improve our community." "We've got to improve the environment, so's the good tenants will stay", says Secretary, Freddy Anderson.

The T.A.'s very own hall is nearing completion. It is licensed, with main hall, stage, lounge, kitchen, committee rooms, toilets. It is being built with a £40,000 loan from Scottish and Newcastle Breweries, to be repaid over 12 years. They hope the hall will bring the community together, on a non-sectarian basis, for the first time in Garthamlock. They plan to have dancing, bingo, a women's night, OAPs in the afternoons, someone to take complaints always there, etc. Long term aim - to extend it into a really big community centre run by the T.A.

The East End Rents Action Committee Was created in 1973, after the Corporation had given in to the threats of the Secretary of State and agreed to put up the rents. The driving force was Garthamlock T.A. and the aim was to create a broad movement of local organisations to encourage tenants not to pay the increases, and to draw attention to the social problems caused by the Housing Finance Act.

A local minister became chairman, and active support was given by Councillor Edgerton, T.A.s in Queenslie, Ruchaizie, Craigend, Lochend, and the White Panthers, a group of revolutionary young folk. They picketed the factor's office for several weeks, collected over 1000 signatures not to pay the increase, held a march from Craigend to Easterhouse shopping centre, sold copies of Scottish Tenant, and ran a 'problems' surgery. They failed to bring about mass rent-withholding, but created a lot of sympathy and gave many people a better grasp of how local authority activities are financed under capitalism, and the underlying causes of the East End's multiple social, economic and environmental problems.

Barrowfield Tenants Association covers a small area of about 500 immediately pre- and post-war houses of low quality in the inner East End—yet it has an average attendance of 40/50 at its weekly meetings, in Camlachie Community Centre. Complaints about repairs not done are written down and a list sent to the local factor, who writes back stating what action has been taken. The Housing Management Department is not popular in the scheme, and officials attend T.A. meetings rarely and **strictly** on invitation only.

The scheme is used as a dumping ground for problem families. A lot of T.A. members are on Social Security or do not have full-time jobs. The T.A. is attended almost exclusively by women, of all ages,and is possibly unique in having a very capable all-female committee (until last year, when one man came on as Secretary). After business, they have tea and buscuits, and play a few games of bingo. Trips are organised, and parties, treats and gifts for children and pensioners. Separate from the T.A. but run by some of its active members are the playgroup and discos. There is also a mothers' group, and this summer a Barrowfield Festival was held.

Mile-end Planning Action Group draws some of its members from Barrowfield, and others from nearby streets. It grew out of events in Janefield Street, a long straight road running behind Celtic Football Park, which was used by motorists to bypass the traffic lights at Parkhead Cross, and by Croft's Garage to test car brakes.

Several children had been hit by vehicles, and after the last incident, in 1972, the mothers and their children with help from Barrowfield T.A. blocked the street. They said it should be closed to through traffic. The Police said it was impossible. One councillor dragged his feet. The other 2 supported the tenants' case. They blocked the street again in the evening, and after several months delay, they won.

Community workers and the secretary of the ward committee used the incident to draw attention to the Comprehensive Redevelopment Plans affecting the area. All local shops and pubs were to be demolished and not replaced. The area was to be cut off on all four sides by fast modern roads. Later a planning action group was formed, bringing together activists and officials. The case for local shops was quickly conceded, but the road plans are unchanged. At least one local member of the group wonders if they are not just being gently coaxed into accepting the planners proposals.

Barrowfield Community School. In June 1972, contact was made through community workers between some lecturers and students at Jordanhill College of Education, and some members of Barrowfield Tenants Association. Truancy and other school problems were discussed, also the idea of a "free" or community run school. After further contacts, trained teacher Brian Addison, along with a handful of parents and some of their children, began to feel their way towards putting the idea into practice.

Eventually in May 1973, Barrowfield Community School started up in Christ Church Hall. In September, they moved to a flat in St. Marnock Street, with 6 pupils, 1 full-time and 5 part-time teachers. Long term aim is to build up to perhaps 4 full-time teachers and a maximum of 40 kids.

> "One must deal with the **causes** of school refusal, truancy, and early leaving ... If schools are perceived as irrelevant institutions by pupils and parents, it is that point at which we have to start. It is useless to simply try ... stricter punishments ... We have tried to provide a school which is perceived as neither alien or irrelevant by those we wish to benefit from it.
>
> "We have accepted the way children in Barrowfield speak, the values they hold, and the kind of behaviour they evidence ... We have our own values and convictions ... The ensuing dialogue we consider an integral part of the educational process.
>
> "We believe it is pretty important that teachers live in the community ...
>
> "The single most important difference between our school and others ... is the commitment of the parents.
>
> "Child A, for example, may spend Monday working in a restaurant, Tuesday in the

school on follow-up work in marketing, economics, and other aspects of the catering trade. Some time on Tuesday there will be an hour or two for close individual tuition perhaps in Mathematics or Reading ... On Wednesday there will be work with the rest of the group on a community project, interviewing the firemen about their strike, for example, or talking to local tenants about the area and its problems. Wednesday afternoon may be spent in the local Corporation nursery working with pre-school children ... on Thursday morning there is work for 'O' level history, in the afternoon perhaps creative writing or more maths ...

"We have seen a change... (the 6 children) are more confident, more articulate, more sensitive, and more knowledgeable... more responsible... This is a school that belongs to its pupils and they enjoy it."

Castlemilk Tenants Association has been going for 20 years, since the scheme was built. It covers nearly 10,000 houses. About 30 attend the monthly meetings in Castlemilk Community Centre, almost all women, mainly middle-aged or elderly. Very few are unemployed or on Social Security. Some of the few men who attend occupy key positions on the Committee, but last year a woman was elected Chairman. Informal extended committee metings take place after the meeting, in the coffee bar.

The T.A. gets on well with the local housing manager, who attends all meetings and takes note of complaints about repairs and other problems. Secretary, Ian Torrill feels this relationship of friendly service on the factor's part is very valuable. On the other hand some women say they're afraid to speak while the factor is there, and that it puts people off coming. This difference of opinion is characteristic of the dialectic between men and women on the committee - the women pushing for a bigger social side, the men emphasising the fight for better services.

Recently they have been working towards setting up local area T.A.s, still linked to the central organisation. Monthly meetings have been held in 2 areas, with attendances around 30, raising issues like vandalism, lack of beat policemen, litter collection, lifts, play facilities, etc. Two site meetings between tenants of multi-story flats and Parks Department officials have resulted, bins have been doubled up, and collection improved, several rubble-strewn areas have been half-landscaped, and kickabouts provided. "We feel you should have some say in what facilities you get and where they go" said Mr. Mann of the Parks Department. In one of these areas, a new independent association has been formed - in the other a local area committee of the T.A. has been set up. More local meetings are planned, possibly in co-operation with the Housing Manager.

Castlemilk Rents Action Committee was set up in Autumn 1972, to develop support for Glasgow Corporation's refusal to implement the Housing Finance Act. The driving force was Castlemilk T.A., the aim to create a united front of local political, social and religious organisations. The T.A., the Communist Party, the Labour Party, the Labour Party Young Socialists, and the Co-op Women's Guild were represented, also the district committee of the N.U.R., Govan Shipbuilders and Sterne's Shop Stewards, with occasional support from Councillors Fitch and Manson.

When the Corporation gave in, they held a 500 strong protest meeting, and called for the increase to be withheld. For 6 months they kept up a campaign of leafletting, street meetings with loudspeakers, sales of Scottish Tenant, and a 2-month picket of the factor's office. The campaign failed to create mass rent withholding, but it put the issue right into the centre of people's minds. and showed the possibilities there are in the idea of co-ordinated local action.

Castlemilk Today is Glasgow's newest community paper, starting in March this year. 2 years ago a local minister and other concerned outsiders started Castlemilk Press, with the minister as editor. It didn't get the practical involvement of enough local people or organisations, the tendency was for contentious material to be edited out, and a substantial debt built up.

A handful of activists from the old paper have been joined by about a dozen new ones, all living in the scheme, mostly young and middle-aged women. Two successful dances were held to clear the debt. Contact was made with The View, and flowing from that it was decided to base the paper on local organisations, which would undertake to contribute monthly reports and sell a quota of papers.

The paper group itself is autonomous - its members are not delegates. It is an open, democratic group, with no editor, meeting weekly and deciding all policy matters, collecting reports from organisations, writing articles, encouraging others to write, doing interviews, editing, typing, laying-out, letrasetting, folding and selling the paper. Net sales have grown from 1500 to 2,200 in 4 issues/months; 400 of these are sold by the group, the rest by organisations and newsagents. The paper is planning a meeting of all organisations in the scheme to discuss the setting up of a community council.

Scottish Tenant first came out in 1973. 3 issues have appeared so far. Sales have dropped from 6,000 to 4,000, mainly through tenants associations, shop stewards committees and trade union branch and district committees. Three-quarters of all sales are in Glasgow.

It is the paper of the Scottish Council of Tenants, and has contained reports from local T.A.s and RACs, campaigning/informing articles on the Housing Finance Act and government white papers, the law affecting private tenants, bits of working class history, contributions by councillors, poems, stories, jokes, cartoons, etc. It is an attempt to create communication between local organisations in different areas, to link in with work situations and the trade unions, to inform activists on issues of interest to them, in general to create of wider perspective than that afforded by local involvement alone. At the moment it is being reorganised to base it more firmly on local T.A.s, so that it will become their paper in a practical participative sense.

The Local Authority

In this and following sections, the aim is to focus on the role of private capital, the local authority, and central government, in relation to the grass roots activity we have been looking at.

Far from merely **responding** to the development of local action, the state is actually **stimulating** it.

First, the local authority. In a document dated October 1973, Glasgow's Chief Constable, Housing Manager, Depute Director of Education and Depute Director of Social Work outline the involvement of their departments in Community Development.

The Chief Constable set up a Community Involvement Department late in 1971. Duties were to include liaison with the Social Work Department regarding juveniles, operation of police warning schemes, crime prevention propaganda, race relations, fostering community activities, contacts with youth, T.A.s, churches, schools, and fostering of police recruitment. 1 Chief Superintendent, 1 Superintendent, 7 Inspectors, 21 Sergeants, 14 Constables, and 8 Clerkesses were assigned to this work. Activities have included helping to set up a tenants' association in Broomloan Road, giving children athletic training, and an involvement in Contact Govan, where all old people living alone in the area have been identified and volunteer wardens keep a friendly eye on them ... "the department have fitted chains in a number of their houses."

The Housing Manager feels his department should be the "instigator of amenity and environmental improvements ... the agent to work out with tenants what is required to make their houses and surroundings more acceptable ..." "While the authority can provide the necessary financial and labour resources ... such work will be abortive .. without consulting the tenants ... Tenants must be given the opportunity to manage their own affairs ... through the activities of Tenants or Residents Associations ..."

"This... can best be achieved by the employment of full-time Community Development Officers..." He has encouraged regular meetings between T.A.s and district office staff. He has organised "meetings with tenants to bring into being Residents Associations... in Easterhouse... it is proposed to introduce similar ideas in Garthamlock, Drumchapel, Castlemilk, Pollock..."

"What is invariably lacking in housing areas is leadership and initiative." Implementation of his proposals is "fundamentally essential if housing areas are to be saved from further blight and degeneration."

The Depute Director of Education outlines the various forms of support given to voluntary organisations - grant to pay the salary of an unattached youth worker in Blackhill ... £80,000 a year spent on paying activity leaders in voluntary youth organisations, £85,000 a year for their premises and equipment.

The most recent initiative is the appointment of Neighbourhood Development Officers - people are looking for "a wider range of leisure opportunities and have more leisure time." They will be based in schools in "a new housing development, an old neighbourhood which is being upgraded, a neighbourhood in a housing estate which has for long been unresponsive to attempts to enrich the quality of life in it." They will "get to know a large number of residents, identify the potential leaders, encourage residents to organise their own leisure time pursuits, make best use of existing facilities, and make good deficiencies as far as possible."

The Depute Director of Social Work writes that "the employment of community workers has been left to various voluntary organisations which have been grant-aided" - YVFF in Mile-End, Park Ward Residents Council, Lochend Neighbourhood Project, Assist, St Andrew's Advice Centre, Gorbals Govanhill Fieldwork Unit, the Glendale Centre, the Community Relations Council. Clearly the local authority's departmental hierarchies have been thoroughly soaked in the ideology of "community", the language of which is intermingling with their specialist jargons and class prejudices to produce some very odd results.

How do Labour councillors see it?

Councillor Rev. Geoff Shaw, Chairman of the new Strathclyde Region, interviewed in 'The View' Dec. 1973:

> "The whole movement towards public involvement in decision-making and making information available to the public, is a fairly new movement - probably within the last ten years ...
>
> "I hope that community councils will be seen as a focus for the community ... possibly they will serve as the middle man between the different departments and the people at local level ...
>
> "Glasgow Corporation ... put a lot of representation to the Government ... that the Community Councils must be stronger, that the District Authority must be **made** to provide the resources ...

(Geoff Shaw has been quoted elsewhere as saying that each Community Council should get an annual grant of £10,000 from its district council.)

Councillor Ronald Young of Greenock, reported in Glasgow News, 16/12/72: "the political role of the local government officer, the accountability concept, political responsibility of the elected representatives, are all part of a pseudo-democratic smokescreen, which can be dispelled by the fresh wind from local grass-roots organisations."

In the same report, Councillor John Hoey of Livingstone: "Participation is a waste of time. What we need is a Cultural Revolution... We must attack the basic social structure, instead of taking toothless bites at the local authority."

Private Capital

It is also interesting to note the involvement of private capital in funding many community projects, usually through a variety of trusts, but in a number of instances by direct grant. Obviously many capitalists see community activity as an antidote to trade union activity, and as a means of reducing government spending on social services.

Small-scale enterprise is the well-spring of capitalism, and it is significant to see it latching onto hints flung up by community activity. Two new commercial newspapers have been started by city landlord Joe Mulholland, alongside existing community papers - West End News alongside Glasgow News, and South Side News alongside The View.

South Side News has used 'View' stories and contacts without any acknowledgement, or getting in touch with the paper itself. It also refused to print a letter from the View correcting a serious inaccuracy in one of the reports, or to apologise.

Under the banner **Welcome to YOUR Paper,** the first issue of South Side News told its readers that it would... "Help to further your involvement in the community... we believe that this local community that is dear to us all will find itself with a new identity and voice... it is our earnest wish to serve you in the years ahead...".." The real face of community capitalism coming into focus?

Reform of Local Government

Reform of local government, in Scotland, as in England, can be seen as part of the long-term trend towards centralization, through the creation of larger and larger units.

The Tory Government's White Paper of 1971 hardly bothered to justify the changes, contenting itself with assertions that "many authorities are too small"; "demands on local government will increase ... this means that local authorities will have to be larger ..."; "the regional authorities ... will enjoy substantial advantages through economies of scale." This was accompanied by bland expressions of concern about the danger of local government becoming remote from the individual - that would be overcome by administrative decentralization. More sugar for the pill was provided by promises that central government control over local authorities would be eased, more financial responsibility would be devolved, and so on. (This was shortly before they took away the power of local authorities to fix the rents of council houses.)

Another theme is connected with the growing influence of the concept of integrated regional planning. In part, this respresents an awareness of the inadequacy of the present system of watertight compartments - housing, parks, education, etc., often not communicating satisfactorily at committee, senior management, or service outlet levels, or operating on the basis of conflicting diagnoses and priorities, or even duplicating provision.

The reform represents a victory for the planners, with the old departments demoted to the level of service administrators, under a top level of policy planning. Strathclyde's new Chief Executive lays it on the line in his advert for a Director of Policy Planning (Glasgow Herald, 17th July, 1974): "The successful applicant ... will work closely with the Chief Executive ... in policy formulation. He will head a small inter-disciplinary team, the 'Policy Planning Unit' ... All plans which involve the commitment of resources (will be) routed through the Policy Planning Planning Unit ... for presentation to the Policy and Resources Committee ..."

Clearly, the bureaucracy is going to get bigger. Instead, for example, of an education department, with a hierarchy of director, deputy and assistant directors and central office staffs, squatting like an idol on top of the hierarchies within the individual service-providing institutions (schools and colleges), we are now going to have a policy planning unit, on top of a regional directorate, on top of a bunch of decentralized directorates (probably at the level of the old authorities contained within the new regions), on top of the hierarchies in the service-providing institutions.

The lines of communication multiply, as do the number of top jobs. The machinery will absorb more and more money simply to maintain itself in existence - more salaries, more offices, more clerical staff, more equipment, so that even with substantial rates increases, given the present rate of inflation it seems possible that the real output of services in quantitative and qualitative terms will fall. Elected representatives will be sucked more and more into the entrails of the machinery, as the committee structure proliferates, and be less available to the people. Confusion will develop about who runs which service.

As for local control, and local co-ordination of services - which to the humble human unit are the real problem - well, the truth is that there is no practical provision in the Act for local control and local co-ordination of local government services. James Kellas (Glasgow News, March 1972): "The Scottish Office is at the root of the local government paradox in Scotland ... The local government reforms fragment Scotland and leave the Scottish Office well clear of democratic controls. No region in Scotland has the financial means to resist central authority. It is time ... that the white-wash about local democracy was put in its true perspective."

Community Councils

It is in the context of the real nature of local government reform that we should consider the cautious and ambiguous provisions for the establishment of Community Councils contained in part 4 of the Act.

The key paragraphs read as follows:

"In addition to any other purpose which a community council may pursue, the general purpose of a community council shall be to ascertain, co-ordinate, and express to the local authorities for its area, and to public authorities, the views of the community which it represents, in relation to matters for which those authorities are responsible, and to take such action in the interests of that community as appears to it to be expedient."

"Regional, islands and district councils may make such contributions as they think fit towards the expenses of community councils within their areas, may make loans to those councils, and may, at the request of such community councils, provide them with staff, services, accommodation, furniture, vehicles, and equipment, on such terms as to payment or otherwise as may be agreed between the councils concerned."

The following timetable is laid down: the district council announces that its going to frame a scheme for community councils. The public has 8 weeks to make suggestions about their areas and composition.

After considering these suggestions, the district sends the scheme, plus objections, to the Secretary of State. He approves it, or holds a local enquiry, or refers it back to the district for further consideration. When they are approved, the proposals are exhibited in each area to be affected. At least 20 electors in each area must then apply in writing for a community council to be set up. Within 6 weeks, elections or other voting arrangements must be organised.

Finally, the district has powers, from time to time, to review its scheme and propose amendments. If these are opposed, the matter goes to the Secretary of State.

The major unanswered questions are:

What size of areas? Local neighbourhoods? School catchment areas? District wards? Regional divisions? Constituencies? The township - "where I come from" - Castlemilk, Govan, Saltcoats, Wester Hailes?

Are community councils to be the single channel of communication with the authorities, supplanting existing organisations like T.A.s, and limiting their right to access and information?

Are the members of community councils to be elected by popular vote? On a party ticket or not? Or are some to be elected and some to be delegates? Or all to be delegates?

Are district and region obliged to provide the community council with information on request - any information? Are community councils obliged to provide district and region with information on request?

The Scottish Development Department's discussion document on **Community Councils:** Some Alternatives for Community Council Schemes in Scotland (HMSO, 1974), published in January 1975, attempts to grapple with some of these problems, "with a view to contributing towards as full and informed a public debate as possible, while the schemes are being drawn up. It does not lay down the law on the ideal patterns for any area (the document states) but offers a large range of possibilities which may be helpful in making a choice locally" (Para. 1.4). The "guidelines" state that "community councils will not be a third tier of local government with legally defined duties and responsibilities". (Para. 1.7).

It is suggested that flexibility in size and organisation depending on community demand would be acceptable, but that "there may well be disadvantages for councils which are beyond the range of 30 members". (Paras. 1.9 and 4.7). The document suggests that "there are three main possibilities for the composition of a community council: entirely of directly elected individual members", entirely of representatives of local organisations, a proportion of both. The Council may wish to co-opt other members for a specific purpose. While some might maintain that only the first type (and possibly the third if directly elected members were in a majority) were truly representative, all three may be regarded as genuine options in that they all ensure, in different ways, that the community as a whole is represented". (Paras. 4.7 and 4.8). On the flow of information required and requested from district and regional government, the document suggests only that "Much of this information will be fed to community councils through contacts with regional, islands and district councillors and officials and through written reports". (Para. 6.5).

Its clear that, although they won't provide any statutory services, Community Councils are a part of the state machinery. Ultimate power to set them up, or not, and to decide their structure, rests with the Secretary of State, through the District Council. Power to give or withhold money lies with the District.

Nevertheless, subject to these limitations, the Community Council has an independent existence. It can do whatever it wants. It need not, therefore, adopt a subservient posture towards the authorities.

Conclusions

I have tried to keep comment to a minimum throughout this article, because I believe the reader must do his own interpretation. These matters have been under-discussed, and no good cause is served by providing instant opinions. The projection of rigid, dogmatic analyses, and closed-minded hostility to other views, has disfigured the left for 50 years. It is time we made serious efforts to overcome it.

But it would be cheating not to say what I think. The following comments are offered, therefore, in an open-minded and tentative spirit.

Open, democratic T.A.s, Residents Associations, Action Groups, and other similar organisations - that is to say, people voluntarily coming together at local level and organising to improve conditions and services, and to provide self-services - these are the growth points for participative democracy.

This is in spite of their reactionary features - the tendency for the platform to dominate the floor, men to dominate women, the old to dominate the young, the danger of a subservient or client relationship with the local authority. It is romantic to imagine that the self-organisation of people at the bottom of the heap in capitalist society will not reproduce many of the features of that society.

We should recognise and work to encourage their democratic co-operative features - sharing out of decision-making, encouraging people to express themselves sometimes at the expense of the orderliness of the agenda, trying new suggestions by new people, a conscious attempt by the key experienced activists to see their job as facilitating the development of younger, newer, less confident people, rather than hogging the interesting jobs, and so on.

I am for complete independence for these organisations from the local authority. Of course they will seek for concessions, improvements, rights - but not as part of a deal giving them policing or minor administrative functions. They should resist incorporation into the machinery.

I recognise the force of Bill Torrill's arguments against neighbourhood T.A.s, but don't agree with him that big T.A.s are what's needed. People must be free to choose the size of the area their organisation covers. The way to overcome the problems of isolation and parochialism is to encourage regular meetings between T.A.s in adjacent areas, to discuss common problems and services, and to co-ordinate campaigns.

We should encourage visits between T.A.s in widely separate areas too. As long as they remain in isolation, they tend to develop distorted views of the causes of their problems, and the system can easily deal with them by occasional concessions. It is no great strain for capitalism to do up the backcourts in Possilpark. What needs to happen now is that every T.A. in the city goes up there and sees for themselves - and start demanding the same for their backcourts.

I also believe it to be important to emphasise the idea of well-publicised direct action, if and when the usual channels fail. Otherwise a T.A. is accepting its powerlessness to change things, when the system does not accede to their polite requests.

95

The importance of the appearance of community newspapers can hardly be overemphasised. Again, the relationship with the local authority must be one of independence - every concession, every grant of resources, must be welcomed and more pressed for, without any compromising deals. Glasgow Corporation's record on this has been very good in recent months.

A word about what I have called self-servicing activities. Many politically conscious activists are uneasy about this - they feel its a trap - the local authority should be providing the services and we should be pressing to get them improved. I agree with that, in a sense.

But in another sense it misses the point. Take playgroups. Its a great thing that mothers in Barrowfield, Govanhill, and so on are running their own playgroups - and fighting to get one of **them** as supervisor, not someone the P.P.A. foists on them. The fact that the (very welcome) new nursery schools now opening are run by 'trained' experts, with mothers excluded - that's a step backwards.

What we should demand is that ordinary working people get more and more control over such resources at local, service-output level.

The same applies to Barrowfield's Community School. The Education authority should be pressed to provide the resources, but not attempt to remodel the school on hierarchical, bureaucratic lines. Control should rest at local level with those involved - teachers, parents, pupils.

. Some socialists may look askance at the direction these comments are taking. Am I suggesting that local authority departmental and service structures be dismantled?

I am not making any such sweeping proposal. What I'm saying is that, just as nationalisation is not socialization, so the social services are not **socialist** services. For them to become that, we will have to overcome the alienating and exploitive characteristics of the present patterns of provision and consumption. This will be a gradual, experimental process. Some experiments will be dead ends. Some, like Housing Associations, can,I think be shown to be reactionary.

Those of us who have worked as local authority officers know from our own experience that the present system of organizing services could not be more wasteful, inefficient and undemocratic. The democratisation of public services is not something to be deferred till "after the revolution". It is part of the revolution, and we should be starting now.

Community councils should not replace or down-value T.A.s, R.A.s, action groups, community papers - or colonize them. They should **not** be elected - that will merely bring so-called representative democracy (which in practice means the dictatorship of the officials, with the ill-informed acquiescence of the elected representatives) into the local arena. The party-ticket electoral charade could set the development of participative democracy back years.

Imagine what might happen in a Labour area, under Labour District and Regional Councils. The Community Council would consist of Labour party folk who would be under pressure to push the line that District and Regional policies were great, don't rock the boat, don't demand too much all at once. The Community Council might become a tame organ of social control, an individual complaints-servicing agency, and a dependence-on-big-brother complex could develop at local level.

In urban areas, Community Councils should cover townships of various sizes, big enough to contain a fair number of T.A.s, political parties, churches, OAP organizations, etc. They should not be forced to fit neatly into administrative boundaries.

The Council should consist of one delegate from each organisation, chosen annually by vote at a well-publicised meeting of members of each organisation. No individual could be delegated by more than 1 organisation, and no-one could be a c.c. member more than once in 5 years.

The purpose of these safeguards would be to ensure that local activists did not become dazzled by the status of being a council member and begin to drop their involvement in their own organisation. (There is already evidence of activists turning their attention away from their T.A. towards participation in the formation of proto-Community Councils.)

As well as delegates, interested members of the public should be allowed to take part in council meetings, but not vote. Local authority officials should not be members nor have standing invitations. The council should be free to invite them or not, and when it wishes. Sending a delegate should be a voluntary act on the part of local organisations. The councils should not be a single channel of communication with the authorities.

The Councils should not be dependent on the district for resources. The provision of resources and services to the councils should be a statutory duty of the district. The Community Council should be empowered to require any information other than bona fide confidential information, from district, region, and central government.

Community Councils might decide to encourage local organisations to report their activities, assist organisations in difficulties, help organisations to expand their activities, provide them with a base, storage and other office facilities, set up working parties, campaign committees, new organisations of various kinds. One organisation I very much hope many community councils will sponsor is a committee to organise non-sectarian working-class adult education in their area.

The reader will by now be pretty clear about the kind of role I envisage for Community Councils. Based on thriving independent organisations, and particularly T.A.s of which we need to see a whole new crop, it would be a voluntary democratic co-ordinating body, independent from the authorities and, in fact, a counter-power against their power, a means, in short, of breeding and feeding popular participative democracy.

Thanks to the following people, who patiently answered all my questions: Isa McCulloch, Eileen and Hugh Thompson, Barbara Holmes, Molly Johnstone, Freddy Anderson (and other members of Garthamlock Tenants Association), Bill Towill, Jimmy Forsyth, Roddy Kerr, Davy McCracken, John Mullen, and Ian Towill.

Industrial Democracy And Workers' Control

Alex Ferry

Foreword

The history of the Scottish Working Class is a proud one and shows clearly the almost fanatical desire of working men and women to control their own destinies and to meaningfully participate in the organisation of the society in which they live. Nowhere is this more clearly seen than in the field of industry itself, where throughout the growth of industry in Scotland workers have constantly battled to establish their rights and not merely to be treated as cogs in the machinery of production units. While it is true that workers in other parts of the United Kingdom have earned their own place in history, no-one could deny that the individual and collective leadership shown in Scotland in the past has paved the way for a positive movement to greater Industrial Democracy and eventual Workers' Control in the not too distant future.

The work done for example by the Clyde Workers' Committee during the First World War and in the inter-war years has made a tremendous contribution, not only in defending and establishing workers' rights in industry, but in creating a self-confidence amongst working people that their class has both the organisation and intellectual ability to control the means of production and create a more just and equitable society from the fruits of their labour.

During that difficult and critical period of the inter-war years the leadership of the Scottish Working Class was probably at its peak, in particular on the Clydeside. Led by people like John Maclean, McManus, Maxton, Gallagher, Kirkwood, Tom Bell and many others, the battle for workers' rights was fought under extreme circumstances and at much personal hardship to the leaders themselves, including deportation, imprisonment and enforced ill health. If it had not been for men like them, together with the unconquerable spirit of the Scottish Worker, it is more than doubtful as to whether or not we would be as advanced in the field of Industrial Democracy as we are at present and would have the right to be highly optimistic as to the future.

The following article is therefore written with a deep sense of gratitude to the long line of Scottish Workers' leaders and to the hundreds of thousands of Scottish Workers who made our present-day demands and aspirations in the field of Industrial Democracy and Workers' Control possible.

Introduction

The terms "Industrial Democracy", "Workers' Participation" and "Workers' Control" have been with us for more than half a century and undoubtedly will create a major platform for discussion among Trade Union activists and politicians during the next five or ten years when it is to be hoped some major progress will be made. Despite the deep and serious discussion there has been among activists and academics, and despite the millions of words that have been written and spoken about this important subject, so far there has not been any real active participation by the average shop floor worker. Why should this be? This is the first important question and one that must be answered if the process of Industrial Democracy is to be speeded up and the eventual objective of Workers' Control achieved in the forseeable future. In trying to find out why there is this apparent apathy among the average shop floor worker two points clearly emerge:

a) That workers clearly believe that the major function of the Trade Union Movement is an economic one which they relate to the rate for the job and the money in their pay packet at the end of each week (or month in the case of salaried staff), and

b) The details of Industrial Democracy and Workers' Control are so complex and deep that the average worker does not find the necessary time to learn the benefits which would be won for all workers by the achievement of the Trade Unions' aims in these fields.

Item a) above is easy to understand in many ways but item b) should cause a great deal of concern to the Trade Union movement as a whole. If we do not have a knowledgeable and willing membership, prepared to campaign, and if necessary involve itself in a struggle for an objective then that objective becomes all the more difficult to obtain.

This paper, therefore, will endeavour to relate the benefits which can be gained by workpeople by greater Industrial Democracy in the first place and by the eventual achievement of Workers' Control. It is doubtful if the paper will in any way resolve the problems of election procedures in a Workers' Control situation, nor spell out in detail the best means of workers' participation through greater Industrial Democracy.

The paper will also look at some of the examples often used when the subject is discussed arising from fairly recent experiences in Scotland, from the "Fairfield experiment" to the current endeavours of the ex-employees of the Scottish Daily Express to form a Workers' Co-operative by the production of the "Scottish Daily News".

It is not thought necessary to make special reference to "Workers' Participation" as this is simply one aspect of Industrial Democracy and should not be seen as a separate phase on the way to Workers' Control.

Industrial Democracy

Public Bodies

The Trade Union policy of workers having more say in their own destiny does not confine itself to actual place of employment. It is much broader than this and calls for representation and power-sharing on all bodies which in some way affect the community as a whole, e.g. Nationalised Boards, Area Boards, Health Councils, Courts of Inquiry, Advisory Committees, Employment Committees, College Boards and many other public bodies. It would be true to say that, particularly in post-war years, Trade Union representation has been obtained in almost all of the areas defined by the T.U.C. although the actual size of the representation has not always been satisfactory. The other unsatisfactory aspect of the T.U. representation from the point of view of involving the shop floor has been that all too often the T.U. representation has been composed mainly of Full Time Officers of the Unions. This in turn has created suspicions in the minds of active rank and file members that the representation is more of a perk than a real movement in the field of Industrial Democracy.

While it is true to say that in some cases appointments are wholly at the discretion of the Government of the day, in many other instances where the T.U.C. or the S.T.U.C. have the right to nominate, the nominees tend to be members of the General Council themselves except in the case of Local Committees such as L.E.Cs or College Boards. It is not unknown for General Council nominees (particularly when they are Full Time Officers) to have a very poor record of attendance on certain minor Boards which means that the opportunity for T.U. representation goes almost by default.

In the Public Sector therefore, where the opportunities are much greater than in the Private Sector, some immediate improvements could be obtained either by Act of Parliament or simply by a greater use of shop floor activists (thus creating a better opportunity for shop floor involvement). These improvements could include:

a) The elimination of Ministerial discretion accorded to certain appointments. Surely if it is decided that T.Us should have representation then they should be allowed to determine who their representatives will be.

b) The greater use of rank and file activists, not only on local bodies but on Regional or National bodies. It would be foolish to argue that Full Time Officers should be debarred from gaining appointments but if Industrial Democracy is to mean anything to the average worker, then he or she must be able to see shop floor participation and this can only be done through shop floor representation, and

c) There should be a complete review of the role of the independent representation, i.e. nominated neither by the Employers nor the Trade Unions. Too often this type of representation has tended to strengthen the establishment or "status quo" type of thought and a reduction of representation in this field could allow greater representation from the T.U.s.

Industry

In its report on Industrial Democracy to the 1968 Annual Conference of the Labour Party, the National Executive Committee of the Party stated—"An extension of industrial democracy, and the effective participation of workers in decision-making in individual industries and firms, is urgent and essential if the nation is to meet the human needs of those confronted by the major structural changes that are now taking place. It is no longer enough for workers and their representatives to treat Management defensively; waiting for them to act and then protesting; asking but rarely achieving some measure of consultation in advance."

The report also stated—"The aim (of industrial democracy) is to extend into the workplace the constructive power the Unions now have in national economic planning. It will mean a new positive role for the Shop Steward or plant official. It will require the closer integration of Shop Stewards into the Unions' chain of command."

The report of the General Council of the T.U.C. to the 1974 Annual Congress opens as follows—"Throughout their history Trade Unions have generated a substantial measure of industrial democracy in this country. All of their activities have served to further this objective. The term industrial democracy cannot be considered outside that context. This report (of the General Council) recognises that collective bargaining is and will continue to be the central method of joint regulation in industry and the public services..."

In an earlier report the General Council of the T.U.C. had stated—"The central feature of all the recommendations (on Industrial Democracy) is that progress in this field can only be made if representation is firmly based on Trade Union organisation. This is why the report comes out clearly against any general system of works councils, as these could only duplicate existing Trade

Union arrangements at plant level or displace them."

While both of the reports referred to above went on in some detail to spell out specific aspects of industrial democracy nevertheless these extracts make certain things clear insofar as the Labour Party and T.U.C. thinking is concerned.

1) That the only successful approach to industrial democracy must be through the single channel system of the Trade Unions.

2) An extension of collective bargaining in industry either by reaching agreement on subjects which hitherto have either not been subject to collective bargaining or where no agreements exist can in itself extend industrial democracy.

3) The role and function of the Shop Steward must be strengthened both in the eyes of the Employers and Trade Unions.

4) Information not previously given to Trade Unions at plant level must be forthcoming from the Employers, and

5) There must be an erosion of powers which previously have been looked upon as Management prerogative.

It is in the context of the five points above that the understanding of workers can be directed and their support obtained. In particular points 2) and 5) are the factors around which many of the everyday problems of workers evolve, i.e. Collective Bargaining and Management Prerogative. It is therefore as well to look at these two aspects in some detail.

Collective Bargaining

The deficiencies of collective bargaining are mainly in its limitations. The main items covered are wages, hours of work, holidays and overtime premiums, and these are much too narrow a field in the context of a modern industrial society. While much has been done to extend the scope of collective bargaining in recent years, millions of workers still do not have agreements covering such things as Redundancy, Sick Pay, Occupational Pensions, Discipline and so on. Is it any wonder therefore that much of industry's problems are found not in items covered by agreements but in matters not covered by them? And is it any wonder that workers in many industries feel that they are still part of the master/servant set up in industry when they are denied the basic rights of participating in matters which can influence their livelihood and affect their future? If we were to use the Engineering Industry as an example we would find that there are no laid down procedures at national level to deal with redundancy or discipline, including dismissal or suspension. So we find in two areas where a worker's job could be taken from him or her there is no procedure which the Employers must honour. More will be said about this in the following section dealing with "Managerial Prerogative". Again in the Engineering Industry we will find a complete absence in the National Agreements to any reference of occupational pension schemes or sick pay schemes. Hundreds or thousands of workers have retired and will retire in the future from the Engineering Industry, many of them having given their lifetime to the industry, without as much as a 'thank you'. Many hundreds of workers are off work every day in any week through illness, many of them through injuries received at work and they will not receive one halfpence from their Employers to offset the hardships they undoubtedly suffer. In actual fact many workers have been known to receive their termination of employment after a fairly short period of illness. In view of this almost Victorian attitude in the Engineering and many other industries is it any wonder that workers themselves feel that the Trade Unions are basically an economic body which deals with wages and hours of work and sets the premiums for overtime working. In other words, workers feel that Trade Unions are only a force in dealing with conditions of work and not as they certainly endeavour to be an organisation concerned with every aspect of a workers' life.

It must be said that in the nationalised industries and the public services the 'fringe' items like those referred to above play an important part in collective bargaining and collective agreements. It is also true that some Employers in the Engineering Industry have come to accept that workers have rights on these very important matters, but very few of these Employers are members of the Engineering Employers' Federation which represents between four and five thousand Companies employing more than a million workers.

We can see therefore the serious shortcomings of the existing collective bargaining machinery in the private sector, excluding those individual Companies which either voluntarily or through pressure have conceded some extension to the traditional subjects dealt with.

The other major area which is hardly covered at all in the whole field of collective bargaining in the private sector (and very often on an individual unit basis in the public sector) is the question of the disclosure of information, such as forward manpower planning (which is so important to redundancy or short time working), the financial position of the Company, forward planning of production processes and production planning, recruitment intentions and procedures, training programmes and so on. The attitude of certain Managements when asked to discuss these items, let alone reach agreements on them, is more akin to 1874 than it is to 1974.

It can only be concluded that collective bargaining, in the main, has failed to date in a very large percentage of industry to provide any real form of industrial democracy in this country. On the other hand, the vast areas which affect workers' lives which are not yet subject matter for collective bargaining shows the tremendous advances that have still to be won in this field. With that thought in mind the proposals contained in the Labour Government's consultative document on the Employment Protection Bill must be welcomed and studied carefully. It includes such items as Guaranteed Week Payments, paid Maternity leave, notice of dismissals, unfair dismissal with written statements from the Employer as to reasons for dismissal, reinstatement on proved unfair dismissal, employees' rights in liquidation including protection for payment of wage arrears, holiday pay, etc., procedures for handling redundancies and the compulsory disclosure of information to ensure effective collective bargaining.

The consultative document will not in itself achieve full industrial democracy (in fact it may be argued that there cannot be full industrial democracy until there is adequate workers' control) but the document itself is to be followed by another consultative document on Industrial Democracy. The importance of the consultative document is that it recognises many areas where workers must be accorded certain rights which they hitherto should have had but in far too many cases have been denied. It will be interesting to see the reaction of Employers when the Employees' Protection Bill receives the Royal assent.

The most important result of the extension of collective bargaining may well be that workers will begin to realise the full purpose of Trade Unionism and may be much more ready to become interested and involved in the whole sphere of industrial democracy. There is nothing which encourages participation more than the knowledge that the result of that participation can be positive and fruitful.

Managerial Prerogative

Possibly the most antiquated, outmoded and trouble-making single feature of modern industry is Management prerogative, i.e. "the divine right of Management to manage." This means to many Managements the right to dismiss without question, to make changes in production processes and techniques without advising workers, the right to declare redundancies without consultation, the right to close factories without good cause, and it goes on and on. It is true that very often they have been halted in their tracks by timely and correct Trade Union action, but nevertheless the belief is still there that somehow or other Management are the only people who have the right to make important decisions and implement them, irrespective of the consequences of their decision on the work force.

Management after Management will throw up their hands in horror and deny that they would contemplate acting in such a way. But the facts are there. They are there in the records of industrial disputes created by the spontaneous reactions of workers in taking action in support of one of their fellow-workers who has been dismissed unjustly; they are there in the history of the breakdown of the National Engineering agreement because of the Engineering Employers' Federation refusal to include a "status quo" clause in the procedures; they are there in the records of the Glasgow District offices of the A.U.E.W. (and no doubt other Districts of the A.U.E.W. and other Trade Unions have similar records) where workers were declared redundant within two hours of their Union offices being advised; and the facts are there for all to see in the derelict factory buildings throughout Scotland and other parts of the U.K. which at one time employed thousands of workers. Yes the facts are there and it is worthwhile looking at them in a little detail.

Discipline. As I have already stated, in the section dealing with collective bargaining, there are far too many industries and individual establishments where there is no agreed procedure for dealing with discipline. As a result Management in such industries feel they have no obligation to either advise or consult the Trade Unions on such matters and even worse don't even give the victim of their decisions the opportunity to involve his or her Trade Union in any appeal to be made prior to the penalty actually being imposed. In other words any appeal has to be made in the background of the decision having been implemented and the worker being outside the factory gate. This inevitably means that no matter how strong a case may be put up for the worker in question or no matter what new or unknown facts can be brought to light, the decision will stand. After all, if Management were to reverse their decision this would be an admission that they were wrong, and that would never do? And so we have the perfect setting for an industrial conflict, albeit a completely unnecessary one if only Management would yield their 'divine right'.

What is required, of course, is an agreement laying down the procedures whereby discipline against workers will be invoked. Such a procedure would contain the need for a verbal warning, at least one written warning and a suspension prior to dismissal, with the right of appeal at every stage. There can be provisions for immediate discipline for such things as proven cases of theft, etc. and the eradication of all warnings after a given period of time.

This basic principle of the accused being innocent until proved otherwise applies in the mind of every fair minded person, but in many fields of industry it is the opposite—the accused is guilty until he is proved innocent. This is extremely unjust and certainly proves that in the field of industrial democracy there is at least one yawning gap.

The Management of Change. It is difficult to believe, but nevertheless it is a fact, that the national negotiating procedure in the Engineering Industry was terminated on this basic argument—"That where Management wished to introduce changes in processes, techniques or procedures affecting the conditions of workpeople in their employment no such change would be made until agreement was reached with the workpeople concerned, or, until such times as the recognised national negotiating procedure had been exhausted and a period of notice given as to the change required."

Months of negotiations took place and literally thousands of words were spoken on details of interpretation, the scope or areas that such an agreement would cover and the meaning of "changes that would affect the conditions of workpeople", but all to no avail. So the Engineering Employers' Federation, rather than give up one of their 'divine rights' allowed the national negotiating procedure to go by the board. Events have shown that their adamance has been a costly one to them but so deep-rooted is their belief in Management prerogative in the field of change that they are prepared to allow the industry to operate on very loose procedures relative to the settling of disputes. It is interesting to note however, that shortly after the breakdown of the national negotiating procedure in general engineering one of the largest groups affiliated to the Engineering Employers' Federation reached a separate agreement with the Trade Unions which incorporated the principle of the Management of Change clause (status quo) sought by the Trade Unions. All concerned in negotiations within that group have appeared to welcome the new agreement as a forward step in Management/Worker relations.

The events in the Engineering Industry have shown how difficult the struggle is to get a reasonable extension of industrial democracy by negotiation especially when the sacred cows of the Employers are involved. Time will show however, that many cows, no matter how sacred, will have to be slaughtered as workers' demands for greater participation grow.

Redundancies and Closures. Unemployment has often been referred to as the curse of Scotland, and rightly so. There is no more sorry a spectacle than to see a fully fit man suffering the degradation which must naturally follow periods of prolonged unemployment. We could expect therefore that in this field the greatest care would be taken by Government, Management and Trade Unions to ensure that all possible avenues were explored on a joint basis before a single worker was thrown on the dole. Unfortunately, this has not been the case. For every Employer who has endeavoured to mitigate the effects of redundancy there are at least half a dozen who have treated it in a completely off-hand manner. For every Employer who has given adequate warning of a potential redundancy at least the same half dozen have endeavoured to implement the redundancies without notice or prior consultation. This also applies to closures of factories and ranges from situations affecting three or four workpeople to those affecting thousands.

The Trade Union movement can do nothing but admit that industrial democracy is only a policy aim until such times as they are fully involved in all aspects of forward manpower planning, involving not only the Employers and Trade Unions but also the Government. Involvement in policy discussions on manpower planning should include abolition of overtime, shift working, re-training, work sharing, or, most desirable of all, the provision of suitable alternative employment as an alternative to redundancy.

It is true that some aspects of the preceding paragraph are controversial within the Trade Union movement itself. For example, re-training of workers opens up the whole question of the protection of skilled trades; shift working is certainly unattractive to most workers and the abolition of overtime, particularly in low earning industries could mean the difference between a reasonable take-home pay and a below the 'bread line' take-home pay. What we should be doing therefore, is creating conditions where the fears and dislikes of these alternatives can be reduced if not eliminated by providing job security, creating the social conditions needed for shift working and creating a national minimum basic pay below which no worker can fall and must be well above the 'bread line' level.

If, as everyone seems to agree, redundancy is soul-destroying and degrading, not to mention detrimental to the wellbeing of the nation's economy, surely it is well worthwhile to create the conditions which will make it more conducive to finding alternatives to redundancy. There must be an abundance of lessons to be learned from all of the conflicts which have taken place on this most important issue, but surely the clearest lesson of all must be, that where we have had any success in stopping closures or avoiding redundancies that success has only been achieved by the fullest involvement of the workpeople themselves.

People's jobs are a great part of their lives and are therefore too important to be left to the whims of any group of Employers, or for that matter, to the decision of a Government Minister. There must be regular and ongoing consultations in all industries involving all parties to ensure that some of the shocking events that have taken place in the past cannot be repeated.

As can be seen industrial democracy can be vastly improved by the extension of collective bargaining and the erosion of Managerial prerogative. One thing must be made clear however on the question of 'Managerial' prerogative. The word 'Managerial' of course means the owners of industry as many managers—who are employees every bit as much as the shop floor worker—have absolutely no say in determining plant policy on such important matters.

It is almost certain that in the next few years, partly through Government legislation and partly through Trade Union pressures that much will be achieved in the field of industrial democracy. It must also be remembered however, that the extension of industrial democracy is only but another stepping stone to "achieving for workers by hand or by brain, the full fruits of their labour".

Workers Control

It would probably be true to say that whilst Trade Union activists have a general idea of what they want by workers' control, relatively few—including myself—have a blueprint in their minds let alone on paper as to how this can best be effected. However certain claims have emerged from the various studies that have been carried out and it may be advantageous if some of of these were listed and some analysis carried out.

1) Workers' control can only operate in a socialist society.

2) That workers' control, like industrial democracy, can only be realised through the single channel of the Trade Union movement.

3) That the German system of Supervisory Boards and Works Councils is not workers' control

and has serious defects.

4) That the T.U.C. proposals re the setting up of Supervisory Boards and Management Board in the private sector with a 50 per cent workpeople representation, while endorsed by the 1974 T.U.C. does not have the wholehearted support of all of the Trade Union movement.

5) That workers must not only control their industry but must also ensure they control their own Trade Unions.

6) That a fair degree of control can be exerted by Trade Unions by the use of collective bargaining.

In briefly analysing these various claims the degree of difference between workers' participation and workers' control must always be borne in mind. If the analysis was on workers' participation then the results would be entirely different. Using the same reference numbers as above experience or logic would tell us the following—

1) It is highly unlikely that true workers' control can operate in the private sector of a mixed economy. Paragraph 86 of the T.U.C. report of 1974 on Industrial Democracy begins:-
"Any method of involvement in Managerial decisions will still raise the issue of who determines the disposition of capital. Ownership of capital confers on shareholders the ultimate right of the withdrawal of their capital."
The T.U.C. having conceded this very obvious fact then goes on to argue the case for Supervisory Boards and Management Boards with direct workers' representation. This at first appears to be a contradiction until it is realised that the T.U.C. are not arguing the case for workers' control but for a degree of **joint control.** (Para.88 T.U.C. Report). It would therefore appear that the T.U.C. concede that workers' control in a mixed economy cannot work and therefore workers' control can only be effective when industry itself is state controlled.

2) There can be no doubt that all the various stages from collective bargaining to industrial democracy and from workers' participation to workers' control must be channelled through the single avenue of the Trade Unions. Any other course would only lead to confusion, duplication and possibly even disintegration in certain areas of Trade Union organisation. The Trade Union movement is a ready-made vehicle to obtain for the workers their aspirations and its whole history proves the effective part it has played in the whole field of worker involvement.

3) The German system, suited to the then needs of the German people when it was established is now recognised as having many defects. For example, the workers' representatives on an eleven man Supervisory Board could contain three non-Trade Unionists and only two Trade Unionists. In fact the constitution of the Supervisory Boards lays down that at least one of the five workers' representatives shall **not** be a member of a Trade Union. There is also a provision whereby the Works Councils may accept certain conditions without consulting the shop floor members which seems to be a contradiction of industrial democracy let alone workers' control.

4) There is a sizeable opposition within the Trade Union movement to the T.U.C. proposals. The main ground of the opposition is that the proposals for **Joint Control** are a recognition that the capitalist system is acceptable and that there should be a joint control and therefore joint responsibility for making it work. The proponents of workers' control and state ownership of **all** industry see this therefore as a possible slowing down of the erosion of capitalism. While it is unlikely that the T.U.C. would accept the latter part of that particular argument nevertheless their proposals are confusing coming from a movement which is wholeheartedly committed to state ownership.

5) If industrial democracy and workers' control are to be operated through the single channel of the Trade Union movement then it must follow that the Trade Union members must control their own organisation. However, in most cases the provisions are already there for such control but unfortunately the members do not always accept their responsibility. If control means anything it

means involvement and also the acceptance of the Rules and Constitution of the organisation which we control. Refusal to accept this is tantamount to abrogating any right to control and providing the machinery for making any desired change is in the hands of the Union membership then the responsibility that goes with control must be recognised and accepted.

6) The length and detail of the preceding section on collective bargaining should illustrate how important this is to the achieving of industrial democracy and therefore **some degree** of control. The effectiveness of our collective bargaining can in many ways determine not only our members' conditions but the degree of interest and involvement which they will take in their Trade Union. In the absence of any short term likelihood of full workers' control then probably our greatest advancements will be in the field of **free** collective bargaining.

However, we should not allow this conclusion to prevent us either from accepting or extending Trade Union participation in the private sector. Workers' control will only be achieved by taking every opportunity to wrest the present almost total control of industry from the private owner. Every experience gained will be helpful in workers playing their full part when total workers' control is achieved, and every mistake made should prevent similar mistakes being made in the future. As stated earlier, the erosion of managerial prerogative can be achieved by collective bargaining and even more progress can be made by fuller participation. This participation can then be used to go forward to help in the complete abolition of the present system and open the road to a real and full system of workers' control.

The last Conservative Government's endeavours through the I.R.C. to impair the effectiveness of the Trade Union movement by its interference in free collective bargaining clearly illustrates the part that this can play in the struggle between capital and labour.

Irrespective of what the final formula will be relative to workers' control one thing is certain, that the formula can only be successful if the majority of Trade Union members can understand it, find it acceptable and participate in it.

In the absence of any tried and trusted form of successful workers' control in this country it is difficult to be positive as to its best form. To date most of the events which have been associated with workers' control, even in its very broadest sense, have tended to be defensive actions rather than positive movements. Whilst in Scotland many lessons were learned through the experiences of the 'Fairfield Experiment', the Upper Clyde Shipbuilders, Govan Shipbuilders, Marathon (U.K.) Ltd., and Plessey, at the end of the day none of them ever came near to being workers' control. But then none of the leaders involved have ever publicly claimed that these actions went beyond the 'Right to Work'. My own opinion is that the unfortunate end to the 'Fairfield Experiment' deprived the Scottish people, and the rest of Britain, from participating to the full in a venture which, if it had run longer would have come very close to workers' control through the Trade Union movement.

The 'Fairfield Experiment' at its time and even to date had some unique aspects to it. It was a venture brought about by a joint rescue operation of a doomed shipyard by a sort of unholy alliance of Government/Trade Union/Private investment. The main Trade Union contributors were the A.E.U. (now A.U.E.W.) and the G.M.W.U. which resulted in both these Unions having members on the Board of Directors. One of the first things to be done by the new Board was to establish the 'Fairfield Joint Council' which was made up of senior Management and senior T.U. officials, who met regularly and discussed manpower planning, orders (both firm and anticipated), production techniques, labour problems, wage structures and all other aspects of running a shipyard. Whilst the T.U. representatives on the Board and on the Joint Council had not been elected by the workers, specifically to fill these posts, nevertheless they had within the rules of the individual Unions been either elected or appointed to represent the interests of workers in the broadest possible sense. In a way, therefore, a form of worker-elected representatives was evolved, not necessarily in the manner which the shipyard workers would have chosen, but nevertheless one which formed the basis for claiming a measure of workers' participation. There is no doubt if the experiment had lasted longer the workers' representation, at least on the Joint Council, would have extended itself to rank and file representation elected direct by the workers in the yard.

The 'Fairfield Experiment' also created some notable achievements in T.U. organisation and working conditions. For the first time in any Scottish shipyard a full time Trade Union Convener was recognised, an office allocated and reasonable facilities agreed to. In all aspects of the running of the yard there was a greater degree of consultation than ever before between Management, workers and Trade Union representatives. Mistakes were undoubtedly made but in any experiment this was to be expected. On the question of conditions the experiment created a reduction of the traditional five year apprenticeship to one of four years, an aim which the Trade Unions had been pursuing with Employers for some time—with little success—although this term of apprenticeship is now generally accepted.

Perhaps the most notable basic achievement in the sphere of workers' conditions was the establishment of a common craft rate for all trades. The question of differentials between trades in the shipyards had been a bone of contention for many, many years and had given rise to industrial disputes and enmity between workers and their organisations. The common rate inevitably spread from Fairfield to other yards on the Clyde and Trade Union relationships are all the better for it.

Many critics have condemend the 'experiment' as a complete failure but such a conclusion was more of wishful thinking than fact. The Trade Union movement learned much from Fairfield's that will stand us in good stead for the future.

One other aspect of the whole situation which is either underplayed or completely ignored, was the subsequent part which the experiment had on ensuring the continuity of shipbuilding as a major industry on the upper reaches of the Clyde. If Fairfield's had not been saved it is doubtful as to what would have happened a few years later when the whole of shipbuilding on the upper reaches of the Clyde (with the possible exception of Yarrow's) faced obliteration.

We must now look to the Action Committee of the Scottish Daily News to provide some more of the pieces that may eventually complete the jigsaw. While basically the S.D.N. was inspired by the right to work, from the very start the workers set out to form and run their own co-operative venture. They are entitled to every success, but if the venture has to be dropped then the most poignant lesson we will have learned will be that our members don't fully understand. From that lesson we will have to find ways and means of involving our members. Without them there can be no industrial democracy or no meaningful workers' control.

Socialists And The SNP

Ray Burnett

Scattered and diffused throughout SNP branches the length and breadth of Scotland are a number of activists who are in that Party because of a genuine belief that active campaigning for the SNP and its aim of a politically independent Scotland is the best way to achieve a radically transformed, or indeed a socialist, Scotland. It is difficult to quantify their numbers or to qualify their notion of the Left and of socialism but it is not difficult to see why they are there.(1) They are there because they oppose conservatism and because conservatism, politically, is not the Tory Party but the Labour Party whose dominance of Scottish politics has long been the biggest single guarantor of the maintenance of the status quo. They are there because they are opposed to the way the physical and material wealth of Scotland—not to mention its human resources—has been consistently and endlessly pillaged by financial and industrial interests who have always shown scant regard for the very real social needs of the Scottish people. They are there because British reformist, social-democratic politics with a series of hollow, unkept promises has failed to fight or control the anarchistic destructiveness of these parasites. They are there because they reject what would appear to be the only two viable alternatives facing the Scottish working class, to be a migrant taking the frustrations and the aspirations elsewhere or to continue as a passive Labour voter awaiting the new dawn that is yet to come. Despairing of these bleak alternatives they are there because the way forward as projected by the SNP with its simple-focusing device 'London-rule' gives, at least to them, a more clearly defined, more identifiable image of the obstacle that blocks the path to social justice and the way it can be removed. Even if it does not completely work, some change, some sort of alternative, they would argue, is better than stagnation. What, they may well ask, have we got to lose?

That there does exist such an SNP 'left' is hardly surprising. It is a position however that needs political justification and what I want to suggest in an argument directed primarily to them is that, however bleak the alternatives may appear to be, the SNP is no haven for a socialist and that on consideration the politics of the SNP offer no way out, no way forward, on the basic, fundamental issue—the struggle for socialism.

But first a clarification. Much of the criticism developed in this essay against the Scottish National Party (SNP) can be applied equally to the policy of the Labour Party (LP)(2) or even to a lesser extent to the policy of the Communist Party (CP)(3). That is to say, I am not presenting a socialist critique in order to justify the LP as the means of achieving socialism. Indeed I would argue the reverse, viz. that the LP is the biggest obstacle to the advancement of socialism in this country. Secondly, I am well aware that the type of society hinted at in my argument has never yet been achieved, that is to say I am not presenting a case which in any way implicitly advocates the creation of a society such as exists in the 'Socialist' bloc where state ownership of the means of production is erroneously equated with social ownership and in which control by the central party bureaucracy is falsely presented as rule by the working class.(4) Clearly, in regard to my fellow-contributors and to the Scottish Left in general, this is a minority position—but it is not a solitary one. It is the historical position of the revolutionary left and it is from this intransigent stance that I take issue with the SNP and not as the champion of any other parliamentary party. The SNP have no exclusive claim to a concern for Scotland. I too would like to see Scotland free—the question is, free from what?

I

By its very nature, the SNP makes a critique of its policies comparatively simple. For convenience, any political organisation's policies can be artificially separated into the political, economic and social though the overlaps and balance can make such an approach difficult at times. With the SNP however, there is much less difficulty because as they have made abundantly clear the political aspect of their total programme far outweighs any other. This is only as it should be with a Party whose first principal aim is: "Self-government for Scotland: that is the restoration of Scottish National Sovereignity...".(5) This is the touchstone to which all other policies are referred and subsumed. There are no deep-seated reasons why 'social justice' should not be available to all, there is nothing intrinsically wrong with the socio-economic structure of our society. What is needed is purely a political change in the narrowest sense of the word. If only we could 'go it alone' in charge of our own affairs then our economic and social problems would be largely resolved.

Would that it were that simple—life would be so much easier. Unfortunately, a reflective pause and an application of the critical, analytical faculties of rational thought, so esteemed in our much-vaunted Scottish educational system and yet so much neglected, would soon suggest that the problems and the solutions lie much deeper. In fact they lie in the very foundation of our complex socio-economic structure itself and it is at this level that any political analysis in the truer, wider sense must begin if it really does seek to clear a path and show the way towards the achievement of a new social order. Obviously in a short essay concerned with the analysis presented by the SNP the development of an alternative approach can only be hinted at through implication or by occasional reference elsewhere. For a Scottish socialist concerned with Scottish society there are certain problems, largely of his own making, because even today after several decades of socialist activity in Scotland the hard documentation vital to a socialist critique of contemporary Scotland remains pitifully weak and scandalously thin. Yet this does not mean that the relevance of broader critiques of a more general nature concerned with Western democracies at large can be doubted or regarded as inapplicable to Scotland. Any honest and enquiring reader will easily see how the general can be translated into the specifically Scottish context and illuminate many of our own dark, under-researched social recesses.(6) How anyone can be acquainted with such criticisms of our **societies** fundamental structures and still, **as a socialist,** be reconciled with membership and advocacy of the SNP is a contradiction that I would suggest cannot be overcome other than by self-deception or by a shift to a non-socialist position.

II

The root trouble in Scotland is economic and as everyone knows the economic problems of Scotland need hardly bear repeating. To decline in the traditional industries have been added sudden, considerable redundancies in the vital 'tertiary' or technological sector. The zero-rate emigration figures notwithstanding, unemployment and emigration together with internal migration continue to inflict considerable social dislocation as they have done for generations. While the North-East experiences the biggest 'rip-off' of Scottish manpower and resources since the first Industrial Revolution, the West Central belt languishes in torpidity, the Borders stumble precariously along, the Highland problem remains as intractable as ever and only Shetland which ironically declines to be a full-fledged part of 'Scotland' would seem to be flourishing. We are indeed an impoverished nation.

To end the grimness of it all the SNP propose one, simple solution:

> "The first major positive step is to make sure that all decisions affecting the livelihood of Scots are taken in Scotland. We have had almost 17 years of London Tory government and almost 12 years of London Labour government since the war. From Scotland's point of view the end result has been virtually the same. Depression."(7)
> "A desirable Scotland will never be created by government from Westminster. In Britain's relatively prosperous days successive Tory and Labour governments completely failed to create living conditions in Scotland comparable to those existing in South-East England or in neighbouring European countries."(8)

In other words the SNP find no fault in the economic system as such; the fault lies simply in its mismanagement—by London. This failure to even query the nature of the 'economy' we live with lies at the heart of SNP thinking and is a failing they share with all the social-democratic parties in Western bourgeois democracy. The difference with the SNP is that this failing masks a reality which is in total and absolute opposition to their stated aims and aspirations for the Scottish people. Whatever they may have promised in the past, the social-democrats of Europe seldom raise the expectations of their supporters beyond the hope of a slow gradual improvement in the condition of the masses. The SNP however, have stalked the land promising "Wealth beyond our wildest dreams"(9) if only the British economy becomes a **Scottish** economy. Yet what is the actual substance of this abstracted, rarified thing, the 'economy' which it is suggested can become the servant of the Scottish people with one bold tick on a piece of ballot paper? In the terms of economists we could say its substance is a complex industrial base with only a small percentage of the GNP derived from agriculture and the primary sector, that this base has a 'public' sector the value of which is greatly overshadowed by the dominating factor which is private ownership of the means of production, and that in the case of the major elements in the productive system this ownership is external to Scotland. But it is only by going beyond this point and considering the social structure on which this floating abstraction rests that its real nature is revealed as a means of organising ourselves towards the maximisation of profit for the benefit of the few through the exploitation of the many, that is to say it is revealed as an economy both Scottish and **capitalist.** It has deep and widespread roots in the social fabric of Scotland and of Britain and of the Western world sustaining not just the social structure on which it rests but permeating and shaping the ethos and ideology of that total society giving it a one-dimensional totality of suffocating self-justification and regeneration. Scottish, British and capitalist, the roots of our economic problems can only be fully discovered and fully resolved by considering the consequences of all three aspects in their interaction.(10)

The SNP's exclusive concern with the 'Scottish' economy and its ill-concealed disdain for the British economy deflects attention away from one of the most significant consequences of a capitalist economy, a consequence that is only properly revealed in the total British context namely the continuance today of the same massive inequalities of wealth and income as existed a century ago. When the Labour Representation Committee was formed in February 1900 it issued a Manifesto with an ironically prophetic comment on the strength and power of capital: "It is on both sides of the House of Commons. It has the ear of Ministers and can control the policy of parties. It frankly uses its powers to promote its own ends."(11) Now over seventy years later with the LRC's progeny as willingly under the thumb of capital as any of its political predecessors that strength and power continues unchecked. The vast majority of the population continue to own very little wealth. In 1966 the 87.9 per cent of the population who owned less than £3,000 had an average holding to their name of only £107. At the same time 7 per cent of the total adult population owned 84 per cent of all private wealth while the richest 2 per cent accounted for a staggering 55 per cent of the total. Property income was even more concentrated than property ownership with the richest 10 per cent of the population actually receiving 99 per cent of all property income. Similarly with share ownership, only 4 per cent of the adult population owned any shares at all in privately owned companies(12). Related gross inequalities also exist in the fields of pensions, redundancy and dismissal compensation, food and drink, housing, leisure, health and education.(13) Where there are figures available there is no reason to doubt that these vast differentials of wealth and comparative poverty are mirrored in Scotland itself. The principal difference from the overall British picture is probably that, in line with the economy itself, those who own and control so much are unlikely to be domiciled here though they may well be Scots and that conversely there will be in our midst a disproportionate number of those most exposed groups recruited almost entirely from the latter, namely the destitute, the unemployed, the aged poor and the sub-proletariat. As if that was not enough we already know that Scotland's record on housing, health, etc. betrays marked inequality.

The point is that the inequalities endemic to Scotland are not peculiar to Scotland. They exist throughout Britain as a consequence and a corollary of British capitalism. What is distinctively Scottish is that at this point in time we constitute a particularly 'distressed' region with certain chronic problems which the currently affluent South-East of England does not face. Yet we are not the only people to face such a problem. Nor have we always been in this situation. About the only thing that is uniform in capitalism is the degree and the extent of inequality, for the most part it is unplanned, uneven and anarchic. It is simply not true to say that in contrast to Scotland, the South-East of England and the European countries have always been prosperous. The Aquitaine region of south-west France, the Walloon area of Belgium, the whole of southern Italy, the north of Ireland are but some of the European areas that have shared Scotland's problem for a number of years.(14) What is more there was a time prior to 1914 when the area of heaviest unemployment was London, and Scotland was the least affected and when the now prosperous south-east of England was second only to London (excluding Ireland) in depression.(15) An exclusivist, non-historical view disguises the fact that the social dislocation we continue to face in terms of massive inequality, unemployment, redundancies, etc are consequences not of a **British** economy but of a British **capitalist** economy.

This is not to deny that today Scotland suffers greatly from the fact that it is British capitalism which is in a crisis and that the peculiar nature of the Scottish economy as a 'branch and subsiduary economy' makes it particularly vulnerable in this crisis. It has been noted that more than half (59 per cent) of Scottish manufacturing employment is located in the 28 per cent of plants that are controlled from outside, and that the vast majority of these are controlled from England.(16) It has also been noted that this integration is likely to increase rather than diminish in the future. The SNP take strong objection to this state of affairs, claiming that the consequence of external control is 'mismanagement' of the Scottish economy to the detriment of the Scottish people as a whole.

Yet this is simply to decry **capital** for following its own logic. The motive force of capitalism as an economic system has always been and remains, profitability. For company men, owners, managers, executives alike, "profits, even though not the ultimate goal, are the necessary means to all ultimate goals. As such, they become the immediate, the unique, unifying, quantitative aim of corporate policies, the touchstone of corporate rationality, the measure of corporate success."(17) Those who take the ultimate decisions on British, American or Scottish capital invested in Scottish industry, be they English, American or Scots and whether their profiles of rising success appear in the **Financial Times,** the **Wall Street Journal** or the 'Top People' column of the **Scotsman's** business pages, they all follow the same guidelines, all follow the same logic. What Western advanced capitalism has consistently shown is that this economic elite have a loyalty to each other and to the system they so devotedly serve and strive to maintain which far outweighs any other consideration of national, moral or even humanitarian responsibility. When the oil giants of the USA faced a conflict between their interests and that of their 'national responsibility' it was the latter they hastily jettisoned just as the memory of thalidomide, asbestos, mercury-poisoning and many other avoidable tragedies go along with the continuing record of British (including Scottish) investment in South Africa as monuments to the flagrant disregard of any moral responsibility and the victims of all the multifarious weaponry of oppression from napalm in Vietnam to CS and CR in Ireland are related testimony to the abandonment of humanitarian principles so long as there are profits in war mongering and a steady market in the hardware of colonial oppression.(20)

In this overall context the decision to 'rationalise' a plant or branch factory which is not fulfilling an adequate role in the overall task of maximising profits is an effortless stroke of the pen and a well-worn brief to the PR consultants. After all, according to the law of capitalism, the 'rationalisation' process is not 'mismanagement' but good management and it is the law which any capitalist worth his salt will unhesitatingly obey without due concern for his 'brither Scot', the worker. Scottish banks and financiers may be leaping over themselves now to put Scotland first but a few years ago when the country was crying out for an economic lift their investment flow was in every direction but homeward. At the moment because of the historical development of British and international capitalism, the decisions with the most adverse effects on Scotland are usually though not always taken outside Scotland, but even if the SNP were to rise to the virtually insurmountable challenge of creating an indigenous elite of Scottish-based industrialists in command of the largest units in the Scottish economy their understanding of their role would in no way substantially differ from that held by the present remote decision-makers.

The SNP believe that independence will "release Scottish initiative and vigour in industry."(21) That may be so. But that initiative and vigour exists already, operating in a broader context but operating according to a logic and single-mindedness which does not alter according to political boundaries. If it is released and **chooses** to direct itself towards Scottish industry then it will only do so to secure its one ultimate aim and all other considerations will continue to be subordinate, including the grandiose dreams held out by the SNP. For capitalism does not operate according to any plan to meet or provide for social needs in any given country. It operates according to the economic forces of the market and it is these forces which will determine the places we will have to work, the nature of the work we will do, the successful and the declining sectors of industry. Furthermore this market mechanism is operated by a search for profit on the part of individuals and companies and as we shall see the slender controls operated by the state are quite unable, nor are they really intended, to prevent the anarchic free-play of these forces. Like many other apologists for the status-quo the SNP may reply that in recent years, since the 'managerial revolution', capitalism has ceased to exist.(22) The logic of this much-quoted argument is, of course, that if capitalism no longer exists then there no longer exists the need for a new social order—for socialism —which makes the SNP a curious place for a socialist to be.

III

The SNP itself, of course, is not socialist; indeed many of its leaders are adamantly opposed to any notion of socialism, one of them, Mr W. Macrae, a member of their National Council, spoke for many when he categorically assured would-be supporters that "certainly the new Scotland will will NOT be Socialist"(23) (his emphasis). They have no wish to replace a capitalist order with an alternative—many of them are doing quite well out of the present set-up already. All they want is an economy more suitable to 'Scottish interests' which they suggest will, by definition, be of benefit to all the Scottish people, serving their needs rather than dominating their lives. Oblivious of the fact that the Scottish working-class spawned a political organisation which was ostensibly to devote itself to the task, a task which is still before us, the SNP reiterate the same promise of a 'new life' but a different route. The Labour Party in Scotland also promised a land of social justice and prosperity, but they based their appeal on 'old-fashioned' irrelevancies like 'class' and the irresponsible notion that bosses and workers do not share the same fundamental interests. The SNP will have none of this; in politics, as in economics, they deny the **fact** of great disparities in power and influence between different social groups and so they are opposed to any attempt to take note of them. They are accordingly proud to be "emerging as the most responsible party in Britain. The most united party in the country—not promoting sectional interest, not pushed around by sectional interests."(24) The route they propose is the path of national unity to achieve self-government. In fact they see it as the **only** route:

> "We will develop the Scotland the majority of us want only by electing a Scottish parliament and by no other means."(25)

This is the cornerstone of the SNP's political programme and the reference point for all else besides. The assumptions implicit to it are important and must be clearly understood. There is the absolute, uncritical fostering of the illusion that in a democratically elected parliament there will be heard the untrammelled, undistorted voice of the people and there is the complete exclusion of the possibility, far less the necessity, of organising around any sort of 'sectional' interest. In other words, in politics as in economics the SNP simply reiterate the operant ideology of orthodox, capitalist political economy and its attendant pluralist theory. The only change they envisage is a mechanical extension downwards through greater devolution.(26) These proposals fit in well with the widespread cynicism and lack of faith in the efficacy of our institutionalised democracy, a cynicism which led many to support the SNP. Well aware of the fact that their rise is based, at least partly, on a rejection of the pluralist democratic structure the SNP seek to restore faith in the structure rather than extend criticism of its workings. They do so by suggesting that present, undeniable failings are due to problems of geographical and administrative remoteness and of size all of which can be overcome in a small, homogenous, self-governing country. But above all they consistently imply that everything will work to the greater benefit of all because with Scottish oil there will be wealth and prosperity in sufficient quantity to keep everyone happy, contented and satisfied with their own share of the poke. In the El Dorado of the future, "where there is full employment and where wealth is distributed fairly to give everybody a decent house and good opportunities for education and employment and contentment—where individuals and communities are protected from exploitation.."(27) oil will lubricate the smooth workings of our democratic institutions. To achieve this heady vision where they will both resolve the old problems and at the same time maximise the benefits of the new opportunities the SNP pin all its policy and its promises on the assumed **ability** of a Scottish government to judiciously control and manage an oil-related economy in the interest of the mass of the Scottish people.

What the sceptic is entitled to ask of the SNP is why and how can they succeed where others have failed. After all, every political party in Western democracy promises to, and when in office claims to, manage the economy for the benefit of all. Yet the tremendous inequalities of wealth and income that were noted earlier continue to persist everywhere, including the Scandinavian countries so often acclaimed as models by the SNP.(28) Adjustments there may have been, but no social democratic government has ever succeeded in significantly and irreversibly altering this general inbuilt inequality. Nor will they ever succeed in doing so. Privilege and power are not forsaken easily, as the tragedy of Chile reminds us.(29) Apart from anything else, to tackle the dominant elite head on in a political struggle for control of the 'commanding heights' of the economy would require, at the very least, an acknowledgement of their power and an awareness of their axiomatic tendency to act in a manner detrimental to the interests of the mass of the people. The SNP acknowledge and are aware of neither.

The SNP are no different from any other bourgeois parliamentary party. They conceive of equality, social justice and prosperity **only within the limits already laid down** by an inherently unequal social system. They are guaranteed to ensuring that the Scottish economy remains a private enterprise economy secure in in the touching belief that what is good for private enterprise must be good for the country at large. Thus when Dr MacIntyre welcomed Sir Hugh Fraser into the SNP in April of last year he did so with the greatest of pleasure because he saw in Sir Hugh one of those "commercial leaders of Scotland who could do, and had done, a great deal for the country."(30) The fact that the Fraser family and their likes represent one of the most glaring examples of the imbalanced dispersal of wealth and power natural to a capitalist economy was never even questioned by MacIntyre or his party. Indeed no sooner was their 'fellow-Scot' into the 'body o' the Kirk' than he was allowed to introduce 170 of his fellow business men to the SNP in order to reassure them that when the SNP successfully gained independence they would all receive a "fair crack of the whip."(31) No one in the SNP saw fit to consider on whose backs the whip would crack. No one saw fit to conceive of a Scotland without 'captains of industry' at the helm. In this the SNP share the failings of all parties committed to a continuation of the present:

> "Liberal democracy has never dared face the fact that industrial capitalism is an intensely coercive form of organisation of society that cumulatively constrains men and all of their institutions to work the will of the minority who hold and wield economic power; and that this relentless warping of men's lives and forms of

113

association becomes less and less the result of voluntary decisions by 'bad' men or 'good' men and more and more an impersonal web of coercions dictated by the need to keep the 'system' running."(32)

In this context, as Professor Miliband has pointed out all the other ends of the leaders and the government are "conditioned by, and pass through the prism of, their acceptance of and commitment to the existing economic system."(33) The result is a foregone conclusion, "for if the national interest is in fact inextricably bound up with the fortunes of capitalist enterprise, apparent partiality towards it is not really partiality at all. On the contrary, in serving the interests of business and in helping capitalist enterprise to thrive, governments are really fulfilling their exalted role as guardians of the good of all. From this standpoint, the much-derided phrase 'What is good for General Moters is good for America' is only defective in that it tends to identify the interests of one particular enterprise with the national interest. But if General Motors is taken to stand for the world of capitalist enterprise as a whole, the slogan is one to which governments in capitalist countries do subscribe, often explicitly."(34)

Certainly there will be talk of government action etc., but if the government ever does encroach on certain rights of private enterprise, the long-term effect is only to further secure the system as a whole. The prolonged phoney argument about government 'interference', and the anguished cries of violated capital at further 'advances' may be orchestrated to sound as if government can impose its will on privately-owned industry, but in reality it can do nothing of the kind. As we have already seen with the present government and the oil-companies, whenever there is talk of action to ensure the better management of the economy in the interest of the population at large, we are talking about the better management of a capitalist economy, "and this ensures that whoever may or may not gain, capitalists interests are least likely to lose."(5)

Undeterred and unseeing, the SNP propose a variety of State institutions whose 'neutral' role will be to ensure that the interests of the business ventures and the country at large will coincide. The flaw with all these agencies, a National Assembly, Land Use Commission, Oil Development Ministry, National Oil Company, Scottish Coal Board, etc.,(36) is the assumption of their 'neutrality' in the 'sectional' conflict between organised labour and industry. Why should such agencies in an independent Scotland be any different in role and function from those already operant elsewhere, not least in Britain just now? In the latter instance we find a multiplicity of social, kinship, financial and business connections which tie those who manage, direct and run the avowedly 'neutral' or 'public' institutions of the State to the top decision-makers of industry in what is best described as a **plurality of elites** or alternatively, a ruling class.(37) From consultants in industry throughout the myriad advisory committees and boards to membership of the Cabinet itself those who are committed to the ethos, logic and advancement of finance capital and its allied interest make themselves heard. Consider the handling of our national fuel policy, in which nationalized coal and all those dependent on the coal industry for a livelihood, including thousands of Scottish miners, was consistently advanced or retarded according to the ongoing needs of business interests such as the oil monopolies or the suppliers of uranium to the Atomoc Energy Authority, RTZ.(38) The post-war history of the governments fuel policy not only shows such a fuel policy is dictated according to the needs of the interests mentioned above, it also shows that "enterprises as aggressive as the oil monopolies having got a foot in the door, proceeded to kick it open."(39)

Yet these are the very interests the SNP suggest they can effortlessly control in the social interest of Scotland. "The enormous wealth of the oil and gas fields off the Scottish coast, allied to our other vast resources, offers **ever improving** living standards to the people of Scotland...(40) (my emphasis R.B.).

"With a Scottish Government exercising effective control over Scottish oil, enormous employment opportunities will be created in Scotland and vast capital wealth will accrue directly to Scotland. This wealth can, and must, be used to secure for all times prosperity, security and a satisfying life style for all the people of Scotland."(41)

The SNP love the mythology of our traditions which perhaps explains their touching Old Testament belief that once again David can slay Goliath—or at least cut him down to size. But the

114

oil industry is no ordinary giant, even by monopoly capitalist standards. What is more, "the record of these companies is one of unrelenting aggression both against producer and consumer countries."(42) There is little doubt that if the SNP made a belated decision to challenge the power of these companies and seriously curb their activities in the interests of the Scottish people then the industry would show the same ruthlessness and naked self-interest as they showed in the Caucusus in 1917, in Mexico 1938, in Venezuala 1948, in Iran 1951, in Iraq 1961 and Algeria and Libya 1970-71.(43) Despite that the SNP are falling over backwards to placate the moguls and to serve their interests. While at the same time castigating Tory and Labour administrations for doing likewise. In Oslo last April, William Wolfe assured the oil industry that the SNP "recognised the valuable skills and functions of the oil companies and are prepared to allow them to earn post-tax capital profits appropriate to capital..."(44) Given the supine attitude adopted to date it would be interesting to see the SNP try and disallow them. The oil companies can rest assured however, that such a likelihood will never arise. Indeed so keen are the SNP to facilitate their new-found friends that they want an expansion of the training and research facilities already given over in our universities and colleges for the benefit of the oil industry(45) regardless of the fact that these expanding departments and institutions are not simply concerned with the exploitation of the mineral wealth of the industry but the exploitation and management of its human wealth, its workforce, as well.

In shop-floor terms it is quite clear where the SNP stand. They want each company operating in the oil industry "to undertake the training of technical and management personnel in all the various skills.(46) "Furthermore: "To complement such 'on-the-job' training, Scotland must have suitable courses for operators and for technical and management staff, at colleges and universities."(47) In industry, technology and managerial skills do not exist in the abstract or in a void. They are used for the advancement of the corporate life of the country and one of the main forces to be 'managed' is the labour force. The SNP may claim to speak for the Scottish people when they talk of 'Scotland's Oil' but in reality they represent the real interests of a very small section of the Scottish people and they have virtually admitted as much: "We must therefore ensure that enough oil expertise is accumulated in Scotland to enable the people of Scotland, through their own corporations and companies, to take part in the search for oil..."(48) Ownership of oil-related companies is not a common phenomena amongst the mass of Scottish people.

Despite the occasional public statement, the total absence of any statement in their major policy documents on the need to minimize the hazards of North Sea Oil exploration for the work-force even though divers continue to die at an average of one a month, or on the need to secure total unionisation of the rigs (far less a school for the training of shop-stewards in their comparable skills), indicates quite clearly what side of the industrial divide the SNP are basically interested in wooing. The conclusion is clear. Unless nationalised without compensation, and under worker's control, the oil industry in Scotland will continue to operate according to a logic squarely opposed to the the very real social needs of the Scottish people. The record and the current practice of the oil companies is there for all to see. If there is the slightest hint of a threat to their overall interest then the cry quickly goes up that 'business confidence' the 'willingness to invest' is being jeopardised, or that in political terms, their 'basic freedoms' are being theatened. Given the terms in which it has chosen to work, government has no option but to retract, as the back-pedalling of the present administration clearly shows. Those who press home their opposition to the will of big business, on the other hand, whether on the picket line or on the streets soon reveal the determination of big business and its cohorts to break no nonsense.(49).

The SNP sum up of the potential of oil for Scotland in. "a simple message to the people of Scotland: DO YOU WISH TO BE 'RICH SCOTS' OR 'POOR BRITISH'?"(50) What they omit to mention is that there **already are** 'rich Scots'—some very rich Scots. And they are growing richer every day on the oil industry and its activities in the North-East, the Eastern Highlands and Shetland. The SNP inform us eagerly that: "Scotland is in the fortunate position of being well-placed in technical skills and native capital resources to take full advantage of the new situation."(51) Involved in a daily struggle for decent conditions, safety and returns while their families try to cope with soaring, inflated prices, inadequate amenities and general social dislocation, it is an observation the isolated workforces in the areas mentioned above hardly need reminding of. As these latest victims of our 'native capital resources' already know to their disadvantage, the vigour and vitality has by no means entirely disappeared from our hard-suffering indigenous entrepreneurs.

A sniff of profit works wonders for a run-down investor or financier. Scottish finance which until recently showed its patriotism by channelling capital out of Scotland has suddenly discovered the virtue in 'putting Scotland first' and is now busy ploughing it back in again while our stalwarts of Charlotte Square are amassing fortunes by advising others on how to do the same. The merchant bank, Edward Bates, for example, expanded its assets from £2.5m. in 1969 to £24.5m. in 1972 principally through its connections with firms like Ivory and Sime.(52) Scottish capitalists are no strangers to the world of finance; one third of all British investment trusts, one sixth of all life insurance companies and a large part of the unit trust and savings movement are located in Scotland(53) though until recently, national identity would seem to have been of little consequence. Although capital raised in Scotland is higher per head than in the rest of Britain(54) our fellow-Scots, the financiers did not hesitate to invest virtually all of it abroad, with no less than one third of the total being invested in the USA.(55)

Such investors like to peddle in trouble-free waters (they leave the real hazards of the North Sea to the workers). To keep things going smoothly and to protect their wealth which lubricates the whole economic system, they like to have a government in the saddle which, far from controlling their interest, will ensure that all their relationships are harmonious and non-antagonistic. In the SNP they see a potential government which they know will be a loyal ally. For their part the SNP have made little secret of the friendships they hope to strike up with big business and its needs. At their Conference in Rothesay (May 1973) the SNP decided to press the government for concessions in their proposed legislation as the party were anxious to keep in with their "support in high places". .

> "If the Government repudiated their share it would help turn their (oil industrialists) minds to self government." (56)

What the SNP make quite clear is that provided they were permitted to allow the Scottish workforce a 'reasonable' and 'acceptable' degree of spin-off benefit then, as a governing party, they would guarantee industrial tranquility. What they find so distasteful in England is the same thing that bothers aggrieved industrialists; the persistent clamour of organised labour who will not just lie down and accept its lot:

> "Scotland by way of contrast is a rich country. The vastly increased prosperity guaranteed by oil will mean that everybody can be better off in contrast to the UK situation where gains for one group can only be made at the expense of others."(57)
>
> "The SNP view the present industrial unrest in the United Kingdom as an inevitable outcome of economic decline. As the economic 'cake' becomes smaller squabbles over relative shares will become increasingly bitter and intractable."(58).

In marked contrast, they hold forth a vision of an independent Scotland which is every employer's dream, a country that will be a paragon of democratic-pluralism:

> "The experience of other, small, prosperous and independent nations suggests that an independent Scotland, with visibly improving living standards and fairer shares for all can expect a high degree of industrial harmony." (59)

Harmony, docility, acceptance of the inevitability of the status quo, this is the 'radical' vision of Scottish nationalism. At the moment this harmony is solicited by the powerful appeals of Scottish management through the Scottish media to Scottish workers to act in the 'national interest'. Indeed so often is the latter catchphrase used whenever steps are about to be taken against either the organisational capacity or the living standards of the working class that Scottish workers have every good reason to greet its pronouncement as a signal for impending class hostilities. Yet this is the very banner the SNP ask the Scottish working class to rally behind, only this time it is in the interests of the 'Scottish' economy as opposed to the British. The conclusion is clear. Nationalism in this sense is the same as it is in current British politics—the mystifying lynchpin of conservative

116

ideology. The political 'choice' offered by the SNP is in reality, no choice at all for the social sytem it holds forth will remain exactly what it is just now and the political structure of an independent Scotland will continue to be a flase plurality masking the influence and power of one economically and politically dominant class over its subordinate.

As one percipient political scientist has observed regarding politics in advanced capitalist societies:

> "... it is no more than a matter of plain political history that the government of those countries have een mostly composed of men who beyond all their political, social, religious, cultural and other differences and diversities, have at least had in common a basic and usually explicit belief in the validity and virtues of the capitalist system, though this is not what they would necessarily call it; and those among them who have not been particularly concerned with that system, or even aware that they were helping to run a specific economic system, much in the way they were not aware of the air they breathed, have at least shared with their more ideologically-aware colleagues or competitors a quite basic and unswerving hostility to any socialist alternative to that system."(60)

For all their avowed 'radicalism', the SNP have no intention of stepping outwith this consensual framework. This is not to deny the obvious; the SNP have several important differences with the other major political parties operating in Scotland. But these differences are differences as to how best to run and organise the **same** economic and social system not the differences between advocates of an alternative form of society and defenders of the present. Even within the present limits, the 'radical' proposals of the SNP have serious weaknesses. It is always difficult to expose the practical weaknesses of a set of political preposals which remain untried in practice. The real politics of the SNP are best seen in their actions and societal allegiances rather than in a static, untested political programme. On paper the SNP attack both bureaucracy and political elites: they are strong advocates of 'participatory democracy' seeing this as part of our mighty Scottish tradition. As William Wolfe put it at their annual Conference in October 1970: "In our heritage we find a key to our outlook summed up in the words 'radical' and 'egalitarianism'. ...We are essentially a democratic people... The outlook of this Party is a distillation of outlooks, essentially radical and egalitarian, in accordance with Scottish humanitarian traditions which have little to do with British party political labels. The mainspring of our dedication is love of humanity in general and of Scotland in particular..."(69)

It is difficult to see how anyone with the slightest knowledge of Scottish social history of current political reality in Scotland can take this sort of stuff seriously. Yet many do. So strong is this love of Scotland that the country becomes an idealised, ethereal wonderland where all would be peace, harmony and fraternity, if only the English disease of class antagonism and social divisiveness could be cauterised and the nation sealed off. This happy belief "that the Scots are essentially a fraternal people"(62) relies heavily on a notion of "collective fraternalism" deriving from our Celtic sources. The Highlands are still regarded as an area exemplifying this innate Scottish, or Celtic tendency to deny social and political emnity because of the bonds of brotherhood. The divide in the Highlands is drawn between the communal, classless, egalitarian tendency of indigenous politics and the divisive, elitist, remote, centralised bureaucracy enforced from outside and maintained by aliens. Thus in the Highlands, the Highland Regional Association of the SNP—one of its more, genuinely radical bodies—calls for the democratisation of the Highlands and Islands Development Councils and the provision of regular consultative channels between the centralised Regional Authority and the communities. By such structural implementations, the innate democracy of the area will flourish free from alien influences.(63)

There is nothing wrong with these proposals as they stand; the HIDB is in grave need of being made publicly accountable and its powers used for the planned betterment of the area. What is wrong is the assumption that such structural changes will thereby result in 'democracy'. It is an integral part of the SNP's master-plan for a democratic Scotland that elitism in government is the consequence of our present party-system, centralism, and sectional appeals.

In the Highlands there is no party-system in local government, there are no overt, sectional appeals, and there is a wide mixture of both local and centralised agencies, elected and non-elected, voluntary and statutory. Thus the Highlands could be said to represent the full diversity of our pluralist society in action amongst a population so scattered and diffuse that for an elite to exist it would have to be introduced. Yet an examination of local government representatives and their social origins, coupled with a study of the composition of the multifarious 'public' agencies with a stake in Highland affairs reveals that it is the same social strata that dominates **all of these bodies**(64), regardless of any differentiating factors. The overwhelming membership of this plethora of agencies, reliably estimated at forty-seven, which look after the Highlands represents a very small band of Scottish society; the same band which produces the managers of the Scottish economy, the owners of the Scottish economy, the administrators and the political elite.

Even in terms of the present, SNP policy has a long way to go before it can seriously be seen as making any sort of radical dent on such inevitable consequences of capitalist society. No matter what new public bodies the SNP propose to set up; no matter how much structural power is devolved and centralism minimised they will not break, nor do they wish to break, the integument of the plurality. Socialism can only be achieved without the consensus; the SNP is locked firmly in the latter's embrace with the same intolerance of those who would step outside. In an independent Scotland the august band of distinguished public servants and responsible people who will manage our affairs are hardly likely to deviate from the tight definitions of what is right and what is wrong that they adhere to at the moment. The socio-political web of the club, the golf-course and the moor is hardly likely to shrivel up and die with the advent of the SNP to power. Indeed, in a homlier atmosphere the consensus may well become even couthier though the Scottish working class and the left should be in little doubt that it will be just as determined as the present to isolate and denounce any would-be dissidents of the left that dare to challenge its legitimacy.

IV

Not much attention is paid to the social aspect of SNP policies. In so far as the SNP themselves place so much attention on the political and economic this is hardly surprising. Unlike the LP they do not have a record to defend or a past legacy of failed promises to justify with the result that they can promise much secure in the knowledge that they will never have to put it into practice this side of independence. Perhaps it is as well for the SNP 'left' that the social programme of their party has received such scant attention. It is clear at a glance that the SNP has no commitment whatsoever to the construction of an alternative social order in Scotland or even to a radically reformed one.

On housing, education, welfare, employment, etc., the SNP's line remains consistently the same: it notes the extent of the problem; chastises the 'London parties' for failing to remedy the situation; promises an improvement of the present, under the SNP; and offers independence as the one and only solution. Thus on housing:

> "In spite of all the fine promises Scotland's housing position threatens to move from bad to worse, from 'critical to catastrophic' "... "Currently the main pressure for rent increases comes from rising interest rates and the high cost of building land. "..."This is one of the most important tasks which has been inadequately dealt with by London governments for generations"... "If there is one area of Scottish life where the case for 'going it alone' is surely stronger than in any other, that area is surely housing."(65)

on education:

> "The key problem in education is lack of finance... At one time Scottish education was world famous with a deserved reputation for its quality, scope and integrity. The SNP believes that Scotland can regain her position as a pace-setter in education only in an independent country."

on welfare:

> "The extent of poverty in Scotland is a national scandal. Nothing short of a comprehensive emergency programme backed by the full resources of a Scottish government will eliminate the scandal. A Scottish state will certainly have the

resources to do the job."

and on employment:
> "Every other country comparable to Scotland in size and resources has expanded... What then is to be done?... The first major positive step is to make sure that all decisions affecting the livelihood of Scots are taken in Scotland." (66)

This is a revealing situation. Nowhere is there a challenge to the social structure, nowhere is there a querying of the presence of privilege and inequality nowhere is there a questioning of the values and attitudes used to justify the present. The opportunities for the money-lenders and land speculators to profit at all in such a key social need as housing are not questioned, we are merely assured that the SNP will try and bring interest rates and land costs "back to within reason". The presence of massive class inequalities in our educational system, the corrosive presence of private education, the extensive links of our 'independent' universities and colleges to big business and the whole anti-working class ethos that permeates the content of so much Scottish education all passes unnoticed. The only threat to the glory of our educational system is 'anglicisation'. The moralistic, punitive attitudes that dominate the present welfare system remain untouched:

> "The introduction of a national minimum wage as proposed for several years by the SNP should minimise the chances of abuse of the welfare benefits scheme. There should be, as a final sanction, powers to direct those who have unreasonably refused offers of employment, to work in the public sector, and to withdraw their personal benefit if this work is refused or if the job is not held for a reasonable length of time."(67)

The social programme of the SNP is a programme firmly embedded in the limitations of the present both as to structure and values and working within a given closed circle. They offer no way out, no way forward. Where does that place the SNP 'left'? The solitary constructive aspect of the SNP's noisy attack on the existing British society is a plea for political nationhood—and that is all. But the Left stands for the construction of a new social order and if what is sought is a reconstruction of the **whole** of society then the **whole** of the present structure must be opposed.

Some in the SNP choose to evade this dilemma by tortuous exercises in political theory which argue that there is a "recognisably different philosophy, one singular in British politics which can in fact provide a readily understandable definitive image of the SNP."

> "The SNP, unlike any of the other major parties, has broken the conformist barrier of being essentially left-wing, or right-wing or centre, or most important, coalition. The Scottish National Party is a Party of 'New Politics' and the key to the SNP's New Politics is the manner in which policy is formed. "The test is... are they the best policies for each issue in Scotland." (68)

In fact, these are but the politics of pragmatism, "of the successful manoeuvre within existing limits." These are not the politics that imply far-reaching fundamental change. Contrary to the hopes of the pundit to avoid political allegiance, such allegiance is unavoidable. To be on the Left is to take up an attitude of negation to the existing world, to "take a position of permanent revisionism to reality". The Right assumes an attitude of opportunism to the world as it is, it is the expression of capitulation to the situation of the moment. For this reason the Left can have a political ideology while the Right has nothing but tactics. It is for this reason also that the Right prefers to deny the necessity for a dividing line which the Left insists on drawing. The SNP deny being Left or Right because they seek both the positive aura of the left and acceptance inside the consensual circle. for to be outside—to hint at the negation of the system and its values is to be ignored. The SNP may be leftish on certain issues, eg, the condemnation of nuclear war, opposition to racism, etc, but this cannot hide the fact that as a movement, the SNP has much more in common with the Right than with the Left.

V

Although, as I have tried to suggest the whole essence of the SNP is tied up with the maintenance of the status quo that does not mean that there are no positive features in its rise to prominence in Scottish politics. There are in fact three strands in the political mood of the Scottish people which have undoubtedly helped the SNP and which I would like to single out.

Firstly, there is an undeniable positive political element, just as in the sixties there was a positive element in the tendency for people to express a disinterest in politics, a healthy scepticism in the remote, illusory promises of remote, professional politicians. The paradox then was that despite the apparent disdain for all things political it was actually a reaffirmation of the fact that politics is but the language in which we talk about the way our community is structured and the rejection of the empty jargon of the professionals was a reiteration of the necessity for politics to relate to reality, to real needs and felt aspirations. The mass of people want the decision making process brought nearer, they want to feel a closer sense of participation so that decisions which so crucially affect them will somehow be more relevant and more appropriate. At its highest such intuitive political yearnings have borne fruit in the creation of worker's councils or soviets and it is but one of the many germinal elements that go towards the development of a revolutionary consciousness. But it can only germinate if it is guided in the right direction which is in the direction of politics based on the reality of class struggle and not the myth of communal harmony.

Secondly, the search for an identity outwith the heavy economism of class struggle and the suffocating cultural plasticity of our society is to be welcomed. The increasing working class awareness that a man as a worker is more than a mere wage slave, that he is both a producer and a creator with traditions and achievements behind him which show the abilities of his class in a creative and expansive sense, is of vital importance. The hegemony of the dominant classes in civil society is much more than economic. It is in fact, "an order in which a certain way of life and thought is dominant, in which one concept of reality is diffused throughout society in all its institutional and private manifestations, informing with its spirit all taste, morality, customs, religious and political principles, and all social relations, particularly in their intellectual and moral connotations. (69). To dispel this hegemony, for the subordinate classes to become themselves the hegemonic social group, is no easy task. However, important it may be, the economic struggle or even the political struggle is not enough. The rottenness, the injustices, the exploitations on which the bourgeois state is built cannot be ended by an insurrectionary frontal assault on the latter—not in the liberal-democratic societies of the West. As Gramsci put it, "the State is merely a frontal trench, an advanced line of defence, and behind it there is a powerful fortress of concrete pillboxes (70). "This 'fortress' consists of the attitudes, morals, habits and general view of the world which most people have absorbed as their education etc. continues to disseminate the prevaling ideology of the dominant class. This ideology must be fought by a new comprehensive view of the world which will dispossess the former in the minds of the people. "The modern prince (the political party) must be and cannot but be the proclaimer and organiser of an intellectual and moral reform, which also means creating the terrain for a subsequent development of the national-popular collective will towards the realisation of a superior, total form of modern civilisation." (71)

The growing working-class awareness that the whole quality of life in Scotland, culturally as well as economically, is not what it could be in terms of creative possibilities related to social needs is a not insignificant stirring against these 'fortresses'. In particular the growing interest being shown in the history of the working masses of Scotland, their past triumphs, failures and sufferings marks an important, even if limited, rejection of the hegemony of the dominant classes. But as with the political stirrings, these developments will not bear fruit unless led into an oppositional stance by forces in no way subservient to the present order. Needless to say this is not the SNP.

Thirdly, the growing national awareness could also be of value in relating different aspects of what is really a common struggle to each other. By seeing things on an all-Scottish bases the essential common cause of the crofter, the oil-rigger, the council scheme tenant and the industrial worker can begin to emerge from the isolation each group is deliberately faced with at the moment. In a similar vien the diverse faces of capitalist exploitation can be exposed and linked from the land-use question of Highland estates to the land-value problem of our big cities. Such connections will never be made by the SNP who see only one connection—the abstracted myth of 'London-control'. I say abstracted because nowhere does such an 'analysis' explore the real world of social relationships to expose the real network of control, a network built on privilege and powered by money.

All these positive features are contained in the resurgence of nationalism. There is nothing inherently wrong with 'nationalism' itself, which is but another way of saying that 'nationalism' as a political force does not exist in a vacuum, it is a social phenomena and is given shape and substance by the social forces which support it. It can be both progressive and reactionary. The positive features of this new, peculiar upsurge in Scotland have already been touched upon. If they are drawn together and developed then national consciousness in Scotland could be an integral part of a socialist consciousness, a revolutionary consciousness. The two are not inherently inimical. But if this consciousness is deflected into the reactionary direction suggested by the SNP then it will be lost. Worse than that, it could develop into a serious threat to organised labour and to the left.

That the British economy is in crisis is not disputed. It is an inevitable corollary of this crisis that there will be a prolonged and sustained attempt to weaken and break the ability of organised labour to protect the working class from the ravages of inflation. Anything which helps to divide and divert labour at this point in time is grist to the mill of those whose interest is the continuing profitability of British capitalism. The SNP assists these dominant interests in attempting both. The focusing of attention on the notion of 'going it alone' without raising the question of who will be going where and at whose expense is diversive just as the focusing of attention on the relatively superior position of south-west of England workers is a classic example of material jealousy being stirred up to divide and rule. It is because of the need to control labour that so many sections of Scottish industrial owners and management are turning to the SNP as a powerful ally. The Scottish Council (Development and Industry) is in favour of devolution—in the UK context and the related Scottish Council Research Institute recently published a report on economic development and devolution which made it very clear that the establishment of a Scottish Parliament was seen as an important step in the improving of Scotland's 'shocking' record in industrial relations and the securing of a "stable and assured labour market".

It is in this context that the possibility of the SNP becoming an agency of extreme Right reaction rather than progressive Left advance reveals itself as a distinct possibility. The social base from which the SNP draws much of its support and leadership is in the main that fickle section of our complex class structures— the petty bourgeois. The SNP is very much the party of the small man, the frustrated Scottish businessman smelling profit in oil yet unable to cash in only to spectate, and the lower-middle class and professional elements watching their hard-won status and security disappear in the furnace of inflation. Trapped between the power of the big, non-Scottish, companies on the one hand and the organised strength of Scottish labour on the other (this is in no way to equate the strength of the two) the small man of Scottish society begins to despair and to nurse his bitterness at the parties he had once put his faith in and who let him down. The perceptive observations of Trotsky have a timely significance. "The petty bourgeois takes refuge in the last resort, in a mythology which stands above manner and above history, and which is safeguarded from competition inflation, crisis, and the auction block. To evolution, economic thought and rationalism—of the twentieth, nineteenth, and eighteenth centuries—is counterposed in his mind national idealism, as the source of the heroic beginning." (72)

The prospects for the SNP 'left' are bleak. To become a radical party, far less a socialist party the SNP will have to drastically revise its policies. The odds on a 'left' faction achieving such a revision are very low. The SNP leadership have been around a long time and they are well entrenched. If they wanted the party to be of a 'radical' nature then they would have made it so some time ago. Any attempt by the 'left' to mount a challenge to their leadership would draw forth their combined animosity and opposition. Nor does the 'left' show any sign of getting together in an organised manner to fight for the soul of the party. There is no apparent 'left' faction, they publish no separate propoganda, they are seldom if ever to be read in the party's official publications, and there was not a shadow of their presence in the list of resolutions put before the last Annual Conference. Even if the SNP 'left' was more successful than the LP 'left' in its similar ambition the fact has to be faced that the social composition of the Party support is not the sort of base that a socialist movement requires or is likely to get.

The alternative prospects elsewhere on the Scottish left may be unappealing and bleak but at least they are all more consistent with the struggle for socialism than the SNP will ever be. Can a socialist really justify his membership of the SNP and yet at the same time stand with John MacLean and say:

"I have squared my conduct with my intellect."

1. For one of the very rare publications emmanating from the 'left' SNP camp see Rob Gibson: **The Promised Land** (Glasgow, 1974) which develops such a position in regard to a particular case of landlordism versus crofters' interests.
2. For critiques of the Labour Party see Ralph Miliband: **Parliamentary Socialism** (London, 1961), Tom Nairn: **The Nature of the Labour Party** in **Towards Socialism** (London, 1965) and Raymond Challinor: **Labour and the Parliamentary Road** in **International Socialism 50** (Jan/Mar 1972).
3. For critiques of the Communist Party see Bill Warren: **The Programme of the CPGB—A Critique** in **New Left Review** 63 (Sept/Oct 1970) and also John Urs: **The British Road to Socialism: a marxist criticism** in **International Socialism** 52 (Jul/Sep 1972).
4. For a very fine critique of the 'socialist' bloc from the inside see Jacak Kuron and Karol Modzslewski: **An Open Letter to the party** published in the UK as **A Revolutionary Socialist Manifesto** (London 1968).
5. **Scotland's Future**—the Manifesto of the Scottish National Party, August 1974, p.3.
6. Thus the relevance of Michael Kidron: **Western Captalism since the War** (London 1968) in economics for example, J.E. Meade: **Efficiency, Equality and the Ownership of Property** (London 1964) in social structures and Ralph Miliband: **The State in Capitalist Society** (London 1969) in politics, to name but three each of which has further copious references.
7. The Scottish National Party General Election Manifesto, February 1974, p.13.
8. ibid. p.4.
9. W. Macrae, prospective parliamentary candidate speaking for Ross-shire at Balmacara, **West Highland Free Press**, 1.3.74.
10. Part of that suffocating ideology is of course the prevailing school of economic theory which consistently treats economics as being abstracted from social systems, economic power and social class. The weaknesses of conventional economics have been taken to task by Edward Nell: **"Orthodox economics tries to show that markets allocate scarce resources according to relative efficiency; political economics tries to show that markets distribute income according to relative power.** It is good to know about efficiency, but in our world, it tends to be subservient to power. By failing to appreciate this, and consequently failing also to accord the distribution of income between labour and capital a properly central role, orthodox economics has become cut off from the central economic issues of our time, drifting further into ever more abstract and ever more sophisticated reformulations of essentially the same propositions. The heart of the matter is the concept of 'capital', and its relation to social class and economic power." Edward Nell: 'Economics: the Revival of Political Economy' in Ideology in Social Science, ed. Robin Blackburn (London 1972). p.95. For two valuable studies of 'the heart of the matter' see Michael Kidron: **op.cit.** and Andrew Glyn and Bob Sutcliffe: **British Capitalism, Workers and the profits Squeeze** (London 1972). For a historical approach see also Eric Hobsbawm: **Industry and Empire** (London 1967).
11. F. Bealey and H. Pelling: Labour and Politics, 1900-1906 (London 1958) p.33.
12. Robin Blackburn: 'The Unequal Society' in **The Incompatibles,** ed Robin Blackburn and Alexandar Cockburn (London 1967).
13. For a convenient brief survey see **The 2 Nations, Inequality in Britain Today,** an LRD publication (London 1973).
14. See the various essays in E.AG. Robinson (ed): **Backward Areas in Advanced Countries**

(London 1969).

15. A.J. Brown: 'Survey of Regional Economics' **Economic Journal** (Dec 1969).

16. See John Firn's series in **The Scotsman** (30-31.10.73 and 1.11.73).

17. Paul A. Baran and Paul A. Sweezy: **Monopoly Capital** (London 1968) p.51.

18. See **Sunday Times** report (24.11.74).

19. For a record of British and Scottish complicity in the South African system see Ruth First, Jonathan Steele and Christabel Gurney: **The South African Connection** (London 1972).

20. The role of the arms economy is of tremendous significance to Western capitalism both as an area of profit in itself and as a technological testing ground. For an illuminating consideration of the latter see the pamphlet **The New Technology of Repression** published by BSSRS (London 1974) and for a powerful reminder of the inhuman consequences in such testing grounds see John McGuffin: **The Guinea Pigs** (London 1974).

21. The Scottish National Party General Election Manifesto, February 1974, p.13.

22. This argument is expounded in C.A.R. Crosland: **The Conservative Enemy** (London 1964). For a rebuttal see Robin Blackburn's essay 'The New Capitalism' in Robin Blackburn (ed) **Ideology in Social Science** (London 1972) and for a lengthier, more extensive argument see Ralph Miliband: **The State in Capitalist Society** (London 1969) especially Chapter 2.

23. Letter to **West Highland Free Press,** 19 July 1974.

24. Dr Robert MacIntyre, **Scotsman,** 10 October 1974.

25. SNP Manifesto, February 1974, page 4.

26. Ibid page 5.

27. Ibid, page 4.

28. See P. Anderson 'Sweden: Mr Crosland's Dreamland', New Left Review, 7 (1961) and P. Anderson 'Sweden II Study in Social Democracy, New Left Review, 9 (1961) and also Therburn: **Power in the Kingdom of Sweden,** quoted in Miliband: **State in Capitalist Society,** page 63.

29. A salutory tale for reformist hopefuls is told in H. Priets: **Chile: the gorillas are amongst us,** London 1974.

30. Scotsman, 9 April, 1974.

31. Ibid, 15 June 1974.

32. R Lynd's Foreword to R A Brade: **Business as a System of Poer,** 1943.

33. R Miliband, 1969, op.cit. page 75.

34. Ibid. page 75.

35. Ibid. page 79.

36. SNP Manifesto, February 1974. page

37. See S Aaronovitch, **The Ruling Class,** London 1961; WL Guttsman: **The British Political Elite,** London 1963; John Urry and John Wakeford (eds): **Power in Britain** London 1973, especially Part Two, sect. B.

38. A Aarenovitch, op.cit. page 169.

39. Ibid, page 170.

40. SNP Manifesto February 1974, page 4.

41. Ibid, p.5.

42. Fred Halliday: **Arabia without Sultans,** London 1974, page 396.

43. Ibid, pages 396-398.

44. Scotsman 30 April, 1974.

45. SNP Manifesto, February 1974, page 12.

46. Ibid., page 12.

47. Ibid, page 12.

48. Ibid., page 12.

49. The case of the Shrewsbury Two makes that quite clear see L.Flynn: **Workers Against the Law,** London 1974.

50. SNP Manifesto February 1974, page 4.

51. Ibid, page 11.

52. **Investor's Review,** Sept. 6-19th, 1974.

53. **The Banker,** May 1974.

54. Ibid.

55. Ibid.

56. Scotsman

57. SNP Manifesto February 1974, page 1.

58. Ibid, page 1.

59. Ibid, page 1.

60. R Miliband (1969) op.cit. page 70.

61. William Wolfe: **Scotland Lives,** Edinburgh 1973, page 147.

62. Ibid, page 34.

63. SNP Highland Regional Association, Election Manifesto, 7 May 1974.

64. M Magnusson: 'Highland Administration' in D C Thomson and I Grimble: **The Future of the Highlands,** London 1968. See also J Hawthorn **'Top Scots'** in **Scotland** (Nov. 1971 pp.17-27), and T Johnston, N Busten, D Mair: **Structure and Growth of the Scottish Economy,** London 1971.

65. George Reid M.P., quoted in **Glasgow Herald,** 16th July, 1974.

66. **SNP Manifesto,** February 1974, p.3, 15 and 13.

67. **ibid.,** p.15.

68. **Scots Independent,** October, 1974.

69. G Williams, Gramsci's Concept of Hegemony, in **Journal of the History of Modern Ideas.** Vol.XXI, No.4 (1960), pp.586-599.

70. A Gramsci, **Prison Notebooks** (London, 1971) p.238.

71. A Gramsci, **The Modern Prince and Other Writings,** (New York, 1970), p.139.

72. L. Trotsky, What is National Socialism, **Fourth International** (1943).

The Left, The SNP And Oil

Bob Tait

The presence of eleven SNP MPs at Westminster is now a constant reminder of theoretical and practical problems that stare the Scottish Left in the face. Staring back at these problems has not solved them in the past, nor has it made them go away, and it won't now. Only action can solve them: action that advances the struggle against international and national capitalist power over people's lives, and which releases the Left in Scotland from dilemmas largely of its own theoretical making.

The choice is between support for the SNP, as a progressive force in our historical context, and continued attacks on/or aloofness towards it, seeing it as merely an anachronistic, populist, chauvinist movement with a leadership that muddles along in a haze of liberal and not so liberal sentiment and "gombeen" capitalist aspirations.

I am arguing for the first choice. It depends on what precisely must count now in Scotland as a "progressive force". Progress, for Left theory, has both local and international connotations; progress is always relative progress—relative, that is, to the forces that dominate our lives in a particular historical context. A force is progressive if it creates at least the preconditions for loosening the strangle-hold of the international and national capitalist apparatus. That apparatus comprises international monopoly finance capital and the nexus of state machines that give it maximum scope for operation. The disturbance of that nexus within the British state, and then Europe, creates a precondition for progress. Neo-nationalist and regionalist movements in Europe highlight people's desperate sense of vulnerability to the concentration of economic power in capital-intensive industries, finance by monopoly capital, and backed up by increasingly centralised and harmonised political power. Neo-nationalism gives political expression to the need to dismantle that apparatus before—in the increasingly beleaguered situation advanced capitalism finds itself in—it declares huge sections of the working population redundant.

As history makes clear, a progressive force is not necessarily a Socialist revolutionary force in its initial stages: at the stage where it merely creates preconditions. The job of the Left is to interpret its potential, however, and act upon it. The alternative is often merely to allow a possible springboard to further progress to go rotten or to be subverted and used as a springboard by others. Failure to recognise progressive elements in the nationalist movement, indeed in the SNP, exposes us to precisely that danger now in Scotland.

I

The case for Left support for Scottish sovereignty, the establishment of a Scottish government, "independence"—however we put it—divides into two: a matter of means and ends, of what might be achieved and how. Fairly obviously, the means at present must involve some kind of active support for the SNP. Equally obviously, many people don't want to commit themselves to at least this aspect of the means, not, anyway, until they are rather more satisfied as to the ends.

As to the question of ends, then, the SNP itself proposes a number of answers, the first and most essential of which is perfectly straightforward, if politically abstract: political independence is the only means of giving the people of Scotland adequate control over their own affairs. It is not an answer socialists can afford to treat lightly, not if they are serious about creating communities based on a socialist distribution of wealth, rights and powers: and hence about transferring control—of economic resources and thus of people's lives—from giant corporations, the capitalist State and its bourgeois hegemony to such communities. It should also be stressed right away that many of the other things the SNP proposes should be achieved by independence, as regards land use, control of industry, general economic and social development and devolution of power within Scotland, are often broadly and sometimes quite specifically compatible with a Left-socialist position (see the SNP election manifesto, 1974; records of, e.g., recent Party conferences). Of course, the actual achievement of such policies in the event of independence would depend on the political power socialists could muster.

Still, it must be faced: many Leftists distrust the SNP and would rather keep clear of it altogether. This effectively means non-support for the basic end: establishment of Scottish government with control over Scottish resources and foreign political and economic alignments. They continue to find justification for this opposition in the political and economic advantages thought to accrue from maintaining British unity, even if it is desirable to manage it more elaborately by allowing restricted devolution of legislative powers to Scottish and Welsh assemblies.

II

The economic objections find supporters both right and left, which is not the main reason for considering them threadbare; but it is a curious fact, in view of what is often said about the odd political coloration of the SNP. More fundamental criticisms of these arguments can be made in the light of post-war experience (to go back no further); and on the basis of the transformed economic circumstances (which are simultaneously advantageous and perilous) resulting from the black, black oil. The Scottish economy has suffered badly from the uneven development of capitalism in the modern industrial state. Successive British governments, responding to the pull of capitalist market forces inevitably exerted by the intensively capitalised industries around which economic policy has been built, have been unable to protect the Scottish economy from recession and high unemployment. The restricted range of regional development incentives available, given overall UK economic strategies, have failed to work as well as expected or hoped for. Given the UK economic development to which they were committed, they have lacked both the means and the motivation to devise economic policies for parts of Britain unlucky enough to lie outside the main centres of industrial energy.

For a long time it was alleged, of course, that the Scottish economy had become so weak that we had no choice but to hang on to the tail of the UK economy in the hope that what we got off it wasn't dandruff or worse. But even before the oil made it possible to question this uncharming piece of advice, in view of the prospects oil held for investment in Scotland, to say nothing for the moment of the ultimate destination of tax revenue and profits, there were those who challenged the underlying economic strategy. Attempts were made, and not only by nationalists, to construct a Scottish budget, to analyse the balance of payments between Scotland and the rest of the UK.

Partly because figures were always incomplete or ambiguous, the debate was conducted in a maze and people had no difficulty finding conflicting paths. Professor Kenneth Alexander, in an article in the magazine **Scotland** (1968), advanced a counsel of caution and pessimism in view of the control of Scottish industry by outsiders. In the same year, the then Chancellor, Roy Jenkins, told a Dundee audience that for the dubious advantage of having a more dominant role in its market of five million people, Scotland would lose a home market of 54 million. Andrew Hargrave, however, then Scottish correspondent of the **Financial Times,** was not the only one to see in this elements of over-caution or scare-mongering; to point out that there was enough evidence to suggest that Scotland did or could pay its own way; and that the fact that we lacked essential means of economic management in Scotland was the key that hinted at the doors that needed to be opened: we needed far more control over our own affairs.(1)

Having granted that the evidence was tangled, it might seem that my summary of the economic debate is rather peremptory. But there is no doubt that the view that we need more control and sensitive management of Scottish resources had gained ground more and more since then over the view that the Scottish economy is too weak to respond favourably to management and stimulation initiated in Scotland. The STUC's Assembly in February 1972 stood firmly on the ground gained by the more optimistic of the two views of the economic case. Representatives of Scotland's political parties and trade unions met then and, remarkably unabashed by each other's proximity, advanced on the road to devolution; not that they took the same road. But the occasion was remarkable not least for the fact that a former national chairman of the Labour Party, John Boyd of the Engineering Union, announced that he was "slowly and painfully coming to the conclusion that the only answer to Scotland's economic problem is Scottish Government."

III

But how much Scottish government? Here we encounter the point at which the economic arguments yield to the political, Having found it possible to envisage Scotland paying its way, the Labour Party and the Left became fraught with anxiety about "seeds of disunity" their own spokesmen helped sow, and particularly afraid that the people of an independent Scotland would suffer if unprotected by representation at Westminster and by a secretary of State, however beleaguered, in the British Cabinet.

There is fear that the Scottish working class would not be able to hold its own. There is fear of dominance by a Tory—rather than Labourite—England. There is fear, indeed, that the English would be condemned to an indefinite period of Tory rule. These are the fears that continue to drive Leftists, despite their reservations, to the support of the Labour Party in Scotland: as the party with a working class base, sensitive to the interests of its working class support, and as the main political arm of the Labour movement. And these inhibitions have deterred the Left from forming a coherent case for devolution.

Yet it is quite impossible to envisage an independent Scotland without a Scottish Labour Party, and one with much of its present apparatus intact. It is also impossible to imagine an independent Scotland without a strong trade union movement. Indeed, it is more possible than not to envisage the Scottish trade union apparatus maintaining almost entirely intact its extensions south, continuing to participate in the congress of British trade unions. For in our case, instead of having to face the difficulties of forging international trade union co-operation, we have a situation in which just that exists. In that respect, as well as in terms of its domestic strength, it is very hard to envisage other than powerful working class organisations in Scotland. The nub of the argument, however, is not the reassuring presence of working class organisations, but their political vision—as distinct, indeed, from trade union consciousness—and the effectiveness of existing political channels.

Disparaging things have been said often enough about the poverty or sheer lack of political vision emanating from the Scottish Labour movement since the heyday of its great pioneering leaders. Critics who have taken that line have met with justifiably tart ripostes: about the masses of work done unsung in the interests of Scottish workers and about the dedicated efforts of Scottish Labour MPs pressing for progressive policies at UK level. The ripostes are not wholly to the point but the critics, on the other hand, have regularly failed to identify their target at source: not so much the failure of the Scottish Labour movement to generate its own political vision, as the system of political representation that ensures the failure. The system is decidedly smothering, and at two levels: at the level of Labour Party organisation in the UK, and at parliamentary level.

The Scottish Labour Party conference operates within a highly unified UK system. The constitution and programme of the Scottish Council is subject to the line of the British Conference. The Scottish conference "does not have any constitutional power to draw up the policy of the party; it remains advisory to the British conference."(2) What weight, then, does Scottish political opinion or vision have at the British conference? By no means all the Scottish constituency parties are even regularly represented: in 1970, for example, only 32 out of the 71 sent delegates; and most Scottish trade unionists were represented by British trade unions.

Of course, none of this is the product of mistake, oversight, or even domination by the English: not, at any rate, in terms of the conditions which these arrangements were originally devised to meet. The union of the British parties in 1909 (the Scottish Council itself was a concession of 1915) did not pass unchallenged in Scotland even at the time. But, **pace** John Maclean, the majority at that time found the case for unified British working class action in the shared economic and political conditions of the period highly persuasive. But the thrust of the economic debate and its implications indicate that it is precisely these conditions that have changed. Consequently, the latent de-merits of the set-up, which have indeed exercised an inhibiting influence on the political fulfilment of Scottish labour culture, become glaring. The perpetuation of the system becomes a mistake. Its farcical nature is illuminated by the irony whereby any decision of the special two day Scottish conference called for August 17th-18th was pre-empted by the (British) National Executive Committee's resolution calling on the Labour Government to declare its support for an elected legislative assembly for Scotland! If John Maclean is turning in his grave, it must now be with wry satisfaction.

In the changed economic and political circumstances in which we find ourselves, then, the political arm of the Scottish labour movement loses more strength than it gains from present arrangements. Its evident inability to generate its own policies with any clarity seriously undermines the intellectual and political potential of the Scottish working class and its representatives. One is driven along similar routes to similar conclusions on the parliamentary level: where the difficulties of successive Scottish Secretaries are legendary and where the Scottish Committee of the House of Commons reproduces the party balance as for the House as a whole and performs wholly subordinate functions in government. Again, as the economic argument suggests, the scant powers of Westminster arrangements to afford protection to the Scottish working class become more blatant. These will not in themselves be enhanced or extended by the granting a Scottish legislative assembly with no overall control over economic, foreign or budgetary policy within the UK framework. As likely as not, the Scottish perch within Westminster would come under greater pressure, in reaction to the new artificial limb installed up north.

The Scottish working class may yet be able to choose to assert itself, rather more effectively and coherently than hitherto, through a re-orientated and autonomous Scottish Labour Party; and the Welsh may yet be able to do likewise. It is often said, with a nice mixture of self-interest and altruism, that that, or SNP success, would sentence the English working class to a long term of Tory rule.

The altruistic element in this surmise is curiously patronising. The English working class is rather large. It is remarkably daring of the Scots to underestimate its resilience and to consider its potential for creative political resurgence to be so low or so predictable. Experience has shown, on the other hand, that the Scots have no power to guarantee socialist respectability to England, however much we may occasionally be inclined to boast about the Scottish contribution to Labour benches, numerically and otherwise. Experience has also sadly shown that the English by no means guarantee the Scottish working class a government that reflects voting in Scotland. So the element of self-interest in the prediction is not based on the idea that political union gives us that advantage. It is based, rather, on the spectre of a Tory England dominating Scotland, through a form of intentional or unintentional neo-colonialist exploitation.

Here is a danger that must neither be ignored nor immediately regarded as overwhelming and insurmountable. The extent of the danger has perhaps been most vividly underlined by the latest data available on the ultimate ownership and control of "Scottish" industry. In a valuable series of articles in **The Scotsman** (3), John Firn, of the Department of Social and Economic Research at Glasgow University, presents an analysis of this data that shows among other things 39.8 per cent English and 14.9 per cent North American control of manufacturing employment as against 41.2 per cent Scottish. He also shows that the proportion of Scottish control has been falling. Even more importantly, "in the five fastest growing sectors, Scottish owned companies only account for some 13.5 per cent of total employment." He concludes that any attempt to run an independent economic policy would be severely constrained—which is certainly one way of looking at it. But there is another way.

The other way is first to recognise that this situation is a large part of the mess that needs to be sorted out: the product of the decline of traditional industries, of general UK economic policies as they have affected Scotland, and of resultant regional development policies that have concentrated on trying to divert externally controlled, fast-growth industries northwards rather than on restructuring the Scottish economy on the basis of indigenously controlled capital. The second thing must be to see that much then depends on the powers summoned up by a sufficiently determined sovereign government in Scotland. To wield its own economic policy while maintaining, and indeed improving markedly on, employment levels would entail having high on its list of priorities the task of redressing the balance of economic control, even though there is at the moment no reason to suppose that "independence" would send externally owned industry scurrying home. The more the Left participated in such a government, the more it would be inclined to redress the balance by controls on the movements of capital in and out of the economy and by acquisition, by fiscal and other means, of capital necessary to restructure an indigenous economy. The range and type of measures meant here are familiar enough. They are to varying degrees open to any government that can muster the political will and seize the opportunities to use them. Naturally, no one is able to predict the specific results of such an attempt; on the other hand, it is unreasonably pessimistic to insist that the inherent dangers foreclose on any possibility of success, particularly since the potential capital accruable from oil, taken as a proportion of the Scottish national budget, and the potential role of oil as a bargaining factor, strengthen the balance on the side of an effort to re-structure the economy. It is just such measures that many have in mind when they turn from the Labour Party to vote for the SNP. The specific SNP proposals on future economic policy are there to be considered on merit. But it must be recognised that the debate can only be finally meaningful in the context of an effective Scottish assembly.

Although there are well founded doubts as to what working class voters would think was an acceptable and effective assembly—"independent" or UK-linked—there is no gainsaying the fact that increasing numbers tend to turn to the SNP rather than the Labour Party. Should Leftists do likewise? Or should they get out such lassoos as they can find? The question has to be answered in terms of the two dimensions of a Leftist position: analysis of basic conflicts under capitalism and the possibilities open for a socialist resolution of the conflicts; and the dimension of political life and method, which hardly ever simply reproduces class conflict and hence enjoys—if that is the word—relative autonomy.

IV

If Leftists have been able to work with the Labour Party despite their reservations because it has enjoyed substantial working class support, it is obvious that they can now consider offering similar support with various other reservations to at least a range of SNP candidates. The same basic reason now holds—plus one other: that, on the basis of the foregoing analysis, the SNP evidently serves legitimate objectives of the Scottish working class which so far the Labour Party has been unable to incorporate. Political choices of this kind, and the reservations that accompany them, are a consequence of the gap between politics and ideological position. But the situation must remain unsatisfactory to Leftists so long as it appears that the element of political action is too far removed from any possible Left ideological position.

The deep-rooted distrust on the Left for nationalism is as understandable as the reasons usually advanced for it are familiar. Nonetheless, this distrust in its frequently undiscriminating form is not substantially supported by any notable body of marxist theory (as Tom Nairn has pointed out (4),). Sometimes people who are otherwise apparently conversant with world developments, including Third World movements of national liberation, are prepared to dismiss nationalism and even nation states as irrelevant to socialist policies and objectives; but this position is untenable because it fails to acknowledge both nationalism and the nation state as products and phases of historical development whether under capitalism or on the road to socialism. As such they are not necessarily either good or bad developments from the socialist's point of view. But at least, or at best, perhaps, they can be vehicles that liberate consciousness and political potential where both have been relatively suppressed, and in this sense provide an essential precondition for further progress.

This being so, another and apparently stronger anti-nationalist argument should be approached somewhat critically and cautiously: the argument that in advanced countries, in Europe, nationalism really is anachronistic, seeing that many of the old national boundaries of the 19th and 20th centuries are themselves disappearing; and considering also that in such a situation, nationalism can only serve sectional opportunism whereas the advance of socialism more than ever requires the furtherance of international working class unity. It draws moral and intellectual strength from the need it implicitly acknowledges to keep a general and long term view of working class interests in mind as a clear guide to socialist movements. It also recognises that capitalism operates on a supranational level and proposes that the Left must respond accordingly. It takes into account at least some elements of the development towards the supranational modern industrial state through the EEC.

Its main weakness is that to be conclusive it would depend on the fulfilment of this European political and economic union, which is indeed foreshadowed, but which has by no means come about. There are reasons to believe that it will not come about—not altogether in the way certain visionaries of the New Order in Europe have hoped.(5) For one thing, it is clear that national governments, to maintain support for themselves domestically, are obliged to assert the "old" national boundaries (as created at an earlier stage of capitalism) against the more advanced interests of capitalism which are now in need of rapid access to cheap labour, resources and a larger market susceptible to monopolistic control. Secondly, this by no means vestigial survival of "old" nationalist bulwarks looks like retarding indefinitely the monetary union that is as essential precondition of political union. The situation in Europe begins to look ambivalent when these factors are recognised. But there are deeper layers of ambivalence still.

The development of capitalism during the post-war European "restoration" period has been dependent on capital-intensive, resource-greedy industries, many of which also require huge and intensively cultivated consumer markets. For both historical and economic reasons the development has also been dependent on international capital, exposing the European nations to the economic overlordship of multinational corporations, both North American and home grown. It has also led to the emergence of political leaderships committed to this general economic strategy and hence to supranational political control of developments. But in facing the problems that have arisen from unevenness of development, disparities in national growth rates, etc., they have responded by encouraging concentration of capital and resources in their own countries, streamlining their economies to make them more intensively and profitably productive. In this way, the machinery of nation-states (the productive, management and governmental apparatus) has been adapted and geared to a new economic geography of Europe; and this has created conflicts with the demands of the old: with the need to protect an older range of industries, to maintain employment, and in general to recognise (or evade) responsibilities to cater for the "old" national populations.

The development creates basic conditions for conflict. In response to these conditions, nationalist or regionalist movements have emerged within the advanced countries of Europe: in Brittany, Sardinia, Wales, Catalonia, Scotland and other areas. There is a clear need to counteract supranational concentration of political and economic power and, correspondingly, to counteract also the parallel concentrations in the "old" but adapted nation states. The various movements are, of course, not necessarily either "right" or "left". But they are recognisably part of the search for alternative means of political and economic control, and attempts to protect people from the ravages of unmitigated super-capitalism.

The neo-nationalist and regionalist movements, precisely because they arise out of basic conflicts under super-capitalism, provide a vital clue to the completion of a Left strategy for Europe: socialist devolutionary policies, comprising devolution of political control and control over resources.

At the moment the positions adopted by various sections of the Left in Britain as regards the EEC are confused. A minority of Leftists are pro-Market, seeing, like Ernest Mandel or Tom Nairn, conditions there for stronger international socialist reaction to capitalism. There is much to be said for this argument.(6)

But what of the political dimension that must form part of a Left position? So far, the soundest foundations for the Mandel/Nairn case are on the industrial front.(7) The idea of European Left unity must amount to more than response to international capitalism by the creation of a parallel international trade union organisation. Is the socialist political response to a capitalist EEC to be the creation of a socialist super-state that inherits the capital-intensive economic structure of the modern industrial state as we know it? Leftists should surely be cautious about committing themselves to that position, both because of the dangers inherent in such economics and because of the dangers of Stalinism involved in that concept of central management of the monster. The alternative is to recognise in the movements for alternative political and economic control phases of an attack of the Super-State. The Left must then contribute, as the necessary political dimension to its activities, socialist devolutionary policies, based on programmes for economic restructuring, which the working class can recognise and respond to.

As we have already seen, the Labour Party in Scotland has failed to produce anyting in this direction. It is convulsed and so, in another sense, is everyone else. Moreover, it supports a UK government which, the elephantine minuet danced by Jim Callaghan notwithstanding, would surely want an arrangement whereby the supranational institutions of capitalism in Europe, ensuring policies of growth **on their terms,** would be substantially maintained. If the Left is looking for betrayals of socialist ideals, they need look no further than that.

V

Which brings us of course to Scottish nationalism. Many a heart has sunk, heavy as the Stone of Destiny itself, at the thought of Scot Nats. The garb which Scottish nationalism often wears, the kitsch, the appeal to revanchist chauvinism: any or all of theses are apt to seem too much. There are fears too about about the socially conservative or reactionary tendencies in the Scottish working class; fears which I have heard expressed by prominent Scottish Labour politicians, and which are by no means unrelated to these other cultural and political tendencies.

A cooler look at the nature of nationalist movements—or of these neo-nationalist movements—and the conditions out of which they spring would indicate that their broad populist nature, mythopoeic aspects, and odd alliance of reactive and radical social and political tendencies are much more to be expected than an unequivocal ideological base.

Although the quite different conditions to which this second wave of nationalism in Europe responds make it different from the 19th and early 20th century wave, which was the aggressive vanguard of capitalism in its time, it has inherited many of the clothes of the older kind while simultaneously building a rather new vehicle for itself. For reasons which cannot be pursued here but which have been very interestingly explored by Tom Nairn (8), Scotland missed out on the earlier phases; and this goes a long way to explain the distortions and gaps in Scottish culture in the widest sense of the word, symptomised by reactionary attitudes to social issues (feared by the Labour people I mentioned) as well as by tartanry and nationalist kitsch.

The "new vehicle" referred to above is the one being constructed by the SNP out of its policies. Regrettably, Leftists tend to be put off so much by their ideas about nationalism that they don't get round to scrutinising SNP constitutional proposals and policies, ro to considering the radical aspects, in social democratic terms, of its leadership; or their presuppositions make them over-sensitive to the limitations of the policies without fully taking into account the distance they cover; and in particular could cover, with Left wing interpretation—and participation in making them effective. The resources policies (including land use), arms policies, industrial democracy proposals, proposals for devolution of powers to the Highlands, Western Isles and Northern Isles are among those that call for close and respectful attention.

True, the SNP uses a language that sounds wrong to socialist ears when they are not so deaf that they cannot hear it. Some SNP spokesmen, for example, are rather prone to imagine that the class war is yet another wicked and diversionary product of Westminster party politics; and they are in general given to "communitarian" myths.

But this can only partly be considered to be a symptom of political naivety; and it is rather more that than political wickedness, a sly new version of Toryism in Scotland. The SNPs political language and style arises out of its being—to use a handy leninist distinction—a vehicle for a movement rather than a fully blown political party, representing a univocal ideological position. As vehicle in this sense, it gives voice to focal issues of regeneration: political, economic, social and cultural regeneration; and the movement brings with it people from across the entire band of the ideological spectrum to these focal points. Such a vehicle performs no more complicated manoeuvres if it can help it while the movement as such is in progress.

What I have been urging, of course, is that at this point in the development of capitalism such developments in Europe are progressive, or, at least, create preconditions for further progress: making possible the release of relatively suppressed political potential and making it available for a socialist devolution of control in the political and economic spheres. Thus the Left has more theoretical grounds for defining a theoretical and practical position within such a movement than it has for evasion or outright opposition. This is not to say that there are no problems as to the uses to which such a movement may from time to time be put and as to the political inheritance it will yield in the event of it achieving its aims. The problems here may be illustrated by two rather dramatic issues which we already face: the role of Scottish capitalists in the SNP and in a future Scotland should they contrive to inherit the mantle of the movement; and the significance of offshore oil as a stimulus to the movement and as a clue to what might follow.

The first problem, of the influence of the Scottish business community has been highlighted by Sir Hugh Fraser's joining the SNP and by his proselytising efforts since. The Scottish end of the CBI seems not to have heard him. In any case, that is less the danger, to my mind, than that too many professional PR men are jockeying for power within the party: a businessmen's wedge if ever there was one. There is reason for concern over this, and over the way in which people from that sector of the party may succeed in establishing themselves within a nationalist parliamentary group in Westminster, using it as a power base increasingly detached from the numerically stronger radical membership (and working class support) within the popular base. The only possible answer to a political problem of this nature is that the Left should make itself strong enough within the nationalist movement to be able to correct the tendency. That is, here is an area where, it seems to me, the Left must consider direct participation, whatever indirect influence on the SNP might be contemplated. For much depends on the candidates the SNP chooses, and on strengthening the party conference as against the relative autonomy of the parliamentary group.

Willie Ross is not the only Labour man or Leftist to pour scorn and indignation on the SNPs appeal to "greed" over the the matter of offshore oil. There have been the most wonderful displays of self-righteous altruism. But to be taken seriously (expecially in Scotland), altruism must have some definable bounds: the most defensible bounds in this case being set by the need to ensure that the people whose land and lives are most affected by oil exploitation do not suffer from it by depletion rather than enhancement of their potential resources, natural and capital. On the contrary, it is clear that a rare historical accident presents a legitimate opportunity for an overdue exercise: general stocktaking of Scottish resources and a coherently planned re-structuring of its internal economy and external relations. Anyone who has examined the progress of oil exploitation so far knows that it has been scandalously managed in Scotland and certainly not managed in the interests of Scottish workers, whether in urban or rural areas; that the way things are going even since February 1974 threatens to create serious imbalances between regions of Scotland, between industrial and agricultural priorities, and within regions. And there can be no guarantee, if anything the reverse, that a restricted Scottish assembly, bound by the overall dynamics of a UK-international-capitalist economy, would have adequate powers to control developments, even if it is allowed to handle a modest capital rake-off (cf. the "disturbance" payments by oil companies to Zetland County Council, which look like being absorbed, very much in the companies' own interests, before they are even done with the place). In this light, a Scottish government adopting at least Norwegian-type powers becomes a stark necessity in practice.

There is yet another way to put all this. The 7:84 Theatre Company's play, "The Cheviot, The Stag and the Black, Black Oil" found it. It found it in a combination of energy and aims: in things to be won, like the power to participate and direct; in things to be resisted, like the daylight robbery of assets. It recognised that a combination of analysis of Scottish history and the inspiration to revolt and seize control is a **sine qua non** of the re-appropriation of assets, rights, dignity and of the revitalisation of a radical socialist spirit in Scotland. It seems to met that it has been in these recognitions that socialists and nationalists have found much common ground in their responses to the play. I have simply tried here to trace the outlines of some of the connecting theoretical roots.

1. Andrew Hargrave: "The Economics of Devolution", November 1968, and "The Politics of Devolution", January 1969, **Scottish International.**

2. Cf. James G Kellas, **The Scottish Political System,** Cambridge, 1973, quoted here, for a much fuller coverage of the institutional arrangements.

3. **The Scotsman,** October, 30th, 31st and November 1st, 1973.

4. The emphasis here is on the undiscriminating nature of Left views on nationalism. Tom Nairn's current work, soon to be published, is on a more sophisticated theory; but see also note 8, below. I do not suggest that he would agree with the line taken here.

5. See, for example, Gunner Myrdal's criticisms of one of the more benign and optimistic visions of the EEC: in **Against the Stream,** Random House, 1973, Chapter 11, **xiv**, discussion of Sicco Mansholt's views.

6. See Tom Nairn, **The Left against Europe?** Pelican, 1973, for a thorough discussion of Left positions in Britain. The positions of the Scottish sections of I.S., I.M.G., etc., as regards either nationalism or the EEC are not markedly distinct from overall UK party positions; the CP in Scotland is an exception in having a positive devolutionary policy. See Ray Burnett, "Scotland and Antonio Gramsci", **Scottish International,** November, 1972, for critiques of the Scottish Left; and the extension of the case by David G Whitfield, "Signposts to Scottish Action", **Scottish International,** August, 1973.

7. **Industry's Democratic Revolution,** Ed. Charles Levinson, Allen & Unwin, 1974, provides some of the evidence (some of it ambivalent) for prospects for unity on the industrial front.

8. Tom Nairn, "Scotland and Europe", **New Left Review,** 1974.

Scotland: Up Against It

John McGrath

There can be few who doubt that capitalism, as a world-wide economic structure, is entering a period of recession of considerable dimensions. There are some on the left who already discern its death-agony, who ecstatically receive every convulsion—(the fall of the Italian Government, the troubles at British Leyland, Nixon's phlebitis)—as fresh proof that the system is shortly to go into a final, mortal, spasm. There are others who cheerfully buckle down to 'social contracts' with the capitalist state, to try to protect the working class from once again bearing the full burden of the system's 'temporary indisposition'. The former joyously prepare to seize power amid violent revolution, the latter ponderously anticipate the opportunity to winkle out a few more concessions for the working-class. Both genuinely act with what they consider to be the 'best interests' of the working class at heart. Both are confronted with the massive propaganda machine for the great Tory-Liberal-SNP fraud: 'national unity'. The basis of such unity appears to be the need for an 'end to divisiveness'—i.e. the unconditional surrender of the Trades Unions. And in this hour of crisis, that surrender becomes more and more urgent for these people.

However, the unions cannot capitulate, wriggle as some of the leaders may. The simple economist base which has propped them up for so long (and clouded their political vision) will not permit them to abandon the immediate interests of their members. So capitalism in the British Isles will continue to flounder for some time, and the spectre of the system's breakdown followed by either a socialist revolution or an authoritarian right-wing takeover will continue to stalk the land. But the greater the problems of British capital, the greater their dependence on gestures of solidarity from international capital. Loans from the Shah of Persia, financial deals with Saudi Arabia, appeals to the EEC, and American self-interested generosity will attempt a rescue. Capital is international, and has its own urgent ideology. There are many on the doctrinaire left who underestimate the efficacy of this, who imagine that capitalism is essentially a system of cut-throat competition, without realising that it also has an over-riding commitment to its own survival. Whether it will survive its contradictions in Britain remains to be seen.

Whatever its prospects, it would seem that neither of the great Communist powers is likely to intervene politically to accelerate its destruction, or even help those who are willing it into the grave. Both Russia and China clearly have strong internal reasons for building their own economies, and have no strong incentive for doing anything to provoke a nuclear confrontation. In fact, both seem to have abandoned an internationalist strategy of any sort. To judge from recent trade-deals, both seem to have a positive interest in maintaining the status quo. So the working classes of the advanced capitalist countries will be facing the recession with only their own strength to rely on. The recession is taking different forms in different countries as usual. But this particular recession coincides with the overwhelming growth to dominance in most western European nations of 'multi-national' capital, and the belated attempts to internationalise, or at least Europeanise, British capital within the EEC.

While the multi-national conglomerates are having their problems much as Basil de Ferranti is, they are in a much better position to survive than any medium-sclae business with plant in Bracknell, Manchester and Edinburgh. Simply by surviving, the multi-nationals will grow. We can expect them to increase their control over the national economies of 'free' Europe during a period of controlled recession. With their ability to switch capital and production from a less profitable nation to a more profitable one, they could well play the key role in the destruction of a weakening national economy. This power, even if never used, is one of immense political significance. We have seen something of its importance in South America. Equally significant, perhaps, is the effect international monopoly capital will have on the interior bourgeoisies of Western Eruope. It will not simply make them mere 'lackeys of American Imperialism'—though in some individual cases it palpably has—it will also alter the way they think and operate.

The nineteenth century 'boss' is going to the wall, and being replaced by a series of management experts with markedly differnet criteria and style. The one constant is that 'boss' and manager both need to screw more production out of the working class for less money. Whether capital intensive or labour intensive, the aim is the same—ever greater profit. But the way the working class will have to deal with the multi-nationals will, of course, have to change. As employers they will be more flexible, expert and ruthless. In a recession their powers will increase as unemployment increases; and as their power increases, so the state will become more obviously identified with their interests; covering up its identification with belligerent noises, and accommodations disguised as 'controls.'

The Common Market, apart from further increasing the opportunities for the multi-nationals, also permits British capital to go wandering abroad more easily in search of the sector of the European work-force that will supply it with the biggest return on investment. This is meant to put the British economy 'on its toes', to make our work-force (and managements) 'more competitive'. The present bungling of the agricultural estimates and price fixing will appear trivial when the industrial working classes of Europe have to go through a prolonged period of recession within the EEC. The only form of real protection they will have, will be genuine internationalisation of their struggle, on a lived community of experience, with highly sophisticated communications and massive solidarity. The size of the task is daunting. The need for its success could not be more obvious. However, it would be a mistake to imagine that **any** political party which is not dedicated to the overthrow of capitalism will remove Britain, or Scotland, from the EEC. The logic of capitalism demands it, and the state will obey that logic, by way of Edward Heath, James Callaghan or Winifred Ewing.

The Demands for Change

This is a crude outline of the international context within which we must examine Scotland's role in the coming years. The questions many people are asking themselves in Scotland are: whether Scotland should constitute itself as a separate state from the rest of the UK, and, if it did, what kind of state would emerge? It is possible to answer these questions emotionally, chauvinistically, dogmatically, even poetically; but many in Scotland would prefer to answer them from the point of view of their importance in the international struggle of the exploited against international capitalism—and to do so rationally and realistically.

First, we must examine why such questions are on the carpet at all as we enter the last quarter of the twentieth century. There seem to be three main reasons. First, the ever-present groundswell of resentment against England, the traditional enemy, which for centuries has dominated Scotland economically, politically, culturally, socially, to the point, it seems to some, of colonial oppression, but without destroying the integrity of Scotland as a nation. England, it is felt, has oppressed Scotland economically, not only directly in the classic manner of imperial power exploiting a third world country, but it has also created a Scottish middle-class, with its own sources of power, but so imbued with 'English' ideology that it has also crushed and distorted indigenous Scottish culture, language, social customs, traditional values, and even changed the physical face of most of the country—all to the ultimate advantage of English Capital, and the English way of doing things. This middle-class in fact, rose to become not a 'third world' subservient class, but full partners with the English bourgeoisie, both in overseas exploitation, and in exploiting its own working class at home. Nevertheless, the model and source of Scotland's oppression is felt to be England, and every Nationalist orator knows how easy it is to arouse the deep resentment of a Scottish audience against the boorish Sassenach.

Secondly, on a more immediate level, the political centralisation of the UK had become intolerable. Not only to Scots, but to Yorkshiremen and Liverpudlians. The South-East of England not only sucked into its maw most of the investment, the talent, the glamour, the wealth of the UK, it was also the source of all political decisions that mattered, and governed apparently in blind ignorance, if not with something approaching contempt, the lives of the people everywhere else. As the Kilbrandon Report says:

> "It appears that whatever other achievements may be credited to the Scottish office and the Welsh office, neither has made a clear impression on the public at large. This finding is significant in two ways. In the first place it provides corroboration in Scotland and Wales of the general conclusion that Government is out of touch with the people. This corroboration must be accounted particularly strong in Scotland."

Obviously the time had come for a change in the political structure of the UK, if normal, manageable, bourgeois consensus politics were not to be challenged by something more frightening to the state. With a minority determinedly confronting the state in Northern Ireland, followed, in the Ulster Workers' Council Strike, by a majority successfully over-throwing a state-imposed system of Government, the London based parties could not afford to resist too strenuously the growing signs of demand for such a change in Scotland.

Thirdly, the sure economic power suddenly imagined to be within Scotland's grasp from North Sea oil, and the simultaneous shakiness of England's fortunes, has reversed a relationship that has remained unchanged for centuries. No wonder many Scots suddenly felt liberation was at hand, and swathed endless halls in yards of tartan to build up the SNP. Little wonder that the SNP achieved a remarkable number of votes in the 1974 elections.

The SNP is, of course, the other reason the question of Scottish separatism is on the agenda. Under the chairmanship of William Wolfe it boomed sincerely and charmingly, drawing together left, right and centre as it grew, successfully postponing all sectional quarrels until the day for independence, forming a brilliant team of publicists, hitting the vote-catching slogans—ruthlessly, at times unscrupulously, undermining opponents. Wolfe has built up a party that has made its impression on Scottish politics, and raises vital tactical questions for the socialist in Scotland. For it has become the major expression, not only of xenophobic emotion, but also of the demand for devolution of power and the final shaking off of England's 'colonial' rule.

These factors: latent anti-English feeling, Westminster's lack of contact, the discovery of oil, and an efficient nationalist political organisation, have put the question of Scotland's 'independence' on the carpet, at this time. The questions we should be asking our selves are:

(i) given the international situation, what would 'independence' really mean if it were achieved, under the leadership of the SNP?
(ii) What alternatives are there for Scotland, either within the UK, or outside it: and
(iii) if one of these is preferable, how can it be achieved?

Independence and Socialism

"The bourgeoisie of the oppressed nations persistently utilize the slogans of national liberation to deceive the workers'—V.I. Lenin.

Elsewhere in this collection, Ray Burnett has attempted an analysis of the class politics of the SNP. To avoid repetition let me simply say that his arguments are clear and beyond dispute: "These are not the politics that imply far-reaching fundamental change... as a movement, the SNP has more in common with the Right than the Left." Furthermore, the SNP intends not only to gain 'independence' for Scotland, but also to run Scotland—it is making, in Billy Wolfe's phrase, "its preparation for taking its chance at the polls in an independent Scotland." No-one even remotely familiar with the history of Ireland's so-called 'independence' can fail to recognise what **that** means. When, in the same speech (Chairman's Address to SNP Conference 1974) Billy Wolfe talks of "our rejection of the bitter expedients of class warfare and bigotry", we can see that his party is "a curious place for a socialist to be." As Ray Burnett correctly points out: "The political 'choice' offered by the SNP is no choice at all, the social system will remain exactly what it is just now, namely a false plurality masking the influence and power of one dominant political and economic class."A brief glance at the results of 'independence' without socialism as it operates in Ireland today will verify this conclusion.

But quite apart from the ideological roots of the SNP, there is another perspective, of grim international reality, behind the strategy of their bid for 'freedom'. There is the recognition of the power of US imperialism. The State Department, the multi-national corporations, the US military arm in Europe-NATO, not to mention the CIA, simply will not tolerate the prospect of a Western European nation that is not very firmly subordinated to the demands of international capital and its imperialist logic. And when that combination of forces, plus the entire apparatus of the British State is lined up against you, you take a look at Vietnam, Chile and what remains of Cuba's hopes, and you modify your stance. No nation of five million people will, alone, defeat that imperialist machine, or defy its wishes, without heroic sacrifice and the risk of total destruction. What makes the prospect even more daunting is, ironically, the presence of that very oil which gave so much hope of 'independence' in the first place.

The new US Consul in Scotland is no affable time-server sent in to fill in a few forms and give a few parties. He is a certain Mr Funkhauser—a geology graduate, who once worked for the oil companies. However, he is now a senior State Department man, with experience in the big embassies, notably Moscow and Paris. In 1970 he headed a 'pacification squad' of 3,000 men in Vietnam, and then became Henry Kissinger's Adviser on oil. On his appointment in Scotland, he pronounced:

"It is time that the Scots realised the heavy responsibility upon them. There is much more involved than Scotland. Not only is the future of Scotland heavily connected to the successful development of North Sea Oil, but the future of Western Industrial life. If produced now, it could help ward off economic disaster. It is a race against time. President Ford gave high priority to this urgent need for production in the World Energy Conference in Detroit."

If President Ford said so, who are a few Scotsmen to insist on regulating the pace of exploitation? This traveller, recently back from Vietnam, went on:

"Scotland is where the action is. Those who will do the work are here, or are arriving. Those who will make the decisions are here, or have their representatives on hand. It is towards Scotland that the forces that will determine the outcome are converging. The stakes are high, and the responsibility heavy."

There are one or two questions that Mr Funkhauser should be in a position to answer, which no one else in Scotland, or even Whitehall, could hope to: such as, how many more CIA men are now working in or on Scotland; what 'contingency' plans does the US Government have for the moment they are politely asked to take their bombs and submarines out of Holy Loch; or even how much state control of Scottish industry would be acceptable to the American corporations. Mr Funkhauser is unlikely to reply, convincingly. His priorities have been spelt out, and the SNP know them very well. Which is probably why nationalisation of the oil companies is now categorically not on when Scotland gains her 'freedom'.

The new Imperialism is not the old nation-conquer-nation stuff of Zululand and the Transvaal: Whether Scotland is in or out of the United Kingdom does not affect it one iota. But a meaningful bid for a Socialist Scotland with a load of commies sitting on all that oil would not be in order for the new Imperialism, which is, after all, the Highest Stage of Capitalism. And don't let us forget that when Gadafi in Libya caused this kind of trouble, it was our own Colonel David Stirling of Kier who tried to burst into his country and create the conditions for his downfall. The new Imperialism is built into Scottish society, in all its naked violence, and is on a short fuse.

Given this perspective, it is not surprising that a 'pragmatic' party with no principles beyond nominal independence would hesitate to adopt a socialist policy. Without such a policy, however, genuine self-government is impossible. So the SNP proclaims itself 'a party of reform', and drags in the optimistic socialists just as the Labour Party has done for fifty years. And it will take them to precisely where the Labour Party has taken **its** socialists: to helping run capitalism more efficiently and humanely. But a long way from genuine socialism.

If a tone of polemical spite has entered this account, it is more from exasperation at the intellectual woolliness and moral evasiveness of the SNP than from a desire to attack the honour of the intentions of its left-wing members. Many genuinely believe that by entering the SNP they can transform it into a Socialist party. They do not take into account the realities behind its policies—not only international, but internal—its petit bourgeois base; its pseudo-pragmatic, unprincipled evasion of class relationships; its anti-socialist failure to analyse in any depth the economic structures and their effect on social, political, and cultural superstructures; and the rapt approval by its supporters of the miserable, reactionary record of its MPs at Westminster.

There are others who joined the SNP in the belief that after independence', Scotland would rid itself of English Tories and assert its true, socialist nature. I have myself subscribed to this myth by writing on this 'radical nation, governed by a pack of floundering reactionaries in Whitehall.' Of course, no capitalist country is 'radical'. Scotland has radical elements, and a dominant bourgeoisie. It has a working-class capable of great solidarity, but also capable of compromise. Sections of that working class are highly politicised, articulate, and have a breadth of vision beyond their immediate demands which should make the 'intellectuals' of Scotland hang their heads in shame. Other sections are subject to antiquated religious sectariansim, or 'estate-worker' mentality, or social-climbing ambitions, or militaristic delusions, or misplaced, dutiful gratitude to their exploiters. Almost all are subject to sexual chauvinism and inter-family oppression. But, in spite of this, class-solidarity and a high awareness of class interest and their own oppression, together with a refusal to be muzzled, make the Scottish working class one of the strongest in Europe, with a considerable experience of struggle and great maturity as a result.

Given this social force, why then are the SNP socialists not attempting to build a strong socialist organisation to confront the reformist and petit-bouregois elements in their own party who intend to 'take their chances at the polls in an independent Scotland.' As Ray Burnett points out: "they publish no separate propaganda, they are seldom if ever to be read in the Party's Official publications, and there was not a shadow of their presence in the list of resolutions put before the last Annual Conference." Above all, there is no attempt to call upon the support of the organised working class for socialist policies within the Party. On the contrary, the effort is to impose bourgeois nationalist policies on a socialist working class.

Perhaps this is tactical cunning. If so, it is dangerous, confusing and diversionary. Scotland abounds with scenarios and prognostications as to what will happen 'after independence'. The most unreal of these—if one of the most popular—is that the day after 'independence' a great socialist upsurge will sweep the land; unprepared for power, it will nevertheless take power; unorganised, it will nevertheless throw up a government, a constitution, and a secure place in a hostile world; with no theoretical grasp, it will nevertheless produce a socialist revolution. If this is the fantasy of the left wing of the SNP, if it is for this that they refuse to 'split' the party, then they are guilty of a massive betrayal of the Scottish working class, whether their intentions are honourable or not.

This is not to deny the force and idealism of Billy Wolfe's genuinely internationalist vision of a community of small nations, his rejection of the Common Market as: "a materialist effort to strengthen centralised capitalism and pressurise it into huge international units, not effectively answerable to the instruments of democracy..... encouraging the exploitation of labour, forcing hundreds of thousands of people to lose their identity and migrate for the sake of a form of so-called progress, which has its roots in inequality and greed." Nor is to question his emphasis on the need for a "legitimate moral force that people can trust." But to fight inequality and greed, the working class needs sound analysis of the realities, and a party determined to overthrow that mausoleum of inequality and greed, the capitalist state. The unfortunate facts are that none of the SNP scenarios contains a realistic possibility of progress to a socialist Scotland, none offers more to the working class than a slice from a bigger cake—with the same old flavour; none shows the remotest grasp of what the building of socialist consciousness really demands.

There are few socialists who would deny the right of Scotland to Self-Determination, to the right to secede from England, even if this did **not** result in a Socialist Scotland. But the duty of any socialist in Scotland is surely to work, now, for the creation of an organisation that is going to have the knowledge, strength, support, wisdom, integrity, determination and principles to create a socialist society in Scotland, in or out of the Union. For none can seriously doubt that Scotland led to independence by the SNP alone would be a capitalist state, neither truly independent nor truly serving the interests of the Scottish people.

> "It is necessary to create sober, patient men who do not lose hope before the worst
> horrors and who are not excited by rubbish. Pessimism of the intellect, optimism of the
> will"—Gramsci.

It is not at all to be assumed that Scotland **will** gain full independent sovereignty. While the Labour Party is very heavy-footed, it marches with a steady tread. Devolution is a game that Waddingtons ought to patent: "You have gained a minor Concession. Collect £50 and wait Five Years before your next throw." "Your Minor Concession produced a boring, incompetent Assembly. Devolution Discredited. Pay £50 back, and lose 10,000,000 Votes." The Devolution game relies on the one hand on the capriciousness of the SNP voters turning to disenchantment somewhere along the line, and on other the other on skillful manipulation by the SNP of the opportunist gestures towards Scotland of the other parties. It is a game the voters, who are going to have other, more serious problems to think about, may well grow tired of—just as they grew tired of Heath's collier-bashing. The question of principled socialist action nowhere enters into it.

If we are looking for that, there are two courses open to us. One is to work for a separate Socialist Republic of Scotland. The other is to work with the English, Welsh and Northern Irish working classes for a socialist Britain, leading to subsequent self-determination of all four constituent elements, or even a federation of more, smaller, regions. Neither will happen overnight, both demand endless hard work of the right kind. To quote Gramsci again: "changes in the mode of thinking, in beliefs, in opinions, do not come about through rapid 'explosions' which are simultaneous and general, they come about almost always through 'successive combinations' according to the most disparate and uncontrollable formulae of 'authority.' "

The difference between the two courses is not one of nationalist v. internationalist socialism. There is nothing internationalist about perpetuating the imperialist web of the UK. There is nothing narrowly 'nationalist' about the concept of a Scottish Socialist Republic. Nor is the difference altogether one of real-politik, or even of opportunism. Because one course is more difficult or less likely to be achieved than the other, can only be **one** element in making an assessment.

There is no easy answer to this question. It is one which was first posed in 1921, when John Maclean rejected Lenin's advice, as transmitted through Willie Gallacher (acting, in Maclean's words, as "Lenin's gramophone"): Lenin advised Gallacher to form one Communist Party for the whole of Great Britain. Lenin's advice was based largely on Gallacher's evidence to Lenin—Maclean having foolishly made it impossible for himself to see Lenin by demanding Government approval. (It was refused; he never saw Lenin; and this particular attempt at a demonstrative gesture backfired on him). Maclean wanted a Scottish Party, independent of London, and of Moscow. Had the full weight of Scottish socialism been put behind such a party, Scottish history would certainly have been very different. But it wasn't. The Communist Party of

Great Britain has demanded 'devolution', and welcomed the Kilbrandon report. Furthermore, it has inherited the taint of Stalinism and is suspected of simply wanting to change the seat of Scotland's masters from London to the Kremlin. This may well be unfair, but it has failed to eradicate the belief from the minds of the public at large. In spite of its hard-earned industrial strength, it performs miserably at General Elections, and has clearly not caught the imagination of the Scottish people.

Nevertheless, one important emphasis emerges from the C.P.'s policies: that nothing should be done to weaken the unity of the trade union movement in Britain as a whole, and, of course, while the same capitalists run both countries, unity is necessary. In fact, with the growth of the multi-nationals, greater and more permanent ties are needed between all the countries of the 'Free World'. To look at Ireland again, its' Trade Union movement does not have the same industrial strength as Scotland's, nor the same history, but it is clear that its separation from the unions of the rest of the British Isles is a serious impediment to effective action against the multi-nationals, even against its own, and our, capitalists.

Is this, then, an argument **for** Ireland renouncing its sovereignty, and **against** a Scottish republic? Certainly not. It is a clear demonstration of the urgent need for a strong, efficient international trade union organisation, with powerful regional councils in permanent session, and an active communications network. (And not an organisation invented and financed by the CIA either, as these things tend to be). But the demand for such an organisation must be made vigorously by any Socialist who also demands Scottish separatism: without it, separatism becomes objectively reactionary.

The way to genuine national independence can only be through greater and greater emphasis on socialist internationalism. Not only in trade union matters. Economically, Scotland may well be about to attain a great deal. But no nation can stand alone, particularly if it is to challenge the might and cunning of American imperialism. The C.P. could mockingly be suspected of wanting to transfer power over Scotland from Westminster to the Kremlin. Mr Funkhauser and his State Department controllers can actually be suspected of wanting to transfer the **real** power over Scotland and its oil from the City of London to Wall Street. Economically, Scotland is at the mercy of international capital: unless Scotland becomes a socialist republic. And Scotland alone can never become a socialist republic. Again, socialist internationalism is the only way. The Scottish working class needs to form the strongest links with all working class movements fighting against American imperialism for the right to determine their own future. That includes Arab oil-workers, South American tin-miners, Cambodian peasants, as well as Spanish chemical workers and French aviation technicians. For they are the people who ultimately will make Scotland "a nation once again."

Cultural integrity, local self-respect, the redistribution of Highland estates, the survival of the Gaelic language, the control of the side-effects of the exploitation of North Sea oil—all those and many more of the dreams close to the heart of many Scottish nationalists all depend on the hard facts of world political and economic structures. They will never become realities unless the struggle for them is seen in the context of world struggle against the imperialism of international, largely American, capital.

This assertion does not answer the immediate tactical problem. It assumes, as any socialist should assume, that Scotland must be free of the UK, the English dominated web of power and exploitation. But it implies that any genuine freedom can only be won through a Socialist Party of Scotland, with the strongest international perspectives. Unless—until, such a party mobilises the people of Scotland, the present wooly, morally evasive movement will remain a serious distraction from the major issues, a hollow laugh in Westminster and a slow grin on the face of Wall Street's money-men.

Capitalism And The Scottish Nation

John Foster

In the 1570s Scotland's population was minute—less than that of present-day Glasgow. Its whole urban population would have fitted into one medium-sized housing scheme. And it was also poor. Even in the relatively settled lowlands, the level of agricultural technique was well behind that of many Asian societies of the same period. In the north and west—where a large part of the population still lived—a money economy had scarcely begun to penetrate.

Yet four centuries later it is Scotland (and not Bengal or Persia) that is overwhelmingly industrial, part of the heartland of advanced capitalism.

The question why is an essential one for Scottish Socialists. Unless we know how Scotland got so (relatively) rich, what its overall relation to capitalism has been—freebooter, favoured colony or merely English accomplice—we cannot define either our attitude to Scotland as a nation or Britain as a state. We cannot even carry through the basic Leninist task of assessing the class content of Scottish culture. Unless we know, for example, whether the forces governing Scotland's emergence as a nation were capitalist or pre-capitalist and how far there existed a specifically Scottish capitalist culture before the merger with England, it is impossible to sort out what elements in it are popular and what anti-popular, to know what to attack and what to develop.

Of course, just to ask such questions underlines how much ground the Marxist study of Scottish history has yet to cover, and what follows can only be a very preliminary look at some of the more vital problems.(1)

A Feudal Scotland

The first (and most inescapable) question is also the trickiest. It concerns the origin and nature

141

of Scottish nationhood, and is to some extent what the whole of this article is about.

Generally speaking, the nation states we know today—with centralised institutions, common languages and cultures—developed in response to the needs of capitalist production. In some cases, like Holland, the new national institutions were the direct result of anti-feudal struggle. In others, like France and Spain, they seem more associated with attempts to reconstruct feudalism in ways that would contain the emerging capitalist forces. But almost always some kind of relationship is clear. Without the free movement of materials and labour and an end to local feudal jurisdiction, the development of a capitalist market economy was impossible, and nowhere is this process more obvious than in the creation of the first irreversably capitalist state, England, and its subsequent transformation into Great Britain.(2)

Seen in these terms, Scotland is definitely an odd man out. Not that its early development differed much from those states that eventually did consolidate themselves. But like other 'proto-nations', the Welsh, Basques, Bretons, its development was at a certain point cut short. In addition, however, Scotland's history presents a still further peculiarity. Unlike the Welsh and Irish (whose independent development ended at a pre-feudal stage) the Scottish nation seems itself to have been an almost entirely feudal creation.

Certainly there can be no doubt that the founding elements of the Scottish language (lowland Scots), of its literature (the Makars) and its legal, religious and educational systems all stem from the last three centuries of the middle ages. All were part of the process by which the lowland and east coast barons (often of Anglo-Norman origin) eventually defeated English dominance and established an independent feudal kingdom controlled to their own advantage.

Nor can there be any doubt that its creation involved much that was destructive. It meant subjecting three pre-existing linguistic groupings (the Norse and the two distinct Celtic peoples that then inhabited much of central and lowland Scotland) to the 'advanced', already feudalised culture of the small Northern English enclave in the Lothians. It meant creating a network of trading centres (the Royal Burghs) and religious communities—both almost exclusively manned with intrusive, non-Celtic populations—to act as control posts for the surrounding areas. It meant eroding an old kinship-based system of property-holding, enforcing primogeniture and establishing a new system of economic relations based on the legal dependence of peasant on landlord.

Admittedly, this process never made much headway in the highlands. Admittedly, too, both the inherited feudal forms and the Northern English language were critically modified in the course of their imposition—thus producing a distinct 'Scots' culture.(3)

All the same, feudalism did take a grip in lowland Scotland, and consequently poses a number of important questions for the historian. The first concerns timing. Scottish feudalism developed relatively late. It imported most of its institutions in an already developed form. We need to know, therefore, how far these institutions carried with them and incorporated the burgeoning class contradictions of late feudal society elsewhere.(4) If the key period of development was the 13th and early 14th centuries (a period marked in Europe generally by the temporary high point of urban challenge and expansion), how far is this reflected in the sceptical, vernacular (or at least linguistically English) cultural traditions of the Scottish court and the persisting strength of the minute merchant oligarchies in Aberdeen, Edinburgh and St. Andrews?

Conversely, we also need to know about the fate of pre-existing cultural traditions. How far did the inheritance of the South Clyde Britons (who had been through a partially violent process of disenslavement from a highly sophisticated slave empire and who afterwards maintained at least some trading and religious contacts with the east Mediterranean) survive amid the totally tribal Gaelic-speaking Scoto-Irish? How far were the traditions of either 'remembered' and embodied in the new society that now engulfed them both?

Most important of all, we need to know whether the new feudal relations themselves generated a popular class struggle, tradition parallel to that produced by the anti-landlord struggles of France and England. Did the destruction of the old semi-communal culture of the Celts at least have the positive by-product of creating a new dimension of **class** opposition— Scottish equivalents of Robin Hood, Wat Tyler and John Ball?

On this the evidence is extremely poor. It has been claimed that there was in fact no such development. Even in the lowlands kinship ties remained important. There was never the English tradition of lost freeholder independence. And throughout the comparatively short life of

Scottish feudalism linguistic and clan rivalries remained quite strong enough to prevent the development of any really large-scale peasant movements.

Yet it would be naive—as well as un-Marxist—to believe that there was altogether **no** peasant-landlord conflict, and it is up to future Marxist historians to document its impact on Scottish culture.(5) In doing this perhaps the most difficult task will be that of placing the apparently 'popular' anti-feudal literature of the sixteenth century, and this brings us to our central problem: Scottish capitalism.

Did Scotland Have A Bourgeois Revolution?

If we want to assess the nature of the English union (to discover at what point and on what terms the independent development of the Scottish nation came to an end), it is essential to determine to what extent Scotland had previously experienced a bourgeois revolution of its own. It is this question that would largely decide whether the forces pulling Scotland into the union were solely external or whether they merged with others originating in Scotland itself. Moreover, the same questions also have considerable implications for our assessment of Scottish culture. If capitalist production was in fact an **alien** imposition on Scotland (as it was perhaps in Ireland and Wales), then the continuing heritage of Scottish culture will have had a quite different role to play in the resulting class struggles than if it was itself—in part at least—already expressing Scottish capitalist control and exploitation.

On the face of it any such development may seem unlikely. Scotland was a very small, very poor country. Its towns and ports had always been less centres of craft manufacture than staging posts for trade between the interior and the continent. Only in the lowlands was there any sort of free market. And the late 16th century attempts to encourage industry—always more heavy handed than in England—bear a strong resemblance to the restabilisation policies adopted by late feudal states on the continent.(6)

Nevertheless it is important to remember the sheer weakness of feudalism in Scotland, and it was often in the system's most marginal areas—Switzerland, Bohemia and the Low Countries—that capitalist methods broke through first.(7)

In Scotland feudally-organised agriculture never incorporated more than a minority of the population (the highland surplus went mostly to the ring of towns that controlled its trade). Even in the lowlands it remained under-developed. A separate, feudally dominated manor system failed to emerge and as a result the privileged, merchant-controlled burghs quickly placed themselves at the hub of the rural economy.(8) Among landlords themselves there were quite a number who were also—as coalowners—interested in the development of industrial markets.

Finally, there was the apparent ease with which new ideas and technology could permeate lowland Scottish society. The east coast burghs were in continual contact with the main centres of capitalist experiment in Holland, Northern France and England. A stream of migrants moved (in both directions) between Scotland and the south Baltic. Inside Scotland itself there was the overextended system of cathedrals, universities and churches—in origin reflecting the late and rather artificial development of Scottish feudalism but which in changed international circumstances could equally lead to a rapid dissemination of anti-feudal perspectives.

There were, therefore, at least some of the conditions needed to induce a particularly strong contrast between new economic potentialities and the bankruptcy of existing social forms.

How far a bourgeois revolution actually occurred is less certain.

There were certainly sharp religious and social struggles in the late 16th and early 17th centuries. There was also a degree of economic growth: coal, iron, salt, flax, capitalist farming.(9) And it is notable that the periods of calvinist ascendancy in the 1570s and 80s and the 1630s coincide with those of economic expansion (indeed in the later 16th century there was an export-boosting depreciation of the currency very much like that under Edward VI in England).(10) It is also clear that the period saw increasing labour mobility and the break up of the old type of feudally-dependent peasantry.(11) There was the spate of emigration (Ulster in the 1610s and 30s, Nova Scotia in the 1620s) and repeated attempts by the coalowners from 1606 to protect their own local labour supplies by legally enserfing miners.

However, it is perhaps what was happening in the lowland countryside that is most significant

143

of all. From the standard histories it might appear to have been a period of feudal resurgence. Yet the significance of the quite real jump in feudal brigandage could well be the reverse: that the real position of the old nobility—like that of their towered strongholds in the age of gunpowder—was more isolated and vulnerable than effectively dominating. There is already some evidence to suggest that their aggressiveness was something of a last-ditch response to a relatively fast commercialisation in which they did not share: a massive (merchant-generated) inflation and the rise of a feu-owning class of farmers, farming lairds and investing burghers.(12) Certainly, the effective exercise of feudal manpower shrank back to the clan-dominated west and north east—with the rise of the Argylls as predictable as was that family's commitment to the defeudalisation of other areas outside its direct control.(13) Already in the 1610s it was to lowland Scotland that the English privy councillors looked for settlers to introduce commercial, non-feudal forms of agriculture to Ulster.(14)

Of course, this does not mean that the question of capitalist dominance is still not very open. Though forms of agricultural production may have changed there is less evidence to suggest any decisive improvement in agricultural technique. Nor is it easy to pinpoint the precise composition of the new capitalist forces. What, for instance, are we to make of Calvinism? One might speculate that as in Switzerland the success of this particular brand of protestantism had something to do with the town-oriented nature of Scottish society:- with the desire of the town merchants to find an organisational form that would cement their alliance with the lairds and gentry and extend anti-feudal discipline over the surrounding hinterland.(15) But as yet we know almost as little about the class base and origin of Calvinism as we do about its populist rhetoric or the (possibly unassociated) spate of witch-hunting (was it, as in England, yet another symptom of commercialisation in the countryside?).(16)

However, despite all this, it does seem possible to draw at least limited conclusions. Whether or not there was a decisive capture of state power, it does seem certain that capitalist forces did exist to a significant degree before union and to this extent the contrast with Wales and Ireland is legitimate. In Scotland capitalism was **not** an altogether alien imposition. Moreover, it also seems possible to make some specifications about the **type** of capitalism. Like Germany and Holland (but unlike England) it developed at a stage when merchant (and not manufacturing capital was unquestionably dominant.(17) The crafts were still strong. There were no **massed** wage-earner populations of a domestic labour type, and it may be this that accounts for the failure of the 1638-60 period to throw up socially radical leveller movements on the English scale (as well perhaps as the Calvinist readiness to experiment in universal education). On the other hand, there does seem to have been fairly radical agrarian change. So unlike Germany and Holland, there were possibilities of non-feudal allies outside the towns, and if (and it is still a big if) agricultural commercialisation really did take place on a large scale one might be able to claim that by the mid-17th century the factors reproducing the feudal base in lowland Scotland had themselves been destroyed.

But the really key feature of Scottish capitalism would seem to lie elsewhere: its external dependence. At almost no point in its development could it survive for very long without outside political support. However commercialised the lowlands, they remained the smaller part of the Scotland land mass, and always open to highland attack. Even in the lowlands some feudal influence survived, and the alliance between the merchant burghers and the lairds remained brittle. From the very beginning, therefore, we find Scotland's anti-feudal forces reaching out for alliance with their counterparts in England: during the 'Rough Wooing' of 1543-50, in the union of the crowns up to 1603 and in the anti-absolutist alliance with the English parliamentarians from 1638.(18) Indeed, the dangerous persistence with which the covenanters intervened in the English civil war stemmed largely from the realisation that their own survival depended on the outcome: that for purely internal reasons it was not possible to withdraw into an independent Scotland. Merely as a result of the structural weakness of the preceding feudalism, the birth of capitalism was in many ways premature and lacked the necessary economic base to sustain its continued growth.

So, in addition to merchant dominance and a degree of agrarian defeudalisation, the third characteristic would seem to be Scottish capitalism's inability to maintain the national institutions it inherited. To this extent capitalist development in Scotland had a quite opposite effect to what usually did elsewhere—which leads us directly to the question of union with

England.

What Sort of Union?

The Union of 1707 has often been presented as the end of Scottish independence. In fact, the first thing to grasp about it would seem to be that it represented just one **stage** (and by no means the least favorable) in a very long and zig-zag process.

Following the 1603 union of the crowns the still expanding and legally independent Scottish economy maintained fairly advantageous relations with England. Despite exclusion from certain monopoly areas, it had access to colonial trade and important allies inside parliament. The Irish Catholic MacDonald presence in the Western Isles—long a ploy of English diplomacy—was ended. In its place the use of Scots settlers and capital in Ulster reveals many of the 'junior partner' features that were to become characteristic of Scotland's overseas role a century later.

However, this period of partnership was short-lived. In the 1640s the economy went into decline. The navigation act of 1651 excluded Scottish shipping from colonial ports. Attempts at political intervention south of the border brought defeat and military occupation. And although the Cromwellian union of 1654 temporarily restored access to colonial trade, its practical operation excluded Scottish interests from any genuine representation in the Union parliament.(19) In this period Scotland's status was not far different from that of Ireland. Nor did Stuart restoration in 1660 bring much improvement. A separate parliament was regained. But the crown appointed Lord High Commissioner retained powers over legislation almost equal to those of a colonial governor general, and Scottish ships were once again excluded from colonial ports.

It was only by exploiting the acute dynastic difficulties that faced English governments in the last few years of the century that the Scots were able to make much headway. 1689 saw the recapture of a large measure of control over legislation. And in 1704 these powers were used to force through the Security Act by which the successor to the English throne could not succeed to the Scottish **unless** there was a complete union of trade, navigations and colonies. So if 1707 marks anything it was not so much the end of independence as the culmination of attempts to end the worst economic side-effects of existing English control.

Nonetheless it does pose a number of problems—especially when compared with developments a century before. In the 1630s Scotland's main allies in England were the anti-monopolist merchants and manufacturers. Yet in 1707 English merchant interests gave only grudging acceptance to what was seen essentially as a matter of state: ensuring the protestant succession against French and Jacobite invasion. And while economic and religious union had been a principal aim of the covenanters, in 1707 it was a proportion of the Royal Burghs that provided the main focus of opposition to a deal that was effectively clinched by the landowning nobility.(21)

Now, this does not necessarily mean that the 1707 union did **not** spring from the logic of capitalist development, but it certainly reflects the very considerable changes that this logic underwent in the latter two-thirds of the 17th century.

Across Europe as a whole these years saw the end of that long cycle of economic advance and population rise that had taken several countries to the point of bourgeois revolution. In almost all there was a decisive reassertion of feudal control. Catholicism was restored. Incipient merchant and agrarian capitalist sectors were reintegrated with the framework of the absolutist state. And while in England the sheer scale of previous defeudalisation plus the logic of the country's rapidly expanding colonial trade prevented any feudal comeback, there was undoubtedly a big change in the balance of capitalist forces. Political and economic initiative swung away from the towns, small-scale domestic industry and smaller rural producers to the great colonial merchants and the (often closely related) big consolidating commercial landlords. Radical elements in the bourgeois tradition were temporarily submerged.

Something similar—though one can only guess—may well have happened in Scotland.

We know that the industry which probably provided what radical impetus there was earlier in the century—coarse, cheap-labour produced woollens—found it difficult to survive, and its contraction would automatically have enhanced the influence of economically more conservative groupings in the burghs.(22) Again in the countryside, if the same economic pressures were operating as in England, one might have expected a passing of initiative from the independent small farmers to large scale commercial estate-owners, and this in turn to have had some effect in breaking or at least transforming the old burgher-laird alliance—maybe as in England inducing a period of landed dominance over the towns. Less speculatively, we know that the economic balance of power among the burghs changed dramatically against the east coast and in favour of the entrepot-oriented Glasgow, already muscling in—illegally but effectively—on the American colonial trade.(23)

So, even if these estimates are only half correct, they go some way to explain why the pro-union forces in 1707 did come mainly from the bigger landowners and west coast merchants (whose interests and attitudes closely matched those of their English counterparts) rather than the more traditional areas of Scottish capitalism. It was these new groupings, representing the only developing elements within the economy, which now dominated what remained of state power and had to face the problems of the country's virtual collapse in the 1690s. All the same, it would be a mistake to write off the older elements altogether. One cannot help being struck by the continuing vigour of the presbyteries (enforcing a massive countryside purge of episcopalians in the 1690s), of the small farmer radical covenanters from the south west—or even of the east coast burghs themselves in promoting the disastrous Darien scheme. To this extent, developments in Scotland may not have been an exact mirror image of those in England. Though the older elements may have been weakened, the new colonial merchants and landowners never achieved anything like the same measure of economic or political dominance of those south of the border— thus explaining perhaps the survival of so many of the **older capitalist forms in the 1707 union.**

Because this is one of its most remarkable features. Not only did it establish a non-colonial **political** relationship—quite distinct from that between England and Ireland or the American colonies—but it also retained separate Scottish legal and education systems (in theory at least providing elementary education for all from 1696), a form of religious settlement not unlike that suppressed in England in 1660, and (springing from this) quite different poor law and social control practices.

This does not mean it was an equal union. No union of one country with another five times as big can be 'equal' in capitalist market conditions. But it does indicate the need of English capitalism at this difficult stage in its development to gain the adhesion of culturally similar forces elsewhere or at least to prevent the inevitable alternative: the precipitation of feudal, highland-based counter-revolution. What is more, the way in which it was achieved does seem to reflect the balance of capitalist forces **inside** the country. If later there was a degree of cultural conflict—between apparently assimilationist 'enlightenment' perspectives and hardline presbyterianism—it was expressed not so much in terms of English against Scottish as between two existing trends within pre-Union development.(24) Even the management of Scottish representation in the Union parliament (which for a generation did involve a substantial infringement of the political, stage power equality of Scottish interests) was handled by the Argyll family within the conventions of Scottish politics as was—as the response to the 1736 Porteous riots clearly demonstrated—by no means one-sided or absolute.(25)

Within the union, therefore, Scotland does seem to have achieved a position of near partnership, the result of a careful grafting of one capitalist economy and culture onto another, and if during the period of competitive capitalism this partnership was in certain ways unequal (as it had to be) the inequality stemmed not so much from political intervention as the pressure of market forces, and it is these that must be examined next.

Market Forces and Economic Subordination

As third world countries have recently discovered 'market forces' can mean all or nothing. In some cases the most extreme economic subordination occurred only after the removal of formal colonial controls, and in Scotland itself one seems to have two opposite poles of experience coexisting side by side.

In the lowlands the pre-existing capitalist sectors diversified and expanded. Agriculture (especially in the Lothians) became a pioneer of new techniques. The Ayrshire coalowners found themselves in a position to become major suppliers to the Irish market. Glasgow's favoured position on the North Atlantic shipping route quickly secured it the bulk of the American tobacco trade. And although there was no great growth in the industries selected for special subsidy under the terms of the 1707 act (linen and fishing) and Border wool production was soon drawn into the orbit of the Yorkshire market, there was a remarkably rapid and successful response to the opportunities opened up in the 1770s and 80s for cotton and iron manufacturing on an industrial, factory basis. While most (but not all) of the technology was English, the money was largely Scottish and already by the mid-1780s Glasgow Chamber of Commerce was taking a lead in developing an all-British cotton manufacturing lobby.(27) Indeed, in Adam Smith Scotland produced a pioneer ideologist of industrial capitalism itself.

Part of this development can be put down to the lowland's natural resources: coal, iron, waterpower and labour (still cheaper than that in England). Yet part also must derive from the prior existence of Scottish capitalist institutions and traditions: institutions that made it risky for an Englishman to invest without Scottish partners but perhaps also traditions in which pre-mercantilist, small-producer practices still survived more strongly than they did in England.

The contrary situation, that in the highlands, amply demonstrates what could happen to an area entering the union without such traditions and at a pre-capitalist stage.

The clearances were only the last act of the story. Long before this highland society as such had been torn apart by the dispersal of the clans, the continuous bleeding of population for soldiers and emigrants and probably worst of all by the establishment of a rack-renting crofting system without security of tenure.(28) This last innovation—by which the chiefs attempted to bring their income into line with English standards—effectively blocked the establishment of developed commercial agriculture until, like Ireland, it had to face impossible competition from elsewhere. This applies even more to other forms of development. By the early 19th century the fisheries and spinning mills set up by the Sutherlands on their north east estates had little chance but to serve as a fig-leaf to cover their economically more viable sheep clearances in the interior. For over a generation the highlands had been a sub-economy to the industrialising lowlands, a virtual internal colony, supplying cheap labour, a few scanty raw materials, kelp alkali and wool but little else.(29)

Yet the most important question about market forces in the pre-monopoly period remains to be tackled.

Given that the lowland economy could benefit from union (and particularly from the imperial parts of it), how far did it still find itself at a regional disadvantage compared with England?

At this stage market disadvantage may seem unlikely. We know that the West of Scotland had a lower unemployment rate and was more industrialised than, for instance, London before 1914.(30) Nor at any time during the period of industrial capitalism were there any significant local capitalist demands for the restoration of separate national institutions. There was no counterpart to the nationalism that erupted in the subject lands of the Austrian and Russian empires when the railways opened them up for commercial exploitation. Nor indeed was there real reflection among Scottish businessmen of the disputes that marked English relations with Ireland and the American colonies: in the 1790s the Glasgow Chamber of Commerce remained firmly wedded to the Dundas interest and British institutions.

All the same, some degree of market disadvantage does seem to have been present, and was perhaps inevitable given the peripheral position of industrial Scotland within the British market. However inadequate the statistics, most indicators for the 19th century (income per head, sizes of urban and industrial populations, letters posted) show Scotland slightly behind England (though may be the most striking feature of such a comparison is how far Scotland was ahead of Ireland and Wales).(31) Looking at industry there also seems to have been a certain structural weakness. Cotton production always remained less capitalised than the English (more dependent on waterpower and retaining its handloom sector far later) and was the first branch of the industry to contract when difficulties were encountered in the 1840s. Similarly with the creation of the hot-blast iron smelting industry in the 1830s. Though run by local capital, its principal result was quickly to exhaust Scotland's ores while maintaining cheap iron supplies for English industry, and it was probably for this reason as much as any that the Scottish railway network was largely financed by capital from the industrial north of England.(32)

Even in shipbuilding—where Scotland might at last seem to have gained an area of predominance—the same pattern recurs. The most detailed available study shows that the move to Clydeside in the 1860s was partly to escape the high wages and strong unions of the south and partly because the profitable exploitation of the new iron-based technology demanded a type of labour force (craft workers **over** labourers) that could be easily built up from Clydeside's culturally split population: lowland Scots against highlanders and Irishmen.(33) Moreover, the whole development of Clydeside's export-oriented heavy industry was ultimately based upon the new capital-export imperialism run (very much to their own profit) by the merchant banks and finance houses of London.

This brings us to the final indicator of Scotland's subordinate position before 1914—the volume and character of Scottish capital export.

We do not know precisely how much went out, but it seems clear that Scotland contributed far more than its share of the British total. It is also clear that it was directly linked to a lack of confidence in the competitive position of Scottish industry. It began with the financing of emigration schemes (largely to Australia and New Zealand) on money coming out of east coast agriculture during the post-Napoleonic depression.(34) However, it only really got going in a big way with money taken out of the Dundee jute industry and Edinburgh shipping in the 1860s and 70s. By the 1890s and 1900s substantial sums were also coming from the heavy industry areas of the west. Most interesting of all is the **form** it now took: the investment trust. When Scottish businessmen started buying foreign stocks and shares it was on the London market: a practice that was generally far more profitable for the banks that issued them than it was for the buyers. The investment trust was a device to get round this further product of Scotland's disadvantaged position—with local businessmen forming their own syndicates for direct intervention in overseas stock markets.(35)

So if Scottish industry was to some extent disadvantaged, we are still left with the question of why there was no significant demand in capitalist circles for home rule, protection or independence. One might point to the original compatibility of the two capitalist cultures and the degree of subsequent assimilation. But a far more plausible explanation can in fact be found elsewhere: in the way in which Scottish industry had sought to compensate for its disadvantage in the internal market by gearing its whole structure to production for Britain's formal and informal empire. As John Gollan put it in his pioneering study:

> 'When textiles...started to give way, first to coal and iron and then later to steel, shipbuilding, engineering and railways, the pattern of modern Scotland was laid. It was part and parcel of the British imperialist system. Scotsmen were enlisted as lieutenants in the exploitation of the colonies and returned with their share of the booty. Out of all this came the Midland industrial belt, the tenements, the slums, the squalid towns...'

In 1914 no area was more dependent than Scotland on the great fly-wheel of capital export, credit and trade centred on the City of London. When that broke under the pressure of war Clydeside's heavy industry crumbled quickly. Within a decade Beardmores, Fairfield, Colvilles, Steel Company of Scotland were all on the rocks. What is worse, there was nothing to take their place. If London had more unemployment before 1914 the balance was more than redressed afterwards. Finally, therefore, we come to Scotland's status during the last, monopoly phase of capitalism.

State Monopoly Capitalism

Among other things this period generally sees a limitation in the role of market forces and a tightening of links between both monopoly industry and banking and the resultant finance capital groupings and the state—with a consequent shrinking of access to state power for non-monopoly sectors. A split of interest occurs within the capitalist class itself.

Accordingly, if interwar Scotland suffered excess unemployment—failed to develop a new generation of high rechnology industries in electrical engineering, petrochemicals and cars—how far was this because it lacked access to the monopoly capitalist state?(37) How far, indeed, did Scotland's problems extend beyond the lack of access suffered by non-monopoly sectors in

England?

At first glance the answer may seem to be no. In terms of personnel Scotland was well represented on the commanding heights. Even discounting politicians like Bonar Law, the Geddes brothers, Steel Maitland and Mackay, there was Sir Alexander Duncan, central figure of the Scottish steel industry, acting as chief industrial adviser to the Governor of the Bank of England, and Scottish businessmen more or less dominating the rationalisation schemes in steel and shipbuilding. Sir James Lithgow and Lord Weir occupied key positions on government committees, and Lithgow was president of the FBI in 1930-32.(38)

Yet on closer examination it is remarkable just how little they got. There was no serious finance for new industry. None of the Bank of England rationalisation schemes in Scotland were made the base for new high technology monopoly. Scotland even failed to get its fair share of state-subsidised factories, and as regards heavy industry the government's main concern seems to have been to maintain just enough of it to provide the basis for a fast rearmament programme—a programme, which, if sited further south, would have seriously disrupted the labour supply (and profitability) of the relatively flourishing consumer durable monopolies.(39)

Part of the explanation no doubt derives from purely market considerations: an intensification of earlier disadvantages as overseas demand dried up and the new consumer market shrunk back to the relatively prosperous south east. But it was certainly made worse by the historically weak links between Scottish industry and the city of London. Interwar state planning, such as it was, tended to operate on an informal basis through the Bank of England and the big merchant banks—granting them statutory powers to rationalise defunct industries and then turn them into adjuncts to existing monopoly sectors. Because so much pre-1914 overseas Scottish investment was routed independently of London (and tended to be of a particularly parasitic portfolio kind) and more important still because even the biggest pre-1914 Scots firms only existed on the periphery of the monopoly sector—Beardmore's armament steel, for instance, had a satellite relationship to Vickers—it tended to be those firms already linked to finance capital groups that got the capital needed to expand in the new conditions of the 1920s. When Weirs tried to produce helicopters and sheet-steel housing and Beardmore's diversified into cars and aircraft, it was largely lack of capital resources that forced them into premature withdrawal in face of competition from better endowed southern competitors.(40)

As a result Scottish industry found itself in a very unfavourable position to meet the new form of state monopoly capitalist planning that emerged after 1945.

This now operated in near full employment conditions through direct investment subsidies and the manipulation of consumer demand in favour of big monopoly producers. As such, the new system positively needed a periphery of unemployment regions to enable the monopolies to escape from the overheating pressures at the centre (and the persistence with which post-war governments have resisted demands for effective regional policies—that is the establishment of new, state-owned industry—would seem to indicate that they were quite aware of this).(41) Certainly, the immigration of non-Scottish big business—either directly or by merger—has been little short of spectacular. The amount of United States investment per head in 1969 was second only to that in Canada and virtually double that for the United Kingdom as a whole.(42) By 1973 only a minority of the Scottish manufacturing labour force was employed by Scottish firms (250 thousand out of 600 thousand)(43) What is more, non-Scottish control was particularly marked among large or even moderately large firms. By then over three-quarters of the workers in concerns with over a thousand employees were employed by non-Scottish companies. Indeed, it is probably true to say that non-monopoly small business is today weaker in Scotland—and the voice of monopoly accordingly louder within its regional business institutions—than anywhere else in Britain.

This subordinate position is most strikingly demonstrated by the response to oil. A century ago there was joint Scottish and English exploitation of Scottish coal and iron reserves. In oil this would be unthinkable. Even on the subcontract engineering side Scottish firms have only picked up the crumbs. And the overall strategy of extraction worked out between the government and the oil monopolies appears designed to maximise immediate foreign currency earnings (to pay for Common Market membership and the accompanying capital export) at the expense of any long-term creation of jobs or downstream industry.(44)

So finally we are brought full circle. The greed of feudal lords first created a Scottish nation.

149

Since then the logic (and greed) of capitalism has progressively eaten its way through those original institutions. At each stage Scottish capital moved further away from its national base: in getting access to colonial markets, in the joint exploitation of Scotland's own resources, in capital export, in the ultimate mergers with external monopoly.

Does this mean, therefore, that a Scottish nationality no longer exists? While this is not the place to go into the problem in any detail, one or two points are directly relevant to the theme already developed.

If one's criterion for a nation is a historically constituted community of culture springing from a period of statehood, then a Scottish nation undoubtedly exists. But it is important to remember the rider that Marxists have always added. The culture or institutions of a nation are not absolute or static. They reflect and record the changing class conditions of its development—including the scale and character of the class struggle within it (it is this that makes certain elements within a nation's heritage worth defending).(45)). On these terms the subsequent post-statehood development of Scottish culture was carried on under very special conditions.

First, the exploiting class remained culturally Scottish. Second, Scottish culture and institutions as inherited from the period of statehood, though basically capitalist, were as yet little modified by the experience of class struggle. Third, that while these institutions continued to be used well into the 20th century as instruments of control (one has only to read accounts of Sir James Lithgow's social activities in the Port Glasgow area), the conditions of effective class struggle demanded that lowland Scots both unite locally with highlander and Irish and on an all-British scale with workers in similar industries in England. So unlike Ireland and Wales (where national culture from the beginning emobdied elements of anti-capitalist resistance) the first task of labour organisation in Scotland was to break the bonds of cultural localism. It was this realisation that brought Scottish workers to take a leading role in establishing all-British unions for the cotton industry (1830s) and coal (1840s) and the united organisation of the British Trade Union Congress in 1868. Similarly with united political demands—from the post-1815 reform movement, from the Chartists, from the Socialist and Labour movements of the late 19th century. To this extent it is no mere rhetoric to claim that the traditions of the Scottish working-class bear within them two centuries' practice of internationalism and have created a separate working-class culture more distanced from that it originally inherited than either the Irish or the Welsh. This does not mean it is 'non-Scottish'. Quite the reverse. Necessarily incorporating the progressive elements of its component cultures, it is—in an age when Scottish bourgeois culture only exists in a totally artificial ersatz form—the one living Scots culture. And, as the STUC has recently made plain, its internationalist logic still retains all its force. In a period when the manipulation of intra-British national differentials is part and parcel of monopoly capitalist exploitation, it remains a paramount need for **all** workers in Britain to ensure that the Welsh and Scottish peoples secure control over their own economies: that the establishment of national parliaments becomes part of the overall struggle against monopoly capitalism.

This is an expanded version of an article that first appeared in **Scottish Marxist** June 1973.

1. H. MacDiarmid, **Selected essays** (1969)—among other writings—and D Craig, **Scottish literature and the Scottish people** (1961) are essential starting points. A pioneering guide to the later phases of Scottish capitalism is provided by J. Gollan, **Scottish prospect** (1948).
2. V. Kiernan, 'State and nation', **Past & Present** 1965 and E. Hobsbawm, '17th ecentury crisis', **Past & Present** 1954 examine this relationship in detail.
3. G. Barrow, **Robert Bruce and the community of Scotland** (1965), K. Witting, **Scottish tradition** (1958) and T. Smout, **History** (1969) chapter 1.
4. For instance V. Rutenberg, 'Revoltes', **Annales** May 1972 examines the question of how far French later medieval culture was permanently modified by internal class struggles.
5. R. Dobson, 'The Robin Hood legend', **Northern History** 1972 provides sources for the existence of Robin Hood tales in south east Scotland by the 1440s at the latest.

6. S. Lythe, 'Scottish economy under James VI', **Scottish Historical Review** 1971.

7. There are certain similarities between Slicher van Bath's description of the Swiss and Friesland rural economies (**Agrarian history** p.191) and that of lowland Scotland.

8. Barrow, **Bruce**, introduction.

9. Lythe, **SHR** 1971.

10. M. Perceval-Maxwell, **Scottish migration to Ulster in the reign of James I** (1973). Prices virtually tripled between 1571 and 1601 and the bullion content of the Scottish pound fell from one fifth to one twelfth of the English. James blamed the merchants responsible for monetary issues (as well as the introduction of coin from abroad).

11. Perceval-Maxwell, **Migration** makes a detailed study of the breakdown of the old type of tied peasantry in the borders.

12. M. Sanderson, 'Feuars of the kirkland', **SHR** 1973 shows that it was resident occupiers of below laird status who formed the biggest single group of purchasers of Church feus in the early and mid 16th century (followed by the lairds and burgesses but with the nobility virtually absent). Perceval-Maxwell, **Migration** (31) talks of a 'revolution' in land tenure in the later 16th century. D. Stevenson, **Scottish revolution 1637-44)** (1973) also gives the impression that the laird estate was strongly increasing its position in the earlier 17th century.

13. E. Creegen, 'The house of Argyll and the highlands', **History and social anthropology** (ed. I. Lewis, 1968).

14. Perceval-Maxwell, **Migration** p.16. Dutch settlers were also considered.

15. Stevenson, **Scottish revolution** presents a noble-presbytery alliance as the moving force behind the covenant. But at almost every stage his own narrative shows the laird and burgess estates together forcing the hand of a divided and equivocating nobility: in the June 1638 protest to the king (p.96); against royal appointment of lay members to parliament (p.176); on the treaty of London and the eventual intervention in the English war in 1642 (pp.236 and 268); and in the exclusion of royalist nobles and the support for Argyll in 1643 (pp.275 and 277).

16. A. Macfarlane, **Witchcraft in Tudor and Stuart England** (1970). C. Larner's 'James and Witchcraft' in A. Smith ed, **The Reign of James VI** (1973), though casting interesting light on court attitudes, fails to provide the necessary evidence on the incidence of local prosecutions.

17. A. Chistozonov, 'Stage and regional study of bourgeois revolutions in the 16th to 18th centuries', **Social Sciences** (USSR) 1973, No.4.

18. M. Merriman, 'The assured Scots', **SHR** 1968 indicates that the **voluntary** supporters of English rule after 1543 were largely drawn from the lairds and smaller gentry.

19. On this particular point J. Casada, 'Scottish representatives in Richard Cromwell's parliament', **SHR** 1972 provides a fairly convincing defence of T. Roper's position in **Religion, reformation and social change** (1967).

20. P. Riley, **English ministers and Scotland 1707-27** (1968) chapter one.

21. Two somewhat differing views of the union are offered by T.Smout and R. Campbell in **Economic History Review** 1965.

22. G. Gulvin, 'Scottish woollen industry', **SHR** 1971.

23. Smout, 'Glasgow', **SHR** 1968.

24. J. Cater, 'Principal Robertson' **SHR** 1970 reveals both the continuing strength of the presbyterian tradition and the deep-laid nature of Bute's politics of cultural assimilation. T. Nairn, 'Scotland', **New Left Review** 83 and D. Craig, **Scottish Literature** also discuss this issue.

25. W. Ferguson, **Scotland 1689 to present** (1968) gives a good account.

26. Smout, **Econ HR** 1965. J. Price, 'Tobacco trade', P. Payne ed. **Studies in Scottish business history** (1967). J. Butt, 'Muirkirk iron works', **SHR** 1966. H. Hamilton, **Economic History** 1963 (for linen industry).

27. Minutes 13th April 1784 (printed goods bounty) and 5 July 1785 for account of Glasgow's role in overcoming disunity between Lancashire and London calico printers.

28. E. Creegen, 'Argyll' as cited. A. Youngson, **After '45** (1973). E. Richards, 'Sutherland and the Industrial Revolution' **Econ HR** 1973 dwells on the Sutherland family's losses in highland industry but fails to provide the much more interesting information on how much they subsequently made on the sheep clearances.

29. V. Morgan, 'Agricultural wage rates in later 18th century Scotland', **Econ HR** 1971 shows that the really big differential between Clydeside and the highlands only emerged after the 1760s.

30. Gollan, **Scottish prospect** p.3.
31. M. Hechter, 'Regional inequality and national integration: the case of the British isles', **Journal of Social History** 1971.
32. W. Vamplew, 'Railways and the Scottish economy', **Econ HR** 1971 and 'Scottish railway capital', **Scottish Journal Political Economy** 1970.
33. S. Pollard, 'Economic history of British shipbuilding 1870-1914', London PhD, 1951, p.207.
34. D. Macmillan, 'Scottish enterprise in Australia', **Studies in Scottish business history.** These early investment companies are to be distinguished from the later investment trusts.
35. W. Jackson, **Enterprising Scot** (1968) is the most detailed study. W. Kerr, 'Scottish investment in Texas', **Studies in Scottish business history** adds some useful details.
36. Gollan, **Scottish prospect** p.211.
37. Detailed figures on the disparities between the development of high technology industries in England and Scotland are provided by Gollan, **Scottish prospect** pp.8-9.
38. J. Reid, **Lithgow** (1964) and W. Reader, **Weir Group** (1971) describes their respective activities.
39. H. Clay, Norman (1959) chapter 6. Gollan. M. Grieve, 'Lowlands' in D. Glenn ed. **Whither Scotland?** (1971) on factories.
40. Interestingly Weirs had links with the French Renault firm. Reader, Weir Group.
41. A. Hargrave, 'Scottish economy' in Glen, **Whither Scotland?** describes this as the main motivation for the GEC/AEI move to Scotland. W. Niven, 'Foreign investment and regional policy', **Scottish Marxist** March 1973.
42. Niven, 'Foreign investment', **Scottish Marxist** March, 1973, pp.6 & 9.
43. J. Firn, 'Who owns Scottish industry?' **The Scotsman,** 31 October 1973. These figures were computed from the Scottish Council's data bank on manufacturing industry. Comparing them with those given in T. Johnston and others, **Structure and growth of the Scottish economy** (1971) one gets the impression of a massive shift towards non-Scottish control in the late sixties and early seventies. Fairly large-scale disinvestment by Scottish businessmen would also account for the rapid growth of the Scottish secondary banking sector in the same period. The indications are that most of the money has gone to short-term speculative uses.
44. P. Smith, 'North sea oil', **Scottish Marxist March 1973.**
45. Engels makes this point to Schmidt, 27 October 1890, Marx-Engels, **Selected Correspondence** (1934) p.481.

External Control And Regional Policy

John Firn

1. Regional Policy

Over the past decade there has developed in Scotland, and indeed in other British regions, a growing disillusionment with the achievements of regional economic policy. Despite nearly 40 years of increasing active government intervention(1), substantial disparities still remain between the expanding and prosperous areas such as the Midlands and the South-East, and the older industrial areas of the North of England, Northern Ireland, Wales and Scotland. Here, despite the expenditure of some £350mn each year by successive UK governments on regional assistance, the continued contraction of the traditional heavy industries such as coal, iron and steel, mechanical engineering and shipbuilding has not been matched by the development of new enterprises and employment opportunities in the newer industrial and service sectors of their economies. The net result is that such regions continue to display above average levels of unemployment and net emigration together with employee activity rates, per capita incomes and infrastructural developments that are all below the national average.

Part of the disillusionment, which in Scotland at least has been translated into political action by the growth of a strong nationalist movement, lies in the failure to understand and appreciate the sheer size and complexity of the economic problems facing the depressed regions, and thus there has frequently been a lack of acknowledgement of the very real achievements that past regional policies have had in Britain. Yet, while it cannot be disputed that the depressed areas of Britain would have suffered even greater economic and social decline in the absence of regional policies, there is a growing realisation that such policies that have been developed have been very much ad-hoc and pragmatic, and have not been based on a full understanding of the components and processes of regional economic development.

The main purpose of this paper is to discuss some of the major economic factors that are important determinants of the long-term viability and prosperity of regional economies. In particular it will focus upon one aspect that has so far been relatively neglected by regional economists, despite its obvious and important theoretical and policy implications, namely, the effects and problems associated with a situation whereby a large amount of the ownership and control of key sectors lies outside the region concerned. Some evidence on the degree and type of external control that exists in Scottish manufacturing industry will be presented, and some comparisions will be made with similar situations elsewhere. The implications that such a situation have for both regional development theory and policy will be discussed, and suggestions made for future research.

2. The Components of Regional Development.

Until fairly recently, economic theorists have not paid much attention to the complex and dynamic problems of regional economic growth and decline. Those who ventured into regional theory have, with few exceptions, concentrated their activity on the formulation of theories of location, which have developed upon the twin foundations of neo-classical economic theory and geographical determinisation in the tradition of Christaller and Losch. More recently, attempts have been made to introduce some of the elements of Keynesian macro-theory into regional analysis, and more technical approaches, such as Growth Pole theory—which mainly seems to offer an ex-post rationalisation of situations that already exist, have also made their appearance, together with the now ubiquitous and almost mandatory econometric and mathematical models. But overwhelmingly, the economic core of regional analysis that is handed down to new practitioners, remains that of the essentially static approach of neo-classical economics.

It does not take a great deal of original effort to discover that the picture of regional development that emerges from the main body of currently accepted regional theory frequently bears little or no resemblance to the organisations, activities and problems of the real world. It is not however, the intention of this paper to pursue the numerous and well-known failings of neo-classical economics(2) and its related regional theories, but rather to examine briefly some of the basic components and processes that underlie regional change, and especially that change that occurs within the manufacturing sector in the regions of developed countires such as the United Kingdom. (This concentration upon manufacturing does not imply that other activities or sectors are unimportant; it merely reflects the existing deficiency of knowledge that exists about the contribution and role of these sectors in modern regional development. The understanding that we have, for instance, about the operation and influence of the service or tertiary sector is still extremely limited, which seems hard to accept given the likely future dominance of this sector in total economic activity. This surely is one area which would repay a much more substantial effort by researchers.)

Regional economic growth is, by definition, simply to aggregate total efforts of the individuals, enterprises and organisations that constitute the economy of any single region. Thus, the only meaningful way that any deep and perceptive understanding of regional change can be achieved is to focus attention on the change that occurs at the level of the individual enterprise or firm(3) What is important is the realisation that a region is composed of a collection of individual enterprises, each one of which is facing certain problems, and each one of which is able to adjust to such problems in a greater or lesser degree. As Nelson noted:

"...what appears important is that individual firms are unique. In short, the firm cannot be viewed any longer as a competent, easily predictable, interchangeable clerk, working in a well-structured environment on well-defined tasks. Rather, the firm must be viewed as attempting to keep its footing and to make progress in a poorly structured, changing environment by trying and doing appropriate new things."(4)

It is simply because of this, that regional analysis needs to become involved with change at the micro level.

During the past five years, members of the Department of Social and Economic Research at the University of Glasgow have been engaged on the first stage of the type of regional analysis outlined above, namely a detailed examination of the components of change at the level of the enterprise, concentrating upon developments in the manufacturing sector in the Central Clydeside Conurbation.(5) This area, which is centred on the City of Glasgow, offers one of the greatest challenges to applied economists interested in regional change, for apart from its constituting the economic core of the Scottish economy, it also represents a possible prototype of the types of change that are likely to affect other industrial regions in the future. The rapid and substantial decline of the area's traditional industries, coupled with the poor urban environment, has presented policy-makers with a regional problem of substantial magnitude, and there can be little doubt that it represents the archetypal industrial problem region in Western Europe.(6)

From the work that has been undertaken so far, two major conclusions have emerged. Firstly, there has been very little development of new enterprises and thus of employment, from within the Conurbation itself. Between 1958 and 1968, the the period covered by the initial study, only some 37 per cent of employment created in new establishments came from local enterprise, against 33 per cent from the rest of the UK and 30 per cent from overseas, mainly North America. Secondly, and this is important in the context of the present paper, the degree of external control of manufacturing enterprises in the Conurbation was found to be much higher than had been previously realised. Indeed, at the end of 1968, 58 per cent of the total employment in the region was in plants where the ultimate control lay outside Scotland.(7) These two major findings, which because of the nature of the data used, were well established, are examples of the kind of initial clues to the nature of the regional problem that can emerge from the use of enterprise-based analytical techniques. They are, however, only the first step, for as noted above they need to be followed through with more detailed investigation at the level of the individual enterprises.

Both of the above two major research findings from the initial analysis of regional change on Clydeside are being investigated in more depth in research projects that are moving on to the second stage of the research strategy outlined above, namely, to examine in detail the nature of the economic transformation process within key areas. The low rate of formation of indigenous enterprise is one aspect of regional change which is of especial interest, for it suggests that there may well be a deficiency of entrepreneurship at the regional level. Yet, even such an intriguing statement as this hides a number of possibilities. Is the lack of entrepreneurship an indication that the area is no longer producing entrepreneurs, or that they are being produced but being prevented from becoming active by the existence of specific local barriers to entrepreneurial entry, or that they are being produced but setting up enterprises elsewhere? It is too early to be able to answer any of these questions yet from the research underway, which is a comparative study of the formation and development of new enterprises in the Clydeside and West Midlands Conurbations, but some early indications seem to point to yet another possibility, namely that Clydeside entrepreneurs are setting up enterprises in declining sectors of the local economy, a highly intriguing situation. These questions will be examined when the relevant research starts its investigations of the development of individual enterprises later this year. What does seem important is that the initial discovery of the low rate of indigenous formation from the structural analysis has turned the attention upon the role of the entrepreneur in regional development, a hitherto neglected but certainly vital issue.(8)

These two findings are related: Manufacturing industry displayed a remarkably high degree of outside control—an important relationship, for if past rates of indigenous enterprise development remain low while those of employment creation by external enterprises remain high, then excluding employment change in existing enterprises(9) the balance must swing further, towards external control. However, as will be shown below, there are a number of definitional and empirical problems associated with the concept of external control, and as yet the picture for Clydeside remains somewhat unclear with regard to the future balance between indigenous and external enterprise. But the initial finding has at least resulted in more attention being paid to the possible implications that a large degree of external control can have on a region such as Clydeside, or indeed for the larger 'region' of Scotland. Thus a research project is underway investigating the components of this switch in control towards external areas, and specifically it is looking at the impact of mergers and take-overs on the long-run economic viability of enterprises in Clydeside. Once again, the initial structural analysis has identified an area of regional change where more detailed exploration is beginning to yield vital information on the major factors lying behind long-term regional economic change. Of even more importance to the present paper is that these particular findings relating to external control in the Clydeside Conurbation raised a number of important issues for the Scottish economy as a whole, and thus it was suggested that there might be a possibility of investigating the degree of external control that existed for the whole of Scottish manufacturing industry. This possibility was investigated, found feasible. and the study which is reported below, put into operation during 1973.

3. The Concept of External Control

Before proceeding any further it is necessary to define exactly what is meant by the term 'external control'. There has been much discussion within management science and business studies as to what the term 'control' means when applied to business organisations, but it is gradually becoming accepted that in both multi-plant companies and/or companies which are members of larger industrial or commercial groups, the ultimate control of the major economic decisions is made by the senior management personnel in the company or establishment at the top of the hierarchy, as distinct from the owners of the equity and the stock of such companies. Thus. ever since Berle and Means first work in this field in the 1930s, the phenomenon of separation of ownership from control has steadily become an established fact of economic life.(10) Of course. such a situation does not arise in the majority of smaller manufacturing units, in which ownership and management are invariably held by the same person or group of people. Our own experiences in talking to management in both branch plants and wholly-owned subsidiary companies confirms the more recent work in this area, namely that long-term strategic decisions on investment, production, purchasing and sales, and to a lesser extent personnel, are being made by specialists in the parent plant or company. Further, with the growing use of telecommunications. even short-term tactical decisions are being referred back to headquarters or to the specialists in the holding company.(11) This constant communication is likely to be even greater in the case of branch-plants than with wholly-owned subsidiaries, and thus a region with a large proportion of branch plants may well suffer a considerable loss of control over its strategic and tactical decisions to other areas. This aspect will be referred to again below, but it can be noted here that such a situation, if existing, would seem to indicate an intra-regional switch from entrepreneurship towards management, which has interesting long-term implications, to put it mildly!

In the study which is currently underway at Glasgow, we have defined the location of ultimate control as being the country (or region) where the headquarters of a branch plant is located, or the country where the headquarters of the senior holding company is located should the company in Scotland be a wholly-owned subsidiary. Where the headquarters of a branch plant is also owned by another company or a hierarchy of other companies, the location of the headquarters of the company at the top of the hierarchy is deemed to be where 'ultimate control' lies. Companies which are owned by two or more separate companies are kept in a separate category, although it is possible to allocate their employment on the basis of shareholdings. The actual information we have had access to is in fact far more sophisticated than the above indicates, but basically the broad categories are as stated.

We realise that the above definitions hide more than they reveal, and accept the fact that ultimately there is no alternative to pursuing detailed studies at the company level. This will come later: what is presented below are merely the first results. Whilst we accept such criticisms as inevitable, the problems above are much smaller than those created by some official UK government statistics.(12) For instance, the Department of Industry classifies any plant which has been in operation in Scotland since before 1945 as 'indigenous'. While there is some merit in this. in that one would expect such plants to be firmly linked into the Scottish economy by now, it does mean that if the Government had not not rescued Rolls-Royce in 1971, the closure of their four factories in Scotland employing 14,000 would have been classified as a decline in indigenous industry! We prefer to retain indigenous to refer to companies that are effectively controlled from within Scotland, and it is interesting to note that the current Government accepts our definition—and indeed our findings.(13)

4. External Control and the Scottish Economy.

Although it would seem on reading this paper, that the question of external control as defined above would be an area for concern within government in the UK, and that therefore, some evidence on its extent must be collected, an examination of the situation reveals that this is not the case. Some data on the ownership of manufacturing establishments is collected during the Census of Production enquiries, but not only is it not checked for accuracy (companies don't always tell Governments the truth!) it is not collected in a format that allows statistical analysis. However, the latter point is very much an academic one, for the legal restrictions on confidentiality are so tight that if there is any chance of identifying an individual firm in the tabulations, the figures are suppressed. Thus only very broad and very old tabulations are released, and indeed even the personnel in the Scottish office of the government department which collects them are forbidden to see individual returns. This would seem to suggest the existence of a statistical 'black-hole' in England, into which everything goes and nothing escapes.

The data employed in this study consists of the answers to a detailed questionnaire that is sent out to Scottish-based manufacturing companies each year by the Scottish Council (Development and Industry), a non-Governmental body which is involved in the promotion of industrial development in Scotland.(14) The survey covers the top 3000 manufacturing enterprises in Scotland, and thus covers the majority of manufacturing plants, and certainly all the major ones. Some checks on its coverage by the Department of Industry have confirmed that it is truly representative of Scottish manufacturing industry, and that the information given is accurate when compared to official returns. During the autumn of 1973, the data on the questionnaires was transferred to computer and a series of analysis undertaken: unfortunately a prolonged strike of computer operators is now delaying the more detailed investigations that are planned, and therefore the information given below represents only the most important parameters of external control. There are six areas which are worth discussing separately: the coverage and accuracy of the data involved; the relationship between enterprises and employment; the relationship between size of plant and external control; the organisational structure of external control; the sectoral distribution of external control; and the intra-regional distribution of external control within Scotland.

1 Distribution of Employment by major industrial sectors: comparison of Scottish Council data for 1973 with Department of Employment figures for 1972.

1968 Standard Industrial Classification Orders	Scottish Council:1973		Dept. of Employment: 1972	
	Number	per cent	Number	per cent
03 Food, drink and tobacco	99,600	16.9	94,600	14.8
04 Coal and petroleum products	2,400	0.4	2,600	0.4
05 Chemicals and allied industries	18,700	3.2	26,300	4.1
06 Metal manufacture	36,700	6.2	42,800	6.7
07 Mechanical engineering	88,400	15.0	84,800	13.2
08 Instrument engineering	17,800	3.0	17,500	2.7
09 Electrical engineering	47,000	8.0	49,500	7.7
10 Shipbuilding and marine engineering	28,200	4.8	43,900	6.8
11 Vehicles	27,600	4.7	35,400	5.5
12 Other metal goods	24,400	4.1	28,700	4.5
13 Textiles	74,800	12.7	71,000	11.0
14 Leather, leather goods and fur	2,800	0.5	3,100	0.5
15 Clothing and footwear	27,100	4.6	32,900	5.1
16 Bricks, pottery, cement, etc.	23,300	3.9	21,400	3.3
17 Timber, furniture, etc.	17,000	2.9	22,700	3.5
18 Paper, printing and publishing	38,300	6.5	49,500	7.7
19 Other manufacturing industries	15,900	2.7	15,900	2.5
Total manufacturing industry	590,700	100.0	642,600	100.0

i. The Accuracy of the Data:

As noted above the information was checked against Government data to determine whether it was truly representative. This was done internally by the Department of Industry, but it was also possible to compare the distribution of employment by major industrial sectors with published employment figures from the Department of Employment (Table 1). Here again the results are reassuring, for the Scottish Council (Development and Industry)—hence SCDI—plants cover about 92 per cent of the total number of employees in manufacturing as recorded by the 1972 Census of Employment. Further, the sectoral distribution of employment in the two sets of data is statistically almost identical, and we can therefore be certain that the analysis, at least in employment terms, is truly representative of Scottish manufacturing as a whole. The information on ownership and plant-type upon which the 'control' variable is based was also checked against other published sources, and in many cases with the enterprises themselves.

Unfortunately, it cannot be checked with **official** information, as this is not something which is **collected, and therefore** it is very much a unique asset: and, indeed, one much in demand by Central Government departments. It should be further added that since the original analysis was undertaken, the sectors where major discrepancies existed, such as shipbuilding, chemicals and paper, have been investigated in order that many of the gaps could be filled in, and with these filled, the basic dimensions of ownership are totally unaffected.

2 Location of Ultimate Ownership of Scottish Manufacturing Plants and Employment: 1973

Location of ultimate ownership	Plants Number	Plants per cent	Employees Number	Employees per cent	Average Size of Plant (Employees)
Scotland	2176	71.6	243,440	41.2	111.9
England	640	21.0	234,990	39.8	367.2
Rest of UK	4	0.1	160	-	40.0
EEC	29	1.0	8,760	1.5	302.1
Other Europe	15	0.5	3,800	0.6	253.3
North America	148	4.9	87,730	14.9	592.8
Other	5	0.2	370	0.1	74.0
Joint-owned	24	0.8	11,450	1.9	476.7
Total	3041	100.0	590,700	100.0	194.2

ii. Plants and Employment:

The situation revealed in Table 2 is of interest in that it shows that although the majority of plants operating in Scotland were domestically controlled, the same is not true for employment, and it is indeed salutary to see that there are nearly as many employees working in plants which are controlled by companies located in the rest of Great Britain as there are in Scotland itself. This would seem to indicate that the Scottish economy is firmly linked to that of the rest of the UK, and this presents economic policy-makers with a difficult situation in that the highly open nature of the Scottish economy cannot be easily isolated from the rest of the UK, which in turn makes it virtually impossible to restrict the operations of regional policy to Scotland, or conversely isolate Scotland from the effects of national economic policies that are more orientated to conditions in the South of England.

It is also interesting to note that although North American plants now occupy a dominant role in the Scottish economy, both on account of the fact that they employ nearly 15 per cent of total employees and that the average size of their plant is very large, the penetration of the European Economic Community has not been very marked so far. Indeed, there are some grounds for doubting whether any substantial increase in direct investment from Europe can be expected by

Scotland during the next decade.

iii. The Size of Plant and External Control:

One of the most important findings that has emerged so far is the relationship between the size of plants and external control. (Table 3) Scotland's industrial structure has always been biased towards large plants, yet the degree of concentration displayed is quite remarkable with nearly 46 per cent of total employment in manufacturing falling within the 110 enterprises that employ over 1000. This would suggest that the Scottish economy is effectively dependent upon the decisions made by a relatively small number of companies, and thus attempts to stimulate the Scottish economy might be more successful if concentrated initially on these particular large companies. The evidence from Table 3 does suggest a clear link between size of plant measured by employment and external control: basically, the larger the enterprise the more likely it is to be controlled from outside Scotland, and further, the more likely it is to be controlled by a North American company. The situation is in fact, probably more disturbing than appears at first sight, for of the 106,000 employees in the 110 largest enterprises, nearly 40 per cent are in externally-controlled branch-plants, where past experience would suggest a relatively low level of autonomy in decision-making. This again would seem to have very important implications for our understanding of long-term economic growth at the regional level, with the leading plants in a region like Scotland being firmly tied in to the national and international economic systems of the multi-national enterprises.

3 Location of ultimate ownership of Scottish manufacturing employment by size of plant: 1973

Location of ultimate Ownership	1—50 Employees		51—100 Employees		101—500 Employees		1001-5000 Employees		5001 and over Employees		Total Plants	
	Number	%	Number	%	Number	%	Number	%	Number	%	Number	%
Scotland	1307	85.6	378	72.8	421	54.6	42	37.5	25	26.0	3	21.4	2176	71.6
England	165	10.8	111	21.3	266	34.4	45	40.2	46	47.9	7	50.0	640	21.0
Rest of UK	3	0.2	1	0.2	—	—	—	—	—	—	4	0.1
EEC	6	0.4	8	1.5	10	1.3	2	1.8	3	3.1	—	—	29	1.0
Other Europe	5	0.4	1	0.2	5	0.6	4	3.6	—	—	—	—	15	0.5
North America	30	2.0	20	3.8	59	7.6	16	14.3	19	19.9	4	28.6	148	4.9
Other	3	0.2	—	—	2	0.2	—	—	—	—	—	—	5	0.2
Joint-owned	7	0.4	1	0.2	10	1.3	3	2.6	3	3.1	—	—	24	0.8
Total	1526	100.0	520	100.0	773	100.0	111	100.0	96	100.0	14	100.0	3041	100.0
Size distribution	50.2		17.1		25.4		3:7		3.1		0.5		100.0	

iv. **Enterprise Organisation and External Control:**

The relationship between organisational structure and external control is another area which is of importance, as the figures on large branch-plants given above demonstrates. It is another area which is comparatively unexplored in UK regional policy, and also one where—once again—comparative statistics for other areas simply do not exist. Although Scottish-owned single-plant companies (Table 4), some of which are subsidiaries of other Scottish companies, form the largest single group when measured in employment terms, they are on average much smaller in size than the externally-controlled plants, and therefore wield less economic power. Even the Scottish-controlled multi-plant companies are smaller than the average English-controlled branch plant when measured in terms of employment, and also smaller than the externally-controlled multi-plant companies that have their 'operational' headquarters in Scotland. This suggests that the bigger the multi-plant company in Scotland, the more likely it is to be a subsidiary of an external group or company.

Apart from the impact of external control on non-branch enterprises, the influence of branch plants is also considerable. From Table 4 it can be seen that non-local branch plants as a whole employ over one quarter of the total manufacturing employment in Scotland. Of this, some 16.8 per cent (96,000 employees) are in branches of English companies, and 8.6 per cent in the Scottish branches of North American enterprises. However an even more interesting insight into the distribution of economic power within the UK can be had by looking at the regional location of the headquarters of the 318 branch plants operating in Scotland. No less than 184 of such headquarters are located in the South-East region of England (overwhelmingly in London), whilst a further 32 have headquarters located in the West Midlands; 30 in the North-West region; and 28 in Yorkshire and Humberside. If these figures demonstrate the monocentricity of the UK, it is even more sharply demonstrated by examining the regional location of ultimate control of all plants operating in Scotland, for 398 of the 422 controlling enterprises involved are located in the South-East region of the United Kingdom.

4 Location of ultimate control of Scottish manufacturing employment by Type of Plant: 1973

Location of Ultimate Control	SINGLE PLANT COMPANIES			MULTI-PLANT COMPANIES WITH SCOTTISH HEADQUARTERS			BRANCH PLANTS		
	Emp	Plants	Average Size	Emp	Plants	Average Size	Emp	Plants	Average Size
Scotland	167,510	1,985	84.4	75.930	191	397.5	—	—	—
England	97,120	369	263.2	41,270	50	825.4	96,600	221	437.1
Rest of UK	90	3	30.0	—	—	—	70	1	70.0
EEC	4,530	18	251.6	2,140	3	713.3	2,090	8	261.2
Other Europe	890	8	111.2	—	—	—	2,910	7	415.7
North America	19,060	64	297.8	17,550	14	1253.6	51,120	70	730.3
Other	255	3	85.0	—	—	—	115	2	57.5
Joint-owned	3,320	14	237.1	850	1	850.0	7,280	9	808.9
Total	292,775	2,464	118.8	137,740	259	531.8	160,185	318	
Percentage Distribution	49.5	81.0	—	23.3	8.5	—	27.2	10.5	503.7

The evidence from Table 4 seems to confirm the earlier assertions that Scotland has been slowly developing a 'branch plant and subsidiary' economy, at least with regard to its industrial structure. Such a development should not of itself be held to be totally contrary to Scotland's economic interests, for it could reflect a much-needed inflow of capital into slow-growing Scottish companies, with little real effect on the autonomy of the enterprises concerned. Further, the take-over of ailing Scottish enterprises by external companies might in many cases be the only alternative to their having to close, with the consequent loss of employment opportunities. Yet the dominance of branch plants is probably a more worrying aspect of external control, and it would seem to suggest that there has been a gradual erosion of decision-making from the Scottish economy. Recent research into multi-company organisation would seem to indicate that this trend is unlikely to be reversed.

v. External Control and Industrial Sectors:

If the external control situation is examined for each of the main industrial sectors (Table 5) then it can be seen that the proportion of employment in each sector that is indigenously controlled within Scotland varies from a remarkably low 7.8 per cent in electrical engineering: 9.8 per cent in vehicles; and 11.8 per cent in chemicals to over 80 per cent in both the leather and timber sectors. In only five of the sectors does Scottish-controlled employment dominate, whereas in seven of the sectors English-controlled enterprises are the major force, with North American enterprises overshadowing both in instrument engineering, a sector which during the 1960s has been the key sector in terms of technological advance. Although such results have great importance for our understanding of the development of the Scottish economy, the analysis ideally needs to be undertaken at a much more refined level, and plans are underway to do this.

However, one very marked feature which does emerge at the broad industrial sector level is the relationship between the growth of output in each sector and the amount of external control. If the growth of output of each sector in the UK over the period 1963-1973 is taken as a fair measure of the overall growth of a sector, then a highly significant statistical relationship emerges: namely, the faster the growth of the sector, the higher the proportion of that sector's employment in Scotland that is externally-controlled.(16) Even more startling is the fact that the level of Scottish control in the five fastest-growing sectors is only some 13.5 per cent of total employment in these sectors in Scotland.

5 Location of ultimate ownership of Scottish manufacturing employment by major industrial sector: 1973

	Scotland	England	Rest of UK	EEC	Other Europe	North America	Other	Joint-owned	Total
	%	%	%	%	%	%	%	%	%
03 Food, drink and tobacco	48.3	44.5	—	0.2	1.3	5.7	—	—	100.0
04 Coal and petroleum products	15.4	80.2	—	—	—	—	—	4.4	100.0
05 Chemicals and allied industries	11.8	63.2	—	2.9	7.8	12.1	0.3	1.9	100.0
06 Metal manufacture	18.3	70.3	0.1	—	—	2.2	—	9.1	100.0
07 Mechanical engineering	39.0	29.2	—	1.1	0.7	29.3	0.4	0.3	100.0
08 Instrument engineering	16.9	21.1	—	—	—	60.7	—	1.3	100.0
09 Electrical engineering	7.8	52.4	—	8.3	—	31.4	—	0.1	100.0
10 Shipbuilding and marine engineering	53.3	29.8	—	—	—	11.8	—	5.1	100.0
11 Vehicles	9.8	53.3	—	—	0.5	36.4	—	—	100.0
12 Other metal goods	58.6	25.2	—	0.3	0.1	10.9	0.1	4.8	100.0
13 Textiles	64.2	28.8	—	3.6	—	3.0	—	0.4	100.0
14 Leather, leather goods and fur	88.0	12.0	—	—	—	—	—	—	100.0
15 Clothing and footwear	48.2	37.7	0.3	—	—	13.8	—	—	100.0
16 Bricks, pottery, cement etc.	37.1	48.1	—	—	—	1.2	—	13.6	100.0
17 Timber, furniture etc.	87.2	12.4	—	—	—	0.4	—	—	100.0
18 Paper printing and publishing	55.0	39.4	—	0.4	0.4	2.5	—	2.3	100.0
19 Other manufacturing industries	28.4	43.2	—	1.3	0.2	26.1	—	0.8	100.0
Total manufacturing industries	41.2	39.8	—	1.5	0.6	14.9	0.1	1.9	100.0

There is also some indication that if the individual enterprises are weighted by an output growth index, then the controlled plants have a lower net output per employee than those of the external enterprises. However, such findings say nothing about the real relative productivity of the domestic and external sectors, and one would anyway expect a higher level of external achievement in the faster-growing sectors, in that it is precisely these sectors that have been generating the new employment opportunities in Britain during the post-war period and which have been major contributors to the movement of jobs to the regions. Because of this, it cannot be argued that such enterprises that have established themselves in Scotland have had unwelcome effects, for they have undoubtedly brought with them new products, processes and technologies that might not have been developed indigenously. What is of importance from the point of view of long-term regional development is whether such innovations have been transferred to the domestic sector or whether they have been retained within the external enterprises.

vi. Intra-regional distribution of External Control:

Finally there is the question as to whether such external-control is evenly distributed within Scotland, or whether there are some sub-regions which are more heavily dependent upon decisions made elsewhere than others. The evidence on this so far is not complete, and analysis is still proceeding. But preliminary figures do seem to show that there are substantial differences in the degree to which industry is controlled domestically, ranging from 36 per cent in the Glasgow Region to 55 per cent in the Highlands. However, it is as yet unclear whether such differences are a function of the industrial composition of the regions in terms of the sectoral distribution of their employment, and the size and organisational type of firms involved.

6 Percentage location of ultimate ownership of Scottish manufacturing
employment by planning region: 1973

Location of ultimate ownership	Glasgow	Edinburgh	Tayside	North-East	Falkirk Stirling	Borders	South-West	Highlands & Islands	Scotland
Scotland	36.2	48.1	55.3	51.1	37.6	39.1	37.6	55.4	41.2
England	42.5	39.6	18.6	38.9	42.0	53.7	53.3	19.7	39.8
Rest of UK	—	—	—	—	—	—	—	0.7	—
EEC	2.0	1.0	—	—	2.1	2.6	—	—	1.5
Other Europe	0.7	—	0.8	1.8	0.8	—	1.9	1.0	0.6
North America	16.7	10.5	24.2	7.0	9.9	4.5	7.2	17.5	14.9
Other	—	—	0.3	—	—	—	—	—	0.1
Joint-owned	2.0	0.7	0.8	1.2	7.6	—	—	5.7	1.9
Total	100.0	100.0	100.0	100.0	100.0	100.0	100.0	100.0	100.0
Total numbers	338,510	98,485	49,290	35.300	34,885	15,865	7,485	10,880	590,700
Percent distribution	57.3	16.7	8.3	6.0	5.9	2.7	1.3	1.8	100.0

It should be stressed once again, that the above dimensions of external-control are very much preliminary, and a much greater amount of analysis needs to be undertaken to uncover the complete pattern of external-control. Yet it cannot be disputed that the results do have important implications for regional theory and regional policy, and thus it is worth simply listing the main findings once again.

1. Only 41 per cent of manufacturing employment in Scotland is controlled internally.
2. The larger the enterprise, the more likely it is to be controlled externally.
3. Over one quarter of total manufacturing employment is in non-local branch plants.
4. 110 enterprises account for 46 per cent of total manufacturing employment.

5. The faster growing the sector the lower is the amount of Scottish participation.
6. The five fastest growing sectors have less than 14 per cent indigenous control.

No matter what the more detailed plant-level studies reveal, the above all add up to an unenviable position for a region to find itself in. Yet, we have no means of knowing whether this situation is unique in terms of regional development, although at a national level—and one should perhaps state here that there are people who regard Scotland as a nation—the experiences of such as Australia, New Zealand and more importantly, Canada do offer possible grounds for comparison. If the problems of foreign ownership in developing countries are excluded as so untypical, then perhaps Canada offers the closest and most useful comparision, for, like Scotland, it shares a common land frontier with a dominant neighbour of about the same relative magnitude. However, unlike a UK region, Canada does have a much greater degree of economic sovereignty, and thus the analogy cannot be taken too far, in that Canada can introduce legislation to control and direct foreign investment in Canada. What is interesting is that the element of external control in the Canadian economy is somewhat similar to that existing in Scotland, and thus the recent Canadian Government investigation into foreign investment in Canada, (the Gray Report) could be profitably examined in the context of regional development.(17) This paper is not the place to do so, but it should be noted that the Gray Report considered the foreign investment situation to be serious enough to require legislation. The British equivalent, namely the report to Steuer et al. for the DTI in 1973, did little analysis on the regional impact of foreign investment, except for a rather disastrous survey of the impact of foreign investment on a labour market in the   West of Scotland, which is well known to be atypical(18). Certainly, the fact that the latest data it had access to was that for 1963 gives little confidence in its bland assurances that there are no real problems at the regional level with foreign investment, provided that the interests of existing firms are safeguarded. Of course, the Steuer investigation confined itself to external control defined as being in non-UK firms, and as we have seen this is the less important of the two categories of external control that we have discussed.

5. The Growth of External Control

So far very little is known about the ways in which the current situation in Scotland has developed, nor even about the relative contribution of the various components involved. Rather haphazard evidence suggests that the impact of mergers and takeovers involving external enterprise might be important, though confirmation of this will have to wait until the results of an associated study are completed. We noted earlier that differential expansion between the domestic and external sectors does not seem to have been very important, if the evidence from West Central Scotland is anything to go by (see footnote 9), and thus we are forced to the (premature) conclusion that the major factors involved have been the different rates of closure and of establishment formation in the two sectors, and specifically, the extremely low rate of new enterprise formation by native Scottish entrepreneurs. This then, would seem to be the key area for future detailed investigation and for policy responses, and it is this precise area that is currently occupying the attention of a major SSRC sponsored research project at Glasgow University. The fact that regional growth and change has not been adequately monitored in the past in Britain, either by the government departments most directly involved or by others such as universities, is perhaps one major reason why the current high level of external control has suddenly emerged as an area of concern.

From the time that the first steps in regional economic policy were taken in Britain under the Special Areas legislation of 1934 until the Industry Act of 1972, the major objective of policy-makers was to encourage the inter-regional mobility of manufacturing plants, using a mixture of carrot and stick techniques. Throughout the whole of this period, comparatively little attention was paid to assisting enterprises already established in the depressed regions and consequently the balance was very much against indigenous enterprise. However, this balance has theoretically been removed with the introduction of the Industry Act of 1972, which gives the Department of Industry very wide powers to assist indigenous industry, and even take equity or encourage mergers. It remains, however, to be seen whether such powers will be used: they certainly have not been so far.

6. The Problems of External Control

The relative absence of previous research into the effects of external control on regional growth means that much of what follows must be considered as speculative hypotheses, all of which cry out for detailed investigation, and all of which will, it is hoped be investigated in the near future.

The major problem with a regional economy that is dominated by externally-controlled enterprises is probably that of the changing balance between innovative, enterpreneurial-type decision making and routine management-type supervision. When major decisions, on such as investment, sales or purchasing are made elsewhere, the plant managers in the regional subsidiaries or branch-plants are reduced merely to what Banmol call "competent calculating machines". Thus much of the drive, enthusiasm and invention that lies at the heart of economic growth is removed, or at best suppressed. Further, when the sales function is centralised, as it is in most major companies, in an environment which is separated both spatially and in terms of organisation from the operating plants, then not only is the competitive element of winning orders removed from the regional plants, it is also possible to be left depending upon what can be termed "allocated growth". This simply means that in a multi-plant company, production or orders are allocated from a central office function, and this in turn puts the onus on the actual production units to achieve good levels of operational efficiency, but yet without it having its efficiency tested in a market environment.

It is also probable that a region that is dominated by branch plants is unlikely to have a large research and development (R & D) component. Research on this aspect has borne such an assertion out, and Scotland has been shown to have a very low R & D component indeed.(19) Thus one would expect that the region will not be a leader in developing new products, processes and technologies, which in turn suggests that innovation will not be a major force in the local economy, which further implies that there will not be a substantial development of new enterprises or of growth within existing enterprises, with the final result being an increased requirement of regional assistance in the future. If this requirement is fulfilled by attracting in further branches or subsidiaries which which have purely manufacturing activities, the vicious circle is set off once again. This again is a major area requiring research, for there are many important questions that are requiring answers.

There is also the likelihood that such a high degree of external control will express itself in terms of producing a very open regional economy, with a high degree of integration with other economic systems. In the the case of Scotland, we know that many of the branches and subsidiaries located in Scotland, purchase most of their requirements from outside Scotland,(20) and while some of these in turn sell most of their output within Scotland, any balance achieved is remitted to the parent plant in the form of interest, profits and dividends. Thus one can expect to find relatively large flows on both the visibles and invisibles account between Scotland and elsewhere, a situation which would make it almost impossible for an independent Scottish government to run an independent economic policy. It also implies that economic fluctuations are transmitted into the Scottish economy relatively quickly, and the large American component in Scottish manufacturing has been a prime point of entry for externally generated economic fluctuations. This particular sector of external control was perhaps the major cause of the big down-turn that Scottish manufacturing industry faced in 1970-71(21), and this situation is also harder to identify let alone control as international trade increasingly becomes a matter not just of trade between large multi-national companies, but of trade between the different operating units **within** multi-national enterprises.(22)

The final problem of external control that will be discussed here is that concerning the type of personnel employed in many of the new external plants that have set up in Scotland during the last twenty years, and which now occupy a dominant place in the Scottish economy, and under this heading it would seem that there are two possible causes for concern. Firstly, because of the large element of branch plants present, there have been very few senior management and professional jobs created per '000 employees. Therefore, young Scottish professionals wishing to enter companies at middle management levels are increasingly forced to leave Scotland thus reducing the potential pool of entrepreneurs, for it is out of this type of occupation that the majority of the founders of new enterprises emerge. Secondly, there seems to have been a mis-match in terms of the male-female ratio between the jobs that have been lost to the region, and those that have replaced them in new enterprises, at least if the experience of West Central Scotland is anything to go by.(23) The nature of new jobs provided by external plants has been principally orientated towards female, semi-skilled assembly operations in such as electronics plants, whereas the jobs lost have been mainly of male, highly-paid craftsmen. Almost certainly, therefore, there has been a net wage-reduction per new job provided, as well as an element of deskilling, but this assertion remains to be proved. What is certain, however, is that the problems attached to external control do require further research, and most importantly of all, a larger measure of quantification.

There can be no doubt, however, that there are advantages connected with external control also, though like the disadvantages, they remain to be provided. First and foremost, non-local enterprises have provided a large number of jobs in Scotland, and in fact, although the jobs might be slightly lower-paid than those they are replacing, they have had so far a greater degree of security and permanence, which is a very important factor in an area such as West Central Scotland where long-term job permanence has perhaps been the exception rather than the rule. External control has also allowed access to larger sources of intra-company finance, to improved management techniques, to advanced technology, and to larger markets, and therefore, very real benefits have been gained. But, as with so many of the other aspects examined in this paper, a detailed study at the level of the individual firm would be required before one could come to any approximation of the costs and benefits of such a large degree of external control.

7. General Conclusions

A substantial amount of further investigation and research is required before the total dimensions and full implications of the situation outlined above can be understood. Such research will not be easy, and will demand a high degree of caution given that the factors determining the development and impact of external control on the Scottish economy are not only exceedingly complex from an economic point of view, but also involve areas of distinct commercial and political sensitivity. Yet the scale and speed of the economic and political changes that currently confront Scotland argue strongly for a high degree of priority and urgency to be given to such research, without which policy formulation will remain a desperately uncertain matter. Even at the present early stages of research, some general points can be made.

Firstly, it cannot be denied that even at the broad level of the results reported above, the factor of external control is an important element in the current debate about Scotland's long-term economic potential and therefore, one which must be taken into account in the preparation of future economic and political strategies.

The central point is that it is no longer possible to assume that the majority of the important strategic decisions shaping the future course of development of the manufacturing sector in Scotland, and especially those made for the important high-technology sectors such as electronics and chemicals, are made within Scotland or indeed are made with Scottish interests predominantly in mind. In large areas of the economy decision-making is being steadily superseded by decision-taking, and this is true for both the public and the private sectors. In turn this means that the power of Scotland to shape or even strongly influence her own economic future has been, is being, and probably will continue to be, strongly eroded. Indeed, it is becoming difficult to talk meaningfully of a distinct 'Scottish Economy' except in a strict geographical sense. Instead, one is seeing the development of increasingly strong links with the world economic system, although these links are often hidden within the global operations of the multinational parent companies of Scottish subsidiaries and branch plants. Thus the old trading ties between Scottish companies and their overseas customers are steadily being replaced by more sophisticated and largely uncharted relationships lying within multinational companies. This in turn raises very substantial problems for those trying to produce estimates of the Scottish balances of trade and payments, in that intra-company flows of goods, services and payments—especially if accompanied by such as transfer-pricing of imports and exports—may well distort the actual flows.

It is also likely that past attempts to solve Scotland's economic problems have unwittingly reinforced the trends towards a higher level of external control. The continued emphasis upon attracting the mobile branch and subsidiary plants from elsewhere in the UK and overseas, whilst neglecting the possibilities of encouraging indigenous enterprise is probably not in Scotland's best long-term interests—nor indeed would it be in the interests of any area or nation faced with similar types of economic decline or stagnation. If one takes as a reasonable objective for regional policy the simple criterion that no policy should be employed that results in the need for continued and often stronger policy measures in the future, then it would seem that the past policy measures and packages have not been an optimal policy-mix from the point of view of encouraging greater self-sufficiency in the Scottish economy, and therefore a growing independence of regional aid. This in turn reflects the relative poverty of much of past and indeed current regional economic development theory, as well as a lack of industrial expertise in many of the governmental agencies responsible for regional development in the United Kingdom. It also indicates that those responsible for the development of policies have not really thought through the long-term consequences of their recommendations. One of the saddest sights in postwar Scotland has been the continual emphasis on attracting external enterprise to locate in Scotland, while domestic enterprises have literally withered from neglect. Yet this dilemma is one which is only now beginning to be appreciated by those responsible for promoting industrial development in Scotland.

Although it is as yet too early to discuss the long-term implications of a high level of external control for the Scottish economy, it does already seem as if the levels reached are sufficiently high as to warrent concern, and to require some remedial action. The Steuer report, whilst finding it hard to place an upper limit on the desired amount of foreign direct investment in the United Kingdom, was sympathetic to the idea of having some overall limit, and noted that as 'the foreign proportion gets higher, say, over twenty per cent, the non-economic drawbacks may become more important.'(24) As the Scottish proportion defined on a broader basis is nearly three times as great, then it would seem that the time is rapidly approaching when this issue will have to be confronted and policy measures to tackle the problems outlined in this paper devised.

It is also clear that neither political devolution nor indeed political independence for Scotland will **in themselves** solve the basic problems associated with a large degree of external involvement in the Scottish economy. However, they very probably will produce the conditions necessary for a reappraisal of economic policies stemming from a greater awareness of the current situation. With one or two notable exceptions, the current debate on devolution and independence has not really confronted the basic economic problems facing Scotland, and thus the advent of oil has come to be seen as the easy solution to our economic difficulties. The hard economic fact is that the discovery and exploitation of oil and gas is not going to solve Scotland's long term industrial problems unless a very carefully thought-out economic strategy is evolved and applied. At the centre of such a strategy there will need to be investment of substantial sums of both public and private sector resources, with the balance probably lying in favour of the former. This in turn argues for some degree of Scottish involvement in the revenues stemming from the North Sea and offshore oil and gas resources. Experience has shown that the past degree of regional financial assistance made available to Scotland has been too small to make a definite impact, and indeed it has been another example of too little, too late.

The sheer size of the oil and gas revenues, even given a relative fall in future oil and gas prices, does give Scotland the opportunity to fundamentally restructure her economy towards the industries and occupations of the post-oil era, and thus become less dependent upon other areas for her prosperity. The degree and type of involvement in the oil and gas revenues will almost certainly become the central issue in the political debate about the future status of Scotland. What is already clear is that the past debates about such as Scottish budgets, or the economics of independence, or indeed the economics of the Kilbrandon Report, are totally irrelevant to the current situation, though interesting in an historical sense.

8. Policy Conclusions

Perhaps the easiest conclusion is that the one policy that is not required is that of having no policy at all, either for economic development in general or towards external ownership in particular. In retrospect, Scotland has suffered badly from the absence of economic policies designed to confront the economic problems present in Scotland, and thus it has been assumed that the policies applied at the United Kingdom level would be sufficient to solve Scotland's problems. Even where distinctly Scottish policy documents have been prepared, as in the White Papers of 1963 and 1966, the emphasis has been heavily on physical rather than on economic planning and policy, and indeed, in the latter area the degree of economic sophistication has been notable by its absence.

Therefore, the first requirement is the establishment of much greater economic—and especially much greater industrial and financial expertise, in Scottish Government departments. Ideally this requires the formation of such as a Department or Ministry of Economic Development, but this is not the place to discuss the type of government institutions that will be required in the future. One of the major functions of such a Department would be the monitoring of economic change taking place in Scotland, and this in turn requires much better economic information to be made available than has been the case so far. It might well be necessary, for example, to insist that all enterprises operating in Scotland keep proper records of their financial and physical activities rather than the cursitory returns which many of them submit at present.

Moreover, it is essential that government attention be brought to bear upon the impact upon Scotland of the growing concentration of economic power that is taking place in United Kingdom industry generally. This is an area which as yet has not been seen as part of the remit of the Monopolies Commission, concerned as it is with the development of Sectoral and financial monopolies rather than with the spatial impacts of such trends. Yet there can be no doubt that the merger and take-over operations by the larger UK and foreign holding companies have been a major cause of the growth of a high level of external control in Scottish manufacturing during the late 1950s and the 1960s. Thus, for instance, by mid-1974, the top 20 UK holding companies which were listed as being prime nationalisation targets by Tony Wedgewood-Benn—none of which incidently, had Scottish headquarters—owned over 150 subsidiaries and branch plants in Scotland, employing some 55,000 persons and producing a substantial proportion of total Scottish output. Whether nationalisation—however defined—would have enhanced the Scottish connection of these companies has never been discussed.

This in turn raises the question of the degree of external control present in the public sector, again something that has not been examined in depth in the debates about devolution and independence that have taken place so far. Certainly there is a good case for taking a public stake (perhaps extending to outright control) in many of the industrial sectors in Britain, especially where the sectors are effectively dominated by a small number of large firms, such as in the aircraft and motor vehicles sectors. But it remains to be seen whether such public sector intervention will conflict with Scottish demands for greater devolution of economic and industrial powers. In some cases, there are sound reasons for establishing separate Scottish public sector corporations, as in Steel and shipbuilding, and perhaps with some reorganisation, motor vehicles. The current proposals for a Scottish Development Agency do not so far seem to have faced up to the issues raised by any extension of the public sector either in the UK generally or in Scotland in particular, neither does the thinking so far reveal any great understanding of the important economic questions raised by the existence of a Scottish manufacturing sector heavily dominated by outside interests.

The oil and gas revenues in the context of the above discussion thus assume an especial economic importance, in that they could provide the scale of funds necessary to achieve some of the policies outlined above. But it must be once more stressed that they must be employed in the framework of a long-term dynamic economic strategy for Scotland, in which the problem of external control is only one of the elements, albeit an important one. The time left to solve Scotland's basic economic problems is short, and therefore both research and debate about the impact of a large degree of external control and possible policy measures to counteract such impacts need to take place now. It is to be hoped that this initial attempt to foster such a reappraisal will be seen as worthwhile.

Note:

An earlier version of this paper was given to the Northwest European Regional Science Association Conference at Louvain-La-Neuve, Belgium, in May 1974. Part of the research discussed above was supported by the Social Science Research Council, and part by **The Scotsman**. I would like to thank the Scottish Council (Development and Industry) for providing the original data and Jean Verth and Marion Firn for technical assisstance. A more detailed analysis of the results of the study of external ownership will be published during the coming year.

1. For a detailed analysis of both regional economic problems and policies in Britain, see: A.J. Brown, **The Framework of Regional Economics in the United Kingdom,** (Cambridge: Cambridge University Press for the National Institute for Economic and Social Research, 1972): and more recently, the evidence given to the House of Commons enquiry into the operation of British regional policy, **Regional Development Incentives,** Report by the Trade and Industry Sub-Committee of the House of Commons Expenditure Committee, House of Commons Paper 85, Session 1973-74.

2. Two of my favourite articles which I think can be read with profit by many regional theorists are: Martin Shubik, 'A Curmudgeon's Guide to Microeconomics', **Journal of Economic Literature,** Vol.8, No.2, June 1970, pp.405-434, and Oskar Morgenstern, 'Thirteen Critical Points in Contemporary Economic Theory: An Interpretation', **Journal of Economic Literature,** Vol.10. No.4, December 1972, pp.1163-1189.

3. One of the best descriptions of the concepts underlying the economic transformation process can be found in Erik Dahmen, **Entrepreneurial Activity and the Development of Swedish Industry, 1919-1939,** (Homewood, Illinois: Richard D Irwin, Inc. for the American Economic Association, 1970), Chapter 4. Dahmen's work, originally published in 1950, is essential reading for applied economists wishing to understand the processes of economic change at the micro level. and deserves wider application in regional analysis.

4. Richard R. Nelson, 'Issues and Suggestions for the Study of Industrial Organization in a Regime of Rapid Technical Change', in Victor R. Fuchs, **Policy Issues and Research Opportunities in Industrial Organization,** (New York: National Bureau of Economic Research, 1972), p.40

5. The data used for the analysis of change in the Central Clydeside Conurbation consisted of over 3,500 manufacturing plants that employed 5 or over, and that were in existence at any time over the period 1.1.1958 to 31.12.1968. For a detailed description of the contents of the databank see John R. Firn, The Glasgow University Register of Industrial Establishments: Metropolitan Industrial Location Working Paper MIL 1.7 (Glasgow: 1970: mimeo).

6. For an analysis of the economic problems of West Central Scotland see: Gordon C. Cameron, 'Economic Analysis for a declining Urban Economy', **Scottish Journal of Political Economy,** Vol. 8, No. 3, November 1971 pp. 315-346.

7. The components of change on Clydeside over 1958-1968 are described in evidence to the House of Commons Select Committee on Regional Development Incentives, House of Commons Paper 85-1, Session 1973-74. pp. 707-708.

8. William J. Baumol, 'Entrepreneurship in Economic Theory', **American Economic Review,** Vol. LVIII, No.2, May 1968, pp.64-71. "The first order of business is an economy which exhibits very little business drive is presumably to induce the appearance of increased supplies of entrepreneurial skills which would then be let loose upon the area's industry", **op.cit.,** p.69. See also: John R. Firn, "Indigenous Growth and Regional Development: the experience and prospects for West Central Scotland", in University of Glasgow Urban and Regional Studies Discussion Papers, No.10, May, 1974.

9. During our analysis of employment change in manufacturing plants in the Central Clydeside Conurbation over 1958 to 1968, there was no difference at all in the growth and decline factors between the locally and externally controlled plants, and the similarity was statistically highly significant! However, the similarity vanishes when one adjusts for the different sectoral distribution of the local and external plans.

10. A.A. Berle and G Means, **The Modern Corporation and Private Property,** (London: Macmillan, 1932). See also C.S. Beed, 'The separation of ownership from control'. **Journal of**

Economic Studies, Vol.1, 1966, pp.29-46.

11. The potential impact of changing managerial techniques and strategies on regional branch-plants and subsidiaries can be seen from the more interesting work that has been done on the multinational enterprise. See, for example, Michael Z. Brooke & H. Lee Remmers, **The Strategy of Multinational Enterprise: Organisation and Finance,** (London: Longman, 1970), especially chapters 3,4 and 12, and John M Stopford & Louis T Wells, Jr., **Managing the Multinational Enterprise: Organisation of the Firm and Ownership of the Subsidiaries,** (London: Longman, 1972), especially Chapter 8.

12. See my review of UK Regional Statistics in House of Commons Paper 85-1, Session 1973-74, pp.708-712.

13. It is interesting to reflect that when the main findings of the above research were first reported in the press in October 1973, the then Conservative Secretary of State for Scotland went to great pains to deny the main conclusions on external control. By May 1974, his Labour replacement was using the same conclusions in a number of major speeches as established facts.

14. A special word of acknowledgement is due to Miss May Sleigh of the Scottish Council (Development and Industry) Information Bank who has patiently and carefully compiled the basic statistics over a number of years. Without her: none of the above would have been possible.

15. M.D. Steuer et al, **The Impact of Foreign Direct Investment on the United Kingdom.** (London: HMSO for the Department of Trade and Industry, 1973), p.197, Table 10XIX.

16. The relationship between net output growth at the UK level and the percentage of the sector that is controlled in Scotland is one that will be explored in more detail later, but even at an aggregated level the relationship is statistically significant at 1 per cent.

17. See **Foreign Direct Investment in Canada. (Ottawa: Information Canada, 1972). In 1967.** the latest year for which statistics are available, 52 per cent of the total capital employed in Canadian manufacturing was owned externally, and 57 per cent externally controlled. **Op.cit.,** p.20. Although it is difficult to equate capital with employment, this overall picture seems to be fairly similar to that for Scotland. See also both: Pierre L Bourgault, **Innovation and the Structure of Canadian Industry,** Special Study No.23 for the Science Council of Canada, (Ottawa: Information Canada, 1972), and J Douglas Gibson, 'Canada's declaration of less dependance . **Harvard Business Review,** Vol.51, No.5, Sept.-Oct. 1973, pp.69-79.

18. M.D. Steuer, **op.cit.,** pp.104f.

19. Very little work has been done on the regional distribution of R & D in the UK, let alone on its importance in Scotland apart from: J.N. Wolfe, et.al,, Regional Aspects of Research and Development Policy., (Edinburgh: Scottish Office, 1970). Confidential and unpublished!

20. William F Lever, "Migrant Industry, demand linkages and the multiplier: some paradoxes in regional development", in University of Glasgow, Urban and Regional Studies Discussion Papers, No.10, May 1974.

21. A Hargrave, 'Feeling the chill of the US climate', **The Financial Times,** August 6th, 1970, p.12.

22. See W.M. Corden, 'The Multinational Corporation and International Trade Theory.' University of Reading Discussion Papers in International Investment and Business Studies. No.10, February, 1974.3. See House of Commons Paper 85-1. Session 1973-74, p.707, Table 3.

23. See House of Commons Paper 85-1. Session 1973-74, p.707, Table 3.

24. M.D. Steurer, **op.cit.,** pp. 14-15.

Finance Capital And The Upper Classes

John Scott
Michael Hughes

The debate on nationalism is in danger of concentrating too heavily upon the political and cultural issues, thereby clouding our view of the economic realities which constitute the environment of the Scottish political system.[1]

This paper attempts to penetrate some of the confusions in the current debate by focusing upon those economic institutions which form the framework within which any independent Scottish assembly will be located, and by which its effective decision making powers will be constrained. Scottish nationalism needs to face the underlying structures of economic power which dominate Scotland today and will dominate any future semi-autonomous region or separate Scottish nation-state.

We must, therefore, be concerned with the character of Scottish industrial and financial capital, and with studying their interpenetration through interlocking directorships and share-ownership.[2] The ownership and control of Scottish industrial, financial and mineral resources is of paramount importance to any consideration of 'devolution' and the political aspirations based in part upon the supposedly redemptive properties of North Sea oil.

We aim to discuss whether a Scottish assembly would constitute an effective redistribution of power and control, which would allow the ordinary people of Scotland to exercise control over the forces affecting their life chances, or whether devolution would constitute a massive deception in which those who gain are those at the top.

When we investigate the structure of the economic power base which is the foundation of the dominant class in capitalist society we realise that it is necessary to modify somewhat the very general and inaccurate assertion that it is the owners of the means of production who comprise the dominant class. In order to grasp the crucial role of this class we must recognise that the **control of significant quantities of capital** is basic. This is the real locus of economic power, and theories of class and class structure must take account of this. It is the control over the allocation and distribution of capital within the economy which distinguishes those who are dominant. It is not necessary to accept naive versions of elitist or managerial theories which do not take account of this central element of control over capital; nor must we fall into the trap of regarding **all** owners as members of the dominant class.

An important distinction must be made between what may be termed industrial capital and financial capital. This distinction was recognised by Marx, but was first systematically investigated by Lenin[3], who examined the trend towards concentration and combination in industrial capital and showed that the outcome of this process was the emergence of holding companies and the dominance of banking capital. Since Lenin wrote, these trends have progressed further and a whole variety of financial institutions have emerged. In an earlier paper we showed the interpenetration of industrial and financial capital in Scotland[4] and showed that finance capital, and in particular Edinburgh finance capital, was the dominant element in the Scottish upper class. In this paper we intend to examine more fully the nature of the financial elite and to discuss the ownership and control of finance capital in Scotland.

It has been proposed by Pahl and Winkler[5] that those who have the power to employ or withdraw capital, as opposed to those who merely have day-to-day use of capital, may be called "allocative institutions". The institutions of finace capital are allocative institutions **par excellence,** and financiers epitomise the allocative controllers.

With this perspective in mind, it is necessary to discuss who comprises the upper class in Scotland. A conventional answer might be that the components of the upper class are based upon landed and industrial property; a more sophisticated approach would add the 'financial bourgeoisie', or 'aristocracy of finance'[6]. This acknowledges the crucial role of capital as a source of independent social power and the important function of directors and managers of financial companies, thereby enabling us to grasp this thorny problem of the ownership and control of capital.[7] Our research has led us to the conclusion that this picture is rather more complex. The various bases of upper class economic power and the categories of individuals possessing the various economic resources are not distinct groups but interact in complex, overlapping circles.

Briefly, and simplifying considerably, it is possible to identify four categories of economic resources:

1. Shareholdings in public and private companies.
2. Directorships in public and private companies.
3. Executive positions in financial companies.
4. Landholdings.

In this presentation we are concerned mainly with members of the first three categories, and particularly those of the second and third which comprise the financial bourgeoisie. Although these groups are not totally distinct we can gain some insights from an analysis of shareholdings and directorships in industrial merchandising and financial companies.

The controllers of Scotland's allocative institutions may be seen as the focus of what Poulantzas[8] has referred to as the 'interior bourgeoisie'. They are that group which is in control of a satellite economy and which have multiple links of dependence with the metropolitan economy. Such a group emerges as a result of the internationalisation of capital and possesses its own economic base and its own basis of capital accumulation. However, owing to their relation of dependence with English and American capital, the interior bourgeoisie are unable to exercise any effective autonomy or independence. The limits and constraints upon their economic autonomy are set by the environment of international capital within which they operate.

Clearly, the prospects of an independent Scotland depend upon the position of this group and their likely role in the future. This paper aims to outline their position as shareholders, directors and executives, in short as allocative controllers, in the Scottish economy and to discuss some prospects for the future.

The Structure of Ownership

In order to discover the pattern of ownership and the relative importance of the various types of economic power an analysis of the ownership of company ordinary share capital is necessary. Studies by Revell and Moyle at Cambridge University show that whilst large quantities of ordinary shares are held by individual persons, these holdings are spread very widely amongst a large number of individuals. Table I shows a comparison of personal and institutional beneficial ownership of ordinary share capital in British industry.

Table I

BENEFICIAL OWNERSHIP OF BRITISH INDUSTRY[9]

	% of market value held		
	1957	1963	1970
Persons, Executors and Trustees	66	54	47
Insurance companies	9	10	12
Pension funds	3	6	9
Investment trust companies	5	7	8
Unit trusts	1	1	3
All Institutions	18	24	32

Thus, the large institutional holders, which today account for a third of all quoted shares, are potentially in a position of effective control. Moreover, institutions are often the single largest holders of a particular company's shares and are, therefore, in a position to influence policy through representation on their boards of directors.[10]

Whilst personal shareholdings have fallen by more than a third in the thirteen years covered by the table, institutional holdings have almost doubled in the same period. The fastest growing groups are the pension fund and unit trusts, both of which have tripled their percentage of the market value; insurance companies have increased their share by a third and investment trusts by a half. The situation in Scotland is somewhat different from this overall picture, although a comparison between England and Scotland is rather difficult since the latest of the Cambridge studies did not carry out a full analysis of beneficial ownership in Scotland. However, some important conclusions can be drawn on the basis of figures for registered ownership.[11] Table II gives some figures for registered shareholdings in 1970.

Before interpreting these figures some remarks must be made about the 'nominee' and 'non-financial companies' entries. Banks and other organisations operate nominee companies in whose name shares may be registered to meet legal requirements (as in the case of unit trusts), as a matter of convenience (as in the case of small investors and some investment trusts), or to prevent disclosure of the identity of the beneficial owner (as in the 'warehousing' of shares prior to a take-over). Revell's 1963 study carried out an analysis of the categories of beneficial ownership into which nominee holdings fell, and it was discovered that whilst in England nominees often held shares for pension funds, in Scotland they were more likely to be holding them for investment trusts. For example, London clearing banks held shares in the proportion of 21% for pension funds. 19% for investment trusts and 2% for insurance companies, whilst Scottish bank nominees held 7% for pension funds, 38% for investment trusts, and 12% for insurance companies.[13] Thus, an analysis of Scottish **beneficial** holdings in British industry would have to inflate the figures given in Table II for investment trust companies. As an example of the importance of this, the large Dundee investment trusts, The Alliance Trust Company and The Second Alliance Trust Company, do not register any share in their own name, but always use nominees.

The entry for non-financial companies shows a substantially higher figure for Scotland than for all holdings, but this can be explained by the operation of only two companies. 80% of the entry is Burmah Oil's quarter holding in British Petroleum which had a market value of £42m in 1970.

much of the remainder is Thomson Scottish Associates' two-thirds holding in The Thomson Organisation. If these two firms are excluded the Scottish figure reduces to about 1%, and this is lower than the overall figure.

Two further points may be made about the character of Scottish shareholdings. Firstly, as compared with English holders, Scots prefer large companies; over 90% of the market value of Scottish holdings is in the 400 largest British companies.[14] Secondly, Scottish holders have a preference for investing in Scottish registered companies; Scottish personal holdings account for 28% of the market value of the top 18 Scottish companies and Scots hold only 8% of the market value of the remaining 290 top British companies.[15] Thus, the Scottish holdings set out in Table II can, to some extent, be seen as showing Scottish investment in large Scottish companies.

Table II

REGISTERED OWNERS OF BRITISH INDUSTRY, 1970[12]

		% of market value held
	Scottish	All holdings
Persons	53.7	46.2
Insurance companies	4.4	10.6
Pension funds	0.4	4.9
Investment trust companies	4.5	4.2
Nominees	16.4	19.8
Banks	0.8	1.4
Non-financial companies	18.9	3.9
Other	0.9	9.0
	100.0	100.0

It can be seen from Table II that, whilst Scottish shareholdings in British industry reflect the overall balance between personal and institutional holdings, there are significant differences in the kind of institutions which are important to shareholding. In Scotland, the proportion of British industry held by insurance companies and pension funds is considerably lower than the figure for all holdings, and, if our discussion of nominee holdings is taken into account, this difference would be enlarged and the importance of Scottish investment trust companies becomes more apparent. Thus, two important conclusions emerge:

1. **Institutions** rather than individuals own the controlling shareholdings in British companies.

2. **Investment trust companies** in Scotland account for significant holdings, whereas in Britain as a whole, insurance companies and pension funds are the most important institutional holders.

Both conclusions point to the central role of the executives and directors of the financial institutions, who comprise the dominant element in the upper class in Scotland. It is therefore worthwhile discussing these people and the kinds of financial institutions with which they are associated.

173

Banks and Bankers[16]

This sector of the upper class is concerned with providing, directly or indirectly, money and credit for industrial investment. Bankers, more than other groups, epitomise the middle-man role of financiers—they neither risk their own capital nor engage directly in production. But, through their control over economic resources and their network of contacts, they significantly effect the pattern of production within the economy as a whole.

The situation in Scotland is somewhat different from the rest of Britain in several respects. There is no central bank in Scotland, i.e. no equivalent of the Bank of England, and for this reason the three commercial banks issue their own bank notes. The first Scottish joint-stock bank, the Bank of Scotland was established in 1695, primarily to promote trade, and the branch system it developed was adopted by other banks. The close and long-standing association between banking capital and the Scottish economy enabled the banks to retain their important position in the Scottish economy until the quite recent expansion of the penetration by the English banking system which reduced the number of Scottish banks and forced the remaining ones to merge.[17] There remain only two significantly Scottish-owned banks: The National & Commercial Banking Group and The Bank of Scotland.[18]

Table 111

STRUCTURE OF SCOTTISH BANKING 1969[19]

	Capital and Reserves	Deposits	Advances	Branches
	£m	£m	£m	
Bank of Scotland		302	142	351
British Linen		144	64	197
Combined Total	28	446	206	548
Royal Bank		187	87	224
National Commercial		324	155	363
Combined Total	30	505	242	587
Clydesdale	13	267	97	350
Overall Total	71	1218	545	1485

Table III shows that the Scottish Commercial banks provide considerable capital for 'local' use—but this is relatively short-term capital lending. For long-term capital Scotland was, and probably still is, a net importer, although this is not possible to assess accurately.[20] Until very recently Scotland had only two relatively small and inactive Merchant Banks, both based in Glasgow[21] This situation has changed rapidly, expanding both the interests of English and Scottish capital, now that "new" opportunities have been realised in Scotland.[22] The British Bank of Commerce was enlarged in 1960 in association with Samuel Montague & Co., and in 1964 Glasgow Industrial Finance was taken over by the Industrial and Commercial Finance Corporation.[23] But perhaps the most significant changes have been the founding of two new Merchant Banks by Scottish investment trusts, demonstrating the response by the 'interior bourgeoisie' to the shift in relations between Scotland and England over the exploitation of natural resources, and its political repercussions in the form of a growing sensitivity to nationalism.

In 1963 Edward Bates,[24] owned by Scottish investment trusts, was set up and was followed by Noble Grossart[25] in 1969. Together, these recently formed banks have quickly taken an interest in North Sea Oil. Pict Petroleum[26] was set up by Noble Grossart as an oil exploration company and was backed by 29 Scottish financial firms (including the major shareholders of Noble Grossart);

the firm intends to convert into a full time oil company something like a mini Burmah Oil. Three groups of fund managers hold, between their trusts, in the region of a third of Pict's capital. On similar lines Edward Bates has set up Caledonian Offshore as an exploration company in which the investment trusts managed by **Ivory & Sime** have a significant stake. Both banks, along with **Ivory & Sime**, floated North Sea Assets, which operates in the supply and service sector of the North Sea operations rather than exploration, and which seeks significant minority holdings in companies.

This recent and dynamic sector of Scottish capital is an excellent illustration of the close co-operation and integration of the Scottish financial elite and of the significance of investment trusts in the expansion and sophistication of Scottish capital.

Insurance Men and Money

Through the medium of the insurance companies the resources of a large number of policy-holders are channelled into profitable and secure ventures. With the growth of pension funds the insurance men are increasingly directing industrial wealth from one part of the economy to another. In Britain as a whole they are of major importance as large investors of funds; in 1968 their assets totalled £15,000m. Scotland has a significant number of large life assurance companies which are shown in Table IV.

Table IV

SCOTTISH INSURANCE CO. (LIFE) IN BRITAIN'S TOP 50[27]

Rank	Name	Life etc. funds (£000)
3	Standard Life	982,127
11	Scottish Widows	477,573
14	General Accident Fire & Life	337,559
18	Scottish Amicable	284,205
23	Scottish Provident Institution	173,251

In 1969 the assets of Scottish Life companies totalled £1,825m (one-eighth of all British insurance company funds) and they hold considerable numbers of shares in investment trusts. The Scottish investment trusts themselves are far more heavily committed to the shares of insurance companies than are the English investment trusts. In this way the Scottish investment trusts exhibit an indirect hand in the vast institutional funds of the British insurance companies.

Investment Trusts and Fund Managers

The men who control the investment trust companies perform a similar function to the insurance men, but are more willing to engage in large holdings in risky ventures, and to take a controlling say in the running of businesses. Investment trust companies may be autonomous, and employ their own executives, but they are increasingly forming tightly knit groups with a common professional investment management.[28] These managers were originally firms of lawyers or accountants but are now increasingly specialised companies staffed by legal, financial and accounting experts.

Scottish investment trusts are the single most important source of institutional finance amongst Scottish shareholders, and in Britain as a whole they control a large part of national investment trust funds. Figures for 1972 show that 22 of the Scottish investment trusts (almost half of the total number in Scotland) were amongst the top 50 British investment trusts. 19 of these Scottish trusts had portfolios of over £50m in 1972. These figures are incomplete, but an analysis of 1968-9 data, for which there are comparative figures with England, shows that the Scottish investment trusts are relatively much larger, having an average portfolio of £33.4m compared with the British average of £26.2m (see Table V)

Table V

SCOTTISH AND U.K. INVESTMENT TRUSTS IN 1969[29]

Portfolio £m	SCOTLAND No.	% of Total	U.K. No.	% of Total
0.20	25	49.0	119	60.7
20-40	9	17.6	37	18.9
40-60	8	15.7	21	10.7
60-80	6	11.8	9	4.6
80-100	1	2.0	2	1.0
100 or over	2	3.9	8	4.1
Total	51		196	

The 196 British investment trusts had holdings valued at £5,134.7m in 1969; one third of this, £1,105.1m, was held by Scottish trusts. These Scottish investments tend to be spread over a wide range of securities and trust companies tend not to be over-involved in one company, group of companies, or industrial sector and have traditionally been heavily committed to North America. In 1968, 37% of Scottish investment trust portfolios were holdings in American stocks and shares, compared with a dollar portfolio for all British investment trusts of 31% In recent years, however, there are some signs of change here, as we have shown: for example, Atlantic Assets, the Edinburgh trust company, played a large part in the flotation of Edward Bates, the merchant banking company, and still has a large holding. In addition, a number of investment trusts are increasingly willing to take significant holdings in companies involved in North Sea oil developments.

Two important points are raised from a comparison of English and Scottish investment trust companies. Firstly, we have noted that Scottish investment trusts are much more heavily committed to the shares of insurance companies than are the English investment trusts. Thus, the predominance of investment trust companies in Scottish patterns of ownership can be seen as an indirect hand in the vast institutional holdings of the insurance companies in British industry. Secondly, Scottish investment trusts are less likely to hold securities in other investment trusts—although this is partly mitigated by the group structure of investment companies, in so far as many groups follow a common investment policy for their trusts and may hold quantities of a particular stock spread throughout the group.[30]

Given this strategic role of investment trust companies in the pattern of Scottish holdings in British industry, and particularly in holdings in large Scottish companies, it is necessary to look in general terms at who owns and controls the investment trusts. Three groups are of importance in this context: directors, managers and shareholders. The board of directors acts as a policy-making investment committee and there tend not to be specialised functions for individual board members.[31] Members of the board are drawn from the company's management and from the wider business and professional community. On the whole, boards of Scottish investment trust companies tend to be smaller than English boards—4.8 against 5.2[32]—and they tend to include more accountants, solicitors and Writers to the Signet than do English boards—74% of Scottish boards have at least one accountant (compared with 47% for England) and 69% have at least one legally qualified member (just over 5% for England)[33]. Managers of investment trust companies, unlike their counterparts in industry, are far more likely to have important executive functions as board members and are frequently partners or directors in the management company to which the trust is attached.

In the majority of investment trusts, as compared with industry generally, a small number of shareholders often have a controlling interest—often the top four to ten shareholders. Their shareholdings follow the same pattern as U.K. industry, in as much as the large holders tend to be insurance companies. Tables VI and VII give some figures for 1964 and 1973-4.

Table VI

Institutional and Company Beneficial Holdings in Ordinary Capital
of large Scottish Investment Trust Companies (1964)[34]

% OF SHARES HELD

	Insurance companies & Pension funds	Investment trusts	Unit trusts	Trading companies
Alliance Trust Co.	2.8	0.5	4.0	7.7
British Investment Trust	6.0	0.8	7.1	2.0
Edinburgh Investment Trust	5.1	0.5	5.0	1.7
British Assets Trust	8.1	0.7	4.7	1.4
Second Scottish Investment Trust	6.4	2.7	6.9	2.3
Scottish United Investments	24.6	1.4	4.6	1.9
Scottish American Inv. Trust	6.1	0.5	1.6	1.2
Scottish National Trust Company	25.1	0.4	5.5	2.0
Securities Trust of Scotland	24.0	2.5	9.8	0.8
Scottish Mortgage & Trust Company	7.3	0.4	2.8	8.7
Second Alliance Trust Company	2.5	0.1	3.8	0.5

Table VII

Registered Institutional Holdings and Large Holdings in Selected
Scottish Investment Trusts (1973-4)[35]

	Percentage of shares held			No. of large holdings	
	Insurance Cos. & Pension funds	Investment Trusts	Banks & Nominees	No. of holdings over 10,000	% of Stock held
Caledonian Trust Co.	16.7	1.5	20.4	44	42.6
Clydesdale Inv. Trust	16.8	0.2	26.1	47	53.9
Edinburgh Inv. Trust	-	-	-	17	22.0
Glendevon Inv. Trust	4.1	0.3	17.4	7	17.4
Scottish & Continental	13.1	12.5	27.7	15	42.3
Scottish Northern Inv. Trust	8.8	2.6	23.5	31	27.0
Scottish Western Inv. Trust	16.0	0.9	29.6	47	44.0
Second Great Northern	15.1	1.2	29.8	16	49.9

On the basis of these two tables and our discussion of the operation of Scottish investment trust

177

companies we can examine what might be called the two faces of Scottish finance capital. On the one hand, the investment trusts are a dominant and active element within the financial sector and have huge funds invested in large Scottish and English companies, and large American and Japanese firms; in this way they are able to exert a not inconsiderable influence on the structure and growth of the Scottish economy. This face of finance capital may appear to offer some hope to those who would place the future of Scotland in the hands of indigenous persons and institutions. Finance capital's second face, however, consists in the fact that controlling holdings in the capital of the investment trust companies are frequently held by English insurance companies. Not only does this second face show the subordination of Scottish capital to 'foreign' capital, it also highlights the importance of the many and complex links between directors of Scottish companies and the English, foreign and multinational firms. Scotland's interior bourgeoisie is in a satellite position with respect to metropolitan capital,[36] and this structure of relations determines the direction and purpose of 'autonomous' Scottish capital.

However, a most important feature of the British and European political economy is the extension of international capital, especially American, and relations of production. From Poulantzas'[37] discussion of the dominance of American capital in Europe and the consequent dissolution of political and ideological autonomy in its wake, we can see the influences upon and changes within those members of the Scottish bourgeoisie who are involved in the financial sector. Table VIII gives an indication of the large degree of penetration by American, English and European capital.

Table VIII

Foreign Ownership in Scottish Manufacturing Industry 1966[38]

Source	No. of Firms	Turnover (£m)	Investment (£m)	Employment (000)
North America	85	247	162	61
England	140	219	119	38
Europe	3	7	7	3
Total all sources	228	473	288	102

The figures in the table must be interpreted in the light of the fact that in 1966 foreign controlled firms, i.e., non-Scottish firms, were responsible for about 16.5% of total turnover and almost 14% of total employment in Scottish manufacturing industry, particularly electronics, business machines and computers.

The extension of American and English capital into Scotland has important implications for the use of local capital. Scottish capital is not likely to be exercised in a 'nationalistic' direction, i.e., it is not likely to serve the interests of a Scottish nation-state or region. The interior bourgeoisie is linked to dominant, internationalised capital and can no longer be characterised as an autonomous national bourgeoisie, if it ever could be so characterised. The prevailing structure of relations between Scottish capital and that of England—that of an interior colony—is reinforced by international capital.

Capital and Company Integration

Now that we have assessed the importance of capital in allocative institutions as a crucial factor in our understanding of power in Scotland, we must look at the structure of relationships between these institutions and industry. These relationships are based upon the interconnections of the controllers of capital through multiple directorships, which perform integrative functions within the Scottish economy.

From a pilot study of top Scottish firms[39] we found that the industrial and financial sectors were tightly interconnected through a small number of men in top positions. These firms included extremely large companies like Burmah Oil, Scottish and Newcastle Breweries, House of Fraser, The Weir Group, Anderson Mavor (now Anderson Strathclyde), The Scottish Amicable Life Assurance Company, The Distillers Company, The Scottish Widows Fund and Life Assurance Society, The Royal Bank of Scotland, and some much less well known firms such as the Scottish Western Investment Company, The Scottish Eastern Investment Trust, The Low and Bonar Group, The Titaghur Jate Factory Company, Scottish and Universal Investments, and The American Trust Company. In total this comprised 69 companies. We found that of the 483 directors in these commanding heights, 60 formed an economic elite of multiple directors— holding 150 directorships between them. The financial firms in this category of top companies were more likely to be interlocked than the industrial firms; of the 38 top industrial and merchandising firms, just under half were interlocked with other firms, whereas amongst the top 31 financial firms, all but one were interlocked. Therefore, this relatively small number of men holding multiple directorships exhibits the important integrative role performed by allocative financial institutions in the network of top Scottish companies. In order to pursue this we analysed multiple directorships in **all** Scottish financial institutions in conjunction with these top firms. We found that there was an overall integration through the 60 members of the economic elite, who were based primarily in financial institutions. The focal point of this being the investment trusts—notably those located in Edinburgh.

This study suggests that the allocative institutions in Scotland are the most significant vehicle for the integration and concentration of capital in Scotland. We noted earlier that the control of significant quantities of capital is one of the factors basic to our analysis of power and its relation to the question of devolution. Therefore it is necessary to look at the connections between Scottish financial institutions, especially the investment trusts, based upon an analysis of multiple directorships. This would complement our analysis of shareholdings in the previous section.

Using figures for 1972 from company Reports and the Directory of Financial Institutions, we find that, of the 73 Scottish financial firms, 64 are interlocked into a network through multiple directorships. The size and distribution of these interlocks are given in Table IX, and the distribution of common-directorships between financial sectors in Table X.

Table IX

Size and Distribution of Scottish Finance

Company Interlocks 1972

Number of interlocks	Bank	Insurance companies	Investment trusts
1—5	2	5	22
6—10	2	3	17
11—15	1	2	6
16—20	3	1	0
Total number of companies interlocked	8	11	45
Total number of companies	8	16	49

These figures indicate the extent to which the allocative institutions are interlocked. They also support our previous suggestion that it is the investment trusts which exhibit, in general, the highest internal interconnections and external interlocks with other financial firms. The investment trusts provide the overall integration of the network. It is not possible to present the full matrix generated by these interlocked companies in this paper, but we can select the five largest investment trusts and insurance companies, and the three commercial bank groups to illustrate the close integration of the larger network. Diagram I is the network formed by these 13 companies.

Each connecting line represents one common director and indicates the closeness of strength of the inter-connections. The network has an integration score[40] of 0.87, suggesting a highly integrated framework, even without accounting for plural connections. Here the role of the large commercial banks is illustrated. The most striking company interlocks are with the National & Commercial Group, and of the other two banks, is not maintained if the companies are placed in a network of **most interlocked** firms,[41] in which case the investment trusts are the firms which draw the network into a tight configuration. This pattern becomes more evident as the number of companies in the network is increased, although the National & Commercial and Royal Bank taken together in this way have the largest number of plural connections and would suggest a high degree of involvement with the companies with which they are interlocked. Diagram I also suggests that the banks and investment trusts draw the insurance companies into the network more tightly and indirectly link the insurance companies to one another, since they are not so tightly internally interlocked as the investment trusts or banks (as shown in Table X).

Table X

Number of Common directors between Scottish

financial sectors 1972

Sectors	Banks	Insurance companies	Investment trusts
Banks	12	14	60
Insurance Cos.	14	6	58
Investment trusts	60	58	160
Totals	86	78	278

A more detailed picture of the structure of the 49 investment trusts reveals the nature of their interconnectedness through multiple directorships and fund managers[42]. Many of the investments trusts form groups whose assets are managed by professional fund managers, the others are independently managed. We find that 37 trusts, 6 independent and 11 groups (31 trusts), are interlocked and integrated into a network of trust groups, as shown in Diagram 2. The remaining 12 investment trusts, 7 independent and 2 groups (5 trusts), remain unconnected with any other investment trust group. Table XI lists these interlocked groups, ranked according to their degree of external integration[43]. There are three 'central' groups each of which is well integrated and multiply connected—**Martin and Currie, Chiene and Tait** and **Baillie and Gifford**. These groups manage a total of 10 trusts, having an average assets value of £43m.

If we now measure the internal cohesion[44] of the investment trust groups we will have some idea of the possible co-ordination of investment policy and an indication of whether a group of trust are likely to act in concert when investing capital. Table XII shows the rank order.

Diagram 1 Connections between Top Scottish Financial Companies[0] 1972

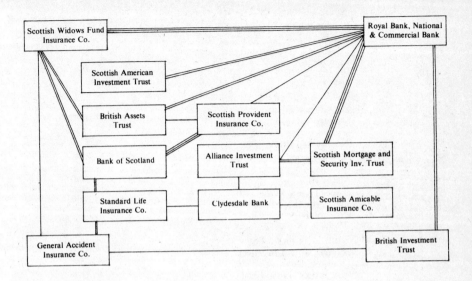

Diagram 2 External Connections between Investment Trusts & Groups 1972

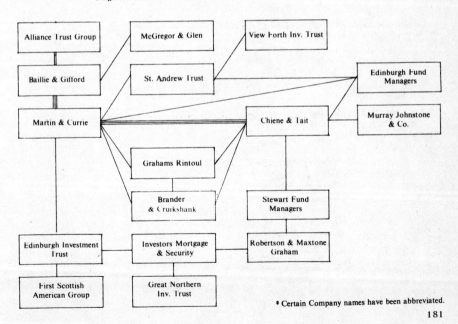

[0] Certain Company names have been abbreviated.

Table XI

Rank		
1	Martin & Currie	4
2	Chiene & Tait	2
3	Edinburgh Investment Trust	1
4	Edinburgh Fund Managers	2
5	Brander & Cruikshank	2
5	Grahams Rintoul	1
7	Baillie & Gifford	4
9	St. Andrew Trust	1
9	Stewart Fund Managers	2
10	Investors Mortgage & Security	1
11	Murray Johnstone & Co.	7
12	Scottish American Group	2
12	Robertson & Maxtone Graham	2
14	Alliance Group	2
14	MacGregor & Glen	2
16	Viewforth Investment Trust	1
17	Great Northern Investment Trust	1
UNCONNECTED	Scottish Heritable Trust	1
	Scottish United Investors	1
	Thomson Mclintock	2
	British Investment Trust	1
	*Scottish Cities Investment Trust	1
	*Aberdeen Investments Ltd.	1
	*Dundee & London Investment Trust	1
	Scottish Northern Investment Trust	1
	Ivory & Sime	3

These three investment trusts are unconnected with any Scottish financial firms. The others are interlocked with other financial institutions - banks or insurance companies.

Table XII

Investment Trust Groups ranked according to internal cohesion

Rank	Group
1	Scottish American Group
1	Ivory & Sime
1	Thomson McLintock
1	MacGregor & Glen
5	Alliance Group
6	Edinburgh Fund Managers
7	Brander & Cruikshank
8	Stewart Fund Managers
9	Murray Johnstone & Co.
10	Robertson & Maxtone Graham
11	Chiene & Tait
12	Martin & Currie
13	Baillie & Gifford

This reveals that the two trust groups which were not connected within the network are highly **internally** interlocked. This is a most interesting situation since it highlights **Ivory & Sime**, a group with assets of £168m, which is heavily involved with merchant banking and North Sea oil developments, as we noted in Section 3. Where groups have a low score, this indicates that they are likely to be merely a convenient umbrella for a number of independently directed trusts. When the investment trust groups are compared according to their rank order on external integration and internal cohesion, using Spearman's Coefficient of rank correlation, we find a small but significant, negative correlation of -0.38. This suggests that there is an inverse relationship between the external integration and internal cohesion for those groups of trusts.

The group's internal cohesion can perhaps be seen as the independent variable. Therefore, we could say **Baillie & Gifford** are less well integrated into the network of trust groups than we would expect from their internal cohesion. This suggests that their trusts have a 'mixed' character. Indeed when we examine their investment trusts we find that two of them are not connected to any other Scottish investment trust; The Monks Investment Trust is not connected to any other Scottish financial institution through a common director, and the Winterbottom trust is connected only to one insurance company. The other two **Baillie & Gifford** trusts account for all the external and internal interlocks: the Edinburgh and Dundee Investment Trust has 4 links with trusts outside the group and the Scottish Mortgage and Trust Company has 5. The **Brander & Cruikshank** group exhibits a similar discrepancy in that they appear to be more tightly integrated than would be expected. This is due to one of the investment trust directors who has a large number of directorships. The recent merger between **Brander & Cruikshank** and **Chiene & Tait** to form **East of Scotland Investment Managers** is most interesting since this would give a composite internal cohesion rank of approximately 10 and an external integration rank of 4, which is consistent with that which we would expect. Another example of a recent merger between The St. Andrew Trust and the **Martin & Currie** group reinforce the inverse relation between external integration and internal cohesion. These changes would seem to indicate a degree of rationalisation amongst the 'umbrella' groups of fund managers and trusts.

This brief overview of the structure of the Scottish allocative institutions illustrates the great extent to which Scottish capital is controlled by a small number of men, who form a tightly integrated network of financial firms. The central position of the investment trusts as a highly interconnected sector is again stressed, this time in their integrative role with respect to allocative institutions. This enables a relatively small number of people to effectively control the distribution of vast amounts of capital invested directly into these trusts, deposited at banks, paid as premiums on insurance policies, or contributed as part of a pension scheme.

It must be remembered that the picture drawn here does not trace out the multiple connections that this web of capital controllers has with America, Europe and England. We would argue that the Scottish allocative institutions are well integrated into the international framework through London, by directorship representations and through shareholdings. This concentration and sophistication of capital control is one sector in which Scotland is certainly not lagging behind, although it is in a peripheral relationship to the large centres of capital such as London. The internationalisation of capital is a phenomenon well understood by the Scottish 'financial aristocracy'. The allocative control exercised by the financial institutions is constrained by an international community of interests[45]. The strength of capital and company integration would ensure a smooth passage by the allocative controllers into a more politically autonomous situation in Scotland.

Some Devolutionary Prospects

The purpose of our paper is to concentrate upon some fundamental economic factors which are of the greatest importance in clarifying the issues of the devolution debate. The ownership and control of Scotland's resources by its interior bourgeoisie has manifest and lasting political consequences. From our analysis, it is evident that a more autonomous Scottish region or nation state would remain in a dependent relationship with England—since the purely Scottish element of the economy is dominated by internationalised capital, which recognises no mere political or territorial lines drawn on a map.

We have shown that there exists a well-integrated upper class in Scotland and that the allocative controllers of the financial institutions—banks, insurance companies, and investment trust companies—are the dominant sector within this upper class. The financial elite brings about an overall integration of the economy, and it is upon them that future prospects for economic growth and industrial development depend. The financial elite constitutes the core of Scotland's interior bourgeoisie: its members are in effective control of local capital but are tied by links of multiple dependency to English and American 'metropolitan' capital—such is the nature of Scotland's satellite economy.

This is the economic environment within which political action in Scotland is constrained. If there are moves towards devolution, or even towards political independence, and the new Scottish political system leaves this environment unchanged in its essential aspects, one of two situations is likely to occur. On the one hand, the Scottish economy could continue more or less as at present—perhaps industry will pay higher taxes on oil revenues etc., so as to marginally reduce income tax and raise the old age pension, but the economy will still remain a satellite economy dependent upon foreign capital and markets. On the other hand a new national consciousness may emerge amongst industrialists and they may voluntarily renounce all their foreign directorships and shareholdings and start to develop an autonomous form of capitalism. In the first case Scotland would continue as a dependent capitalism; in the second case it would attempt to become an independent capitalism. Even if this latter, highly unrealistic, case does come into existence the important point is that **Scotland would remain basically a capitalist society,** and this would perpetuate the social, political and economic inequalities of Scotland today.

Of course, a possible alternative is that an independent Scottish government would radically alter the whole basis of the economy by increasing public ownership and public intervention so as to limit the social power of private property. Such an alternative would certainly place devolution in the wider context of a socialist strategy—but it is necessary to point out that it is not a very likely alternative. Ralph Miliband and others[46] have shown how the framework of a capitalist society limits and constrains the possibilities for political action which aims at changing that framework. One persistent criticism of the British Labour Party is that throughout all the years of its existence it has never effectively challenged the power of private property. If this is the case, what chance would there be in Scotland with a Scottish assembly as a pale reflection of Westminster? The Scottish Conservative and Liberal parties would promote policies designed to make Scottish capitalism work a little more effectively and the Scottish Labour Party would find itself unable to change the basis structures of a capitalist society. The only prospect for really radical change would be the emergence of a totally new political grouping: and the issues of devolution and independence are largely irrelevant to the emergence of such a movement.

We do not argue against devolution—but we do wish to expose the illusion that constitutional restructuring will alter the situation of the Scottish people in a dramatic fashion.

The success of a socialist strategy for Scotland depends upon its being able to counter the economic power of the upper class in Scotland and its links with international capital. A socialist strategy must take account of the particular nature of the financial elite in Scotland—especially the investment trust and fund managers—and must advocate and support policies designed to move Scotland towards socialism. But not just this. A policy, no matter how radical, could not be counted as a socialist policy if it pursued the interests of a part of the British Isles at the expense of, or without regard for, the rest of Britain. Such a policy would constitute a particularly nasty form of national socialism. Socialists in Scotland should be aware of this possibility and should ensure that the policies they advocate are part of a wider international strategy for socialism—a strategy designed to match the nature of international capital.

A socialist strategy involves a struggle against the power of private capital. Devolution may or may not contribute to this strategy, but on its own it provides no panacea. As socialists we would support all measures designed to give people more control over the forces that influence their lives, and one such measure may well be the devolution of central government power to smaller and more meaningful territorial units. But one question which is rarely raised is why such devolution should start and end with the present geographical boundaries of modern Scotland. Scotland has always been an area in which many different peoples have coexisted or come into conflict with one another. What basis for unity is there today between the Edinburgh lawyer, the Orkney crofter and the Border farmer? There is no reason to believe that 'Scotland' is the most

184

meaningful social unit for all these people, or that a government in Edinburgh will be any more responsive to the needs of the people of Kirkwall or Hawick than a government in London—although a Scottish assembly may be more responsive to the people of Charlotte Square.

Greater political autonomy will not **necessarily** benefit the Highlands and Islands, the unemployed, or the low paid worker. Social and regional exploitation will not disappear when Scotland has its own national assembly and national anthem.

The central issues for socialists to face in the devolution debate are: to what extent does a territorial redistribution of political power contribute to an overall socialist strategy, and to what extent are the territorial boundaries of modern Scotland an appropriate finishing point for such devolution? When there is a call for 'self-determination' in Scotland we must ask: who will determine Scotland's future, in who's interests, and what direction? Only by facing these questions can we prevent devolution from being a massive deception.

1. See 'The Scottish Ruling Class', J. P. Scott and M. D. Hughes, in **Social Class in Scottish Society**, edited by A. Allan MacLaren, Routledge & Kegan Paul, in press. Also relevant is **The Scottish Political System**, James Kellas, Cambridge University Press, 1973.
2. This data has been collected as part of a pilot study on the Scottish ruling class which reveals the structure of latent economic power within Scotland and the relationship with English and international capital. For some initial results see Scott and Hughes **op cit**.
3. See **Imperialism: The Highest Stage of Capitalism**, V. I. Lenin, 1917.
4. Scott and Hughes, **op. cit.**
5. 'The Economic Elite: Theory and Practice', R. E. Pahl and J. T. Winkler, in Stanworth and Gidders (eds), **Elites and Power in British Society**, Cambridge University Press, 1974, especially pp. 114-9.
6. **The Eighteenth Brumaire of Louis Bonaparte**, K. Marx, in **Selected Works**, Lawrence and Wishart, 1968, p. 158.
7. See **Capital**, Volume III, Lawrence and Wishart, pp. 264, 606-7, 386-89.
8. 'The Internationalisation of Capitalist Relations and the Nation-State', N. Poulantzas, **Economy and Society**, Volume 3, number 1, 1974.
9. Adapted from: **The Pattern of Ordinary Share Ownership**, J. Moyle, Cambridge University Press, 1971, p. 18.
10. See the following section which analyses interlocking directorships in Scottish industry. The ownership of company loan stock is also of considerable importance in this respect but has not been studied in any depth.
11. The registered holders of shares need not be the beneficiaries of share ownership, for this reason share registers include many nominee and trustee entries. It is thus rather difficult if not impossible, to identify major shareholders. With the increased internationalisation of relations of production it is not always possible to accurately assess the structure and degree of capital dependence of companies.
12. Adapted from Moyle **op. cit.** p.6. 'Scottish' refers to all registered holders with an address in Scotland. It will be seen that the category 'unit trusts' does not appear. This is because unit trusts are not permitted to register shares in their own name—shares are held by trustees for the benefit of unit holders. Management of the assets of unit trusts is in the hands of management companies whose ownership follows the same pattern as other companies.
13 **The Owners of Quoted Ordinary Shares**, J. Revell, Chapman and Hall, 1966, p.18.
14. Moyle, **op. cit.** p. 12.
15. **Ibid** p. 19.
16 For an illuminating account of banking capital see Lenin, **op. cit.**, sections II and III.
17. English banks bought the British Linen, National, Clydesdale and North of Scotland banks between 1918 and 1923. The mergers in English banks during the 1960's were followed by the

mergers of the Royal and National and Commercial banks in 1968 and the British Linen Bank and the Bank of Scotland in 1969.

18. The Clydesdale Bank is a subsidiary of the Midland Bank. Barclays have a holding in the Bank of Scotland and Lloyd's in the National and Commercial group.

19. Source: **Scottish Bankers Magazine**, August 1969.

20. See: **The Economic Effects of Scottish Nationalism**, Stage I, The Economist Intelligence Unit, 1969.

21. British Bank of Commerce, founded in 1935 and Glasgow Industrial Finance, founded in 1946 by a number of Glasgow and Edinburgh investment trusts.

22. E.G., regional development, North Sea oil and gas, and allied industrial expansion, increases in the number of Scottish businesses going public. Previously, long-term capital was supplied by the City, but Scottish financiers now regard this as geographically remote and therefore there has been an expansion of local long-term capital.

23. We are using a relatively loose definition of 'merchant bank' and it could be argued that Glasgow Industrial Finance, particularly, because of its investment trust background is not a true merchant bank. However, the growth of various sorts of investment companies and of secondary banking has shown that such hard and fast definitions are now outmoded.

24. Most of the companies in the Edward Bates group are registered in London, although they operate mainly in Scotland and are mainly Scottish-owned.

25. Initially financed by Ian Noble and Angus Grossart together with four investment trusts (Scottish American Investment Trust, American Trust Company, Scottish Northern Investment Trust, and Stenhouse Investments Ltd.). Initially these four trusts held 54% of the capital, but changes have occurred and now Stenhouse Holdings and Sir Hugh Fraser Bt., hold 33% between them.

26. Pict has a 12% holding in the Total gas discovery in the Frigg field and an interest in Oil and Gas Enterprises, another exploration company.

27. Adapted from **Times 1000**, 1973.

28. We discuss the form and significance of some of these groups in the following section.

29. Source: **The Structure and Growth of the Scottish Economy**, T. Johnston et al., Collins, 1971.

30. On both of those points see **Investment and Unit Trusts in Britain and America**, D. C. Corner and H. Burton, Elek books, 1968, p. 138.

31. In contrast to the industrial decision-taking boards discussed in Pahl and Winkler, **op. cit.**

32. Corner and Burton **op. cit.**

33. **Ibid.** p. 116

34. Adapted from Corner and Burton, **op. cit.** p. 158.

35. Based on the Annual Reports of the companies.

36. On the nature of metropolis—satelite relations see **Capitalism and Underdevelopment in Latin America**, A. G. Frank, Monthly Review Press, 1967.

37. Poulantzas **op. cit.**

38. **The Structure and Growth of the Scottish Economy**, T. Johnston et al, Collins, 1971.

39. See Scott and Hughes **op. cit.** for details of this pilot survey and an account of the selection of these top Scottish firms.

40. The integration score is a measure used by R. Whitely for a similar purpose. See his paper 'The City and Industry'. in Stanworth and Giddens **op. cit.**

41. This network includes Second Great Northern, Scottish Western, Scottish Eastern, Caledonian, and Scottish and Continental Investment trusts and various insurance companies.

42. Further research is intended to fully analyse these relationships in conjunction with the interpenetration of capital and the distribution of assets within Scottish allocative institutions.

43. Degree of external integration is based on calculations of minimum distances between all pairs of trusts of groups.

44. It is possible to develop an **Index of Internal Cohesion** for any group of 2 or more trusts.

45. For example, **Ivory & Sime** the Edinburgh based investment fund managers, have recently bought the Slater Walker Securities 26.6% interest in Haw Par, based in Singapore for £10m.

46. **The State in Capitalist Society**, R. Miliband, Weidenfeld and Nicholson, 1969.

The Political Economy Of North Sea Oil

Peter Smith

Ever since the discovery of gas and oil in the waters off the east coast of Britain, claims about its impact on the British economy, on living standards and on the general conditions of life, have been many and mostly highly optimistic.

The Scottish Council of the Labour Party, in its document 'North Sea Oil and the Scottish Economy' (February '73) argue that "this new oil ... is significant - its currently known scale and proximity to major oil-using countries have already made it so" and imply that, given certain policies, "job-starved Scotland (can) reap truly important benefits."

Gordon Wilson, Scottish National Party M. P., claims, again given certain policies, that ... "to a small country like Scotland (oil) represents the opportunity to transform the whole economic future in a relatively small space of time." ('Scots Independent' - June '74).

The 'Investors Chronicle' of May 3rd '74, against the background of the recent oil crisis, states that:-

> "Only Britain of all the industrialised countries outside the United States has a panacea to this new balance of payments sickness.
> It is the oil that will come from the North Sea, first a trickle, then in a stream and finally in a flood. The North Sea adventure could become Britain's greatest industrial revolution."

The aim of this essay (1) (2), is not, in the first instance, to get involved in a polemic with the three claims outlined above, but to assemble the factual material (Sections 1 - 5); to evaluate the impact of North Sea oil and gas developments on the political economy of Britain and Scotland, and to attempt to outline the ruling class strategy giving rise to this impact (Section 6); to give some idea of future trends in world oil prices and industrial structure and to propose some ideas on an integrated fuel policy for Britain (Section 7).

Only after this has been carried through can the political arguments be undertaken and a Socialist perspective outlined in the final section, Section 8.

Nevertheless, the conclusions arrived at with respect to the overall economic impact, given present trends and stated party policies, can be given here briefly.

Firstly, **there is no indication that a major economic expansion based on oil or on oil revenue will take place over the next 5 - 8 years.**

Secondly, **Government policy over the past 10 years,** (by pushing up the rate of exploitation of the fields), **has directly created this minimal economic expansion and has been directed at achieving Balance of Payments savings as quickly as possible in order to prop up the domestic economy, while at the same time providing some of the capital for export to the Common Market which is seen as the main "saviour" of British capitalism.**

This strategy of rapid exploitation aimed at early B.O.P. savings and at the expense of new industrial expansion in Britain, and in particular, in Scotland, can be called the ruling class "option". Generally speaking, it is supported by the right-wing leaders in the Labour Party and the T.U.C. - though, of course, there are some differences.

Another "option" is that put forward by the S.N.P. which contains a number of different strands - oil financed social security increases, high grants or allowances to private industry in Scotland, etc., though the oil companies are to maintain their independence and thus, as in other spheres, their ability to control.

Leaving aside the obvious electoral propaganda contained in this "option" it does not guarantee economic expansion in Scotland nor real control over the rate of exploitation of the fuels, and profit repatriation abroad.

The dominant trend, given the "defection" of leading Tories to the S.N.P. , is either a split between certain sections of the British ruling class and Scottish "ruling class' or a reinforcement of the right-wing trend in the National Party - this latter is more likely, though these two trends are not, of course, mutually exclusive.

That is that the support given to the S.N.P. by leading Scottish industrialists and in particular the Edinburgh-based finance capitalists, may represent an attempt to gain further monopoly profits at the expense of the English industrialists and in particular the London-based finance capitalists   More likely, however, taking together the support given to the S.N.P. by industrialists, leading Tories, the junior and middle management personnel who provide many of its parliamentary candidates and certain sections of the media, is an attempt by the British ruling classes to build a tactical second line of defense given the series of electoral defeats and their need for B.O.P. savings in line with their aspirations vis a vis the Common Market.

The other major "option" is complete nationalisation of the fuels operated within an integrated fuel policy, initially as part of a "mixed" economy, transferring eventually to a full Socialist economy. Complete nationalisation would give both the control and the revenue to build and expand new State-owned industries in Britain, but in particular in Scotland, which is the only guarantee of full employment and rising income.

Only on such a foundation can a realistic and realisable Socialist strategy be placed before the working class.

It is perhaps worthwhile, given the static and isolated nature of much that has been written on North Sea oil and gas, to round off this introduction with a brief statement of the longer-term economic analysis which underlies the approach of the author to this subject.

That is, that any estimate of the overall political and economic impact of North Sea developments on the British economy, and in particular on employment and real wages, must be set in the framework of the recent historical development of world monopoly capitalism and of the peculiar place of Britain in this development. Generally and briefly, the framework would seem to be as follows:

The restructuring and restabilisation of the capitalist world in the post-1945 period rested mainly on United States political and economic strength, and international trade and financial arrangements and institutions reflected this fact. U.S. "aid" was concentrated in the main on those nations at the monopoly capitalist stage of development and within this concentration two economies in particular were singled out as front-line "stabilisers" against the Socialist States, i.e. West Germany and Japan.

By 1956 and the British/French/Israeli aggression in Egypt and then retreat under U.S. pressure, U.S. hegemony seemed assured and British and French imperialist comebacks seemed a thing of the past. Superficially, given the historically high levels of employment and rates of growth in the monopoly capitalist countries, coupled with the apparent success of the propaganda effort against the Socialist States, world capitalism seemed stable by the late 50's and early 60's.

In fact, the fundamental instability inherent in capitalism still existed as exemplified in the rapidly changing structure of world trade (in favour of the imperialist countries and against the colonial and ex-colonial countries, and trade between the various imperialist countries growing at vastly different rates), in the differential rates of growth of the monopoly capitalist countries, in the continued growth of the 'multi-national" companies, resulting inter alia in massive flows of "hot" capital, etc., in the increasing difficulties arising in the domestic economies of the two main "defenders of freedom"—the U.S. and the U.K.—and all this in the context of stable and growing Socialism and massive gains by national liberation movements.

By the late 60's the two "strong" economies were Japan and West Germany- both the U.S. and the U.K. had major domestic economic problems- the international financial structure had collapsed- what had previously been "creeping" inflation became "rapid" or "hyper" inflation in all capitalist countries- and the threat of a capitalist world-wide depression appeared.

The British ruling classes' answer is the Common Market, an entity they tried to control for 20 years from the outside and into which they are now forced to crawl, hoping, as will be shown in this essay, to carve out for themselves some semblance of a world imperialist role using North Sea Oil and Gas as a major source of finance at the expense of the British, but in particular the Scottish, working class.

All this is surely classic evidence of the correctness of Lenin's **famous law of the uneven development of capitalism** and must lead on to the question of the **weakest link in the capitalist chain.**
It is not argued here that this "weakest link" role yet falls to Britain, though it does seem to be the case that the depth of the crisis is greater in Britain as against the other monopoly capitalist countries as measured by one indicator, the Balance of Payments deficit.
That is that the international capitalist institution, the Organisation for Economic Co-operation and Development (O.E.C.D.) predicts that France will be some £2,750 million in the red by December '74, Italy and Japan will be £3,500 million in the red, while Britain will have "the biggest deficit of all the O.E.C.D. member countries - that is, of all the major countries of the non-Communist world", a massive £4,500 million in the red, more than three times the 1973 deficit of £1,468 and only 25 per cent of this year's deficit is directly related to oil price increases!
This growing deficit, in the context of the important position Britain plays in the capitalist world in financial and military terms, coupled to the growing strength and class consciousness of the organised working class, is nevertheless salutory in terms of the "weakest link" theory.
Thus, the overall impact of North Sea oil and gas developments on the British nation must be set within a major international crisis of capitalism which may lead to new international alignments and must take into consideration the dominant strategy of British monopoly capitalism - supported by the ruling groups in the Tory, Labour, Liberal and Scottish National Parties - within the Common Market. The really important questions to be asked in relation to North Sea oil and gas are: How far does North Sea oil and gas offset the tendency for British capitalism to become the 'weakest link'? and: What policies should the Labour Movement pursue with respect to the North Sea fuels in order to advance the struggle for Socialism? While this essay does not answer either question directly it is hoped that it points the way to answers.

Finally, given the tremendous upsurge in working class political and industrial action over the past few years, with new sections and strata being drawn into and around the industrial working class, this introduction can perhaps be usefully concluded by a quote from Lenin:

> "The continuing economic crisis, unemployment and (inflation) show that the (ruling classes') latest policy cannot provide the conditions necessary for (further) capitalist development. This policy is unavoidably leading to an intensification of the conflict between the democratic masses and the ruling classes, to increased discontent among new strata of the population and to the accentuation and intensification of the political struggle between the different classes. This being the economic and political situation, a new revolutionary crisis is inevitably maturing".(3)

1. The Chronology of North Sea Oil and Gas

In the late 50's and early 60's large gas fields were discovered at Groningen in Holland, and these proved to be the world's largest exploitable gas fields outside the U.S.S.R., exceeding in size the largest of the Texas gas fields. Following these discoveries, interest was stimulated in the possibility of finding natural gas and oil in parts of the North Sea with similar geological conditions to those existing at Groningen.

The discovery of the Groningen gas fields had been preceded by an agreement in 1958 between some of the countries bordering on the North Sea which divided the sea into territories in which the various states would have the exclusive right to search for and exploit any mineral resources under their portion of the sea. In 1964 the British area was sub-divided into blocks of 100 square miles and under the terms of the 1964 Continental Shelf Act the British Government issued licenses to companies wanting to explore and, if found, produce oil and natural gas. Under the terms of the licenses, the initial 24 groups of companies agreed to carry out their promised exploration programme and then surrender at least half the areas involved within six years.

Further allocations of licenses on similar terms followed in 1965, 1970 and 1971/72, and apparently the Labour Government is contemplating a further round of licensing in the fairly near future.

In 1965 the first U.K. gas fields were discovered 40 miles offshore from the mouth of the Humber. Subsequent gas discoveries have been mainly scattered off the Norfolk coast. Most of this natural gas is piped ashore to Bacton, in Norfolk, while the gas from the West Sole field off the Humber comes ashore at Easington, and gas from the Viking North field at Theddlethorpe. From these points the gas goes into the national natural gas grid. The British Gas Corporation, supposedly the monopoly buyer of all gas found in the British area of the North Sea, negotiates a fixed price for the gas with the oil companies concerned in gas production. By 1975 virtually all of Britain will be converted to natural gas.

In addition to exploration offshore, substantial areas of Britain have been licensed for onshore oil and gas exploration and so far some small fields have been discovered, e.g. under Lockton, on the Yorkshire moors.

In 1969 Philips Petroleum discovered the Ekofisk field in the Norwegian sector of the North Sea. This discovery precipitated a spate of subsequent activity in the North Sea, and by the end of 1973 about 565 exploration and appraisal wells had been drilled in the North Sea with 335 of these in the U.K. sector.

The average success rate for exploration wells in Northern waters (above the 56° parallel) where the bulk of oil exploration is at present taking place, has been 1 to 8 and, as of the end of January 1974, production plans for 10 "economically viable" oil fields in the U.K. sector had been announced.

Exploration is at an all-time high during this year's drilling season and further commercially exploitable oil fields are bound to be discovered during the rest of 1975.

2. North Sea oil and the world's oil supplies

The pace of exploration for oil in the North Sea, from the point of view of the oil companies, is directly linked to the growing ability of the oil producing countries and their cartel, the Organisation of Petroleum Exporting Countries (OPEC), to enforce their terms on the oil companies that operate within their State boundaries.

The dramatic rises in the price of crude oil from the OPEC countries which occurred at the time of the last Arab/Israeli war needs to be examined in the context of the workings and structure of the world's largest industry - the oil industry.

Outside of North America and the Socialist States the 'international majors' dominate oil production and distribution. (4)   Five out of seven of these giant monopolies have their headquarters and almost all their shareholders in the United States. They are Standard Oil of New Jersey (Esso), Standard Oil of New York (Mobiloil), Standard Oil of California (Chevron), Gulf Oil and Texaco. The other two 'international majors' are the Royal Dutch/Shell group and British Petroleum. Shell is owned 60 per cent by Dutch shareholders and 40 per cent by British shareholders and although its operational and commercial headquarters are in London, there is a 4:3 split of managing directorships in favour of the Dutch. BP is almost entirely British owned, and the British Government has a 49 per cent shareholding in the company which dates from 1913. The Government nominates two directors to the seven-man board but does not control their actions.

In 1970 the 'international majors' were responsible for about 80 per cent of all oil production outside of the Socialist States and North America and in the same area they owned or controlled over 70 per cent of the total refining capacity and operated either directly, or indirectly, through long-term charter, well over 50 per cent of the tonnage of internationally operating tankers. These percentages were slightly smaller in 1970 than a few years previously, and since 1970 they have diminished further owing to nationalisation measures in the Middle East and the growing activities of State capitalist and 'smaller' capitalist oil companies, such as Compagnie Francaises des Petroles (CFP), Ente Nazionale Idrocarburi (ENI) and Burmah/Castrol.

Assets in excess of £5,000 million are invested in oil abroad by U.S. companies, and this accounts for around one-third of total U.S. foreign investment. In 1969 oil industry earnings sent back to the U.S. were estimated as being in excess of $1,750 million. This was about $400 million more than the total cost of the country's oil imports and the outflow of funds to finance further overseas oil investment.

The OPEC countries are now squeezing the oil companies in three ways. Firstly, prices of crude oil have been raised- secondly, far harder terms are enforced on the oil companies' production facilities, which in some cases have resulted in the outright nationalisation of western-owned companies, such as the Iraq Petroleum Company- and, thirdly, the OPEC countries' aim to permanently cut back the growth of oil production from their States.

The cutbacks mean that other, generally new, sources of oil must be found or the growth of the world's capitalist economies will be (given present technology), constrained by oil shortages. In this situation North Sea Oil is "manna from heaven" to the 'international majors' and the 'independent' oil companies.

The Secretary-General of OPEC, Dr. Abdurraham Khene, has stated that projected world consumption of oil and natural gas on present trends is, in millions of tons a year, as follows:-

Table 1

1970	1975	1980	1985	2000
2,500	3,300	4,150	5,100	10,000

and he said that:

> "Known world reserves are estimated at the equivalent of 1,000 billion (thousand million) barrels of oil (130 to 140 billion tons) of which gas accounts for approximately

one-third.

Calculations based on these figures show that the world has a maximum of 30 years oil left, assuming that no more reserves are discovered (an assumption which is fortunately rather improbable)." (5)

The OPEC cutbacks in production in the context of a continuing increase in the demand for oil by the capitalist economies, firstly raises the price of crude oil to the oil companies, and, secondly, **stimulates the oil companies' efforts to obtain alternative sources of supply at lower 'well-head' prices.**

3. How Much North Sea Oil and Gas?

To date production plans have been announced for 10 fields in the U.K. sector. This includes the new B.P. Ninian field, announced on 25.1.74, but excludes the Frigg field which lies mainly in Norwegian waters.

In a report to Parliament by the Minister for Industry in 1973 entitled 'Production and Reserves of Oil and Gas on the U.K. Continental Shelf', the following statement occurs:-

> "Estimates of North Sea Oil production in 1980 are, therefore, found to have a wide margin of error. We can be reasonably confident that production in that year from the five fields already established as commercial will be between 40 and 50 million tons. Some at least of the additional fields mentioned in the report will also be established as commercial, and it is reasonable to assume that further discoveries will be made during the next year or two, in time for production of oil by 1980. It is very hard to fix an upper limit to the possible level of production in 1980, since it depends so much on discoveries not yet made. If things go well, it could exceed 100 million tons; any figure much above this would, however, involve a rate of future discoveries which, while possible, cannot be counted on. Our best judgement accordingly is that total production of oil in that year should be in the range of 70-100 million tons. There is also uncertainty for gas, even though the major gas fields in the southern basin are already producing. Production in the mid 1970's seems likely to be in the range 3,500 - 4,000 million cubic feet a day. Its level after that depends on the size and pace of further discoveries and on the extent to which finds already made prove commercial, and the timing of their coming into production.",

The Dept. of Political Economy at Aberdeen University quote estimates of recoverable oil reserves in the U.K. sector of the North Sea as between 8,000 and 9,000 million barrels (i.e. 1,150 million tons) which by 1980 could result in the production of two million barrels of oil per day (100 million tons per year). They note that these estimates compiled at the end of 1973 are 30 per cent higher than those of 12 months previously. They make the following assumption: that if the present average success rate for exploration wells of 1 to 8 falls to about 1 to 16 for future finds, then this would increase recoverable reserves to around 18,000 million barrels (2,500 million tons) by 1980 and increase production to about three million barrels per day (150 million tons a year) by 1982.

Britain's oil needs have been estimated as around 150 million tons by 1980 (Varley, Secretary for Energy - 'Financial Times', 22nd May, 1974).

In December 1973 a Conference on offshore oil and gas resources was held. The following information comes from an article entitled - 'North Sea Oil slow to yield' - in the January 1974 edition of the Petroleum Economist (formerly the Petroleum Press Service).

> The Conference heard various estimates put forward as to the amount of oil and gas under the North Sea. Dr. J. Birks of B.P. foresaw a production potential for all North Sea areas (U.K., Norwegian, Denmark, West Germany and Holland) of about four million barrels of oil a day (200 million tons a year) by 1980, with three million of these (150 million tons a year) coming from the U.K. sector.

Professor Odell (author of the book 'Oil and World Power'), who is Professor of economic geography at Erasmus University in Rotterdam, held the view that by 1982 the North Sea would be yielding six million barrels a day (300 million tons a year). Assuming a 5 per cent annual growth rate in energy consumption he forecasted that on and offshore oil and gas would be capable of supplying 45 per cent of the total energy demand of Western Europe by 1982.

For the first time, figures on potential gas production from the North Sea were disclosed at the Conference. Birks estimated for an offtake rate of 4.5 billion (thousand million) cubic feet per day during 1980/82 from fields already proven in the southern North Sea, with two-thirds coming from the U.K. sector. Assuming 17 trillion (million million) cubic feet for proven non-associated gas (found separately from oil) in the northern North Sea, he considers that the offtake rate could rise to around seven billion cubic feet per day by 1980/82.

Finally, with the addition of the discoveries of proven associated gas the figure could rise to gas offtake rates of 9 to 9.5 billion cubic feet per day in 1980/82. Hazier assumptions on the possibility of further discoveries would lead to an offtake rate of around 13 billion cubic feet per day by 1982.

Clearly it is important to be as accurate as possible as to the amount of North Sea oil and gas and the likely rate of extraction. It is worth indicating some of the problems in doing this:

a) The selling price of crude oil on world markets: The recent quadrupling, of the price of crude oil must provide a substantial stimulus to speeding up exploration and production in the North Sea, but by how much?

b) The oil companies' exploration programmes have to contend with the weather and deep water in the northern North Sea and possible delays in obtaining necessary machinery and equipment.

c) The figures of oil and gas reserves in the North Sea given out by the oil companies are conservative, but it is difficult to estimate by how much.

To expand on these points: the report in January's Petroleum Economist on the offshore oil and gas Conference said that:-

"Short of co-ordinated measures by governments, oil companies, industry and research organisations comparable with those of the American space programme, there is no way of securing a substantial flow of oil from the North Sea before 1978. For the oil companies and manufacturing industries are already operating to the limits enforced by the availablility of supplies of materials and components, technological know-how, skilled labour and finance."

With regards to the figures given out by the oil companies as to the amount of existing proven oil reserves, a commentator writing in the October 1973 issue of Petroleum Press Service stated that:- "There is a natural tendency within operating companies to use minimum estimates of recoverable reserves when assessing the return to be obtained from the very large capital investment required to put a field into production."

Apart from any political and economic reasons the oil companies might have for doing this, there are also technical reasons. In an article in the June 1973 issue of Petroleum Press Service called "North Sea's latest estimates" the writer, commenting on the Department of Trade and Industry May report to Parliament, said that:-

"The reserve figures give an output to reserves ratio of about 1 to 11, which at first glance seems low. However, with a not uncommon build-up period of 3 years using 20 per cent of reserves, followed by a 5 year plateau output period using 30 per cent, and by 8 years of declining production using the final 50 per cent, the production life of a field can be programmed over 16 years.

While the field is producing, reserves are as a rule continually updated on the basis of the latest field data obtained and its production life is then often extended beyond 20 years."

At the December 1973 conference the Editor of the Petroleum Times said that:

"with the value of crude oil rising at such a fantastic rate, the need to provide oil resources and the profit motive will see to it that undoubtedly the North Sea programmes of the large range of 150 groups comprising some 500 companies, will be stepped up. As a result there will be in the very near future more business accruing to European suppliers who can offer equipment, materials or services to this country."

And, commenting on another aspect of the rising price of crude oil, he stated that: "The important effect is that it will possibly make the marginal fields such as Maureen and Josephine and the other small fields economically viable."

Whereas in 1971 an oil industry estimate reckoned that to be viable, a field had to be capable of producing a plateau output of 200,000 barrels a day and have reserves of 1000 million barrels before the high cost of development and exploitation could be considered.

since these estimates were made, further oil strikes in the North Sea have made it clear that **not only can Britain attain self-sufficiency in oil by 1980/2, but also become a net exporter of oil in the early 1980's.**

Indeed, considerable areas of the North Sea which may contain oil (and gas) remain to be explored, as do the sea areas to the west of Britain. **There is, however, a tendency to underplay the gas finds in the North Sea. These, according to the "Sunday Times" of 9/6/74, may become Britain's "biggest single supplier of energy to the home market."**

Nevertheless, no matter which estimate is taken for Britain's likely production of oil by 1980 (70-100 million tons p.a. minimum to 200 million tons p.a. maximum) - **it is virtually certain that Britain will be the major West European producer, with some 50-60 per cent of total North Sea output,** so that there can be little doubt that the economic and political impact of oil and gas on Britain's international relations are likely to be massive and complex.

4. Government Policy on North Sea Fuels

The summary of the main conclusions of the first report from the Committee of Public Accounts, produced in the 1972-73 Parliamentary Session on the question of North Sea oil and gas stated,

Paragraph 97:

"(1) We regard it as unsatisfactory that U.K. tax revenue from continental shelf operations should be pre-empted by the tax demands of administrations elsewhere in the world- and that for tax purposes capital allowance on extraneous activities, such as tanker operations elsewhere, should be used to offset profits on continental shelf operations.

(2) Under the present arrangements the U.K. will not obtain either for the Exchequer or the balance of payments anything like the share of the 'take' of oil operations on the continental shelf that other countries are obtaining for oil within their territories .....

(4) We consider that, even disregarding the taxation points referred to in sub-paragraph (1) of this paragraph, there are grounds for considering that the U.K. terms have tended to lag behind those of other countries right from the start ....

(13) We are concerned that so many production licenses have now been granted with the result that the most promising areas of the North Sea have already been allocated on the original terms.

(14) The most striking fact to emerge from our review of the four rounds of licensing is that the terms for each, apart from the limited tender experiment, have remained

virtually unchanged since they were fixed in 1964, before any discoveries had been made and when the potentialities of the shelf were unknown.

(15) We are concerned that the licenses granted remain valid, without a break clause exercisable by the Department, for 46 years; and that there is no provision for variation or re-negotiation of the financial terms, however large the finds, or for obtaining a degree of Government participation.

(16) We were surprised that a thorough examination of the opportunities for British industry and employment had not taken place much earlier than 1972 (when the International Management and Engineering Group report was commissioned) as the full opportunities of the discoveries became apparent."

Recommendations

Paragraph 98:

"(1) The Government should take action substantially to improve the effective tax yield from operations on the continental shelf - and should consider, among other methods, the possibility of imposing a system of quantity taxation.

(2) Before any further licenses are issued all aspects of the regime for licensing, especially as regards oil, should be reviewed in the light of this report and the conclusions in paragraph 97 in order to secure for the Exchequer and the economy a better share of the take from continental shelf operations." (Committee of Public Accounts - 1972/73).

A number of issues need expanding on. Firstly, how much the Exchequer make from North Sea oil; secondly, how much of it is owned by foreign companies.

On the first issue, note the first two points in the main conclusions of the Public Accounts Committee. The Department of Trade and Industry supplied the Committee with data and some of their leading personnel were available for questioning by the Committee. Quoting from the Report:

> "The financial package decided upon to suit the U.K.'s particular circumstances, in conjunction with the tax position, comprised a royalty rate of 12½ per cent and initial payment, covering the first six years of a licence, of about £6,250 per average block of about 100 square miles, followed by an annual payment of £10,000 per block in the seventh year with annual increments thereafter of £6,250 a year to a maximum of £72,500 per year."

These royalties and licensing fees are to all intents and purposes peanuts. The royalties are computed on the value of the crude oil at the wellhead. The refining process greatly enhances its value. So the important financial gain to the U.K. Exchequer will come from the levying of U.K. Corporation Tax - or will it?

The Department of Trade and Industry (DTI) implied that it would, but the Committee pointed out that owing to the disparity between 'posted prices' in the OPEC countries (in effect, it is nowadays a tax reference price in the country of the oil's origin) and the 'market price' of crude oil, the production companies were being overpaid for the crude oil.

The production companies pay local taxes to the country from which they obtain oil and so, although the profits on the production stage are large, local tax liability wipes out any obligation to pay U.K. taxation as the oil companies are not taxed twice; say in Iran and then the U.K. (or USA). Now, the crude oil is sold by the production company to the marketing company (although both are part of BP, etc.) at the posted price, and if this outstrips the market price, then the paper losses of the marketing company increases. This is precisely what has been happening in recent years. Quoting from evidence to the Committee by Mr. Lord, the Deputy Chairman of the Inland Revenue:

> "One of the best indications of the growing divergence between posted prices and market prices is, in fact, I suspect, the losses of oil companies which, looking only at the

companies which are resident in the U.K. for tax purposes grew from £90 millions in 1966 to an estimated £470 millions in 1972. The total accumulated losses which are available for relief against profits of these companies is now £1,500 million."

Note, this was stated in January 1973. With the recent massive increases in posted prices by the OPEC countries the accumulated losses of the oil companies must have sharply risen. For oil companies active in OPEC countries and in the North Sea, and having a U.K. subsidiary or being U.K. based firm, these losses can be offset against any tax liability (i.e. U.K. Corporation Tax) they might encounter in making profits from North Sea oil.

In addition, oil companies active in the North Sea receive assistance with capital investment. As Mr. Lord, of the Inland Revenue, remarked:

"The tax revenue in 1975 plainly will be nothing at all, but this is merely because of the effect of the extremely favourable tax treatment of capital investment which now exists in this country. All capital investment in plant and machinery and in some other things too, like exploration expenditure gets what is known as free depreciation. That is, it is all written off against the first year's profits and so tax does not really begin to bite until the pay back period is over."

Later on in the proceedings Mr. Dell, M.P., asked Mr. Lord:

"You were talking about the existing tax losses, which are very large in amount, and indicating that Parliament might be unwilling to take retrospective measures to deal with this?"
- "Yes, I was."
"But these tax losses are so large that they might, in fact, eliminate liability to tax for a significant number of years to come?"
- "That is true."
"As it is clear that little will come into the U.K. Exchequer in the way of tax revenue from North Sea oil in the early 1980's, and perhaps later as things stand at the moment, maybe there will be benefits because the oil firms are British?"
- "Well, no - most of them are not."

From Table II which is taken from the Report it can be seen that the total British interest in territory at present licensed in the U.K. sector of the North Sea is 32.0 per cent (Shell is taken as being 40 per cent British).

TERRITORY HELD BY

| Licensing Round | PUBLIC SECTOR | | | | OTHER BRITISH INTERESTS | TOTAL BRITISH INTERESTS |
| | GAS COUNCIL | NCB | H.M.G. Share 48.6% of BP | TOTAL | | |
	Per Cent	Per Cent	Per Cent	Per Cent	Per Cent	Per Cent
1	4.5	2.1	2.6	9.2	13.5	22.7
2	7.6	4.5	3.4	15.5	18.1	33.6
3	10.1	4.5	5.4	20.0	16.5	36.5
4 Auction	2.1	6.2	1.7	10.0	10.0	20.0
Discretion	3.0	2.3	4.3	9.6	25.1	34.7
TOTAL	2.9	2.5	4.2	9.6	24.4	34.0
OVERALL	5.0	3.0	4.0	12.0	20.0	32.0

There is only one stipulation as to the destination of North Sea oil and that is laid down by the Government. That is, all oil extracted in the U.K. sector has to be landed in Britain - it can then be exported without any further restraint. Even this provision can be waived by the Secretary of State!

A final point which deals with the rate of exploitation of North Sea oil.

Mr. Dell, M.P., putting a question to Sir Robert Marshall, Secretary of the DTI:

> "Nevertheless, whatever may be the actual facts so far, it was clear to the Department from the beginning that the policy of speeding exploitation of the North Sea was bound to reduce the opportunities of British companies as suppliers?"
> - "Yes, I have previously said that. The bulk of the oil industry is foreign. Next to the Americans this country has the largest single stake in it, but simply following the great emphasis of American enterprise in the petroleum industry established across the world, American suppliers are the most prominent and **it was quite clear that the faster one went and the less notice that was given towards exploitation and exploration plans in the North Sea, the less the immediate share of British industry.**"

In effect previous Tory and Labour Governments have carried out a bi-partisan policy on the exploitation and production of North Sea oil and gas which has been highly favourable to the U.S. dominated 'multi-national' oil companies in particular and to the British and foreign industrial firms which are shareholders in the various consortia of companies which have acquired licenses for offshore exploration. At today's prices, the 'Sunday Times' on April 28th estimated that £3,000 million worth of oil will be coming ashore each year in the 1980's. **The bulk of profits will go, as things stand, into the coffers of international (mainly U.S.) monopoly capital.**

5. Ownership of the Onshore Oil Engineering and Construction Industry

The geographical locations of onshore oil engineering and construction sites raises in very sharp relief the complete anarchy of capitalist enterprise; the spoilation of areas of natural beauty, the overcrowding in certain towns and cities, high rents and over-burdened social services, the 'shanty' work camps, the probability of future 'ghost towns', the wasteful duplication of onshore facilities by local authorities, the encroachment of democratic rights with respect to public inquiries into planning requirements, etc. All these - and more - are the outcome of monopolicy capitalism's drive for profit at local level, under acquiescent governments.

The present Section deals, however, with the question of ownership (and hence, control and destination of profits) in the main, rather than with the problems outlined in the last paragraph. These latter are dealt with more fully in Section 6 below.

Rigs and platforms - manufacturing location

At present there are 40 **drilling rigs** under construction for intended service in the North Sea. It is possible that a majority of these will be operating in the U.K. sector. Only two of these rigs are being built in Britain, both at Marathon Limited on the Clyde.

The most popular rig is the Aker H - 3 semi-submersible of which twenty-four are being built either at the Aker yard in Norway or elsewhere under licence.

Twenty-eight **production platforms** are being constructed for service in the North Sea. Ten are being built in Britain, eleven elsewhere and seven are out for tender. Of the ten being built in Britain, four are at yards either wholly or mainly owned by U.S. companies, and a further two are being built by a French/British consortium. The remaining four are under construction by two British firms.

The principal drilling contractors are U.S. comapnies; South Eastern Drilling Services and Offshore Drilling Services have opened offices and factories in Aberdeen.

There companies have been established to produce oil tools and all are U.S. owned. Baker Oil Tools have set up their first factory outside the U.S. to manufacture offshore equipment, and VETCO has also set up a factory and warehouse on the same industrial estate outside Aberdeen.

The third company, Weatherford Oil Tools, is setting up outside Aberdeen in the course of this year.

Steel production platform sites exist at **Ardersier** near Nairn (Ray McDermotts - a U.S. company); at **Nigg Bay** (Highland Fabricators, two-thirds owned by the U.S. Brown and Root and one-third by Wimpeys)- at **Methil** in Fife (Redparth, Dorman Long) (and at **Graythorp** in England (Laing Pipelines)). Concrete platforms are being built at **Ardyne Point** by the Anglo/French firm, McAlpine/Sea Tank.

A considerable build-up of manufacturing and construction work is continuing around the **Cromarty Firth** and apart from Highland Fabricators, includes a pipe-coating yard at **Invergordon** owned by an Anglo-American firm, MK-Shand, Taylor Woodrow intend to build concrete production platforms on Cromarty Firth at **Alness.**

(Cromarty Petroleum Limited, a wholly-owned subsidiary of the massive U.S. shipping concern National Bulk Carriers, are seeking planning permission to build a £100 million refinery at **Nigg Point** on the Cromarty Firth - one of the very few projected 'downstream' operations, i.e. one which **uses** oil rather than being involved in its primary production. (See Section 6 for further analysis)).

North of the Moray Firth at **Brora,** Carpet Operations International of Canada are to put up a £2.5 million factory for the production of modules for production platforms and pipelines.

On the West coast of Scotland, Sea Tank/McAlpine (French/British) are aiming to build two concrete production platforms at a time, at **Ardyne Point,** Argyll. Several other attempts to establish sites to build concrete production platforms along the West Coast have been made, although most of these have run into problems in getting planning permission, due to opposition from local residents.

At **Burntisland** in the Firth of Forth, the Anglo-Dutch Offshore Concrete consortium is also intending to construct concrete platforms.

In the Islands, Fred Olsen (U.K.) Limited, which is a Norwegian firm (and builds the Aker H-3 semi-submersible rigs), intends to spend £6 million on a base outside **Stornoway.** This project could include the construction of oil rigs, the building of pontoons for semi-submersible rigs and the fabrication of steel decks for offshore concrete platforms. As a rig supply base, Fred Olsen (U.K.) Limited will be ideally situated for any oil which may be discovered and exploited West of the Shetlands.

The **Shetlands,** unlike the rest of Scotland, have attempted to gain some control over the activities of the oil industry through a parliamentary Act which will perhaps enable the County Council to plan an integrated development at **Sullom Voe** in conjunction with the oil Companies that intend to land oil at this deep water inlet.

This cursory examination of the ownership of the onshore oil engineering and construction industry tends to neglect the British firms which are moving in on the oil boom.

This applies to British companies active in rig supply operations and engineering companies which supply components and materials for offshore activities.

Whereas it is fairly easy to assess the ownership of the oil and gas by British and non-British companies, it is more difficult to do this in the field of engineering and construction.

However, from the information presented above, it is clear that foreign, and in particular U.S. companies, are already strongly entrenched in the onshore activities geared to the offshore industry. Indeed, that this follows direct from Government policy with respect to fast exploitation of oil and gas has already been indicated.

British participation tends to be concentrated in the 'servicing' side of the industry where much smaller amounts of capital seem to be required and where advanced technology and skills are not needed, although of course British firms reap some demand from work sub-contracted to them from the foreign 'giants'; detailed employment effects are fully considered below.

However, **unless a radical change in the approach of the State to North Sea Oil and Gas occurs, then this situation of foreign monopoly capitalist domination of the onshore industry is likely to continue,** thus reinforcing the similar position with respect to ownership of the offshore industry, **which will undoubtedly lead** - as it has in the past in other industries - **to major social problems and major problems of control of the economy, profit repatriation, etc.**

6. Impact on the Scottish Economy

This section is concerned to evaluate firstly, the likely overall effects of North Sea Oil and Gas exploitation on the development of the British economy **given the present political and economic system.**

Secondly, it is concerned to evaluate the effects on the employment prospects and living standards of the Scottish working class given the same assumptions.

The specific impact of North Sea developments on the nationalised (fuel) industries is treated separately in Section 7, and an alternative, socialist perspective is outlined in the final Section - Section 8.

By way of introduction, it should be noted that little information has been forthcoming on projected effects on the overall employment situation from the two usual research sources - government departments and universities.

This lack of projections may by itself be indicative of governmental expectations arising from the bipartisan policies pursued - that is, that few jobs will be created! If a 'jobs explosion' were expected, particularly in Scotland where both main parties have political difficulties presently, then it may be assumed that it would have been used as political propaganda.

This dearth of (published) research material presents major problems in carrying through the first aim of this section. All that can be done is to construct a number of hypotheses based on the meagre information available coupled to major trends within British monopoly capitalism.

Fortunately, however, a fair amount of published material is available on the North East of Scotland and this is presented and evaluated later in this Section.

Firstly, other things being equal, there will overall be **substantial savings to the Balance of Payments by 1980** (given the estimates outlined above), whether or not North Sea oil (and gas) is processed in Britain or is directly exported in crude form

However, the saving will be greater:-

> A. the more Britain becomes a net exporter of the fuels (which depends largely on the rate of exploitation) and in particular the greater the proportion of the net export which is refined and processed 'downstream' in Britain, i.e. the value of refined and processed fuels being very much greater than that of crude fuels, (which will depend largely on the rate of expansion of the petro-chemical industry in Britain),
>
> B. the less is the profit repatriation from Britain to other countries, (which will depend largely on the proportion of the petro-chemical industry which is British-owned and on the governmental policies pursued), and
>
> C. the more positive the overall impact of the North Sea fuels and their developments on the net export position of other industries.

In more concrete terms the position seems to be as follows.

There is presently no indication of either an expansion of the petro-chemical industry or the re-location of parts of it nearer the fuel fields.

The **expansion** programmes announced so far refer to refineries only, five in total, and **no announcements have been made on 'downstream' processing activities whatsoever.** For an international industry which prides itself on 'capitalist forward planning' and expects oil to be coming ashore in significant quantitites by 1978-80 and given the construction times on new plants, this lack of announcements on new plants may well be very significant.

Neither have there been announcements with respect to **relocation** of parts of the petro-chemical industry.

The present distribution of the industry tends to favour England and there is no reason to suppose that if North Sea Oil replaces imported oil this distribution will substantially alter.

Transport costs probably represent such a small fraction of total costs that there will be no impetus to re-locate nearer the fuel fields. Indeed, any expansion of the British-based industry which may yet take place will, if left to the monopoly-dominated market, probably follow the past trend of expansion alongside existing facilities (mainly in England) since the necessary social and industrial 'infrastructure' already exists, as do the mass markets and transport facilities to continental Europe.

Further, those terminal facilities which have been announced e.g. Sullom Voe in the Shetlands, incorporate tanker-loading facilities and it is just as easy to 'export' to England and continental Europe as to elsewhere in Scotland.

There is one major technical consideration which links the tanker-loading facilities and direct export with the lack of expansion and re-location of the petro-chemical industry. This is, that the present petro-chemical industry in Britain, being based on imported oils, conforms to the chemical composition of these oils while North Sea Oil differs significantly in chemical composition and further that a heavy industrial economy such as Britain requires a high proportion of heavy oil, whereas North Sea Oil is relatively light. (The Institute of Petroleum estimates that North Sea Oil could only be substituted for 50 per cent of Britain's present needs due to this heavy/light differentation.)

It might have been thought therefore that this forced 'surplus' of North Sea Oil over and above domestic requirements would lead to the expansion of the petro-chemical industry (even allowing for some spare capacity presently), based on the light chemical composition, and the high-value products exported, thus substantially benefiting the Balance of Payments while at the same time adding a very modern industry with all its ramifications to the industrial structure of the economy. The arguments of the previous paragraphs show, however, that this is almost certainly not to be the case. From the point of view of the oil companies it would seem that they prefer to export the light crude oil, more than likely to Western Europe. Perhaps this is because continental Western Europe refines 28 per cent of the world's oil supplies, a greater capacity than that possessed in the U.S.A., and thus is the 'centre of gravity' and of high profits for the international oil industry!

On the **construction and servicing** side of the industry there is again little indication that new modern export-oriented industries, which will make a major impact on the economy, will be built up. The detailed position on the Scottish economy is given below but it can be noted at this stage that the estimates for direct employment in the North East of Scotland range from 9,000 jobs in 1981 to 20,000 jobs in 1980-85, substantial perhaps but not overwhelmingly so.

Table III : Present and Forecast Employment of Companies
Engaged in North Sea Oil
Activities, June 1974

Area	Present Employment (1)	Forecast Increase (2)	Total (1) and (2)
(1) Inverness & Easter Ross	4,860	1,245	6,105
(2) Remainder of Highlands & Islands	470	270	
(3) North East	4,545	3,690	8,235
(4) Tayside	270	355	625
(5) East Central Scotland	2,275	100	2,375
(6) West Central	2,785(1)	235	3,020
	15,205	5,895	21,110

(1) Including Marathon

Source: Department of Employment

The overall employment impact has been patchy. The 'Investors Chronicle' of 3rd May, 1974, notes that offshore suppliers have so far won orders for some £35 million worth of work, the biggest employment concentration arising from it being 4,000 jobs in the North East of **England**, much of it accounted for by the Graythorpe operation of Laing Pipelines. On the other hand it has been estimated that total expenditure on U.K. North Sea development was some £300 million in 1973 and will be of the order of £500 million in 1974, with British firms supplying less

200

than 50 per cent of the total (Strang, Min. Oil, 18th July, 1974).

Estimates as to the total number of British firms involved in supplying the North Sea oil and gas industry vary from Department of Energy estimates of fifty-five major contractors, eight hundred sub-contractors and two thousand other companies involved in supplying "thirteen priority shore projects" to a Petroleum Times estimate that more than one thousand companies have derived work due to the North Sea development (Report from the Select Committee on Science and Technology, 1974).

Nevertheless, individual firms, rather than whole industries, seem to have benefited. For example, four tug-supply vessels valued at £1.8 million each have been ordered by Seaforth Marine (a Scottish Company) from British yards while on the other hand, a Scottish yard felt compelled to build a supply ship on spec - hardly an industry-wide impact.

Other examples of orders are for **modules** by Lummus of the Construction Engineering Group, by Press and by Whessoe, **pipeline work** by Land and Marine Engineering and by Turriff Taylor, John Laing Construction and CBI Constructors, **compressors** by Broom Wade and Bellis and Morcom, **navigation equipment** by Decca, **floodlights** by Thorn, **corrosion prevention** by BKL Alloys, and **fire protection** by Chubb.

While no estimate can be given of the employment effect of all the orders placed with British industry it is clear firstly that the impact is not great and secondly, that no important new industries are being built up and no important new technologies are being utilised.

The real industrial disaster which can be laid at the door of British capitalism and in particular at the Wilson government's role on capitalism's behalf, is surely the weak position of the British iron and steel industry with respect to the North Sea fuel industry. The Government-commissioned International Management and Engineering Group (IMEG) report of 1972 concluded:-

> "Considering that the quality and competitiveness of steel supply are fundamental to the success of British industry in gaining markets in the offshore oil and gas industry; that more than half the value of equipment and materials supplied to this industry comprises steel itself; **and that the advanced technology required offshore corresponds also to the requirements of other important expanding markets for steel, we therefore recommend:**
>
> IV. The B.S.C. should be strongly urged to establish the present and future requirements of the offshore oil and gas industry as one of the principal targets for the B.S.C. in respect of both investment and research and development effort.
> V. A continuing interest should be taken in the relationships betwen the steel industry and the offshore oil and gas equipment suppliers.
> VI. The B.S.C. should be encouraged to keep in closer touch with its customers at both the commercial and the technical level, so that the latter are fully aware of progress made and problems overcome.'

Now while this advice is presently necessary it really represents the closing of the stable door after the horse has bolted, for this advice, rather, **a directive**, should have been given to the B.S.C. on its establishment in 1967, in order to allow it sufficient time to develop the technologies required and lay down new manufacturing capacity. **In fact between 1967 and the present a whole British industry -advanced technology steel pipe-making - was gifted to foreign manufacturers, in particular the Japanese, who provided almost all the pipes for the under-sea lines!**

It would seem, however, that 20" - 44" dia. pipes can be produced at the Clydesdale, Scotland, works of B.S.C. so that it should be possible to maintain and perhaps expand employment in central Scotland.

On the "thick plate" side of the steel industry, B.S.C. have been caught short on capacity and IMEG noted that B.S.C. has continued to be diliatory in developing facilities for volume production for this product. An example of the imported steel content of North Sea development is that of the approximately 40,000 tons of steel required for the first two Forties field platforms B.S.C. will supply 42 per cent, Japan 18 per cent, and Sweden, West Germany and France 40 per cent between them.

Again the Dalziel and Clydebridge, Scotland, works of B.S.C. can produce "thick plate" and if B.S.C. are prepared to invest the time, effort and capital, employment could be expanded.

From all this it can only be concluded (in line with the conclusions on ownership of the oil and gas and ownership of the oil engineering and construction industries) that Labour and Tory Governments were more interested in rapacious exploitation of the fuels rather than industrial expansion and restructuring of the British economy. Indeed this unplanned and very fast exploitation will result in general terms in minimum Balance of Payment savings unless the net export of oil is so vast as to be suicidal!

So that while much more research needs to be carried out on the employment effects of North Sea fuels than has been undertaken here, it nevertheless seems safe to conclude that the employment effect in a British context will be minimal!

If this conclusion is anywhere near the mark then a conclusion on wages necessarily follows; that there will be no general rise in real wages due directly to oil-related developments. It is possible of course, that certain sections of the working class and in particular certain sections of the middle class will receive rises in real income when the B.O.P. savings start to work through in the late 70's and early 80's as part of a political re-stabilisation policy on behalf of the ruling class (analogous to the labour aristocracy payments of earlier periods) and this would be in line with the bipartisan approach of the two main political parties.

The North East

Much of what remains of this Section is concerned with the North East of Scotland for the simple reason that there is more printed material on the North East than on the Highlands, (or for that matter on Scotland as a whole).

A Government-commissioned report (the Gaskin Report) which got under way in October 1966, estimated that the North East contained a population of just under 450,000 with 210,000 of these living in and immediately around the City of Aberdeen. A circle around the City with a radius of 16 miles which encompassed the burghs of Stonehaven, Banchory (18 miles away), Inverurie and Ellon, boosted this figure to a total of 240,000. The other sizeable population zones were Elgin and its surrounding region, a circle with a radius of 16 miles enclosed a population of 66,000 and the same measure applied to the Buchan region which included Peterhead and Fraserburgh covered 47,000 people.

The report states that:

> "The North East of Scotland presents a particular variant of the difficulties besetting all the economically 'lagging' regions of Britain. The problem, which is basically one of 'growth', has two outstanding symptoms. The first is a relatively high rate of unemployment. The second is a level of outward migration - both to the rest of Britain and overseas - which is so high as to exceed the natural increase of the population. It must be stressed that these are symptoms of the same malady- they are connected with other significant conditions arising from the basic slowness of growth."

The report goes on to suggest that the North East was losing 4,500 people a year net. Further:-

> "A significant feature of employment in the service industries is the predominance of female labour. Women account for about 51 per cent of service employment compared with only 37 per cent of the regional labour force as a whole. Moreover, women predominate most in the fastest growing categories, e.g. professional and scientific services and miscellaneous services- while the sectors relying most on male labour are either declining (e.g. transport) or are regionally under-represented (e.g. National Government service, insurance, banking and finance). Expansion in service employment will be associated with a continued rise in the proportion of women; and although new male jobs will be created on some scale in a few sectors, e.g. motor repairers and garages, the service industries as a whole are unlikely to create substantial additional demands for male labour. Thus while expansion in service sectors can make

a valuable contribution to the region's future development, by generating income and by raising activity rates among women, it cannot replace an inflow of manufacturing as a means of reducing net migration rates."

"Finally, wages in the North East. It has already been stated .... that the region is a low-wage area. This is a view which is widely accepted though hard evidence to support it is lacking. It is, however, almost certainly true. For one thing, such low-wage industries as agriculture, textiles, food, drink and tobacco, construction, miscellaneous services and distributive trades are heavily represented in the region. Indeed with the exception of paper and shipbuilding, the North East is poorly supplied with high-wage industries. Secondly, not only is there this predominance of low-wage industries, but evidence suggests that wages in the North East are below the average even for these industries. This is to be expected since there is a lack of competition from high-paying industries. The manufacturing questionnaire showed that in October 1966 out of twelve of the Standard Industrial Classification categories for which there was information, in seven categories every firm was paying its men an hourly rate below the British average. For women, the situation was better in that only in four out of the twelve industrial groups did every firm pay below the British average. For eleven of the twelve categories, however, at least 70 per cent of all firms paid below the national average for women."

Thus the North East of Scotland and the Highlands, etc., suffered acutely from the general malady afflicting the Scottish economy. Stripping the Gaskin Report of its empiricism which describes but does not explain, the North East suffered from a net outflow of capital, both financial and human, the former in search of higher profits, the latter a consequence of the financial outflow. The industrial structure was anything but modern, wages were in general below the Scottish average for most industries, unemployment was high, living conditions were generally poor and the social 'infrastructure' (housing, roads, social services, communications) left much to be desired.

On this foundation North Sea Oil and Gas developments have been superimposed in a completely unplanned fashion.

Eastern Scotland since the discovery of oil

During 1966-71 there was a continuing decline in the numbers employed in primary industries. The main loss of labour occurred in agriculture. In the manufacturing industries the two main areas of expansion were in food, drink and tobacco and in the category termed 'other manufacturing industries'. One estimate is that during the last three years both oil related development, and food, drink and tobacco, have each created approximately 1,000 new jobs a year. This is a considerable increase in employment and it is clear that with increasing momentum, oil and oil-related developments will become the 'motor' of economic change along the East Coast of Scotland, though much of this will be short-term and perhaps in decline by 1978-9 (see Table IV below).

Although it can be accurately estimated how many people are employed in the oil industry at present, extrapolating from present trends is difficult as the pace of exploitation of the North Sea Oil resources is not an even one.

The North East Scotland Development Association estimate that the following numbers were employed in the oil industry in N.E. Scotland at the end of 1973:

MALE	FEMALE	TOTAL
3,649	302	3,951

NESDA state that:

"**By 1975** with exploration running at a high level and oilfield development and production under way, **the number employed is certain to rise again, probably**

exceeding 10,000...... This kind of rapid expansion has naturally had a secondary effect right through the local economy. There has been an influx of new commercial and professional offices as well as an expansion of established firms benefiting from the new industrial and consumer markets. Any estimate of the multiplier effect can only be a guess, but it is likely to have increased from its previous levels to between 1.5 and 2, meaning that 2,000 to 4,000 jobs have already been created by the spin-off from the offshore industry. This indirect employment could have risen to between 5,000 and 10,000 by 1975. **The industry would then account for 15,000 to 20,000 jobs."**

However, the Department of Political Economy at Aberdeen University, which is doing continuing research into the effect of oil developments on the economy of the North East, has come up with a set of figures different from those of NESDA. The figure are pitched on the conservative side. Firstly, because they reckon that services (such as housing) will lag behind demand and this will create unnecessary labour shortages and secondly, extracting oil from the North Sea will be a more prolonged process than some of the optimistic forecasts floating about would lead one to believe.

They reckon that virtually all the new directly oil-related jobs will be in the Aberdeen areas with the exception of 500 in the Peterhead area and a smaller number in the Elgin area which will be connected with developments in the Moray Firth as people commute from Elgin to the Firth to work.

The University have identified three phases in the oil developments. Exploration (using various types of rigs), construction, and production (when the platforms are fixed in position and the oil is flowing). Clearly there will be overlap in these three phases. When some fields eventually start producing others will be only newly discovered. Their figures for employees directly employed by the oil industry are:

Table IV

	1973	1976	1981
H.Q. Administration	1500	1500	1500
Exploration	1500	1500	2250
Construction	500	1500	2250
Production	500	1000	3000
TOTAL	4000	7000	9000

The University reckon that employment in the North East may develop in the following way:

Table V

	1971	1976	1981
Primary Industries	22,000	19,000/20,000	16,000/18,000
Manufacturing	45,000	52,000/53,000	56,000/58,000
Oil		7,000	9,000/10,000
Construction	17,000	19,000/20,000	16,000/19,000
Services	89,000	100,000/102,000	108,000/111,000
TOTAL	173,000	197,000/202,000	205,000/216,000

This total includes the self-employed. In the period 1972/76 of the possibility of between 24,000 and 29,000 additional jobs the preferred forecast lies in between at 26,000 new jobs. Similarly, in the period 1977/81 the preferred forecast is 11,000 new jobs in a range that could be between 8,000 and 19,000 jobs. In the period from 1977/81 the ratio breaks down to 4,000 male jobs and 7,000 female out of a projected total of 11,000 new jobs.

In the Grampian Region the distribution of the employed population in the University's estimation could be as follows:

Table VI

	1971	1976	1981
Aberdeen City	109,000	120,000	126.500
Kincardine & Deeside	6,000	6,500	6.500
Banff & Buchan	25,000	28.500	30.000
Gordon	10,000	9,500	9,000
Moray	23,000	24,500	26.000
GRAMPIAN REGION	173,000	199,000	208.000

It can be noted that Aberdeen City, Peterhead and Fraserburgh and Elgin will be the main urban areas to benefit from the creation of new jobs.

Little information is presently available on the Orkneys and Shetlands, HIDB areas or the Angus area, though it is doubtful if the employment effect will be substantial.

Thus although the University's estimates are lower than those of NESDA, there will still be considerable employment impact but it will tend to be centred on a few urban areas. **Already this concentration has led to major social problems in these areas - lack of adequate housing, rapidly rising rents and house prices, over-burdened social services, etc.**

On the wages front there can be little doubt that the average **money wage** in the North East must have risen considerably in the last few years. **This does not mean, however, that particular wage rates are equivalent to those paid for equivalent work elsewhere in Britain, indeed there is much evidence to suggest that 'cheap' labour is a feature to N.E. oil industry.** (See the Morning Star). It is much more difficult to assess the position with respect to real income given the announced rate of inflation in the N.E.; nevertheless it seems certain that those employed in the old low wage industries and those on fixed incomes, e.g. OAP's, widows etc., must have suffered a relative decline in recent years.

The West-Central industrial belt

Sufficient has been said above to indicate that little economic expansion can be expected in the economy as a whole and this holds true for the central belt of Scotland which is at the heart of Scotland's economic problem, with unemployment higher than the Scottish average and certainly the highest migration rate of any region of Britain.

It is estimated that a minimum of 35,000 male jobs will be lost in this area over the next five years exacerbating an already appalling economic situation. Indeed, it is no exaggeration to say that West Central Scotland faces a regional economic problem the like of which is not found anywhere else in Europe as a whole, let alone in Western Europe!

Of course, some engineering firms in the central belt have received orders for equipment and the effects of this local 'sub-contracting' may continue for some years though would seem to be related to the construction side of the industry and thus of no likely long-term importance. Indeed if these orders are being taken at the expense of other markets then the long-run effect may be negative. Some examples of such orders are **pumps** by Weir in Glasgow, **deck modules** by Foster Wheeler John Brown in Dumbarton, **generators** by Parsons Peebles in Edinburgh, **compressors** by Howdens in Glasgow and **cranes** by Carruthers in East Kilbride. Nevertheless the employment impact has so far been slight on the Scottish engineering industry.

There are two other factors which have undoubtedly affected the economic impact on the Central belt, but both are difficult to quantify.

Firstly, it is almost certainly the case that the pace of exploitation has necessitated both rig and platform builders requiring (because of present designs) deep water construction sites which are only available outwith the central belt coast-line. Planned exploitation almost certainly would have allowed rig and platform designs to be developed such that a greater proportion of the construction work could be located and sub-contracted in the central belt, particularly around West Central Scotland. Thus not only are areas of great scenic beauty being spoiled and Highland communities disrupted - at great social costs, - but democratic rights of public inquiry are also being eroded in order to facilitate the needs of the construction companies.

There is, of course, the suspicion that some sites outwith the central belt were chosen in order to by-pass the wages and conditions imposed by the unionised working class.

Secondly, and a subject which requires much more research not only with respect to North Sea developments, is the effect on the Scottish economy of the vast capital-raising operations of the Edinburgh-based merchant banks, insurance companies, etc. If capital is being raised in Scotland for North Sea purposes at the expense of presnet Scottish industries, then it can be expected that some presently declining industries, including those in the West Central belt, will decline even more rapidly. It does not follow, of course, that the profits from capital invested in the North Sea by Scottish merchant banks, etc., will be used to finance old or new industries in Scotland!

One other point may be made. To the extent that it was ever Labour or Tory government policy to build up a Scottish oil industry technology (and there is little indication that this was ever so) then their approach to the provision of the necessary academic and technical education leaves much to be desired. Once again they imposed much less severe conditions than did other governments. Quoting from the Fabian pamphlet 'Oil for the Highlands' (June 1974):- "Education at all stages was part of the bargain between Norway and the oil companies. They have to train their Norwegian counter-parts so that at every stage in technology and management there are as many Norwegians as foreginers - often more. On the ground most of the top level engineers are Norwegians and even on the rigs more and more Norwegians are taking over. There the colonial situation has not arisen because of government foresight and toughness. There has also been much more educational investment in Norway than ever before.

Finally with respect to the S.E., S.W. and Borders of Scotland, little if anything will be forthcoming from a progressive economic point of view for these areas.

Conclusion on the economic impact

It is difficult to escape the conclusion that the underlying economic strategy of the ruling class - supported by both Tory and Labour Governments - with respect to North Sea fuels must be seen within the context of short-run B.O.P. savings and the political perspective of membership of the Common Market. On the evidence to hand, while the B.O.P. savings will be substantial they are likely to be the minimum possible (unless the fuel offtake rate is astronomical) and no evidence is available that a major immediate and positive restructuring of the domestic industrial economy is foreseen. Rather the past trend of unplanned development at a rapid rate is likely to continue with the consequences already noted with respect to living standards and working and living conditions in order to re-build the British ruling class's dominant position in the capitalist world as the major Common Market member. Whether the North Sea fuels will provide sufficient finance to carry this ruling class strategy is open to some doubt when set against (for example), Governmental international borrowing requirements, estimated by the Godley-Cripps team at Cambridge at some £11,000 millions by 1977 costing some £1,000 million in interest charges on the B.O.P.

Thus this major economic resource is to be squandered and the British working class subjected to a further period of economic and social stagnation!

7. The Requirements of an Integrated Fuel Policy

By way of introduction, two areas of the international oil industry are briefly discussed - both bear on the future world price of oil.

Firstly, the success of the OPEC countries has forced **the international 'majors'** to tighten their overall monopoly grip on refining and distribution. Thus, Professor Odell has argued that there has been "the apparent move towards the re-establishment of an international oil cartel, such as existed in the 1930's, by the companies responsible for most of the trade in world oil. Their motivation is clearly profit protection ..." Further: "Though not openly declared the 'arrangements' also imply inter-company agreement not to undercut each other in the market place - particularly in Western Europe, where all the twenty or so companies involved have marketing interests. Price increases already achieved by mid-1971 indicate the quick success of these arrangements, with fuel oil in particular available only at twice the price charged a year previously." No sign, therefore, that world oil prices will fall due to the actions of the international 'majors' - indeed, the tendency is likely to be for prices to rise due to their monopoly profit maximisation activities!

Secondly, the actions of **the producing countries grouped around OPEC,** through continued moves towards full nationalisation or majority state participation, guarantee firstly that they intend to reap substantial revenues in the future as against the economic imperialist low pricing of the past and, secondly, that they intend to limit the rate of off-take of their fuel. Both actions will, to say the least, tend to maintain oil prices at their present level.

(The following countries have, in recent months, taken steps towards nationalisation or majority participation - Venezuela, Saudi Arabia, Kuwait, Abu Dhabi, Quator, Iraq, Libya and Nigeria).

Thus it seems safe to conclude that world oil prices are unlikely to drop markedly over, say, the next ten years; already the recent price increases have completely altered the relative costs of (domestic) primary fuels in a very marked manner and attention can now be turned to overall domestic energy policy.

Two problems stand out in the consideration of the viability of an integrated fuel policy. To some extent they relate to the political and economic environment within which such a policy is pursued. Firstly, with a **"mixed" fuel economy,** with portions of it in State and the rest in private capitalist hands, it is impossible to work out the best long-term policy for utilising these fuels. Secondly, owing to the **cyclical nature** of capitalist production, planning for future domestic and industrial consumption is always a hazardous affair, particularly for an economy that is likely to be tied for some time to international capitalist trade and payments systems.

The first problem can, of course, be solved by the complete nationalisation of the oil industry in Britain, so that by the early 1980's the country could obtain almost all its requirements for energy from State-owned gas, hydro-electricity, oil and coal. This would leave nuclear fuel, such as uranium, to be obtained on the world market - though it is possible that the development, economically, of the fast breeder nuclear reactors will assist in slowing down the long-term tendency for the price of uranium to rise.

The second problem cannot be completely eliminated this side of taking State power and integrating the economy into the other planned Socialist economies (both present and future). But a powerful anti-monopoly offensive, which among other things nationalised the oil industry, could increase the influence of the organised Labour and Trade Union movement in bending the machinery of the State towards a policy of regulating the activities of the monopolies, **in particular holding down the price of energy to the mass of the people.**

This could result in better investment fore-casting for the energy-producing industries as well as other areas of the nationalised sector, but obviously could not insulate Britain from the full effects of a widespread recession in the economics of the capitalist world.

It should be borne in mind, however, that there will be real and complex forecasting and planning problems even under Socialism. Nothing more is attempted in this Section than a brief look at some of the current problems and a suggestion about the scope of nationalisation, with respect to energy.

It is accepted here that the nationalised (fuel) industries have to date been operated, in the main, for the benefit of the monopolies. (For example, the under-pricing of coal in the 40's and 50's, leading to low wages and low investment and, eventually, the run-down of the industry; the excess profits made by Coal Board suppliers and, one suspects, the excess profits made by the companies responsible for the work entailed in the nation-wide conversion to natural gas, etc.). Even given this, the recent massive increase in the price of oil and the likelihood of further price increases, now make the other fuels much more attractive since their prices can be allowed to rise and output expanded. It is unlikely that there will be attempts to do a major "hiving-off" operation, since there is much accumulated experience at milking nationalised industries while at the same time discrediting them in the eyes of the working class. This latter exercise may now be much more difficult than in the past, given the likely "profitability" of the nationalised fuel sector due to increased prices, and it is possible that this "milking"/"discrediting" exercise may become the "Achilles heel" of the present British form of State monopoly capitalism - the "mixed-managed economy".

Nevertheless, the major problem remains - what rates of expansion are to be applied to the coal industry, the nuclear power industry, the gas and oil industries (i.e. the primary fuel industries) and how much should be spent on research and development on other energy sources, e.g. tidal energy, and what effects would such expansion rates have on the major final supplier of energy, the Central Electricity Generating Board?

Some indication of the massive revision of estimates for future primary fuel consumption arising from the oil crisis can be obtained from Table vii below, which is taken from a European Communities Commission Background Report of June 12th 1974:-

Table VII Total primary Energy needs of the Community in 1985 (1)

	1973 (estimates)		1985 (initial fore-casts)		1985 (objectives)	
	Mill. toe	%	Mill. toe	%	Mill. toe	%
Solid fuels	227	22.6	175	10	250	16
Oil	617	61.4	1160	64	655	41
Natural gas	117	11.6	265	15	375	24
Hydro-elec. power & other	30	3.0	40	2	35	2
Nuclear energy	14	1.4	160	9	260	17
	1005	100	1800	100	1575	100

(1) Internal consumption and exports and bunkers.

History has, in a very positive manner, vindicated the position taken up by both the miners and the Communist Party with respect to the role of coal as a primary fuel in the British economy. Against the prevailing trend in the '60's - held by the Tories and the bulk of the social democrats, that coal should be run down - both the N.U.M. and the C.P. argued that coal output should be maintained at mid-1950 levels (240 million tons) perhaps even expanded, that investment should be substantially increased and some concentration of output should take place, but that coal as the major indigenous fuel at that time should provide the major energy source.

So now - belatedly, to say the least - and with massive quantities of oil and gas available domestically, coal output is to be expanded.

The N.C.B. has argued that output should be expanded from the 1970 figure of 140 million tons to 150 m/t by 1980. The N.U.M. argue that output should rise to 200 m/t by 1985, and this latter would not seem unrealistic against the European Communities Commission's argument that "present levels of coal production in the Community ... must at least be maintained. (This means maximising production in Germany and the United Kingdom)." Further: "To achieve this will require rationalising production; developing improvements in mining techniques; achieving a manpower policy based on attractive remuneration, secure career prospects, and improved working conditions for miners."

The Commission argue that coal imports will still be necessary; thus the British coal industry could perhaps become a major net exporter, particularly if present oil-fired power stations are converted to coal, and coal gasification is once more utilised in a major way, as the Commission suggest.

The resurgence of the gas industry in the last few years probably points the way to future trends. The use of gas will certainly continue to increase and it may become the major fuel for domestic heating use.

Given present estimates of world oil reserves and the reserves in the U.K. sector of the North Sea, it seems obvious that the growth of domestic oil consumption should be constrained where appropriate domestic substitutes such as coal are available. Given the downward revision in oil consumption asked for in the Communities' estimates in Table VI on the previous page, and their request that coal replace oil in power stations, etc., the same logic seems applicable to Britain.

Nuclear power is taken in conjunction with the generation of electricity because of the very close relationship between the two.

Nigel Hawkes, writing in the Business Section of the "Observer" on 5th May, 1974, drew attention to a number of problems that have affected the Central Electricity Generating Board. He indicated that the recent 30 per cent increase in electricity prices only reflected the increased price of oil and coal and would not cancel out the deficit which the C.E.G.B. is running and which will amount to an estimated £200 million during 1974. This will be met by a Government subsidy. He estimated that an additional 20 per cent on the latest tariffs would be necessary to bring the C.E.G.B. into financial balance and that this took no account of a further increase in the price of coal promised for autumn, 1974. He identified a number of specific planning and investment errors, some of which are as follows:-

(1) That nuclear reactors selected by the C.E.G.B. in 1965 are now more than £750 million over their budget and have not yet generated a single kilowatt of electricity. In that year the C.E.G.B. did a deal with Atomic Power Constructors (one of the then three nuclear consortia) to build four Advanced Gas-cooled Reactors (AGR) at a cost of £625 million, but now they will cost at least £875 million.

The South of Scotland Electricity Board (SSEB) ordered a single AGR, bringing the total to five. All are way behind on their initial completion date, and Hawkes estimates that the ensuing cost of replacement power from older stations will add a further £500 million to the costs of AGR programme by the time the fourth is on stream in 1980. The SSEB AGR is also running late and adds £150 million to this figure.

He says that:-

"Not all these problems can be laid at the C.E.G.B.'s door. The Nuclear Installations Inspectorate contributed by demanding changes to make the stations safer, and the consortia, with complete design and construction responsibility have failed to conquer an unending series of problems.

Even when the AGRs are finished, the industry concedes, operating them is going to be a tight-rope balancing act."

(2) On the general question of building and commissioning nuclear plant, Hawkes says:-

"Nor is there much sign that the C.E.G.B. has learned wisdom with the years. It is now pressing the Government to allow it to go ahead with a huge programme of nuclear ordering. Whatever the merits of the 18 machines chosen - the Westinghouse designed pressurised water reactors - they will be wholly new to the C.E.G.B. And yet, the Board intends to go ahead with a £2,000 million reactor programme without even building a prototype to find out the snags."

The pressure to adopt the Westinghouse design comes from G.E.C. which owns 50 per cent of the National Nuclear Corporation. The other big shareholder is the

Government with 15 per cent. Westinghouse own 45 per cent of Framatome, the leading French vendor, and these three monopolies, G.E.C., Westinghouse and Framatome, are clearly aiming to carve up the market for nuclear reactors in Western Europe with an American design which will effectively knock out all other competition.

On 4th February 1974, the Select Committee on Science and Technology of the House of Commons issued a report which found unproven the C.E.G.B.'s case for buying reactors of U.S. instead of British design. On the evidence publicly available, it concluded that the Government should withhold approval of the C.E.G.B. Proposal. As the Financial Times of 5th February, 1974, put it:-

"The report puts its finger on the weaknesses in the C.E.G.B.'s case; the contrast in its evidence on electricity demand forecasts, between the pessimism of August 1972, and the optimism of December 1973; the uncertainties in the data on costs submitted for a type of reactor of which there is, as yet, virtually no operating experience; the acceptability or otherwise of its proposals to the Government's nuclear safety authority".

The recent Government decision to back the British design is, therefore, to be supported. However, it does not remove the difficulties inherent in the C.E.G.B. or the construction industry, both of which in reality are still in private hands.

Nationalisation and an integrated fuel policy

We must therefore consider the areas of the economy that will need to be taken into public ownership to provide the necessary material basis for an integrated fuel policy. It is not intended to delve deeply into the economics of such a programme.

It can be noted here, however, that even the Tories may go for an "integrated" fuel policy (given the trend of the last 15-20 years towards a corporate state) if this should bolster their class and its interests.

Thus a clear distinction is necessary between a class collaborationist "integrated" fuel policy which operates against the interests of the working class, both in terms of the cost of energy to the working class as consumers, and in terms of the longer-term employment and income prospects, and one which operates against the monopolies which involves the working class in its operation in participatory control, which reduces the price of energy to them as consumers and which leads on in a positive way to a broader anti-monopoly offensive.

Such a progressive nationalisation programme would consist of the nationalisation of the offshore oil and gas resources, with compensation for the licensees extending only to their development costs (minus Government grants for plant and machinery) and leaves the problem of refining of offshore oil and its distribution, and for some of the production its possible export, to be dealt with.

The private sector of British Petroleum (the most substantial capitalist shareholder in the company is Burmah), the 40 per cent of Shell owned by British shareholders and the Burmah/Castrol group will need to be nationalised to provide what the Labour Party have called a National Hydrocarbons Corporation with a network of refineries, tanker fleets and distribution points.

Additionally, both Shell and B.P. have extensive interests in the chemical sector, where crude oil is the major basic foodstock.

I.C.I. - the dominant chemical concern in Britain - has a share of the Ninian oil field in the North Sea and, again, if nationalised could, with B.P.'s and Shell's chemical plants, become part of a massive State-owned chemical corporation inter-linked with the National Hydrocarbons Corporation.

Chemical companies like I.C.I. are taking steps to integrate backwards into the heavier end of the oil business, while the oil companies may have to develop their downstream activities (that is, petrochemical schemes).

Diversification by the major oil companies also includes the Shell Group's agreement to invest an initial 200 million dollars in a joint scheme with Gulf Oil to produce high temperature gas-cooled nuclear reactors, and Exxon's (Esso) £85 million research and development programme, which stretched over the next six years, will examine the conversion of coal into oil.

On the nuclear side, G.E.C. which owns 50 per cent of the National Nuclear Corporation, is an obvious candidate for nationalisation. As well as occupying a dominant place in the nuclear energy field, it is also a substantial supplier to the G.P.O.

In the coal industry the Left's long-existing aim of nationalisation of the mining machinery suppliers and the coal distributors, would need to be carried through.

The carrying through of these nationalisation measures would mean that a number of the most profitable monopolies would be brought under State control, which would be a substantial step forward in exerting control over 'the commanding heights of the economy.'

Such a struggle, if carried through to success, could take the Labour Movement further into the anti-monopoly phase of the struggle for socialism.

8. A political perspective

This final section is simply intended to outline - **in brief form** - some ideas on the prospects associated with the availability of North Sea oil and gas. It is hoped nevertheless that these ideas will help point the way to a political and economic programme around which leading sections of the Labour Movement can be drawn.

There is no intention, however, to offer in any way a supposedly complete economic programme for the total problem of the British economy - though at one level the "British" problem and the problem associated with the availability of North Sea fuels are one and the same, an insufficiency of domestic capital investment.

In the introduction to this article three "options" were noted. The first of these - the ruling class option - has been adequately dealt with in previous sections, and little more need be said here. The second "option" - the Scottish Nationalist one - is dealt with here in contra-distinction to the third - the working class "option".

The real and very present needs of the British working class are - income, security and steady economic growth; increased democratisation at almost every level, and world peace. These issues are, to a greater or lesser degree, interconnected. Any economic and political programme must, therefore, encompass them to a greater or lesser degree.

It should be apparent, therefore, that the Nationalist "option" in no way matches up to such a programme. To take only one strand of the foregoing needs - the economic one - the Nationalist programme would leave the bulk of the oil industry in U.S. hands and, as history has shown, U.S. capitalists operate on behalf of U.S. capitalism rather than, as a minimum, on behalf of the specific domestic ruling class. Further, the accompanying idea that oil revenues to a Scottish Exchequer can somehow induce foreign capital to come to Scotland is by no means new- indeed, it has been tried with no success for at least the last 15 years, and if the 1964-70 investment grants of 45 per cent were not inducement enough (coupled to all the other paraphernalia of "regional" policy) - and, as Benn has pointed out, it means State subsidy without State control - then anything above that figure surely entails full nationalisation and new State-owned and controlled industry.

However, nationalisation and new State industries in a purely Scottish context, while possible, can in no sense be seen as progressive, as the examples given illustrate. Such an idea or variations on it, must be treated with the same contempt that should be levelled at past "regional" policies - that is, they were never really meant to work, they were only intended to con the Labour Movement into thinking that they would work!

This is not the place to treat the national question fully, but it should be obvious that only an all-British approach to the controlled exploitation of the North Sea fuels offers any solution, and this against a background of withdrawal from the Common Market.

It should be noted at this point that the present Labour Government's initiative in setting up Scottish oil development offices, etc. and majority State participation, coupled to transfers of Civil service jobs to Central Scotland, is very much in line with past "regional" policy and nationalisation measures and offers little hope that Scotland's - let alone Britain's - employment and income needs can be met.

The real question to be posed about North Sea fuels is this: what advantages does the

availability of the fuels give to the working class in terms of the needs outlined above?

Firstly, in terms of both employment and general consumption, North Sea oil and gas ensure a supply of raw material for one of the world's fastest growing industries - the chemical industry. Now, while it may be true that the recent massive increases in oil prices will slow down the expansion of the chemical industry, this may be offset to the extent that other feedstocks, e.g. coal, are developed, so that while the following figures were compiled prior to the recent oil crisis, there is little danger that they vastly over-estimate the future growth of the chemical industry.

Table VIII. Output Forecasts of Petroleum-based Organic Chemicals (Mill. Metric Tons)

	1960	1969	1975	1980	1985
U.S.A.	10.0	24.5	45	65	90
Western Europe	2.3	15.5	35	60	100
Rest of Western World	0.7	11.0	25	40	60
TOTAL:	13.0	51.0	105	165	250

Even if the estimated annual growth rate for Western Europe which underlies the above figures is reduced from 13 per cent to 8 per cent, production would still double between 1970 and 1980. Plastics alone, which take over 40 per cent of total organic chemicals in their manufacture, would reach a world figure of 100 million tons by 1980 as against 30 million tons in 1970. Other "end products" are resins, solvents, detergents, fertilisers, pharmaceuticals, etc., and all are likely to be subject to growth rates similar to the above.

Britain and Scotland within it, must obtain a major share of this expansion, using North Sea oil and coal as feedstocks, rather than such expansion taking place in continental Western Europe.

To take but one example, the pharmaceutical industry in Britain, presently dominated by foreign, mainly U.S. monopolies, and selling almost wholly to the National Health Service at monopoly prices, could be nationalised and its expansion controlled in the interests of the working people.

Coupled to North Sea Oil as a feedstock, this would give Britain not only a better Health Service and expanded employment, but also a major exporting industry in world terms.

If the Nationalist programme were to be followed, however, it is difficult to see how these foreign monopolies could be controlled, since Scotland itself does not have a sufficient market to absorb the output of a modern pharmaceutical industry and would thus either need to compete with them internationally, which is unlikely, or capitulate to them!

One final example can be given—the fertiliser industry, presently dominated by a few massive companies. **If the political battle can be won to take Britain out of the Common Market, then the whole question of British agriculture comes directly onto the agenda.** Though British agriculture is highly capitalised, much would need to be done to ensure a greater self-sufficiency in food supplies (even in a Left government/private agriculture transitional period) and the fertiliser industry would have an important and expanded role to play.

Thus, once again, Britain would benefit not only in terms of domestic food supplies and employment but also in terms of export earnings, since world demands for food and hence fertilisers will continue to expand rapidly. Only if such domestic industrial expansion takes place can the working peoples of Britain be assured of high future income and employment. Since there is no indication that this will happen if present policies are continued or if the Nationalist "option" is pursued, then the only viable and realistic solution is State ownership of North Sea oil and gas and new chemical-based industries set up and run by the State. Within a framework of increased democracy and control within the present Nationalised industries as advanced by the Left, an expanded State sector based on North Sea oil and operated on behalf of the masses rather than the few becomes a distinct possibility.

The ideas outlined in the previous sub-section, coupled to the proposals for an integrated fuel policy and further nationalisation outlined in Section 7, perhaps lay the basis for the economic component of a strategy for moving towards Socialism—the anti-monopoly alliance—which draws around the working class other strata in society who also suffer at the hands of the monopolies. The present demands of the Health Service workers on the future development of the N.H.S. are but one indication of new strata being drawn into struggle and fighting for class policies as well as wages.

That this and many other such struggles need a broad yet detailed class programme and perspective is not open to question. The Left's role is a crucial one in the building of such an anti-monopoly alliance, in giving the movement a class programme and perspective, and much more detailed work needs to be undertaken on both the political and economic aspects of the relationship between North Sea fuels and an anti-monopoly alliance.

(1) This essay was originally prepared as a discussion document for the Scottish Committee of the Communist Party.
(2) The author wishes to thank his friend, Gary Morton, for the provision of some of the material for this essay.
(3) V.I. Lenin **Collected Works** Vol.15, pp.293-6.
(4) See in particular C.I.S. Pamphlet, **The Oil Fix** (1974).
(5) **The Observer,** 21.4.74.

Regional Policy & The Scottish Assembly

Bill Niven

INTRODUCTION

One aspect of nationhood which the Scottish working class has always used to advantage has been the existence of a T.U.C. in Glasgow with a degree of autonomy over Scottish affairs, including a separate General Council, acting as a quite distinct pressure group on Government, such as it exists, in St Andrew's House, Edinburgh.

Any further measure of devolution of power from Westminster to Edinburgh, therefore, opens up new possibilities for the S.T.U.C.—and certainly the proposals contained in the White Paper on Devolution, published just before the October election, would seem to confer on St Andrew's House power to deal with a substantial area of important business.

The emergence of a Labour-controlled Scottish Assembly linked to an already left-orientated STUC General Council would form a powerful axis, capable of implementing many resolutions emanating directly from T.U. Congress over the next five years.

There are strong historical and personal links within the Scottish Labour Movement based on a broad Left-unity—spanning the Co-operative Movement, Labour Party, Communist Party and STUC—which is of a quite different political complexion to, say, the T.U.C. General Council in London, which is still Right-orientated, and the amorphous Parliamentary Labour Party. Are we then entering a new era in the role of the STUC which will see a vast increase in its power and stature and which will make Annual Congress much more meaningful in terms of its economic and political demands as expressed in resolutions from affiliated bodies?

What's good for the STUC may well be good for Scottish Government—within the confines of the devolved powers, of course. What changes in economic and political demands should be raised in readiness for the Assembly? What refinements, if any, will be required in Left strategy and organisation?

The Economy and Regional Policy

Whilst Regional Policies have become increasingly sophisticated, they have also become increasingly costly. The best that can be said of them is that they have helped. They have created jobs but failed to prevent jobs disappearing. The tendency for capital accumulating in some areas to the deprivation of others, is a fundamental law associated with the dynamic of Capitalism.

It has never been easy to calculate the total amount of Government assistance to industry in the creation of jobs in Scotland, but examining investment grants, regional employment premiums, S.E.T. additional payments and grants under the local employment Act, and other grants (including S.E.T. refunds by hotels, D.E.P. training assistance and payment by the Highlands and Islands Development Board), we find that in 1968-69, government assistance amounted to £128.3m. Assuming 1968/9 as a mean point between 1966 and 1971, then the expenditure over that five year period would be £641.5million. The STUC estimated that 105,600 new jobs were provided (it works out at over £6,000 per job) but that there was a corresponding loss of 156,000 jobs.

If we examine total public expenditure on trade industry and employment in assistance of private industry in Scotland between 1964-5 and 1972-3, then we find that government assistance has amounted to £951.9million. In 1972/3 alone this was £192.3m. (Table 1).

Table I

Public Expenditure on Trade, Industry and Employment

£ million		1972/3			1964/5-1972/3	
Private Industry	Scotland	G.B.	Scotland per cent	Scotland	G.B.	Scotland per cent
Investment Grants	34.6	295	11.7	326.4	2565	12.7
Selective, Regional & Gen. Assistance	3.1	18	17.2	3.1	18	17.2
Local Employment Act	26.2	69	38.0	165.8	528	31.4
REP and SET (additional payments)	37.2	101	36.8	248.0	811	30.6
Shipbuilding Industry	(29.5)	81	36.4	(44.0)	148	29.7
Employment Services and Redundancy Fund	21.7	200	10.9	79.6	942	8.5
Aircraft and Aerospace projects		(126)			(729)	
National Space Programme		(4)			(78)	
General R and D Support	(10.0)	(5)	8.1	(55.0)	(108)	5.1
Other Assistance (incl. films, tourism IRC, general investment, cotton		(-11)			(157)	
Refinancing Export Credit	(30.0)	297	10.1	(30.0)	297	10.1
TOTAL:	192.3	1185	16.2	951.9	6381	14.9

It cannot be said any longer that the jobs being lost through the hole in the bucket are those in the old heavy industries. During the '50s and '60s the cry from the Labour Movement in Scotland was for a fair share of the new science-based industries with growth potential to replace the "dying industries" which constituted such a large proportion of Scotland's economy. The problem was one of structure, said the pundits; what was required, they said, was a better balance between the old and the new, the heavy and the light, labour intensive and capital intensive, skilled and unskilled, and so on and so forth.

Today, however, the problem of redundancy and closure covers the whole spectrum of the economy, including so-called growth sectors, such as computers, tractors and agricultural equipment, aero-engines, electric motors, valves, earth moving equipment, carpets and foodstuffs.

Since 1971 redundancies have occurred in such stalwart growth companies as Honeywell Controls, Burroughs Machines, N.C.R., Rolls Royce, Massey Ferguson, Caterpillar Tractor, General Motors, Singers, Veeder-Root and G.E.C. (Satchwell Sunvic).

More recently, there were complete closures at Grays Carpet Factory, Robertsons Jam Factory and two companies in the East Kilbride growth centre, Hilti Equipment and Tolland Engineering, and Beaverbrook closed the "Scottish Daily Express".

None of the above companies readily falls into the category of the "old dying industries". Indeed, there is a strong suggestion that the number of foreign-owned companies, mainly U.S. Corporations, operating in many different countries, plays a significant role in the level of employment in Scotland at any given time.

On a per capita basis, Scotland occupies the second top position in the league table of countries receiving U.S. capital investment. (See Table II below).

Table II

Country or Area	Investment Per Capita 1969 (mid-year estimates)
Canada	439.48
Scotland	143.20
Australia	126.63
UK	81.65
Belgium/Luxembourg	69.58
Switzerland	60.63
Netherlands	50.59
Germany	46.77
Venezuela	40.80
Argentina	32.67
New Zealand	31.54
France	30.00
Sweden	22.33
Mexico	22.27
South Africa	18.83
Norway	16.04
Italy	13.41
Brazil	12.06
Denmark	11.76
Colombia	10.58
Spain	8.90
Peru	7.25
Philippines	7.14
Chile	6.70
Japan	6.21
India	0.26
EEC	34.11
World	8.22

It may well be that with world 'markets in a state of perpetual fluidity due to intensifying competition, output from the large Corporation needs to be flexible; and it is much easier to expand or contract in the branch-plant rather than the parent-company. So that, although foreign investment may provide some relief in the short term to those who need it most, in the long term the new structure created is highly volatile with employment prospects ebbing and flowing in an extremely sensitive way as world demand (or that company's market share) increases and decreases.(1) So while the structure may be different and the balance may have altered after decades of incentives, the percentage level of unemployment in Scotland remains double that in the U.K. The new structure with multi-national corporations, science-based and all, far from balancing the Scottish economy, is probably just as unstable as ever; more so when one takes into consideration the further employment problems in the basic industries of steel and shipbuilding. It should be stressed that neither steel nor shipbuilding can be described as "dying industries"—both are reckoned to be "growth centres".

The proposals for the steel industry (although currently under review by Wedgewood Benn) would mean an improvement in Scottish steal output from three million tons currently to four and a half million tons, but with a corresponding reduction in the number of jobs from 26,000 to 19,000.

Given a 1:1 multiplier effect, the total loss of jobs in West-Central Scotland would, therefore, be 14,000.

The Shipbuilding Industry is less advanced in terms of forward thinking, but the Booz Allen Report, commissioned by the Tories and published in 1973, emphasised that world merchant shipping was once more a growth industry and argued the case for an increase in U.K. output up to 2½ million tons, but again this was to be achieved with a corresponding reduction in the U.K. labour force of nearly one half, from 61,000 to 35,000.

Given the distribution of shipbuilding, ship repairing and marine-engine manufacturing throughout the U.K. and its heavy influence on Scottish employment, then the reduction in the labour force should be of the order of 15,000 directly and indirectly affected, **thus making a total loss of jobs in Steel and Shipbuilding of nearly 30,000 by 1977.**

Were this to happen as predicted, it would certainly compare in magnitude with the catastrophe which hit the Scottish economy during the 1960's, viz. 16,000 redundancies in the Coal Industry and a further 13,500 redundancies coming from Beeching's Rail rationalisation and closures.

The Labour Movement in Scotland failed to respond to the loss of jobs in the sixties; it would be a pity if there were no lesson to be learned. Yet, even now there would appear to be a fairly casual approach to the Steel proposals.

A number of meetings have been organised by the STUC and the Steel Unions where angry noises have been made, but the great problem will lie in trying to sustain any sort of campaign of resistance over such a long period. (Open hearth furnaces are to be phased out between now and 1980).

The 1974 Congress Resolution states..."This Congress notes with approval the policy of the affiliated Steel Unions to resist closures and redundancy, and to insist that no such closures shall take place until satisfactory alternative job opportunities have been made available in the locality for all those who will be made redundant. The Congress pledges full support to the affiliated Unions for any action taken to assert that policy."

The attention of Benn, Heffer and Gregor McKenzie has already been drawn to it. The Left should demand that they carry out their part.

A New Approach

If these were the only aspects of the Scottish economic scene to be considered, then there would be little chance of unemployment dropping below its present level of around 100,000 before the 1980's, given predicted redundancies in both the private and public sector.

As an aside, it should be noted that in line with the national trend, the peaks and troughs in the level of unemployment are becoming less exaggerated and there is a trend towards a consistently higher level of unemployment; for example in Scotland out of 90,000 unemployed in December, 70,000 have been out of work for more than four weeks.

In reality, however, the situation is less bleak. The prospect of another 5 years of Labour Government—with Wedgwood-Benn and Eric Heffer in control of Industry and Regional Policies and committed to an extension of State intervention and public ownership, opens the way for a new approach to the question of high unemployment; and then, of course, there is the job opportunities arising from North Sea Oil and ancillary industries.

The STUC General Council is certainly ready to admit that during the 1974 period, Government and Ministers have been more willing to listen to Congress resolutions seeking to remedy Scotland's economic problems.

Indeed, many of the demands in this year's resolutions have already been implemented or there is a committtment from the Government to do so. For example, the first three clauses in the Resolution on the Scottish Economy are as follows:-

"Congress demands...

a) The Government play a specifically interventionist role in the financing and management of industry including, where necessary (1) the direction of industry to areas of persistent unemployment and low growth performance;

b) The establishment of a Scottish Development Authority to co-ordinate planning and initiate through a Scottish State Holding Company, the compulsory purchase of equity in firms and to establish enterprises where necessary;

c) The establishment of a West Central Scotland Development Authority charged with the responsibility of, and having the resources necessary to promote maximum development of (1) existing indigenous industry, and (2) of new male employing industry."

The White Paper on Industrial Regeneration published in August, contains proposals on all aspects of the above demands. Legislation is, however, still required for the setting up of such bodies and pressure must be applied at all levels to ensure that even with the slender majority which the new Government has, top priority is given to implementing the necessary legislation.

It appears as if the Scottish Development Agency will be responsible to the Government through the Secretary of State for Scotland. The precise nature of the Agency's powers has still to be determined, but there is a committment from Wedgwood-Benn and Willie Ross that consultation with the STUC will take place beforehand. It would be as well if during that consultation, the General Council of the STUC were to repeat Harold Wilson's statement during the election campaign, when speaking at the Apollo Centre, Glasgow, on 23rd September, that "in time the Scottish Development Agency may become responsible to the Scottish Assembly."

This seems a legitimate demand around which a campaign could be built in readiness for the setting up of the Scottish Assembly over the next two years.

This would put an entirely different complexion on that part of the White Paper on Devolution which ruled out the whole section on Trade and Industry as appropriate subject matter for the devolution of power, (the new powers passed to the Secretary of State for Scotland in December 1974 did, of course, help in this regard).

The Left view in Scotland on the devolution proposals was that the demand for a Scottish Assembly was basically an economic demand concerned with jobs and economic prosperity and, therefore, almost by definition, a Scottish Assembly must have some economic control over Trade and Industry.

In evidence to the Kilbrandon Commission, the Communist Party argued strongly for the devolution of economic powers, and the Eadie/Ewing/Robertson/Sillars pamphlet, which represented the focal point for Left Labour Party pressure on devolution, contained the following:-

"With the exception of the Highlands and Islands Development Board, no economic powers are to be vested in the Assembly. This is a serious error of judgement, especially when the Commission itself identified the dissatisfaction arising in Scotland from an inability even marginally to effect decisions about the Scottish economy."

The STUC argued less so. It said... "Accepting as we do the main recommendations of the Kilbrandon Report, we consider that there will be comparatively little devolution of power in the fields of trade, industry and employment. We believe that the Assembly should only have direct control over those matters which at present are administered through the Scottish Office and the Secretary of State for Scotland."

This standpoint is uncharacteristically negative, considering the degree of pressure which the STUC itself is able to generate across the whole front of Trade, Industry and Employment. The General Council position, therefore, must be sharpened, bearing in mind the Resolution passed by the rank-and-file at the 1974 Congress (passed almost unanimously, the only major exception being the General & Municipal Workers' Union) which spoke of the "**economic** and social malaise" in Scotland and demanded that there ought to be "**adequate** measures of self-Government."

218

The Role of the Public Sector

Another prospect which must brighten the horizon is the possible dominance of the public sector in Scotland in terms of numbers employed. For the first time in history it may well be the case that the public sector has a higher number of employees than the private sector.

At the moment there would appear to be just over 650,000 employees in Scotland in the public sector, which is approximately 30 per cent of the total. If the Labour Government carry through their proposals for State intervention, particularly in the Regions, and with particular regard to the North Sea Oil industry, then these figures will obviously increase.

In the nationalised industries, for example, there is a disproportionately high number of employees in Scotland, compared to that in the U.K., in rail, coal, steel, shipbuilding, atomic energy, telecommunications. Added to this there is the Local Government sector of the economy, including Health, Education and Public Transport employees.

On the East Coast, the North Sea Oil industry will, now that Labour is returned, have a substantial State involvement which spills over into ancillary industries; also on the East Coast there is the B.P. Petrochemical Industry at Grangemouth, partially State owned and also, now, the Ferranti enterprise, B.L.M.C., and Burmah with state involvement.

In West-Central Scotland, there are already three Rolls-Royce factories, publicly owned and employing approximately 8,000 people, allied to what was U.C.S. (now Govan Shipbuilders) which also has a majority state holding, and State involvement to the tune of £1.75m, in the ex-Beaverbrook "Scottish Daily Express", which is enough to ensure state control.

Further, the dispersal of 7,000 Civil Service jobs (to begin with) can only help the Scottish economy, even if it poses problems for the Civil Service Unions and the individuals concerned. Finally, the regeneration of demand and investment in Coal and the recanting of Beeching's policies due to increasing private transport costs, will all add to the number of employees in the Public Sector.

In total, then, one can see emerging a public sector dominance which may well provide an effective countervailing power to the previous dominance of U.S. multi-national concerns, especially if Government is prepared to adopt a position of utilising the public sector in a social-sense, using "social-cost" as a factor.

Even if the vague preliminary parts of the Labour Party's nationalisation programme are implemented, involving shipbuilding, ports and parts of the agricultural, forestry and fishing industries, then this in itself would raise the percentage employment in the public sector of the Scottish economy to just over 40 per cent.

Returning to the theme of the STUC Resolution on the Scottish Economy and the above references to State intervention and public control, even those aspects of the Resolution relating to the private sector have had some considerable attention from the Government.

Not only have the existing incentives been maintained but a number of steps have been taken to increase them.

The rate of Regional Employment Premiums has been doubled, thus pumping an additional £100million into manufacturing industry in the development areas, and this is now available to eligible firms throughout the whole of Scotland as a result of the decision to upgrade Edinburgh, Leith and Portobello to Development Area status.

Both the above points were given prominence in the STUC resolution, and so too was the demand for the tightening up of the issue of Industrial Development Certificates. Here too, the Government have acted by reducing the exemption limits to 5,000 square feet in South East England and 10,000 square feet in the rest of England.

So, all in all, there is a remarkable degree of unanimity in what should be done with regard to Regional Policies in the private sector insofar as the attraction of industry is concerned.

It would appear as if the D.T.I. officials over the years and through successive Governments, have got the incentives policy nearly right.

Criticism could still be levelled at the Department, however, for its failure to prevent jobs leaving. There is currently no dis-incentive to any employer to pack up and move to greener pastures.

It is perfectly feasible that a penalty of some sort could have been levied on such companies as those mentioned previously, namely Grays Carpets, Tolland Engineering, Hilti Equipment,

Beaverbrook Newspapers and Robertsons Jam, by virtue of the fact that they left Scotland, not because they were broke, but to make higher profits through economies of scale and rationalisation of the enterprise in England.

The D.T.I. officials would be entitled to reply to this criticism with the retort that the Trade Union Movement, at Joint Shop Stewards' level, has done little itself to prevent redundancy and closures, and with the exception of U.C.S. and Plessey as notable examples, this criticism would largely be correct.

The Movement has never really come to terms with the effect which Redundancy Payments has had on the resistance to redundancy and closures.

Even the relatively limited amounts of money which are dangled by the employer are sufficient to divide the workforce into those who are prepared to struggle and those who are ready to accept short-term benefits, and this in itself makes it an uphill struggle to develop any campaign of resistance.

Given this dilemma, the Labour Movement should perhaps begin to think about an increase in the level of redundancy payments, particularly the employers' contribution to the fund, such that it becomes prohibitive for the employer to engage in what has become known as a "cost reduction exercise" as distinct from a genuine reduction in the work load. The recent T.U.C. statement on redundancy, which in effect makes it illegal unless alternative work is made available is, of course, an even better proposition.

At a different level and in the atmosphere generated by the establishing of a Scottish Assembly, an alliance could be formed of M.P.'s, Ministers and D.T.I. officials, and an STUC Sub-Committee, to permanently monitor closures and redundancy, with proper powers to gain access to company finance. This "watch-dog" effect might dissuade employers from phoney redundancy attempts.

Finally on the economic front, two aspects which may be of significance but which can only be dealt with briefly; in the period 1961/71, the net emigration figure for Scotland was minus 380,000, whereas the figures issued in October 1974 show that, for the first time in 40 years, there was a net increase of 5,000. Emigration has had a crucial effect on the level of unemployment. Had it not been for emigration during the '60s, the real futility of Regional Policies would have been more evident, with the level of unemployment never less than 4½ per cent and rising cumulatively within the '60s to almost 8 per cent.

The change from net outflow is almost certainly as a result of North Sea Oil and the inflow of experienced foreign labour, taken together with the rising hopes of the indigenous population in the gold rush atmosphere. Secondly, all of the references to Regional Policies above might well turn out to be a macabre joke if the discussions earlier this year within the E.E.C. on regional development have to be taken at their face value. Since there is no guarantee that separate regional proposals can be applied within national frontiers on top of the regional proposals of the Community, the finesse and sophistication of British Regional Policy built up over the years, may well be sacrificed.

The "Financial Times" of 7th January, '74 made what was perhaps the most apt comment of all in regard to the E.E.C.'s Regional Aid Fund when it said:

..."The money in dispute, it is worth remembering, is derisory in absolute terms, a total sum of less than one ten thousandth of the combined G.N.P. of the Nine is involved, less than 0.25 per cent of projected British Government expenditure this year."

The Politics of the Scottish Assembly

There is an undeniable Left balance, politically, within the General Council and within the delegations to Congress. The policies of successive Congresses, whether in regard to Public Ownership, Incomes Policy, the Industrial Relations Act, or wider issues such as Chile, Apartheid, Nuclear Bases, have been Left by any standard; indeed, some people have seen the STUC, which meets in April, acting as a spur and a forerunner to the B.T.U.C. which meets in September. Likewise, the rank and file who attend the Scottish Labour Party Conference have voted overwhelmingly for Left policies on such subjects as Rents, Land Nationalisation, Polaris

220

bases, Vietnam, etc.

The dominance of these Left policies, however, does not exclude a Right-Wing existence at all levels in the Scottish Labour Movement.

Will the setting up of a Scottish Assembly affect the traditional authority of the Left in Scotland, whether in the Unions or in the Labour Party?

There can be no doubt that the chance of a right-wing revival in Scotland centres on SNP hopes of a massive majority in the Assembly, which would create the necessary political confusion on which the Right Wing thrive and could gain a new foothold. But what are the chances of the SNP achieving this?

The October election results showed considerable SNP gains, but only at the expense of the Conservatives and Liberals. Labour held its ground in so far as the number of MPs was concerned. But more important, however, it is to analyse the results earlier this year for the new Regional Authorities where, faced with the removal of Nationalism as an issue, the SNP made little impact. Is it the case, then, that when the Nationalist aspect is no longer in contention, the Scottish people return to basic class instincts in their approach to Elections? And, if this is the case, what class does the SNP represent?

This unanswerable question is precisely the reason why the political complexion (in terms of number of seats) of the Scottish Assembly is unlikely to be radically different from that which exists currently in the distribution of the 71 Scottish seats.

With the removal of the emotional base on which the Nationalist vote has been built, given Scottish Government, where else can the SNP extend their influence?

There is no connection between the SNP and the Trade Union Movement in Scotland; they have no roots and no organisation at important levels in the Unions on which to extend their vote. There is an idealogical gap which is unbridgeable. Despite Wolfe's waving of a fairly sizeable "olive branch" at the STUC General Council at the time of the February election, the General Council feels only animosity towards the Nationalists—and that is a unanimous feeling which spans Left and Right in the General Council.

The historical and very personal links within the Labour Movement were responsible for a unified attack on the SNP at the February and October elections in the shape of leaflets issued to all Joint Shop Stewards' Committees throughout Scotland; combined meetings of Labour M.P.'s and STUC General Council members at factory gates and in Constituencies; and a common line of attack on the SNP when using the media.

The obvious identification of Jimmy Jack with Willie Ross and vice-versa was picked up by the vast majority of Trade Unionists (there is reputed to be a telephone "hot-line" between the two at all times); and Wilson's readiness to meet the General Council on all occasions is of mutual benefit, insofar as it raises the stature of the STUC.

For example, on the eve of the October election, a promise was given by Wilson to spend a full weekend with the General Council at a sort of "Scottish Chequers" meeting to discuss the problems of the economy and to have the appropriate Ministers present (probably Benn, Foot and Ross) for questioning. Given all of these factors, is there any possibility that the SNP is anything but a superficial challenge to the authority of the Left and when deprived of its Nationalist emotional appeal, is it incapable of further advance?

If Left-STUC policies are fed straight through to the floor of the Assembly, there will be those SNP representatives who will suffer mild forms of schizophrenia; and one suspects that the further Left the discussion is on Scottish policy matters, the more the SNP will be likely to split themselves into two camps (for example, Sir Hugh Fraser, arch-typical member of the Scottish ruling class as distinct from, say George Reid M.P.) Reid, who claims to be a Social Democrat, was the only SNP representative in Westminster who abstained from voting on the issue of the return of £10¼million to the Trade Unions—money previously filched by the Tories from those Unions refusing to register under the Industrial Relations Act.

All other SNP representatives voted against, and their numbers were critical in the decision not to return the money to the Unions. From this example it can be seen that, faced with class issues, a polarisation of view amongst those elected representatives of the SNP must take place.

Therefore, the setting up of the Assembly, far from being grist to the Nationalist's mill, is an opportunity for the Left to expose and isolate them.

The Broad-Left task must be to utilise the setting up of the Assembly as an extension of democracy to the rank and file, who through their affiliated organisations, should be encouraged to see the direct connection between—Branch Meetings, individual Conferences, the Scottish Trades Union Congress, the Scottish Labour Party Conference, and the Scottish Assembly.

The limited powers, to begin with, which will be conferred on the Scottish Assembly must never be decried by the Left, but rather should be built upon in order to raise the stature of that Assembly.

It is here that the political, economic, social and cultural aspirations of the Scottish people can best be expressed in the long term, and where a modest step may be taken towards Socialism, which can only act as an inspiration to the working class throughout the United Kingdom.

(1) A paper produced by D.T.I. officials last year analysed employment trends in multi-establishment plants to see whether the parent establishment or the branch-plant suffer worse from upswings and downswings in total company employment. The analysis showed that branch-plants came off no worse, and in some cases slightly better, than the parent, but the Report covered only **British firms,** operating in **Britain,** and I believe my point to remain valid for the Multi-National Corporations, operating across national frontiers with different monetary and fiscal policies.

The recent Honeywell redundancies throughout Scotland would appear to substantiate this. Despite the fact that management seek to justify the Scottish redundancies by quoting the numbers similarly redundant in Oklahoma (500); Phoenix (400) and Boston (300), which on the surface looks fair—1,200 in America and 1,150 in Scotland—but since 1971 in Scotland, additional redundancies have occurred as follows:-

1971 - 350
1972 - 250
early 1974 - 250

No such redundancies in U.S. plants during these years were reported and, further, within the context of this redundancy exercise, it is the intention of the Company to transfer the production of all ancillary equipment connected with the magnetic tape storage equipment to the Oklahoma establishment.

In parallel with the above, there is the increasing political awareness of the American worker to be contended with—for example, the Nixon regime in the early '70s came under considerable pressure to end the export of the U.S. dollar in view of the high level of unemployment that existed there which, if examined, is another way of saying no further redundancies or closures would be acceptable to the American Trade Union Movement.

In any case, it is better to dirty someone else's doorstep rather than your own, and the current mania amongst large corporations in the U.S. to talk in terms of the "Corporate Image" and "Stability" demands a defence of that image in the parent company rather than abroad.

The Scottish Development Agency

Frank Stephen

In this paper the case is advanced for the establishment of a wide ranging development agency for Scotland(1). The approach leans towards the discursive rather than the statistical, emphasising the need for a new approach to development. The substantial maldistribution of economic activity in the United Kingdom, and in particular, the poor performance of the Scottish Economy as measured in levels of unemployment, net emigration, activity rates etc. is discussed elsewhere in this collection. The proposal of a development agency is not original (indeed the Labour Government has proposed the setting up of a body with such a title) but the extent of powers suggested here may be wider than previously suggested. My proposal is essentially a synthesis of a number of disparate suggestions.

It will be useful, I think, before outlining these proposals to set out the basis on which I as an economist can make them. It is inevitable in framing proposals such as these that value judgements are made. In most of my work as analyst and teacher of economics I strive to maintain the utmost standards of objectivity and halt when the precipice of value judgement is reached. However, the range of problems which can be dealt with in this way is severely limited as anyone who has read Little's "Critique"(2) will know. At some stage in economic policy formulation value judgements must be made. Often this is where the economist leaves off and the politician takes over. Thus I am writing this not solely as an economist but also as a social and political animal. Some might argue that an economist's value judgements in this context are more weighty than anyone else's. I would not be so arrogant as to suggest that.

On the other hand my conclusions are based very much on my training as, and prediliction to be, an economist of the non-Marxian variety. This leaves me with an appreciation of the signals of markets and a tempered respect for economic efficiency. Some might feel that this precludes my using the title "socialist". I would disagree. Socialism is in my eyes about ownership and control, amongst other things, of wealth. The removal of all markets is neither a necessary nor sufficient

223

condition for achieving socialism.

The major premise of this paper is that the free play of markets cannot be left to allocate economic activity spatially in the U.K. Some economists would argue that the drift of people and jobs to the S.E. and Midlands of England is economically desirable since it is an indication of the higher level of efficiency obtaining in these areas, in large measure, arising from the proximity to the major home markets and ease of communications with overseas markets. These influences are reinforced by the general non competitiveness of peripheral regions under a regime of "nationally" negotiated wages. This relocation of economic activity would result in an increase in National Income and by implication economic and social welfare.

It is then argued that a point will be reached where further agglomeration will be inefficient and the drift will cease. This will arise because of factors affecting individual firms and the increased cost of social overhead capital, that is to say diseconomies of agglomeration will occur. However, the recent campaign for an increased "London Allowance" tends to suggest the market will not be allowed to provide such corrections.

Another group of economists argue that this labour migration approach is not the most desirable. They argue that the Government should come to the aid of peripheral regions by supporting existing industry, encouraging the settlement of new industry or stimulating demand in the "peripheral" regions. This can be thought of as the spatial equivalent of neo-Keynesian full employment policy. Thus the Government should not only maintain full employment at the macro level but also at the disaggregated level of the region. Thus regional policy instruments such as investment incentives, allowances, R.E.P. etc. are analogs of the various instruments of discretionary fiscal policy.

It is not my intent to deal at length with the pros and cons of these two views (it will rapidly become obvious which I support). Such a discussion is available in a recent paper by J.A. Trevithick[3]. Suffice it to say that in a dynamic context with a non-zero time preference Trevithick has shown that the pure migration solution does not maximise social welfare. He concludes that the optimal policy will be one that combines both the migration and neo-Keynesian strategies, the relative importance of each being determined by the particular situation and society's rate of time preference.

An intuitive explanation of this result is that since it takes time for adjustments to occur via the market disruptions will take place, output will be lost and social costs incurred before the "optimal" position is achieved. The longer this lag the further will the static optimum be from the actual (dynamic) outcome.

This conclusion is still based on a pure economic efficiency approach i.e. the combination of the two policies will be that which maximises national income over time. It might still allow the rundown of a region. The problem is that we do not know whether maximisation of national income necessarily maximises social welfare. This problem is not new to economists. It is one aspect of an area of great controversy over a number of years, the problem of interpersonal comparisons in welfare economics.

A policy designed to maximise national income does not necessarily maximise social welfare. It will do so if everyone is better off and no-one is worse off. Even if there are some gainers and some losers it may be possible to judge a change socially desirable if the marginal utility of income is constant. This would be a case of the aggregate of gains outweighing losses (which would mean higher national income). Except where there were extensive interrelated utility functions these two cases would be examples of where maximising national income and maximising social welfare were synonymous.

If however, as is more likely, the marginal utility of income declines as income rises it is conceivable that an increase in National Income could result in a decrease in social welfare. This would be so if the increase in national income was brought about in such a way that those who benefited were the rich whilst those who bore the cost were the poor. In such a case because marginal increases in income afforded little increase in utility to the rich their welfare might not increase by much whilst the loss of income to the poor would result in a substantial drop in their level of welfare. The net result would be a decrease in social welfare. This result is theoretically possible but we cannot measure the effect on social welfare because we do not know the form of the Social Welfare Function i.e. the relationship between economic and other variables on the one hand and the level of welfare of society on the other.

However, a number of economists have accepted the proposition that a change should be sanctioned if national income is increased and the distribution of income is better (i.e. less skewed). We can get this far without value judgement (or at least by a widely acceptable value judgement). To go beyond this however does require a value judgement i.e. that it would be desirable to redistribute income even at the cost of a reduction in national income. This is a judgement which many, if not all, socialists would be prepared to make and it is one on which this paper is predicated.

This digression into the murky depths of welfare economics is not entirely irrelevant to a discussion of regional policy. Any attempt to redress the imbalance in economic activity between regions will result in a redistribution of regional incomes. Thus I am saying that, at the limit, I would be willing to sanction regional policies which brought about a more equitable spatial distribution of economic activity even at the cost of a lower overall national income. Ideally I would like to see it achieved within the context of an increased national income: however, forced to choose between a policy which increased national income by promoting growth in the S.E. and one which produced a more equitable distribution of economic activity I would choose the latter. I believe that most socialists would do the same. It is inequality which is the indictment of capitalism not slow growth. Socialists in the S.E. of England might care to ponder on this.

The Failure of Regional Policy

I hope that the foregoing has been adequate ground-work for a discussion of the failure of regional policy in Scotland and a possible new arm for that policy. However, lest the reader think that it is inevitable that a redistribution of economic activity from the "centre" to the "periphery" inevitably means a reduction in national income it is worth mentioning the case of office employment.

Much of the office employment currently located in London could operate at least as efficiently outside the metropolis. It is possible that there might be some increase in communications costs but these would be likely to be marginal when compared with the savings in terms of office costs and wages. This would be equally true of almost any part of the country. There are two possible reasons why such economic factors do not lead to a natural dispersal of office employment. One is the purely psychological and the other the actual cost of transfer. The latter may well be removed by the increased level of grant now available in such cases. For grants to be effective the psychological problems must be overcome, particularly straightforward inertia. This will be all the more so if the firms are not profit maximisers but satisficers, with the decision to remain in London being an aspect of managerial discretion. Furthermore the decision makers often have a very strange idea of what life North of Watford is really like.

Therefore, it may not be solely economic factors which are the main determinants of office location. Economic measures designed to relocate offices would, therefore, be neutered from the start. In such circumstances a much more positive form of direct intervention may be required. Not just strangling office expansion at birth but "diverting" some office activity to the regions in the interests of **both** economic efficiency **and** social welfare.

Both of these objectives could be met by the dispersal of Government Offices from London. The Hardman Report recommended a measure of dispersal of such jobs but a large precentage of this was to remain within the South East Region and very few were destined for Scotland. Much of the subsequent discussion of the Hardman recommendations has been in the context of a political campaign to increase the number of jobs going to the regions (in particular Scotland). This has missed the fact that the conclusions of the report are not borne out by a careful economic analysis of its methodology. A detailed analysis of the Hardman Report's methodology and the logic of its conclusions is available elsewhere.(4),(5). My analysis suggests that the dispersal of Government offices from London to the development areas would be economically efficient.

During the post-war period private and Government office employment could have provided a large number of jobs for the regions at little or no cost to the community at large. In the period 1966-71 341,000 new office jobs became available. There was however no appreciable shift in the location of office employment with 42 per cent of the total still remaining in the South East. In the private sector even of these moves which took place out of London 80 per cent (according to the

Location of Offices Bureau) moved to a new site in the S.E.

Why have Governments not intervened more directly in the office sector in the past? The answer is not clear. Their vision may have been clouded by the fact that the declining areas were losing manufacturing employment and they wanted to replace like with like. It might also have been to some extent the result of a lack of pressure on Government by the "Regional Lobby". Since that is in no small measure based on the Labour Movement, there may have been a desire to maintain "productive" jobs rather than go for the "non-productive". We must realise that the pattern of employment must change over time even if we can maintain the geographical balance.

Regional Economic Policy has been with us since the 1930s but it has really only been at its height in the '60s and '70s. Whilst there has been a different emphasis placed on direct incentives by Labour and Conservative Governments (with the latter laying more emphasis on infrastructure and the former on grants) political considerations have necessitated the adoption of policies which have attempted to "steer" industry to the development areas.

Labour administrations have tended to favour grants towards the capital costs of new plant, machinery and industrial buildings in these areas whilst the Conservatives up until their volte-face of 1971 when they were forced to return to grants, have tended to favour allowances against tax. These capital grants (or allowances) have often been accompanied by accelerated depreciation, training grants and a direct labour subsidy in the form of the Regional Employment Premium. These "carrots" have been accompanied by a "stick" in the form of constraints on expansion in the S.E. and Midlands Industrial Development Certificates have to be obtained before expansion of premises can take place. The policy was to limit the size of expansion in terms of square footage in the developed areas with no limit in the development areas. Labour administrations have tended to be more stringent in the application of I.D.C. policy than Conservatives. One study(6) of the period 1960-69 clearly shows that the attraction of industry to the development areas was more successful in the latter half of the period when a Labour Government applied the restrictions more rigidly.

What then has the effect of this expenditure of a vast amount of public money achieved by way of reducing regional imbalance? Moore and Rhodes(7) intimate that between 1963 and 1970 regional policy was responsible for "creating" 220,000 jobs in the development areas. The extent to which the policy has been effective (or not) can be seen from comparing the levels of employment, unemployment and migration for the assisted areas as against the U.K. as a whole in Table 1.

Country or Area	Unemployment monthly average			Net migration 1951-1969 as a percentage of population in 1951.	Employment change	
	1971	1972	1973		59/68	68/71
	%	%	%		%	%
Scotland	6.0	6.4	4.7	-11.3	0.6	-3.3
W.C. Scotland						
Special Dev. Area	7.1	8.4	5.9			
Northern England	5.9	6.3	4.8	-4.2	-0.8	-1.0
Northern S.D.A.	6.8	7.8	5.7			
Northern Ireland	8.0	8.1	6.3	-11.1	9.0	0.4
Wales	4.7	4.9	3.8	-1.9	2.8	-2.0
Wales S.D.A.	5.6	6.8	4.3			
Yorks — Humberside	4.0	4.2	2.9	-3.1	4.2	-3.9
N.W. England	4.1	4.8	3.6	-3.1	-0.1	-4.1
Merseyside D.A.	5.2	7.1	6.0		6.5	-7.4
U.K.	3.7	3.8	2.7		5.2	-2.7

Source: Table 2.1. West Central Scotland—A Programme for Action.

From this table it can be seen that the position of the peripheral regions and Scotland in particular has not improved relative to the South East and Midlands and a lot remains to be done.

It is always difficult to judge the success of policies when they are continually being ammended and adapted. This is particularly so in the case of regional policy. Firms have often complained that the uncertainty surrounding the continuance of various grants or allowances has not helped firms to make rational investment decisions. Similarly it is difficult for the economic analyst to assess the efficiency of a particular policy when it is superseded or augmented after a few years. This is certainly an area where "ceteris paribus" cannot be assumed.

Nevertheless one can see that the position of Scotland and particularly the West Central Industrial Belt has not radically improved vis-a-vis the S.E. and Midlands of England. It may be argued by some that this position would have been much worse in the absence of regional policy and that this contribution should not be underwritten. However my case is that the required policy is one which will achieve an improvement of the Scottish position vis-a-vis these other regions. I do not think that regional policy has been satisfactory in this respect. The question is what can be done to improve the situation.

A Development Agency

Regional policy has up to the present consisted largely of tinkering with the market mechanism by offering various financial incentives to firms in order that they might perceive their operating in a development area as being economically efficient. As was said above, this "carrot" approach has been most successful when accompanied by an element of "stick" (i.e. when Industrial Development Certificate policy has been stringently applied in the "prosperous" regions).

But we must conclude that this type of policy has not been wholly successful in Scotland's case. If regional imbalance is to be removed a much more radical approach requires to be taken. I have never been a great supporter of the "direction of industry". This has often been the Labour movement's ultimate solution to the regional problem. At its crudest such a policy would have the Government instruct firms to move plants to development areas or insist that any new plants must be built in such areas and not in the prosperous regions. I do not believe that such a policy is acceptable or even possible in our mixed economy. (I confess perhaps to using the most extreme version of such a policy but I think the point worth making). The Government can stop expansion in a given place but it cannot direct privately owned firms to set up plants where in their opinion they would be uneconomic. It is an entirely different matter to direct state owned industry or to bring about such a locational change by increasing the degree of state participation in the running of a firm. We are then not changing the rules of the game but the game. This approach will be taken up again below.

One problem I have always seen inherent in the operation of regional policy is that it is simply one aspect of a whole range of government activity. I do not seek to malign either Ministers or Civil Servants but it strikes me that the real problems of developing industry and bringing about changes in industrial structure etc. are not really suited to the talents of parliamentarians and mandarins. Civil Servants may be good at drafting policy statements but the extent to which they are equipped to reorganise a region is dubious. In this respect I have always favoured some form of agency outwith day-to-day Government control, in many ways simply because those working in such an agency can clearly see for which purpose they are there. Undoubtedly, there are many people within the Scottish Office and other Departments capable of doing this, but as Civil Servants they are not in the appropriate atmosphere.

The type of agency I favour has its genesis in a number of sources—the Labour Party's Scottish Enterprise Board(8), the West Central Plan's Strathclyde Economic Development Corporation(9), and the various proposals of the Scottish T.U.C. for Regional Development Agencies down the years. I begin by reviewing each of these precursors of my proposal.

The S.T.U.C. has had a long history of advocating the setting up of interventionist agencies to promote regional economic development. Indeed Congress started the campaign for the establishment of a Highlands and Islands development agency in the early 50s. In the 1970s its campaign initially revolved around the Scottish Economic Planning Council and the establishment of Regional Development Boards (c.f. H.I.D.B.) in each of the Scottish sub-regions. The first plank was to invest the S.E.P.C. with executive powers so that it might commission its own surveys of Scottish economic activity and investigate the viability of new expanding industries being brought to Scotland. This would have been an important departure from the Council's purely advisory role. These proposals together with an analysis of the then current regional policy is contained in the General Councils Evidence to the Select Committee on Scottish Affairs in January, 1970. However, the most interventionist aspect was their proposal for Development Boards for each sub-region carrying out functions similar to the H.I.D.B. This policy has been slightly modified over subsequent years but the S.T.U.C. is probably due the credit of having been the earliest and most consistent proponent of the "Development Authority" approach to the problems of the Scottish Economy.

The S.T.U.C. policy has been modified over the years and the 1974 Resolution on the Scottish Economy contained, inter alia, a "demand" for

"...(b) the establishment of a Scottish Development Authority to co-ordinate planning and initiate through a Scottish State Holding Company... the compulsory purchase of equity in firms and to establish enterprises where necessary;

(c) the establishment of a West Central Scotland Development Authority charged with the responsibility of, and having the resources necessary to promote maximum development of (1) existing industry; and (2) of new male employing industry;"

The call for a number of Development Authorities has been dropped. The link between a Development Authority and a State Holding Company will be developed below.

In September 1973 the Scottish Council of the Labour Party issued a paper entitled "Scotland and the National Enterprises Board". The document outlined the role which a Scottish subsidiary of the proposed National Enterprises Board could play in the development of the Scottish Economy. The National Enterprises Board has been characterised in the press as simply a modernised vehicle for nationalisation, taking holdings in the largest companies as opposed to simply taking over whole industries. The Scottish document certainly includes proposals for such state take-overs but the emphasis is much more on the role which such a body could play in regional policy.

The document outlined five functions which a Scottish National Enterprises Board could perform:

1. **Acquisition** of U.K. companies in order to direct their growth north of the border;
2. **Reorganising and restructuring** Scottish industries in order to "preserve employment" (in which respect a social cost subsidy might be appropriate);
3. Establishing **new enterprise** in Scotland;
4. Acting as a **Development Bank** promoting small and medium size enterprise;
5. **Taking-over** firms under special circumstances (e.g. where under investment has resulted in bottlenecks, high cost technologies and research requirements);

The role envisaged is obviously much more than that of a holding company for state owned shares in private enterprise. The S.E.B. would have a much more positive role in the righting of regional imbalance and promoting the growth of the Scottish Economy. The document did suggest that there was also a case for allowing the S.E.B. to allocate the discretionary grants and loans presently administered by the Industrial Development Executives.

The Strathclyde Economic Development Corporation (SEDCOR) was proposed by the West Central Scotland Planning Team as being the most appropriate means of bringing about the economic development of the region. They confined themselves to a consideration of a regional authority because of the restricted nature of their remit in this respect. The case for establishing a public corporation to discharge a range of duties in the field of regional development is most cogently outlined by the Team.

They stress the need to be free from the day-to-day pressures which would apply in a Government Department. This would allow for a greater flexibility of operation. The corporation would however through a Minister still remain ultimately responsible to Parliament for fulfilling the **long-term** objectives set out for it. One of the most important advantages of being a para government agency would be in staff recruitment. It is more likely that staff of appropriate industrial and economic experience would be attracted to such a body than to a Government

Department. There would be a much more outgoing and forward looking approach from the staff of such a body.

The proposed form of SEDCOR is such that it should only be responsible for indigenous industry. It would have no responsibility for the attraction of industry to the region. In other words it would not have responsibility for discretionary or non discretionary grants and allowances presently used to attract industry to the region. It would in total be responsible for:

1. providing an advisory service to existing industry;
2. helping to bring about a better climate of industrial relations;
3. promoting new industries within Scotland (including financial aid and technical and commercial advice);
4. assisting with the reorganisation of industry to provide a more viable basis for future development;
5. administering selective financial assistance for existing industry in accordance with a long term industrial development strategy.

There are therefore both similarities and differences between the SEDCOR proposal, the S.E.B. proposal and the suggestions of the S.T.U.C. In part at least the S.T.U.C. seems to be asking for the establishment of an S.E.B. and SEDCOR although the S.T.U.C. does seem to differentiate between a Scottish Development Authority and a Scottish State Holding Company. It, however, seems to me, as in the realm of regional government, there is no room for both a Scottish Agency and a West Central Scotland Agency of the same type. The earlier S.T.U.C. proposal of a Scottish Economic Planning Council with a small range of executive authority and a number of sub-regional Development Agencies with considerable resources was feasible simply because of the small role proposed for S.E.P.C. However the demise of the S.E.P.C. (and the possibility of some form of Scottish Assembly) open up the possibility of a substantial Scottish Development Agency responsible for the development of the country as a whole. There is no scope for a two tier development agency system without one of the levels having to bow to the other in terms of executive function and left to perform only an advisory role. Nor do I feel is there a case for simply adding SEDCOR to the H.I.D.B. and having only two agencies. All the sub regions of Scotland require a development strategy, if perhaps for different reasons. Thus I conclude that there should be established a Scottish Development Authority.

The S.D.A. should be "at arms length from Government" i.e. it should not be accountable to a Minister for its day to day operations but should have its policy objectives laid down by Parliament (or a Scottish Assembly) from time-to-time. Ideally the objectives should be spelt out in a White Paper at intervals of say five years. It might be ambitious to think that there would be no political tinkering in the intervening period but the job of the S.D.A. should be seen as long term.

In response to such a White Paper the Development Authority would be required to publish a strategic plan outlining how these objectives might be met and incorporating strategies for each sub-region. This should be a rolling plan and certainly not a list of hopes and aspirations (these would be in the White Paper). The Development Authority would then be free to initiate any action, which legislation permitted it to, in pursuance of the strategy. At the tactical level the Development Authority would have to liaise with physical planning authorities, the employment service etc. Given this overall strategic responsibility there would have to be an involvement by the Agency in the attraction of industry from outside Scotland. It would be the Development Agency which was responsible for the promotion of Scotland as an industrial location because it would have identified the desired industries and the appropriate locations. It would also have to be responsible for the discretionary grants and allowances for mobile industry and might act as agent on behalf of the D.T.I. for administering the non discretionary payments (since it would be inefficient to require two sets of applications to be made). In this respect therefore I would go beyond the SEDCOR-type powers.

The other functions would largely be those proposed within the West Central Scotland context for SEDCOR. In summary then the functions of such a Scottish Development Authority would be:

1. In the light of the objectives laid down by the Secretary of State for Scotland, and approved by Parliament (or Scottish Assembly) draw up a strategic plan for the economic development of Scotland.
2. Ensure, in co-operation with the appropriate statutory authorities, that the means for pursuing the strategic plan are provided.

At its own hand the S.D.A. would pursue the strategy by a number of avenues:

a) the attraction of industry from outside Scotland:
b) the reorganisation and rationalisation of existing industry:
c) the establishment of new industries (see below for relationship with N.E.B.)
d) the provision of financial, technological and commercial advice to existing firms or potential new enterprises, including the provision of risk capital where appropriate (again see below):
e) the stabilising of employment in areas where decline of particular firms would have severe social and economic consequences:

The Agency's funds should be provided by the U.K. Treasury and should not in any way be tied to the revenue from North Sea Oil. Ministerial responsibility should be vested in the Secretary of State for Scotland or an appropriate minister in the Scottish Assembly.

What then of the H.I.D.B. and the imperative needs of West Central Scotland. I have already argued that there is no room for two levels of Agency. However, if it is to make a real contribution the S.D.A. will have to concern itself with the problems of the regions within Scotland. Within the S.D.A.'s structure there should be scope for teams working on the particular needs of such areas. The H.I.D.B. functions would then be incorporated within a sub-unit of the S.D.A. and such units would be created for West Central Scotland, the North East, South West, Borders etc. etc. The "industrial attraction" function of the New Towns should also be incorporated in the S.D.A. and administered by specialists there.

Whilst being ultimately responsible to a Minister it is desirable that such an agency should allow for the representation of the various interest groups in the Scottish community. There should be a Board including both executive members (e.g. a Director and those in charge of specific functions) and representatives of both sides of industry and the community in general. This should be a fairly small **working** body. It should not be a talking shop. At a lower level there should be advisory committees for each of the sub-regions again representing all sections of the community. This would allow for an element of feed back on the Agency's proposals for a particular area.

A Scottish Development Authority would, I think, remove the need for a Scottish Enterprise Board. Most of the functions proposed for a S.E.B. should be performed by the S.D.A. The acquisition functions of the proposed S.E.B. were not seen as being the holding of Scottish Assets of firms acquired by the National Enterprise Board but simply whether the acquisition of a firm was in the interests of Scottish economic development. This latter function would be better initiated by the agency responsible for economic development and carried out via the agency responsible for state holdings in industry. Thus the S.D.A. would identify the firms requiring an element of (or total) state holding which would be acquired under the N.E.B. legislation and be vested in the N.E.B. However, the N.E.B. would be under a statutory obligation to carry out any management function it exercised over such firms with due regard to the strategy of the S.D.A. which prompted the acquisition.

As I write the Labour Government has announced that a Scottish Development Agency is to be set up. The announcement was made in the context of the proposals for a greater state participation in Offshore Oil developments. The exact nature of the Agency has not been outlined, but may of course be known by the time this paper is published. However, I will be pleasantly surprised if the role is as great as that which I have suggested here. It seems likely that the function of the Agency will be simply to direct a limited amount of money to particular areas of the country to promote their economic development.

The type of Agency proposed in this paper will involve the transfer of extensive financial resources from Government to the Agency. It will be the main instrument for planning and ensuring the long run economic development of Scotland and its regions. These proposals go further than anything which has existed hitherto (much further, for example, than the powers of the H.I.D.B.) for they would provide for a planned development of Scotland rather than the scrambling take-what-we-can-get approach. This is surely an approach which most socialists would welcome.

1. I am indebted to Professor K.J.W. Alexander for reading the draft of this paper and making a number of important suggestions. The remaining errors or illogicalities are, however, my sole responsibility.
2. I.M.D. Little: **A Critique of Welfare Economics**; Oxford University Press, 1950.
3. J.A. Trevithick: 'The Theory of Discretionary Intervention in Regions', mimeographed.
4. F.H. Stephen: 'The Hardman Report: A Critique', **Regional Studies**, 8(4), 1974
5. F.H. Stephen: 'Government Office Employment and Regional Policy', **Public Enterprise**, No.7, 1974.
6. R.A. Hart: 'The Distribution of New Industrial Building in the 1960s, **Scottish Journal of Political Economy**, Vol. XVIII, No.2, June 1971.
7. Moore & Rhodes: 'Evaluating the Effects of British Regional Economic Policy', **Economic Journal**, March 1973.
8. The Labour Party: Scottish Council: **'Scotland and the National Enterprises Board'**, September 1973.
9. 'West Central Scotland—A programme of action'. Consultative Draft Report, West Central Scotland Plan Committee, April 1974.

Glasgow: Area Of Need

Vincent Cable

"Scotland is a divided land. In the East the arrival of oil has produced the country's biggest boom. In the West there is still doubt, even depression... The Clyde Valley is Scotland's greatest weakness and the source of its deepest inferiority complex."

A. Neil and S. Milligan **"The Two Nations",** The Economist, Sept.29, 1973.

The Economist's thesis of the emerging 'dual economy' is likely very soon to be put to the test. 1975 will almost certainly see a significant recession in the U.K. economy to which Clydeside is tied. Even a conservative projection of 4 to 4½ per cent unemployed, means 9 to 10 per cent in Glasgow; 13 to 15 per cent amongst men; 40 per cent or more in Blackhill, Barrowfield and parts of Springburn and Maryhill. Emigration from the city will rise from the regular 20,000-25,000 persons, surpassing perhaps the all time high of 39,000 in 1971/72. This will lead in industry to strikes, factory occupations, and general bloody-mindedness; and on a personal level to financial instability, insecurity and neglect of family and environment. This in turn will lead to a dearth of new investment to replace the ageing capital stock. Local firms will be forced into liquidation, or take-over; or 'rationalised' and stripped of decision making functions, shedding management and skilled men to swell the outflow of population.

The reason for predicting this scenario so confidently is that it is precisely what happened in the (relatively mild?) recession of 1971/72. While the prospects for the East of Scotland have now improved sufficiently to insulate it in part from U.K. trends, this is not true of Clydeside. There is now a great deal of documentary evidence available which indicates all too clearly that despite many years of active 'regional policy' and of comprehensive urban redevelopment, Glasgow's economic and social problems still remain second to none in Britain. The most important of these contributions have been the West of Scotland Central Plan(1), produced by planners and economists of the Scottish Development Department; and the Second Review of Glasgow's

Development Plan (the first being in 1960). From these reports has flowed not only a monitoring of trends but a welcome departure from the traditional mainstream of town planning and its preoccupation with land use, densities and physical standards. The W.C.S. Plan is very largely concerned with economic policy; the Glasgow Development Plan review, in some of its subsidiary reports, with social deprivation.(2) The purpose of this paper is to review these studies for the insights and recommendations that they contain particularly as they effect the city's economic prospects, to relate them to other research, and to assess their political significance.

The Economy

It is a reasonable working hypothesis that most of Glasgow's social problems can be related back to unemployment, job instability and an unbalanced occupational structure. The city's economic base, then, seems a good point from which to start.

Net employment fell in the city between 1961 and 1971 by 78,000 (diagram below); 61,000 from manufacturing, the bulk of these in engineering.

Diagram 1. Total Employment in Glasgow: changes 1961-1971.

	1961	1971	Change
Metal Manufactures	13,152	6,994	-6,158
Engineering and Electrical goods	46,955	32,788	-14,167
Shipbuilding and marine engineering	26,013	14,261	-11,752
Vehicles	19,326	11,814	-7,512
All Manufacturing	215,656	154,778	-60,878
Distributive Trades	85,128	67,952	-17,176
Professional and Scientific Services	60,406	68,571	8,165
Public Admin. and Defence	12,542	17,171	4,629
All Services	300,832	283,746	-17,086

Note: Only firms over 5 employees.

Source: Glasgow Development Plan Review: Employment Report 1972.

The mechanics of this contraction have been the closure or contraction of local plants, some well publicised (Tollcross Foundry; Davy Ashmore; MB Loco Co; Sterns; Nobel-I.C.I.; Pilkington Fibreglass). The rate of decline was proportionately twice as rapid as for Scotland as a whole, then one of the least successful and promising areas of the U.K. The consequence was, partly, out-migration and partly unemployment. The migration question will be taken up again later, but in the decade 1961-71 it is worth recording that about 190,000 Clydesiders left Scotland (out of 215,000 from Scotland as a whole), 55 per cent of whom went overseas. As a consequence, even the relatively high birth rate has been outstripped so that the population of the conurbation is falling by 8,000 per annum and of the City by 17,000 p.a. Of course, this is not necessarily undesirable if it led to less overcrowding and a better life for those that left and stayed; however migration has been significantly selective of the young and economically active leaving a higher proportion of dependents to be supported by a weakening economic base.

Moreover, residual unemployment also rose; and the differential between the City and the rest of the U.K. has remained large. The position is particularly serious for men, though the problem is largely confined to unskilled work since there is a serious labour shortage for many skilled jobs.

On the other hand, collective bargaining has been able to keep money wages in most manufacturing industries on par with comparable jobs elsewhere in the U.K.

The extent of the employment problem has been widely recognised but the causes are less obvious. Indeed Glasgow Corporation launched a full scale day conference last year to obtain

233

from academics, businessmen and others a clear prescription: and received a plethora of conflicting views.(3) There used to be two fashionable explanations; one being Clydeside's relatively 'backward' industrial structure with its preponderance of slow growth, low productivity industries, the other being the region's geographical isolation from the main markets in England.

Diagram 2: Unemployment Rates in Glasgow

	August 1974		August 1972	
	Male	All	Male	All
Glasgow City	8.1	5.5	12.0	8.3
Scotland	5.8	4.3	8.5	6.6
Britain	3.9	3.0	5.2	3.9

The West Central Scotland Study concluded on the basis of research by Cameron and others(4) that they had "largely discredited the argument that the poor performance of the region is solely the result of a concentration of nationally declining industries"(5), and they suggested that less than one-third of the relative job deficiency could be explained in this way (the equivalent of 43,000 jobs for the West Central region). Similarly, the transportation factor has been dismissed as significant(6) for the vast majority of goods, in determining competitiveness on a U.K. level, though the car companies gave this as evidence for problems at their Scottish plant(7) and the academic studies which discounted real transport costs did nonetheless attribute some significance to the psychological effects on management and their families of relocating long distances.(8) Certainly there appears to be no significant problem as regards intra-regional transport costs, despite the agitation of the roads' lobby, and successive governments have created significant excess highway capacity.(9)

Indigenous Industry

The W.C.S. Plan commented that "the major emphasis of this report is on the problems and potential of indigenous industry" (p.51) and it is the poor performance of this sector that explains very largely the lack of new job creation. Any new net employment growth has in fact come from migrant companies. The weakness of indigenous Scottish industry is traced back by the W.C.S. Plan to low labour productivity; in turn a product of low quality management, defensive labour practices, and the outflow of skilled workers and management stimulated by the significant gap in executive salaries between Clydeside and other regions.(10) But this still leaves us with a near-insoluble chicken-and-egg problem, since these 'causes' are effects of the same process of decline. It is thus not at all clear what at all is to be done and the reports are correspondingly unsensational in their recommendations.

Two specific factors that one might isolate are the local capital market and planning policy: Cameron and the W.C.S. Plan regard both as unimportant but this may not be entirely valid. The deficiencies of the U.K. capital market as it affects small firms have been well documented by the Bolton Report(11) and there is no reason to suppose that any regional differential exists: the increasing concentration of ownership and problems of small enterprises are universal. But in Scotland this has to be set against the fact that Glasgow and Edinburgh are well developed centres for financial institutions, in a way that Newcastle, Manchester and Cardiff are not. Glasgow houses the Scottish Amicable Life Insurance Company with assets over £2000 million; the Scottish Mutual and Scottish Legal Life; several leading investments trusts; and several major industrial holding companies are registered in the city (Burmah, Grampian, Wm. Baird, Lindustries, Stenhouse). Yet relatively little investment flows from these bodies into Clydeside industry and in the case of the financial institutions, savings are channelled elsewhere.(12) Conversely bodies like ICFC and NRDC which are supposed to provide venture capital for the growing and insecure small company have only had a modest role to play in the West of Scotland.(13) It would, of course, be naive to expect private capital to flow automatically to a

234

relatively low profit location anymore than water can be expected to flow uphill; but it is worth noting the cleavage between unsuccessful 'industrial capital' and successful 'offshore finance capital' which mirrors that of the U.K. as a whole.

On a more parochial level, it is undoubtedly true that Corporation planning policies have done a great deal in certain areas of Glasgow to inhibit indigenous firm activity. "Blight" and the subsequent casual monitoring of firms in redevelopment areas has wiped out many, especially in the service trades and small manufacturers, who cannot afford the rents of redeveloped sites or the cost of dislocating production. Some dislocated firms go to the estates provided notably by the former Lyon Group but they catch only a fraction of loss. This process has been recorded in the Glasgow Cross, Bridgeton and Anderston areas.(14) The East Flank of the Inner Ring Road, if ever built, will directly result in the loss of nearly 1,000 jobs in the next decade. By contrast, the Corporation has given only one loan under its 1964 Act powers to aid indigenous industry.

The deficiency of indigenous industry has created expectations that the gap might be filled by immigrant firms.

Migrant Industry

While much has been expected of 'regional policy' to induce new 'foot-loose' industries to settle on Clydeside, in the past this source has only accounted for 20-30 per cent (gross) of new manufacturing employment and the W.C.S. Plan argued that "even on the most optimistic estimates of the potential inflow of mobile industry to the region in the future, it is clear that only a fraction of the jobs can come from that source. Between 1958 and 1968 only 2,000 new jobs were provided in Glasgow by incoming firms, male and female, as against 25,000 to the rest of the conurbation."(15) In the short-term, a depression situation is unlikely to make even past levels of foot-loose capital available.

The reasons for Clydeside, and particularly Glasgow, being unable to attract their share of mobile capital are normally advanced on two levels. First it could be assumed that businessmen are rational profit maximisers who do not invest because "efficiency wages" are out of line, (a polite piece of jargon which implies that relative wages be cut to a more competitive level, to compensate for lower productivity). One way of countering this would be direct incentives to subsidise labour and/or capital but the present differential incentive under the Special Development Area provision is so derisory as to evade the attention of most businessmen. Another difficulty encountered is the generally recognised deficiency of large, serviced industries sites in the city, now being remedied in part.(16)

But the problem runs deeper. Increasing scepticism exists over the effectiveness of regional incentives and indeed over whether many firms are not so much interested in maximum profits or in 'satisficing' behaviour; settling for an easy life in a convenient location where diseconomies are not too great.(17) Firms so motivated are likely to be very conscious of the "image" of any new location and here Glasgow scores badly. The Corporation Planning Review refers to "the record of difficult labour relations and strikes, recalling the Red Clydeside reputation " (18), and "unsettled labour relations" emerge as chief villain of the W.C.S. Plan, but tactfully attributed to "inflexible" and "conservative" management.(19) Glasgow Corporation has responded to this problem by developing an obsession with public relations. Motorway approaches are tidied up and buildings cleaned. Significantly; Glasgow has a very expensive P.R.O.—but has never felt the need for long range corporate planning or economic intelligence.

Ownership and Dependency

One of the consequences of a weakening indigenous sector and increasing dependence on new immigrant enterprises, combined with continuous merger activity, has been to create what many Scots see as a 'branch plant economy'. The number of employees in Scottish-owned production establishments is now (1971) about 40 per cent or less.(20) This is almost certainly a symptom rather than a cause of the area's problems since "establishments owned from outside Scotland had better closure records than locally owned firms"(21), but the W.C.S. team added "the long term effects of decreasing local control may still be important." As the Scottish Council and others have argued this results in a draining away of decision-making functions, of R. and D. activities and white collar work.(22) This can be seen by looking at the ownership of Glasgow's leading manufacturing establishments: only the Weir Group of the big ones is predominantly locally owned (Diagram 3). A similar picture emerges from the tertiary (services) sector (Diagram 4). The author compiled rateable values for the city centre for the 1971/72 valuation. The largest owners of commercial property were, excepting British Rail, Strathclyde University and the Corporation, London-based insurance companies (notably the Prudential, Legal and General, and Guardian) property companies (e.g. Stock Conversion and Investment, Artagen, Ronex) and chain stores, notably the Wolfson Group. Only the Fraser Group and Scottish Metropolitan Properties are 'local' of those in the really big time. Even of companies registered in Glasgow their role in the city's economy is generally negligible: Burmah Oil and Lindustries and Grampian Holdings do not even have a nominal headquarters in the City. The only sector where there is much evidence of successful local entrepreneurship is amongst small building contractors, and in what is sometimes euphemistically called the "leisure industry"—in practice, pubs and betting shops. But even here the large nationals dominate (Scottish and Newcastle, and Tennants of the brewers) and local interests tend to be disproportionately composed of ex-sportsmen and friends or relatives of city councillors. The Stakis Organisation is the only one in recent years to have progressed from a small private outfit to a successful public quoted company (turnover £13 million in 1973 from restaurants, hotels, property, pubs and betting shops and casinos).

Recommendations

To summarise the basic argument of these reports is difficult since it is basically circular. Clydeside industry suffers in general from "inefficiency" and a "bad image" caused by bad management, bad labour relations, and low morale caused in turn by bad management, labour relations, etc., and by the loss of ownership and control caused in turn by relative "inefficiency" etc. But so what? What is one to do about it? It is at the level of recommendations that the W.C.S. Plan and Corporation Planning Review are seen at their weakest, once they have got past the obvious, if relatively minor, points (industrial sites; improving S.D.A. grants).

Two basic approaches could have been adopted. One was to restore full blooded capitalist incentives: to encourage wages to go down, and top salaries to go up, to internationally competitive levels; to break up work-sharing manning arrangements; to rationalise industrial structures so as to clear away the 'lame duck' enterprises; to relate industrial incentives to profit and efficiency; and to provide in education, housing and transport the kind of services which the managerial and entrepreneurial classes expect. This approach was momentarily tried in 1971/72 and has helped create folk memories of class benefit warfare to last a decade. It belongs to the realm of political fantasy on Clydeside. Anyway even in its own terms it would probably not work since under a free market the East of Scotland will tend to retain an increasing attraction for private investors not to mention the higher profits of locations in Brazil, South Africa or Southern Europe for the totally, foot-loose firms.

The alternative approach is to acknowledge that the private sector is unable, or will not be allowed, to deliver the goods; and this has led to the idea of 'state entrepreneurship' as well as more radical solutions.(23) Moving some way in this direction the W.C.S. Plan suggested the formation of a Strathclyde public development corporation (S.E.D.C.O.R.) which could channel funds and advice towards indigenous firms, and work out a long run industrial strategy for the region. It is seen as a parastatal body in the mould of the·Highlands and Islands Development Board though a closer analogy could be drawn with the Northern Ireland Finance Company which has acquired a reputation for successfully reorganising some medium-sized Ulster industries; and with L.E.D.U. a small firm agency, also in Ulster.(24) Italy has also developed a range of institutions like G.E.P.I. with this function. The Government has in effect accepted the general trend of the argument, through its proposal to set up a Scottish Development Agency though we know few of the details of this idea. In effect, the state is now being required to take an active promotional role as well as merely grant giving.

On this level the proposals so far advanced are sensible, avoiding controversy but tending to be somewhat innocuous. By contrast, the rationale behind the government's National Enterprises Board (at least in its preemasculated state)(25) was that 'state entrepreneurship' was needed in respect of migrant capital; and by considerably extending public enterprise new investment by

DIAGRAM 3: LIST OF MAJOR MANUFACTURING FIRMS IN (OR ADJACENT TO) THE CITY OF GLASGOW 1973.

Firm	Owned By	Ultimate Control H.Q.	Employment
Rolls Royce (Hillingtom)	Rolls Royce	Derby	5000 plus men
Govan Shipbuilders (all divisions)	Govan Shipbuilders	Scotland	"
Weir Pumps (Cathcart)	Weir Group	Glasgow	"
Beatties Bakeries (Rutherglen)	Rank Hovis MacDougall	London	"
Scottish Co-op Society	C.W.S.	Manchester	"
Yarrows (Scotstoun)	Yarrows	Glasgow	4000-5000 men
Hoover (Cambuslang)	Hoover Co.	Ohio (USA)	"
Wills (Alexandra Parade)	Imperial Tobacco	London	3000-4000 men
United Co-op Baking Society	U.C.B.	Glasgow	2000-3000 men
United Biscuits	United Biscuits	Edinburgh	"
Tennant Caledonian Breweries	Bass Charrington	London	"
Wm Collins	Wm Collins	Glasgow	"
Caterpillar Motors Co.	Caterpillar Tractor (Illinois)	USA (Glasgow- UK H.Q.)	"
Albion Motors (South St.)	British Leyland	London	"
Barclay Curle (Scotstoun)	Swan Hunter Group	Wallsend	1000-2000
Barr & Stroud (Anniesland)	Barr & Stroud	Glasgow	"
Wm Beardmore (Parkhead)	Thos. Firth & John Brown (Sheffield)	Sheffield	"
D M Cohen	D M Cohen	Glasgow	"
J Howden (Scotland St)	J Howden	Glasgow	"
Kings & Co (Nithsdale Dr)	Tarmac	Wolverhampton	"
John Laird	Dickinson; Robertson Group	Bristol	"
George Outram	Suits	Glasgow	"
Goodyear (Drumchapel)	Goodyear (Ohio)	USA (Stafford UK H.Q.)	"
John Player (Alexandra Parade)	Imperial Tobacco	London	"
Templeton Carpets (Bridgeton)	Guthrie Corporation	London	"
Bilsland Bros.	Spillers	London	750-1000 men
S & P Harris	Wm Baird	London	"
Gray & Dunn	Rowntree McIntosh	York	"
Milanda Bread	Rank, Hovis, MacDougall	London	
Rawplug (Thorniebank)	Burmah Oil	London	"
Scottish Brick	NCB and T Tillings Co	London	"
Beattie's Biscuits (Drumchapel)	Rank, Hovis, MacDougall	London	500-750
Bowater, Stevenson Containers (Milngavie)	Bowater Ciro.	London	"
British Olivetti (Queenslea)	Olivetti (Italy)	Italy (London- UK H.Q.)	"
British Oxygen (Polmodie)	British Oxygen	London	"
Brownlee (Sawmills)	Brownlee	Glasgow	"
City Bakeries	George Weston	London	"
R.J. Geyer	A J Geyer	Glasgow	"
John Horn Ltd.	McCorquodale Holton	Basingstoke	"
John Lyle Carpets	John Lyle	Glasgow	"
Mine Safety Appliances (Queenslie)	MSA (Pennsylvania)	U.S.A.	"
Prestcold (Queenslie)	British Leyland	London	"
Wm Teacher	Teachers	Glasgow	"
T Tunnock (Uddingston)	Tunnock	Glasgow	"
White Horse Distilleries	Distillers Co.	Edinburgh	"

Note: Information applies to 1973, is not comprehensive and in some cases employment figures relate to those outside the city itself.

(social and Economic Research Dept., Glasgow University)

NOTE: Diagram 4, Commercial Interests in the City Centre of Glasgow by Rate Valuation, p.246

acquired firms could be directed to Development Areas. However, the W.C.S. Plan avoids this approach, favouring more general incentives. And even in the case of indigenous industry, will the new agency have compulsory acquisition and equity holding powers to sort out industries? Or will it, like the late I.R.C., concentrate on informal pressure and voluntary assistance? What relations will it have with the Scottish Office, the Strathclyde Region and the D.T.I.? To whom will it be accountable democratically? Will it aim to make profits? And if it is to avoid being accused of bolstering inefficiency what will be its approach to redundancy in plants with low productivity? These questions and others need to be answered before one can be clear whether the new agency is a serious attempt to deal with the problems, or a mere slogan.

But even if it is successful, its effects will not be felt for a long time. Both the W.C.S. Plan and Corporation Planning Review project a continuing decline in jobs in the City—estimates ranging from 10,000 to 70,000 in the next decade. Both studies argue that this process might be arrested by cutting back on planned overspill notably at Stonehouse New Town. However, even if this is successful there is no guarantee that the frustrated overspill will not go outside Scotland altogether.

One final recommendation, that is now being implemented, is to press for a larger allocation of Civil Service jobs. Glasgow now seems likely to get 7,000 to 10,000 from the Ministry of Defence and O.D.A. and offshore supplies office. The reasons for this are sensible enough if sometimes overstated. Half the jobs will go directly to local people (though this has to be substantiated) and then there are multiplier effects. In addition Glasgow school-leavers get the benefit of a better spread of jobs; with some expectation of reaching a responsible post. At the moment Glasgow has only 2 per cent of all Civil Service jobs, a considerable underrepresentation: and there is need to counter the decline in service jobs caused by the diminishing requirements for city centre shopping provision as population declines(26), redevelopment and suburbanisation take their toll.(27) The relative success of the National Savings Bank relocation to Cowglen is another plus factor.

On the other hand there will be additional pressure on private housing, road space and schools at some cost to local inhabitants. It is argued that this is an acceptable price to pay for a better "social mix" though it is not at all clear how several thousand English civil servants living in suburban ghettos are likely to have any noticeable effect on the quality of life of the rest of the city; especially since the main dormitory suburbs have been allowed to secede from Glasgow in the course of local government reorganisation, and since most will apparently be coming very reluctantly. More fundamentally, it should be stressed that proportionately Glasgow already has more service jobs (64 per cent) than Leeds (56 per cent) or Birmingham (44 per cent) and most other cities, while 60 per cent of its unemployed are unskilled. It is in industry, and in the area of male, manual employment that the main priority still lies.

As the 1975 depression looms, the government has shown greater inclination to roll out the pork-barrel than was ever felt necessary before the political base of the major parties in Scotland was so vulnerable; R.E.P. doubled, the go ahead for Glasgow's big construction and rail expansion plans, civil servants for Glasgow, and a Scottish development agency financed by oil revenues. This may help in a small way to cushion the West of Scotland as the oil boom is protecting the East.(28) But Clydeside is still closely tied to the level of demand in the U.K. as a whole and with 15 per cent inflation and massive balance of payments problems no British government is going to be able to stimulate demand sufficiently to prevent painful unemployment on Clydeside. If that happens many electors will conclude that an economically independent Scotland with North Sea oil to finance its balance of payments and its Treasury could be at least partly freed from these constraints. Others will conclude that unless a badly functioning mixed economy is replaced by a totally controlled economy, problems like unemployment and inflation will never go away. If either of these views prevails in the next two or three years, and the first may well do, then Clydeside's long term prospects may be very much changed. But in the short term, say to 1980, one can predict declining economic activity and population, and to the latter problem we now turn.

Population

Population decline has not until very recently been seen as one of Glasgow's problems except by those who equated numbers with power and wealth: a falling population would in fact lead to less

238

pressure on housing and land, removing Glasgow's basic historic planning problem, overcrowding. The basic assumption behind the 1960 Quinquennial Planning Review was to relocate 16,000 people per annum by planned overspill (10,000 p.a.) and unplanned suburban movement (6,000 p.a.) in order to reduce residential densities in 29 Comprehensive Development Areas. It was implied that ultimately an 'equilibrium' would be reached, and outmigration would fall.

The population has certainly declined, but the overspill has been largely unplanned, in excess of expectations, and the rate of emigration has increased, not decreased to an equilibrium level (see below). In fact, in 1971/72 a record figure of 40,000 left the city. The rate of loss of population has far exceeded the additions from immigration and birth. Between the 1961 and 1971 Census, population fell by 165,000 which, at 6.3 per cent per annum, is twice the percentage rate of decline of even the next most unpopular place—Merseyside. The pace of decline is now such that by 1978 Glasgow (on its pre-1974 boundaries) will be down to 750,000 people, the figure which the Clyde Valley planners considered optimal thirty years ago.(29) But all will not then be ideal; even if, against all evidence to the contrary, the population stabilises at that point.

	Quinquennial Review Projecting (1960-70)	Actual (1960-70)
Planned Overspill (gross)	100,000	70,000
Population Loss (gross)	160,000	240,000

First, all the City's housing transport and other plans have been consistently based on population projections, even in the last few years, which have been excessive (see Diagram 5). So the City will probably be left with many small houses built on high densities, while central gap sites go unfilled—a scenario first painted by Peter Norman in 1971(30); with underutilised motorways but a dearth of parking in residential areas; and a good deal of unviable city centre shopping that will close, leaving blight.

Second, the City has been losing disproportionately large numbers of young people of working age. In 1951 the age structure of the City was similar to that of Liverpool, Manchester or Birmingham, However, by 1981, it is projected that the number of dependents per 1,000 of working population age will be 912 (from 557 in 1951) and for Scotland as a whole 714 (from 589).(31) If trends continue, by 1981 19.5 per cent of Glasgow's population will be pensioners, over 65, as against 16.2 per cent in 1970, 13.5 per cent in 1966 and 11 per cent in 1951: "it can be shown from a comparison of dependency ratios of other cities that Glasgow has moved towards a rather more extreme position in the last few years and is probably more susceptible to further deterioration."(32)

Diagram 5: Population Projections for Glasgow

Population Projections	Date	Base date of Population	1980 Projected
Glasgow 1st Development Plan Review	1960	(1961)	900,000
Lothians Regional Study (McLellan)	1966	(1966)	890,000
Greater Glasgow Transport Study	1969		844,000
Joint Working Party	1970	(1969)	761,000 to 807,000 (1981)
Registrar General	1970		722,000
Glasgow 2nd Plan Review	1973	(1971)	700,000 to 750,000 (1981)

However, the population decline has had one significant side effect: that by 1981, the City will have "solved" its housing problem at least in crude quantitative terms. Below can be seen the supply and demand changes implied by the trends incorporated in the Corporation Planning Review(33); and which lead to predictions of a "surplus".

Diagram 6: Supply and Demand for Glasgow Housing

Supply	(1971-81)	Demand	
New houses planned and under construction	33,000	Loss of population	-62,000
Improvements	30,000	Improvement in occupancy rates	19,000
	63,000		
Less slum clearance	-45,000		
Houses required for improvement	-38,000		
Loss for roads etc.	-10,000		
	-93,000		
Net Decrease in Supply	30,000	Net Decrease in Demand	-43,300
Therefore, Surplus supply is	13,000		

Stock in 1971: 303,000; Stock in 1981:273,000; of which 3 per cent are void.

It is in fact very unlikely that improvement can be effected on this scale; at the moment only several hundred are being improved per annum. Also many houses presently classified as "fit" may very well be unacceptable by 1981. Even then there is a more than reasonable expectation that well within a decade the "housing problem" as traditionally understood in terms of sanitary conditions and overcrowding in slum tenements will have disappeared. Whether this will have produced better environmental conditions and greater consumer satisfaction is, however, a completely different matter.

Areas of Need

Although uncontrolled mass emigration seems as one of its biproducts to be solving Glasgow's traditional planning and housing problems, there is mounting evidence of real and large scale poverty which is disguised by the conventional planning indices. Amazingly, perhaps, less serious research has been carried out into poverty in Glasgow, than in York, or Edinburgh, or Oxford: in the last decade only scattered academic work(34), or as a biproduct of medical work(35), or research into crime.(36) This has now been remedied in part by the 2nd Planning Review with its survey of 'Areas of Need' and of the East End.

These studies show that in almost every respect Glasgow has greater deficiencies than other British cities. In part, these deficiencies are residual features of the remaining slum housing, now fast being eliminated, but they also cover indicators of community health, mortality rates, for example. Glasgow is also shown to be 'deficient' in professionals, managers and executives, and much has been made of this including the campaign to attract civil servants. However, most other British cities appear to have the same 'deficiency', perhaps simply explained by the general process of suburbanisation.

The second major disparity lies in living standards between different parts of the City. The 'Areas of Need' Report showed 13,000 acres to be 'multiply deprived' (though the arbitrary use of five indicators means that no intrinsic significance attaches to this figure). The main conclusion drawn from the study was that serious 'deprivation' problems extend far beyond the 4,000 acres originally designated as Comprehensive Development Areas in 1960; and include prewar and postwar council housing of good structural standard. Perhaps the key indicator is unemployment. Three of the city's employment exchanges—Parkhead (the East End), Springburn and Maryhill—account for half the unemployed. A recent S.D.D. analysis(37) showed that in 14 out of 86 zones of the city there was a staggering total of 22.5 to 40 per cent male

Diagram7: Showing Indicators of Comparative Deprivation between Cities (Glasgow (G), Edinburgh (E), Manchester (M). Liverpool (L), Sheffield(S), Aberdeen (A)).

	G	E	M	L	B	G.L.C.	S	A
Population Density (per hectare)(1971)	55.7	31.8	49.2	54.2	47.4	45.6	27.7	34.4
Percentage of Population living in over 1.5 persons per room (1971)	26.0	10.7	5.8	5.5	6.4	5.0	2.9	6.4
Percentage of Households with no fixed bath or shower (1971)	22.3	14.3	11.1	17.0	8.3	9.1	16.3	22.4
Active male unemployment excluding sick (1971)	16.8	6.3	7.2	9.5	5.2	3.6	3.9	5.0
Infant mortality per 1000 live births (1966)	27	22	29	20	21	-	-	17
T.B. per 1000 population (1966)	.09	.02	.04	.03	.03	-	-	.02
Bronchitis per 1000 population (1966)	.84	.56	1.20	.63	.74	-	-	.50
Percentage male employees: professionals; managers and employers (1966)	8.7	17.3	10.7	9.3	10.2	-	-	14.0

unemployed in 1971. In part this is due to a geographical mismatch of residential and industrial zoning: due to localised closures (as in Bridgeton and Maryhill) or the absence of adequate nearby industrial estates (as for Easterhouse). But it is frequently aggravated by concentrations of people with personal inadequacies, difficult family conditions, or just low incomes; which tend to make the deficience is self-perpetuating. When the effects of concentrating the unemployed and poor people generally are compounded by overcrowding, lack of play space and squalid communal facilities, there are slum conditions regardless of the sanitary inspectors' assessment of 'tolerable standard' under the Housing Acts. However, let us look at the progress in the C.D.A. redevelopment areas defined essentially by planning and sanitary standards. The 29 C.D.A. programme, spanning 20 years, was initiated largely because of peripheral area land constraints and since comprehensive rather than piecemeal clearance would enable "more detailed plans to be prepared to provide overall improvement to the general urban environment." The programme is by now well behind schedule and has in effect lapsed as a rigid policy framework. Several C.D.A.'s have been   finished or are well under way (Anderston, Hutchesontown Gorbals, Pollockshields, Royston, Cowcaddens, Townhead Gorbals, Woodside and after a long delay in 1972 and 1973, several others were approved (Govan, Bridgeton, Dalmarnock, Whiteinch).

This is not the place to review the history of this exercise, already done elsewhere(38), but a few points are relevant. First, the process of clearance is very advanced in all areas but construction of new buildings is very far behind, of housing and schools, but even more of community services and shops; leaving a patchwork of gap sites, remaining slum dwellings and badly serviced new houses. Given the declining population trends these gap sites may well acquire a semi-permanent character though in other cases lack of co-ordination is to blame. Bad planning may also explain the neglect of provision for industrial premises and employment generally; with the loss of local firms due to the redevelopment of low rent sites, falling population and poor monitoring. Only with the publication of the Bridgeton and Kinning Park C.D.A. proposals did there appear to be adequate provision for industrial land in these C.D.A. areas.

Secondly, both inside and outside C.D.A.s many housing developments were executed at higher densities than that originally intended (150 persons per acre). This means that in practice 80 per cent rather than 50 per cent of dwellings were multistoreys with the deficiencies which these

241

buildings are known to have, but in an attenuated form (39). Third, in the large residual areas not yet comprehensively developed, there is widespread blight and growing disamenity as blocks of houses are cleared by the Sanitary Inspector, but nothing replaces them (e.g. N. Kelvin, Partick). It is now intended that some of these areas will see more of a 'cellular renewal' rather than comprehensive development, by house improvement rather than demolition. However, Glasgow so far has a dismal record in this field, largely due to the multiple ownership problems of Scottish tenements and of communal backcourts. There have been a few successful but very small voluntary schemes, as in Govan, and several larger, and so far abortive efforts by the Corporation. The ability of the new Glasgow District Authority to increase drastically the amount of improvement is the key factor determining the city's ability to meet its housing demand by 1980, to provide inner city working class housing for renting and buying, and to arrest the continuing environmental decline of the residual older housing areas. Otherwise, by 1980 a large number of the C.D.A. areas will still be characterised by decay rather than renewal.

But the most disturbing problem is the deterioration of many corporation housing schemes. The problems fall into two parts; first, the interwar tenemental rehousing developments such as Possil and Blackhill; second, the postwar perimeter schemes, Easterhouse, Pollock, Castlemilk and Drumchapel. In the first case there may well be overcrowding and environmental deficiencies but the key factor is that certain areas have by design or neglect become what the Corporation itself describes as "ghettos" or "dumping grounds" for problem families.(40) Because these houses have been regarded from the outset as slum redevelopment they acquired a 'name'. They were then classified as the lowest of the Corporation's eight amenity grades which by a process of self-selection (rents are lowest in Grade 8) and segregation (the Corporation 'grades' tenants by cleanliness, housekeeping standards etc. in order to protect the 'good apples in the barrel from the bad ones', to use a favourite housing management metaphor) has led to an extreme concentration of unemployables, large families and families with antisocial habits.(41) This is clearly brought out by the census data below. (Diag.8) The effect has been not only to create areas of intense social stress but to create what amounts to a segregated labour market since school leavers and men from these areas find that discrimination against them compounds their other problems.(42) Indeed there is an argument to be made that Glasgow's unemployment problem is due to these 'structural' barriers as much as lack of demand. Attention has been drawn increasingly to Clydeside's serious labour shortage for skilled and semiskilled workers.(43)

Diag. 8: 1971 Census Figures: East End Study (Aggregation of Districts)—Indicators by Percentage of Households

	Unemployment Rate Male (per cent)	Occupancy 1.5 person per room (per cent)	Social Work Refusals
Amenity Groups 2 and 3	4.7	3.1	.7
Post War Amenity Group 3	9.4	16.0	2.1
Post War Amenity Group 4	13.2	28.3	5.8
Intermediate Amenity Group 5	15.0	21.0	2.6
Intermediate Amenity Group 6	17.0	27.3	4.5
Rehousing Amenity Group 7	21.0	20.7	4.4
Rehousing Amenity Group 8	34.0	39.2	11.5

In the lowest amenity group (Blackhill) male unemployment is 34 per cent, nearly 40 per cent are living in seriously overcrowded conditions, and 11.5 per cent are annually referred for help to the social work department. Crime figures reflect these other tendencies. The Corporation's response is totally inappropriate. There is a large scale programme of 'environmental improvement' for which the pilot project is in the Possil scheme, and ambitious plans to improve the plumbing of all prewar houses. Apart from the fact that the Possil approach is very expensive (£800 per house) and was insensitively handled, it operates on the entirely false premise that physical layout, and better space provision, will 'solve' social problems of multiple deprivation.

Even where amenity gradings are not at their lowest, as in the postwar perimeter schemes, there is still intense dissatisfaction. Over one third of Easterhouse tenants want transfers out of the scheme (about 25 per cent in Castlemilk, Pollock and Drumchapel). These almost entirely working class suburbs have suffered deficiencies in transport, shopping, local employment and community facilities. The cost of this imposed isolation is reflected in the extremely high rate of social work referrals. But the general phenomenon was eloquently described by Donnison(44):

"We have too often tolerated or unwittingly exacerbated social traps.....cities have replaced one class slums with another one class council estates, served by one-class (and possibly one denomination) schools and readily accessible only to one-class jobs. If rents are then increased to levels which compel the successful to escape to owner-occupied estates, leaving behind only those who get special help from rent and rate rebates and supplementary benefit, social segregation may grow more destructive. Developers may fear with good reason that rents on such estates will be pushed to a level that only leaves tenants enough to buy the essentials of life. Hence they will not be prepared to provide shopping and recreational opportunities in their vicinity and the horizons of aspiration for tenants and their children will be restricted as a result."

Glasgow's corporation housing schemes are replete with 'traps' of this kind. Yet the favoured solutions fail to match the problem. The 'Areas of Need' Report recommended an essentially 'physical' approach to the problem—thinning out housing to provide more open space, and providing major sports complexes in the main schemes.(45) These things are very desirable in themselves but, reducing the density of the schemes will further reduce local purchasing power and thus the local demand for transport and shopping facilities. And it is not so much major prestigous capital projects that are required as generally improved services; cheap, reliable and frequent buses, reliable cleansing, teachers, and above all a housing management policy that ensures a better mix of tenants, and greater mobility in and out. The other approach pressed on the corporation—and now partly accepted(46)—is to try and incorporate a bigger element of private housing in the overall stock; since present trends indicate that the corporation will soon have over 60 per cent ownership in the city. But the sale of council houses would do nothing to alleviate the deprivation problem, merely taking out of the letting pool houses that are already in high demand; and building new private houses would be irrelevant too, merely offering an alternative to suburbanisation for the middle classes. The improvement and sale of the older tenement houses could open up better opportunities. But for the existing stock of 160,000 council houses, if there is to be greater sense of tenant responsibility, less bureaucracy and more participation, it will have to take into account the communal nature of the multistorey and tenemental housing. Glasgow could well try to pioneer some form of co-ownership of the kind that is more common in Scandinavia and Eastern Europe; and which gives tenants a financial and democratic stake in the future of their homes. More directly, Glasgow's 'areas of need' require two things; better management and more resources.

Glasgow Corporation is frequently upbraided as being "the worst run city in Britain"(47). But as with New York, the administration finds itself the chief butt for the exceptionally difficult problems which are not national or international in character and cannot be solved by the city alone. Certainly if plans were a yardstick, or even major projects completed, Glasgow could not be faulted for its effort. It has successively launched the largest programme of any British city for comprehensive redevelopment, and for the improvement of council houses.

However, there are several specific deficiencies. First the level of interdepartmental co-ordination is very poor, particularly as it affects welfare services (Housing Management and Social Work) and planning (the Planning Department, the Sanitary Inspector, and house building); though this deficiency is by no means unique to Glasgow.(48) Unfortunately local government reorganisation will compound its problem by allocating these functions to different tiers. Second, the response to innovation is slow. The reform of local government management, incorporating corporate planning techniques, is years behind most other cities; similarly the multistorey housing and urban motorway programmes have ground on for several years after circumstances invalidated the original strategy. Third, there is a deep suspicion of genuine public participation—as opposed to the presentation of agreed policy—and this has tended to mean that many of the corporation's well intended policies, in environmental improvement, district plans, house improvement and demolition, have become the subject of increasingly acrimonious debate.

Finally, and surprisingly considering the city's political tradition, there is relatively little interest in the seriously deprived family. This shows itself only too clearly in the city's attitude to the problem of rent arrears cases and problem families who are recycled in and out of slum tenements and the lowest amenity council schemes. Rents have to be paid, with few exceptions monthly; there are minimal safeguards in the eviction procedure; there is no mechanism for co-ordinating and simplifying the mass of local and national selective benefits: model lodging house provision has declined drastically, for the really 'down and out'.

However, the city's main problem is one of resources. It has had to be rebuilt on the cheap because of lack of funds to do anything else. Many of the deficiencies of the new housing developments—lack of or delay in providing community centres, libraries, municipal offices—are less a product of bad local planning than of government public expenditure policies which used this 'non priority' sector of spending as a tool of stabilisation, even as late as the cuts of 1973. And as the final arbiter of planning and housing standards, the central government had as much responsibility as local government for any mistakes.

The response to the fiscal problem has been to draw in the surrounding Strathclyde region to help foot the bill, as will likely happen after reorganisation is effective. But the game has now changed. The lure of oil revenue and independence has suddenly given Clydeside as a whole a bargaining power that it previously lacked. The test of the strength of Strathclyde's leaders is the extent to which they can use their new political importance to reverse the process of cumulative decline into which Clydeside has fallen, by attracting public and private investment on a scale far beyond previous experience. If this happens, then the vicious circle could become virtuous, and the West of Scotland will then no longer limp along behind the East and behind the rest of Britain.

Political Conclusions

1. The main problem to be resolved on Clydeside is the "national" question. Scotland could, in all probability, expect in the 1980's to be more prosperous as an independent country. Growing agitation in industry, the bitterness of the autumn strikes of teachers and other public service employees are surface manifestations of this new consciousness. Until a few months ago Glasgow had mainly stood back from the growing national mood, partly because of the political discipline of organised labour and partly because of scepticism that the new wealth and associated influence would merely move from London to the East of Scotland with little spillover elsewhere.

2. This reserve is unlikely to survive a slump. By the end of 1974 the full force of the impending recession had not hit Scotland, notably in the East, but even on Clydeside where layoffs were not as serious as feared, and it is possible that the West Midlands rather than the West of Scotland may bear the brunt of unemployment. But that is optimistic and Clydeside has so far received very little of the oil related industrial development, nor adequate public investment to counter national trends. If unemployment and short-time working do rise to or beyond 1971/72 levels under a Labour Government, the cause of U.K. integration will suffer a serious and perhaps irreversible blow: a fact that seems not to have been fully understood by the "sound money fraternity" in London.

3. The political "left" is on the defensive in this situation. A generation of particularly sensitive Labour dominated local government has destroyed many illusions and left a vacuum of local leadership. Parties further left have even less grip in the public imagination. The stage is set for a major political struggle such as has not been seen since the "Red Clydeside" days of over fifty years ago. It is perhaps unfortunate that the main battle to persuade Scots of the advantages of remaining in the U.K. should have to be fought in Scotland's most deprived area.

1. West Central Scotland Plan **"West Central Scotland—a Programme of Action"** Consultative Draft Report. April 1971.
2. Second Review of the Development Plan **"Areas of Need in Glasgow"** June 1972, Vol.1 East

End District Study: **"Family Circumstances and Location of the Socially Deprived"** April, 1974.
3. City Hall, November 29th, 1973.
4. G. Cameron **"Study of a Declining Urban Economy"** Scottish Journal of Political Economy, Nov. 1971, pp.315-346.

5. West Central Scotland Plan: **"Economic Background Report"**
6. G. Cameron, **op.cit.** G. Cameron & B. Clark **"Industrial Movement and the Regional Problem",** Oliver & Boyd, 1965.
7. House of Commons Expenditure Committee (Trade and Industry sub-Committee) Chrysler, U.K. H.M.S.O. 1972.
8. G. Cameron & B. Clark **op.cit.**
9 V. Cable: **'Glasgow's Motorways and Technocratic Blight'** New Society, 5th September, 1974.
10. May—M.S.L. Survey 1970 (A. Hargrave: Financial Times 26th June 1970).
11. Small Firms: Committee of Enquiry Report, Cmd. 4811, 1971.
12. J. Walker, 'Business Finance in the West of Scotland' Dept. of Accountancy, Glasgow 1970.
13. V. Cable **"Indigenous Industry, Regional Policy and the Role of Local Authorities"** Unpublished conference paper, University of Glasgow, 1973.
14. e.g. E Anderson **"The Effect of Planning on Inner City Commercial Areas and Small Firms with special reference to Central Glasgow"** M.Sc. University of Strathclyde, 1974.
15. **"West Central Scotland—a programme of action"** op.cit. p.50.
16. Development Plan Review Report: **"Industrial Land"** 1972.
R. Henderson **"Immigrant Industry—Locational Preferences and their Relevance to West Central Scotland"** unpublished conference paper; University of Glasgow, 1973.
17. This term is taken from the jargon enveloping the modern 'theory of the firm': to which contributions have been made notably by Simon, Marns, Baumol, etc.
18. Development Plan Review Report **"Industry"** 1972, p.10
19. Development Plan Review Report **"Industry"** 1972, p.9.
20. G.U.R.I.E. (Glasgow University Register of Industrial Establishments) G. Cameron & J. Firn.
21. West Central Scotland Plan: **Economic Background Report.**
22. Scottish Council **"Centralisation; Scotland's 20th Century Mine of Diamonds",** Edinburgh, 1969.
Scottish Council, **"Economic Development and Devolution",** 1974.
23. S. Holland (Ed.) **"State Entrepreneurship",** Weidenfeld, 1972.
24. T. Wilson: **"Venture Capital and Scotland's Economic Development"** University of Glasgow, Conference Paper, August, 1974.
25. Labour Party (Scottish Council) **"Scotland, and the National Enterprises Board",** 1973.
26. Development Plan Review Report: **Shopping,** 1973.
27. General argument developed in J. Rhodes and A. Kan **'Office Dispersal and Regional Policy .** Cambridge, 1971.
28. The latest Scottish Economic Bulletin, Summer 1974, indicates that only about 10 per cent of work stemming from oil suppliers accrues to Clydeside.
29. Sir P. Abercrombie and R. Mathew: **The Clyde Valley Regional Plan** H.M.S.O. Edinburgh, 1969.
30. P. Norman: **"A Derelict Policy"** Built Environment, January, 1972.
31. Scottish Development Department **"Aspects of Population Change in the City of Glasgow"** (C.R.U.) 1972.
32. Ibid, p.13.
33. Development Plan Review Report **"Population and Housing"** 1973.
34. I. Sumnall: **"Planning and Deprivation"** M.Sc. Thesis. Strathclyde University, 1971.
35. G. Arneil **"Rickets Return to Glasgow",** The Lancet, Vol.2, 1963, pp.423-5.
G. Home, **'Some Recent Developments in Disease Mapping'** Royal Society of Health Journal. January, 1970.
36. Institute for the Study and Treatment of Delinquency: Glasgow Working Party, 1920.
G. Armstrong & M. Wilson in **"Delinquency and Some Aspects of Housing"** in Colin Ward (Ed.) **Vandalism,** 1973.

37. P. Levein, C. MacDonald, A. McKenzie, **"Urban Deprivation in Scotland: Planning Options"** Glasgow University Conference on Metropolitan Labour Markets and Poverty, 1973.
38. P. Murnaghan: **"A Review of Progress in Glasgow's C.D.A. programme"**, Diploma in Town and Regional Planning, Glasgow, 1972.
T. Hart: "The Comprehensive Development Area", University of Glasgow, Oliver & Boyd, 1968.
39. A. Sutcliffe (ed.) **"Multistorey Living"**, 1974.
P. Jephcott: **"Homes in High Flats"**, Oliver & Boyd, 1971.
40. East End Study, Vol.II (Strategy) p.19.
41. Discussed in B. Cullingworth **"Problems of an Urban Society"** Vol.I pp.33-54.
Sean Darner, **"The Broombran Road Housing Scheme"**, Trinity College, Dublin, 1972.
T. Brennan **"Reshaping a City"**, 1959.
42. P. Levein, C. MacDonald, A. McKenzie op.cit. also paper by Alan MacGregor (University of Glasgow) at the same conference.
43. C. Baur, Financial Times, September 17th, 1974.
44. D. Donnison, **"Ideologies and Policies"** in Journal of Social Policy 1972, pp.97-117.
45. **Areas of Need,** Report op.cit. Vol.II Revised Standards, Aims and Costs, 1973.
46. Development Plan Review Report **"Housing"** 1974.
47. Brian Barr, Scotsman, 17th June, 1974.
48. Kay Carmichael: **"A City in Need"**, Scotsman, 7th June, 1972.

DIAGRAM 4: COMMERCIAL INTERESTS IN THE CITY CENTRE OF GLASGOW
(A) BY RATE VALUATION   (B) L = London; M = Manchester; G = Glasgow

Company (C) (Main Glasgow Subsidiaries & Main Activities)	H.Q.	App. G.A.V.(D)
Prudential Assurance (Shops)	L	£550,000
Wolfson Group (Cavendish Woodhouse, Morrison's Associates (Hector Powe), G.U.S., Wolseley T.V. Aerials - Shops)	L	£320,000
Legal and General Assurance (Shops)	L	£310,000
Scottish Metropolitan Property Co. (Northrent; Fairlight—Shops)	G	£300,000
Stock (Scottish Site Improvements; Intercourt Prop.; Gleniffer Finance Corp—Offices)	L	£300,000
S.U.I.T.S. (Outran, Wylie & Lochhead; House of Fraser—Shops)	L/G	c£300,000
John Lewis Partnership (Lewis—Shops)	L	c£300,000
Guardian (Royal Exchange) Assurance Co. (E) (R.E.A. Properties— (Offices and showrooms)	L	c£150,000
Artagen Properties (Offices and Showrooms)	L	c£150,000
Scottish Amicable Life (Offices and Shops)	G	c£150,000
Ronex Properties (Offices)	L	c£150,000
C.I.S. (Coop Insurance) (Offices and Shops)	M	c£150,000
Capital and Counties (Offices)	L	c£125,000

(A) The City Centre was looked at as bounded by the line of the Ring Road in the N.E. and W., and by the river in the south
(B) Rate valuation relates only indirectly to property values. It excludes properties built or constructed since.
(C) The coverage is very crude but includes the main firms: it excludes nationalised industries (British Rail's property ownership seems to be more extensive than any mentioned here), the University of Strathclyde and the Corporation itself.
(D) Valuation aggregates, 1971-72, are approximate and are probably understated.
(E) The Scottish Met Property Co. and Guardian are closely linked financially

A Socialist Strategy For The Highlands

Ian Carter

It is odd that one should have to think about socialist strategies for the Highlands in 1974. Almost a decade ago the millenium seemed close at hand. The New Statesman heralded the Highlands and Islands Development (Scotland) Bill as a measure "which, if properly applied, paves the way for revolutionary change in the seven crofting counties."(1) When that Bill duly became law there came into being the Highlands and Islands Development Board. The potential implications of the HIDB were not lost on those who failed to share the New Statesman's enthusiasm for revolutionary change:

"As briefed by the new Secretary of State (Willie Ross), the Board is identifiable as the army of the anti-laird crusade.(2)"

Who would say such outrageous things about the HIDB today? As a harbinger of socialist change in the crofting counties the HIDB has changed from a great white hope to a duck that is less lame than dead. I will argue that this outcome was inevitable, if not from the time that the Highlands and Islands Development (Scotland) Bill was drafted, then at least from the time that the first professional staff were recruited in 1965. The existence of the Board is irrelevant, if not directly antagonistic, to socialist change in the Highlands. We must return to first principles.

The 1965 Act establishing the HIDB gave the new agency a very wide remit. It was to assist the people of the Highlands and Islands to improve their economic and social conditions and to enable the Highlands and Islands to play a more effective part in the economic and social development of the nation. In order to pursue this remit the Board was given powers—on paper—which were unparallelled in their breadth for British regional policy.(3) Two elements of these powers merit discussion. Firstly, while the HIDB was **enabled** to do a large number of things, the one thing that it was **required** to do was to run a grants and loans scheme in order to provide financial assistance to new and existing firms within the crofting counties. Secondly, the Board was given an enabling power, subject only to the consent of the Secretary of State for

247

Scotland, to acquire land by compulsory purchase, and to hold, manage, and dispose of land. It was this power, in the situation where landholding was the hot potato of Highland history, that gave rise to such extremes of hope and fear for the radical potential of the HIDB. In operation the Board has placed very heavy emphasis on its grant and loan function and, as we will see in more detail below, has never sought to use its power over land. The HIDB likes to see itself, and to project itself to others—the public relations puffing of its activities is much the most competent part of the whole exercise—as a thrusting research and development agency on the model of the Tennessee Valley Authority. With a couple of honourable exceptions—fishing is the most notable—this pose is a sham. The overriding importance of the grants and loans scheme in the Board's operation means that a much more apt analogy is a milch cow. The extraordinary amount of money which went from the Board to Shetland between 1965 and 1970—before the intrusion of the oil industry—shows that those who understood this fact did very well, for Shetland was not an area to which the HIDB intended to give especial favour in grants and loans.(4)

Thus the requirement to operate a grant and loan scheme, which would involve a great deal of administration, meant that the immediate likelihood of the Board bringing about socialism in seven crofting counties in 1965 was dimmed. What finally killed the possibility was the staffing of the new agency. The first Chairman of the HIDB, Professor Robert (now Sir Robert) Grieve, was a distinguished town and country planner, and he gathered around him a team who, in the main, shared his professional origins. This team shared more than educational experiences—it had a common view of the way to go about 'developing' an area like the Highlands. It had an ideology of regional planning.(5) On to a town planning ideology, an idea long familiar to sociologists and planners alike, was grafted a particular theory of development. From town planning ideology was taken the the idea of the planner as impartial professional—'the master allocator' in David Eversley's recent olympian phrase. This was an extremely convenient pose in the mid 1960s, after the debates on the revolutionary potential of the HIDB while the 1965 Act was going through Parliament. It kept the Board out of overt political conflict with those who had political and economic control of the Highlands, though at the expense of an acceptance of the status quo.

The regional planning literature typically identifies three types of problem regions: poor rural regions, declining industrial regions, and congested conurban regions.(6) At first sight it is not too difficult to slot the Highlands in to this typology. The Mezzogiorno, North Norway, parts of Holland and Eire, and the Highlands share common features. They are all "areas of their countries that the various revolutions in agriculture, industry and technology have passed by."(7)

The Board's staff thus held—and hold—an implicit theory of development in which the Highlands are obdurately 'traditional' and must be made 'modern'. That means bringing the area within the market economy, for hitherto market forces have passed by the Highlands. The consequence of this for the operation of the HIDB is that the forces of modernity must be drafted into the crofting counties as fast and as heavily as possible. And nothing is as modern as manufacturing industry. Hence the heavy emphasis in the early annual reports of the HIDB on manufacturing industry as the only safe long term let for the regeneration of the Highlands. Hence the Board's utterly uncritical welcome to any and all aspects of the oil industry. There have been two public enquiries into plans to establish facilities to build oil production platforms within the crofting counties. At one enquiry, into the rather inane proposal to build platforms at Dunnet Bay, Caithness, the Board gave evidence in support of the American-based multinational developer, Chicago Bridge. The other public enquiry eoncerned the proposal to build platforms at Drumbuie, Wester Ross. So keen were the HIDB to see several hundred unattached men brought to the sparsely populated Kyle peninsula, there to live in a labour camp and labour at constructing platforms at Drumbuie to the greater profit of the British balance of payments, that they retained their own QC for the entire—interminable—length of the enquiry. This from an agency whose remit places equal weight on economic and social development! But in the view of the HIDB, expressed recently by Sir Andrew Gilchrist, "The best hope for the Highlands lies in keeping step with the future."(8) Onwards and upwards to modernity through industrialisation, and the higher the technology the better.

And in class terms, onwards and upwards to a bourgeois revolution. For a corollary of the view that the Highlands are premodern is that they are precapitalist, a lagging 'peasant subsistence' sector of a dual economy.(9) Thus if the HIDB's implicit dual economy thesis were valid, then their development strategy might have radical effects within the Highlands, for industrialisation would bring in its train a rising bourgeois class which would challenge, and eventually destroy, the hegemony of a seemingly feudal landowning aristocracy who currently dominate the Highlands and disburse public money to their mates to provide by-passes for their castles. (Hereward the Wake, thou shouldst be living at this hour). But the Board's dual economy thesis is not valid.

The economic history of the Highlands since 1700 can be told as a story of successive booms and busts. The Hack cattle trade, kelp, sheep farming, deer forests, herring fishing, the Caithness flagstone industry, the garrisoning of the north in two world wars, and now the latest boom—oil. The fact that such a story can be told shows that the idea that the Highlands have been unaffected by market forces is utterly mistaken. The Highlands as we see them today are the result of precisely those forces. But the crofting counties look different from places which we would take to be unambiguously modern-like Birmingham or London, god help us-because of the mode of incorporation of the Highlands into the national, and later the world, capitalist economy. The Highlands have always been **dependent.**(10) They have provided low value primary products—food, raw materials—which were converted to higher value finished goods elsewhere, to the profit of non-Highlanders. Thus a boom has come to the Highlands when a local resource—kelp in the Napoleonic Wars, oil today—came to have value for the metropolis whose satellite the Highlands were or are at the time. Once the resource was worked out, market conditions changed, or the herring ungratefully decided to go and live somewhere else, then the metropolis lost interest in its Highland satellite and the boom went bust, leaving dereliction and decay in the former boom area. Without a historical perspective it then becomes all too easy to see such areas as precapitalist, still stuck in a feudal slime. In fact, however, they are as much the result of capitalist development as in Birmingham. The kelp industry in the Hebrides and the West coast not only tied those areas into the market economy in the later eighteenth and early nineteenth centuries; it also marked a decisive transition to capitalism in the west, for the mode of production in kelping was unambiguously capitalist, and so were the relations of production derived from that mode of production. If we look at South Uist today the relations of production may appear to be precapitalist, but that does not mean that the system is precapitalist. All the models of development which we have, from the liberal economist's shift from a subsistence economy to a market economy to the Marxist feudal-capitalist shift, are evolutionary and cannot handle regression. If the mode of production is transformed from a feudal mode to a capitalist mode, then this means the birth of a higher order of productive forces and relations. Under certain conditions the relations of production may appear to be more appropriate to an earlier stage of societal development; but this appearance is misleading. The underlying structure remains at the higher level.

The Weakening of Dependence

The HIDB's development strategy looks rather quaint in this light. The crofting counties are to be developed by opening them up to the very forces which actively generated the 'underdevelopment' from which the area is perceived to suffer today. If the dependence thesis is correct, then this is a recipe for disaster. The uncritical welcoming of all manufacturing industry will merely satellise the Highlands more firmly than they are at the moment, particularly since most of the companies involved in, for example, production platform construction are multinationals. The assiduous creation of a branch plant economy in central Scotland in the 1960s is now increasingly seen as a less than perfect solution to the problems of the area. Any socialist strategy for the Highlands must oppose a deepening of satellisation in the area through an uncritical implementation of a similar policy. 'A job is a job is a job' is not a good development strategy, particularly when a high proportion of the jobs created go to non-Highlanders (and almost all the good jobs, at that).

So what might a socialist strategy for the Highlands look like? Two immediate tasks present themselves: the weakening of dependence and the raising of consciousness. If it is true that a satellite can enjoy 'authentic development' only when its controlling metropolis is engaged elsewhere—as in the case of Latin America between 1914 and 1945(11)—then it is clear that the oil industry, in all its current manifestations, is precisely the kind of operation that the Highlands do not need. Questions about whose oil it is, whether Exxon's, Britain's, or Scotland's, become irrelevent—one is merely discussing different sources of metropolitan control. Those who see political nationalism as the answer to the problems of the Highlands should ask themselves whether a parliament of Edinburgh lawyers would have any more beneficial effects for the satellised Highlands today than had the rule of Edinburgh lawyers as estate factors in the eighteenth and nineteenth centuries. So we should strive to cool the oil boom and, since the Highlands are inevitably to be involved in the exploration for and extraction of oil, the best short-term way to do this is by radically cutting the extraction rate. Let the British national bourgeoisie handle its balance of payments problems at the expense of others apart from northern Scots.

The weakening of dependence also involves resisting the blandishments of non-locally owned and multinational companies wishing to locate in the Highlands. The public relations of these companies frequently emphasise the social responsibility which they feel for the inhabitants of the Highlands. At the Dunnet Bay enquiry Chicago Bridge waxed lyrical on their wish to bring jobs to Caithness and to help the fine people living there. Profit appeared to be an insignificant element in their essentially philanthropic plans. Then they discovered that large as their profits would be if they 'developed' Dunnet Bay (for which they received planning permission) their profits would be even greater in County Mayo. Caithness saw them no more. More recently an application was made by another 'developer' to build production platforms in Argyll. The proposed site inexplicably included a number of fairly recently built houses. An explanation was soon forthcoming, however; the company had drawn up their proposal solely on the basis of out of date maps. In the depth of their social responsibility they had not even bothered to send someone to look at the place.

The weakening of dependence also involves the raising of consciousness. Fanon argued in Algeria that the most profound effects of French colonialism lay in dehumanising the indigenous population, in working through a multitude of means—with the education system as a prime means—to make those indigenes acquiesce in their own dependence and exploitation.(12) The systematic denigration of Gaelic in the Highlands from the eighteenth century, carried on primarily through religious and then state schools, shows the same process; an acceptance of the legitimacy of the Lowland and English control of the Highlands through a forced acceptance of the language and culture of the metropolitan power. It is a pattern which was repeated again and again in the expansion of the British Empire, with Nigerian children being taught English fairy tales and being left in ignorance of the history of their own country.

But the Highlanders never lost their history. Academics provide ideological justifications of the actions of landowners in the nineteenth century—a classic example is a recent account of 'improvement' (sardonic phrase) in Morvern:

> "But although it was a situation in which the rich and the ruthless had the best chances of survival, it would be mistaken to put the blame for the resulting clearances simply upon greedy or malign landlords, for they were really the results of impersonal forces beyond the control of either landlords or tenants, of 'the total impact of the powerful individualism and economic rationalism of industrial civilisation on the weaker, semi-communal traditionalism of the recalcitrant fringe.' "(13)

Against this there remains a widespread popular view in the Highlands that the clearances, still a significant political issue, were a scandalous abrogation of customary obligations by landlords. To see this one needs only to look at the extraordinary success of the West Highland Free Press (given financial aid by the HIDB, to the credit of the latter) whose philosophy is built around the articulation of opposition to landowners, whether the scions of ancient Highland families or newcomers (like the exquisite tale of Sir Hereward Wake and his bypass or the tale of Dr No of Raasay). The barnstorming success of the 7:84 Company with John McGrath's, 'The Cheviot, the Stag and the Black, Black Oil' shows the same continuing interest in and   concern with the land issue. Indeed, one could argue that both the Free Press and 'The Cheviot' have made important contributions to the raising of the consciousness of the Highland people. That this is a very fruitful line for further action is shown by the experience of the Federation of Student Nationalists' Skye Crofters' Scheme. This scheme started as a simple attempt to help crofters by, for example, assisting elderly female crofters to get in their hay harvest. Before long, however, the members of

250

the scheme found themselves involved in protest action by crofters against the depredations of landlords. It is significant that they did not instigate this protest, but rather provided specialist skills which allowed the crofters to articulate their previously inarticulate opposition.

This kind of community development strategy(14) has enormous potential in the Highlands. Its potential is enhanced because the land question is so intimately linked with the structure of power, economic and political, in the Highlands. An attack on landlords is an attack on the national bourgeoisie of the Highlands. The use of improvable Highland land for sport rather than for agriculture or forestry is a scandalous misuse of resources.(15) The newly-established HIDB was put on this particular spot by the Advisory Panel on the Highlands and Islands, which in 1964 demanded an investigation into the development potential of the island of Mull. Mull is notorious for the underuse of land resources in sporting estates, and for the dominance of immigrant landowners, mostly retired military gentlemen, in the political and economic life of the island. The HIDB duly carried out a highly competent survey of the development potential of Mull, recommending a considerable increase in agriculture and forestry; but:

> "Some estate owners drew attention to points concerning their own estates that were at variance with the report's general philosophy on optimising land productivity. It is clear that sport, and in particular deer stalking, is regarded as being of considerably higher importance relative to agriculture and forestry than indicated in the report, and it has to be recognised that some estates will not be in favour of exploiting the indicated agricultural potential to the extent recommended."(16)

Such obscurantist and reactionary attitudes need not, of course, prevent the Board from pursuing its aim of comprehensive development on Mull. It will be remembered that the 1965 Act gave the Board powers of compulsory purchase over land subject only to the consent of the Secretary of State. It is inconceivable that Willie Ross could fail to give consent to the compulsory purchase of the estates of these antediluvian landlords, when he himself said that "Anyone who denies the Board powers over land is suggesting that the Board should not function effectively at all."(17)

But of course it won't happen. The HIDB will not try compulsorily to purchase the offending Mull estates because it has shown a consistent pusillanimity on the land question over the years. The Board has been negotiating with that extraordinary Highland landlord, Dr Green of Raasay, ever since 1965. Neither in this amazing case, nor in any other, has the Board ever used its compulsory purchase powers over land. When Green was finally cornered, and a compulsory purchase order for land on which to build a ferry terminal on Raasay was pushed on him, it was not the HIDB that produced the order but Inverness County Council—led by such notorious anti-landlord fanatics as Lord Burton. By thus accepting the extraordinarily inequitable landholding structure of the Highlands the HIDB has reinforced the political and economic power of the great capitalist landlords who form the Highland bourgeoisie.

Land and Intermediate Technology

An emphasis on land as the central element of a socialist strategy for the Highlands might seem perverse. Everybody knows—don't they?—that development means a move from subsistence based production to specialised production; and that industrial development, preferably high technology industrial development, is the real way forward. Two arguments can be put against this line. Firstly, if the power of the Highland bourgeoisie is based on land, then a socialist strategy should seek to challenge that landed hegemony. Secondly, however, the notion of what constitutes development is not that simple. It has been argued recently that high technology, far from releasing one from dependence, binds one ever more tightly into a dependent position.(18) And Jack Gray's recent work on Maoist China(19) shows the working out of a development strategy for a rural society which decisively rejects the conventional wisdom on the nature and process of development which has guided attempts to solve 'the Highland problem'. Gray emphasises Mao's preference for intermediate technology to high technology; among other things this reduces dependence on a central source of technical skills like a tractor station, and so promotes the decentralisation of decision making and the development of new skills—and new small-scale industrial processes to complement agricultural production—at the village level. Rural cooperatives were given a considerable degree of autonomy in productive decisions in the 1950s; the overriding policy aim was that each unit should at least become self sufficient in food production—if it produced a marketable surplus, so much the better. But units which were deficient in food production were strongly exhorted to become self-sufficient.(20) The principal means by which self-sufficiency was to be achieved was not mechanisation, but more intensive use of underutilised labour and land resources. Orchards were underplanted with vegetables, flax and melons grown on banks, and so on. The increased labour inputs in this more intensive agriculture made up for deficiencies of capital.(21) Ultimately, this strategy could provide "both the demand **and** the savings for gradual mechanisation and diversification of the village economy, it could spiral out to reach in the end the full modernisation of village life."(22) But this development strategy differs from current Western (and Soviet) ideas of development in being very highly decentralised; it is the village co-operative that decides what is to be done, which non-agricultural enterprises are to be started, and so on. The central state apparatus plays very little part in the determination of these productive decisions. It is development from below rather than above, and what constitutes development is to be decided in a thousand villages rather than in one air-conditioned 'expert's' office.

It may be that such a strategy is inappropriate in any conditons other than those of Maoist China. But so much of what we know about the Highlands suggests its applicability. There is the same shortage of capital and underutilisation of land and of labour resources (particularly if we bear in mind the continuing net migration loss of the 'remote' areas of the Highlands). There is a communal tradition to build on, if somewhat attenuated by two centuries of attack by an aggressively individualistic dominant culture. The preconditions for this kind of strategy do seem to be present. And Mao's strategy is not even a desperately new idea; in one sense it may be seen as a differently expressed and unusually successful version on a huge sclae of the kind of community development project that has been peddled around by international agencies ever since the war. But where such projects typically fail is in trying to pursue this kind of strategy without at the same time trying to change the wider structure of inequality in the society. And then one finds, as in Huizer's El Salvador valley, that the community development project becomes assimilated to the local power interests and it is the landlords, not the peasants, who derive the benefit.(23) Thus this kind of strategy does have a great potential in the Highlands, I would argue; but it can only be a socialist strategy if it goes along with an attempt fundamentally to alter the structure of inequality that is so obvious in the Highlands today.

1. **New Statesman,** 12 March 1965, p.386.
2. J. Holburn, 'The troubles of the Scottish Tories', **Spectator,** 23 April 1965, p.529.
3. I. Carter, 'Six years on', **Aberdeen University Review,** 1973, xlu, pp.57-8.
4. **Ibid.,** pp.63-4.
5. For a more extended account of the idea of an ideology of regional development see I. Carter, 'In the beginning was the Board: the ideology of regional planning', **Policy and Politics,** forthcoming.
6. See, for example, G. McCrone, **Regional Policy in Britain, London, Allen and Unwin, 1969.** One of the quaint features of regional planning is that the solution for all these different kinds of problem regions is the same—the establishment of growth centres. Someone has found the philosopher's stone at last.
7. HIDB, **First Annual Report,** Inverness, HIDB, 1965, Foreword.
8. **North 7,** December 1973, p.2.
9. For criticisms of the dual economy thesis in the Highland context see I. Carter, 'Economic models and the recent history of the Highlands, **Scottish Studies,** 1971, 15, pp.99-120; I. Carter, 'The Highlands of Scotland as an underdeveloped region', in E. de Kadt and G. Williams (ed),

Sociology and Development, London, Tavistock, 1974, pp.279-311.

10. The idea of dependence increasingly preoccupies the sociology of development. See A.G. Frank, **Capitalism and Underdevelopment in Latin America,** New York, Monthly Review Press, 1967; A.G. Frank, Latin America: Underdevelopment or Revolution? New York Monthly Review Press, 1970; H. Bernstein, 'Introduction', to H. Bernstein (ed), **Underdevelopment and Development,** Harmondsworth, Penguin, 1973, pp.13-30; de Kadt and Williams (ed), **on cit,** pp.229-311.

11. Frank, **Latin America,** Ch.2.

12. F. Fanon, **The Wretched of the Earth,** Harmondsworth, Penguin, 1967, p.29.

13. P. Gaskell, **Morvern Transformed!** Cambridge, Cambridge University Press, 1968, p.26, quoting M. Gray, **The Highland Economy,** Edinburgh, Oliver and Boyd, 1957, p.246.

14. A. Varwell, 'Highlands and Islands communities', in M. Broady (ed), **Marginal Regions: Essays in Social Planning,** London, Bedford Square Press, 1973, pp.67-77.

15. G.R. Miller, 'The management of heather moors', **Advancement of Science,** 1964, new series, 21, pp.163-169.

16. HIDB, **Island of Mull-Survey and Proposals for Development,** Inverness, HIDB, 1973, p.137.

17. Speech on the second reading of the Highland Development (Scotland) Bill, 16 March 1965.

18. D. Dickson, **Alternative Technology and the Politics of Technical Change,** London, Fontana, 1974.

19. J. Gray, 'The two roads: alternative strategies of social change and economic growth in China', in S. Schram (ed) **Authority, Participation and Cultural Change in China,** Cambridge, Cambridge University Press, 1973, pp.109-158; 'The economics of Maoism', in Bernstein (ed), **op.cit.,** pp.254-273; 'Mao Tse-Tung's strategy for the collectivisation of Chinese agriculture', in de Kadt and Williams (ed), **op.cit.,** pp.39-66.

20. Gray, 'Mao Tse-Tung's strategy...' p.41.

21. Ibid., p.44.

22. Ibid., p.61.

23. G. Huizer, 'Community development, land reform, and political participation', in T. Shanin (ed) **Peasants and Peasant Societies,** Harmondsworth, Penguin, 1971, pp.389-411.

Land Ownership And Land Nationalisation

Jim Sillars

The Scottish Labour movement requires a land use policy based on the principle of public ownership but which takes into account current political and economic realities. This contribution sets out my views and thoughts on how to put together such a policy, which I regard as a matter of some priority.

There is no doubt in my mind that if democratic socialist land policies are to be applied in Scotland sooner rather than later, then we must have devolvement of legislative power from Westminster to a Scottish Parliament. As the tempo of oil and related development increases and the pressures on land intensifies, and the profit taking from land multiplies, we need a socialist based land policy sooner than either the British Labour movement or the Westminster set-up will provide it, if they ever do provide it.

Landownership has always aroused much stronger feelings in Scotland than in any other part of the United Kingdom. Perhaps this is partly because the Clearances, when a small group ruthlessly employed the power inherent in great landholding to decimate a whole people, have left an indelible mark on the Scottish mind and a permanent scar on the Scottish conscience, Highland or Lowland. Anyone who viewed audience reaction to the 7:84 Theatre Group play, 'The Cheviot, the Stag, and the Black Black Oil', will know that the Clearances still hurt.

Whatever the reasons, and they are many, the case for public ownership of land always finds a receptive hearing in Scotland, and there is no doubt that if the Scottish socialist movement could ever achieve the power to act within Scotland, through a socialist majority on the proposed Scottish legislative assembly, then the land question would be among the first to be tackled.

Scotland's mainland and islands are made up of 30,000 square miles of land through which flows many a river rich in game fish. It is as well to understand that these rivers form an important and lucrative part of a landowner's so-called rights, and that their transfer to public ownership and their exploitation for tourism would make a not insignificant contribution to the national

254

purse. Away back in the early 1960's the then Earl of Home turned down an offer of £47,000 for two miles of salmon fishing on the Tweed, and the Daily Telegraph reported in 1963 that charges of between £150 and £250 per week for grouse shooting were not uncommon. No doubt charges made today for shooting and fishing over Scotland's land and rivers reflects the inflation since the 1960s; but hardly a dribble of this large cash flow finds its way into the pockets of the Scottish people.

Of the Scottish land mass mentioned above, part is owned by the public already in the shape of the Scottish Office and public agencies like the Forestry Commission. The local authorities are landowners, as are Scotland's 900,000 owner-occupiers. The rest of the land is held by private landowners.

No-one is willing to provide an accurate estimate of how much land is held by big private owners, because the establishment has made sure that no modern register of landownership exists and have successfully resisted all pressure to create such a register. Time and again Labour MPs have been rebuffed by successive governments. In the opening weeks of the Parliament elected on 28 February 1974, Mr Peter Doig, MP for Dundee West, asked the new Labour Government, to produce an annual landownership register. Replying for the Government, Mr Bruce Millan, Minister of State at the Scottish Office, said no, and justified his decision by claiming that such a register would be difficult to compile and that it was not needed. Some of us cannot take no for an answer and continue to press for this necessary information to be made public.

When I served on the Select Committee on Scottish Affairs which dealt with land use (House of Commons Session 1971/72) I found it impossible to get the facts of landownership in private hands. Up against muddle and vagueness it was possible only to extract the odd piece of information such as that the Countess of Seafield held 216,000 acres, Lord Lovat 200,000 acres, the Duke of Buccleuch 500,000 acres, and Sir Alec Douglas Home about 60,000 acres. These figures were the product of private digging by socialist groups and individual journalists, and they serve only as pointers to the extent by which a still small group of people control vast areas of Scotland.

Land is a basic commodity and its retention in large scale private ownership will remain a major obstacle to the implementation of sensible comprehensive policies for economic development, housing, recreation, and the redistribution of wealth and power, which must all be undertaken if Scottish society is to improve its social condition and the quality of its democracy.

The principle underlying the case for public ownership of land is the same as that for public ownership of oil, gas, coal and electricity generation—that basic resources essential to the life of the nation should be in the hands of the nation. Land, along with water and air, is our most basic and necessary resource. It is impossible to conceive of and then carry out plans for economic, social and recreational development, making full use of resources and having complete regard to environment, unless we control the land upon which all development is based. Anyone with local government experience will know that unless the community has ownership of land, despite its town and country planning powers, it does not have full control over development decisions.

This principle of public ownership is an important one for the Labour movement to grasp and advocate, and for Labour legislators to act upon. That would seem to state the obvious, but it is far from obvious that the political wing of the movement knows the importance of really getting to grips with the land question.

Until now Labour's whole approach to the subject has been marred by timidity, resulting in policies which led the 1964-70 Labour Government to create the quite hopeless Land Commission, which had no obvious effect on either land ownership or land prices. Present Labour policy has carried us a little way forward from the bad old days of 1970, and Labour's 1974 election programme aimed at taking into public ownership that land which is required for development. Progress has been made, but the new policy will in no way break the landowner's grip in Scotland, especially where it should be broken, in the rural areas, and the new policy will not succeed in transferring much of private land into public hands.

That is not an unfair judgement on Labour's current outline of land policy, which I welcome so far as it goes. Let us take an example of an Easter Ross landholding of considerable acreage, part of which is to be zoned for industrial or social development. Under our new policy the part zoned for development will be brought into public ownership, but the rest of the landholding will, presumably, be left in private hands. That is bound to be the case, because our current policy is not intended to shift land from private to public ownership but to concentrate only on development land.

To push the Labour Party into a more radical land policy we have to understand and then overcome some of the difficulties which lie in the way of that objective. We have to accept that many people seriously question the relevance of public ownership and many are puzzled as to the motives of those who advocate such a policy. We cannot brush these matters aside as of no consequence, for we need to carry the majority of people with us if we are to succeed in a democracy. It is a simple truth, often overlooked, that we cannot build socialism in a democratic society unless we first make a substantial number of socialists from among the population.

So the first task is to set out our guiding principles on this particular issue: establish the worth of our motives- and show the relevance of our policy in that the practical points we espouse relate to our basic beliefs while taking account of reality. To do that is to take the first essential steps in creating socialist attitudes in the minds of people, and to winning electoral support for policies of fundamental change.

The argument for public ownership of land, that is the motive, should not arise out of spite or envy of the landed class, irrespective of historic or present day provocation, but out of recognition of the truth of the simple proposition that until the people own the land they can never claim to own their own country. It should not be the purpose of the democratic socialist movement in Scotland to correct the wrongs of history by policies of malicious expropriation, by a modern clearance of the landowner as ruthless as that by which past landowners removed the common folk from the Highlands.

Expropriation has never been the policy of the socialist movement in Scotland, because our case rests on a desire to extend public ownership for sound democratic and economic reasons and not out of revenge on the landed class, and not from any compulsion to humiliate and humble that class in society.

Of course I realise that critics of the 'no expropriation' policy will be able to advance sound arguments proving that much of the land of Scotland went into private ownership, and into the hands of certain families who are still in benefit, by foul or shady means; and that from this base the critics will be able to mount a good case, at least in principle, as to why it would be quite proper to place the land back into public ownership without a penny changing hands. Tom Johnston's 'The History of the Scottish Working Class' deals extensively with land theft by the nobility, and Ramsay MacDonald in his 1913 foreword to Johnston's 'Our Scots Noble Families', launched a superb attack on the myth and majesty which has kept the landowners out of reach of the common people.

MacDonald's words are worth quoting:

> "Show the people that our Old Nobility is not noble, that its lands are stolen lands — stolen whether by force or fraud; show people that the title deeds are rapine, murder, massacre, cheating or Court Harlotry; dissolve the halo of divinity that surrounds the hereditary title; let the people clearly understand that our present House of Lords is composed largely of descendents of successful pirates and rogues; do these things and you shatter the Romance that keeps the nations numb and spellbound while privilege picks its pockets."

Few in the contemporary scene could put the matter so forcefully and well, and the fact that Ramsay MacDonald committed a political sin by ditching the movement in 1931 in no way invalidates the worth of his deeds and words, such as those above, during the period when he led the Labour movement with courage and distinction.

But even when taking into account all that has happened in the history of Scotland, we have to ask the expropriator what is to be gained by a policy of expropriation other than revenge for history. Attempts to right historical wrongs by wreaking revenge on descendents of our old nobility, or on those who have inherited from them by one means or another, is not the way to create a balanced, tolerant, civilised society. Taking land from the landed class will of itself be a traumatic event for them, and the compensation we pay will be worth the price for getting the land and a small price for easing them and theirs into the modern Scotland in which power and wealth will be more equitably shared than at present, and in which there will be no place for the semi-idle rich. The price of compensation is of the utmost importance, and I will put a suggestion on this a little later.

Taking a lesson from MacDonald's words we have first to convince the public that our case is right. To do this we need to promote the democratic argument, produce an economic and social case to which the public can respond, and then put forward a comprehensive scheme of compensation that will be regarded as fair but which will not impose on the community a financial burden it cannot bear.

First to the democratic argument. The pre-requisite of a democracy is a free people unhindered in seeking to extend the public weal. The fight for democracy has been the fight to take power from an elite group and those who serve them, and to spread that power widely among the people. We can measure the quality of our democracy by considering just how widespread is power and just how free are the people to take decisions affecting their communities.

The truth is that so long as a small group of large scale landowners hold exclusive rights to such a vast natural national resource, Scottish society will be ill-divided in terms of power distribution, and so seriously deficient in democracy. While the landowners are in their present position they will continue to wield an influence over events which is quite disproportionate to their individual worth or contribution to society. Large scale landownership is still a source of enormous power, either in controlling public institutions in certain areas of Scotland or in frustrating local and nation public policy objectives. That power must be broken and transferred to the public. There is a conflict between the needs of the people and the interests of the landed class, and this must be resolved to the satisfaction of the people. A first step is to persuade the people that their true interests and needs will always be frustrated and thwarted by allowing so much of Scotland's land to remain in private ownership.

The debate about landownership will not be a cosy chat between us and the people: our advocacy of public ownership will provoke a strong response from the vested land interests. They will not choose the issue of land democracy around which to rally their forces, because that is weak ground for them. They will concentrate instead on practical issues and argue that present planning powers and fiscal measures already give the public all the power that is required over land use. Another argument will be that present landowners have a deep regard for the contribution their estates make to enhancing landscape, and that things might go to pot without their guiding hand. A further point likely to come from landowners is that to pay their notion of fair compensation would be a truly ridiculous price for the nation to pay for control which, through the planning acts and fiscal weapons, it already has for next to nothing.

This kind of rebuttal of the public ownership idea was much in evidence during the proceedings of the Select Committee, with the Landowners' Federation obviously to the fore in protecting their members' interests. Surprisingly, or perhaps not surprisingly, we also had the Highlands and Inslands Development Board deliver a staunch defence of highland landowning interests.

The HIDB evidence is worth referring to. The Board's written submission stated that: "Rational criteria for land use, however, are notably absent from the present system of land allocation", and that for example, "Forestry Commission planting targets for the country are not related to land suitability or its assured availability." That particular paragraph rounded off with the important assertion that: "Fiscal concessions are over-riding factors in determining the location and rate of private planting."

All that amounts to is a tacit admission that forestry policy in Scotland is based on the unsound principle that the Forestry Commission get land not necessarily where it needs it but where it can get it, even if it is second best land in a second best place.

However, instead of supporting public ownership to which the logic of their memorandum seemed to point, the Board simply insisted that the best way to implement rational plans was by "way of financial inducements" although they followed up this gem by pointing out that such bribery had little or no effect on certain people. As the Board put it, there are a minority of "landowners who are not personally interested in such development", and that "quite large areas of potentially useful and improvable agricultural land could effectively be sterilized as a result of landowner disconcern." I suppose it is true that people like the Countess of Seafield and Col. Whitbread are immune to most financial inducements calculated to persuade them towards a policy of land use to which they are opposed.

When pressed in Committee during oral evidence the Board's Chairman, Sir Andrew Gilchrist, was unrepentant as the following passage shows:

Sir Andrew Gilchrist:

Before I was Chairman of the Board I was conscious of the fact that the Board was by no means popular with land proprietors in the Highlands. We have had no difficulty at all. I think the unpopularity of the Board arose partly out of original misunderstandings. It was appointed by a Labour Government, and also because of the Invergordom planning procedures for the smelter in the course of which a lot of people were defending their land bitterly and to the last ditch, and the impression was created that the Board was behind everything evil in stealing the land. That impression has now been eliminated and some of the farmers have done well out of Invergordon so the position of the Board is easier.

Mr Sillars:

I am interested in the issue of resolving conflict by persuasion. In your evidence, you single out the fact that there is a minority of landowners not presently interested in certain development who are themselves immune to an offer of financial assistance—not open to bribery to put it at its crudest. It is possible in the Highlands that a minority owns a substantial area of land and it must loom significantly enough in the Board's future thoughts on land use for it to be planted inside the evidence to us. Do you foresee any real difficulties in future, and would it not make the Board's job much easier as a dynamic institution of the Highlands if land was publicly owned?

Sir Andrew Gilchrist:

I doubt if that would necessarily be the right solution. We planted that little time bomb, and it is a little one, as you say, we are not yet at the stage where we are in any conflict of policy with Highland landlords. Most of the landed estates in the Highlands, a good many, are managed on excellent principles. I would regard the Secretary of State, who is a big landlord in the Highlands as managing his estates no better than a dozen or so others, and that applies whichever Government is in power.

So there we have it all in a nutshell. The HIDB spotlight the problem posed to the community by rich landlords and then lamely say that, despite their own written words to the contrary, financial inducements are the best means of winning rational land use plans. And the Chairman of the Board himself goes on record as saying that there is no conflict between landowners and the Highland communities, and that, anyway, it is all a question of management and private interests do this as well as public agencies.

Later in his evidence Sir Andrew acknowledged that the Board could seek compulsory purchase of land in the Board's area, but he did not dwell overlong on this aspect of the matter. There are some, however, who leap in at the mention of 'compulsory purchase' and argue that its availability to local authorities is an adequate method for the public to control the use of land. But they are wrong in believing that CPO procedure is adequate and that it provides the community with the power to pursue comprehensive land use policies. Compulsory purchase orders, important though they are, are only ad hoc instruments used for ad hoc land use development purposes. Admittedly some of the developments which flow from compulsory purchase orders are on a large scale, but those who believe that these procedures give back to the public a truly decisive measure of power and control are fooling themselves.

Two cases fairly illustrate that even with CPO powers the public good can meet with damaging delays. These are the saga of the proposed Tweedbank development and the scandal of the Isle of Raasay. The Tweedbank scheme was devised as an essential part of the answer to the economic and social problems of the Borders. The development plan was subjected to considerable public scrutiny and gained massive public support. The key to its success lay in the 297 acres required for development, but this land was denied by a decision of the landowner who managed to impose several years delay despite the local authority's recourse to CPO procedure. People with local government experience could cite other examples, perhaps not simply of delay but of the Council choosing to develop poorer or less suitable sites for housing and schools, because to have chosen the best site would have meant facing serious delay in the face of landowner resistence to compulsory purchase.

The other case, Raasay, is a classic of its kind. Early in 1972 it came to light that a vital ferry development for this small island, two miles off the east coast of Skye, had been vetoed by a landowner, Dr John Green of Sussex, England, who refused to sell the 1.5 acres necessary for the terminal project. The local authority threatened compulsory purchase and were rebuffed when Dr Green, in a Glasgow Herald interview on 14 March, 1972, described such action as "a monstrous intrusion of my rights as a property owner." Had the land at Tuerdbank and at Raasay been in public ownership no such problems would have arisen.

Of course not all landowners are as blatantly obdurate in resisting development as were those involved in these two examples. Many are, but show more resilience and public relations skill in disguising that their objection to development is in fact development. Some are more progressive than others.

At its best however large scale private landownership is akin to benevolent dictatorship. There is no guarantee that the benevolence will continue, and as the Tweedbank and Raasay examples show, compulsory purchase procedure is not a sufficiently powerful influence working on the public's behalf. Indeed this view of compulsory purchase was backed up by evidence to the Select Committee from the Association of County Councils. The closer one looks at compulsory purchase the more one comes to appreciate that it will never be a substitute for the control which the public can exercise only when they own the land on which they wish to develop. The closer the examination of CPO procedure the stronger becomes the case for outright public ownership. What we have to get clear as a movement is what exclusions if any there are to be from a policy of publicly owning the land. It is to this matter, a politically crucial one, that I now turn.

A Plan for Public Ownership

First there is the group known as owner-occupiers. In keeping with the new Parliamentary practice of the day let me declare an interest and identify myself as one of them. Most owner-occupiers own only the small plot of land upon which their family home is built, and they should be specifically and emphatically excluded from any plan to take land into public ownership. Neither individually nor when taken as a complete group do they pose any problems for society in land use terms, and it would be a nonsense to attempt to take their small bits of land away from their ownership.

Next there are the owner-occupier and tenant farmers. I happen to believe that our farmers are highly efficient producers of food, and that one reason for this is that they feel they have a stake in the land, and that this is especially so with owner-occupiers. In Scotland owner-occupier farmers have relatively modest individual landholdings and they rarely if ever thwart development which is in the public interest. It would not be for the benefit of the community's food policy for us to destroy the farmers intimate link with his land by taking it from him, whatever the level of compensation. Tenant farmers are not of course owner-occupiers, but many of them have farmed the same land for generations and have an attachment to it no less strong than that of the owner-occupier for his land. Any sensible scheme of land reform would guarantee tenant farmers security of tenure, and moreover would ensure that the guarantee covers the family and not only the male head of the household.

That leaves us with the Highland and Lowland urban and rural landowners. Land in urban areas, with the owner-occupier exceptions already mentioned, should be taken into public ownership. Land in the Highlands and rural Lowlands should be treated differently and in accordance with the principal aim of breaking the power grip of the big landowners, without starting a wholesale clearance.

There are those with big estates and those with small estates. Many with great estates have at best an arms length relationship with local people; some are absentees; and still others have an old style baronial relationship with local communities. Those with smaller estates often have a deep involvement with and form part of the viable element in the life of local areas. Socialists may not share the smaller landowner's view of life, nor particularly like his influence on the politics of rural Scotland, but it is true to say that this group does not pose the same obstacles to rational land use and the spread of democracy as do the huge vested land interests. At any rate I see both political and practical advantage in clearly differentiating between the large and the small, and I would concentrate legislative action on defining the maximum permitted estate holding, and taking all above that size into public ownership. The definition of maximum holding would have to bear relation to agricultural economics, and therefore the maximum would vary from one major geographical area to another.

We are next required to turn to the issue of compensation, which is no small matter. Conventional notions of what are correct levels of compensation, and methods of assessing compensation, should be rejected. These methods usually mean paying at either current market value or current use value, but compensation awards based on these ideas would be clearly unfair to the public and would place an intolerable burden on the public purse.

In the first place it has to be borne in mind that landowning families have extracted considerable wealth from the land over many years, and have seen the value of land rise through inflation without any work on their part. Also to be borne in mind is that in many cases the increased market value in land has been due entirely to public policy decisions and public investment in agricultural support, housing, roads, schools, and industrial developments. Current use value is also affected by public policy decisions, and it would be ludicrous to suggest that the public pay a price for land which has been commercially enhanced, directly more often than indirectly, by public action.

Taking all these factors into account it is obvious that we require a new approach to compensation: one that is both fair to the public and is fair and non-punitive to the dispossessed landowner. During my time of service on the Select Committee I gave this a lot of thought and finally produced an unorthodox but fair scheme, unhappily rejected by a majority of the Committee. Nothing that has happened since then has shaken my view and for what it is worth I now set it out again.

In considering compensation policy it has to be recognised that there are two groups to be examined, and two situations to be considered. The large landowners, who are our target, can be divided into two groups, the landowning families and organisations such as companies which own land. The two situations are urban and rural. Any compensation scheme must take account of these differences.

For the purposes of the compensation scheme Scotland should be divided into designated urban and rural areas. Owners in urban areas, whether landowning families with long title to the land or people who belong to some other category, will transfer land to the public and will then make application for compensation to a new body—The Urban Land Compensation Board. This Board would be an appointed body with nominees drawn from local authorities, trade union and industrial organisations. Its duty would be to pay out fair compensation to applicants within a scale of minimum payments and a variable supplement up to a certain prescribed level.

The minimum payment should be the price paid for the land acquisition, with that price upvalued to take account of the dipping value of the £ in intervening years, with the same formula to be applied to any property on the land which might have been purchased under separate arrangements.

The variable supplement in any one case would be a sum of money equal to from 1 per cent to 25 per cent return on the original capital expended in the purchase of the land and property, plus a sum of money equal to from 1 per cent to 25 per cent return on capital invested in the land or property since the date of original purchase.

Applicants for compensation would be guaranteed the minimum compensation price as described above, but they would have to prove their case when seeking supplementary benefit. The Urban Land Compensation Board would need to exercise discretion within the limits prescribed, and they would be required to pay particular attention to the applicant's ability to prove his need of supplementary payment.

In dealing with the designated rural areas the suggestion is that a Rural Land Compensation Board be appointed from among similar kinds of people nominated for membership of the Urban Board. When dealing with organisations which own land, as distinct from individuals or land-owning families, the Rural Board should operate the same formula as applies in all urban situations, including supplementary benefits on the 1 per cent to 25 per cent scale. Individuals and landowning families, as has already been implied, would be treated somewhat differently.

What I suggest for individual and landowning families is a pension scheme. Those affected by public ownership would apply to the Rural Board for compensation and this would be awarded in the form of a pension. People in this take-over category would also have the inalienable right to retain their family home and a sufficient part of their land to make up a viable farming or commercial unit, thus providing them with continuity of residence and the means of earning a living.

The pension part of the deal would take account of the problems which would confront the Board because of differences in size and quality of one landholding compared to another. The needs of one individual or one family will vary one from another also. We therefore need a flexible pension plan based on fixed minima and maxima, with the Board having discretion in awarding a pension within these fixed limits. The Board's primary conern would be to ensure that the applicant could face the future with an income adequate to his or the family needs.

The outline of the pension plan is as follows:-

	Minimum	Maximum
Individual owner	£3,000 p.a.	£6,000 p.a.
Spouse	£800 p.a.	£1,500 p.a.
Elderly dependent relative	£800 p.a.	£2,000 p.a.
Young dependent relative	£500 p.a.	£1,000 p.a.

(these scales to be uprated every two years to maintain the real value of the award).

In the event of the owner dying before the spouse the owner's pension would transfer to the spouse, and the spouse's pension would cease.

The pension would cease on the death of both owner and spouse, except that the owner pension would be paid out for the benefit of any dependent children until they attained the age of 18 years. The young dependent relative pension would continue to be paid in these circumstances.

On the death of both owner and spouse the pension of the elderly dependent relatives would be increased at the discretion of the Board by the award of a special supplement on a scale going from £1,000 to £2,000 p.a. Any pension payable to any dependent relative would cease on their death.

All pensions would be taxable

In my view this set of new compensation proposals has two outstanding merits. First it ensures that the public would not have to pay a ransom for land taken into public ownership, the value of which has been inflated principally because of progressive public policy creating pressures on land resources. Secondly, it ensures that no landowner, individual or organisation, is deprived of either a return on capital invested or an adequate income for a lifetime. Some landowners would be bought off, and others pensioned off with their home and its immediate surroundings intact. The policy is a blend of financial sense with a generous splash of humanity: something the working class, to its credit, has always been willing to give, but rarely itself receives.

In reaching the conclusion of my contribution to this book, my thoughts are that some will regard my proposals as not red enough for a Red Paper. I can understand that view, although I doubt if the Scottish Landowners' Federation will see it quite that way. But what I have tried to do is not so much to retreat from sloganising, as to show how we might turn the slogan 'public ownership of land' into a legislative reality fully acceptable to the Scottish electorate.

Highland Landlordism

John McEwen

The degraded condition of the Highlands of Scotland, in the hands of powerful, often anti-social landlordism, has worried me for years. The secrecy surrounding many of the major holdings is, I think, a public scandal.

In 1874, the government managed to produce a return of all land owners, entitled "Owners of Land and Heritages".(1) It showed that 106 people owned half the country. Since then, many changes have taken place, a major one being the steady depopulation of the Highlands until, today, these areas resemble a vast green desert, but alas, in 1974, we do not have a land register in Scotland. We do not know who owns our land.(2)

The Perth and Kinross Fabian Society decided in 1967 that it would be of great interest to discover who owns Perthshire, and a project with this aim was embarked on. "The Acreocracy of Perthshire"(3), published in 1971, gives an account of the incredible obstacles we found in our way. After four years' struggle we were able to record the estimated size of only the 31 largest estates (10,000 acres and upwards) in the county and compare them with the 1874 position.

A parallel piece of research was being carried out by Dr Roger Millman of Aberdeen University who was endeavouring to mark the "marches" of all highland estates. (He has now extended this to the whole of Scotland). This involved placing on 1" ordnance survey sheets the boundaries of all estates and compiling index sheets naming the owners (but in no case examining acreages).

Millman himself concluded his work by saying "It should be stressed that the publication of the map and inventory is in no way intended to prejudice the concept or tradition of the private ownership of land in Scotland which, despite many defects in both the attitude of the workers and the management of estates, continues, in the opinion of many rural management consultants, to be the most expedient form of land occupancy."(4) Personally, I am under no such illusions. My objective is to see the stranglehold of our mainly absentee landlordism destroyed, to see cap-in-hand servile flunkeyism replaced by dedicated workers reclaiming our desert lands. When

I heard of Dr Millman's work, however, I realised that this was the breakthrough I had been awaiting for decades, and, when, in 1972, I discovered that his maps and "index sheets" had been lodged in Register House, Edinburgh, and that copies were available for purchase, I immediately sent for the Perthshire sections, and, by planimeter, was able to ascertain the acreages of all estates down to 500 acres or so, and pair them with the names of owners on the index sheets. This set me on fire, and finally I bought all 87 maps covering the Highlands plus the 396 index sheets.(5)

Work on these 1" maps and index sheets has been going on steadily since then, and I feel that a summary of the main findings is of sufficient interest for publication now, before I complete further research, particularly into the fantastic family links between ownerships, their interlocking interests with banking, insurance, high finance, drink, tobacco, the car industry, and so on.(6)

I am beginning to find out some of the people who do, in fact, now own our Highlands. I can now record that three hundred and forty—private families or companies own just under 6,500,000 acres of 9,985,300 acres—the total acreage of the Highlands and Islands (Caithness, Sutherland, Ross & Cromarty, Inverness, Argyll, and Perthshire). One hundred and forty individuals or companies own just under half the Highlands and Islands. Four individuals own just under half a million acres of the Highlands (6 per cent of the land); ten own nearly one million acres (12 per cent of the land) and 56 people own 3,044,300 acres—just under one third of the land. 0.1 per cent (340) of the population of the Highlands and Islands (375,668) including Perthshire own 64 per cent of the land.

Seventeen individuals or companies own 69 per cent of the land of Caithness. Thirty eight own 84 per cent of the land of Sutherland. Eighty own 57 per cent of the land of Invernesshire; sixty seven own 48 per cent of the land of Argyll; seventy six own 80 per cent of the land of Ross and Cromarty; and sixty three own 62 per cent of the land of Perthshire. (7). Just over one and a half million acres of the Highlands and Islands is publicly owned and estates under 5000 acres account for just over two million acres of these counties.

The Highland and Islands

Various public bodies have been formed to deal with the run-down of the Highlands, and I refer to them briefly as follows:-

The Highland and Islands Development Board, since its inception, has not shown itself capable of standing up to the landlords.

The Forestry Commission had had a much longer run in these benighted areas, having been in direct and very considerable contact with landowenrs since 1919, but again, in my opinion, this Lord Lovat militarily-planned body, with its officers and ordinary workers (P.B.I.) has not made adequate impact. This Government Department is now being run into the ground for lack of sufficient decent plantable land, yet it has all along had powers for compulsory acquisition of land-powers never used. Why? Your guess is as good as mine. In any case, land which they could have bought for around £5 per acre 7/8 years ago now costs ten times as much.

The Red Deer Commission is a body of 13 men until recently led by Lord Arbuthnot. It costs us around £30,000 p.a. for its services in controlling the Red Deer population. When it began work a few years ago there were about 120,000 animals. Today the figure is nearer 200,000. First class conservationists, but what about the severe losses suffered by farmers and foresters?

The Crofters' Commission. This body seems to have had no great success in bettering the lot of crofters. The hard line taken by the 1884 Napier Commission in restricting any increase in croft size and stopping the uniting of existing tenancies may have hampered the present Commission.

As a contrast, the **Hill Farming Research Organisation** (H.F.R.O.) in its work at Lephinmore (Argyll) and other centres has, in my opinion, come to grips with the desperate soil degradation in the Highlands brought about in the last hundred years.

Acreages of Estates of 5,000 acres & upwards within the Five Main Crofting Counties plus Perthshire Based on Millman's "Estate Boundaries", 1969

Size cat. acres	Caithness E.	Caithness 1000s acres	Sutherland E.	Sutherland 1000s acres	Ross & Crom. E.	Ross & Crom. 1000s acres	Inverness E.	Inverness 1000s acres	Argyll E.	Argyll 1000s acres	Perthshire E.	Perthshire 1000s acres	Totals E.	Totals 1000s acres	Running Totals E.	Running Totals 1000s acres
100,000	—	—	2	236.5	—	—	1	103.2	—	—	1	130.0	4	469.7	4	469.7
80/100,000	—	—	1	81.4	—	—	3	276.4	—	—	—	—	4	357.8	8	827.5
70/80,000	—	—	—	—	2	144.2	1	76.0	2	147.8	—	—	5	368.0	13	1195.5
60/70,000	—	—	2	112.3	2	125.4	1	62.5	—	—	1	65.0	6	365.2	19	1560.7
50/60,000	1	52.6	—	—	2	109.8	2	102.7	1	51.0	1	57.9	7	374.0	26	1934.7
40/50,000	1	48.0	3	124.1	4	177.8	2	84.7	2	82.2	1	45.0	13	561.8	39	2496.5
30/40,000	1	33.8	4	145.1	6	203.9	1	34.5	3	95.9	2	67.6	17	580.8	56	3077.3
20/30,000	1	27.5	6	145.9	10	245.3	7	162.0	3	63.3	4	85.4	31	729.4	87	3806.7
15/20,000	3	49.9	6	110.2	17	236.5	13	227.9	6	100.0	8	137.3	53	861.8	140	4668.5
10/15,000	4	50.5	4	55.8	17	213.9	14	166.2	17	209.4	18	213.9	74	909.1	214	5578.2
5/10,000	6	41.4	10	73.7	16	118.5	34	233.8	33	213.2	27	184.4	127	865.0	340	6443.2
Totals	17	303.7	38	1085.0	76	1575.3	79	1529.9	67	962.8	63	986.5	340	6443.2	340	6443.2
Official acreages of these counties		438.9		1297.8		1977.3		2,695.0		1,990.5		1,595.8		9,985.3		
State owned land		303.7		1085.0		1575.0		1529.9		962.5		986.5		6,443.2		
		22.1		173.6		.139.4		619.9		492.3		100.0		1,546.5		
Area left for estates under 5,000 acres		13.1		39.2		262.6		546.0		535.4		509.3		1,993.6		
Pop. of counties (1971)		27,781		13,055		58,287		89,659		59,780		127,106		375,668		

E = Estate

264

But H.F.R.O. findings and suggested remedies have been largely ignored.

Speaking of the biological resources of the Highlands at the recent B.A. meeting at Stirling, Dr Cunningham of H.F.R.O. said: "There are some who regard the Highland region as little more than a wilderness and consider that agriculture, especially hill-farming is of no consequence (and should be substantially abandoned). We may be discussing an underdeveloped area, but certainly not one in which the spectre of starvation haunts the inhabitants, but rather one which could make an increasing contribution to the National larder for the teeming millions packed into the S.E. of England. The view has been expressed that the Highland area is the only unspoilt region in Europe and should be kept in its present state. This implies that the presence of man and agriculture is in some way undesirable, and this I would question."

This long quotation shows the aims of H.F.R.O.. I fully agree with them. In conclusion, I have been asked to say what I would like to see done in the Highlands.

1. An official register of estates, owners and acreages should be made.
2. A complete survey and classification of the land is necessary. This could be done quickly by the combined efforts of the following bodies, each of which holds a mass of dormant information: The Department of Agriculture for Scotland, the Forestry Commission, the MacAulay Soil Institute, the Hill-Farming Research Organisation, and the three agricultural colleges. However, I have just learned that land classification for these areas has been compiled but is strictly confidential in St Andrews House.
3. The land must all be nationlised (and I can see this happening only in a U.K. context). Crofters and farmers would be tenants of the State. In the final analysis, the full development of the Highlands depends on agriculture, forestry and small industries, including the processing of all state-grown timber in state owned sawmills and pulp mills. Agriculture, in the form of crofting, small farming, a very limited amount of ranch farming and deer farming, should be given priority.

1. "Owners of Land and Heritage" H.M.S.O. 1874.
2. Today there is no officially provided comprehensive register of landowning. The assessor's Valuation Rolls on which taxation is based list properties and give gross annual values as well as rateable values but very little idea at all can be obtained from them of the total extent of landed estates. The Register of Sesines, kept in Register House, Edinburgh, is the chief security for title to land in Scotland but there are now 700,000 research sheets which frequently do not include acreages.
3. **"Acreocracy of Perthshire"** Perthshire Fabians' Pamphlet.
4. **Scottish Geographical Magazine.** Dec. 1969.
5. I should like to record the help I have received from my wife, Margaret, and her patience. She has been responsible for at least 50 per cent of my absorption in this work.
Can I further add my indebtedness to my friend Keith Openshaw, Forestry Consultant, for his intensive work on tables and histograms and also for his advice in many other directions.
6. I have no desire to stress the difficulties I had to face, in fitting maps together (there was much duplication) defining county boundaries, identifying and classifying estate boundaries, and finally, by far the most time consuming, making allowance for the unexpected fact that these photostat maps were not true to the 1" to the mile scale stated on them, but ranged between 13/16 and 14/16 of true scale, in which case my planimeter had to be're-adjusted to suit.
7. I cannot absolutely guarantee the figures I have produced, because of the complicated methods entailed but, as we say in measuring standing timber they are "not guaranteed but reasonably correct." In fact Keith Openshaw thinks I have erred on the side of underestimating private estates.

Argyll: Estates of 5,000 acres upwards (from Millman's Maps, 1968) (7)

Owners	Estates	Acres
Islay Estates Ltd.	Islay Estate	74,400
Duke of Argyll	Argyll Estate	73,400
R. Fleming	Blackmount	51,000
Lady Wyfold	Glen Kinglass	41,200
Jura Ltd. (London)	Tarbet (Jura)	41,100
Ardtornish Est. Ltd.	Ardtornish	34,400
J. M. Guthrie	Conaglen	31,000
Noble Family	Ardkinglass	30,500
Mrs. A. R. Nelson	Ardlussa (Jura)	22,000
Miss C. MacLean	Ardgour	20,700
Mrs. Faller-Bell	Dalness	20,600
Viscountess Masserene	Knock (Mull)	18,700
Bruno L. Schroder	Dunlossit (Jura)	17,700
J. T. Thomas	Ardnamurchan	17,100
Campbell Preston	Ardchattam	16,200
Craignure Est. Trust	Torosay (Mull)	15,500
Western Heritable Inv. Ltd.	Kintour (Islay)	15,300
Tr. of C.A.M. Oates	Loch Buie (Mull)	14,900
Sir L. T. Lithgow	Skipness	14,700
J. Maxwell McDonald	Ormsary	14,400
Maj. O. B. Clapham	Largie	14,400
Hon. Mr. Dalness	Laggan (Islay)	13,100
Arthur Strutt	Altnafeagh	12,600
C. K. M. Stewart	Coll (island)	12,300
F. A. Riley-Smith	Ardfin (Jura)	11,900
Simon Fraser	Glenure	11,500
R. M. Abel-Smith	Laudale	11,300
M. W. Brand Aitken	Auch	11,200
Lt. Col. & Mrs. Nicholl	Black Corries	10,800
Fenton Barns (N. Berwick)	Ardlarig	10,800
Rt. Hon. Lord Strathcona	Colonsay (Isle)	10,500
V. P. Hardwick	Pennyghae (Mull)	10,400
H. M. Speirs	Glenborrodale	10,300
R. M. Malcolm	Poltalloch	9,500
D. H. Rogers	Ellary	9,000
MacKie Campbell	Stonefield	9,000
M. J. Micholls	Killean	7,900
Atlas Investment Co.	Castles	7,700
A. C. Farquarson	Torfoisk (Mull)	7,700
Mrs. Hester Sassoon	Ben Buie (Mull) or Cameron Est.	7,300
Tr. of late Holman	Acharacle	7,200
Sir I. M. Campbell	Cumlodden	7,200
Fitzroy MacLean	Strachur	7,200
The Chalmers Property	Killiechronan (Mull)	7,000
Schuster and others	Duillater	6,900
—	Glenlonan	6,800
	Edderline	6,800
Mrs. V. I. Montgomery	Kinnabus (Islay)	6,800
British Aluminium Ltd.	Brit. Aluminium	6,300
R. M. B. McAllister	Glenbarr	6,300
G.R. Kickman and M.S. Wilson	Leanganbeach (Jura)	6,000
Sir Wm. J. Lithgow	Inver (Jura)	6,000
Mrs. Pollok	Ronnachan	5,900
John McPherson	Ballimeanach	5,500
C. S. Bailey	Inversanda	5,400
Brig. R. W. L. Fellowes	Cladich	5,400
J. H. C. Crerar	Breckley	5,400
Economic Forestry Group	Knockdow	5,400
Tr. of the Late J. MacRae Gilstrap	Ballochyle	5,400
Tr. of Wallbrook	Ballimore	5,400
A. B. MacArthur	Carskiey	5,400
Hugh MacPhail	Arnicle	5,200
H. L. MacDonald	Achnashnich	5,100
Mrs. Billimeir	Barguillen	5,100
A. Colville	Melfort	5,100
	Ráhoy	5,000
		5,000
		5,000

Sutherland: Estates of 5,000 acres upwards

Owners	Estates	Acres
Countess of Sutherland	Sutherland Estates	123,500
Duke of Westminster, Lady Grosvenor	Reay, Kylestrome etc.	112,700
Edmond H. Vestey	Lochinver, Assynt	81,400
Michael Berry	Altnahaven	62,300
T. G. Moncrieff-Mrs Gow etc.	Strathmore, Benroyal etc.	60,000
Benmore Estates Ltd	Benmore	44,100
J. E. Elliot (Langholm)	Dunfelling, Balnakeil etc.	40,000
Mrs. J. B. W. Tyser	Gordonbush	40,000
Liberton Properties	Bighouse	38,300
V. G. Balan	Forsinard	37,800
R.F.T. Foljambe	Hope and Malness	34,500
Mrs. E.M. Jonson	Dalnessie, Ben Armine etc.	34,500
Lt. Com. H. V. Bruce & Mrs. E. E. Bonnington Wood	Sallachy	26,700
Tr. of R. Midwood	Syre	25,400
Auchentoul Est. Co.	Auchentoul	24,100
Sir Adam Wigan	Borrobol	23,700
Ch. H. Garton and Mrs. Garton	Loch Merkland	23,200
Viscount Leverhulme	Badanloch	22,800
Kinlochbervie Hotel	Kinlochbervie	19,700

Mr. and Mrs. Price Jenkins	Kilouman	19,700
Lord Roborough	Shelpick	19,500
Lady Balfour of Inchyre	Tressary	17,600
Lady Paynter	Kildonan	17,500
Mr. and Mrs. Balfour	Scourie	16,200
Gen. Osborne	Rhiemich	14,400
Torrish Co. Ltd.	Torrish	14,300
M. A. H. Fletcher	Shinnes	14,100
R. M. Abel Smith	Cambusmore	13,000
Mrs. Amy M. Mance	Glen Casslay	9,500
P. Robinson	Smoo Lodge	9,000
Miss Upwhat	Inchnadamph	8,600
Mrs. Fergusson	Gualin	8,200
Sir R. Rootes	Rispond	7,500
Miss Nancy Bradford	Tumore	7,500
Tr. of Lt. Col. Negus	Invernaver	5,500
W. Palmer Sankey	Loch Assynt Lodge	5,100
G. T. Roberts	Morvich	5,000
Miss M. G. Dudgeon	Crakaig	5,000

Inverness: Estates of 5,000 acres upwards

Brit. Alumin. Ltd.	Brit. Alumin. Co. Ltd.	103,200
Lord Cameron	Lochiel	97,600
S. Uist Estates Ltd.	S. Uist & Islands	92,200
Countess of Seafield	Seafield Estate	86,600
Lord Lovat	Lovat Estates	76,000
Maj. Hereward Wake	Amhunnsuidh	62,500
Lord Dulverton (Wills)	Glenfeshie	52,700
N. Uist and Benbecula Est. Ltd	N. Uist & Islands	50,000
Sir Oliver Crosswaithe-Eyre	Knoydart	43,000
Lord MacDonald	Sleat Estates	41,700
John MacLeod of MacLeod	Dunvegan Estates	34,500
Wm. G. Gordon of Lude	Arrisdale	27,700
Capt. Sandison (Mrs. Hume)	Glentromie	27,000
M. J. Beecher	Arisaig	22,500
Taylor Bros.	Abernethy	22,000
Th. Girvan	W. Ceannacroc	21,500
M. N. C. Ford	Meoble	21,300
J. P. Grant	Balmacaan	20,000
	Rothiemurchus	19,800
P. H. Byam Cook	Stocknish	19,500
Lord Burton	Ben Alder	18,900
Robert Ellice	Dockfour	18,300
	Glenfarrar	18,000
Glendale Crofters Ltd.	Glendale Crofters	18,000
The MacNeil of Barra	Barra & Islands	17,200

W. MacKenzie Goodman	Glendoe	17,100
J. C. Wilson, P. Wilson	Garrogie	17,000
R. J. & A. Trapp Ltd	Braeroy	16,700
D. Cameron	Glen Nevis	16,300
Tr. Late D.I.C. MacLaren	Clune & Cluny	16,200
J. L. Macdonald	Skebost (Skye)	16,200
M. A. Johnston	Strathaird (Skye)	15,000
Hon. P. M. Samuel	Phoine, Etteridge	14,400
J. M. Grant	Glen Morriston	14,000
—	Ralia, S. Drumochter	13,400
D. R. MacDonald	Waternish (Skye)	13,100
Sir J. Fuller	Cozac	12,300
Nether Pollok Ltd	Bheinn Bhinc Deer Forest	12,200
Mr. Hayward	Newtonmore	12,200
Mrs. L. P. Cameron Head	Inverailort	11,600
Sir J. Barber	Drumnaglass	10,800
Maj. Gen. MacDonald	Braes (Skye)	10,700
Forbes Leith	Dalraddy	10,600
	Dunachton	10,400
Sligachan Hotel	Sligachan	10,200
J. C. Cremer	Pitmain	9,900
G. M. Tunline Pretyman	Corrygarth	9,500
Col. Eliot Holt	Corryborough	9,500
Mrs. Wilkie Griss	Guisachan	9,000
Lord Bildland	Kinrara	9,000
E. K. MacLeod Hilleary	Edinbane & Lyndale (Skye)	9,000
Tarbert Estate Dev. Co.	Glenmazeran	8,300
Lt. Col. L. G. Gray-Cheape	Glenaladale	8,100
Westminster (Liverpool) Trust Co. Ltd.	Dorlin	8,100
Earl Bradford	Culligram	7,700
Wm. I. Bruges	Dell	7,600
Mr and Mrs. J. Lees-Millais	Tulloch	7,600
A. McKelliag	Glenmoidart	7,500
R. Morrison, Harwood Evans	Glenforman	7,200
A. Spencer Nairn	Eigg	7,000
Lewis Briggs	Struy	6,700
F.T. Davies	Cullachy	6,700
—	Aberarder	6,600
G. Forbes	Glenspean	6,400
D. J. Wilson	Balayil	6,300
H. Birbeck	Moy	6,000
—	Kinlochourn	6,000
Moray Estates Dev. Co.	Vallay (N. Uist)	6,000
T. C. Cunningham	Castle Stewart	5,800
A. Dunbar	Inverarne	5,700
Ballindalloch Estate	Achlarn	5,400

Owner	Estate	Acres
—	Dalnagarvie	5,400
General Martin	Husabost (Skye)	5,300
Tr. T. H. Hatford	Scalpay	5,200
MacDonald	Strathconnon	5,100
E. D. H. MacRae	Clava	5,000
Eagle Star	Knockie Lodge	5,000
Col. R. Swire	Arbost	5,000

Perthshire: Estates of 5,000 acres upwards

Owner	Estate	Acres
Duke of Atholl	Atholl	130,000
Earl of Ancaster	Drummond Castle	65,000
Sir Ed. Wills Bt.	Meggernie	57,900
Brig. Colvin	Camusericht	45,000
D. S. Fothringham	Murthly	33,800
Earl of Mansfield	Scone	22,400
E. J. & R. N. Lowes	Glenfalloch	21,600
Capt. A. A. C. Farquharson	Invercauld	21,200
Visc. Wimbourne	Craigenour	20,200
Capt. I.C. Sales, I. Terriere	Dunalastair	19,600
R. W. Pilkington	Dalnacardoch	18,400
Water Board	Loch Katrine	18,300
Ben Challum Ltd.	Glen Lochay	17,700
Mr. & Mrs. D. S. Bower	Argaty & Auchlyne	16,400
Keir & Cawdor	Quoigs	16,300
Moray Estates	Doune	15,500
Th. Lord Roots	Glen Almond	15,100
Mrs. M. E. Stroyan	Boreland	14,700
Mrs. Molteno	Glen Lyon	13,000
Lt. Col. I. Hornung	Dalnaspidal	13,000
Alex. Spearman	Fealar	13,000
I. J. McKinlay	Auchleeks	12,500
W. S. H. Drummond-Moray	Abercairney	12,400
W. J. Denby Roberts	Strathallan	12,100
Marquis of Lansdowne	Meikleour	12,000
Lord Forteviot	Dupplin	11,800
A. R. Ward	Kinnaird	11,800
Wills Estates	Innerwick	11,700
Sir J. Whitaker	Auchnafree	11,700
Mr. McNaughton	Inverlochlaraig	11,500
H. S. Fothringham	Graudtully	10,700
W. G. Gordon	Lude	10,700
J. F. Priestly	Innergeldie	10,200
Sir J. Amory	Glenfernate	10,200
Mr. Curzon	Dunan	10,000
J. Cameron	Glenfinlas	9,800
Glen Devon Estates Ltd.	Glendevon	9,300
Sir W. P. K. Murray	Ochtartyre	8,900
Maj. N. C. Ramsay	Farleyer	
Mrs. Mary Constable	Glasclune	8,900
Sir M. G. Nairne	Pitcarmick	8,300
Mrs. B. M. Hatford	Moness	8,000
National Trust	Lawers	8,000
W. Taylor	Ardeonaig	7,900
Maj. D. H. Butter	Cluniemore	7,300
J. D. Miller	Remony	7,300
W. J. Christie	Loch Dochart	7,200
Lord Dundee	Kinnell	7,200
Lord Cadogan	Glen Quaich, Snaigow	6,900
—	Stronvar	6,600
D. Winton	Dalmunzie	6,200
W. J. Webber	Kynachan	5,800
The Master of Kinnaird	Rossie Priory	5,700
More Farm Prop. Ltd.	Ardtalnaig	5,700
Stewart Duff	Strelitz	5,700
Dr. Watters	Edinample	5,700
Hon. R. J. Eden	Cromlix	5,400
Mrs. Joynson	Ledard	5,300
Sir R. Orr Ewing Bt.	Cardross	5,100
Sir Stanley Norie-Millar	Murrayshall	5,000
P. Rattray of Rattray	Rattray Castle	5,000
Gleneagles Estate Trust	Gleneagles	5,000
Wild Life Trust	Coire-Bhachaidh	5,000

Ross and Cromarty: Estates of 5,000 acres upwards

Owner	Estate	Acres
Col. Wm. H. Whitbread	Letterewe etc.	73,100
A. J. MacDonald-Buchanan	Strathconon, etc.	71,100
Stornoway Trust	Stornoway Est.	64,300
Ross Estates Ltd.	Balnagowan	61,100
Sir H. P. MacKenzie	Gairloch	57,600
Galson Estates Ltd.	Galson Lodge	52,200
Uig Crofters Ltd	Uig Crofters Estates	46,300
Maj. John. Capt. And. Wills	Applecross	45,700
Eishken Lodge Ltd.	Eishken	43,900
Barvas Estates Ltd	Barvas	41,900
Mr M.H. & F.H.D.H. Wills	Torran etc.	37,400
Ian McPherson	Attadale	35,700
Benmore Estates	Benmore	35,200
A.S., A.F. & M.M. Roger	Dundonnell	32,700
Miss E.J.M. Douglas	Killilan	31,500
J. F. Robinson (Bristol)	Morsgail	31,400
Lochluichart Estates Ltd.	Kinlochuichart	28,700
A. B. L. Munro-Ferguson	Novar	28,700
Carloway Estates Ltd.	Carloway	26,600
Maj. I.M. Scobie	Rhidderoch	25,200
Lady McCorquodale	Gruinard	24,300

R. Williams	Strathvaich	23,000
A. Carlton Greg	Loch Carron	23,000
Parc Crofters Estates Ltd.	Parc Crofters	23,000
Mrs. Barker, Mrs. Kershaw	Soval	22,800
Lord Burton	Dochfour	20,000
Ex. of Visc. Mountgarret	Wyvis	19,800
Visc. Portman	Inverinate	19,400
Maj. & Mrs. Braithwaite	Ben Damph	18,800
A. M. Hickley	Glencalvie	18,800
Grimerston Estates Ltd.	Grimerston	18,800
Tim W. Sandiman	Fannich	18,700
Muriel Calder	Braemore	18,700
Dorothy A. Balcan	Aultbea	18,500
C. S. R. Stroyan	Monar	18,500
Mr. McDonald	Inverasdale	18,200
	Kildonan	17,000
Dr. S.M. Whitteridge	Inverlael	15,900
The Polly Estate Ltd.	Inverpolly	15,300
John Wills	Grudie	14,800
A. L. Sladen	Glen Carron	14,800
L. W. Robson	Inverbran	14,400
Major J. P. Harrington	Strathrusdale	14,100
Kenneth MacKenzie	Aline	13,500
P. Wilson	Loch Rosque	13,200
P. S. Henman	Benmore Coigach	12,600
Ian S. Smilie	Langwell Lodge	12,600
Sir John Brooke Bt.	Midfearn	12,600
	W. Benula	12,300
G. E. Ruggles-Birse	Ledgowan	12,200
G. & B.H.C. Van Veen	E. Rhidderoch	12,200
E. H. Vestey	Assynt	11,700
Lewis Crofters Ltd.	Lewis Crofters	11,200
The Corriemulzie Estate	Corriemulzie	10,800
Hon. P.J.W. Fairfax (London)	E. Benula	10,700
National Trust	Kinlail	10,200
Sir John Stirling	Fairburn	9,900
	Luberoy	9,800
H. & R. Combe	Scandroy	9,400
Marq. de Torrehermes	Starbran	9,100
Chairman Langstaff	Badentarbet	9,000
	Big Sands	9,000
	Corriehallie	7,200
Com. C.G. Tyner	Strathkinnaird	6,700
Ch. M. Beattie	Leckhelm	6,700
G. S. Richardson	Gladfield	6,700
	N. Chuaine	6,700
Maj. Botley, Maj. Dea	Arnacraig	6,300

Tr. of Late Lord Seaforth	Brahan	5,800
J. D. Laurie	Little Gruinard	5,700
Mrs. Dunphie	Eilea Darroch	5,500
Eagle Star	Rosehaugh	5,000

Caithness: Estates of 5,000 acres upwards

Sinclair Family Trust	Ulbster Estates	52,600
Duke of Portland	Wellbeck Estates, Langwell	48,000
M. S. M. Threipland	Waas, Dale, Toftingall	33,800
Harry & Helen Blythe	Dunbeath	27,500
Tr. of D. C. Duff Sutherland Dunbar	Hemprigs	17,700
	Glutt	16,900
Sir R. H. Anstruther	Watten (Dunn)	15,300
Sir R. & Lady I. Holmes Black	Shurrery	14,500
Lt. Col. H.B. Taylor	Sandside	12,600
Clare College, Cambridge	Mey	10,800
Former Crown Lands	Dorrery, Scots Calder	9,500
Thrumster Estates Ltd.	Thrumster	8,100
John Sinclair	Clyth Mains	7,700
Mrs. A. B. Pottinger	Greenland	5,500
J.W. & Mrs M.H. Sutherland	Granton Mains	5,500
E. & J. Darmaday	Camster	5,100

Twenty One Selected Land Ownerships

S (Sutherland); R (Ross & Cromarty); I (Inverness); A (Argyll), P (Perthshire).

		1967/68	1872/3
Wills family	R & P	193,700	Nil
Duke of Atholl	P	130,000	194,600
Duke of Sutherland	S & R	123,800	1,300,000
Duke of Westminster	I & A	120,800	Nil
British Aluminium Co Ltd	I & A	103,200	Nil
Sir D. Cameron of Lochiel	I & A	97,600	125,600
Mr. E. H. Vestey	S & R	93,100	Nil
Earl of Seafield	I	86,600	160,200
Col. L. H. Whitbread	I	80,000	Nil
Lord Lovat	R & I	80,000	162,000
Duke of Argyll	A	73,400	68,365
Ross Estates Ltd.	R	61,000	165,400
Col. Moncrieffe	S & P	60,000	Nil
Robert Fleming	A	56,000	Nil
Rt. Hon. Lady Wyfold	A	45,000	Nil
Mr. W. G. Gordon	I & P	38,400	165,600
Lord Burton	R	38,300	Nil
Noble family	A	33,800	Nil
Rootes family	S & P	23,000	Nil
Mr. Campbell Preston	A	17,900	Nil
Lord Forteviot	P	12,100	Nil

The Social Impact Of Oil

David Taylor

Up until recently the man in the street's interest in the oil industry would vary only with the price of a gallon of petrol. Now the reason for concern is much nearer home. Towns and villages in Scotland are already being changed out of recognition by the immense and uncontrollable pressure of the world's most powerful industry, the oil multi-nationals. The contrast between the monolithic powers and speed of activity of the oil multinationals operating in the so called national interest and the slow and inadequate political leverage of affected communities appears obvious—yet sparse attention has been paid and little documentation still exists of the social impact of oil on Scottish communities, of the diversity of local reactions to the incursion of oil related development and of the inadequacies of present national and local planning and consultation machinery to cope.

It is necessary first to draw attention to the sheer vastness of the modern US dominated oil industry. Medvin has written that "it is their global scale of operations coupled with less than ardent passion for revealing details, which gives the oil industry the ability to fragmentise and conceal its endeavours so that no single co-ordinated picture can be drawn of its mammoth affairs"(1) Even the industry's general title, the oil industry, is a general misrepresentation of fact. The U.S. domestic experience has proven conclusively that this is a multinational energy industry: investing in and dispensing the most appropriate energy commodity according to the most favourable market situation, with sole consideration for profits—and none for the countries of their operations.

Many of the observations documented in recent reports on the US activities in the Middle East confirm conclusions my own group has been reaching in our study of oil companies' early activity in Scotland: they also confirm the need to learn from the experience of others whose proximity to oil company actions gives them an insight that we could only gain from bitter experience.

The most damning recent evidence concerning the US oil cartels's real aims, to produce dividends as opposed to energy for the consumer, came in the months following the Arab-Israeli War. In a brilliant exposure, the New York Post published secret documents from the files of AMACO (the Arab American Oil Company) which proved that the major U.S. companies played a paramount role in encouraging the quadrupling of world oil prices. The motive was clear—make hay before the sun disappears for good. While their public relations men screamed indignation on the public's behalf, at 400 per cent price rises, hundreds of millions of dollars poured into oil company coffers. Yet while the millions continued to pour in, the companies knew that this was a massive but temporary bonanza. It would only be a matter of time before the Arabs assumed total control of Arab oil and the focus of oil company operations would have to change. New price levels made many new sources of 'energy' much more viable than before. One such viable energy source lay beneath the North Sea. As Professor Odell has written that "it is very largely the very rapid deterioration in the international oil scene that has made the North Sea activity centre number one for the large international oil companies..."(2). The new American Consul in Edinburgh summed it up when he said that "It is towards Scotland that the forces who will determine the outcome are converging. The stakes are high and the responsibility is heavy". But perhaps the most damning comment has come from John Singer, Chairman of the Rockefeller Chase Manhattan Bank, "It is important to develop North Sea oil reserves as soon as possible in order to alleviate the ominous energy shortage now facing America."(sic)

Economic Background

Much has been written which needs no repetition here of the performance of the Scottish economy over the last decade, since regional policy got off the ground in earnest. Reports, predictions and policies abound but three factors stand out: the inability to create a new economic base for sustained economic growth, the failure to create much needed jobs and to eliminate the disparities between Scottish and general UK rates of employment, and the increased level of external control over Scottish manufacturing industry.(3) The discovery of oil appeared as a panacea to all three ills. But recent evidence confirms that oil and oil related industries are unlikely to provide the long term sustained economic base for a major structural shift in economic activities, that jobs are few and far between and allocated disproportionately between areas and that British and Scottish companies are merely picking up the crumbs in terms of contracts related to oil activity. Cameron and Hunter recently argued that "the oil development will still leave the economy in need of strong assistance from a regional policy and from other sources which offer a possibility of growth." McKay has suggested from government statistics that "it would seem that direct employment might amount to 25,000-30,000 jobs at its peak, which will probably be sometime in the late nineteen-seventies... employment in services and in the construction industry is likely to be on a 1:1 ratio with primary employment, so that total employment creation might be in the range of 50,000-60,000."(4)

But it is the distribution of oil related activity and the disproportionate effects on Scottish communities which must cause the greatest concern. Generally speaking there are four types of direct activity—headquarters based activity concentrated in Aberdeen; service based activity concentrated in Aberdeen, with Dundee, Montrose and Peterhead in supporting roles; platform construction mainly in the East with signs of activity now, belatedly, in the west of Scotland; and component supply activity for exploration rigs, drilling rigs, service vessels, specialist well equipment, pipeline coating and so on. "The Scotsman's" recent conclusion on the distribution of such work showed how unplanned and unco-ordinated activity has been in terms of Scotland's social requirements. Alistair Balfour wrote: "At the end of last October 14,140 people were employed in North Sea oil projects in Scotland, an increase of more than five hundred in three months. However, the depressing truth becomes clear with a closer examination of the latter figure, revealing that just 855 of these jobs are located in West Central Scotland compared with nearly 2,500 in East Central Scotland and 5,500 in Aberdeenshire and Buchan. Apart from Aberdeen—ideally placed and equipped for a sea-based industrial revolution—the West is the area of Scotland which might have been thought to gain most from such a boom. In the early 1970's spare capacity abounded in heavy engineering, shipbuilding and manufacturing,

271

traditional industries for the Greater Glasgow area and ones suffering sadly from decline. Yet the harsh fact is that the main work of offshore oil production—the design, manufacture and installation of systems to bring oil and gas ashore—is still dominated to a large extent by US and continental interests. There is still no major British—let alone Scottish—interest in the ultra-sophisticated fields of pipeline laying and platform installation."(5)

The juggernaut has arrived: but what of the "countervailing powers of public authorities?" For the most part there is little countervailing about it. Even the feeble light of a parliamentary investigation was enough to show that, although few took much notice at the time, the first report of the Public Accounts Committee revealed the ludicrous sums for which offshore concessions had been given to the oil industry and the incredible tax loopholes they had engineered. Even the revelation that the oil industry had paid less than £5m in corporation tax since 1965 did not get much attention from the Great British press.

At no stage was clear overall responsibility for the assimilation of the oil industry allocated anywhere. Most frequently the buck has had to rest with St Andrews House and the Scottish Development Department in particular. That body had for so long adopted a begging posture in the name of new jobs, new activity, that it could hardly be regarded as a countervailing power. Nor were its early attempts at producing planning documents a notable success. One of the supposedly most important was called "North Sea oil and gas—interim coastal planning framework." It had strong claim to being one of the most inadequate planning documents ever to emerge from a government department.

The hapless showing until recently of the Scottish Office however, reflects not just its lack of skills or critical faculty. It reflects also the ludicrous nature of the Scottish Office's position in the whole game. This was to be revealed dramatically when, as over Drumbuie, St Andrews' House was supposed to be 'holding the ring' whilst its big brother paymasters, the London superministries were parties to the dispute on the same side as the oil companies.

For most of the last four years, then, inadequate 'central planning bodies' have been overwhelmed if not outright compromised, but in addition, the onslaught has come in the middle of the reorganisation of local government in Scotland, thus adding to the incoherence of public authority response. It has taken a determined local authority even to try to hold the line, as we shall see in the case of Shetland.

Now the record is available to anyone who cares to read it—a good many studies have been done and a brief reference to some of them seems timely. The Church of Scotland has had the services until recently of John Francis and Norman Swan. They produced the general survey of the social and environmental impact of oil and gas on Scottish Communities, "Scotland in Turmoil" and followed it up in January 1974 with a detailed report on one area in the north east: Peterhead and district.(6) The Cromarty Firth too has had its chroniclers. These include the Easter Ross case study, "The Objectives of Highland Development"(7) and George Rosie's perhaps better known "Cromarty—The Scramble for Oil".(8) The Shetland saga has also been traced. These areas tended to feel the impact of oil earliest—they may act as beacons for the others. In Wester Ross the classic "struggle for a site", discussed below, was well documented at the time by Neil Ascheron in "The Observer" (March 1974) and by the West Highland Free Press. The turn of the Clyde has yet to come; but it is clearly not far off. On January 11th, 1975, the Scottish Daily Express blazoned uncritically, "Oil Boom on Clyde", and the troika, Campbeltown—Portavadie—Hunterston was on its way. The "Architect's Journal" of 26 June, 1974, was devoted to the oil impact in most of the affected areas of Scotland.

Academic research at the time of writing is only just beginning, Professor C.F. Carter of Aberdeen University recently pointed to both the lack of, and the urgency for detailed investigation. Aberdeen has just launched a centre for the study of sparsely populated regions one of whose researchers, James Hunter, has worked on the development of the crofting community; the SSRC and the HIDB have now also funded research projects on the social impact of oil. We await the forthcoming study "The Political Economy of North Sea Oil" by Professor Donald McKay and Tony McKay of Aberdeen University, to be published in the spring.

In the following pages, I propose to devote some attention to the labour problems associated with oil; and to a discussion of the impact of oil on certain communities, in an effort to show the weak and unco-ordinated response of government, local authorities and communities in face of the monolithic pressure of the energy cartel.

Pressure on Existing Communities

North East Corner

As the Boom got underway those onshore were also feeling the first of the pressures, the North East being the first to experience the jarring gear changes. To suggest that all the effects were adverse would be unfair: emigration of population from Aberdeen almost ceased completely. But it can be argued that without oil, the local economy of the North East would have grown at a high rate. McKay suggests that since 1968 there was a reduction in the rate of decline of agricultural employment, increased fishing prosperity, increased employment in food processing, and a rapid growth in jobs in the service sector. However, when all the excitement about the granite city becoming the new 'Texas of Europe' had subsided, few people can actually have found themselves much better off. The value of property had trebled, fine for those with property but not much consolation for the young married couple with no roof over their heads. The cases of interest are too numerous and complex to detail. I would like to illustrate effects with one or two examples. One such case concerns the fate of Torry Village, one of the original settlements from which Aberdeen grew and designated by the Corporation for conservation. Shell Exploration (U.K.) Ltd, however, had other ideas: their harbour development plans required the total demolition of the village. The proceedings of the public enquiry which followed produced the following 'newspaper headline': "Provide land for base or we move on, oil firm tell inquiry." This approach bordering on complete blackmail had the desired, if somewhat inevitable, effect. Within a short space of months, the village was cleared of its 350 population, including many old people, and bulldozed. Aberdeen has not been the only community in the north-east to experience the "capitulate-or-we-move-on" tactic. Indeed, for an industry which is so fond of claiming that its every demand on space must be met because the constraints on suitability are so exacting, it is curious how often this ploy is invoked. Peterhead experienced the pressure also. Its harbour of Refuge had hardly got used to the good fortune of attracting the Aberdeen seine-net fleet than it found a bigger cuckoo wanting room in the nest. Deep water and short steaming distance to the best fields made it an obvious target. And once again, the timetable was hectic once things began. Francis and Swan have chronicled the saga. The sequence, they comment judiciously, "illustrated the rapid flow of decision-taking events and the mild concessions to public participation in the planning processes." In the spring of 1972, it was clear "that development of any kind of the Bay... was prohibited under the terms of the 1886 Peterhead Harbour of Refuge Act... May 1972... the Secretary of State introduced an amending Bill into Parliament enabling him to undertake developments... July 1972... The final committee stage of the Bill in the Commons was completed... August 1972... The Harbour Development (Scotland) Act received the Royal Assent."(9)

The North East may well achieve more stable employment from oil than other areas although the bulk of exploration and drilling activity is likely to move further northwards in the next few years. Francis and Swan suggest that while the oil industry is gregarious, the main loci have already established themselves in the north-east and that growth is likely to take place around these centres. But if the north-east is more fortunate in this respect, the colossal social problems remain as daunting. Francis and Swan conclude that "after a long hard look at the gathering storm in and around Peterhead there is a consuming sense of desperation about the sheer inertia surrounding critical events... it is when the prospects for community developments are considered in this light that there is an ominous silence: the application of our newly qcquired planning skills for the creation of an attractive social environment begins to sound ridiculous in places where the sudden influx of industry has taken everyone by surprise... nobody really appears to reflect any confidence in being able to get the machinery to work effectively." Events in Peterhead, they say, "serve to illustrate the mismatch between scale and timing of industrial investment and the corresponding factors in community development... while the central planning machinery is limbering up for a marathon, the explosive events on field and track are already indicating that this contest is null and void. Without some properly managed team effort, it will become increasingly difficult to bring his community together on important matters concerning its future."(10)

Cromarty

Cromarty, Caithness, Shetland, the West Coast and Argyll have been subject in turn to similar pressures often from a much greater scale of development where the issues are more complex and more difficult to understand. In his study of Cromarty Rosie remarks that "of all the rural areas of Scotland the deep water anchorage of the Cromarty Firth has been the most sought after, the most hotly disputed and perhaps the most deeply transformed"... in the space of a few years an economy which had coasted along very modestly on a mixture of farming, the aluminium smelter, some light industry and small scale navy servicing has been transformed. Hotels in Dingwall, Invergordon, Tain, Balintore, and Evanton were suddenly frequented by some of the sharpest business heads in Europe, competing with each other for the best sites, the best conditions and the best options around."(11)

If there is one enterprise which can be said to have transformed the Cromarty Firth, it is the platform construction on the Nigg point. Nigg was to be Scotland's new twentieth century "Europort". Today no long term industry independent of oil has established itself. Within two weeks, late in 1971, two applications were made to construct platforms in Scotland—one in Cromarty Firth and one in Fife, both receiving planning permission. In a statement made previous to securing permission to build oil platforms in Easter Ross, Brown and Root, the US combine concerned, urged a quick negotiation "to avoid the necessity of considering alternative sites on the other side of the North Sea". The platforms themselves over 600 feet high, to be installed over oil wellheads, must be built on land and it is the introduction of this industry to north Scotland which has been one of the most controversial of recent times. Three years later, in 1974, one year behind schedule, Brown and Root's first platform in Cromarty was launched, heralded in a special Highland News Group supplement as "The most gigantic achievement ever known in the Highlands. The story is fantastic. Here is that story. Read it with pride." As well as heralding a new all-time low in press coverage of oil related matters, the supplement found no room in its 16 pages of advertising and inane journalistic flag waving to mention that 800 men had just been paid off.

They were right about one point, the story is 'fantastic'. Brown Root paid off almost double the amount of permanent jobs they had promised to bring to the area. In October 1971 they stated they would create 400-600 jobs for local men for a period of fifty years. Few questions were asked and since they had good friends in people like local councillor John Robertson and Scottish Secretary of State, Gordon Campbell, it was not long before the bulldozers were preparing the Nigg site. Such was the rush that almost no conditions were attached to the development. Within two years the workforce had soared to just short of 3,000, totally overwhelming attempts to deal with the population increase, consequently most men had to live in filthy conditions on **two** battered old Greek cruise liners. Another US controlled development, a pipe coasting yard run by MK Shand followed a similar employment pattern. They promised 200 jobs, took on 600, completed the contract well ahead of schedule and payed off most of their workforce. A training school opened at Nigg to teach the 'locals' to be welders in the short space of six weeks, but this venture ended in predictable failure.

The unstable atmosphere of the 'Boom' prevails with hundreds of single men living and working in dangerous and dirty conditions. Yet none of this was to stand in the way of the ultimate industrial accolade 'The Royal Visit'. Another press bonus eagerly lapped up. This time with a Press and Journal supplement "Queen meets the oilmen", four pages of Liz and the family decked out in safety helmets and safety glasses. Perhaps if the management were as careful with their own workforce the yard might not have such a disgusting reputation for working conditions.

Meanwhile, work on two other platform yards for which planning permission has been granted could go ahead any day, and the construction of a refinery next to Brown and Root's yard looks inevitable. Brown and Root themselves plan to double the size of their yard. Yes folks, its Klondyke in Cromarty and the UK taxpayer is doing his bit to assist these kindhearted US businessmen with development area grants worth **over £5 million.** Most of that, however, will go to the 'real Texas' back home, where the cover of Brown and Root (i.e. the Halliburton Group) annual shareholders' report announces "another record year for a billion dollar company serving the energy industries world-wide." Hardly surprising that the editor of the American oil magazine 'Drilling' wrote at the time, "We think the oil industry is going to be a good citizen of Scotland. We think the people of Scotland are the oil field's kind of people... the kind of people you can talk to, the kind who can get a handle on your problem. We believe that, in the oil industry, Scotland has a friendly and responsible guest." But it does not have to be like this. Rosie concludes his study of Cromarty by saying that "there is no way of preventing the oil industry moving into Easter Ross. The oil must be exploited and the people of the area need the prosperity it will bring. But it is in everyone's interest that what has to be done should be done properly. It is important that the men who work at the yards should have decent working conditions, reasonable wages, and decent places to live in. There must be enough schools, hospitals, clinics, doctors, policemen and facilities for entertainment and recreation—everything needed by a community to thrive. It is important that the minimum of valuable farmland is swallowed up, that areas hospitable to wildlife are maintained and disturbed as little as possible... if the problems of the Cromarty Firth are not resolved satisfactorily, it is Scotland as a whole which will suffer."(11) But the more pessimistic conclusions reached by the Easter Ross Study Group in 1973 are based on hard realism:

"For Easter Ross the immediate prospect is bleak. The County Council is struggling to make good the inadequacies of the present infra structure for the benefit of development which may well prove to be of far from permanent duration... an examination of the problems from the experience of Easter Ross in the Highland Board's growth centre policy and from the first phase of oil development may forewarn and forearm the Highlands and Islands for the potential disaster of the second." (12).

While Cromarty is more conducive to economic development, doubts remain about the wisdom of large scale development in Wester Ross. Yet probably the most controversial and publicised aspect of oil development resolved around the proposed construction of 'all concrete' production platforms at Drumbuie in Wester Ross—a vital test case in the industrialisation of the rural Western Highlands. Two firms, Taylor Woodrow and Mowlem, had applied separately to build on the site in question at Port Cam, Drumbuie, one of the deepest inlets in the west coast, comparable to the depth of water to be found east of Shetland where massive oil fields were being found. The Norwegians had devised an all-concrete design suitable to their fjord terrain, Mowlems had secured the U.K. licence rights, but were encountering considerably more trouble in locating a Scottish fjord. The developers case rested on two major points. The first, to be expected, was the well-worn national interest. The second, that "if the U.K. is to produce these platforms it can only be done at Loch Carron." The enquiry which followed was at best a charade, at worst a network of lies and deceit with no holds barred.

On the opening day the competing developers announced, that they would contest the case together and develop the site together. In the days which followed a number of interesting points came to light. First, Mowlems admitted that they had experienced considerable 'pressure and encouragement' from the D.T.I. to develop the Norwegian design from no less a person than Peter Walker, the Tory minister. Both D.T.I. civil servants and HIDB, so-called impartial bodies, gave evidence on behalf of the developers. Under cross examination the government spokesman was rather embarrassed to admit that his his evidence was founded on figures supplied by Mowlem. As the enquiry progressed pressure mounted for the enquiry to give way to a broader commission investigating the whole question of industrialisation and the west coast. When a second developer arrived at Loch Kishorn only six miles away this seemed the only option, but still no reaction from the Administration.

However, the Friday before the objectors were due to open their case the Tory Government upstaged the whole proceedings by announcing their infamous land grab Bill. Secretary for State, Gordon Campbell, made up for months of silence and inaction with one short comment. "I am certain it is necessary to have one site in Loch Carron if we are to have oil as quickly as possible, whether the people like it or not." The enquiry was allowed to continue but it was external events which really made a farce of the whole proceedings. Shell/Esso had negotiated a £25m. Christmas present with Sir Robert McAlpine in the form of orders for 'all concrete' platforms to be built in their Argyle yard and installed east of Shetland, making nonsense of the 'only site in the U.K.' claim. And as far as the 'national interest' was concerned these were at the times of the enquiry no less than five sites with planning consent where work had not started. At one of these, Dunnet Bay in Caithness, a U.S. construction combine had come, pleaded U.K. national interest , been given swift approval and thereafter the site stood empty for six months before they left for a site in Ireland (probably in the Irish national interest.).

However, and probably most important, one of these firms who had planning approval for a site was none other than Taylor "the only site in the UK" Woodrow in the Cromarty Firth whose plans to develop an all concrete platform (Duplex) Yard are now well advanced. The final proof if any was needed of the deceit came in November 1974 when the same combine of 'Woodrow and Mowlem' applied to build the same platform, 'Con-deep' in a completely different site at Campbeltown. No doubt the cash will soon be pouring into help them maintain their position as top contributor to Aims of Industry. But the most revealing evidence came in the confidential minute of a meeting between the National Trust for Scotland and Taylor Woodrow on the 14th of March 1972. Asked whether major concrete construction operations could not be done on the Clyde, Taylor Woodrow replied that "they would prefer not to work near to the major constructions because of possible labour disputes which could not be tolerated in their tight schedule."(13) This ability to escape the obvious area for major constructions—the Clyde—is shown by the few jobs projected for that area.

With the conclusion of the enquiry, the Secretary of State has stepped in to complete the final act of the farce. First, "The developers will not be allowed to ravage Drumbuie." Second, they can do what they like at Loch Kishorn only six miles away.

As a member of the South West Ross Action Group, Ray Burnett has chronicled the diversities in local organisation in fighting the Drumbuie case—and his remarks as to what happened in Drumbuie serve as a warning to those who will be active elsewhere. He echoes much of what George Rosie has written of public opinion in Cromarty

> "Faced with the collusion of Government and business, local tenants grew closer together. For the action group (fighting development) desperate to be the true voice of local feeling this was disastrous. The National Trust for Scotland, the county council, the outraged letter writers to the national press are not indeed noted for their working class composition. This point was not lost on the working inhabitants of the area especially when the action group joined with the NTS etc., in the collective voice of an influential minority whose most salient features were their external relationships to the area, their detachment from the process of having to live and work in it and above all their overwhelmingly middle class background." It was a rehearsal of the classic pattern which seems to be repeated wherever development is proposed... there is a pronounced variation in local feeling... they may still want the few schemes that might come their way; they may hope it never happens; but whatever stance they adopt the oil plans for Loch Carron have already been a profound and instructive example of the extent to which any of us who actually lives here will; have any real say in his own future."(14)

Shetland

One such area which was already feeling the increasing pressures of oil development was the Shetland Islands; an area which had little in common with Scotland other than a history of recurring 'boom and bust' economies and continuing maladministration from central government.(15) Despite this, Shetland was one of the only areas in the Highlands and Islands region to successfully combat insidious decline and migration of population. The post-1945 economy had been built on a diversified base. Confidence was high and early in 1972 a local author claimed "unprecedented expansion in the basic industries of fishing, agriculture and knitting are taking Shetland to an all-time peak of prosperity." In July of that year while drilling a trial hole in Block 211/29, 125 miles north east of Shetland, Shell/Esso struck oil and all hell was let loose.

There had already been some early activity in the form of oil rig servicing but this strike confirmed Shetland as a major oil development area in the eyes of the industry. At this stage the Council, with no Planning Department or no development plan, found itself ill-equipped to deal with the pressures. However, a development plan was hurriedly drawn up and further studies commissioned from consultants, engineers and planners, who put a respectable face on what I believe was the basic mistake. That is, from July 1972 until now, almost every aspect of this

276

massive development programme has been accepted as inevitable (all be it with slight physical amendments).

Some indication of this 'inevitable' tone may be had from part of the public relations hand-out from Livsay and Hendersons' conclusions on possible oil development which stated, "Until the position becomes clearer, a site must be planned for gas liquification plant." This seems to be a direct contradiction of even basic commonsense, let alone advanced planning theory, a contradiction which can only aid the speculator. If the scale of development has seemed inevitable from the start then the location of this development has been equally inevitable. It seems that most parties officially involved agree that Sullom Voe is the most expendable in scenic terms and also technically viable. This area was not only central to the Council's development plan but also to the first development storm which created deep divisions in the community. A substantial area of land was designated for oil development here and called The Nordport triangle. It was in the week following the publication of the Council's intentions that the first oil development bombshell was to rock the Islands. It was revealed that a private development company not only had the audacity to adopt the Council's name of Nordport Limited but more important it had already secured 5,000 acres at Sullom and had options on not less than 40,000 acres of land, a massive area in a restricted group of islands. Within weeks the company announced their intentions thinly disguised in the form of a planning strategy. They proposed a massive port complex to include almost every oil-related activity imaginable, a complex which, if realised, would have been one of the largest new industrial developments ever proposed in Western Europe. It was very obvious that Nordport saw itself very much in the Europort league. A massive public relations exercise provoked little sympathy within the County Council, but the fact was that this group controlled the land and any potential developer would first need to approach them.

The pressure for development continued to increase and in April 1972, the Milford Argosy Corporation of Oklahoma City filed an application to build an oil refinery. To facilitate this one development, the total population of the island might need to increase by one-third since a refinery could require a construction force of at least 5,000 men. The speed of events at this early stage was staggering, and in August, Zetland Council appointed their first ever County Planning Officer. Within the same week Nordport published their second major planning study for the Baltasound area—a blatant example of the lag between commercial intentions and public control. All this came on the night of the Council's first public discussion on the future of Sullom Voe. On that same night, Shell announced their own intentions for a £20 million crude oil terminal, the synchronisation making something of a mockery of the Council's genuine attempts to inform and involve local people in the future.

In this atmosphere of overwhelming commercial pressure, intensified by the abdication of responsibility by the then Conservative administration, the local authority deserves much credit for its reaction. When County Councils could, and indeed in other oil development areas had, opted out of the responsibility and started to hand out planning permissions, they bravely attempted to take control. In November, 1972, the Council announced its intention of promoting legislation in Parliament with a view to retaining ultimate control over all oil developments. This legislation was to become 'The Shetland Bill.' The most controversial proposal was the question of company purchase powers. This was to cause a storm of protest not only from speculators who already had a finger in the pie, but also, and more important, from those living on the land. It was in this atmosphere of fear and mistrust in May, 1973, that the Council was thrown out at the polls. The new Council soon found its private bill firmly enmeshed in the democratic process and was still in receipt of absolutely no central government support. It was forced to take two immediate steps, the first to set up an 'oil liaison committee' in partnership with the four major oil companies. As a communication link this made good sense, however, this committee was to become a combined development partnership. Despite the County convener's statement that, "the industry has found we are responsible people, if uncompromising in our demand for ultimate control of our own destiny"—it will be more than surprising if four major multinational oil companies will be prepared to give a small County Council ultimate control of major development decisions. The second, and much more worrying, step was taken after an 'approach' to the Council by Rothschilds, the international bankers who offered 'to back and advise' the Council. The offer was accepted and in this way the Council had little option but to allow the commercial sector to take up the role the government had abdicated. They should, however, be well aware of the

277

dangers.

On the 3rd of September, 1974, almost every UK paper carried headlines concerning a joint seventeen company joint pipeline venture for Sullom Voe in Shetland with Shell and Esso retaining 34 per cent each. The Express headlined it as a great deal for "a surging Scotland" but failed to add where we were surging to. The "Medvin" report on US oil companies identified one of the major anti-competitive practises as the "joint venture, particularly in pipelines. "Shetland County Council as partners in the deal were dealing on one hand with Rockefeller, controlled Chase Manhattan Bank and relying, on their backers, Rothschild, for financial advice—yet they still insist they retain control of the situation. But the Labour government's 'Off-shore Petroleum Bill' has completely upstaged the steps which Zetland Council have taken, scant thanks for three years of hard work and hard bargaining. When the chips are really down big business or government does not hesitate to bring out the big stick. So who is in control now? It seems that no matter who wants to develop, somebody has a legal mandate to force it through, yet if one dares to allege "steamroller' tactics there are screams of indignation from all sides.

To take the question of refineries, for instance, it would be disastrous if Milford Argosy, Shell, or any other company were allowed to proceed with refinery proposals in Shetland. Required refining capacity is a finite figure which must be calculated in a national (U.K.) context. Only if it can be substantiated that an increased capacity is required should new or extended refineries be constructed, and only then should a decision on location be made, again within a national context. The fact that currently nine new oil refineries are proposed in Scotland alone may give some indication of the need for much stricter government control of the industry. Particularly in relation to two of these proposals (Milford Argosy in Shetland and National Bulk Carriers in Cromarty) where there can be little doubt that they are manifestations of the U.S. need for an increased refining capacity and have little to do with North Sea Oil

Yet, even at this early stage the advance pressures of the oil industry are causing disproportionate social upheavals. The most important single element of Shetland's economy is its intermediate scale industries which give that economy its diversified base. Ironically these industries are to become victims of the very factor that makes them so different from the standard industrial production line treadmill. They are industries where the individual still matters, where nearly every person employed is a key worker. The loss of just a few of these workers can bring such an industry to its knees in a very short time. Coupled with this is the almost inevitable accommodation crisis, rapid deterioration in road networks, and almost complete breakdown in delivery runs of essential commodities such as coal and milk. A local columnist wrote "I find it galling to be constantly confronted with schemes reckoned in millions while the few thousands we need for our own projects still elude us", indeed, it is always those who can least afford it who must pay the price of progress.

In a very short period of time the predicted 'peak of prosperity' has materialised into ominous question marks for the people of Shetland and their way of life. I have listed a few of the bigger factors yet it is now, in 1975, that the real impact of large scale development will be felt when construction of the Sullom Voe complex gets underway. Yet, even the compensation for this impact has been called into doubt. Iain Clark, the Chief Executive of Zetland Council speaking at the Financial Times North Sea Oil Conference in December, 1974, said, "While it is true that my Council will be recompensed in millions of pounds we must also reckon our problems in terms of millions of pounds." This confirms that Shetland fits the oil development picture perfectly, slightly behind Easter Ross yet more advanced than the West coast development areas, where local people or the imported work force of thousands will continue to be losers.

Pressures on the New Industrial Work-force

The North Sea is acknowledged to be one of the worlds wildest and most dangerous seas, hence drilling for oil in depths of water up to 600 ft in all weathers is a very hazardous process. Yet the financial risks seem to be of much more interest to the media than the daily risk to human life. The toll in life and limb has already been intolerably high yet only a few months ago two significant events achieved almost no national press coverage. In October 1974 a rig collapsed in the Gulf of Suez killing eighteen men. Both the oil company Amoco and the rig operator Offshore

278

Incorporated of Houston are currently operating in the North Sea. In the UK drilling sector a less dramatic, if more insidious record of one diving death a month was achieved. Neither event seemed to merit the attention of the Great British press despite their obvious relevance to the issue, but then too much talk about the victims of the boom might call into question certain aspects of the boom, particularly the hysterical speed of operations (which might not suit the Scottish press Barons and their oil interests). It is now estimated that 800 men will lose their lives as a result of offshore activities.(16)

The scale of the operations is considerable. Even modest government oil reserve estimates would necessitate a build up to 200 offshore installations, 100 fixed platforms and 100 rigs, at peak production. Controlling this potential workforce of thousands there are twelve drilling contractors plus Shell and BP who operate their own rigs. The conditions under which these men work are probably among the most hazardous of almost any job anywhere, yet attempts to unionise the rigs have been met by almost continued hostility from the predominantly American contractors.

The plight of these men is best illustrated by taking the case of a Rigger working for one of the independent contractors in the East Shetland Basin during late October. A high tension hawser snapped and the recoil killed the rigger instantly. The contractor's liability to the man and his family also terminated at that instant. The following extracts are taken from a standard contract form:

> "In the event of the Employee being unable to perform the duties of his job classification because of sickness or accident his employment shall terminate. No payment will be made by the Company to employees absent through sickness. Employees absent through injuries sustained in the course of duty will be eligible to make claim for compensation through the Ministry of Social security. Any additional insurance left to the Employee **not** Employer."

All this for a basic weekly rate of £27, the big cash is made during the exhausting hours of overtime in excess of the standard 84 hour week. And for his troubles he will be lucky to qualify for more than 24 hour notice of contract termination. No workforce in British labour history ever needed the protection of trade unionism more than the offshore oil industry.

The problems of mounting pressure for unionisation are immense, the nature of the work attracts an itinerant work force, the atrocious conditions force a massive labour turnover, and open union membership also leads to instant dismissal. In an attempt to combat this situation the seven unions involved formed the 'inter-union off-shore oil committee' aimed at recruiting over 2,000 members, but with anything up to 300 miles of sea between the Aberdeen based committee and the factory gate the task was a formidable one.

The situation has been remarkably similar on shore—at Nigg Bay for example. In August 1972 the 'White Book', officially called the 'Workers Handbook of Terms and Employment' was signed by representatives of the AEUW and the Boilermakers. The White Book's basic agreement was nothing new—high productivity at any cost, iron discipline and low pay rates. Shop stewards are still having to battle, two years later, to win 100 per cent union membership. Not only this. The 'Observer' of January 25th, 1975 records that "shop stewards representing 4,500 workers threatened a strike in protest against the failure of their employers and the government to secure more North Sea Orders for them". Orders are in fact flowing abroad. At the Redpath-Dorman Long Methil yard there is no other major work on hand. There is also a bleak outlook at Burntisland and Dumbarton. At Leith, Bredcro Price, which set up a pipe coating yard in 1972, 250 workers were paid off at the end of January this year while at Motherwell Bridge, a six week strike for parity by rig modules' workers led to the cutting of the workforce from 180 to 70. The one day strike which ensued, organised by the Oil Rigs Liaison Committee, showed how weak the bargaining position of the union is. It has been said that "the committee sees its role, not as a focus for independent activity of the construction workers in rig construction but as a "ginger group" to put pressure on the unions (17). There is an urgent need for full unionisation, for co-ordination of activities to avoid inter-union disputes such as the recent one at Ardyne, and as contracts move abroad, an increasing urgency for co-ordination with European workers.

279

Conclusions

But what is to be a co-ordinated response to oil development, sensitive at one and the same time to community life and to economic and social needs. As this survey has pointed out, we have had so far half-hearted governmental guidance whether by design (in the hope that minimal government involvement would speed oil development) or through sheer inexperience. The result is one of inefficient extremes. At one end a national administration remote from the realities of the situation is unable to respond to the needs and fears of those intimately affected. At the other the small local authority on its own turn remote from the context of national priorities is ill equipped to deal with the massive changes thrust upon it. And at a community level there is uncertainty and cynicism—the anti-development lobby embracing a variety of (mainly middle class) conservationists, as in the Cromarty and Drumbuie cases, and the pro development lobby attracting the most avaricious of local entrepreneurs and councillors. Concluding their Easter Ross case study, Andrew Currie and associates stress rightly the need for community participation in decisionmaking—and they argue how this might be achieved within a Highland Regional Authority.

> "The centralisation of the planning function at a regional level in the Highland region poses a threat which can only be overcome by the Regional Authority making a conscious and sustained effort to pursue a community centred development strategy... it will be critical to maintain predominance of social and community goals over the economic means of their attainment... it will be essential to be thoroughly discriminating between potential industrial developers. Realistic population targets and rates of growth should be set and adhered to. Developments should be actively sought which are of an appropriate scale to the area in which they are to be sited. Developments offering secure employment and a balanced variety of jobs suited to local needs should receive preference... If economic growth is to aid the regeneration of the Highlands, it is essential that the methods of public consultation are developed to a fine art... Community growth requires community involvement.(18)."

Francis and Swan reach rather different conclusions in their study of Peterhead. After outlining four options which may be considered as viable for planning the future of Peterhead—open ended development aimed at full economic exploitation, a stabilisation on the basis of presently agreed development, a build-up only of indigenous industries and a moratorium on all developments—they argue that there is a case for bringing in specialist project groups to form a single planning centre at a community level on the lines of new town development authorities. Their aim would be "to initiate and supervise crash programmes on housing, education, medical and social services, in conjunction with the local planning authorities." In particular "the overall object of a project group in a particular area would be to prevent any slippage on construction programmes already under way, to assist in land acquisition and with tender assessments for community housing, social amenities etc...".(19)

But a planned and co-ordinated approach is clearly required also at a national level. Rosie's suggestion that while oil development is inevitable, the material problems could be solved by the harnessing of adequate resources to planning and good will is not enough. There is no lack of official committees on oil related subjects but they have little power and are confusingly responsible to two government ministries, the Department of Energy and the Scottish Office. A plethora of over lapping committees has led to many conflicts between local and national interests with neither government or local authority being served properly. What is needed is an intermediate administration to replace rather than supplement the current inefficient network. This must be part of an overall strategy which has as yet not been forthcoming for a National Hydrocarbons Authority and a concerted energy policy, with short term, medium term and long term strategies. Were the North Sea considered in this context then guidelines for a production rate of oil related to needs would emerge. Briefly, I suggest that the Government forms a strategic oil related development authority. This authority should be responsible to the Scottish Office supervised at ministerial level, administering all oil-related activities, thus clarifying the situation in particular for local authority and local action groups. This authority should be a strategic oil planning authority and an oil related development authority. The planning authority limb, immediately and in consultation with concerned bodies, should instigate the preparation of a Scottish structure plan as part of an integrated approach to oil related development. (20)

1. N. Medvin, **The Energy Cartel** (1974).
2. P. Odell, in SCDI, **Investing in Scotland's Future** (1974) p.28.
3. See articles in this collection by Niven, Firn and Stephen.
4. D. MacKay, **North Sea Oil and the Scottish Economy,** North Sea Study Occasional Paper No.1 (1975) p.10.
5. **Scotsman,** Oil Supplement, January 1975, p.2.
6. Francis and Swan, **Scotland's Pipedream,** Church of Scotland (1974).
7. A. Currie & Associates, **The Objectives of Highland Development** (1973).
8. G. Rosie, **Cromarty: The Scramble for Oil,** Canongate Press, Edin. (1974).
9. Francis and Swan, **op.cit.**
10. **ibid.,** p.78.
11. Rosie, **op.cit.**
12. Currie, **op.cit.,** p.24-25.
13. **West Highland Free Press,** July 14th, 1972.
14. **Architects' Journal,** June 29th, 1974 pp.1459-60.
15. A fuller study in **A.J.** pp.1446-1449.
16. **Scotsman,** 20th January, 1975.
17. Red Weekly, 24th January, 6th February, 1975.
18. Currie, **op.cit.,** p.27.
19. Francis and Swan, **op.cit.,** p.76-77.
20. The Offshore Petroleum Development (Scotland) Bill illustrates well the strong arm tactics of government. Its inspiration sprang from the D.T.I. and Drumbuie. The only point at which meaningful opposition can occur is over the initial granting of planning permission. In its latest shape (Feb. 1975) the Bill specifies that an acquisition, if approved by both Houses, would cut out the right of an individual for an ultimate appeal to a committee of the House. The Bill has not yet become law and it is impossible to comment further, while it is being amended.

The Rise Of Scottish Socialism

James Young

The rise of Scottish socialism in the early 1880s coincided with the emergence of similar movements throughout the world. The socialist parties engendered by capitalist society in the late nineteenth century came together to form the Second International: an International whose formation was influenced, if not dictated, by the solidarity of international capital.

In a Scotland that provides a historical illustration of Antonio Gramsci's conception of 'a hegemonic society', a minority of workers and intellectuals played an outstanding part in creating the traditions of modern socialism. It is important to stress that the socialists in Scotland were a small minority, and that they had to face day-to-day inertia, or at best indifference, from the majority of working people. Moreover, a critical analysis of the cultural attitudes and social values of the 'masses' was not provided in Tom Johnston's classic study, **A History of the Working Classes in Scotland**; and the persistence of the myth that 'Scotland has always been a radical country' - a myth reinforced by the superb 7:84 company - has simultaneously contributed to the decline of labourism and the rise of Scottish nationalism.

I

In the opinion of G.D.H. Cole the intervention of the Scottish Land Restoration League in the general election of 1885, together with John Burns's contest at Nottingham, represented 'the pioneer battles for independent labour representation'. Certainly something significant had happened in Scottish politics, and Dr Fred Reid has argued that in the late 1880s 'the discontent of the working class provided the main basis for divergence between Scottish and English politics'. As H.M. Hyndman put it:

Scotland was the country in which the independent labour movement began... it seemed probable that Scotland, by far the best educated portion of the United Kingdom, would come to the front and take the lead in the political arena on behalf of the disinherited class. That I know was the hope and ambiton then, not only of Graham and Hardie and Burgess, but of many who have since fallen into the muddy ways of capitalist Liberalism.

In practice the break with Liberalism in 1885 was not so complete, either organisationally or ideologically, as has often been imagined.

There was in the English labour movement from the 1860s onwards a conflict 'within individuals as well as within movements' between 'the desire to be assimilated and the urge to independence' from Liberalism. So Royden Harrison. In Scotland, too, there were very few individuals who were untouched by inconsistent and 'contradictory' attitudes towards Liberalism. In 1885 J. Shaw Maxwell, at the same time as he was fighting as a Land and Labour candidate in Glasgow, told the Linlithgow Liberal Association that 'the present century would be remembered because of the great legislative achievements of the Liberal Parliament'. During the course of a long address on the programme of advanced Liberalism in which he ignored any reference to socialism or even land nationalisation, he emphasised the need for land reform. Then in 1895, when he was fighting in the same Glasgow constituency as an I.L.P. candidate, he said he had been fighting the cause of 'aggressive democracy' since 1885. By then he was arguing that 'both parties were capitalist', and that the fight was now between 'those who had property and those who had none'. Yet by the turn of the century, he would again evoke the example of Bright's aggressive democracy.

Moreover, such apparently contradictory attitudes towards Liberalism were not confined to 'soft' socialists of the I.L.P. variety. In March, 1885, William Small, a man who was to remain a Social Democrat until his death, formed a branch of the Social Democratic Federation in Cambuslang; then a few months later Small, Shaw, Maxwell and other working class leaders joined the new Glasgow Radical Association which had been organised by Dr Charles Cameron and the advanced Liberals. Chisholm Robertson, the miners' leader also displayed 'contradictory' attitudes and ambiguities in his relationships with middle class Liberals. During his election campaign in Stirlingshire in 1892, where he was standing as a Labour candidate, he made a blistering attack on A.J. Mundella. Yet he had just previously told a working class audience that: 'Mr Gladstone's whole sympathies were with the workers, but he was hampered and crippled by his colleagues, who were less in sympathy with the aspirations of the workers.' Then in 1900, by which time the Scots were to the 'left' of the English and when John Weir was standing in West Fife as a Labour condidate, Dr Bell, a leading figure in the I.L.P. in Glasgow, told a meeting of Fife miners that, by sending Weir to Parliament, they could 'foreshadow the better times prophesied by John Bright.' Clearly, there were many socialists and Lib-Lab leaders who did not regard political independence from the Liberal Party as being incompatible with adherence to some Liberal values and traditions; and in 1892, when Chisholm Robertson was fighting as a Parliamentary candidate, he told one audience that he had been asked 'by his fellow working men to go to London to work for them, to raise them in the social scale'. Trade union agitation and the fight for Parliamentary representation dovetailed, and both forms of agitation were seen as aspects of self-help. And such conceptions of self-help were compatible with Liberal values and ideology, at least theoretically.

In the 1880s the English leaders of the S.D.F. saw Gladstonian Liberalism as the main obstacle to an independent workers' movement and 'the leaders of trade unionism' as 'the main working class allies of Gladstone'. By 1900 the English leaders of the S.D.F. were less intransigent towards the advanced Liberals, or Radicals as they were sometimes called, and H.M. Hyndman wrote a letter to the **Ethical World** announcing his opposition to the decision of the S.D.F. to 'support certain Radical candidates'. In Scotland, where Liberalism was to remain a formidable force after 1900, the socialists were a bit firmer in their opposition to the Liberal Party. J.A. Tait, the secretary of the Socialist League, wrote to the secretary of the League in London after the general election of 1885:

The mob here as elsewhere are, of course, no use at least at the present stage and in Edinburgh the class we want to get hold of just now seem from the results of the recent Parliamentary elections to be far back indeed and hopelessly out of reach. Edinburgh is still the home of Whiggery and orthodoxy: Socialism is not yet respectable enough for it I fear.

The same inconsistent attitudes to Liberalism prevailed as in England; but the Scottish socialists were confronted with a much more powerful and socially insensitive Liberal Party.

In 1895 Keir Hardie told the Scottish District Council of the I.L.P. that they ought to use their votes to 'sweep away from their path the one obstacle which stood in their way - the historic Liberal Party'. A Parliamentary by-election in Edinburgh in 1899 provided the socialists with an excuse for asking working people to vote for the Tories:

> The policy of sacrificing a minnow to catch a salmon is as old as the hills, and is well understood by the Liberal Party... large numbers of the working class have been led to believe in it as the Party of progress.

And in 1900 Robert Brown, a Lib-Lab miners' leader, who had evoked the example of John Bright while justifying John Weir's claim as the Labour candidate for West Fife, said the miners in the Lothians would 'vote Tory because the Liberals in Fife had opposed Weir'.

Peter Burt and David McLardy simultaneously belonged to the Socialist League, the Scottish Land Restoration League and the Liberal Party in the 1880s, and they frequently lectured for the Scottish Land and Labour League branches on 'the nationalisation of the land' and 'the nationalisation of society'. By 1895 they had become fairly orthodox Georgeites and they opposed the socialist and Lib-Lab candidates by campaigning for orthodox Liberals. It would, however, be a mistake to assume that the middle class Liberals were exempt from the process of social change, or that they were not influenced by the pressures exerted by the labour movement. In 1892, for example, Robert Brodie, the I.L.P. candidate in the College constituency, told an election meeting that the Labour Party 'had helped Dr Cameron to make up his mind on State interference with labour'; and, while, Cameron's conversion had taken a long time since he had first been pressurised by the Glasgow Trades Council in the 1870s, his new attitudes to labour questions were a reflection of the changes in the composition of both the labour movement and Liberal Party.

Nevertheless Scottish Liberalism was to the 'right' of the English, and Scottish Liberal-Unionism also leaned to the 'right' rather than the 'left'. A few Scottish Liberals were aware of the fact that they were to the 'right' of the English; but, when they lamented over this fact, they blamed the social conservatism of the electors rather than their own lack of a 'left-wing' programme. R.B. Haldane, a leading Scottish advanced Liberal wrote to a friend from Baden in Germany:

> To an English (sic!) politician one of the regrets of whose life is the difficulty of stirring the working classes in a free country into action, it would be amusing were it not pathetic to observe the terror of the educated classes at the Social Democratic movement in Germany. The university has no notion apparently of throwing itself on to the forward movement with the hope of winning the confidence of the people and guiding them aright... Yet after all what is the good of all our reading to us who are in public life if we cannot use it in the effort with all the strength we possess to guide the current of opinion among our constituents.

He later wrote to A.J. Balfour: 'I am not sure I do not agree with a good deal of what you concluded on the subject of Liberalism (I hate the name and call myself 'Progressive') in Scotland. But this, not because I disbelieve in what ought to be the cause of my Party, but because I have not a high opinion of my Scot as a social reformer'.

R.B. Haldane saw himself as one of the most progressive of the Scottish Liberals, and he was indeed to the 'left' of many of his contemporaries. Haldane and Dr Cameron were both advanced Liberals, but some advanced Liberals were more advanced than others. Dr Charles Cameron was more advanced than Haldane so far as labour questions were concerned; but Haldane, who had successfully contested Lord Elcho's old constituency in 1885, did not have to confront a militant or well-organised labour movement in his East Lothian constituency.

For the Scottish advanced Liberals in 1885 and in constituencies where there was no organised labour movement, land reform and later the disestablishment of the Church of Scotland were the main planks of the programme of advanced reform. Henry Calderwood, a Liberal official who had an office in Edinburgh, wrote to reassure Haldane who was worried about how he could best capture and hold the constituency of East Lothian:

> I think the line you propose for yourself is the right one: a clear, quiet, decisive utterance on Disestablishment as **the expression of Liberalism** in the Church question; and a leading, strong, and earnest pleading for reform of the land laws, as the main questions for East Lothian.

Yet even Haldane's Liberalism changed slightly under the impact of events, and in an article he wrote in 1888 he stressed 'a fulfilment of the just obligations of property'. Nonetheless 'the obligations of property' did not include support for the legal eight hour day. Indeed Haldane thought that the real aim of the advocates of 'the Eight-Hours question' was to 'raise wages rather than to regulate hours'; and he reminded the readers of the **Contemporary Review** that 'politicians must be not only idealists but men of business.'

For many working class activists the disestablishment of the Church of Scotland was still an important question, and farm servants, who were invariably Liberals, were particularly interested in disestablishment and land reform. Like the majority of the miners they only gained the franchise in 1884, and they were not influenced by the Liberal-Unionists. In 1892 farm servants had played a decisive role in defeating Arthur Elliot, the Liberal-Unionist candidate in Roxburgh, and in July T.S. Snail wrote:

> We are very disappointed, and exceedingly for Mrs Elliot and yourself; but the Hinds (in return for all you did for them) seem to have gone solid for Napier. After all, it is not a very big beating—if 80 of them had voted for you instead of Napier you would have gained the election.

Then a Liberal-Unionist in Elgin wrote to express the hope that Elliot would be able to reverse the Roxburgh verdict; but he wondered if 'the amount of trouble involved in getting at the rural voters' was 'worth the candle'. The agitations for the disestablishment of the Church of Scotland and land reform were considered vital by many working class electors, and these particular agitations which had been formulated by the Scottish Division of the Reform League in the mid-1860s were given a new impetus by Henry George.

II

An activist in English politics recorded his impression that Henry George, though not a socialist himself, had done more 'than any other single person to stir and deepen in this country an agitation which, if not socialist, at least promises to be the mother of socialism.' In contrast to the English Land and Labour League the Republican elements in the Scottish Labour movement in the 1870s had not agitated for land nationalisation, and George's subsequent agitation for land nationalisation had an explosive impact on Scottish politics. There were no Scottish social investigators comparable to Charles Booth or the author of **The Bitter Cry of Outcast London,** and George made an important contribution to the growth of socialist sympathies by rediscovering the poverty of the labouring population. By dramatically directing attention to the hopelessly inadequate living standards of crofters and industrial workers, he challenged the implicit assumption of the ruling class that the poverty of the working class was an inescapable consequence of thriftlessness and indolence.

By tracing poverty, unemployment and inadequate wages back to structural factors within capitalism, Henry George helped to give the labour movement's agitations a more militant edge. The accusation that poverty was created by capitalism struck at the cultural, psychological and spiritual roots of the hegemony existing in Scottish society, and James Leatham, a leading young socialist in the labour movement in Aberdeen in the 1880s, subsequently recalled this forgotten aspect of Georgeite propaganda:

> Like Henry George at a later date and from a different opening Marx taught La Misere—the intensification of misery, or as George called it, the increase of want side by side with the increase of wealth.

The Georgeites were important catalysts in the growth of socialist trends in the Scottish labour movement, and in the early 1880s the Georgeites and the socialists often worked together. In Edinburgh Andreas Scheu, an Austrian emigre, concentrated on influencing George's supporters. In a letter to Miss Reeves, a member of the Edinburgh branch of the Scottish Land Restoration League, he argued:

> Not that I believe you to be a socialist; but I am aware that you are supporting a movement which goes very far in the direction of socialism. Two years ago I heard Mr Henry George admit that himself by saying he knew full well that the nationalisation of the land would not solve the social question; but he was convinced that it was a sure step towards bringing that solution about.

The Third Reform Bill had created a larger working class electorate, and the local caucus-dominated committees of the Liberal Party had now to confront the challenge of some trade unionists and middle class radicals who were pressing for the acceptance of certain socialist demands. **Laissez-faire** Liberalism, with its 'night watchman's idea of the functions of Government', was henceforth questioned by permeationists who were committed to collectivist solutions to the social problem. The propertied classes had already been frightened by the spectre of German social democracy, and labour radicals, who belonged to the Scottish Liberal Association, played on these fears in order to persuade the middle class Liberals to accept a radical programme of social reform.

A profound fear of social revolution was deeply rooted in the consciousness of the propertied classes, and in 1887 a member of the Glasgow branch of the Socialist League described the response of one influential Liberal academic to the new threat to social stability:

> I have just come in from the (Glasgow) Philosophical (Society) where I heard Smart deliver a lecture on Factory, Industry and Socialism. Marx almost from beginning to end—vigorous and outspoken—conclusion of the whole matter something like this: 'If we who call ourselves the upper classes do not take Carlyle's advice and become real Captains of Industry and organisers of the people working not for gain but for the good of all, so as to open up to every man the opportunities for the higher life of culture at present the possession of a very few—if we do not do this within a very few years, then we shall have to prevent Revolution by leading it.'

Nonetheless the Scottish Liberal Association repeatedly rejected the demands of the labour radicals and the Georgeites for land nationalisation and a legal eight hour day, and the Liberal-Unionists like Lord Melgund, who had just recently left the Liberal Party in 1886, criticised the agitations for the disestablishment of the Church of Scotland and Irish Home Rule. In his election address to the people of Selkirk and Peebles, for example, Melgund attacked the 'Irish-American agitators' who were working for 'the creation of a self-independent, disaffected State close to our own shores.'

Moreover, Scottish Liberal-Unionism, in contrast to its English variety, was a conservative rather than a radical social force, and the Liberal-Unionists were frightened by the land agitations in the Highlands where the Whig elements had been challenged by the Crofters' Party. And by then John Murdoch, the crofters' leader, who had obtained financial assistance from Dr William Carroll, of Philadelphia, to prevent the collapse of his weekly agitational newspaper, **The**

Highlander, was agitating among the coal miners in the west of Scotland. Land and labour agitations were converging, and what Professor Hanham has perhaps erroneously called the porridgy uniformity of the 'sixties' had been watered down by the stirrings of discontented socialists and radicals.

If Dr Cameron and the advanced Liberals in Glasgow had been compelled by a militant labour movement to view the labour question more sympathetically than they had done earlier, the Liberal-Unionists sometimes chose to champion a radical programme of reform in order to attract votes. Scottish Liberal-Unionism was shaped by the initial leadership which included Sir Edward Colebrooke, and, while they were to the 'right' of their English equivalents, they were capable of promising a legal eight hour day and other reforms in order to attract the votes of working class electors. Haldane's Liberal-Unionist opponent in East Lothian in 1895 promised the working men old age pensions, poor law reform, a fixed number of holidays for ploughmen, temperance reform and a legal eight hour day for miners. The Liberal-Unionists did not, however, think of themselves as being to the 'left' of the Liberals, and in 1900 W. Stroyan, (a Liberal-Unionist who was standing as a Parliamentary candidate in Stirlingshire) told electors that 'the Radical remnant which today calls itself the Liberal Party is not the old Liberal Party'.

The almost impregnable electoral dominance of Scottish Liberalism had been the key factor in pushing the labour movement to the 'left' of the English one from 1868 onwards, and this continuity was unbroken as a result of the Liberals uncompromising refusal to make sufficient concessions to the labour movement. A large number of Scottish labour leaders were ambiguous about their attitudes to the Liberal Party and Liberal values, and Dr James Kellas has used this fact to prove his argument that the middle class liberals were to the 'left' of the labour movement. But the ambiguity of the labour leaders did not prevent them from opposing Liberal candidates in Parliamentary elections, and even when some middle class advanced Liberals paid lip service to the agitation for a legal eight hour day their hearts were not in it. In 1981 Dr Cameron's **Glasgow Weekly Mail attributed working class poverty to drink and improvidence and denied the need for** old age pensions by drawing attention to the large amount of money invested by the working classes.

Moreover, there were other signs in the late Victorian period illuminating just how far the Scottish labour movement was to the 'left' of the English one. The Scottish Trades Union Congress had been under 'left-wing' influence since its foundation in 1896, and it was later to the 'left' of the British Trades Union Congress. In 1897 and 1898 the socialists in the British T.U.C. had failed to persuade a majority of delegates to support resolutions committing the delegates to pay a political levy, and 'even in 1899 the socialists were not strong enough to carry such a scheme.' In 1897 only four of the seventy-four delegates to the Scottish T.U.C. opposed a resolution on collectivism in which it was stated that the workers would not obtain 'the full value of their labour' until 'the land, mines, railways, machinery and industrial capital' were 'owned and controlled by the State'; and in 1898 only nineteen of the sixty-nine delegates opposed a resolution urging Scottish trade unionists to 'morally and financially support the working class Socialist Parties already in existence.'

A majority of the delegates to the British T.U.C. in 1899 supported the following resolution which gave birth to the Labour Representation Committee:

> This Congress, having regard to its decisions in former years, and with a view to securing a better representation in the interests of Labour in the House of Commons, hereby instructs the Parliamentary Committee to invite the co-operation of all the co-operative, socialistic, trade unions, and other working class organisations, to jointly co-operate on lines mutually agreed upon in convening a special congress of representatives from such of the above-mentioned organisations as may be willing, to devise ways and means for securing the return of an increased number of labour members to the next Parliament.

Though this resolution had been drafted in the office of the **Labour Leader,** a number of historians have pointed out that it made no reference to political independence from the Liberals or a socialist basis for the new Party.

By contrast the Scottish T.U.C. in 1899 accepted unanimously a resolution calling for a new working class Party to fight for socialism:

> That this Congress, viewing the present economic and political situation, with the break-up of the Liberal Party, consider the time ripe for the consolidation of all working class movements, whose ultimate object would be the nationalisation of the land and the means of production, distribution and exchange, and looks to the closest union of the Trade Unionists, Co-operators and Socialists to form the nucleus of this Party.

The Scottish Co-operative movement, too, was 'much more socialist and much less adverse to political action than the parallel movement in England.' In 1900 the Scottish T.U.C. not only adopted a resolution supporting the Scottish Workers' Parliamentary Election Committee, but also accepted their leaders' recommendations that:

> If there were a second Ballot, electors would have no objection, after the obnoxious candidate was eliminated, in supporting the Labour candidate.

Clearly, then, the Scottish labour movement was to the 'left' of the middle class Liberals as well as to the 'left' of the English labour movement. The fact that Scotland was excluded from the MacDonald-Gladstone entente in 1905 was another sign of the traditional emnity between the Scottish labour movement and the middle class Liberals; and the two Labour candidates who won seats in Dundee and Glasgow in 1906 did so in the teeth of Liberal opposition. And this Liberal hostility was behind the labour movement's failure to gain Parliamentary representation between 1868 and 1900; for Scottish Liberalism, as G.D.H. Cole put it, 'would have no truck with Labour, even of the old-fashioned "Lib-Lab" brand.'

In England the mining constituencies, except in Lancashire, provided the Liberals with their 'firmest' seats; but in Scotland the miners were in the forefront of the struggle for independent labour representation. The miners were also the main force within the Scottish Workers' Parliamentary Representation Committee, and in the general election of 1900 their five candidates polled an aggregate vote of 14,878. But if the Scottish labour movement was to the 'left' of the English one, it was also to the 'left' of the majority of working class electors. A vital factor in the persistence of working class electors in voting Liberal was the character of the Scottish community, a community which, if we may borrow the formulation of Dr Christopher Lasch, possessed 'the cohesiveness and sense of shared experience that distinguish a truly integrated community from an atomistic society.'

III

In his brilliant but neglected book, **Flashlights of the Amsterdam Congress,** Daniel De Leon made the perceptive comment that 'a ruling class dominates not only the bodies, but the mind also of the class that it rules.' The insight was, and is, central to an understanding of the origins and weaknesses of the modern Scottish working class movement. Yet it would be a profound mistake to assume that there was a correlation between the voting behaviour of the Scottish working class and their **apparent** adherence to middle class social values. For industrial militancy did not only expose the existence of social tensions and class conflicts: it also led some working people to recognise the need for real community life and humanistic social values.

Moreover, the Socialist thermometers for registering social tensions in the eighteen-eighties and eighteen-nineties were restricted to parliamentary elections and institutionalised conflict. Outside these institutionalised arenas of class conflict, social tensions were manifested in a variety of ways Scottish socialists had not envisaged. Indeed the subterranean forces of opposition—e.g. in the School Boards, in the Highlands and in the poaching activities of the miners—were not utilised until after the collapse of the Second International.

The Radical Literary Tradition

David Craig

By radicalism I mean the frame of mind of someone who sees to the roots of the human condition in his or her time, is honest with himself about his dissatisfactions, and works with whatever forces in society bid fair to win forwards to a better way. Trying to be radical inside your head, with little effort at concerted action, will not do. Partisan activism (whether socialist or nationalist) without care for our psychological depths will not do. The great radicals don't separate the historical and the personal. I mean Burns, as much concerned about the hardening-over of vital feelings by a puritanical repression as he was about the destroying grind of poverty. I mean Dickens, to whom that last sentence exactly applies. I mean Gorky, feeling in his own flesh the pain and yearning of the under-man. I mean Brecht, who ended his major **credo** poem 'To Posterity' with these lines:

> You, who will get out of the flood
> In which we are sinking,
> Think
> When you mention our weaknesses
> Also of the dark time
> That engendered them ...
>
> For we knew too well:
> Even the hatred of squalor
> Distorts the features.
> Even anger against injustice
> Makes the voice harsh. Oh, we
> Who wanted to lay a base for friendliness
> Could not ourselves be friendly.

But you, when at last it comes about
That man is a help to man,
Think of us
With understanding.

And I mean MacDiarmid, who has thought harder than any other modern poet about the need for the human species to better its living in every way from the most cerebral and individual to the most public. And I mean Arthur Miller, who almost alone among recent Western writers of the front rank has made himself at home in the working conditions where most people spend their lives, who knows the human nature of industrial man.

There are two Scottish writers there. But the supporting cast is thin. Our radical literary tradition has been intermittent - barely a tradition. To make plain the sort of touchstone I am working with, and to articulate the historical sequence in which these writers belong, it is necessary first to say as shortly as possible what the radical tradition in world literature has amounted to.

There seem to have been six main phases: the French Revolution, the Hungry Forties, the Great Unrest, the Great War and the October Revolution, the Slump and the Popular Front, and the present with its mixture of radical trends that include youth revolt, the peace movement, and the resurgence of nationalism. Radicalism has to be seen as starting in the 1780s, when the breakneck growth of the cities began to bring the have's and the have-not's into stark confrontation. To reach much back beyond that point thins out the notion until it loses its specific reference to revolutionary movements that seriously challenge the ruling class. From 1789 onwards the French artisans and intellectuals were raising the cry for freedom, equality, and brotherhood that has never since died away. The English artisan Tom Paine writes his fearlessly candid, trenchantly reasoned attack on privilege and tyranny and it circulates hugely in the Scottish Lowlands from Paisley through to Dundee - the working men who are looting the meal shops for the food they needed to prevent starvation are reading it aloud to their illiterate comrades. The most creative poets of the time are either from the artisan class (Blake, Burns) or are striving to base their art amongst working people (Wordsworth, Shelley). For a time radical literature loses force and momentum as the war against Napoleon's empire eats up social energies - the Gagging Acts, the police spying, and other forms of governmental terrorism bite deep - the best poets all die young - the Reform Acts of 1832 seem goal enough for a time. But the men and women in the new ironworks, deep coal mines, spinning and weaving sheds, and docks are feeling their own needs and envisaging their own rights more than ever before, and the first deep slumps of capitalism in the 1820s and 1840s cause another radical wave to gather. The novel that goes deeply into the workings of society comes of age with **Dombey and Son**, just before the Year of Revolutions in 1848, and **Little Dorrit** and **Felix Holt the Radical**, a few years after Chartism and the middle-European revolutions have collapsed. As Britain settles into the role of workshop of the world and the middle-class grows ever more comfortable on trading and manufacturing profits, a generation of apparent calm elapses. Barracks are built in the cities to 'contain' any 'insurgents': the soldiers stay inside. Miners and weavers are grinding small their shot-firing powder and melting down the lead weights that keep their looms true, to make small-arms for a rising: they never use them. In literature, creative drama barely exists - stage versions of the Waverley Novels run and run. Poetry is escapist or weakly classical (Tennyson, Arnold, early Yeats). Folksong starts to wither and is replaced by music-hall. Fiction concentrates on a massively complex analysis of the self-conscious upper-middle class (Tolstoy, Balzac, George Eliot, Henry James). But life in the actually festering slums of Glasgow, Manchester, and London must make itself heard. Experts study it (Marx, Beatrice Webb, Charles Booth, Rowntree). Activists strive to organise it politically (Tom Mann, Keir Hardie, Eleanor Marx, Debs, Lenin, Trotsky). Poets and novelists fulminate against it (James Thomson, William Morris, Jack London, Gorky). A comprehensive analysis of what capitalism is doing to civilisation is taking shape in the work of Zola and Shaw and Wells when the first World War breaks out. Conscription and the arms boom nip revolutionary movements in the bud, as they were to do again a generation later. But the hereditary ruling class is blackly discredited by the course the war takes. In the Trench poetry of Owen, Sassoon, and Brecht, the elders are accused of murdering "half the seed of Europe, one by one". In Britain, France, Germany, Italy, Hungary, Bulgaria, Russia, capitalist governments are shaken to the foundation. In the latter five countries they fall. In Russia it is permanent. The break-up of the old system is dealt with by the writers in many different ways - the nightmare poetry of **The Waste Land,** Sholokhov's epic prose in **The Quiet Don,** the reborn popular theatre of Brecht's **Threepenny Opera.** Crises now follow each other with sickening speed. The radical writer is he who can say with Victor Serge:

> For my part, I have undergone a little over ten years of various forms of captivity, agitated in seven countries, and written twenty books. I own nothing. On several occasions a Press with a vast circulation has hurled filth at me because I spoke the truth. Behind us lies a victorious revolution gone astray, several abortive attempts at revolution, and massacres in so great number as to inspire a certain dizziness. And to think that it is not over yet.[1]

The radical writer now has to strive to keep his head amidst hideous dangers, civil wars, the houndings of Fascist policemen; and he has to steady his style and keep it clear and popular in the face of temptations to go in for crazy and violent experiments in the way of the **avant garde.** In Germany, Brecht does it by modernising a wide range of popular modes - hymns, cabaret songs, blues, the songs and sayings of peasant almanacs. In Scotland MacDiarmid does the same. In Italy Silone is using the anecdotes and the blunt speech of the hill farmers to write his revolutionary fables. In China Lu Hsun is using the economy of mandarin Chinese for the first time to write stories of everyday life and militant commentary on current politics. In America Dos Passos and Farrell, and in Scotland Grassic Gibbon, are doing what was no longer possible in England, with its dwindling energies - writing large fictional series which make up a panorama of an entire nation with its variety of mingling, conflicting peoples. The second World War seems from the Western-European point of view too stale and foregone an experience to stimulate creativity, although in America it is felt to be enough of an outrage to give rise over the next twenty years to three different sorts of masterpiece, **The Naked and the Dead, Catch-22,** and **Slaughterhouse Five.** Peace, in the teeth of the nuclear arms race, now engrosses a generation of writers none of whom had seen war at first hand and a wealth of remarkable poems, songs, films, and plays on the theme are made by artists eager to abandon elite modes and work in the popular media (John Arden, Adrian Mitchell, Peter Watkins, Ewan MacColl, the Ian Campbell Group, Bob Dylan).

Burns and Revolution

If that very summary account of the radical tradition is about right, we have to see that a Scottish contribution of remarkable quality is limited to three phases - although there are worthwhile talents at other points, as will appear shortly. There is no point in being crestfallen about this - there are historical reasons for it, as we'll see. Equally there is no point in dressing up our contribution as more than it is - the old national vice of plying away at the handle of the parish pump and producing little but the usual hollow sounds from somewhere below ground. The positive point is that from time to time radicalism in Scotland has spoken out in a distinctive and wholehearted voice that has a claim to be heard by the world at large for the validity of the message it utters.

From 1785 onwards, Burns was writing in the full spirit of that revolutionary dawn. Blake in the 'Songs of Experience', dating from the same years, was protesting against both the needless deaths of those whose cries 'run in blood down palace walls' and the more psychological tyranny of the 'priests in black gowns who bind with briers our joys and desires'. Burns was creating savage and ludicrous images of the agents of unfreedom wherever he met them. His call for liberty is heard in the 'Address of Beelzebub', for equality in 'To a Louse', and for brotherhood in 'A man's a man for a' that'. Of course these values are scarcely separable, and of course they are in many other poems of his. In them we see how his democratic militancy fed his most creative self. In the spring of 1786 he heard that some big landlords from Wester Ross were getting up a fund to improve the crofts and fisheries of tenants from the Glengarry area who wanted, so it was said, to emigrate to Canada. This philanthropy was a bit late in the day. Four years before, the Glengarry estates had begun turning over their land to sheep farming. Their rents rose 700 per cent in thirty years. In 1785 520 sub-tenants and cotters were evicted from beside Loch Quoich and sailed for Canada in the poisonous holds of a ship named after the laird's family, Macdonald.[2] This mixture of the carrot and the big stick so angered Burns that he rose to his most biting stretch of satire. His stance is to pretend to take the landlord's part. 'Well done!' he seems to say, 'more power to your elbow! high time you showed these yobboes who's the boss!' It is the crafty pretence at complicity with the snooty, the bigoted, the tyrannical which he uses in all the best satires of his heyday in the middle 1780s. First he simulates delight that the 'Highland boors' are being kept from running off to the free lands of Canada where

> up amang thae lakes an' seas
> They'll mak' what rules an' laws they please.

He names George Washington and Benjamin Franklin to show his approval of the American leaders in the freedom struggle against Birtish rule. He exhorts the estate management to still greater zeal in hounding their tenants, and then, as his actual solidarity with the 'wretched of the earth' rises to boiling-point in contemplation of their sufferings, he releases it into his lines in the guise of a sadistic frenzy very similar to what we must imagine a Patrick Sellar as psyching himself up to in order to go through with the genocidal clearances in Sutherland twenty years later:

> Your FACTORS, greives, TRUSTEES an' BAILIES,
> I canna say but they do gailies;
> They lay aside a' tender mercies
> An' tirl the HALLIONS to the BIRSIES;
> Yet, while they're only poin'd, and herriet,
> They'll keep their stubborn Highlan spirit.
> But smash them! crush them a' to spails!
> An' rot the DYVORS i' the JAILS!
> The young dogs, swinge them to the labour,
> Let WARK an' HUNGER mak them sober!
> The HIZZIES, if they're oughtlins fausont,
> Let them in DRURY LANE be lesson'd!
> An' if the wives, an' dirty brats,
> Come thiggan at your doors an' yets,
> Flaffan wi' duds, an' grey wi' beese,
> Frightan awa your deucks an' geese;
> Get out a HORSE-WHIP, or a JOWLER,
> The langest thong, the fiercest growler,
> An' gar the tatter'd gypseys pack
> Wi' a' their bastarts on their back!

This passion of anger on behalf of the downtrodden is the spirit in which the Bastille was stormed and the ancien regime in France brought down. And the downtrodden are not some cowed mass, seen vaguely from a distance, they are known at close quarters, with the grey lice on them, and carrying their children on their backs. Without such detailed knowledge, protest is an empty noise. Burns knew what was coming. From his place away down in south-west Scotland, he anticipated our worst single disaster of modern times, the clearances in the far north during the first few decades of the 19th century.[3]

'To a Louse' isn't radical in a usual or obvious sense. The point is that Burns' radicalism pervades his imagination through and through. The least domestic item reminds him of the hunger and shortages of poor folk, the unfeeling above-it-all stance of the well-to-do, the need to expose the shams of finery and what was then called rank. For Burns, the louse is an underdog and all his complicity is with it.

> How daur ye set your fit upon her,
> Sae fine a Lady!

> Gae somewhere else and seek your dinner,
>> On some poor body.
>
> Swith, in some beggar's haffet squattle;
> There ye may creep, and sprawl, and sprattle,
> Wi' ither kindred, jumping cattle,
>> In shoals and nations ...

Already the louse has come to stand for all the dispossessed and propertyless who one day will come and **squat** in the big houses when the upper-class nightmare of a **jacquerie** comes to pass. The beauty of this poem is that it insinuates its radical challenge to the unequal nature of class society into a perfectly observed comic scene. The social point makes itself. It is the kind of piece we need when answering the usual conservative objection that radical literature tends to blare and tub-thump.

'To a Louse' has got too much of its currency from the moralising couplet "O wad some Pow'r the giftie gie us/**To see oursels as others see us!**" 'For a' that and a' that' is likewise best-known for the harmless liberal idealism of its close, written more or less in English, "Man to Man the warld o'er,/Shall brothers be for a' that". The previous verses of the song concentrate the essence of democracy, and especially its equality and brotherhood, into masterly lyric phrases which are rich in life and hit hard, especially when taken with their tune (as all songs must be).

> Ye see yon birkie ca'd, a lord,
>> Wha struts, and stares, and a' that,
> Though hundreds worship at his word,
>> He's but a coof for a' that.
> For a' that, and a' that,
>> His ribband, star and a' that,
> The man of independant mind,
>> He looks and laughs at a' that.

The tune is:

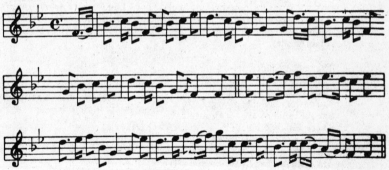

Burns has matched the two perfectly. It is a sturdy, treading tune, not a flowing one. At each point where a peak in the tune goes with a key word ("lord", "struts", "word"), the ring of emphatic and convinced opinion is perfectly got. In the second half of each verse, the climax of the tune in terms of pitch goes with the effect of a speaker drawing himself up to deliver a clinching point ("the guinea's stamp", "though e'er sae poor", "the warld o'er") and the whole thing then steadies itself on the last two level notes.

Burns said with a tone of mock self-criticism that the song expressed "two or three pretty good prose thoughts". The said thoughts were the pith of the republican ideology then being carried out in France. Paine published the **Rights of Man** in March 1791 and February 1792. Its finest satirical flight against the **image** of the ruling-class and the tyranny that it implies would seem to be the source for Burn's imagery in his song.

> Titles are but nicknames, and every nickname is a title. The thing is perfectly harmless in itself, but it marks a sort of foppery in the human character, which degrades it ... It talks about its fine **blue ribbon** like a girl, and shows its new **garter** like a child ...It is, properly, from the elevated mind of France that the folly of titles has fallen. It has outgrown the baby cloaths of **Count** and **Duke**, and breeched itself in manhood... Even those who possessed them have disowned the gibberish, and as they outgrew the rickets, have despised the rattle. The genuine mind of man, thirsting for its native home, society, contemns the gewgaws that separate him from it.[4]

It was dangerous to think those thoughts. Burns subscribed to an Edinburgh reforming paper called the **Gazetteer**: its editor, William Johnston, was imprisoned in 1792. Burns and his radical friends in Dumfries had to meet behind locked doors when they wanted to discuss politics. It is thought that many of his 'democratic poems' will have been suppressed or destroyed for safety's sake.[5] But the wholeheartedness with which he voiced the experience of his class was irresistible. They needed his jokes, his tunes, his thoughts. A weaver poet from Aberdeenshire, William Thom, describes this at first hand. He was working in a spinning mill at Woodside, near Aberdeen, during the bad times of the slump during the 1820s, when the war contracts had finished.

> ... when the breast was filled with everything but hope and happiness, and all but seared, let only break forth the healthy and vigorous chorus 'A man's a man for a' that', the fagged weaver brightens up. His very shuttle skytes boldly along, and clatters through in faithful time to the tune of his merrier shopmates!

Thom himself was one of three Scottish contributors to a narrow but distinct vein of poetry that expressed the poisoned life of the city poor through the 19th century. Their lurid, heartfelt titles epitomise the mixture of bitterness and incoherent culture which the industrial system at its most cancerous was then engendering - Thom's 'Whisperings for the Unwashed', James Thomson's **City of Dreadful Night** (1874), Francis Lauderdale Adam's **Songs for the Army of the Night** (1890). Thom's poem wavers from speaking Scots to book English, from detail to abstraction; but in its best passage it moves from an echo of one of Shelley's great 'anthems' for militant labour, the 'Song to the Men of England', to the most scathing protest written by a Scottish poet between Burns and MacDiarmid:

> The nobler Spider weaves alone,
> And feels the little web his **own**,
> His hame, his fortress, foul or fair,
> Nor factory whipper swaggers there.
> Should ruffian wasp, or flaunting fly
> Touch his lov'd lair, 'TIS TOUCH AND DIE!'
> Supreme in rage, ye weave, in tears,
> The shining robe your murderer wears;
> Till worn, at last, to very **'waste'**,
> A hole to die in, at the best;
> And, dead, the session saits begrudge ye
> The twa-three deals in death to lodge ye;
> They grudge the grave wherein to drap ye,
> An' grudge the very **muck** to hap ye.

Nothing else of Thom's actually expresses his radicalism. Local landed families (the Forbeses, Gordons, and Lummsdens) hindered his career because he had exposed how "they debauched and starved their workers", and the Chartist leader, George Julian Harney, apologised to Thom for keeping his name out of a report of a left-wing meeting in his paper, the **Northern Star** for fear it harmed Thom's literary reputation.[6]

So all the evidence is that interference to the point of victimisation helped to choke the radical literary tradition in Scotland. But the dearth from the Hungry Forties onwards to the Slump in the 1930s is too complete for that to be the main cause. The only notable things throughout that time are Hugh Miller's political and social essays - if indeed they are radical - and some snatches of poetry by Adams and John Davidson, the former an emigre in Australia, the latter in England. Emigration was robbing us of talent of every kind, whether radical or not. The facts of this are too notorious to need detailing her.[7] The loss involved, the sense of gutted barrenness it left behind are put memorably in the best lines from MacDiarmid's 'The Glen of Silence':

Where have I heard a silence before
Like this that only a lone bird's cries
And the sound of a brawling burn to-day
Serve in this wide glen but to emphasise?

Every doctor knows it - the stillness of foetal death,
The indescribable silence over the abdomen then!
It stands out in the auscultation of the abdomen.

Here is an identical silence, picked out
By a bickering burn and a lone bird's wheeple
- The foetal death in this great 'cleared' glen
Where the **fear-tholladh nan tighem** has done his foul work
- The tragedy of an unevolved people.

A silence burdening two-thirds of Scotland now!
While, in our belt of mining-towns and the like,
There is an awful sense of the presence of death ...

All sucked away - and on dumps round our ghost towns laid
A rusting wreckage of machinery, like hopes betrayed.[8]

Hugh Miller was a quarry worker from Easter Ross who became a kind of progressive-Christian journalist. He saw at first hand the early stages of the process and put his observations into his essays on 'Our Working Classes', 'The Franchise', 'The Strikes', 'The Bothy System', 'The Highlands', 'The Scotch Poorlaw', 'Pauper Labour', and 'The Crime-making Laws'. As a social observer he challenges comparison with Cobbett and Engels in point of detail, he is closer than Mayhew to the mainstream of working life, his thinking is much more sensible than Carlyle's. He knew the rotten premises in which the workers lodged, the routine slavery of their manufacturing work, and the vengeful bitterness felt by many of the 'hands' towards the 'masters'. Is he finally radical? Hardly, because when it comes to ways of solving the social problems, he always favours containing, educating, and moralising the 'disruptive' forces at work rather than going through with them towards some further stage of social evolution. In 'Our Working Classes' he regrets the destruction of the family by the factory system because it "prepares the way for theoretic socialism of the direst and most disastrous tendency, atheistic and material" - he is as far as could be from Marx's realisation that industrialisation, if lived through and controlled, could create "a new economical foundation for a higher form of the family and of the relations between the sexes". In his article of January 21, 1854 on the Lancashire mill strikes which gave the material for Dicken's **Hard Times**, Miller only perpetuates the smear that militants are wreckers foreign to your real, sound working-class. And in 'Pauper Labour' all his sharp observation of how poor folk live goes for nothing when he recommends, by way of solution, the purely conservative stop-gap of "compulsory imposition of labour on every pauper to whom God has given, in even the slightest degree, the labouring ability."[9] Miller - like Disraeli in England - shows how, at an early stage in the factory system, the best observers of industrial living were liable to waste their evidence by reacting back and away from the main trend in history and especially from the evolution of the working-class.

During the Great Unrest from 1887-1914, militant organisation was achieved for the first time by the worst-off (match girls, gas workers, dockers) but the literary work we think of as typifying the smouldering spirit of those years deals more with the skilled and white-collar workers, the house painters of Robert Tressell's **Ragged Trousered Philanthropists,** the shop assistants of Wells's **Kipps.** John Davidson, an emigrant from Renfrewshire to London, knew at first hand the scraping, anxious life of the poorly-paid clerks and teachers in a huge, jostling city and in the one poem, 'Thirty Bob a Week', he brought off the feat of breaking out of his usual flowery rhetoric and writing in the **persona** of a Londoner who is having to pinch and make-do to survive.

> And it's often very cold and very wet,
>   And my missis stitches towels for a hunks;
> And the Pillar'd Halls is half of it to let -
>   Three rooms about the size of travelling trunks.
> And we cough, my wife and I, to dislocate a sigh,
>   When the noisy little kinds are in their bunks ...
>
> It's a naked child against a hungry wolf;
>   It's playing bowls upon a splitting wreck;
> It's walking on a string across a gulf
>   With millstones fore-and-aft about your neck;
> But the thing is daily done by many and many a one;
>   And we fall, face forward, fighting, on the deck.[10]

What makes it authentic, and saves it from the sobstuff the Nineties usually made of the lives of 'the poor', is the sharpness of the domestic detail that comes over naturally on the speaking idiom. Francis Lauderdale Adams, in **Songs for the Army of the Night,** is more literary - his 'Evening Hymn in the Hovels' echoes, yet again, Shelley's radical 'Song'. But Adams has his own way of keeping his poetry buckled to hard facts and saving it from the sighings and sonorities that make most poetry of that age ring hollow. He writes quatrains with the shortest of lines, which he then end-stops, as though biting off his words in anger.

> Where is poor Jesus gone,
>   The lamb they sacrificed?
> They've made God of his carrion
>   And labelled it 'Christ'!
>
> Take, then, your paltry Christ,
>   Your gentleman God.
> We want the carpenter's son,
>   With his saw and hod ...
>
> We want the Galilean
>   Who knew cross and rod.
> It's your 'good taste' that prefers
>   A bastard God!
>
> Her shrunken breasts were dry;
>   She felt the hunger bite.
> She lay down in the night,
> She and the child, to die ...
>
> She took a jagged stone;
>   She wished it to be dead.
>   She beat it on her head;
> It only gave one moan.[11]

The nearest poem to that, in its subject and its stripped-down style, would be Brecht's 'Concerning the Infanticide, Marie Farrar', and the difference brings out how, finally, Adam falls a bit short of the radical as I have used it so far. Brecht casts his story of an unmarried mother in the style of a police witness and so brings us up against the stony face of the state-machine. He also glances sharply in the direction of the privileged through the repeated appeals to "you who bear pleasantly between clean sheets/ And give the name blessed to your womb's weight" not to write off those whom poverty forces to crime. A similar point could be made about 'Thirty Bob a Week': Davidson is with the undermen and under-women in the very language of his poem, but he apparently lacks a sense of how they might take a grip of social life and bend it to their own advantage.

War and Socialism

The first World War rolled over Europe, the Russian army walked home from the Eastern Front to make the revolution, in France the left-wing mutineers who ran up the red flag over the barracks and arsenals were massacred by their own artillery, in Scotland the villages never recovered from the loss of the men, the boats that could no longer be got down to the water rotted on the tidemark, the war memorials reared up ugly and pompous, their polished granite faces crammed with names, or as Grassic Gibbon put it in **Cloud Howe**, "an angel set on a block of stone, decent and sonsy in its stone night-gown, goggling genteel away from the Arms". There was apparently nobody in Scotland to write down the poems, songs, and stories of all those dead. MacDiarmid was in the army during the War and wrote his first publishable poetry in Salonika. But pieces like the 'Annals of the Five Senses' show little sign of the time and place of their origin. In January of 1919, the year MacDiarmid left the army, Karl Liebknecht, a leader of **Spartakus**, the forerunner of the German Communist Party, was murdered by soldiers in the putting down of the German revolution. The first distinct mark left on our literature by the great European shake-up seems to have been MacDiarmid's version in Scots of a poem for Liebknecht by Rudolf Leonhardt. The poem isn't overtly political and is 'radical', from a Scottish viewpoint, only in its use of city imagery (the bloodstained squares and streets, the crowds of workers coming off the shift). Yet it is a trailer for the Communist-revolutionary programme which MacDiarmid was to adopt six or seven years later when he took stock of how capitalist boom-and-slump, geared to Britain's managing of her armed forces and her empire, had laid waste Scotland's countryside, population, and pool of talent.
MacDiarmid's radicalism is belittled if it is seen as mainly nationalist/Marxist. It is these and at the same time it is existential. He is always striving to get at the essence and the conditions of being fully human at a particular time and place. When he says in the 'Second Hymn to Lenin' that "An unexamined life is no' worth ha'in", he is as near the core of his concern as when he writes in **To Circumjack Cencrastus** -

> Whiles
> I look at Scotland and dumfounded see't
> A muckle clod split off frae ither life,
> Shapeless, uncanny, unendurable clod ...[12]

In the book that marked his coming to Communism, the **First Hymn to Lenin** (1931), he both endorses the worst severities of Stalinism and gets deep into what I am calling the existential: for example, in 'Charisma and my Relatives' he imagines what it would be to live as oneself, freed of the usual props and appendages -

> But naewhere has the love-religion had
> A harder struggle than in Scotland here
> Which means we've been untrue as fechters even
> To oor essential genius - Scots, yet sweer
> To fecht in, or owre blin' to see where lay
> > The hert o' the fray ...

> A fiercer struggle than joukin' it's involved.
> Oorsels oor greatest foes. Yet, even yet,
> I haud to "I" and "Scot" and "Borderer"
> And fence the wondrous fire that in me's lit
> Wi' sicna barriers roond as hide frae'ts licht
> > Near a'body's sicht. [13]

But MacDiarmid was not a mere moralist, speculating about some 'human nature' outside specific conditions. In the same book he writes what I take to be the classic poem of socialism in Thirties Britain, and the only one to speak easily and directly, in a spirit of natural brotherhood, to working men at the point of production - 'The Seamless Garment'. He says to 'Wullie', his cousin in the weaving shed at Langholm:

> Are you equal to life as to the loom?
> > Turnin' oot shoddy or what?
> Claith better than man? D'ye live to the full,
> > Your poo'ers a' deliverly taught?
> Or scamp a'thing else? Border's claith's famous.
> Shall things o' mair consequence shame us?[14]

MacDiarmid was more conscious than any other writer I have read - except perhaps Lawrence - of the creative duty to get to the root of things, of each experience and each phenomenon. This is explicit in the verse of 'The War with England' that starts

> Now I deal with the hills at their roots
> And the streams at their springs

and ends with the heartfelt frustrated appeal of

> **When was anything born in Scotland last,**
> **Risks taken and triumphs won?**

To win the independence needed for this sort of creative effort, he felt he must break out wholly from the usual roles and identify (as Burns had done in a different way) with the vermin and the outcasts on the 'underside' of society:

> And yet - there's some folk lice'll no' live on,
> I'm ane o' them I doot. But what a thocht!
> What speculations maun a man sae shunned
> No' ha'e ...

He quotes, clearly thinking of himself, a sentence from Petronius: "you might without difficulty recognise him as belonging to that class of men of letters who are continuously hated by the Rich".[15] From this position he can reach his final revolutionary vision of his country - the middle verses of the 'Third Hymn to Lenin', where the life-destroying mess, the needs, and the possibilities of urban civilisation in Scotland are implacably set down:

> ... first of all - in Cranston's tea-rooms say -
> With some of our leading wart-hogs calmly sat
> Watching the creatures' sardonically toothsome face
> Die out in horror like Alice's Cheshire cat ...

> Clever - and yet we cannot solve this problem even;
> Civilised - and flaunting such a monstrous sore;
> Christian - in flat defiance of all Christ taught;
> Proud of our country with this open sewer at our door,

Come, let us shed all this transparent bluff,
Acknowledge our impotence, the prize eunuchs of Europe,
Battening on our shame, and with voices weak as bats'
Proclaiming in ghoulish kirks our base immortal hope.

And what is this impossible problem then?
Only to give a few thousand people enough to eat,
Decent houses and a fair income every week.
What? For nothing? Yes! Scotland can well afford it.

It cannot be done. The poor are always with us,
The Bible says. Would other countries agree?
Clearly we couldn't unless they did it too.
All the old arguments against ending Slavery![16]

MacDiarmid's work was always remarkable for the utmost clarity of thought along with rather a want of the solidly-realised situations in which the thoughts originated and had their being. Almost the opposite is true of his counterpart in prose fiction, Lewis Grassic Gibbon. Between them they gave Scotland a voice again, after the century and more of near-silence, and did so by laying bare the roots of the cultural tragedy - the dispossession of the 'peasantry', the raw exploitation of the city workers, the allowing of the native languages to wither under the shadow of the metropolitan-English culture.

Gibbon's base was among the small tenant-farmers of the North-east and this helps to give **A Scots Quair** its quality of epic lament. The first book of the trilogy, **Sunset Song**, ends with the funeral sermon on the war dead from the parish:

> we may believe that never again will the old speech and the old songs, the old curses and the old benedictions, rise but with alien effort to our lips.
> The last of the peasants, those four that you knew, took that with them to the darkness and the quietness of the places where they sleep. And the land changes, their parks and their steadings are a desolation where the sheep are pastured, we are told that great machines come soon to till the land, and the great herds come to feed on it, the crofter has gone, the man with the house and steading of his own and the land closer to his heart than the flesh of his body.

In 1821 half a million or 1 in 4 of the people were on the land, by 1911 200,000 or 1 in 20. "Hill pastures, rough grazings and woodlands had everywhere encroached on the farm-land ... (It) was a tragedy for the whole nation." The price of corn dropped from 70s a quarter in 1918 to 20s 6d by 1933 '(the year of Gibbon's middle volume, **Cloud Howe**) and the ploughman's weekly wage dropped from 53s 9d in 1920 to 37s in 1932 (the year of **Sunset Song**). "The farmer now stood on the brink of despair."[17]

Gibbon's heartsick exile's passion for his country suffused his reaction to this situation with a nostalgia that spoils his work with patches and streaks of unreality, especially at the close. But the book is irreplaceable, and pioneering in the most important way, because it is the first modern work of any size that lets the whole life of the mass of the people express itself **in their own voice**. It is a voice that carries fleering gossip, argument, abuse, details of a weather that matters to the speaker, reminiscence and history, all urging themselves along with the vital energies of working and sexual life. The whole of human nature is felt to be present and this includes—from the small holder's viewpoint—a natural, scathing disrespect for one's 'betters', a natural egalitariansim.

> You could go never a road but farmer billies were leaning over the gates, glowering at the weather, and road-menders, poor stocks, chapping away at their hillocks with the sweat fair dripping off them ... the hill springs about a shepherd's herd would dry up or seep away all in an hour and the sheep go straying and baying and driving the man fair senseless till he'd led them weary miles to the nearest burn. So everybody was fair

snappy, staring up at the sky, and the ministers all over the Howe were offering up prayers for rain in between the bit about the Army and the Prince of Wales' rheumatics. But feint the good it did for rain; and Long Rob of the Mill said he'd heard both Army and rheumatics were much the same as before.[18]

After the War and the lament for the crofters, Gibbon has to face the contemporary world of drift from the land and slump, General Strike and hunger marches. His view is mixed. In **Cloud Howe** Chris Guthrie's second husband, the minister Robert Colquhoun, is bent on cleaning up the small mill town of Segget in a Christian--Socialist kind of way, and is supposed to be in alliance with the radical spinners, though this is rarely shown close up. When 1926 comes, local activists plan to blow up a bridge to stop a train that is bringing in blacklegs. What else could have saved the Strike from the sell-out that ushered in the next twenty years of stagnancy and compromised socialism in British politics? Yet the minister rushes off with the most 'responsible' of the activists and prevents the sabotage. And immediately afterwards Chris has a miscarriage. And Robert is never the same again - he collapses into a smush of evangelism. In this mess of half-buried implications Gibbon has lost touch with the radical drive in contemporary life. But in **Grey Granite**, in which he reaches up to his present and beyond, he is again at one, or very nearly, with those of the working-class who were struggling to break out of the capitalist paralysis. The hero, Chris's son Ewan, is dangerously near the stainless-steel activist of a hundred hack-revolutionary novels. But he is given many interesting and burning thoughts (the great protest at suffering through the ages on pp 54-5) and he lives his life of hard work, busy political talk, demonstrating in the rain against the savagery of the police, amidst a living city that moves and talks under our eyes with an actuality which I consider little different, in terms of achieved art, from the panorama of the hill-farms in **Sunset Song**.

    A Scots Quair belongs to the family of novels about crisis on the land which make up the most coherent trend in world radical literature between the Wars.[19] It has hardly been noticed as such. The limelight has been hogged by the work of the English poets whose socialism was temporary where MacDiarmid's was durable. The cruelly testing events of that time reached so far in the imagination of Western writers that they even brought modern politics for the first time into Gaelic poetry, in the Communist lyrics of Sorley Maclean.

> My een are nae on Calvary
> or the Bethelehem they praise,
> but on shitten back-lands in Glesca toun
> whaur growan life decays ...
>
> Can beauty and the mendacity of verse
> deceive the patient with its transient cures
> or hide the Spanish miner from his doom,
> his soul going down without delirium?
>
> What is your kiss, electrical and proud,
> when valued by each drop of precious blood
> that fell on the frozen mountain-sides of Spain
> when men were dying in their bitter pain?...
>
> I who avoided the sore cross
> and agony of Spain,
> what should I expect or hope,
> what splendid prize to win?
>
> I who took the coward's way,
> the mean road of the slave,
> how should I expect to meet
> the thunderbolt of love?[20]

Maclean's radicalism has lasted into the present as a grief at the tragic aspect of recent history. Only nine years ago he could write:

> It was not the brutal Nazi madness nor the miserable slavery
> of France that closed the vice on my heart but a poor object
> of pity, a woman who bared to me the sharp novelty of her anguish ...
>
> Little did I know of her sore wound: that it was only a kind
> of trial that comes from adultery and lies.
>
> I have long since learned the opposite, with bullets, mines,
> deathly shells, with defeat in victory and despair, with
> famine of the spirit and of the flesh: that worse than the
> baseness of a silly woman is the stench from the gas-chambers
> of Europe.
>
> If I go someday to Richmond and see the shapely strong Castle,
> it will only make me smile if I remember my agony at all.[21]

Such veterans of the pre-War radical movement include men who had learned through Army service and writing for workers' theatre that committed literature demands the use of modes rooted in the culture of the working-class. So Ewan MacColl has worked in the modes of folksong, pop, and radio and has been able to make the juke-boxes and the charts with songs that bring the unheard- of qualities of candour and subtlety into the love 'ballad' and even pass on a radical message in a sweetly-singable style:

> The first time ever I lay with you
> And felt your heart beat close to mine,
> I thought our joy would never end
> But last till the end of time, my love,
> And last till the end of time...
>
> I met my love by the gasworks croft,
> Kissed my girl by the old canal,
> Dreamed a dream by the factory wall,
> Dirty old town, dirty old town...
>
> Going to make me an axe of shining steel,
> Good sharp steel tempered in the fire,
> Going to cut it down like an old dead tree,
> That dirty old town, dirty old town.

MacColl is writing as an emigrant from Lanarkshire to Salford in the thick of industrial Lancashire. Hamish Henderson has stayed close to the Wellsprings of folksong, whether among the travelling folk in the Perthshire berry fields or in the pit villages of Midlothian and Fife. It is his knowledge of the vital buoyancy of that tradition that manages to make his revolutionary optimism ring true in the eloquent lyric he wrote to the pipe tune, 'The Bloody Fields of Flanders':

Roch the wind in the clear day's daw - in Blows the

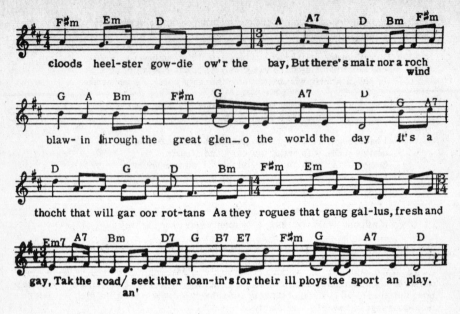

cloods heel-ster gow-die ow'r the bay, But there's mair nor a roch wind blaw-in through the great glen—o the world the day it's a thocht that will gar oor rot-tans Aa they rogues that gang gal-lus, fresh and gay, Tak the road/ an' seek ither loan-in's for their ill ploys tae sport an play.

'The Freedom Come-all-ye' ends:

So come all ye at hame wi freedom,
  Never heed whit the hoodies croak for doom;
In your hoose aa the bairns o Adam
  Can find breid, barley bree an painted room.
When Maclean meets wi's freens in Springburn
  Aa the roses an geans will turn tae bloom,
An a black boy frae yont Nyanga
  Dings the fell gallows o the burghers doon.[22]

That is a song for the marchers to the submarine base on the Holy Loch or the thousands who demonstrated to save the Upper Clyde Shipyard. Radical literature fails its potential unless it rings out amongst and is taken up by the many on whose behalf it is written. It is for this reason that John McGrath's play for village hall, television, and theatre, **The Cheviot, The Stag, and the Black, Black Oil** (along with such kindred pieces as **Willie Rough** and the 7:84 company's John Maclean play), strike me as much the most fertile recent work in the radical tradition of Scotland or any other country. It combines 'everything' - the funny monologue, the poignant lyric, the satirical sketch, the historical film, the documentary interview...in its television version as a 'Play of the Week' on BBC-1 (June 1974) it even became the first piece ever to bridge the gap between the large-scale electronic medium and the live audience by cutting with perfect adroitness between film of the audience (in a Highland village hall) and the show itself. (It was fitting that the beautifully economical and lifelike film sequence reconstructing the Sutherland clearances should have owed much in style to a BBC film by an Englishman on a Scottish subject, Peter Watkin's Culloden). I first read about the play in the Kyleakin paper, the **West Highland Free Press**, when I was in Wester Ross last summer, and I saw it on TV in my home in Lancashire. By that time it had been round the Highlands and Islands where it had brought out the buried history of that region and re-enacted it for the people whose forebears had suffered it. So it spanned the radical tradition in Scottish literature from the time of Burns, who protested against the plundering of the land by semi-absentee capitalists, to the present, when new representatives of the same class are threatening, against ever more effective resistance, to despoil our seas and coastline in new ways.

1. **Memoirs of a Revolutionary, 1901-1941,** trans. Peter Sedgwick (1967 ed.), 9-10.
2. **Life and Works of Burns,** ed. Robert Chambers, revised by William Wallace (1896), I, 347; G.D.H. Cole and Raymond Postgate, **The Common People, 1746-1946** (1956 ed.), 7; John Prebble, **The Highland Clearances** (1969 ed.), 137-8.
3. The poem is social dynamite and Burns left it out of his first book in 1786. **The Mask of Anarchy** was not published till ten years after Shelley's death. Blake stopped writing **The French Revolution** when police spying became dangerous.
4. Part the First: **The Rights of Man** (Everyman ed., 1966), 59.
5. Chambers-Wallace **Burns,** III, 374; IV, 132-3.
6. Thom, **Rhymes and Recollections of a Hand-loom Weaver** (1845 ed.; 1st ed., Aberdeen, 1844), 14, 74; Robert Bruce, **William Thom** (Aberdeen, 1970), 100, 108.
7. I reviewed them fifteen years ago in chapter 9 of my **Scottish Literature and the Scottish People.** The annual loss of people by emigration was then 22,000. In the latter Sixties it had risen above 44,000. Now, the North Sea oil boom has dropped it again to about 25,000.
8. This poem is scattered through several places: **The Voice of Scotland,** June-August 1938; MacDiarmid, **Lucky Poet** (1943), 296; MacDiarmid, **A Clyack-Sheaf** (1969), 17.
9. Miller, **Essays** (Edinburgh, 1869), 144, 179, 236; Marx, **Capital,** I (1867), Part IV, sect. 15, ch.9.
10. **The Poems of John Davidson,** ed. Andrew Turnbull (Edinburgh, 1973), 63, 65.
11. **Songs for the Army of the Night,** which was published in Brisbane as well as London, is unobtainable, and I have seen these poems of Adam's—'Jesus', 'To the Christians', and 'Hagar'—only in the **Oxford Book of Scottish Verse,** ed. John MacQueen and Tom Scott (1966), 456-8.
12. The Hugh MacDiarmid Anthology (ed. Grieve & Scott) pp.105-120, (London, 1972).
13 . **ibid.,** pp.123-4.
14 'Charisma and my Relatives': **Selected Poems,** ed. David Craig and John Manson (Penguin, 1970), 57; 'The Seamless Garment': same place, 60.
15. **Selected Poems,** 84, 85, 86.
16. **Selected Poems,** 106-7.
17. Both the facts and the comments are taken from a conservative historian, G.S. Pryde: **Scotland from 1603 to the Present Day** (1962), 232, 293-4, 296.
18. **Sunset Song,** in **A Scots Quair** (1950 ed.), 33.
19. The group includes Sholkohov's **Quiet Don and Virgin Soil Upturned** Silone's **Fontamar** and **Bread and Wine,** Anna Seghers's **The Revolt of the Fishermen of Santa Barbara** and **The Price of a Head,** and Steinbeck's **In Dubious Battle** and **The Grapes of Wrath.**
20. My knowledge of Sorley Maclean's poetry in the original tongue is unavoidably second-hand and scrappy. The poems excerpted are 'Calbharaigh', trans. Douglas Young, in **Modern Scottish Poetry** ed. Maurice Lindsay (1946; 1966 ed.), 93; **Poems to Eimhir,** 1943, trans. Iain Crichton Smith (Newcastle, 1971), 20, 33.
21. This is Maclean's own translation of his 'Coig Bliadhna Fichead o Richmond, 1965', in **Contemporary Scottish Verse** ed. Norman MacCaig and Alexander Scott (1970), 165-6.
22. The text is from **Ding Dong Dollar** (Glasgow, 1961) and the arrangement of the tune from **Sing Out!** (New York, Feb./Mar. 1964). The best recording is by Gordon McCulloch on the Exiles' LP **Freedom, Come All Ye** (Topic, 1966). It is also on the Dubliners' **Revolution** (Major Minor, 1970).

Scotland: Lessons From Ireland

Owen Dudley Edwards

The issue of Scottish nationalism has taken most commentators by surprise. It is, indeed, one of the arguments for Scottish nationalism that London-based political analysts and politicians should demonstrably be as destitute of a Scottish awareness as they are showing themselves to be. Until the Scottish National Party succeeded in transforming Scotland in politics from the Metternichian level of a geographical abstraction, the Westminster Metternichs could get by very nicely with a few vague mouthings about such traditional Scottish figures as Keir Hardie and Queen Victoria. But with Scotland on the agenda, it becomes painfully evident that the defenders of the Union know far less about its component parts than do its opponents. It is possible that, a century ago, the British defenders of the Union with Ireland may have known more about the smaller partner than do their counterparts today. The readiness to substitute condescension for knowledge has lost none of its vigour in 100 years, as may be judged by anyone who scrutinised the Prime Minister's references to his token Scot, the Rt. Hon. Wm. Ross, PC, MP, during the last campaign.

Even in Scotland, the debate has proceeded somewhat opaquely. The Scottish National Party, notably in its journal, the **Scots Independent,** has an irritating habit of preaching to the converted, and of arguing as though its audience was in thorough agreement with its every cliche. Only a very few commentators—Professor Hanham, the McCormick brothers, Tom Nairn, John P Mackintosh are examples—immediately come to mind as students of the rise of Scottish nationalism in any depth.(1) The cultural dimension has been the most poorly assessed or celebrated of all. The SNP is probably right to claim that its grasp of most Scottish questions is superior to that of other political parties, but in the cultural sphere it has work to do aplenty, all the more ironically given its own birth during a Scottish cultural revolt. How many SNP candidates let alone party members, during the last election were aware that the main office of the Edinburgh Festival is in London?

The relevance of Ireland to the Scottish question is quite another matter. It is mentioned about as frequently during the debate as a clergyman mentions his experience of Paris: often enough to make it sink in as a dreadful warning, but not so often as to suggest that any contamination or addiction has affected the speaker. Public reference to Ireland in this context usually occurs in inverse proportion to the speaker's mastery of the realities. Indeed, however widespread the revival of jokes about the stupid Irish, the one point on which most British statesmen are prepared to assert invincible ignorance for themselves is on Ireland. Perhaps not many would go as far as Mr Tam Dalyell, MP, who has assured us that no British person can ever understand Ireland. I would not doubt his word as far as he himself is concerned, but my experience of British students would suggest that others are more educable.

Professor A.P. Thornton, in his **The Habit of Authority,** has argued that unacknowledged guilt feelings concerning Ireland led until recently to a general belittlement of Irish studies in Britain.(2) There may be other reasons: in the 1880s, for instance, Irish nationalism and its agrarian concomitant proved highly infectious in both Scotland and Wales, and Irish history may subsequently have been discouraged in Scotland for much the same reasons as, previously, Scottish history had been discouraged there. No British political party has much to cheer about with respect to Ireland. Occasionally they try. Mr Jeremy Thorpe makes bland references to what he appears to think of as Swinging Billy Gladstone. Mr Edward Heath actually referred to Mr Whitelaw during the February election as the man who had solved a 700-year-old problem: he probably meant an 800-year-old one, nor should he have left it there, considering the bad relations between the two islands when Ireland was making slave raids on British coasts during the first millenium A.D. He is probably more concerned today at the possibility that Mr Whitelaw may be thinking of solving a ten-year-old problem—the Heath party leadership.

There is complacency also in Mr Harold Wilson's most frequent private references to Ireland, viz. his assertion to each Irish politician he meets that, "I get more Irish votes than you do". But however gratifying the ethnic composition of his Huyton majority may be, the Labour party under him and before him shares the discredit with Tories and Liberals of leaving the powder-keg of Northern Ireland to smoulder unobtrusively until it exploded. Indeed, the first parallel to be made between the Irish and Scottish questions is that each testify to the failure of politicians to concern themselves with questions of importance until they are hit over the head with them. Scotland has not, so far, had to pay so bloody a penalty for Westminster indifference. Yet the response of Scotland and Northern Ireland to the blundering of the successive Westminster governments has been comparable in one respect: archaic and tribalistic voting patterns are being finally swept aside in both countries. The SNP has nothing in common with the political attitudes of Dr Ian Paisley, and shares surprisingly little ground with Mr Gerry Fitt. Yet the SNP represents a revolt against Pavlovian voting behaviour which led Scotland to the polls for Tories, Labour or Liberals as a matter of traditional loyalties, and in Northern Ireland the UUUC and the SDLP constituted similar revolts against the traditional Unionist and Nationalist establishments.

The Scottish National Party is no more in search of Irish parallels than anyone else. In Ireland we are as anxious for Irish angles on news stories as are the Scots—SNP or not—for Scottish ones: and I recall at the SNP Rothesay conference asking the then press officer, Mr Douglas Crawford, now MP for Perth and East Perthshire, "what is your party's policy on Northern Ireland?" To which he replied all too appositely: "Jesus Christ!"

It is untrue to say, as many of the SNP's opponents do, that underneath the surface of Scottish unity the party is split between Orange and Green, any more than it is sensible to talk of a Left-Right split. By the standards of most political parties in this island, the solidarity of the SNP is something for the British Left to envy and for the British Right to ponder with incomprehension. I have been much exposed to stories of SNP Orangeism so much so, indeed, that I have derived some curious insights into the degree to which Labour party supporters seek to prompt elbow-jerk responses to tribal totems and taboos. "You know", a Labour party MP told me, "Billy Wolfe is an Orangeman". I cited some evidence which contradicted this. "Well, he's a Mason, then." I observed rather coldly that my being a practicing Catholic did not mean that I thought the worse of persons for being Masons and that I met my wife when I was best-manning a 33 degree Mason. The episode was instructive, suggesting that Orange and Green tints in the SNP image have been placed there by opponents in no casual way. (Incidentally, Wolfe later told me he is not a Mason, although he added with a grin that there had been much pressure on him to

305

become one.)

There certainly were one or two vehemently anti-Catholic publicists floating about the fringe of the SNP, but they are probably more rather than less discouraged by the present situation. After all the SNP in the House of Commons has as large a percentage of Roman Catholics among its ranks as any party in the House (apart from the SDLP which is, in the person of its only MP in Westminster, 100 per cent RC—but had Ivan Cooper been elected, as he nearly was, that percentage would have halved). The high proportion of Catholics among the party's founders has no greater significance than the Paisleyite crank element. Where there is a problem, as Douglas Crawford was eloquently testifying, is that Scotland itself retains much ethno-religious division among the **emigre** Irish and that this often expresses itself vehemently if confusedly. However, Scottish the SNP likes to be, it doesn't want to absorb the Celtic-Rangers confrontation into its own annual convention. Hence Tam Dalyell might shout to his heart's content in West Lothian about the need to pull the British troops out of Northern Ireland. His closest rival for the seat, SNP chairman, William Wolfe, could never afford to discuss such an issue at all. Ironically, it follows that if the Wolfe programme—the SNP programme— is implemented, the troops in Northern Ireland will be reduced to English and Welsh. Still more ironically, the voters of Irish descent in West Lothian who normally flock to Mr Dalyell's colours might well desert them if they realised that a British withdrawal would almost certainly mean a massacre of Nigerian proportions in Northern Ireland—but Mr Wolfe still dare not use such an argument. Whether the Northern Ireland issue was a factor in Mr Dalyell's loss of support in West Lothian at the last election is as yet unclear.

In political terms the SNP is no doubt right to be circumspect, and the other parties are wise to eschew overmuch Irish reference, but the student of politics would be wise to think about Ireland. And even if the SNP feels it unwise to refer to Ireland, its spokesmen would be well advised to reflect on the Irish experience. In certain respects this should not give the SNP too much trouble. Despite its opponents' claims, it is a much less parochial party than almost any other in Britain. It does not face a problem in educating itself on Ireland, given its success in coming to terms with the examples of Norway and Canada. By contrast, the other parties look insular in the extreme. Geoffrey Rippon could say on TV during the last election that a referendum was incompatible with democracy. It is possible that he was working on one of the political principles enunciated by H.L. Mencken—"bosh is the right medicine for boobs"—but it is only reasonable to consider the possibility that he believed what he was saying. It follows from his remarks that he believes any country which employs a referendum—of the kind that Norway, Denmark and Ireland (unlike the U.K.) invoked on the question of entry into the EEC—is not a democracy, nor is a country (such as the U.S.A.) which uses a reasonable facsimile thereof, such as ratification of constitutional amendments by popular vote in each state, to be regarded as one. Mr Rippon (unless he is purely cynical) stands as a parochialist of a dangerous kind, nor is he alone. His colleague, Sir Keith Joseph, in his recent attack on universities, directly stated that England (or Britain—it was not clear which) defeated Napoleon, Kaiser Wilhelm II and Adolf Hitler and destroyed them. It is evident that Sir Keith has achieved a parochialism which can visualise Waterloo without Blucher, World War I without British allies, and World War II without USA or USSR. His additional intellectual acrobatics, which included British destruction of Philip II of Spain and the reduction of early Roman history to about one-twentieth of its duration, merely go to prove that he dislikes universities in the way that a dung-beetle dislikes spring-cleaning. He is currently spoken of as a front-running contender for the leadership of Her Majesty's Opposition.

As to the former internationalism of the Labour party, let the reader who needs enlightenment on its present position on this, or on any other question which involves self-effacement, examine Harold Wilson's memoirs. The world exists while he watches it, whether it is a business of seeing that the imprisoned Mr Sithole in Rhodesia eats a breakfast on one day out of 365 or whether Mr Kosygin is to annoy people by whispering in the theatre. His awareness of foreign influences shows less respect for them than General Weydemayer exhibited to the cabinet of Chiang Kai-Shek when he pointed out that Confucius had been in favour of the good old free enterprise system as practiced in the U.S. The student Left, in and out of the Labour movement, has shown a good deal of responsiveness to international influences: its difficulty has been to acquire some originality of its own in response to specifically British problems. The SNP has a cause which enables it to be internationalist without merely being imitative. I recall once asking Mr Paul Foot, when he was speaking at this university, where the British student Left had made a contribution to compare with those of the brave struggle of American students for civil rights or against the war in Vietnam, or the student protests in Japan, Germany or France. He answered my charge of imitative insincerity and concentration on trivialities by pointing to the example of the courageous work for civil rights in Northern Ireland undertaken by the People's Democracy and the Northern Ireland Civil Rights Association (these were the days before the Provos had come into their own and the PD was still a non-violent, socialist, non-IRA body). He completely silenced me by adding "and that's a British example, isn't it, since Northern Ireland is a part of Britain". As Paul Foot must be one of the most incisive as well as one of the best writers on the British Left, I doubt if Scotland will find too great a challenge in acquiring a better Irish consciousness than obtains among the best minds in the London area.

The fact remains that while the SNP is ready enough to cite international arguments and examples to prove its case, it will want to retain an international awareness on a more general level. Ireland, in its time, showed an international consciousness. Ulster Protestant and Irish Catholic glorified their American **emigres.** Irish nationalism grew on a cultural foundation partially systematised by German and Swedish scholars. The Irish renaissance grew in part from a refusal by the Yeatses and the Joyces to be hidebound by the London-dominated metropolitan culture, and insistence on looking to the continent and beyond.(3) Even the most lively popular religions, Roman Catholicism and Presbyterianism, were necessarily very responsive to counterparts overseas, however noticeably they developed distinctively Irish versions of of their faith. Yet despite all of this, and despite the surprising extent to which Galwaymen and Dubliners can prove much more aware of the U.S.A. or of Europe than their London opposite numbers, there remains an insistence on the Irish implication of any story with a suggestion that if none can be found the story is of no value. My own work on Scottish nationalism for the **Irish Times** was always slightly inhibited by awareness of the editorial insistence on Irish relevance. The only real exception to this has been my work done directly for the present foreign editor, who is a Norwegian.

But in fact Irish nationalism itself, even in its most cosmopolitan moments, has succumbed to self-obsession. Its theoretical founder, Theobald Wolfe Tone, was more or less the spokesman in Ireland for the ideals of the French Revolution. The constitutionalist leader, Daniel O'Connell, the first real mass leader in the world—he could obtain a million Irish signatures for a petition against American slavery within a few weeks—was a forceful part of the crusade for reform that swept across the north Atlantic. Yet their internationalism is forgotten in their own country while their nationalism is glorified in its narrowest aspects. Thomas Davis and his "Young Ireland" movement testified to the influence of the ideals of Mazzini's "Young Italy" and comparable causes; Davis urged the study of foreign institutions and cultures on his countrymen. But what is remembered is the specifically Irish morals Davis drew from such study. Fenians and Parnellites fought for the rights of the people of India: if remembered at all in Ireland, such activities are dismissed as part of the necessary tactics of agitation. Roger Casement's absurd intervention in World War I is remembered where his great work in the Congo and in South America wins little more than a courtesy mention. James Connolly's work as an international Socialist received so little recognition that up to a few years ago it was always denied that he was a Scot and his experience in the I.W.W. in the USA won no response at all.(4) Scotland will, in a way, move to cast off parochialism in seeking independence. An assurance of identity should be the means of dispelling the need for a reassuring constant local reference. But it would be easy to find a new parochialism on the Irish—or the English—model.

It is curious that one of the least parochial sides of Irish nationalism has been that connected with the Irish language. I do not allude here to the governmental policy of compulsory Irish. This reduced stress on Gaelic culture to arid grammar, imbecilic texts and the strokes of a cane. It also brought in requirements for the civil service which called for proficiency in Irish: but civil service Irish was a language of barbarous, artificial bureaucratese foisted on a vocabulary intended for a rural and somewhat nomadic people. But the Irish language was revived with a great emphasis on the other Celtic tongues and peoples, as well as with assistance from European and American scholars. Even today, the **Irish Times** is at its most cosmopolitan in the Irish-language sections. Irish speakers can in some way digest foreign news without a need for constant deference to totems of Irish relevance. It strikes me that the linguistic features of Scottish nationalism, Gaelic and Lallans, are likely to move the same way. Those involved will seek comparable international experiences, and will have less necessity to reassure themselves that they are carrying the correct cards of Caledonian identity.

English Nationalism

One reason why both Irish and Scottish nationalism face this danger of parochialism is that both are in some respects children of an English nationalism whose cultural expression has simply invited a mirror-image response and rejection. This is, I think, less true of Scotland than of Ireland. The late emergence of Scottish nationalism has meant that specifically English influence is much more remote. Some aspects of Scottish nationalism involve long memories of the old imperialism of 1900—John Buchan writ small, so to speak—but this is far less evident than can be found by a dispassionate comparison of Irish nationalist thought and British imperial thought at the commencement of the century. Henry Cowper of the Open University has well said that much of Patrick Pearse could pass for British imperialistic propaganda with the alteration of a few names and the reversal of a few expressions of opinion. Pearse and his siblings read a children's diet of imperialistic magazines and the Hibernia they came to imagine bore a sinister resemblance to her old enemy Britannia. With it came an obsession about Britannia which was, as George Washington remarked in another context, as enslaving as perpetual obeisance would be. Scottish nationalism may be as yet exempt from this danger—but it cannot be too self-satisfied.

In comparing Irish nationalism in, say, 1920, with Scottish nationalism in 1974, a couple of important differentials suggest themselves. My remarks about Pearse suggest a fairly arid basis for his doctines. He was not, of course, the only prophet of Irish nationalism at that time and his writings in Irish are certainly much richer and more positive than the imitative post-imperial work in English. A vast complex of conflicting nationalisms went into the Irish renaissance, a complex which demands mention of Yeats and Synge, Shaw and Wilde, Somerville and Ross, Corkery and George Moore, Michael Cusack and Douglas Hyde, D.P. Moran and W.P. Ryan, Tom Clarke and Thomas MacDonagh, James Connolly and Jim Larkin. **But somebody won.** Of the huge variety of conflicting nationalist ideologies, whose combat and controversy had produced such cultural richness and intellectual excitement, one group ultimately became the political and cultural establishment. It made occasional efforts to harness the work of some of its old rivals—e.g. Yeats was made a Senator of the Irish Free State. But that didn't work. The refusal to ask Yeats to serve a second term was symbolic. The rather narrowly anti-English nationalism that became the official state religion, carrying with it a reactionary social policy and a Draconian standard of cultural censorship, could not afford a Yeats. As it stands now, Scottish nationalism is fortunate in its comparative immunity to anti-Englishness. It is fortunate also that environmental questions and social concerns have forced it towards a sense of community and its material needs which the Irish nationalists lacked. It may be felt that the SNP is too materialistic: but it is talking about realities. The Irish Free State was materialistic also, but its materialism was based on imagined assets and liabilities. The partition issue gave a permanent lease of life to the doctrine of nationalism by grievance, which in its turn provided alibis against the need for solving social problems of the people. Scottish nationalism has shown itself far more concerned with social questions than with repetition of grievances. It may be that the oil has forced it to this situation, but its answers are certainly not in the airy-fairy realm where so much official Irish Free State nationalist propaganda spent itself.

It may be argued that the militaristic traditions of the Scots could result in a dangerously militaristic form of nationalist establishment. The Scots, after all, received better terms of unequal partnership in the empire than did the Irish. One could say that Scottish nationalism is among some folk the vestigial remnant of a Scottish version of British imperialism as it existed seventy years ago. John Buchan's novels and the song "The Scottish Soldier" convey the tradition. But in fact there is less to this than appears on the surface. No doubt one origin of modern Scottish nationalism is the simple fact that the British empire's claim on Scotland was its economic and social benefits and its psychological boost, and that the loss of these things removes the motives for participating in any "British nationalism". But the Buchan style involved too much servility on the part of the bourgeoisie, let alone the working class. His well-set shopkeeper,

Dickson McCunn of **Huntingtower,** must needs become a monarchist with the aid of such members of the old Gorbals "die-hards" whom the author has not forcibly emigrated. (But at least Buchan was a Tory who was not afraid to like Glasgow street-gangs; in the more fearful, class-divided situation today, the authors of **Scotch on the Rocks** present a pattern of murderous hostility. The collapse of the Buchanism confidence, of which Buchan's last work offers a foretaste, symbolises the general collapse of Scottish conservatism and the deference vote). Moreover, Buchan was the poet of the grouse-moor class, and the force of environment on the SNP has been to make Scottish nationalism mean the end of the grouse moore "if it means anything", as Douglas Henderson, one of its more conservative MPs, has observed. In that sense we can point to an Irish parallel. The Irish tenant-farmer revolt of the 1880s, which had its own Scottish spillover, played a critical part in the emancipation of Irish nationalism from servility, something that on its own Irish nationalism could never have achieved. (Compare the insistence of William Smith O'Brien during the 1848 revolt that trees not be felled for barricades without the permission of the landlord.)

As for the more formal militarism, whether in ballads or in appeals from Colonel Colin Mitchell and other gifted statesmen to save the Argylls, it has much more in common with the Irish experience than we might think. The Republic of Ireland, and its predecessor The Irish Free State, in a rather dishonest act of oblivion, have officially discouraged any acknowledgement of Irish participation in British military service. There was in fact an enormous amount of it, with participants ranging from the strolling agricultural labourers who found the Saxon shilling preferable to Irish wage-slavery, to the General Wolseleys and General O'Dwyers who ordered the destruction of wogs with an assurance their more squeamish brother officers from Britain could hardly muster. It certainly was dangerous. British culture as transmitted to Ireland was saturated with militarism; so Irish nationalism in its turn was preached in a highly militaristic fashion. The Irish national anthem, "The Soldier's Song" (by an author of much better work), is a nasty performance mingling vain-glory, racial complacency and bathos in more or less equal proportions. Irish nationalism as described to young people was conveyed very often primarily in violent terms. In particular, the fact that the final settlement of 1921 had been preceded by considerable bloodshed was stressed, with the result (especially in the Christian Brothers' schools) that simple children assumed it was their duty to be the Robert Emmets and Patrick Pearses who would liberate Northern Ireland. Today Ireland is paying a frightful penalty for this indulgence in militaristic nationalism, whether of the Irish variety, or of the archaic post-imperial British version peddled in Unionist and Orange circles north of the border. But as yet Scottish nationalism seems unrelated to Scottish militarism; the SNP is—fortunately—100 per cent opposed to violence in its every statement; and if there is an influence from British culture at large it is more in the rejection of nuclear weapons and Polaris bases. Should the nationalist struggle assume a violent turn, then Northern Ireland remains an example of what can follow.

It has rightly been pointed out that Scottish nationalism has risen to its present formidable strength in very different economic circumstances to those in which other nationalisms have emerged. Tom Nairn in particular has made much of this point. Yet some of the greatest advances of Scottish nationalism which have been made in the arena of parliamentary conflicts lie in run-down and poverty-stricken regions. Argyll, the Western Isles and comparable regions are victims of bureaucratic indifference to non-industrial society. SNP victories in East Aberdeenshire, Banff and Moray and Nairn constitute virtually the first electoral step from feudalism. Ross and Cromarty, and Inverness, which contain features of both areas, seem on the verge of declaring for the SNP also. Accordingly, in this pattern of nationalist advance, it is possible to see the many points in common with the Irish experience. But it may be that the nationalism of these areas will be based on a wiser reading of history than was the case in Ireland. Much of Irish agrarian woes derived from Irish landlordism but were ascribed to British or English oppression. Scots would be foolish in the extreme merely to lump all grievances on Whitehall's plate: many of Scotland's ills are those of other client states of the great American empire, while many more are specifically the kind contributions of Scots. It might be that the SNP in its earlier phases was insufficiently aware of the role of Scottish oppression of Scots tenants and fishermen in the past, but the work of the 7:84 Theatre group and others have made its members aware of it. And in a major particular, of course, the Scots land struggle was far worse than the Irish. In Scotland, what happened was done by chieftains to their people, kinsfolk to their kinsfolk. The SNP victors in formerly Tory seats have overthrown Gordons and Campbells, however anglified. All circumstances combine to remind them that Scotland needs no new editions of the laird class, and that they have not been elected to create such. In Ireland, the lesson did not sink home, and even from the early nineteenth century the bourgeois rack-renter was moving in to take the place of the degenerate aristocrat.

Without becoming unduly sentimentalist about it, both Scotland and Ireland after independence will possess a common series of obvious post-colonial problems. The most obvious one relates to democratic institutions. Britain successfully (if often involuntarily) exported the idea of democracy to various colonies, including Ireland. From an early stage, however, it became clear that the concomitant blessing of civil liberties was emphatically not intended for export. **Habeas Corpus** was at many epochs of Irish history much more the exception than the rule, and the British administrative experience of Ireland was all too faithfully modelled elsewhere, to say nothing of being implemented by **emigre** Irishmen in imperial service. Irish nationalism in opposition seemed to pick up something of the lesson of civil liberties: contemplation of injustice or hard treatment meted out to fellow-Irishmen led them to sympathise with fellow-victims of other races and nationalities. Shaw, in his preface to **On the Rocks,** spoke of flogging which he claimed was now being revived in Britain (1933).

> though thirty years ago there would have been a strenuous outcry against it, raised by the old Humanitarian League, and voiced in Parliament by the Irish Nationalists. Alas, the first thing the Irish did when they at last enjoyed self government was to get rid of these sentimental Nationalists and put flogging on their statute book in a series of Coercion Acts that would have horrified Dublin Castle.

Nor was it the only way in which the new Irish inheritors made far more of the precedents of British administrative repression and its justifying statutes than their forerunners would have dared to do. The case of the Irish Civil War, also, where a much rougher justice was meted out to prisoners by the Irish Free State than had been the case when Britain governed, is instructive. (Admittedly, the Free State forces do not seem to have made the most of the considerable latitude in precedent provided by the Black and Tans and Auxiliaries: over the decades it is the IRA which seems, in its various manifestations, to have learned those lessons.) Scotland, with a separate legal system, escaped so obvious a colonial legacy. But she cannot hope to remain immune from comparable pressures, especially of the populist kind. In one way the answer may be a more thorough de-anglicisation than poor Pearse ever envisaged. We need to ponder lessons of the American experience of more profundity than those induced by an admiring or a hostile contemplation of American wealth and power. The U.S.A. has all too frequently departed from the principles of civil, religious and communications freedom to which she is supposed nominally to adhere. This makes her no more hypocritical than other national defectors from their holy traditions. But when she stands by the freedom she possesses, she is an example for other nations. **The Pentagon Papers** revealed part of the truth behind a peculiarly foul war which was a crime against humanity committed by the U.S.A. But if anything comparable to **The Pentagon Papers** had been published in the U.K., the U.S.S.R., France—or the Republic of Ireland—the editors who published such material would promptly find themselves in jail. President Nixon, indeed, tried to bring his countrymen to European standards in this respect, but he was unsuccessful. Again, Watergate has involved much sneering at the U.S.A., but in fact there is little reason for self-congratulation elsewhere. The U.S.S.R. may very well have suppressed the Dubcek regime primarily for fear that the principle of public accountability by bureaucrats should become contagious. France has never stilled the suspicion of high official involvement in the Ben Barka affair. The political consequences of Mr Poulson have so far produced more whitewash than investigation; meanwhile Mr Wilson's attacks on the communications media are reaching a Nixonian vehemence, although he faces far less searching media enquiry than did Mr Nixon. As for Ireland, the discovery in 1970 that half the cabinet was involved in gun-running led to botched investigations. Reporters and editors simply gave up the quest for the truth, although a politician against whom the gravest of suspicion in the matter existed—Mr James Gibbons—remained a member of the cabinet until the government fell three years later.

I have simply chosen the example of American traditions of press freedom and press investigative zeal to show one area in which Scotland must look farther than British traditions and precedents. Above all, there must be no truckling to chauvinistic blather about the superiority of British institutions and the necessity to maintain them. An extremely dispassionate assessment of existing institutions is needed. Scottish nationalism should neither reject English precedent because it is English nor accept it because it is. Ireland, bluntly, did both. On the one hand no child under the age of 15 was permitted to be taught British history: Irish and European alone were studied. It was a childish response to the old imperial parochialism which taught nothing but English history, and it paid the compliment to that parochialism of preserving its idiotic standards while affecting to displace it. And on the other hand, Irish criminal law was for decades maintained in the unreformed state that it was when it passed out of the jurisdiction of the Westminster legislators and the Whitehall-dominated civil servants. We showed our independence by holding to English traditions with an obstinacy which by contrast makes screaming Socialists of the Monday Club. Clearly an independent Scotland will be immunised from following the latter example because Scots law, unlike Irish law, is not a mere extension of English law. From this fact much also follows to give separate destinies to Scotland and Ireland in a state of independence. But there exist many obvious parallels to the examples I have quoted. There exists much popular annoyance about the way Scottish history has been slighted in the past which has led, among contemporary Scottish nationalists, to very narrow expressions of opinion about the situation in the present. Some of the best recent work on Scottish history is unfriendly or critical with respect to Scottish nationalism. That is no reason for ignoring its suggestive insights and its stimulation. And more of the best recent work is decidedly friendly to Scottish nationalism: yet popular spokesmen for the nationalist cause continue to bewail the grievance of bad history with no admission that any improvement has taken place in fifty years. The SNP must remember that it can no more justify a claim to be the only custodian of Scottish nationalism than could the Government of Ireland in 1923 or that in 1933 justify similar claims for Ireland. (They made such claims nonetheless.) Indeed, there is evidence that Scottish nationalism may be much more powerful than current SNP voting strength suggests—it is simply that up to now Scottish nationalism has not been political. It may have been instinctively suspicious of politics and politicians, and it may continue to be so. Indeed many of the staunchest Labour supporters are highly nationalist in non-political terms, and several distinguished Tories show the same quality. It is a little alarming that the SNP remains so weak on the cultural and intellectual dimension. There is a parallel here with the fact that Irish cultural nationalism was so powerful at the beginning of the century, but that much of it withered away later under the dead hand of an anti-intellectual official nationalism.

The Irish Crisis

One of the disturbing responses of both Irish and Scottish nationalism to intellectual questions lies in the way in which cultural giants are so frequently cited for tribalistic reassurance. Yeats, as presented by official school certificate programmes, was firmly reduced to his status as the bard of Father Gilligan, the Lake Isle of Inishfree, and Cathleen the daughter of Houlihan. It is perhaps a little unfair to cite the case of Hugh MacDiarmid (who was more or less expelled from the SNP before it was founded), but how few SNP men know his political writing at its greatest, as in such works as **Scottish Eccentrics** where he forces his readers to re-examine innumerable aspects of the Scottish heritage and opens up highly positive methods of investigation and celebration of the Scottish past. MacDiarmid often amuses himself by an impishly negative nationalism—he has been pulling everyone's leg too long to be worried about censure for his irresponsibility by sombre academics—but in fact his great achievement has been a superbly affirmative form of nationalism. It is precisely this kind of affirmation for which Scotland must seek. I suppose it will be hopelessly misunderstood if I say we need to be as affirmative as Molly Bloom at the close of **Ulysses.** At least the misunderstanding will be in good company.

Clearly the kernel of any assessment of Irish lessons for Scotland must lie in the Northern Ireland crisis. The situation could not be more urgent. The first assertion about it must be that any assertion has to fail because of its simplicity. I look back wryly to the innocence with which I wrote of it in the past. But we can see one evil at the heart, which is that of the monolith. Neither in the six counties nor in the twenty six was anyone really prepared to seek to build a heterogeneous society. Ireland as an island is ethnically, linguistically, religiously composed of very diverse groups. Each group has maintained that it is "their" country, whether they lay claim to the whole island or merely to part of it. Each group has fostered its own ideology with no concessions to that of anyone else. The Irish nationalist insisted that every Irishman owed a duty to a concept of the national heritage forcefully rejected by two-ninths of the island's inhabitants. The Irish unionist (a nationalist in a different suit of clothes) said exactly the same thing, save that it was a different concept and its opponents were more numerous: but the unionist of the six counties and the nationalist of the 26 were alike in their utter contempt for minority hostility to their doctrines. The Irish Catholic—and while many Irish nationalists are Catholic it is important whether Catholic priorities surpass nationalist—was ready to speak of his "Catholic" country without qualification. The Ulster Protestant acted as his counterpart. Nobody was ready to contemplate an acknowledgement of diverse heritage. Nobody would give up their tribalistic ego-trips. Nobody would deny themselves the pleasure of insisting on one belief alone for all Irish people in this world, the failure to adhere to which meant inevitable consequences in the next. It is, of course, easy to censure. Catholics and Protestants had ugly traditions in history of wrongs and grievances. Ghosts would not be silenced, with the result that they bred more ghosts. Liberal gestures, even when they commenced from generous motives, quickly were reduced to bargaining ploys. The intoxication of the tribes with the need to maintain their numbers led to intransigence on questions of educational **apartheid** and the hatreds were communicated **sub specie aeternitatis** to the next generations.

I do not advocate that Scottish nationalism should take cognisance of the Irish situation for the purpose of sniffily drawing its skirts up and passing by on the other side, or even of more handsomely proclaiming that there but for the grace of God goes it. All parties in Ireland have been free in their assertions as to the disposition of the grace of God, and Scotland would be very unwise to assume it is free either from direct contagion or from comparable situations. But it should be made clear that whatever may be the nature of the Irish tragedy, it need be no indictment of nationalism. On the contrary, it is an indictment of its enemies. A nationalism which demands that one section of the community have its beliefs, totems and taboos, aggrandised at the expense of the rest of the community, is no nationalism at all. A nationalism which seeks to coerce its community members into violation of thei their own beliefs is no nationalism. A nationalism which perpetuates divisive tribalism is no nationalism. Fortunately for herself, Scotland is a country of such incredible diversity that no one faction has so clear an opportunity for coercion of the rest—except, to be sure, that men of property and wealth can combine against the rest of the community if it is foolish enough to let them. But Scotland in its ethnic plurality, its religious multiplicity, its linguistic diversity, its geographical fragmentation, presents a far more complex picture than Ireland. And there lies Scottish strength. Moreover, the very weakest areas in the Scottish economy were among the first to declare for Scottish nationalism, and thereby have won an additional insurance against coercion from the more potent sectors. The credentials of the Western Isles cannot be dismissed by Edinburgh. Glasgow can expect no truckling from Dundee. In this sense the defeat in Hamilton and the victory in the Western Isles in the 1970 by-election may have been the greatest piece of good fortunate imaginable for Scottish nationalism. At one blow it got rid of fair-weather friends, of an excessively urban emphasis, of a preoccupation with victories of the Orpington type, and instead focussed attention on a Scotland that the urban SNP leaders hardly knew. Thereby it may help to deliver Scotland from the fate of Ireland. But the advocates of Scottish independence should never allow themselves to relax from the need to guard the ideal of a pluralistic society.

The Northern Ireland crisis obliges us to examine some further points. Conor Cruise O'Brien in his **States of Ireland** has done a masterly job in bringing the more unpalatable truths of the situation in Ireland to the eyes of his people, but since it appeared he has raised yet another. He has denounced the selective indignation which leads Irish liberals to deplore internment while remaining silent about IRA murders.(5) It is the kind of point which is all too often made by interested parties. The Tory who finds cultural and other benefits from friendship with South Africa accuses the Socialist enemy of **apartheid** of selectivity in his failure to attack repression in the USSR. The defender of Israel sees only Arab outrages, and **vice versa.** But the unsavoury associations of such a point rob it of none of its validity. (After all, **Encounter** was in the past a great denouncer of the Left for its "selective indignation" until Conor Cruise O'Brien proved that (a) **Encounter** was highly selective in its own indignation, and (b) **Encounter**, despite its protestations of disinteredness, was founded by an organization whose own origins lay in CIA finance.) We may feel that Scottish nationalism is mercifully free from having to face moral questions of this magnitude. But in fact they are the same moral questions. Whatever our tribe may be, be it religious, ethnic, class, theological, if we are not prepared to denounce its sins as we denounce those of others, then we are qualitatively no different from any other apostle of selective indignation. And there is a danger that Scottish nationalism, like every political doctrine under the sun, will have its undesirable friends from the ranks of the selectively indignant. Already we are seeing signs of this during the last election. Labour party workers speak of cars broken open by nationalist slogan daubers in Glasgow. SNP activists recall old shopkeepers being bullied to remove SNP posters or put up Labour ones by thugs in Edinburgh. The beam in the eye of the speaker is not only more of a subject for his attention than the mote in his brother's: it is also capable of mortal injury to him and his cause unless he removes it now.

It is worth remembering too that Macchiavelli was in some respects the founder of modern nationalism, and his hand lies heavily on some of its practitioners. If the SNP is to justify its existence to ushering into being an independent Scotland worth living in, it cannot be a Scotland whose independence has been achieved by dirty tricks of any kind, whether murder or petty chicanery. I alluded earlier to British and Irish failure to look to Watergate for lessons. In one sense, it seems, there has been a readiness to accept instruction. Certain British politicians have given close study to that episode with a view to repeating the sort of tactics involved without, of course, risking exposure. No SNP person has done so, to my knowledge, but it is worth stressing that no political movement can regard itself as immune to outriders of this kind. It is one of the terrible effects of Macchiavelli that his ethics are easily accepted by such outriders in the name of sophistication, superiority to textbook moralism and devotion to the larger cause. In fact, the larger cause is destroyed by all activity of this kind and what arises in its place is a hideous and mocking parody. And as Watergate pointedly emphasised, the dirty tricks department was inextricably interwoven with the John Ehrlichman type of morality, where the activity of espionage on a political rival with a view to discoveing his personal habits in the manner of sex, drink, etc, was defended before a nation-wide TV audience as vital for the public good. Scottish nationalists would do well to remember that their beloved Robert Burns knew this type of Macchiavelli well, and immortalised him in "Holy Willie's Prayer". If they keep that example in mind they may avoid yet another reproach that has been justly visited on Irish nationalism—that of indifference to the suffering caused to others if the ends of the cause are served. For all of Tennyson's Toryism, his bitter lines denouncing cattle-maiming and livestock-burning in the Irish land war still carry their own integrity and their unanswerable accusation. Their force is no less powerful despite the other fact that English indignation often seemed more easily roused for animals than human beings. It may be that in concern for either the SNP will have to sustain charges of sentimentalism from its Macchiavellian (and Nietzschean) critics from Left and Right. It will be an attack well worth receiving, and a charge of which to be proud.

The Left and Nationalism

It must be said that I am leaving it to my colleagues, Tom Nairn and Robert Tait, to examine the direction relationship between Scottish Nationalism and the Left, although I am to be taken as feeling, much as Robert Tait feels, that the initial work to be done in any such investigation is to ponder the plays of John McGrath and their performance by his comrades of the 7:84 group, to say nothing of the inspiration of Hugh MacDiarmid. I am also inviting my readers to be realistic, and accept it that Scottish nationalism', like sex, is here to stay and has to be lived with. And it does seem to me that we on the Left in making that admission would do well to think of certain more bourgeois questions which in our desire to establish our Left-wing credentials we are a little inclined to ignore. The values to which I alluded earlier are values which the Left has in the past sometimes chosen to ignore, and whose violations we have often politely overlooked in people we are unwise enough to call our friends.

There is in fact a peculiar and rather conservative timorousness of the Left with respect to nationalism, despite the rather formidable remarks on the subject which have been produced by socialists in such relatively good standing as V.I. Lenin, James Connolly, John Maclean, Ho Chi Minh, Mao Tse-tung and (in rather more noisome odour) J.V. Stalin. The student body at Edinburgh, and presumably other Scottish universitites, tends to fight shy of Scottish nationalism with a terror which recalls to me Irish Catholics of my youth on being invited to turn Protestant. I notice, however, that graduates of two or three years standing are much more likely to be caught up in the SNP, once the totems and taboos of the student herd have been lost to their sight. My own view of the Labour party is that a false friend is not preferable to an unconverted neutral; it is easier to convert Scottish nationalism to Socialism, because it thinks it is not Socialist, than to convert the Labour party, because Socialist is what it believes itself to be (although Tories term the Labour MPs Socialists much more frequently than they themselves do). There is certainly no point in disguising the fact that the SNP has quite some way to go, although it should equally be acknowledged that some of its policies, notably land, defence and certain other items, are considerably better from the Socialist standpoint than the theory and practice preferred by Labour. Nor can it be denied that in certain respects the SNP has house-cleaning to do. One position which I regard as far to the Left of anyone else is pacifism. An absolute refusal to take human life, or to will that it be taken, is a position so radical that most Socialists recoil from it. On this issue the SNP has distinguished itself by producing a majority of MPs present and voting in favour of capital punishment for terrorists. That is a sin whose stain will long remain on their political and actual souls. Mr Iain MacCormick, MP for Argyll, has for the future forfeited respect for his arguments as to the sanctity of human life when he preaches against abortion, for he himself has by his vote on capital punishment committed the crime of consenting to the taking of human life. It is to be hoped that SNP members with more respect for that sanctity than its ostensible defenders will lose no time in dissociating themselves from so dreadful a blemish on their party and that Mr MacCormick and his friends will learn of their anger and dismay.

The immediate and ugly relevance of the foregoing remarks is that the vote was for the hanging of terrorists of the murderous kind operating in Birmingham, that these were presumably Irish and that a motive for the action of the SNP members was to answer any assumption that their nationalism was of the IRA kind. To be fair, interested critics of Scottish nationalism did move in to exploit the Birmingham murders by such remarks, which only goes to show that the enemies of Scottish nationalism can essay some profit from murder as well as the IRA without doing the bloodletting. But it is no answer to such critics to show an indifference to the sanctity of human life ourselves. It is no answer to say "to show my horror at the taking of human life, I will take some more." And while the indifference of some Irishmen and their British friends to human life may suggest Irish nationalism is a poor precedent on this one, in fact some of the finest moments in the tradition of white non-violence were provided in Ireland. Daniel O'Connell, faced with the prospect of the slaughter of a huge crowd by government troops, had the greatness to think of the safety of his followers rather than his own vulgar glory and cancelled his monster meeting at Clontarf in 1843. The great weapon of the boycott, which has time and again achieved results where hotter spirits sought bloodshed, is an Irish tradition and its name comes directly from the land struggle of 1879-82. Francis Sheehy-Skeffington, the greatest advocate of pacifism and of women's rights in the Ireland before the Easter rising (in which, trying to avert the effects of slaughter he was murdered), was a socialist of such standing that the great James Connolly named him as his ideological heir. The men and women who struggled against violence and its use may have all too much relevance for Scotland in the future. If the cry "the oil is ours" is to be answered by bloodshed from the English, then no Scottish nationalist has the right to endanger his fellow-Scots or to lead them into temptation by advocating or employing the use of arms. But he has weapons of non-violent resistance at his disposal, and these, if necessary, we must be prepared to use. In doing so we will need to study the precedents of Christ and Ghandi, King and O'Connell, Parnell and Sheehy-Skeffington.

But if we study these men and their movements, we must beware of falling into one of the great traps into which Irishmen of all denominations have so regularly fallen—vulnerability to the personality cult. Time and again Irishmen and Irishwomen have elected to abdicate their reason and conscience before the force of a dynamic personality, whether O'Connell, Parnell, Carson or de Valera. In a sense it was understandable: popular unity in politics on a mass activist level began in Ireland with O'Connell's movement. But however much Ireland may have led the world in this respect to the extent that Macaulay could describe Daniel O'Connell as "the greatest popular leader the world has ever seen", its personality cult was but a stage on the road to true democracy. A sensible Communist may feel that the USSR could not have survived without Stalinism, but he cannot justify it on any other basis than as an ugly short-term necessity. Unfortunately, neither the personality cult in Ireland nor its Russian equivalent are showing much signs of losing force. There may be a dearth of personalities, but the machinery of such cults remains in existence. Scottish nationalism at the present moment is blessed with nominal leadership from such figures as the extraordinarily humble William Wolfe and the retiring Donald Stewart: they offer a pleasing contrast with the publicity-grabbing approach of the cult high priests of the other parties who substitute personality for policy. But this does not mean that Scottish nationalism can stand immune from this desease. Ireland exhibits it in virulent forms, as did Russia, because of the pioneer status of both countries in their different forms of political activity. But Right and Left are riddled with it. Paul Foot's **Politics of Harold Wilson** writes brilliantly on his subject's nauseous readiness to wrap the mantle of Nye Bevan round himself ("Nye as ever had a word for it: 'rubbish' ", and similar banalities). But not only is Wilson's cheap prostitution of Socialist idols evident here: his stress on the implicit desirability of a personality cult is evident. Personality cults are dangerous short cuts which inevitably reduce the thinking powers of their votaries. The fact that they also emerge from generosity and loyalty makes them all the more insidious.

Connolly and the Challenge

I have, I hope, made a case for a critical reading of Irish history by the Left on the issue of Scotland. I have to apologise for a twice-told tale for some, such as for John McGrath and the 7:84 group who have shown themselves well aware of the interaction of Scottish and Irish land struggles no less than their comparability. It is essential that such a reading divest itself of sentimentality and of censure and that it look for what is not there as well as for what is. In this connection one welcomes the present reflection on the history of Anglo-Irish constitutional relations which some SNP leaders are engaging in, but they would do well to remember that in reading, say, Desmond Williams's collection on 1916-26 **The Irish Struggle** they ought not to skip Patrick Lynch's essay in it "The Social Revolution that Never Was". If Scotland is to become truly independent, it is essential that there be no similar chapter-title in a future history of the victory of Scottish nationalism. Above all, they should read the Edinburgh-born James Connolly who brought to such a fine art the combination of socialist, syndicalist and nationalist theories and who has left us such rich writing on them. Connolly defended nationalism, but he never ceased till his death denouncing that nationalism which proposed to continue the exploitation of man by man under the green flag. Nor would he have liked it better under the Saltire. And Scotland, which first taught him what exploitation was, has as great a duty to listen to him as Ireland. The street of his birth, the Cowgate, mean, dark, harsh and rat-haunted runs today as it ran then below the proud drives and fashionable thoroughfares of North and South Bridges and George IV Bridge. The boy had the facts of the class system imposed before his gaze before he could even read. If we propose to continue the indifference to human suffering which drove his parents into those rat-holes and underground refuges, we may as well pack Scottish nationalism in. Nor is it enough to cite progress since Connolly's day. The divide between privilege and property is as vivid as ever, as every pup of a lecturer who gets called "sir" by far more hard-working office-cleaners should be able to tell us. And we may be about to learn how paper-thin that progress is, and how many of us will be left behind when its major beneficiaries save themselves.

As for the Left, the Connolly legacy is also very relevant. I have to appeal here to what I may call the Broad Left, by which I mean Socialists and Anarchists of independence of mind rather than of Pavolvian reaction. I am not attempting the hopeless task of appealing to, say, the **Workers' Press,** excellent and worthy of examination though it often is. Its discovery that the SNP controls the Scottish Communist Party and most of the Scottish Labour Party was certainly a beautiful thought ("McGahey, this is William Wolfe" ... "yes, comrade chairman" ... "I want the following orders carried out in double-quick time ... and now put Willy Ross on ... Ross, I want five more stupid decisions this week, you're falling behind on the job" ... mind you, there may be **something** in the Ross theory). But it is a little difficult to carry the debate much further. I think the basic discovery was of importance, viz. that Wolfe possesses a great admiration for Jimmy Reid and for the 7:84 show. But that simply indicates that Wolfe, and, one hopes, some of his colleagues, has a refreshing independence of mind, being more concerned by the quality of the ideas he discovers than the labels attached to them.

The basic message is that Scottish nationalism is the wave of future politics here. But it remains open to influence in certain vital ways. The Left can either avert its eyes, put a clothes-peg on its nostrils, retire to its pubs, congratulate itself on its ideological virginity and settle for doing sweet damn all apart from writing about occasional deviations and conspiracies, or the Left can come in and help to make this a truly Socialist party. If the Left will come inside, there is a world to be won. Allies await you, men and women of receptivity await you, you may find you are not the only respository of truth and wisdom and may learn something in return. You will have to settle for independence; there can be no ultimate arbiters in Transport House, Downing Street or Brussels (the SNP being a far more stern, unbending foe of the EEC than the quick-change artists of Downing Street). And in the world of the future, we would be wise to settle for decisions taken for smaller units. Even at its most Socialist, the Labour government never seems to have enough Socialism to go round. The supply runs out on the way to Scotland, as the teachers are discovering and as so many citizens of Glasgow learned. Moreover, as Socialists or nationalist outlook such as Keir Hardie, James Connolly and John Maclean well knew, Socialism is a thing to be taken seriously here, and not reduced to a permanent Punch and Wedgie show for the benefit of a Fleet Street which has forgotten what investigative journalism is in its fascination with name-calling and gossip.

The lesson of Connolly's life was a readiness to work out his own ideas, but to take them into the largest arena into which he could go without the sacrifice of his ideological integrity. In the end, he took the risk of seeing his Socialism sabotaged by the heirs of the nationalist allies he found. And this, too, is the risk Scottish Socialists take today in joining the SNP. But they will find, as Connolly found, the prospects for conversion and for self-education through ecumenical discussion are great. And if the Left will come in, with enough numbers, its views cannot be overwhelmed, or else politely discarded as Connolly's were. The decision is that of Scottish Socialists. It is a difficult one to make, especially for the student Left, often unable to cut the umbilical cord binding them to the centres of Left-wing student opinion in London or, to be frank, from all of those exciting people in Carnaby Street and Grosvenor Square. It will not, of course, be a cut off. But it does mean accepting a centre of emphasis in one's immediate neighbours, instead of in some far off vogue culture of exciting rhetoric and inchoate content. It means hard work and an acceptance of colleagues whose dialect may be nearer to one's own but whose cliches are different. It means emergence from a comfortable herd and a warm womb. Yet to ignore the opportunity, and to continue the present policy of no relations with Scottish nationalism, is to convict oneself not only of sloth but of cowardice. And it is not by such qualities that the giants of Socialism lived and died.

1. H.J. Hanham, **Scottish Nationalism** (London, 1968). Neil MacCormick, "Independence and Constitutional Change" and Iain S.M. MacCormick, "The Case for Independence", both in Neil MacCormick ed., **The Scottish Debate.** (London, 1970).
2. (London, 1964), p.10.
3. Holbrook Jackson, **The Eighteen Nineties** (London, 1913) on this as on so much else is extremely thoughtful and suggestive. I am at the moment engaged on a book whose working title is **The United States and the British Isles 1875-1935** and in which I hope to explore in depth the revolt of London's cultural provinces on a comparative basis.
4. Desmond Greaves's useful **Life and Times of James Connolly** (London, 1961), was the first work to establish Connolly's Scottish origin which is examined in detail in Bernard Ransom's dissertation "James Connolly and Scotland" to be presented for the Ph.D. degree in 1975.
5. I am clearly following Cruise O'Brien's views very closely in this article. For his controversy with Senator Mary Robinson, see the **Irish Times** for October 1974.

Poverty In Scotland

Ian Levitt

Today in Scotland there are over a million poor—even though we are generally better housed, clothed and fed than ever before. (1). What this means is that one person in four has not shared the new prosperity that has come in the last decade. (2). While most people assumed that the changing structure of Scottish industry had gone a long way to wiping out the inequality and poverty of the last fifty years, a new class of poor has been created—and because we have been blinded by outward manifestations of growth, the new poor have been ignored.

This is the paradox in the Scotland of the affluent society. In the late fifties, Scotland suffered from a chronically deteriorating employment situation and an endemic low wage structure. In the sixties Scotland's industrial base shifted from the traditional heavy to new technologically based industries (3). Moreover the general level of real wages increased and largely wiped out the Scotland/U.K. wage differential. The political and social repercussion of a new "middle income" class of Scotland has, as yet, not received the kind of attention from political and social scientists that one might expect. At the same time unemployment, the numbers with low pay, and those on supplementary benefit have all grown. I estimate that there are half a million people wholly or partly dependent upon supplementary benefit and another half a million people at or below the poverty line because of low pay. Another quarter of a million are in poverty because they are pensioners or unemployed not in supplementary benefits. Again the paradox-national economic growth linked with an increase in poverty.

The future can only be viewed with apprehension. Even with continued economic growth the scale of poverty will remain constant as long as the mechanism for distributing wealth and income remains the same. If we are to avoid a continuation of the present situation, then two related aspects of wealth, income, and welfare must be considered. Firstly there is the overall amount of wealth; secondly there is the method of its distribution. In many respects the second is now more important than the first; a solution to poverty is not found by merely increasing the total stock of wealth. So what we must have is an appreciation of the real distribution of wealth and how that distribution now causes poverty (4). For any method of distribution is not something which is "supra-rational", whose criteria for deciding the level of minimal help and the method involved has some inner inbuilt logic. Rather it is built around our own prejudices and moral assumptions about who should benefit and at what level. Thus, as the first section will show, there is a gigantic means tested system which seems capable of self-perpetuation beyond the purposes for which it was originally intended, and is capable of hiding behind its own self-made rules, regulations and pseudo-judicial morality. But this particular system results from a public unwillingness to come to terms with growing categories of poor persons (and in supplementary benefits this means the elderly, the long term unemployed and the single parent family in particular). A double bind therefore operates: the poor are defined as poor by virtue of public assistance—yet remain poor because we do not consider that they are worthy of greater assistance on a less punitive basis (5).

This paper will look at three dimensions of poverty—the supplementary benefits system, the unemployed and low pay and income distribution. These do not exhaust all the dimensions of poverty nor all who are poor. But any discussion of poverty in Scotland today must start somewhere—and these are three large and distinct areas (6). Where possible, purely Scottish evidence is used, but it is in the nature of much of the data that the more reliable and exhaustive material relates to Britain as a whole. The publication of regional and local data is becoming more of the norm but there are still some very large gaps which hinder accuracy. Some of the data presented here may seem provocative and lacking in complete accuracy. There is no apology for this: it is up to the relevant authorities to produce better, more reliable and exhaustive material.

The Supplementary Benefits System

When the present system of welfare (7) was introduced by the Labour government between 1945 and 1948 an archaic system of Poor Relief was swept away. (8) However rather than scrapping the means tested philosophy, which was based on the Poor Laws, the new "philosophy" of social insurance continued the means tested system. It was continued to act as a "safety net" for the so called "residual groups not covered by the insurance based welfare state. In 1948 these groups were thought to represent 3% of the U.K. population; today this picture has altered completely.

TABLE 1. No. of Means-Tested Social Security Payments 1947-72 (Scotland)
in thousands

	1947 P.L. & A.B.	1961 N.A.B.	1972 S.B.
Retired	40	108	184
Unemployed with National Insurance Benefit	8	8	16
Unemployed without National Insurance Benefit		28	57
Sick and Disabled with Nat. Ins. Benefit	18	18	15
Sick and Disabled without Nat. Ins. Benefit	15	19	19
Nat. Insurance Widows under 60	7	5	7
Other Women with Dependant Children	4	10	24
Others	-	2	2
	91	190	324

(Sources: Report of the Dept. of Health Scotland 1947) Report of the Assistance Board 1947. D.H.S.S. Social Security Stats. 1972. Scottish Abstract of Stats (1973).

Notes: P.L. = Poor Law; A.B. = Assistance Board; N.A.B. = National Assistance Board; S.B. = Supplementary Benefits, The 1947 data are the author's estimates, based on the D.H.S. and A.B. Those receiving "outdoor" Poor Law Medical Relief (about 6,000 mainly the elderly) and homeless children (about 7,000) have been excluded. The figures, of course, refer to a count on one particular day in their respective years. Consideration has to be given to "throughput"—the number of payments made in any one year.

What was once thought to be 3% has now grown to about 10% of the U.K. population. The biggest increase being amongst the retired, unemployed and women with dependent children. (In the case of women with children a flat rate benefit was considered by Beveridge, but eventually rejected (9). After all, how can you expect a man to plan for his family's breakdown!) The one time residuals are now, clearly, the new poor. In Scotland the National pattern has been followed, although always slightly ahead.

TABLE 2. Total number of Scots receiving Means Tested Social
Security Payments (recipients and dependants) 1947-1972

Year	(Thousands)	% of Population
1947	150	3.0
1961	268	5.2
1972	536	10.3

(Sources. As above)

Note: These figures, apart from the Poor Law 1947 figures are all estimated; The estimates being produced by taking the number of dependants to recipients in each group for the U.K. and multiplying the resultant figure with the corresponding Scottish total.

Table three shows the trend more clearly. From 1962 when compared with the rest of the U.K., the increase in the number of Social Security payments was dramatic.

TABLE 3. Increase in No. of Social Security Payments 1961-66-72
Scotland and in the U.K. (Index; 1961 = 100)

	1961		1966		1972	
	Scot	(U.K.)	Scot	(U.K.)	Scot	(U.K.)
All Payments	100	(100)	139	(132)	172	(158)
Retired (Supplementary Pensioners)	100	(100)	160	(140)	171	(147)
All other Supplementary Allowances	100	(100)	111	(121)	173	(182)
of which						
Unemployed with National Insurance						
Benefit	100	(100)	112	(171)	200	(208)
Unemployed without Nat. Ins. Benefit	100	(100)	110	(119)	285	(369)
Sick and Disabled with Nat. Ins.						
Benefit	100	(100)	111	(123)	83	(102)
Sick and Disabled without Nat. Ins. Ben.	100	(100)	100	(105)	111	(119)
National Insurance Widows under 60	100	(100)	140	(102)	140	(107)
Other Women with Dependant						
Children	100	(100)	132	(164)	240	(300)

(Sources: As Above)

Notes: Since the 1966 Social Security Act, the Supplementary Benefits Commission took over the functions of the National Assistance Board. 1961 is the earliest year of published regional statistics under the N.A.B. While the unemployment rate was low in 1961, it was much higher in 1972. As unemployment decreased in 1973, the unemployment groups in these tables will decline rapidly, particularly those with National Insurance Benefit. Consequently the number of Scots on S.B. at the end of 1973 will be fewer than in 1972.

In 1948 the National Assistance Board made, roughly, 8500,000 weekly payments to 'residuals'. At the end of 1953 the weekly payment had doubled to 1,760,000·by 1965 there was a gradual increase to two million. When the Supplementary Benefits Commission (SBC) replaced the NAB under the 1966 Social Security Act, the number of payments reached 2 million in 1966. In 1972 there were 3 million weekly payments by the SBC

	1961			1972		
	U.K.	Scot.	Scot/U.K.	U.K.	Scot	Scot/U.K.
ALL	100	100	10.3	100	100	11.1
Retired	70.2	56.8	8.3	65.2	56.5	9.7
Unemployed with N.I.B.	2.4	4.2	17.8	3.2	5.0	17.2
Unemployed without N.I.B.	4.7	10.5	23.0	10.8	17.5	18.0
Sick and Disabled with N.I.B.	7.3	9.5	13.4	4.7	4.6	11.0
Sick and Disabled without N.I.B.	7.3	10.0	14.0	5.5	6.1	12.4
N.I. Widows under 60	3.1	2.6	8.6	2.1	2.1	11.3
Other Women and Dependt. Child	4.1	5.3	13.2	7.8	7.4	10.6
Others	1.0	1.0	10.3	1	1	10.3

(Sources: As above)

From the Annual Reports of the NAB in the 1950's it can be deduced that the Scottish rise in assistance payments followed the general upward trend, but that the number of retired was considerably less than the U.K. average (due perhaps to higher mortality among the elderly), The unemployed was considerably greater (Table four—1961). As each economic recession in the 50's caused increasing industrial displacement and "technological" unemployment the experience of the older industrial regions was similar—more unemployment. In 1961, with 10% of the U.K. population, Scotland had a quarter of the long-term unemployed.

From tables three and four interesting trends can be seen for the 60's and early 70's. Overall the number of payments made rose faster in Scotland than in the U.K. and whereas in 1961 the number of payments made in Scotland would be about average for the U.K., in 1972 more payments being made in Scotland than would be expected given the population. Since the introduction of the S.B.C. in 1966, the largest rises in Scotland occurred in three groups, the retired, national insurance widows, and 'other women' In the U.K. the largest rises occurred, again in the retired and 'other women', but also in the unemployed with national insurance benefits. Whereas benefits to the retired in Scotland rose faster than in the U.K., the reverse was true of 'other women'.

Today the three groups receiving or eligible to receive supplementary benefits who should be causing most concern are the pensioners, the single parent families and the unemployed—either through the phenomenal increase in their numbers of claimants during the last decade or through their high absolute numbers. (Discussion of the long term unemployed follows in the next section). The remainder of this section examines some of the characteristics of the other two groups, pensioners and single parent families, and links them with the general nature of this means tested system.

About one in three of Scottish pensioners receive supplementary benefits. Supplementary Benefit payments to pensions accounted in 1972 for 56.5% of all supplementary benefit payments. Social security payments to pensioners in Scotland actually increased by 71% between 1961 and 1972, but the rise was most dramatic—60% between 1961 and 1966, the year when Supplementary Benefits were first introduced and claimed. One writer has claimed that between a half and two thirds of the increase of the retired group after the introduction of the S.B.C. was due solely to changes in the scale rates (10). If this is so, then in Scotland, many retired persons must have been living just above the previous "official" definition of poverty. An official survey conducted prior to the ending of the N.A.B., found fewer elderly Scots entitled to assistance, and of those entitled proportionately fewer applied (11). The official survey concluded with three main reasons for non-application in the United Kingdom. One, many people did not think that they were entitled. Two, others thought the amount to which they were entitled was too small to bother about. Three, some disliked the red tape and petty officials.

Two studies in 1972 carried out in Coventry reached similar conclusions; they stressed how disadvantaged the elderly were in understanding the rules, regulations and discretionary nature of the payments, particularly where exceptional needs payments could be given (12).

The problem of women with dependent children on Social Security was, of course, the major consideration of the recently published 'Finer Committee on One-Parent Families'. There are in the region of 55,000 mothers with dependent children in Scotland who claim supplementary benefit. This amounted in 1972 to over 7% of recipients of benefit. The following tables show some of the characteristics of the group.

TABLE 5. Fatherless Families receiving supplementary benefits in the U.K. and Scotland at the end of 1972

	Single	Widowed	Divorced	Prisoner's Wife	Separated	Total
U.K. %	25	10	18	2	44	252,000
Scotland %	20	11	17	3	48	28,000

(Source: The Finer Report 1974)

TABLE 6. Fatherless families receiving supplementary benefits in Dundee 1972

	Single	Widowed	Divorced	Legally Separated	Estranged	Total
Dundee %	14.5	11	24.5	9	40	143

(Source: A Hunt, Families & Their Needs O.P.C.S. SSD 1973)

Note: Dundee was one of five U.K. areas chosen for this social survey. The legally separated and estranged groups are estimates based on information from the survey. The survey showed Dundee had twice as many 'estranged' as the other areas, and correspondingly less legally separated, apart from one English rural area.

Table 5 shows fewer single and more separated fatherless families in Scotland. These figures may not be statistically significant because some other U.K. regions show a similar pattern, particularly the north-west. There are about 500,000 children in this U.K. group, 55,000 of them are in Scotland. Evidence to the Finer Committee by the S.B.C. indicates that the majority of these families have been on benefit for a considerable length of time. 10%, at the end of 1972 had been on for less than 2 months. 50% for more than 1 year and 10% for more than 7 years. Apart from the prisoner's wife group, time on benefit did not vary greatly between groups.

The material and financial circumstances of fatherless families has now been the subject of a number of enquiries (13). The basic conclusion from all of them is similar: that the group is placed towards the lower end of the income scale, but that the position of those on supplementary benefit does not differ markedly from two-parent families on benefit. The group which suffers least are the widows because they have other state insurance which bolster their income (and no earning rules are attached to them whereby benefit is reduced). But fatherless families tend to be on benefit for a longer period and their resources are often at a lower level. In consequence, they are more liable to require exceptional needs payments (covering the costs of bedding, clothes, etc.). The following table shows the various sources of weekly income for those in the Dundee survey.

It is clear that the lack of a reasonable weekly wage is the most important factor in causing these mothers to be in poverty. The younger the children are, and the larger the family, increases the inability to find cheap or free child day-care, and the low level of part-time earnings, disregarded by the S.B.C., prevent many of them from working. The authors of the Dundee survey also considered that fewer of these mothers worked by choice, but that most regarded it as essential in maintaining their independence.

321

TABLE 7. % of Fatherless Families in Dundee in Receipt of Various Sources
of Income

	Separated	Divorced	Widowed	Single	All
Wages	38	46	50	58	46
Insurance Benefits etc.	1	-	99	4	23
Supplementary Benefits	73	56	26	45	51
Maintenance Payments	55	51	3	20	36
From children	12	16	19	7	14

(Source: As above)

Much attention of the Finer Report is devoted to family law. While public welfare law is common to both England and Scotland, family law is different. The Report states that "... in the course of our enquiries we have come to suspect that in Scotland, as in England, the general law as it effects one-parent families is capable of much improvement (14). This is emphasised by the evidence from table 5 which shows that about half of the Scots fatherless families receiving benefit were families where husband and wife are separated. In Dundee nearly four fifths of this group do not have a legal separation order. The reasons for this have been attributed to the difficulties in obtaining separation orders in Scotland, an unwillingness of aggrieved parties to have anything more to do with their partners, and common law marriages (thereby avoiding the necessity of divorce and separation courts) (15). In the Dundee survey the average maintenance/payment, either voluntary or through a court order, was about a quarter of the average supplementary benefit payment. Such a low payment reflects the inability of one man to support, as is often the case, two families.

The system of insuring that maintenance payments are actually made is again different in Scotland. In Scotland, it is a private system, usually through one's own solicitor. The Supplementary Benefits Commission in Scotland pursues far more "liable relatives" (husbands, fathers) through the criminal courts to ensure payment than in England. This, they concede in evidence to Finer, is due more to the unsatisfactory nature of the court procedures, than a simple desire on their parts to prosecute (16). It is a sad reflection on Scots law.

The unsatisfactory legal situation, the inability of a working man to support two families, and of the lone mother with young children to work, the rules and regulations of the S.B.C., the employment and housing discrimination against women, the lack of child-care facilities, the general lower financial position of the single parent and the expected increase in the numbers of single-parent families due to increased marital breakdown led Finer to a number of conclusions. Firstly Finer wished a new family court to be established, with both cheaper and easier access. Secondly, all one-parent families, as soon as reasonable proof is ascertainable of one-parentness, should be given a Guaranteed Maintenance Allowance, though an "administrative order" of the S.B.C. would then have the responsibility of assessing and collecting maintenance payments, where appropriate, from a liable relative. Other welfare rules, like disregarded income and the cohabitation rule, would either be amended or abolished to substantially improve the financial position of these families. Although they liken their G.M.A. to the proposed tax-credit scheme, they state that if this does not materialise, then family allowances ought to be improved, or Family Income Supplements amended to incorporate non-working one-parent families, or the G.M.A. rate raised to their designated new minimum support level above the current Supplementary Benefits scale rates. They also recommend improvements in the housing and employment position of women (such as right of tenure) and child-care facilities.

However, it should be stressed that with the exception of the child's allowance portion of G.M.A., this new benefit is still means-tested, albeit on a different and substantially improved scale.

Finer concedes that the S.B.C. would continue to have a role to play in the income—maintenance of the single-parent families, particularly when the family splits, or when there is acute financial hardship. Moreover, although it is suggested that the application of the cohabitation rule be eased, there would still be cases, particularly where two unmarried persons were cohabiting prior to the family break down, when immediate benefit could be withdrawn.

The S.B.C. has not put many of Finer's recommendations into practice, and they appear to be attempting to offload those whose benefits are stopped or refused to the Social Work Departments (17). It also seems that, whatever present practice, in the past, the S.B.C.'s officers have made the situation of the single parent whose benefit was stopped or refused, worse than under the Poor Law. Under the Poor Law in Scotland any claimant whose benefit was cut off, could apply to the Sheriff for an interim relief order. This was guaranteed under the 1845 Act and gave the poor a legal right to relief.

> "When an applicant is refused relief he may apply to the sheriff, who after hearing his statement may either confirm the refusal or order the Inspector of the Poor to grant interim relief and instruct him to lodge within a specific time a detailed statement in writing of his reason for refusal. After the statement has been lodged, the case proceeds as an ordinary action at law... the applicant... continuing... to receive interim relief until final judgment is pronounced. If the Inspector of the Poor does not lodge the statement as directed, judgment is given against him by default, and the poor person becomes entitled to permanent relief. It should be observed that the Sheriff can only decide the question of whether the applicant has a legal right to be relieved. It is for the parish council to determine what shall be the amount of relief. (18)

However, the claimant could appeal to the Central Scottish Poor Law Authority on this matter. (19)

Today it can take weeks before an appeal is heard (20). Supplementary Benefits Tribunals are not courts of law and have few legally trained members. Each case is heard in private and supposedly on its merits without reference to any other case. This system, which in reality emphasises the discretion of the supplementary benefits system, has come under increasing attack, not only for its treatment of those unlucky single parent families forced to appeal, but also for its treatment of all the other applicants (21). Yet the critics' schemes for reform seem to have little in common. Some wish to establish social courts with easier access for the appellant but operating on a more informal basis than traditional courts and offering a legal framework based on principle and precedent. Others seek to have better trained members of tribunals with the tribunals more independent of the general administration of Supplementary Benefits and a second tier appeal system (22).

Indeed one thing that can be said about social policy at the moment is that there is little consensus as to what its direction should be. Although the Labour Government set up the Finer Committee in 1969, the new Labour Government, in receiving the report, accepted the need for increased aid but greeted its financial recommendations with caution. But the Finer Report itself, while apparently radical, in fact falls short of a total non-means tested benefit system for the single parent family. The history of such provision from 1911 onwards, emphasised in today's trends, is that the use of a discretionary payments system increases with the failure to extend universal welfare provision.

What is needed now is decision on how to overcome this chaotic system of means tested benefits, which has continued to grow both in numbers and in scope (23). The failure is only partly the failure of governments: the blame lies in a society which has refused over the past two decades, to recognise that increasing material affluence leaves in its tracks a destructive path of poverty. It is clear that the means test will remain politically acceptable into the foreseeable future, for neither Conservative, Liberal, Labour nor SNP in Scotland and in Britain have promised an end to it.

A resolution of this problem involves a total strategy for removing inequalities in society and attacking wealth and power. In the meantime however there is a crying need to ensure that the intention of the 1966 Social Security Act of "benefit as a right" is established in reality and not in bureaucratic fiction. The establishment of a legal right, and in Scotland this might be achieved by re-establishing the Sheriff's interim relief order (or by a modified scheme based on it) should be the first step.

There are inherent dangers to a democratic state which allows growing numbers of its citizens to apply for relief of need on a discretionary, and some would say punitive system of relief. The obstacle to reform in the fifties and sixties was partly the widespread belief in the infallibility of the general provisions of the Welfare State, and partly the very nature of the welfare provision it entailed. Poverty was only considered to exist at the margins and social policy was directed to supplementation of welfare provision (such as graduated pensions). The dawning of the seventies has revealed the truth that like the Poor Law before it, our own present system of supplementary benefits has created its own category of poverty, its own poor. Once this becomes central to our social and political thinking, then like the Poor Law, its days will be numbered.

Unemployment

The reasons for Scotland's high rate of unemployment are too well rehearsed to be detailed here. Yet it is by no means obvious to all that the unemployed are poor. Many assume that redundancy and earnings related payments ensure that the unemployed are well catered for in our welfare state. This is by no means the case. The restrictions on the eligibility for these payments and their ultimate exhaustion over time for those unlucky enough not to be re-employed means that for a large number the only reliable state support is flat rate insurance benefit and supplementary benefit either to supplement or to replace insurance benefit when it runs out. The rise in the numbers being supplemented and the numbers without insurance benefit can be seen from tables 1, 3, and 4 in the last section. Whereas the intention of national assistance at the beginning of the welfare state was to cater for the few (residual) unemployed, it now caters for all but the few. We have had an inversion of rates as between insurance and supplementary benefits. In this section, attention will be primarily focused on that aspect of unemployment giving considerable concern, the rising numbers of long-term unemployed. Long term unemployment is usually defined as being unemployed for over a year. Obviously many of those out of work for less than one year will have low levels of resources to meet their basic needs, and the large numbers having to supplement their unemployment benefit by supplementary benefit has been noted in the last section.

The Department of Employment, in their 1973 report on the characteristics of the unemployed, noted, as expected, that long term unemployment was primarily linked to age, previous occupation and general ill-health (24). The likelihood of long term unemployment increased with age, but in Scotland's case, as we shall see below, Scotland has a high percentage of young persons unemployed than the U.K. as a whole. Table 8 shows both the occupational and regional bias of unemployment.

TABLE 8. The Occupations of the Male Unemployed,
as % of Total Regional Male Unemployment, June 1974

	General Labourers	Clerical Workers	Total	Unemploy-ment Rate
Scotland	58%	6%	(63,000)	3.9
North of England	59%	6%	(44,000)	4.4
South-East England	32%	17%	(88,000)	1.5
U.K.	48%	11%	(453,000)	2.5

Source: Department of Employment Gazette, July August 1974

From the D.E. survey it can be seen that labourers who are the largest single group of unemployed tend to have poorer prospects and be out of work longest. Clerical workers however tend to be older and less likely to be re-employed. On a follow up survey, the group reckoned to have at least reasonable prospects of jobs were more likely to have found employment or be in employment. But in all cases the limiting factor was not employability but opportunities, with the result that Scots who had poorer prospects were far more likely to remain out of work than their comparable U.K. groups. The present situation can best be summed up by the Department of Employment's own Gazette which stated that, "whilst duration rose and fell with changes in the business cycle, there has been an underlying upward trend since the late fifties in the duration of unemployment, with higher percentages of persons experiencing longer duration spells... (the data) shows that males experience longer duration of unemployment than females and duration increases with age" (25). But while the duration of unemployment increases with age, it is also worrying that for those under twenty, the rate of increase has been twice as fast (26). Taking occupations, the rate of increase in duration of unemployment has been fastest among the skilled, and while the "older" regions of the U.K. had more than their fair share of long-term unemployment in the 1950's, by the late 1960's the differential between regions was narrowing.

In highlighting what has been said above in the Scottish context, Tables 9(1), 9(2), 9(3), show that at any one time about one third of the Scots unemployed have been out of work for more than a year and although unemployment has doubled between 1961 and 1973, the long-term unemployment rate has increased faster. The rate of increase of long term unemployment among the two younger age groups is in excess of the older age groups itself above that for all the unemployed. From 1961 to 1973 it has more than doubled. The number of those up to nineteen who were unemployed for more than one year has risen from 2700 in 1961 to 10,190 in 1973.

TABLE 9(1) Duration of Male Unemployment; by Region (%)
June 1973

	Unemployed up to 4 weeks	Unemployed over 52 weeks
Scotland	19.4	33.5
North of England	14.9	37.9
South-East England	24.9	21.3
U.K.	19.6	30.9

Source: Department of Employment Gazette, June 1974

TABLE 9 (2) Scottish Male Unemployment 1961-73, by Age

	up to 19	20-34	35-49	50-65	Total
June 1961	2,700	11,400	11,200	13,400	38,800
July 1973	10,100	24,500	19,100	22,600	76,400

Source: Scottish Abstract of Statistics, No. 2 1972 and No. 3, 1974

TABLE 9(3) Nos. and Rise in Scottish Long-Term Unemployment
1961-73, by Age (1961 = 100)

	up to 19	20-34	34-49	50-65	Total
Unemployed over 52 weeks at July '73 (with inc. over 1961 in brackets)	600(600)	4,600(307)	7,300(232)	11,500(211)	24,000(238)
Total Unemployed at July '73	10,100(370)	24,500(215)	19,100(171)	22,600(167)	76,400(197)

Source: as above

Generally, therefore, Scotland has more unemployment, more long-term unemployment, more unskilled unemployment and more young unemployment relative to the U.K. as a whole, and in the long-run unemployment appears to be rising. Both the welfare institutions and the social policy we have to mitigate the effects of unemployment are increasingly inadequate. The Department of Employment Survey previously mentioned shows that in Scotland only 36% of the unemployed were actually receiving unemployment insurance benefit. 50% were receiving supplementary benefits (and this figure is increased to 60% if unemployment benefit supplementation cases are added). It is a nonsensical situation where "the safety net" caters for more than the supposedly main statutory unemployment benefit. Yet the public view (and indeed political) view of most of the unemployed on supplementary benefits is that they are scroungers or "work-shy" who deserve all the social security harassment and stigma that can be offered. To classify half the Scots unemployed in this way is nothing short of ludicrous. Even the Fisher Committee on Social Security Abuse, set up under the last Conservative Government, found it hard to quantify "scroungers" beyond a miniscule few per cent of all those receiving benefit. What Fisher didn't do, though, was to examine the problem from the other way round and look at the abuse of claimants by the system.

Despite reforms there is little indication that serious attempts will be made to destroy the prejudices which have developed. Job centres and extended re-training schemes while being welcomed by a particular sector of the unemployed will largely help only those most likely to find employment. At the same time, the implication is that available resources will be shifted away from the long term, hard core. (27) Certain alternatives have been suggested. Sir Keith Joseph who has something of a following for his proposals would like to see the hard core treated on a case-work basis (28). While the SNP, in their War on Poverty programme want to step up the retraining programmes and have more sheltered work-shops. These, and similar proposals, besides smacking of a return to the Indoor Relief of the Poor Laws, cannot work because on the one hand they do not attack the roots of unemployment but the symptoms, and on the other because in the case of re-training, to be serious about it in terms of Scotland would mean establishing three units with places for ten thousand persons in each.

If we wish to find the roots of long term unemployment we must look at the educational system and the employment structure. 55% of young people now leave school without qualifications. Without skills, or the access to employment which can provide such skills, the possibility of eventual unemployment on a long term is obvious. What is required is not re-training when unemployed but continual education or training of workers to prevent them from reaching this status. Only when it is realised that there must be a radical extension of education beyond school can the rapidly growing problem of unemployment be seriously tackled.(29)

In any human society unemployment can only be seen as the malfunctioning of the economic system, and any such system which relegates the basic right to work to the alleged "needs" of an omnipotent economy will result in social callousness towards unemployment provision. To correct this situation two fundamental steps are needed: one, better more humane treatment for unemployment; two, overcoming our present callousness to unemployment by understanding not just the fluctuations of the economy from time to time but the long run creation of unemployment in our economy and society. That requires a fundamental redistribution of power in our society.

Low Pay

Some people consider it axiomatic that Scots are low paid. While it is true to say that incomes in Scotland are, as a whole, lower than in England, it should not be forgotten that the distribution of incomes within Scotland is vitally important in determining who shall be really low paid and who shall not. Therefore any discussion of low pay must start with the distribution and structure of incomes; for it is that which determines the crucial element of pay differentials. Age, sex, occupational and regional differences all play a part in determining this distribution and structure. As Scotland is not an industrially homogeneous country quite wide divergences of regional incomes can be expected, and by beginning with regional aspects some overall nature of Scottish incomes can be grasped.

The table produced here correlates three aspects of regional differences; average incomes, the distribution of incomes and an index of income inequality.

Thus acute inter-regional differences are observable along these three statistical measures, with Ayr and Argyll at opposing ends of the inequality index and average incomes. But while the distributions of incomes in the middle range is comparatively small in Ayr, it is correspondingly large in Renfrew. It can also be seen that the upper decile incomes in Dumfries, Dumbarton, Lanark, Midlothian, Renfrew and Stirling exceed the comparable Scottish deciles, and match, if not exceed the comparable U.K. deciles. In comparison, lower decile incomes in Aberdeen, etc.,

Angus, Argyll, Caithness, etc., Fife and Midlothian are comparatively worse than both Scottish and U.K. lower decile incomes.

TABLE 10: The Distribution of Incomes and Income Inequality
within Scotland by Region 1970-71

Deciles	1	2	3	4	5	6	7	8	9	Gini Coeffi-cient
				Yearly income in £s						
U.K.	607	779	963	1140	1327	1529	1760	2069	2709	.336
Scotland	591	711	917	1084	1270	1481	1708	1978	2641	.334
Aberdeen, Banff, Moray & Nairn	566	717	890	1006	1240	1423	1624	1896	2726	.354
Angus & Kincardine	616	691	880	1016	1121	1293	1621	1913	2595	.348
Argyll & Bute	464	540	703	905	964	1068	1257	1486	2033	.394
Ayr	696	1007	1394	1535	1583	1583	1531	1680	1728	.216
Caithness, Inverness, Orkney Sutherland Zetland Ross & Cromarty	583	684	825	936	1075	1259	1426	1691	2043	.328
Clackmannan & Kinross	708	798	1083	1246	1336	1426	1524	1658	1879	.252
Dumfries, Kirkcudbright & Wigton	591	715	917	997	1373	1563	1713	2059	2767	.363
Dumbarton	685	838	1068	1225	1449	1659	1931	2343	2780	.310
Fife	567	705	852	1034	1168	1369	1581	1810	2445	.316
Lanark	597	754	937	1103	1283	1512	1771	2007	2623	.329
Midlothian	578	704	850	1042	1276	1500	1713	2903	2768	.357
Perth	629	791	939	1149	1301	1427	1597	1886	2591	.341
Renfrew	710	830	1023	1228	1440	1725	1983	2391	2811	.329
Stirling	613	935	1132	1352	1550	1700	1858	2072	2678	.302
West Lothian	549	832	963	1097	1262	1478	1627	1786	2193	.276
Berwick, East Lothian, Peebles, Roxburgh & Selkirk	604	737	975	1047	1216	1377	1551	1784	2400	.328

Source: Inland Revenue, "Survey of Personal Incomes 1970-71" (1973) Regional table. pp. 122-123

Notes: Figures subject to high sampling error. The data are based on the source table above, as published. Statistical terms: Decile—a positional measure of data analysis. Thus the first decile can be interpreted as 10% of cases lying below this point and 90% above. The second decile as 20% below and 80% above, and so on. The fifth decile is the median, which is used as the average in income analysis. The Gini Co-efficient is a statistical measure of income inequality. A value of 1 means absolute inequality. The closer the value is to 0, the greater the amount of income equality, i.e. there are few people with very large and very small incomes (30). (The author wishes to acknowledge the assistance of C. L. Jones and T. W. Jones (Dept. of Sociology, Edinburgh University) in the computation of this table).

But note should also be taken of inter-regional differences. Aberdeen, etc.. Dumfries, etc., and Midlothian, all have higher upper deciles (in real terms) and their gini co-efficients are comparatively large, indicating greater degrees of income inequality in these counties. Although Argyll has the highest gini co-efficient, its upper decile incomes are low in real terms, indicating, of course, that real incomes through the distribution are very low.

The next unit of analysis is age. From tables produced by the D.H.S.S. it is possible to break down earnings into age groups and sex (31). In 1970/71 the D.H.S.S. data shows an average of £1,547 for males and £790 for females (both figures relate to those who have been in continuous employment for at least a year), so some general comparison with the Inland Revenue data is possible.

The D.H.S.S. produced two sets of statistics from their source data; one includes those who have been, or are in employment, but have had, or are having spells of illness or unemployment, in the last employment year, the other excludes these groups. Consequently, although the data used here are of the latter set, it must be remembered that it will favour Scotland because unemployment affect-proportionately more wage-earners here. The first set of statistics show that from 1964/65 to 1971/72 that Scottish male average income rose 77% as compared with 72% for Great Britain. This compares with the second set which shows figures of 81.5% and 74%. The following tables relate to this second set.

TABLE 11 Scottish Male Average Annual Earnings as % of Great Britain
by Age Group, 1971/72—1964/65

All	18-19	20-24	25-29	30-34	35-39	40-44	45-49	50-54	55-59	60-64
1971/72										
94.5	95.0	96.0	96.5	97.0	95.5	93.0	92.0	95.0	95.0	95.5
1964/65										
90.5	93.5	93.5	93.0	90.0	92.0	89.5	90.5	91.5	92.5	85.5

Source: Scottish Abstract of Statistics No. 3 1973.

TABLE 12 % Increase in Male Average Annual Earnings by Age Group
Scotland and the U.K. 1964/65 to 1971/72

	18-19	20-24	25-29	30-34	35-39	40-44	45-49	50-54	55-59
Scotland	72.5	80.0	85.0	92.0	83.0	83.0	75.5	80.5	79.5
Gt. Brit.	69.5	75.5	76.5	78.5	77.0	76.5	72.0	75.0	70.0

	60-65	All
	90.0	81.5
	70.5	74.0

Source: as above

TABLE 13 Age Group Average Annual Earnings as % of the Scottish
and Britain Average, 1971/72

	18-19	20-24	25-29	30-34	35-39	40-44	45-49	50-54	55-59
Scotland	52.0	79.0	98.0	109.0	112.0	110.0	106.5	109.0	102.0
Gt. Brit.	51.5	77.5	96.0	106.0	111.0	111.5	109.5	109.0	101.5

	60-64
	93.0
	92.0

Source: As above

Table 11 shows each Scottish age group as a percentage of the comparable Great Britain group and it can be seen that the age groups 20-34 are nearest to their British averages, while the age groups 40-49 are the furthest behind their averages. In Table 12, only the under 20's in Scotland failed to increase as fast or faster than the overall British average. In fact, large increases were recorded for 25-34 and 60-64 age groups, well surpassing their corresponding British age group increases. Table 13 shows the distribution within Scotland, with age groups 30-59 having earnings above the average and age groups 18-29 and 60-64 below the average.

In conclusion, although average earnings have risen faster in Scotland than in Britain, and the earnings differential has narrowed, there has been a marked variation in the distribution of this increase between age groups. By and large, the best earnings performance has occurred amongst the young to middle-aged earner (25-44) and the high average earnings are associated with the middle band of earners (30-54). Correspondingly the incidence of lower pay can be linked partly to age, with both the young and old worker being the most affected.

The same data source also provides information on female and regional earnings. Unfortunately the sub-samples in both are rather small to be statistically acceptable, but if we are prepared to examine them the Falkirk/Stirling region shows an above average increase (89.5%), while the Tayside and Edinburgh regions show a below average increase (67% and 62%).

Average female earnings rose by 75% in Scotland as compared with 71.5% for Great Britain, so that the Scottish/G.B. differential moved from 96.5% to 98%. But this increase was largely due to married women whose average earnings rose by 81.5% as compared with 73.5% for Great Britain, cutting the differential from 94% to 98.5%. Again, "speculatively", the figures show a similar age pattern to Scots males.

Sex also plays an important part in the distribution of earnings, and the differential in average earnings has already been given. But there is a problem. At least half of women who work, only work part-time, compared to under 10% for men. Although Equal Pay legislation is having a beneficial effect in reducing discrimination, many women do not work in "comparable" occupations (32). Nevertheless for those in full-time work, according to the New Earnings Survey in 1973, over 90% of women in Scotland earned less than the male average wage of £36 a week. Moreover 75% of women earned less than the bottom 10% (the lowest decile) of male earners, often taken as the boundary of low pay (33). In April 1973 there were roughly 100,000 adult male and 450,000 adult female Scots earning less than this weekly wage of £23.70.

The New Earnings Survey was instituted in 1968, and apart from 1969, has been conducted every year by the Department of Employment. From the mass of published tables it is possible to construct certain information on pay, and more particularly, low pay in Scotland. The following tables summarise some of this information.

TABLE 14: Scottish Average Earnings, as % of G.B. Average
April 1973

	(% increase of differential from 1968)	1973
Male Manual Glasgow Region 104%	(0%)	£37.7
Falkirk/Stirling 103%	(-4%)	£37.2
Edinburgh Region 97%	(-2%)	£35.1
Tayside Region 90%	(+6%)	£32.1
Border Region 87%	(+2%)	£31.4
South-West Region 94%	(+8%)	£33.8
North East Region 97%	(+4%)	£34.9
Highland Region 95%	(+6%)	£34.4
Scotland Region 98%	(+2%)	£36.1
Male Non-Manual Scotland Region 96%	(0%)	£46.6
Female Manual, Scotland 100%	(+7%)	£19.0
Female Non-Manual, Scotland 93%	(-5%)	£23.5

Source: N.E.S. 1968, 1973 (Regional Tables)

TABLE 15 Scottish Lowest Decile Earnings September 1968 and
April 1973

		% of G.B. Average	G.B.L/D
1968 Male Manual	£14.3	64%	£15.1
Male Non-Manual	£16.3	59%	£17.0
Female Manual	£7.6	70%	£7.7
Female Non-Manual	£9.1	65%	£9.3
1973 Male Manual	£23.7	65%	£24.4
Male Non-Manual	£25.3	59%	£26.4
Female Manual	£12.9	68%	£13.1
Female Non-Manual	£13.9	62%	£14.6

Source: as above

Note: These tables refer to men in full time employment over 21 and women over 18.

Table 14 emphasises the regional differences in Scotland of manual men. But it is interesting to note the reversal of female average earnings, with manual women matching the British female manual earnings and non-manual falling behind sharply. The latter is almost certainly due to faster increases in middle range earnings in the South-East of England. Table 15 indicates that for low paid men, no real gain has been made. Manual women, who are low paid do not appear to have gained anything unlike the middle range earners. In fact there has been a small deterioration. For non-manual women, who are low paid, they too appear to have suffered, although not to the same extent, from faster increases elsewhere in Britain.

Generally in the last few years, despite marginal yearly movements, the low paid have remained low paid and their earnings are roughly about one-third or less below average earnings.

The N.E.S. is, of course, conducted at one period in time. But from N.E.S. data gathered over the past few years the Department of Employment has been able to analyse movements by individual workers in and out of these low pay margins (34). Whereas non-manual male workers show little fluctuation in earnings, manual male workers show quite marked fluctuations, indicating that for many workers the threat of low earnings sometime over a short period is a living reality. Even so over 8% of manual workers were shown to be continually low paid.

One of the problems in considering low pay is that there is a six-way split of groups of low earners—adult male/female, juvenile male/female and part-time male/female. Unfortunately most of the data which is available concerns full-time wage earners, but previous tables in this section show that considerable numbers of low wage earners can be found amongst women and the young. The usual explanation is that the young can't expect to earn great amounts as they are at the beginning of their "career", and for women, particularly part-time women, their income is secondary to the family income, and consequently less important for "poverty" (35). Yet this hides the fact that for many young people their first job is not the first step on the ladder of their career, but is the first dead-end job of an intermittent series of low paid jobs in their working life. The section on Supplementary Benefits has shown the increasing number of single-parent families, most of whom are women, and the importance of wage especially if it is part-time, is only too great. More attention in official circles is needed to collect and then analyse movements in these groups earnings for it will be shown below, not only are these groups among the lowest earners but the wage differences between them and the others may be growing.

From all the data that is available it is possible to say that in Scotland over half of low paid adult men can be found in four industries, Distributive Trades, Miscellaneous Services, Construction and Public Administration. But half of low paid women are in just two industries, Distribution and Miscellaneous Services (catering, laundry, pubs, etc.). The N.E.S. also shows that about 20% of male manual workers in local Government are low paid, that nearly 40% of Agricultural workers are low paid, that about 20% of Government Clerical workers are low paid, and that about 25% of male nurses are low paid. Recent C.I.R. reports have shown that over 40% of adult males are low paid in the Retail Trade (covered by Wages Councils) and that substantial packets of low pay can be found in Licensed Non-Residential Establishments (pubs) and the Clothing Trade (36).

By amalgamating all this information together it is possible to construct the following table of low paid.

TABLE 16 Nos. of Adult Men Low Paid in Scotland

Retail and Wholesale Distribution	15,000
Agriculture	15,000
Construction	7,000
Pubs, Catering, etc.	6,000
Local Government	5,000
Clerical Workers, National Government	4,000
Food Industry	3,000
Post Office	3,000
National Health Service	2,000
Manual Workers, National Government	1,000
Railways	1,000
Clothing Industry	1,000

Total 90,000—100,000

Source: N.E.S. Surveys, C.I.R. Reports 56, 77, 89, 1966
Sample Census, Abstract of Scottish Statistics 1973.

This table, of course, refers to those earning below the male lowest decile earnings, yet in all of these occupations substantial numbers can be found just above this line.

As previously mentioned there have recently been reports on three areas of low pay, pubs, the Retail Trade and the Clothing Trade. All are covered by Wages Councils, and are illustrative of the magnitude of the low pay problem. Low earnings in them, are endemic, and compounded by large numbers of women, part-timers and juvenile workers. The earnings of those in pubs are of the lowest in any industry and it is no compensation that rates of pay in Scotland are marginally higher than in England. Scottish earnings in the other two industries are roughly comparable to Provincial English wages. But it is notable that in all three full-time adult males do better than all other groups. Moreover in Scotland this differential is greater than in England. Women, part-timers and juveniles all have very large numbers of vulnerable minorities whose basic rates come very close to their Wages Councils Statutory Minimum Rates. For those in the Retail Trade the earnings differential between them and others has been increasing, that is, over the last few years their earnings have not risen as fast as other workers. What is perhaps more disturbing is that in the Retail Trade covered by the separate Scottish Wages Councils (Bread, Flour, Confectionary, Food and Newsagents) there is a higher percentage of low paid workers than in the other all-British Wage Councils. Again it is no compensation to know that the same is true for the comparable English only Wages Councils.

The C.I.R. reports makes startling reading. The following quotation from their Retail Trade report sums up the general situation—"... wages councils settlements are unquestionably of relevance to the earnings of large numbers of retail employees but the machinery for enforcing and publicising the settlements is not working satisfactorily" (37). With large numbers of women, part-timers and juveniles working, these Wages Councils industries are not really conducive to Trade Unionism. Although Trade Unionism is higher amongst Scottish Retail workers, it is still only about 15%. The C.I.R. stress the need for the development of voluntary collective bargaining through a greater degree of trade unionism. But they also suggest that employers organisations should be better organised and cover more employers. No doubt this suggestion is due to poor membership amongst employer's organisation and can be partly reflected in the ludicrous situation in one separate Scottish Clothing Wages Council where a very small and unrepresentative minority of employers have twice sought (unsuccessfully) in recent years to reduce their employees wages. C.I.R. also propose amalgamating some Wages Councils and generally streamlining the whole system, including better notification of statutory minimum rates amongst employees.

The whole subject of Wages Councils and low pay is at the moment the subject of a general Government review, but over the past few years various groups have suggested the need for minimum wage legislation. It is interesting to note that these groups, for instance the Liberals and Scottish Nationalist Party, tend to seek a weekly minimum wage. There is evidence to suggest that without further controls on the employment of workers in low paid industries, such legislation would not necessarily mean in increase in the wage level for all these workers. One of the Retail Trade studies previously mentioned has indicated that employers use their hiring flexibility to reduce total wage costs. More youngesters are employed at base minimum rates. Part-time workers (usually women and week-enders), are also paid at minimum hourly rates. This means a reduction usually in full-time men. At the moment half the men working in this industry are under 20. This suggests unless legislation covers hourly rates of pay and concomitant conditions of employment, wage legislation in a period of rising labour costs could be counter productive and produce more unemployment amongst adult men.

The history of minimum wage legislation, via Wages Councils, has shown that it is no substitute for free voluntary collective bargaining. For the low paid worker, better legislative provision can only be half the answer. The C.I.R. reports indicates that employer hostility to trade unionism and voluntary collective bargaining is reducing. So much the better, for so long as the Scottish low paid worker remains unorganised no amount of Government regulation of wage levels can substitute for the day to day organisation at the shop-floor level. Only when this occurs can greater control over working and wage conditions be exercised by the workers.

Over the last decade Scottish earnings have increased to reduce the U.K./Scottish wage differential. It is obvious, though, that this increase has not been equally distributed. If Scottish poverty amongst low wage earners is to be reduced then in the next decade more attention must be given to the distribution of earnings. Without poistive measures to do this then it will remain axiomatic that the low paid in Scotland will remain low paid.

1. The most commonly accepted definition of an income poverty "line" is that of supplementary benefits. The S.B.C. scale rates, of course, vary, from person to person, and from "need" to "need". If we take this "line" as the public definition of subsistence then there are about 1.2 million Scots on, below or just above this line.

2. The Child Poverty Action Group argued—1969-70 that the position of poor families deteriorated under the Labour Government of 1966-70. Other aspects of the increase in inequality can be found in Townsend (et al) **"Labour and Inequality"** (1972) Bull D., **"Family Poverty"** (1972).

3. See Firn in this collection of essays, and Johnston T.L. (et al), **"Taxation Policy"** (1973).

5. Simmel G., "The Poor".. Translation in **Social Problems, Vol.13,** 1965-66, p.40.

6. Other aspects not touched upon include housing and health. For the operation of social work in Scotland, see Bryant in this collection of essays. One important area which has been ommitted in this discussion is the operation of Section 12 of the 1968 Social Work Act. This allows for monetary payments to those in "need" in "emergencies" etc., by Social Work Departments. The disturbing aspect of these payments, totalling £250,000 in 1971, is that the S.B.C. has also the statutory duty to assist with monetary payments in emergencies, and does operate a twenty-four hour emergency system, which theoretically is open to all. Clearly the S.B.C. is failing in its statutory duty. It would seem that the S.B.C. is attempting to reduce its financial and obligatory duties by off-loading "difficult" or "welfare" cases onto Social Work Departments.

7. "Everyone aged 16 and over is entitled to supplementary benefits if his resources are less than his 'requirements'. People who are in renumerative full-time work or involved in a trade dispute or still at school are normally excluded..., although the (Supplementary Benefits) Commission is given power to make payments to such people in cases of urgency." **The Supplementary Benefits Handbook** (1972), p.5. Although there are sclae rates of benefit and such benefits are considered as a "right", the system is administered on a discretionary basis. There is a procedure for appeals against an S.B.C. decision, but in real terms the officers of the S.B.C. have considerable scope for discretion. See the Handbook mentioned above and; "Exceptional Needs Payments", the Supplementary Benefits Administration Papers No.4, (1973) "National Welfare Benefits Handbook" ed. Lister R., the **Child Poverty Action Group Poverty Pamphlet 13,** 1974; **"The Penguin Guide to Supplementary Benefits"**, by Lynes, T. (1972). Examples of this discretionary system can be found in many of the references given below and the C.P.A.G. quarterly publication "Poverty" has useful information on poverty in Britain today.

8. The Welfare State was really the conjoining of disparate systems of social welfare that then existed. It should be noted that Scotland had its own separate system of Poor Relief dating back to the sixteenth century. As the Poor Laws became politcally redundant in the early twentieth century, newer forms of social welfare were instituted on an ever widening scale, e.g. old age pensions and insurance benefits. But the inter-war depression increased the tensions within this chaotic system. The unemployed looted and rioted Port Glasgow in 1922 over Poor Law relief. The Parish of Bonhill which was Labour controlled was surcharged for too liberal relief in 1923. Relief to strikers dependants in 1926 was held to be illegal and the Conservative administration had to pass retrospective legislation legalising payments made by Parish Councils. Incidentally

9. See the D.H.S.S. **Report of the Committee on One-Parent Families** (The Finer Report) 1974

10. A. B. Atkinson, **Poverty in Britain and the Reform of Social Security** (1969).

11. Ministry of Pensions, **Financial and Other Circumstances of Retirement Pensioners,** H.M.S.O. (1968).

12. **Community Development Project** (Coventry). Occasional Paper No. 10 "Exceptional Needs Payments and the Elderly," No 14, "Knowledge of Rights and Extent of Unmet Need amongst recipients of supplementary benefits" (1972).

13. D.H.S.S., Statistical and Research Report Series No. 1 (1972), Population Censuses and Surveys, Social Surveys Division. A. Hunt, **Families and their Needs** (1973), and Finer

14. Finer, **op cit,** Vol. 1 pp. 223-224.

15. Hunt, **op cit,** Vol. 1, Chapter on Dundee.

16. See also D.H.S.S., **Cohabitation** (1971), R. Lister, **As Man and Wife.** (C.P.A.G.)

17. **New Society** December 12th, 1974.

18. **The Royal Commission on the Poor Laws,** Report on Scotland, (1909). Cd 4922, p.84.

19. **op cit,** pp. 442-43. The Poor Law (Scotland) Act 1934 amongst other provisions actually

extended "the rights of those who are refused relief or granted inadequate relief to appeal against the decisions of the local authority". Briefly, the right of appeal to the sheriff was extended to the unemployed on the Poor Law and the Department of Health for Scotland could now award interim relief to those who they considered had inadequate relief pending appeal to the Court of Session or further investigation. In the year ending 15th May 1935 there were 46 Sheriff interim relief orders and in 1934 there were 667 complaints of inadequate relief

20. **The Supplementary Benefits Handbook**, Chapt. 7, Lister, **loc cit.**, Part 6. Lynes **loc cit.**

21. Two other more renowned areas of discretion surround the Four Week Rule where some unemployed can have their benefit stopped unless they prove they cannot get a job, see Meacher M., "Scrounging on the Welfare" (1974), and the Wage Stop where recipients are kept in "poverty", i.e. below their official needs line because the wage they would most likely get if in employment would be below that needs line, see Ministry of Social Security **Administration of the Wage Step** 1967 and 1972. (S. B. Admin. paper no. 1), Lister R., **The Wage Stop** C.P.A.G. Poverty pamphlet 17 (1974), **Below the Poverty Line**, Edinburgh Poverty Action Group In January 1974 out of 9,500 cases in the U.K. there were 2,500 unemployed wage-stopped in Scotland. This reflected a high proportion of unemployed men who had a family and the generally low wages of unskilled workers in Scotland. It may also reflect a desire by the Scottish regional offices of the S.B.C. to cut down on Social Security payments in an area of high payments. (See Meacher above).

22. Fulbrook J., et al, **Tribunals: a Social Court?** Fabian Tract 427 (1973) Lister R., **Justice for the Claimant** C.P.A.G. Poverty research series 4, (1974). For a defence of the S.B. appeals system, and a critique of American experience of a Legal appeal system see, Titmuss R.H., "Welfare, 'Rights', Law and Discretion," **Political Quarterly** 42 1971.

23. There are around 50 means tested benefits of varying categories today.

24. **Department of Employment Gazette** (March, May, June 1974), "Characteristics of the Unemployed". For further survey of the unemployed see, Hill M.J., (et al) **Men Out of Work** (1973).

25. **Department of Employment Gazette** (February 1973) "Duration of Unemployment". See also Baxter J.L., "Long-term Unemployment—Great Britain 1953-71" in the **Bulletin of the Oxford Institute of Economics and Statistics,** Vol. 34, 1972.

26. **Department of Employment Gazette** (March 1973), "Trends in the Composition of the Unemployed".

27. Hill M., **Policies for the Unemployed: Help or Coercion?** E.P.A.G. Poverty Pamphlet 15.

28. See, for instance, his letter to 'New Society', 26th September 1974.

29. Bosanquet N. and Doeringer P., "Is there a Dual Labour Market in the U.K.?", **Economic Journal** Vol. 83 No. 330, 1973.

30. A. B. Atkinson, "Poverty and Income Inequality in Britain", in D. Wedderburn, (Ed): **Poverty, Inequality and Class Structure.** (1974). Atkinson discusses the problems of using various types of income data, including that of the Inland Revenue used here. T.L. Johnston (et. al) **The Structure and Growth of the Scottish Economy** (1971), chapter 6, gives a breakdown of income movements within Scotland through the 1960's.

31. **Scottish Abstract of Statistics No. 3** 1973, tables 96, 97, 98.

32. O. Robinson, "Part-Time Employment and Low Pay in Retail Distribution in Great Britain", **Industrial Relations**, Vol. 5 No. 1 1974, O. Robinson and J. Wallace, "Equal Pay in Retailing", **Retail and Distribution Management,** Nov./Dec. 1973.

33. N.B.P.I. **General Problems of Low Pay,** No. 169 Cmnd. 4648. This report gives a useful historical analytical perspective to the field of low pay. For more radical discussions see N. Bosanquet and J. R. Stephens, "Another Look at Low Pay", **Journal of Social Policy,** July 1972; and F. Field (ed) **Low Pay** (1973; and A. Fisher and B. Dix, **Low Pay and how to end it.** (1974).

34. **Dept. of Employment Gazette,** April 1973; and D. Layton "Low Pay and Collective Bargaining", in F. Field, **op. cit.**

35. This point is stressed in the N.B.P.I. report.

36. **C.I.R. report No. 77** Clothing, Wages Councils, (1974). Also No. 36, Hotel and Catering Industry, Part 3; Public Houses, Clubs and other Licensed, Non-Residential Establishments No.

37. Annual Report, No. 89, Retail Distribution (1974). On retailing see Robinson and Wallace, above, May/June, July/August, September/October 1973.

Scotland's Housing

Robin Cook

Stop any politician on the hustings and ask him what is Scotland's first housing problem and he will tell you it is our slums. And he will have a point. There is no shortage of housing units in Scotland. On paper we are in surplus. The surplus, and the illusory concept of "the appointed day" when each local authority achieves a housing sufficiency, only recede out of sight when we reckon up that about a tenth of our housing stock falls below the standard of what is tolerable for human habitation. Few local authorities in Scotland have no slums; many have far more than their fair share. The 1971 Census found 28,000 households in Glasgow who lack an internal toilet, and 46,000 households who have no hot water. The households who have to live in these conditions represent populations the size of Motherwell and the whole of Midlothian County respectively. The epic scale of such figures defies the efforts of the imagination to grasp their significance. Who can hope to comprehend this arithmetic of deprivation, representing such a multitude of households who face the daily irritation of the shared toilet and the absence of hot water, or who have to resort to the constant shifts and expedients through which a family with young children tries to dull the stress and tension of living together in a room and kitchen.

The absolute dimensions of Clydeside's problem are so colossal that it blinds us to the housing difficulties of other areas which in relative terms have an even worse problem. The 1971 Census reveals that in Galashiels, 19% of all households lacked an internal toilet, compared with only 10% in Glasgow. Even predominantly rural areas such as Bute or the Shetlands actually had a higher proportion of households lacking an internal toilet, hot water or a bath than Glasgow itself. As Cullingworth said, "We ourselves have seen families inhabiting rural cottages in unbelievably squalid conditions—without water, electricity or sanitation. These may have been isolated cases, but we were shocked to discover the extent of the rural problem.....Indeed the landward areas of several counties appear to have proportionately a bigger problem than that which appalled us in Glasgow."[1]

Cullingworth also pointed out that the really insidious feature of the Scottish slum tenement is that it is stone built, and even the most overcrowded, damp and insanitary warren of alternating single-ends and room-and-kitchens can be concealed by a towering facade of dressed sandstone or ashlar. Engels long ago described how the English middle-class instinctively designed their thoroughfares so that they need not be distressed by the sight of working-class housing.[2] For the Scottish middle-class there has been no need for such subterfuge, as they can protect their innocence simply by refraining from opening the closed door. Behind the Georgian facade of a building within sight of the modern university buildings of Edinburgh, I have found a flat so damp that the lobby floorboards had rotted away, and fungus the size of a man's fist hung from the ceiling. The ashlar gable of a tenement which could be seen daily by the commuters through the Queen's Park concealed a stair in which some tenants walked a quarter of a mile to use the nearest public convenience. Symbolically, Edinburgh's post-war slum clearance programme only really began after one night in 1958 when one such gable end peeled away into the street, leaving fifty families homeless, and exposing the rotting housing it had hidden.

It is insane to blame this legacy of sub-standard housing on English domination. All our slum tenements were erected in the last century by Scottish builders on behalf of Scottish landlords. They have survived through the present century in which housing legislation was drafted by Scottish Secretaries of State, debated by the Scottish Grand Committee, and administered by Scottish local authorities. Housing at least is one issue for which Scots have had total responsibility, and if our policies have failed to achieve a solution, then we must carry out a rigorous re-appraisal of these policies. There is no sign of such a fundamental re-examination coming out of the S.N.P. Their official spokesman on housing has spoken once on the topic in Parliament in his five months there, and even then saw his single speech refuted by the Leader of his group. Instead they now content themselves with the simple assertion that after independence non-Scots will be compelled to sell their homes and land to Scots although nowhere do they make it clear how they imagine this will increase the stock of available fit dwellings. The desire to blame housing shortage on someone else is a timeless failing. Long ago the Rev. George Bell, in his genuine horror that Edinburgh could contain such slums as he found in the wynds off the High Street, sought an escape from his moral responsibility by blaming the Irish and demanded that they be "wafted back" to Ireland: "The migratory Irish are a pestilence as well as a pest. This country both desires and deserves to be protected from them".[3]

The English have not yet wholly replaced the Irish as the favourite fall guy for our housing problems. Only five years ago Dr. Malcolm Slesser, a one time S.N.P. candidate for South Angus wrote; "Labour won the Gorbals at the expense of the Scottish people, for it is we who pay for the massive unemployment benefits, the family allowances, and the public assistance for the Irish immigrants and it is the people of Glasgow who pay for their subsidised housing."[4] The search for an external scapegoat is a perfectly understandable, indeed predictable, reaction to our failure to solve our own problems. But all it does is interfere with the rational analysis of why we have failed, distract us from the pursuit of constructive policies, and rouse passions of xenophobia and chauvinism which threaten the liberal values of a free society.

In any event it is not our legacy of sub-standard dwellings which differentiates Scottish housing from English housing. Those English towns, such as Salford or Liverpool, which went through the same experience of rapid expansion in the last century in response to the Industrial Revolution can now boast an inheritance of slum housing which is as bad as anything we can point to in our Central Belt. The most depressing concentration of slum housing I have yet seen was not in the Gorbals or St. Leonard's but the row upon row of drab brick terraces which make up the Byker Ward of Newcastle. What makes our housing stock markedly different is not our slums, but the solution our major local authorities have adopted—the vast estates of high-density and frequently high-rise, council housing to which we have transferred our urban population. It is a phenomenon which is by no means unique to Scotland, but we have adopted it so widely that it has become the distinctive feature of our housing stock. And with it has come a whole new generation of housing problems, for which we have no-one to blame but ourselves.

Of course, we must recognise the virtually heroic building achievements of our local authorities who are responsible for 85% of all houses built in Scotland since the war, the great majority of which has been wholly successful, particularly in the small burghs. Even at their worst, the problems which have been created on our largest estates are preferable to the immense housing stress which would have arisen had they never been built. One Glasgow politician, whenever he is challenged as to why the Corporation rushed through vast barrack estates of repetitive housing such as Castlemilk without pausing to reflect on the environment they were creating, has the novel response of producing his chest X-ray, which shows the shadow of tuberculosis that few who were brought up in the Gorbals slums could escape. Nevertheless, we cannot conceal from ourselves the uncomfortable truth that the syndrome of social deprivation and a depressed environment has emerged as forcibly as it ever did among our Victorian slums on some of the estates which we have built within the past thirty years. The universal provision of sound plumbing has not enabled these estates to achieve a balanced and cohesive community, and it is hard to share the confidence of those who now put their faith in the provision of some trees and shrubs.

Nearly every urban centre in Scotland can produce its own depressed council estate: Craigmillar or Pilton in Edinburgh, Blackhill or Easterhouse in Glasgow, Fintry in Dundee, Bowhouse in Alloa, Ferguslie Park in Paisley. The reader can extend the list according to his own first-hand experience. In each of them we can find the same cyclical experience of a depressing environment first repelling all families other than those that are desperate for any house, and then a further decline in the estate because of the unbalanced community which results, with a consequent reduction once again in the families who will consider living there. The harsh truth is that estates such as these are now the largest areas of housing stress in Scotland. The latest census reveals one clear index of this stress. The alarming increase in overcrowding since 1966 which is revealed by the census appears largely attributable to an increase in the council sector, mainly on such estates. In both Edinburgh and Dundee the council sector contains a higher proportion of families living at a density of over 1.5 persons per room than any other sector, including the private tenants who live in the Victorian tenements in the heart of the cities; indeed in the Craigmillar and Pilton Wards the rate of overcrowding is double the Edinburgh average. The SHELTER Housing Aid Centre used to keep a map of the city on their wall to which they added a pin to represent each new family seeking help. The effect was a graphic illustration of the astonishing number of homeless families sharing houses with relatives in Craigmillar or Pilton. Notoriously, a clear majority of all children admitted to emergency accommodation in Scotland are from households evicted from council houses, mostly on these deprived estates.

And yet Parliament remains preoccupied with plumbing standards. The current Housing (Scotland) Bill has 50 clauses, of which nearly all are concerned with unfit housing, specifically with their plumbing arrangements, and only a couple of clauses with the rest of our housing stock. It is not even a preoccupation which is shared by most residents of our substandard tenements. For the last three years I have represented many of them on Edinburgh Town Council and I spent much of that time trying to persuade residents with genuinely distressing housing problems to move out to one or other large estate where a house is available. Most often they refused for the perfectly understandable reason that they considered what they would undoubtedly gain in terms of a house of adequate size and sanitation would not compensate for the social and environmental deprivation that went with it.

Housing and Social Justice

I do not want in any way to diminish the urgency with which our remaining slums must be tackled. I have seen too many of them to wish that. But before we can formulate a programme to deal with our stress areas it is as well to realise that not only have our past efforts failed to eliminate them, but that some of our attempts at a solution are now themselves stress areas which any comprehensive programme must also tackle. Let us now try to paint in broad strokes the general principles which should govern such a programme.

The first essential is to rid ourselves of our absurd notion that we can divorce housing stress and the solutions to it from all other social issues and community provisions. This attitude has been with us for a long time and in one sense it is a product of over-reaction to bad housing. The Victorians had every reason for seeking an improvement in sanitary standards on medical grounds, but naturally wanted also to see such reforms as increasing virtue and saving souls. Thus Robert Foulis—in a passionate plea for better sanitation of the tenements in Edinburgh's

Grassmarket enlists temperance in his cause: "If cleanliness is next to godliness, unquestionably filthiness is next to the dram shop."[5] Even Marx in writing of the Victorian slums feels obliged to raise the spectre of incest as the major objection to overcrowding.[6] Today the danger of early educational failure as a result of overcrowding is invoked to rouse the same frisson of horror in the modern bourgeoisie which drink or sex provoked in their forebears. This fundamentally patronising attitude has always met with the most bitter resentment among the objects of such concern. As long ago as 1858 the Edinburgh Courant carried a report of a meeting of working men to press for better housing at which a resolution was passed condemning the bad housing in which they had to live but rejecting allegations as to the "concomitant moral contagion".[7]. In fact little attention has been paid to the views of such residents and it has taken us over a century in which to learn the lesson that bad housing may not necessarily produce moral contagion and that certainly the implicit corollary that good housing will of itself make for a healthier community is fallacious. Two consequences flow from this belated discovery.

Firstly we must recognise that a strong community is a priceless asset which cannot easily be replaced and must therefore be conserved wherever it exists. This means that we must halt the destruction of settled communities in our city centres. These areas are the result of organic growth over centuries, the product of a myriad of individual decisions on the opening of a corner shop or the siting of a new pub. No single team of planners could hope to replace the multitude of judgements which have been taken by several generations of residents, builders, and businessmen in the creation of a mature urban neighbourhood. No attention to the details of soft landscaping or provision of an institutional community centre can provide a substitute for the natural affection which residents feel for the streets in which they grew up, or spin the fragile thread of friendship and acquaintance which hold together a society which can support its weak members and preserve a community ethic. It therefore must be our policy to conserve as many of these neighbourhoods as possible through their modernisation and conversion. We must resolve to take baths to the people, not people to the baths.

Of course many of the buildings in such areas are so far gone as to require urgent demolition— not least because both owners and tenants have been often led to expect demolition any time these past twenty years. This is not necessarily inconsistent with our policy of preserving the local community. A static neighbourhood is one which is in decay; only a dynamic community which is constantly renewing itself can achieve stability. We need new housing within our urban centres to provide purpose-built homes for the elderly who now cannot cope with tenement stairs, to attract young families to maintain an age-balance, and to ensure the long-term survival of the community. Thus we can even welcome demolition of the worst dwellings, provided that the cleared site is swiftly brought back into use for modern housing.

This has many far-reaching implications which have yet to be grasped by many of our local authorities who have still to complete a single major public programme of renovation in any Scottish slum clearance area. We must firmly reject any housing programme in which the proposals for demolition happily coincide with the alignment of the next road or the proposed expansion of business or university premises. We must insist on officials reversing the habits and training of a life-time and embracing conservation with the same enthusiasm that they currently devote to demolition. In particular we must firmly inform tidy-minded planners obsessed with the separation of residential dwellings from everything else above ground that we do not have the time to wait on the final perfected version of their comprehensive plan, but intend to encourage small-scale local improvements on a flexible basis, in order to revive the organic development of our urban communities. For instance Glasgow might well ask itself whether its housing stress is really best relieved by covering its central area with no fewer than thirty Comprehensive Development Areas, of which only half-a-dozen look like ever nearing completion.

The second area where we must apply the lessons of recent decades is in the preparation of future council estates, which will continue to provide the bulk of all marginal additions to Scotland's housing stock for the foreseeable future. Here we must make it a categorical imperative that no new scheme is to be of such a scale that it dwarfs each individual family and thereby denies them any sense of identity with a local community. And we must ensure that our new smaller estates contain a mix of housing tenure and of social class. It is precisely this mix of owner occupation and tenancy from a variety of landlords that gives the central urban communities their balance and resilience to the colossal strains of redevelopment under which they have been placed. In filleting out the owners from among the tenants and consigning them as sheep and goats to different pens in our suburban areas we have laid the foundation of much of our social stress. It is sad that these lessons have still to be grasped by the countrymen of Patrick Geddes who over fifty years ago was telling us that an essential objective of a new construction should be to provide an interesting and distinctive environment for small, integrated communities. Ramsay Garden, in the heart of my constituency, remains as a monument to his ideas put into practice.

Lastly we must pay much more attention to the form of housing we build. We have been slower than the English in recognising the limitations of multi-storey blocks. As late as the period 1970-72, the last three years for which figures are available, 16% of all council houses in Scotland for which tenders were approved were in blocks five or more storeys high, compared with only 9% in and Wales. This lingering affection for the multi-storey might have been predicted given the obsession of our politicians with the simple provision of dwellings in isolation of all other amenities. Tower blocks are more expensive than other forms of housing, and by the time one meets all the requirements of the building regulations they actually take up more land than an equivalent number of homes in an intensive low-rise development. There only advantage is that they can be bought off the shelf from the package dealer and thrust up quickly—they give the right political results for those who measure success by statistics. This is not to say that multi-storey buildings are always the wrong solution. Anyone who has visited the Callander Park estate at Falkirk cannot but be impressed by its successful use of high flats. But it succeeded because of the very generous provision of a strikingly beautiful landscaped open space, the use of the ground floors for shops and other amenities, and a consistent policy of letting few flats to families with young children. As a rule local councils have erected these monolithic monsters without any recognition that their form required more intensive provision of amenity or more sensitive management policies.

There has of course always been a strong temptation on architects to use council housing as an opportunity to experiment with new methods which they find "exciting" since they are rarely expected to live in them. I vividly remember visiting one planner who displayed on his desk a model of some futurist housing design in which each flat formed a polygonal ball and fitted in with its neighbours to a continuous arc that only touched ground at either end. The chief defence which he adduced for this brave new venture was that the standard form of the brick built house with an upper and lower floor and a ground floor entrance to front and rear can be traced back as far as the Romans and must therefore be hopelessly outdated. On the contrary, any feature of human society which has survived for that length of time must successfully meet some very basic human aspirations and should not be lightly abandoned. The most pathetic comment on the drive to multi-storey living was the discovery that most children living in a multi-storey if asked to draw a house would produce a detached house with a garden.[8]

The truth is that with the advent of higher statutory building standards the modern council flat has more space, higher specifications and a better quality of finish than most houses built speculatively for private sale. The private builder, however, has long understood that his shoddy specifications will not stop buyers so long as he offers a house on a small estate of low-rise, low-density housing and with immediate access to private open space. Ordinary familes now place a higher value on such environmental benefits than the quality of internal finishing, but to suggest that these might be extended to working-class tenants is to meet with the derision heaped on those who last century demanded a bath for every household.

In Edinburgh we are nearing completion of the vast new Wester Hailes estate. When fully occupied it will contain the same population as towns such as Hawick or Renfrew. It will be a town without any middle-class, without any owners, and with only one monopoly landlord. Yet crazily the Housing Corporation is developing at Corstorphine, only two miles away, an estate almost a third as large, solely for middle-class housing associations and co-ownership schemes. Half of all the flats at Wester Hailes are in multi-storey blocks, some of them vast slabs containing 150 flats and towering against the horizon on an oppressive and inhuman scale. Walk down the main streets of Hawick and the whole of its long length you will find shopping facilities, recreational amenities, and community buildings which have developed organically over the life of the burgh. Visit Wester Hailes and you will find only the new district shopping centre providing branches of the national chains. Even it has only opened this summer, five years behind the first residents. Two years ago, when there were only two shops for half the eventual population, the Housing Committee divided on party political lines over the provision of a separate door to the butcher's shop to enable him to open a Post Office counter. There remains a total absence of leisure facilities and a desperate shortage of meeting places for community organisations. The only amenity which the middle-class planners have systematically built in to the estate is the provision of 1.5 car spaces per dwelling on the droll idea that some day every tenant will have a car, and every household may be at home, and half of them will have visitors in to dinner. Thus residents of the high-rise flats deprived of access to any private open space can look out on an ocean of unused tarmacadam which laps the base of their cliff-top eyrie. They are, of course, forbidden to own and park a caravan on these areas, which are designated only for cars—no doubt lest they attempt an escape.

It can surprise no-one, except perhaps the planners, that Wester Hailes already exhibits all the early symptoms of social malaise. One recent report produced the revelation that at some of the local primary schools a staggering 86% of all children came from families so large or so poor that they were eligible for free school meals.[9] There are encouraging signs that the tenants themselves are now organising to demand better provision, but it will take considerable determination to overcome the environment which we have created for them. It must never happen again.

It need never have happened in the first place, if we had paid more attention in Scotland to the development of a properly recognised cadre of housing managers with a professional ethic and standards. Schemes such as Wester Hailes are only possible so long as building policy originates in the Architect's Department since its staff are shot of the job once the houses are handed over for occupation. No Housing Director would countenance the creation of Wester Hailes because his problems only begin once the tenants move in. Three years ago Edinburgh Corporation had 50,000 council houses but no Housing Department, and only one man on the entire staff of the Corporation had a qualification in housing management. When we created a Housing Department to provide a comprehensive housing service, we had to recruit five out of the six members of its directorate from English local authorities, because Scottish authorities, including ourselves, had failed to train an adequate pool of qualified managers from which we could recruit. Even today, only two further education colleges in Scotland provide courses leading to membership of the Institute of Housing Managers.

A co-ordinated approach

How many local authorities still run housing from within their Architect's or Chamberlain's Departments? How many other local authorities have a Housing Manager whose functions are basically those of the old factor—giving out keys and taking in rent? In Glasgow itself the Housing Manager has no locus in the slum clearance programme, a responsibility which is jealously disputed by the Master of Works, the Director of Environmental Health and the City Planning Officer, and none of these officials controls the programme of new construction which is in the hands of the City Architect. The number of Scottish housing authorities who have achieved an integrated housing department such as Edinburgh and Dundee is probably still in single figures. The Scottish Development Department have been exhorting local authorities for some time to develop proper housing management, but they themselves hardly set a particularly glorious example. At present they employ in their housing section forty-five architects, surveyors and engineers to get in the way of local authority proposals for new developments, but employ only one single man with a qualification in housing management to advise on a part-time basis.

This neglect of housing management is hard to understand since our proportion of council housing is twice as high as elsewhere in Britain, but it makes it more easy to see why so much of housing hardship in Scotland, particularly in county landward authorities, is not the product of physical shortage but of management policies. Despite the report on this topic by the Scottish Housing Advisory Committee seven years ago, the system of housing allocation of many local authorities remains frankly inscrutable.[10] In one Lowland county, the system is reduced to the simple policy that each councillor is credited with a dozen keys each year for his personal allocation. In another county, one of the largest council landlords in the country, all new lettings are decided at a meeting between the housing manager and the county councillor within whose ward the vacant dwelling falls. It cannot be said too forcibly that, other than as a court of last appeal, councillors have no more business choosing who is allocated a council house than they have in selecting who gets a rent rebate. Under the influence of its new Housing Department, Edinburgh last year completed a review of its allocation rules. Among some of the absurd regulations which were until then enforced, although long forgotten by the committee which instructed them, was a requirement that unmarried daughters could only inherit the tenancy of a council house in which they lived if they gave an undertaking they would not marry. No officials with a proper professional training and ethic would lend themselves to such petty practices.

Much of our mounting problem of rent arrears can also be traced to inadequate housing management and the refusal to see that every failure to pay rent is a failure in the system for the collection of rent. This latter problem would not be so severe if it were not for the punitive attitude which our society displays towards the tenant who falls into arrears, and the penal nature of the emergency accommodation which is available to his family after eviction. Midlothian have refined all these points to an illustration of awesome symmetry. If you are in arrears to Midlothian County you are liable to summary eviction. Unfortunately for you, the only emergency accommodation for the homeless which is maintained by the authority is in Peebles, and once there you lose your residential qualification for the Midlothian waiting list.

There is an overwhelming case for taking into social ownership those privately let dwellings which yet remain in our urban centres in response to the collapse of the private landlord. Nevertheless we must recognise that the privately let sector does provide refuge of a sort for a number of vulnerable social groups such as the unmarried mother, the adult single homeless, or those with a history of rent arrears, who are at present frequently rejected by local authorities. Unless these authorities adopt a comprehensive housing management service we might question whether it is wisdom to give them a monopoly of rented accommodation. It is currently fashionable to answer this difficulty by reference to the expansion of housing associations, but it must be said that only a few of them have a better record of management than their local authority, and most are even more selective as to their tenants.

Clearly we must give priority to the development of housing management in Scotland. However, the creation of a professional class of housing manager does not mean that we must perpetuate the present arrangement in which the tenants as such have no say in the administration of their estates. Of all the distinctions between the owner-occupier and the council tenant none is more marked than the fact that the owner has total control over improvements to his home and an ability to affect its environment, whereas the tenant can only hope to influence either as a voter at local elections. This distinction is yet another example of radical politicians unwittingly re-inforcing the power imbalance of our society through well-meaning policies intended to redress it. I have sat on Housing Committee through lengthy debates on topics which need never have come up at elected member level but could have been resolved perfectly appropriately by local tenants' associations, co-operatives, soviets or whatever. The aim on the smaller cohesive estates which we propose for the future should be to devolve management functions as much as possible to local offices controlled by a local tenants' committee. Unfortunately if you do not have an integrated management department, if your allocation system is based on no rational principle, and if your repairs service is collapsing about your ears, then you are in a weak position to talk about devolution. A professional class of housing managers is a precondition to tenant participation, not an alternative.

I have avoided discussion of specific targets because I firmly believe that our obsession with the annual figure for housing completions is largely responsible for the policies which have purchased quantity at the expense of quality. Moreover it has also contributed to our concept of housing programmes as a spasmodic activity—in other words if we build a specified number of houses for this and a few other years, then we will have met a fixed housing need, or if we thoroughly modernise an aging council scheme then we will have set it up for the next thirty years. In real life our housing programme ought to be an on-going dynamic activity, through which we annually increase the housing stock as part of a process of organic renewal, and constantly improve individual dwellings. It was precisely because local authorities regarded housing as a spasmodic rather than a dynamic activity that they build their pre-war estates and then forgot about them until forty years later they discovered that predictably these schemes required a complete modernisation, which has involved a major disruption of both the lives of their tenants and the new construction programme of the authority, and, will take until the end of the present decade by which time the post-war schemes will require similar attention. However, having made all these caveats about the dangers of playing the numbers game I will say that I believe we should reject any programme which at the end of ten years will leave us with a housing shortage, or a single house below the satisfactory standard, or any major pre-war council estate which has not been upgraded. But it is idle to talk about such objectives unless we are prepared to release the resources which such a programme could require, and I will conclude by examining the resources we must make available.

Firstly we must have land—and we must have it at a reasonable price. This is not a new cry. When we look over the surviving accounts of Victorian housing movements in Edinburgh, we find that time and time again a succession of philanthropists are driven to complain about the extortionate price and feu they had to pay to the Heriot Trust, which had then the stranglehold on suburban building land which is now enjoyed by two or three firms of speculative builders with impeccable Scottish credentials.

In 1861 the building trade operatives in Edinburgh struck for a maximum working day of nine hours. Out of the agitation which accompanied the campaign there was formed the Edinburgh Co-operative Building Company, partly to provide good houses for the skilled artisan at a cheap price and partly to provide employment for the men on strike. The first of their schemes which actually was built during the strike was the Stockbridge colonies on land they purchased at Glenogle Park. The chairman of the nine-hours movement in Edinburgh Mr. James Colville, was appointed manager of the new company. When he appeared before the Royal Commission on the Housing of the Working Classes in 1885, Mr. Colville commented on his difficulty in obtaining building land at a reasonable price, "That is the worst thing in the whole affair; you could not build houses for the poorer classes unless you got cheap sites." Mr. Telfer, President of the Trades Council, who gave evidence on the same day had found the price and feus of building land so "outrageous" that he urged the Commission to "give up the corporations the power to acquire compulsorily the land surrounding a city".[11] His advice fell on deaf ears and in the event the four acres of land adjacent to the development at Glenogle Park were acquired by a brewery which built a maltings on them. Nearly a hundred years later, in 1972, Scottish and Newcastle Brewers Ltd put this now derelict site on the market and sold it for £137,500 to a 'development company', whose directors displayed a fine sense of humour when they registered its title as Highlife Investment Developments Ltd. The very next day the land was sold again for £220,000. No local authority could hope to match that kind of price. To do so would mean charging £3 per week on the rent of each house simply to cover land costs alone. The result is that we have to build even more houses on the city outskirts, throwing perhaps even greater expenditure on other local authority accounts such as highways, transport, education and social work. As it is the profit of £82,500 which was picked up on this site within 24 hours has added £800 to the cost of each house now being built there. The 'development company' concerned has since been involved in a very interesting deal with Ayrshire County Council over land at Bowhouse which increased from a purchase price of £35,000 to a selling price of £230,000 over eight weeks.

A century ago, Telfer and Colville were already making the case for public ownership of land. Our experience in the years since then has simply confirmed how right they were. Unfortunately, although the Labour movement has generally favoured public ownership of land, particularly in recent years, we really have not given serious consideration to how it should be achieved. This is not the place to discuss land nationalisation in detail, but it must be said that the prime question is not how the land is to be purchased but what body is going to hold it on behalf of the public. If all land is vested in central government, public ownership will simply become yet another device by which St. Andrew's House can control the programmes of local authorities.

The second resource we will need is an adequate building industry. In practice we are precious close to having none left at all. The primary task of the building industry is to produce buildings, and in this context it should be the primary task of government to see that it is capable of producing those buildings efficiently. God knows but we need such an efficient industry to provide the houses, schools and hospitals which are essential to our programmes of social reform. In fact successive governments of both colours have been unable to resist the deduction that since just over half of all construction orders are placed by public bodies the building industry is particularly sensitive to changes in government policy. They have therefore ruthlessly used the building industry as a regulator of the economy to be thrown into action in the first-line of any switch in economic policy. Whenever the economy is cooling down and government wishes to reflate it they exhort public bodies to rush out and place building orders. But as soon as the economy is overheated they announce they are clamping down on borrowing consent. In the past ten years there have been no fewer than nine circulars issued by St. Andrew's House ordering yet another alternation in government policy towards new building.

The effect of this openly cynical treatment of the industry is that neither management nor labour have any confidence that any expansion will be sustained for a period of more than a couple of years. The former group have therefore failed to invest in the industry which is now chronically undercapitalised. The latter group have simply withdrawn from the industry. I recently spent some time studying the United Nations statistics on Housing and Construction in Europe, and the point which most struck me was that Britain is the only country in Europe whose building labour force shows a consistent and significant decline over the past decade. The figures for new apprentices to skilled trades such as joiners and electricians are particularly depressing and now run at less than half the level of five years ago—partly because of the lack of confidence in the industry and partly because of the pernicious system of the lump. The supply industries are now, if anything, even more retrenched than the actual construction companies and are incapable of meeting any increase in demand. The current boom in modernisation has produced the remarkable result that most council houses in Edinburgh which are part of the upgrading programme are being fitted with baths from Belgium.

There are a variety of policies with which we can respond to this situation. We must expand training for the building trades and we ought to introduce some form of national planning for the supply of materials so that we can foresee demand and aim to meet it. We could also do with at least one major public building corporation which would have the scale to achieve the benefits of industrialised building which largely eludes local authority direct labour departments who are too small in this respect. Such a corporation could also act as a pacemaker in setting decent standards within the industry in training, research and not least safety. And of course we must abolish the lump. But what the construction industry needs more than anything else is a sustained period of steady assured growth, free from retrenchment every time the economy hiccups, and it is hard to believe they are going to get that because it implies a recognition that the building process is longer than the period from one General Election to the next.

Land, men and materials are the raw input of the construction process, but they must be paid for, and the last resource we will require is finance. I have refrained from discussion of housing finance because I have written at length on it elsewhere and the the field has been fully contested for the past four years. Moveover, I firmly believe that a major effect of that debate has been to emphasise the distinction between owners and tenants, whereas in reality there is a wide degree of common interest between then. Both groups suffer in time of inflation, and those households who wish to join either group face equal hardship in time of housing shortage or decline of the building industry.

But one point cannot be repeated too often. However we choose to divide subsidies between owner and tenant as a nation, we spend too little on housing construction and improvement. This has not been changed by the recent exponential curve in house prices, because the increased expenditure on mortgage repayments which it has compelled, reflects the increasing value of this form of investment, and whilst only marginally increasing actual construction it has excluded a large number of families from even the hope of home ownership. That Britain comes bottom of the international league in the proportion of G.N.P. which is spent on housing construction is well known. Indeed we devote to this end only half the proportion which is allocated by our major Common Market partners. However, an even more illuminating guide to the priority which we attach to housing is the proportion of public expenditure allocated to housing, which has at best remained stagnant whilst expenditure on all other social services has more than doubled. In 1951 both housing and education received 6.9% of public expenditure. By 1978 it is anticipated that public expenditure on housing will have dwindled to 5% of the total, whilst expenditure on education will have expanded to 14%. I do not make this contrast in order to suggest that expenditure on education could be in any way reduced, but it is instructive to note that for all our fine talk of treating housing as a social service, it has not shared in the increased resources made available to toher forms of social services.

The tragedy of this missed opportunity is that the universal provision of good housing is just as much an impetus to an egalitarian society as universal education. Nothing better reinforces existing inequalities in society than tolerating the expression of those inequalities through differing standards of environment which ensure that each successive generation gets off to an unequal start. Good housing is an integral part of a decent environment, although as we have seen it is foolish to isolate it from the other components. If however we are genuine in our repeated demands for universal access to good housing then we must be prepared to make the necessary resources available

I will not pretend that these resources can be made available painlessly. They can only be found if we cut the resources we devote to other items of government expenditure, or if we are all prepared to cut our personal expenditure by accepting higher taxation or greater housing expenditure. But it is not a decision which will become any less painful by the simple expedient of transferring it to a Scottish parliament. The idea that if only Mick McGahey and Sir Hugh Fraser could be persuaded to lie down together like goods Scots in a Scottish assembly, a patriotic solution to our housing problems would somehow emerge is a delusion. Nationalism is only a romantic escape from the blunt truth that only a major re-ordering of the priorities of our society will provide a decent environment for every citizen within the foreseeable future. The challenge of achieving such a major redirection of our priorities is great. It is up to us to prove that only socialism can meet that challenge.

1. **Scotland's Older Houses,** A Report by a Sub-Committee of the Scottish Housing Advisory Committee, chaired by Professor Barry Cullingworth (1967), Chap.2
2. Frederick Engels, **The Condition of the Working-Class in England in 1844** (1845), Chap.3
3. Rev. George Bell, **Day and Night in the Wynds of Edinburgh** (1849).
4. Quoted in **Glasgow Herald** 21st January 1970.
5. Rev. Robert Foulis, **Old Houses in Edinburgh** (1852).
6. Karl Marx, **Capital** (1867), Chap. 23.
7. **Edinburgh Evening Courant,** 18th September 1858.
8. Gilloran A. Rapoganti **House form and Culture** (1969).
9. **The Scotsman,** 7th June 1974.
10. **Allocating Council Houses.** A Report of a Sub-Committee of the Scottish Housing Advisory Committee, chaired by Mr. John Kay (1967).
11. **Royal Commission on Housing of the Working Classes,** 2nd Report (Scotland), 1884-85, XXXI.

Social Work: New Departments And Old Problems

Richard Bryant

Over five years ago, in November 1969, Scotland's social work services were reorganised. The fragmented, and separately organised services, on minimal budgets, for child care, welfare and home helps, mental health, day nurseries and probation and after care were brought together into one single local authority department. The prison welfare service was added in 1973 and the hospital social work service will be a logical addition during 1975. Essentially, it was a fundamentally different sort of integration than that experienced some eighteen months later south of the border. On paper, the Social Work Scotland Act 1968(1) was a much more thorough—and more radical—piece of legislation than the English integrating Act.

The Scottish Act set out to do more than simply bring together the varied personal social services. The Act widened the scope of social work investing in the new departments a responsibility "to promote social welfare by making available advice, guidance and assistance on such a scale as may be appropriate for their area."(2) It stretched the traditional boundaries of social work beyond the individual and the family to the community-at large.

The Act, too, introduced a new approach, through children's hearings, to dealing with children in need of compulsory measures of care. An emphasis was to be placed on "care and treatment" rather than "correction and punishment" and a locally recruited panel, of lay people were to be involved, talking over with parents, child and social worker what should be done in the child's best interests.

Social Work has developed in recent years into a major undertaking, commanding more resources and a position of increasing importance (albeit a poor third to education and housing) within the structure of local authority services. There has been a notable expansion—revenue expenditure on social work has grown in the last four years from £20 millions in 1969/70 to £24.3m. in 1970/71 to £31.2m. in 1971/72 to £34.7m. in 1972/73.(3) A budget of £45 million is estimated for 1976/77, with half being spent in the new Strathclyde region. But, for comparision,

344

the expenditure in Scotland on the police force or the Scottish Universities both exceed the total social work outlay; the local authority education expenditure in Scotland is about ten times that of social work.

The expansion has taken place behind the backcloth of the Social Work Scotland Act 1968 and not necessarily because of it. Scotland is spending less per head than England and Wales and there is evidence to suggest the differential is increasing. In 1972/73 the Scottish social work expenditure per head was £6.62(4) compared to £6.58(5) in England and Wales excluding the separate Probation and After Care expenditure which apportioned would be an addition of 45p per head(6) . Therefore, some 41p less per head was being spent on the social work services in Scotland: the reason was not that the need was less.

It has been suggested that Scotland's social work has been "haunted by a tragic history of parsimony", partly the result of weak Scottish committees for children's and welfare work prior to November 1969, an accompanying degree of ignorance and a smack of meanness.(7) Certainly Scotland's infrastructure—the homes, the day centres etc. and the personell—was skeletal and Scotland's directors of Social Work time and time again have admitted that this area required immediate attention. The Act itself cannot, of course, be blamed for the earlier failures.

The Act brought in its wake no easy solution. The much needed resources were not immediately forthcoming; but hopes for the much needed finance were dashed by the Labour Government in 1968 in an explanatory memorandum to local authorities. It saw the Act as solely an organisational change, increasing efficiency, yet involving only minimal extra expenditure. "The creation of social work departments", the memorandum bluntly spelt out, "and the general provisions of the Bill (The Social Work Scotland Bill) are not expected in themselves to give rise to appreciable extra expenditure in relation to the general expansion of welfare services."

Such a guideline was inappropriate, especially as the resources necessary for the Act were widely recognised as wanting. In those early, yet critical, days the guideline was unquestionably observed by the new social work committees, where the parsimonious attitudes of the separate committees were carried over and entrenched by government memoranda. Consequently, there was little enthusiasm for development. Interestingly, the new social services departments, as they were called, were better received in 1971 in England and Wales.

Ronald Young, Vice-Chairman of Greenock and Port Glasgow's Social Work Committee and Director of the local government research unit at Paisley College of Technology, has argued(8) that the slowness to implement the Social Work Scotland Act was because there was a "poorly articulated philosophy of social work in our (Scottish) political culture". The absence of a document similar in status to the English Seebohm report is a relevant factor in explaining, says Young, the slow way elected members responded to the new social work philosophy. He suggests the councillors saw "the 1968 Act as leading primarily to a more effective delivery of service to the consumer in terms of the one-door philosophy. The two other elements—namely the 'preventive' aspects and the 'strategic planning' requirement (with the concurrent need for co-ordinated policy planning with other departments whose decisions interrelate with social work)—were not really appreciated by the political system in Scotland."

But there were other factors. The social work professionals themselves (and in particular their separate professional organisations) exhausted themselves in their pre-Act battles; there was no emerging common identity or social work voice for the post-Act situation. Individuals obtained promoted posts and there was a dearth of enthusiasm to apply the Act's philosophy into practice.

A limiting factor was the size of many of Scotland's departments—over half of which were serving populations of less than 50,000. This was as a direct result of the Act being rushed through parliament and to appease the burgh lobby, almost double the number of social work departments were established than originally envisaged. With the inevitability of regionalisation at a later date, the large number of smaller departments ensured that the social work services would never be developed rationally. Consequently, expenditure per head (a reflection of resources made available) varied considerably in, for example, the Glasgow Area. Airdrie spent £4.65 per head, while in adjacent Coatbridge it was £6.93, Greenock £8.71, Paisley £9.19, Rutherglen £5.58, Motherwell and Wishaw £6.30. Glasgow's expenditure was £10.08 and Lanark County's was £5.76.(9)

The lack of trained personell was a further factor. Since the Act there has been a spawning of training in the colleges and the universities. This training unfortunately has tended to concentrate

345

solely on producing social workers (the great majority of whom will be graduates) because the shortfalls tended simply, but naively, to be measured only in terms of the professional caseworker. The acceleration of a graduate social work profession is being achieved at the expense of the overall social work service—the bulk of staff in the social work departments are home helps, care assistants, in residential or day care settings, nursery nurses. Training opportunities for them have not really increased since the Act. It is an indictment of a social caring service to concentrate on an elite, to the almost neglect of the majority who to departments are seen as numbers of hours not people.

It was never intended that the shortcomings of other local authority departments—education, health and housing—in particular, or the D.H.S.S. can be redressed by the new Social Work Department. The emergent S.W.D. has too often been a dustbin for the Local Authority's problems, individualised for comfort. Its role has consequently been confused—an additional weakening factor. Efforts to change this are long overdue.

Rhetoric and Reality

The acid test for any social service in Scotland is presented by those areas which suffer from a history of economic decline, unemployment and environmental dereliction. It is in these areas like many within the industrial belt of the west and central Scotland that the rehetoric of intent is confronted with the hard realities of economic and social deprivation. The new departments which tend to be under the greatest strain are invariably those departments which are located in areas with a concentration of social and economic problems. It is in those areas like Glasgow which are most in need of fully functioning social services that the new social work departments are tending to fare badly. Within social work the symptoms of stress and strain are often defined in manpower and administration; a shortage of trained staff, excessive caseloads, a lack of supervision for trainee and inexperienced staff, cramped work conditions, difficulties in establishing area based teams of field workers and an overall shortage of financial and technical resources. In 1973 James Johnston, the Director of Social Work in Glasgow, spelt out some of the repercussions which can result from a shortage of staff, which at that time totalled sixty fieldworkers or 25 per cent of the Glasgow department establishment.(10) The repercussions included:

(1) Youngsters coming before the Children's Panels could not be given the supervision they needed. Some youngsters went to List D schools because they could not receive adequate home supervision.

(2) It took months even to make the first visit to a disabled persons home to report on the need for facilities, such as bath handles and ramps.

(3) In many cases children were in residential homes because there were not sufficient social workers to carry out the necessary visits to their own homes or those of foster parents.

(4) In only a few cases could the department follow up a contact with a family after an immediate crisis—such as a court case—had been dealt with.

As these examples clearly indicate the people who bear the ultimate social costs of a manpower shortage are the clients. They are at the receiving end of an inadequate and inferior service, a service which is unlikely to improve their already disadvantaged life chances. A shortage of manpower may also diminish the quality of services in other less direct ways. The scope for experimentation in the development of services tends to be limited, promotional work in the wider community setting can be delayed because of other more immediate demands and attention can be deployed away from any systematic assessment of the broader political and economic issues which confront clients. Departments which are hard pressed can not afford to aim for an optimum level of service provision. They avoid taking risks and engaging in projects which may increase their workload and staff commitments.

A picture emerges, in some areas, of social work departments which appear to be struggling to survive, struggling to avoid a breakdown in their basic services. Within social work the standard response to these issues has been to press for more staff and resources.(11) But is this the only or the most valid response to the situation which exists in many areas? Although an increase in staff resources would certainly relieve some of the pressures which are on the social work departments, it is naive to suppose that they would resolve any of the more deep seated dilemmas which confront these departments. The problems which social work departments and their clients face need to be viewed within a broader framework of reference, one which takes account of such factors as the structural nature of poverty in Scotland and the authoritarian attitudes towards disadvantaged groups which informs much of the thinking about social policy and public administration in Scotland.

Poverty

The majority of social work clients are working class and many are drawn from amongst the most vulnerable and impoverished sectors of the working class; large families living on low incomes, single parent families, old age pensioners, the physically and mentally ill, the disabled and the long-term unemployed. Individual expressions of need vary widely but certain material issues recur with monotonous regularity in the social worker's caseload; this applies particularly to problems of financial insecurity, which are often manifest in such difficulties as rent arrears, hire purchase debts, problems of paying electricity and gas bills and difficulties in managing household budgets. As a consequece of this financial insecurity social workers may spend a considerable amount of their time and energy in handling financial problems and dealing with requests for financial assistance. For instance, recently in Glasgow the social work department, within the space of a fortnight, paid out £4,842 to corporation tenants who were threatened with eviction because of rent arrears.(12)

As has been frequently recorded financial insecurity is often linked with a wider set of social and environmental problems. For many of the clients of social work departments their lack of money is part of an all embracing condition of deprivation, which may also include living in sub-standard housing, poor physical health, difficulties in obtaining employment and a lack of local access to decent recreational and social amenities. This condition of deprivation may also be reinforced by an isolation from those political and organisational supports which are available to the more economically secure members of society.

The sense of powerlessness which is felt by some social work clients—and which is frequently mistaken for apathy—is often a very rational expression of political isolation which they experience. Social work clients have no trade union to represent them and few of them are in regular contact with community organisations which might support them in their dealings with the statutory services and help guide them through the complex labyrinth of the welfare bureaucracy. For many social work clients a contact with a social work department forms only a part of a wider range of transactions they may have with different public and social services. These transactions often comprise a formidable obstacle course, which they have to negotiate unaided and with little or no bargaining power at their command. In theory social workers could act as advocates for their clients and assist them in their dealings with the different services. This sometimes happens, but in many areas the pressure of other demands pre-empts the sustained involvement which is necessary for the social workers to act as an advocate for the client. It should also be noted that much of the conventional theory and tradition about the practice of social work discourages the social workers from adopting an openly partisan stance on behalf of clients.

Many of the problems which are experienced by social work clients can not be defined and understood in terms of pathological or or deviant behaviour. Their private troubles are often an expression of public ills, they are symptomatic of the inequalities which exist in the distribution of income, power and opportunities in British society.

The Poor Law Ideology

The structural nature of poverty imposes a critical set of constraints and burdens upon social work departments. These constraints and burdens are often reinforced by the negative and punitive attitudes towards the poor which inform much of the thinking about social policy and public administration in Scotland. The old poor law ideology of the 'deserving and undeserving poor' has not disappeared. In an article, published in the 'Scotsman', Kay Carmichael identified this ideology as exercising a considerable influence upon the attitudes expressed towards groups in need in Glasgow—her remarks could well apply to other areas in Scotland.(13)

'A persistent theme in Glasgow's attitudes to those in a relationship of need with the city has been that in some undefined way it is that person's fault that they do need help. While we talk about social problems this has continued to mean people are problems unless they come into a clear category of being deserving of help... To be deserving means that the situation for which you are seeking help was to be very clearly not of your own making, but equally important it has to be borne with fortitude and if help is given it has to be received with unquestioning gratitude. To be ungrateful, resentful or aggressive is to abdicate your role as deserving, although technically you qualify. The most unacceptable position of all is to think you have the right to help and to expect to be consulted about the kind of help you would consider most appropriate, is just not to be thought of... There has in fact been very little difference in the philosophy of the Labour and Tory members of the Local Authority to those in 'undeserving need.'

We could note many examples of how the old poor law ideology, under various disguises, informs social policy and public administration. One classic illustration—which would warm the hearts of 19th Century workhouse guardians—is provided by a housing visitors form which, until recently, was in use in Glasgow. This form was used by the housing department to assess the type of rehousing offer which would be made to people who were living in areas which were undergoing slum clearance or redevelopment. The majority of Glasgow residents obtain a corporation property as a result of clearance or redevelopment. The assessment which is made of the tenants is an important influence in deciding the type of housing offer they receive. The form was administered by housing visitors, who visited the residents in their homes.(14) In some cases these visits lasted no more than five minutes. The assessment made by the housing visitors was based on the following three criteria;

Type of people:	Very good/Good/Medium/Fair/Poor
Cleanlinesss:	Very good/Good/Medium/Fair/Poor
Furniture:	Very good/Good/Medium/Fair/Poor

According to how people fared on this arbitary set of criteria they were recommended for a house in districts which were, predictably, graded:- Very good/Good/Medium/Fair/Poor neighbourhood.(15) Apart from providing an illustration of the poor law ideology at work in the 1970s, this assessment procedure may also help to explain how so called 'difficult' or 'problem' housing estates can be created. They are the product of a rigidly stratified and judgemental system of allocating corporation houses. This illustration may also enable us to understand why relations between social work and housing departments are often strained. The casualties of housing management policies often end up at the door of the social work department. In fairness to Glasgow it should be noted that the arbitary grading of tenants also operates in other local authorities.

Apart from increasing the workload of social work departments the poor law ideology also effects social work practice in a variety of other ways. In particular it can generate resistence to policies which attempt to move beyond controlling disadvantaged groups and seeks to involve them in change centred activities. For example, attempting to promote and organise client organisations which will represent the needs and interests of their members. As Kay Carmichael has indicated the poor law ideology defines certain groups in passive and subservient terms.

They are expected to receive services and assistance with gratitude and not to make demands or critically voice their grievances. As a consequence of this any action which encourages collective activity, the expression of needs and the positive value of criticism is likely to encounter' considerable resistance. Projects and policies which are concerned with unleashing the potential for action which exists within disadvantaged groups challenge existing stereotypes and carry with them the threat of disturbing a well established pattern of power and status relationships. It is not surprising that a number of newly formed client and community groups have been received with a defensive, and even an openly hostile response, by some councillors and local government officials.

Social Work in an Unequal Society

It has been suggested that the problems faced by social work departments, particularly those in the West and Central belt of Scotland, cannot be fully understood in terms of manpower shortages and the lack of organisational resources. Although additional staff and resources are needed they will not resolve the deep seated dilemmas which are generated by material deprivation and the persistence of a poor law ideology which labels disadvantaged groups as being 'undeserving'. In short the new social work departments are confronted with an old set of problems. The key question which these problems raise also has a familiar ring about it—what is the role of social work within an unequal society which rewards its members according to the principles of a market economy and not on the basis of human need?

In the 19th Century the pioneers of British social work had little or no doubt about the answer to the above question. They accepted the established social and economic order without question and concentrated their energies upon helping the poor to adjust and cope with their circumstances.

The outstanding Scottish pioneer of social work, Dr Thomas Chalmers, was no exception. In the Glasgow slums of the 1820s Chalmers, who was later a prominent figure in the Free Church Secession from the Church of Scotland, established many of the guidelines for the development of social work in Britain. Working from his Church, in the then St John's district of Glasgow, he organised a system of poor relief based on local fund raising and visits to the poor made by church elders and deacons. The tasks undertaken by these elders and deacons included many activities which are now familiar in modern day social work; investigating the social and economic circumstances of the poor, encouraging people to 'help themselves', providing advice and assistance on the management of family budgets. For Chalmers poverty was essentially a problem of individual failure and solutions were to be sought through the encouragement of self help efforts and an improvement in the moral and social habits of the poor. Underpinning this approach was the assumption that inequalities in society were natural and immutable.

"The inequalities of condition in life are often spoken of as artificial, but in truth they are most thoroughly natural... the superiority of one man to another in certain outward circumstances of his state are not artificial but natural and the consideration in which occupiers of the higher state are held is natural also.(16)"

It should come as no surprise to learn that Chalmers was hostile to any collective organisation of the poor and that he ridiculed the early trade unions and other working class associations for their 'grotesque committees' and 'curious machinery'. Chalmers has been described as the 'patron saint' of the Charity Organisation Society (C.O.S.)(17) the organisation which, from the 1860s, was to become the major focus for the development of British social work.

The leading figures in the C.O.S. shared Chalmers 'natural' model of society and they viewed the rise of socialism with considerable distaste. C.S. Loch, who was a leading figure in the C.O.S. from 1875 to the 1920s, wrote in the aftermath of the Russian revolution:

'The antidote to Bolshevism is good casework'.(18)

The C.O.S. philosophy still forms one current of influence within social work. Although the language of social work has changed and the anti-socialist sentiments are now more muted, there are still today many social workers who accept the status quo without question and are suspicious of any initiatives which seek to connect social work with broader based political action. For these social workers the crisis which confronts many Scottish departments is viewed essentially in administrative and professional terms. The problems which social workers encounter are not defined within the context of social and economic inequalities. However, within social work there have always been some social workers and educationalists who have questioned the conventional theory and practice and have sought to provide alternative definitions of social work goals. In 1920 Clement Attlee, then a lecturer in social administration, provided a view of the social workers role which was sharply at odds with the tradition of the C.O.S.

"Every social worker is almost certain to be also an agitator. If he or she learns social facts and believes that they are due to certain causes which are beyond the power of an individual to remove, it is impossible to rest contented with the limited amount of good that can be done by following old methods."(19)

This broader conception of the social workers role would find considerable support within some quarters today, particularly amongst many of the younger generation of social workers who have recently completed their training. On occasions social workers in Scotland have acted collectively to voice their concern about social and economic issues which adversely affect their clients and the wider community.

In 1972 a group of social workers in Clackmannanshire voiced their concern about unemployment in the county and called for government intervention to prevent a decline in local employment opportunities.(20) During the previous year the Glasgow branches of the British Association of Social Workers (B.A.S.W.) had expressed their concern about the possible social repercussions which would result from a close down in the Upper Clyde Shipyards. The B.A.S.W. branches submitted evidence to the Scottish Trade Union Congress inquiry into the U.C.S. crisis(21) and some of the more active members helped raise funds for the U.C.S. work in and joined the various demonstrations which occurred.

These examples are important for two reasons. Firstly they indicate that, on occasions, social workers in Scotland have defined their roles within a broader socio-economic framework. They have at times made a basic and critical connection between social work and the workings of the market economy. Secondly, the action taken in Clackmannanshire and over the U.C.S. crisis indicate that social workers are not always prepared to accept the traditional C.O.S. role of dealing only with individual consequences of unemployment. However, employing authorities may not share this position. When the social workers in Clackmannanshire made their representation on unemployment they were severely criticised by a number of councillors for 'gross inference in county council business'. One councillor, in a reference to the social workers concern about the threatened closure of a paper factory at Tillicoultry, commented:

"I think we should leave the social work department to deal with the effects of the closure and not allow them to try and find a cure."(22)

Attempts to redefine the traditional roles of social work inevitably involve risk taking and conflict. Those social workers who recognise that they must also be agitators have to be prepared to upset many of the conventional wisdoms which surround social work and public administration in Scotland. They must also be prepared to forge links with groups and organisations which operate outside of the limited boundaries of professional social work, such as trade unions, tenants associations, client and other community organisations. This risk taking and conflict pales into insignificance when it is weighed against the daily humiliations which are suffered by many social work clients. The social worker who explains away his political inactivity on the grounds of organisational constraints, is often as guilty of underwriting the status quo as is the social worker who is only content to encourage his clients to cope with unacceptable circumstances.

1. Social Work Scotland Act 1968, Section 12.
2. Reports on Social Work in Scotland 1970, 1971, 1972 (HMSO) and 'Rating Review', Feb 1974
3. **Rating Review** (February 1974) Aggregated Average.
4. 'Local Health and Social Services Statistics 1972/73' **The Chartered Institute of Public Finance and Accountancy**, November 1974.
5. **Social Trends** 1974. Table 196 1972/73 plus AC exp. was £22m.
6. "The five-year countdown", John Brown **Community Care** 16th October, 1974.
7. "An experiment in Social Policy formation in Greenock and Port Glasgow" **Working Paper III**/April 1973
8. **Rating Review** February 1974.
9. **See Housing and Social Work—a joint approach** HMSO 1974 and **Fieldwork Staffing (Scotland)**, Advisory Council on Social Work (of relevance is Appendix 1)
10. Reported in the **Glasgow Herald** 4th September, 1973.
11. 'The lack of a good supply of trained social workers was the biggest obstacle in the way of new services'. Comment made by Mr. John Murphy in his presidential address to the Association of Directors of Social Work, St. Andrews, 1971. Reported in the **Guardian** April 7th, 1971.

12. Reported in the **Evening Times** August 19th, 1974.

13. C. M. Carmichael 'Glasgow and Social Problems' **Scotsman**, 1972.

14. For an examination of this assessment procedure and the role of the housing visitors see; Sean Damer and Ruth Madigan 'The Housing Investigator' **New Society** 25th July, 1974.

15. With the exception of the 'type of people' criteria the form now in use is similar to one described above.

16. N. Masterman (ed.): **Chalmers on Charity** Constable 1900 pp. 166-167.

17. Charles Loch Mowat: **The Charity Organisation Society 1869-1913** Methuen 1961. p.10.

18. Quoted in an article by Jim Kincaid 'The Decline of the Welfare State' in a book of essays edited by Nigel Harris and John Palmer: **World Crisis—Essays in Revolutionary Socialism** Hutchinson, 1971, p. 69.

19. Quoted by Adrian Sinfield in 'Which Way for Social Work?' Fabian Tract 393, 1969, p.35.

20. 'The Social Consequences of Industrial Recession'—A statement on unemployment in Clackmannanshire issued by local social workers (1972).

21. See B. Challoner and J. McLaughlan 'Unemployment: Urgent Concern for the Social Implications' **Social Work Today,** September, 1971.

22. Reported in the **Scotsman** 20th June, 1972.

Public Health In Scotland

Donald Cameron

Health in Scotland is a difficult subject to discuss. Health is a difficult concept. You recognise it when you see it, for example, in a first-class football team or in a group of children playing in a field. However, to define it we need to say what it is not.

A discussion of health inevitably ends in a discussion of ill-health. One looks for its absence. Health statistics are ill-health rates and indices, mortality rates, rates of absence from work or school, disability rates. When planning for health, we plan to minimise these. In a better society in the future in which the social integration of mankind is recognised and exploited we may be able to talk positively about health and regard ill-health as an unfortunate accident, which it certainly is not just now. The best we can do in the meantime is say what health is not.

The number of babies dying in the first year of life, calculated for every thousand live births, the infant mortality rate, is generally reckoned one of the most sensitive measures of ill-health in a country. It reflects social conditions as well as services for the care and cure of sick children. In the 19th century in Scotland it fluctuated around 126/1000 live births. In some large towns it was as high as 250-300/1000. That is, 1/4 to 1/3 of all babies failed to survive their first year of life. This is the sort of mortality we find today among babies in some parts of Asia, Africa and South America. In 1949, the first full year of the National Health Service, Scotland's infant mortality rate so improved that of western European countires, only Norway, Sweden, Denmark, the Netherlands, Switzerland and England and Wales had lower rates. Although infant deaths have vastly declined, and the rate of death in Scotland now stands at only 19/1000, relatively, we are not doing at all well. Of Western European countries, now only Belgium, Italy, Portugal and Austria, have worse records. (1) Table I.

Table I

Infant Mortality—Deaths per 1000 births—(1973)

Netherlands	11
Findland	11
France	13
Luxemburg	14
Japan	14
Malta	17
England & Wales	17
GDR	18
Scotland	19
Spain	19
Belgium	21
Austria	25
Portugal	41

It might be thought that, now that we have a comprehensive national health service available to all, free at the time of need, infant mortality rates would become more uniform throughout the various income and occupational groups. This, however, has not happened. The better-off continue to enjoy the same relative advantage in lower infant mortality as they did when the service was started. This is due to a number of factors: good housing and nutrition are important to protect infants from infections and accidents, smaller families and better educated parents leads to higher standards of infant care. Ann Cartwright has shown an additional bonus: the better educated professional workers make better use of and get better treatment from the various facilities of the national health service. They are more likely to complain when facilities are not up to standard.(2)

Table II shows how, in respect of infant mortality rates, the relative positions of the Registrar General's five social classes have remained the same over the last 25 years. It should, however, be remembered, that there is wide variation with these 'classes' and also that they are not within "classes" in the political sense but more or less arbitrary groups of occupations. The main criteria for classification are education, training and skill.

Table II Infant Mortality rates among various Social Classes in Scotland

1950-52 and 1970-72 (3)

RG	1950-52			1970-72		
Social Class	plus I I	III	IV plusV	I plus II	III	IV plus V
Infant mortality per 1000 live births	22.2	34.3	43.0	12.7	18.1	24.1

It is not only among our children that ill-health should give cause for concern. Older people too, suffer more than they need because of conditions in Scotland. For example, our death rates from coronary thrombosis, lung cancer and bronchitis, are among the highest in the world.

Ill-health is socially caused. It is due to under or bad nutrition, to overcrowding in houses and the consequent spread of infections, to habits which are forced on us by the desperate conditions we live in: the abuse of alcohol, tobacco and other drugs. The so-called accidents at work, on the roads and at home, are of course no accidents. They are due to the willful neglect of simple precautions by a society for which a human life is considered a mere production unit. Perhaps most important of all the causes of disease and premature death are the poisons and radiations which we breath in by the lungful, absorb through out skins or consume with our food and drink. Almost all diseases are produced by the various causes mentioned above. Only some of them we can cure, but nearly all are preventable.

The National Health Service

Our means of cure is the National Health Service. It has provided Scotland with a very good system for treating sickness and disability since 1948, but it could be vastly improved. It has for instance a completely undemocratic structure. Health Boards run the hospitals, General Practitioner and other domiciliary services in each area. Their members are all nominated by the Secretary of State for Scotland. They are few in number and are overwhelmed by an amount of work which, in the administration which ran the service before 1974, was done by many times their number of Regional Board, Executive Council and Local Health Authority members. They, therefore, leave important decisions to the senior officers of the Board who are often out of touch with the needs of the local people. Priorities in the provision of treatment services are determined by professionals. They are too often based on what the experts enjoy doing best rather than on what patients need and want to have done for them. This results in an imbalance which creates long waiting lists for simple but rather boring operating procedures, such as varicose veins, hernias, prolapsed wombs, piles, etc. Another defect, is the almost complete neglect of patients' thirst for knowledge, for information about their illness: how to overcome their difficulties, how to avoid making their condition worse, how, after they are cured, they can prevent such a thing happening again. These are some of the questions patients need answered. Medical advice should provide patients with knowledge that will allow them to take part in promoting their own recovery. Medical workers must learn to treat patients as intelligent people rather than as objects to whom something is done. This kind of change will be brought about partly by a change in teaching medical and other students and partly by demands for better treatment by patients themselves.

Priorities

If we want a first class curative service we must do several important things very urgently. First, we must change the Health Service Act so that the Boards are democratically run for securing the health needs of the people of Scotland. There must be many more members of boards so that they properly supervise the work of the various parts of the service. The purpose of the recent change in the administrative set-up was to make things more efficient! But, for the ruling class efficiency has a different meaning than it has for us. It means cutting down expenditure on things that we need and cutting out services that make life tolerable for sick and disabled people. Board members must be chosen by the working class to carry out policies which will best promote cure and relieve suffering.

Secondly, we must spend much more money on the health service. Hospital workers and ambulance drivers have recently had strikes. Nurses are demonstrating now. We need much more of this if the health service is to be saved. It is not hospital workers, ambulance drivers and nurses who have the responsibility for running the service. It is the government through the Secretary of State for Scotland. All Secretaries of State in recent years have neglected this statutory duty with the result that equipment and rates of pay have so deteriorated that many devoted workers have been forced to leave. The remaining staff have had to work in desperately undermanned situations. Instead of abusing the Secretary of State, newspapers—other than the "Morning Star"—and television have abused the strikers and demonstrators. It is they, in fact, who are promoting the interests of the health service and the nation by drawing attention to an imminent collapse. In addition to more nurses and other hospital staffs we need new and up-to-date hospital buildings. There is no kind of hospital of which we in Scotland can be proud. If you compare hospital buildings with those of insurance offices you will see what I mean. Worst of all are psychiatric hospitals. Most are over 100 years old, with 'temporary' buildings erected in 1914 and 1939 to house air raid and other casualties, still in use. Psychiatry is a service which has thoroughly broken down. Chronically ill patients are being refused admission even when they urgently need and want it. The old humane function of asylum has been abandoned and many desperately ill people are a burden to themselves and to their relatives. Quite a few are in prison.

General practice needs more manpower of all kinds, doctors, nurses and receptionists. All must be housed in health centres. We should not tolerate makeshift premises in doctors' houses or in old shops. Health centres should have adequate surgeries and waiting rooms and accommodation for nurses, laboratory and X-ray and there should be a pharmacy on the premises. Much of the work that is now done in hospital could take place in a properly equipped health centre thus cutting down distance travelled and waiting time. With many more General Practitioners and smaller lists more effort could be given to patient education.

Preventive Medicine

The National Health Service needs to be expanded in a number of new ways. We need a comprehensive pregnancy advice and family planning service which will allow women to have the children they want, when they want them. The Lane committee showed that the Glasgow area had far fewer abortions than one would expect from the population of the area, and from the number of unwanted births there. This was not because abortions were not wanted, but because powerful professional people refused to provide a service.(4)

We need an occupational health service, based on, and responsible to the National Health Service and not the individual industries and factories. It must be clearly for the benefit of workers and not of the management. We also need a vast development of rehabilitation services and sheltered workshops for the long-term disabled.

Most of what I have mentioned so far are services which try to rectify the situation after health has already broken down. Unfortunately our health service is like that. It has been called our 'National Ill-health Service', and there is a lot of truth in the joke. It is only a small part of the fight against ill-health. The bigger part is played by these organisations in society which protect us from the adversities of the environment. First, the Trade Unions, we must thank them for their part in the fight for National Health Insurance and later for the National Health Service and for the enforcement of legislation for safety and for an environment free from pollution. The political parties of the left and other democrats took part in the same struggles. They were responsible for the passing of factory and sanitary legislation and the setting up of the Factory Inspectorate, the Mines and Quarries Inspectorate, the Alkali Inspectorate, the local sanitary authorities and their Environmental Health Inspectors. The Inspectors, the men and women employed by these bodies, examine and probe into safety in factories, mines and home. They investigate mechanical structures that might lead to accidents and chemical, bacteriological, radiological and biological hazards. They protect us at work, in the home, in cafes, restaurants, food shops and generally in our environment from dangers that we often do not imagine exist.(5)

These workers are all working in conditions of understaffing, partly for the usual reason that they are underpaid, and partly because the ruling class would like to see their services run down anyway. The factory inspectors are so few in number that workplaces can only be inspected every three to four years. In the case of the building industry, sites are up, the building completed, and the contractors are away before the site is properly inspected. This results in the notoriously high number of deaths and maimings in the industry. Other dangerous industries are mining, which is improving, thanks to the vigilance of the N.U.M., and fishing, which is not improving. The police, who proclaim an interest in law and order, completely fail to carry out their duties to enforce the safety laws in industry.

There is one part of Scottish industry that is completely without protection: the off-shore oil drilling rigs. Oil workers are toiling in some of the worst conditions of all industry. Their particular risk from wet and cold, which saps their strength, alertness and morale, making them prone to accidents has been well described by A.D.G. Gunn.(6) The numbers of these workers who present themselves at hospitals round the east coast of Scotland has not so far been estimated but it is certainly an intolerable proportion of the men involved. Of all these men, divers are most at risk. They are often inadequately trained and medical and other support services are rudimentary. This year 11 divers have died. As their most common and disabling injuries take some time to develop their numbers are completely unknown.

Employers' bitter resistance to trades union organisation prevents a proper investigation of the causes of accidents and keeps conditions of work at what would, elsewhere, be an unacceptably low level. Furthermore, the rig workers do not have the protection of British Law, Scottish or English. These rigs are outside British legal and administrative jurisdiction. They are not, therefore, inspected by factory or environmental health inspectors.

Legislation is urgently needed to make these rigs part of one of the Regions of Scotland and subject to all the factory and public health legislation. The workers must be unionised and a proper industrial health service introduced.

The Environmental Health Inspectors of the local authority have duties under the Public Health, Food and Drugs, Housing and Shops Offices and Railways premises Acts. They supervise the cleanliness and safety of the general environment, including: the air, food, ports, offices. They are responsible for the inspection of insanitary housing and many other things. The law is seriously behind the times and neglects our needs. What law there is the magistrates will often not enforce. The result is that we in Scotland have some of the worst and most overcrowded houses in Europe. We have the dirtiest food and the dirtiest city streets. We need new laws. We need magistrates who will apply them on behalf of the people and many times more inspectors who will be able to devote some of their time to education.

Although government and local government inspectors are an essential part of any preventive service and make a great contribution to health, they are not enough. The miners have shown us the way to genuine improvement. We need workmens' inspectors: men appointed by their workmates through the union, with a right of access to all plant, and to all documents about production processes. They should have a right to publish their findings and a direct access both to the plant boss and to the responsible minister. Only with these facilities will working men and women be able to protect themselves against sickness and injury. There are some causes of disease so subtle that they take many years to show their effects. For this reason there should be medical follow-up of workers for long after they have left an industry in which such risk is great to make sure that there is no disease attributable to it.

We as a community neglect our health in other important ways. In Scotland the chief negligence takes the form of poor housing. Overcrowding prevents the proper emotional and intellectual as well as physical development of children. Lack of sanitary facilities puts lives at danger from infection. Council house building is a form of health service.

In Scotland we have low wages, high unemployment, fewer professional, technical and managerial jobs and higher food prices than in England and Wales. This means a lower standard of living: poorer nutrition. Recent reports have shown a return of rickets in Glasgow children, and malnutrition is quite common in old people. A demand for higher wages and higher pensions is a form of health service.

As I have said, most of the ways we can protect our health lie outside the hospital and other treatment services. However, people continue to fall sick and we need hospitals to care for them, but the sickness services must be supplemented by facilities for rehabilitation to help restore the individual to the fullest possible state of health. Where there is some residual permanent disability, hostels, day centres, sheltered workshops, are needed to support the patient and allow him a reasonable life with dignity, and without putting intolerable financial and other burdens on members of his family. The treatment and rehabilitation services should provide a comprehensive support in sickness and disability. We must fight against what is once more being imposed on us by the ruling class: the placing of the responsibility for the care and treatment of the sick on their friends, relatives and immediate family. The struggle for health is a political struggle. Gains made in this field are steps on the road to socialism.

1. See various of the annual reports of the Registrar General for Scotland.
2. Cartwright, Ann **Patients and their Doctors,** London, (1967)
3. Registrar General for Scotland **Annual Report** (1972) Edinburgh H.M.S.O.
4. Report of Committee on the Working of the Abortion Act. Vol.1 London (1974)
5. See the various annual reports of the Chief Inspector of Factories.
6. Gunn, A.D.G., (1974) Safety in the North Sea, **Nursing Times. 70:** 1924 - 1925

Scottish Education: A Socialist Plan

Nigel Grant

It is easy enough for a socialist looking at education in Scotland today to say what is wrong with it. The inequities in the present system are glaring enough; and although the private sector is less dominant than in England, in Edinburgh at least it is still strong enough to distort the entire school system by creaming off a quarter of its pupils. In spite of the reforms of the sixties, higher education is still a privileged enclave, internally divided by an elaborate hierarchy of institutions. The school system can not even claim the justification that it works; on the contrary it seems near the point of collapse. Schools are often ill-equipped and understaffed with teachers who are badly paid, angry and demoralised, feeling that society expects more and more of them without either defining objectives or willing the means to realise them. The school regime has changed but is often still authoritarian to a degree that outsiders find scarcely credible. At all levels the examination reigns supreme, and one does not have to go all the way with the abolitionist lobby to recognise how far examinations can distort the whole learning process, to the point that what is not examined is unlikely to be taken seriously. Class snobbery is less evident than south of the Border, but obsession with formal status is, if anything, greater. There is a good deal of soulless pendantry too. It would not be true to say that no children enjoy their schooling. But a great many do not, and it is significant that many Scottish teachers are convinced that this is how it should be. There is also a good deal of smugness, based on the notion that because Scotland was once in the lead it must inevitably still be there. Contrariwise, this ethnocentrism is balanced by frequent and uncritical importation of English practises, often to the point of caricature (like the Edinburgh four-plus).(1) Similarily staid conservatism has its opposite in the anxious gimmick-hunting that can give genuine reform a bad name. Above all, the system is heavily weighted against the have-nots: in a society which traditionally places a high value on self improvement through learning, the kind of schools many have to attend kill all desire and block all opportunity to achieve it.

357

Many of these defects are not, of course, peculiar to Scotland, but are to be found in most urbanised societies. Many must be unacceptable to anyone, socialist or not. For a socialist, the difficulty is not in finding things to denounce, nor even in relating them to a critical analysis of class society. Nor is it in proposing improvements, whether short term or utopian: anyone can see that something must be done about the supply of teachers, for instance, and most would agree that the conditions under which many of our children are taught are not tolerable in any society. The socialist concerned with improving the system needs not only goodwill and a sense of justice—though these must be the mainspring of his concern—but also a clearer view of the system he wants to transform it into. He must try to clarify basic principles, and to relate them to practical objectives.

Ironically this is a difficulty which conservatives do not have to face. Having a conceptual model to hand already, they are under no obligation to construct one. If content with things as they are, they can concentrate on keeping the system as it is, and dismiss attempts at fundamental reform as "unrealistic". Or they may feel that change has gone too far, and seek to re-establish a more acceptable state of affairs. (Whether it ever existed is immaterial, for the creative power of myth is rarely affected by facts) (2). They may even accept the need to correct the grosser inequalities while leaving the essential structure untouched. In each case, the model is the familiar system or a variant of it.

There are many educational systems considered by those running them to be socialist, and there may be a temptation to rely on these as models. There is a wide choice—from social democratic systems like the Swedish, through orthodox communist systems, like the Soviet Union—Eastern Europe, to the more thorough-going Chinese model with its emphasis on work-experience and ideological committment: there are also the more eccentric cases of Yugoslavia with its preference for decentralisation or Tanzania with its stress on rural self-sufficiency. But quite apart from the question of the acceptability of any of the particular brands of socialism professed in any of these systems, it is doubtful if straight borrowing can be of use. Past experience of wholesale importation has not been altogether encouraging even when the importing or exporting countries have been ideologically close. The Soviet system is not only Marxist-Leninist but also Russian, and even the Chinese system while setting its face against much of its cultural past, is still influenced by it. Scotland is not Tanzania or China, or even Sweden. Of course, much can be learned from the experience of other countries committed to fundamental social change, and, some practises, suitably adapted, can be judiciously borrowed: but the socialist in Scotland has to take the Scottish system as his starting-point(3).

Lacking ready-made models, we have to determine the principles with which objectives can be framed, firm enough and flexible enough to avoid the twin dangers of sloganising and dogmatism, The basic principle can be described as humanism, concern for the completeness and integrity of the human being. This, surely, is what socialism is all about. It can easily be lost sight of in the necessary pursuit of the means to the end: but socialists seeking to alter the disposition of wealth and power in society are trying to create a social order in which people can develop their full potential to the benefit of their own lives and those of their fellows, can be fully human rather than mere economic units diminished by privilege and division. All else follows from this: socialists oppose political injustice, class privilege, economic exploitation, ignorance and discrimination by race, nationality, class or sex, because these are dehumanising, making people into something less than they can be. The difference between socialism and some other forms of humanism is that it is concerned with all members of society, and seeks to create a society fit for people to live in through collective action and social control of wealth and power.

It is well to restate such fundamentals, otherwise there is the danger of letting dependent principles turn into a set of unexamined assumptions. It is true that socialists believe in equality, but it is also true that equality is not a simple concept. It is **not** a matter of trying to make everyone the same, since people are not and cannot be identical: rather socialists are opposed to systems which permit privilege and deprivation, and impose restrictions on developments and opportunities that have nothing to do with peoples' needs or contributions. Again, democracy is not a socialist preserve, nor need socialists argue that the counting of heads is necessarily the best way of solving any problem: but it follows from their belief in the importance of human beings that those who are affected by decisions have a right and a duty to participate in taking them. Further, belief in social responsibility does not mean a preference for herd behaviour, but a recognition that the social order necessary to secure the main objective is possible only in co-operation with others. Finally, socialists have to be rational. This is not to say that reason is a peculiarly socialist quality or that other facets of human nature can or should be ignored: but if we believe that man can be the controller of his own state (and to believe less is to be less), we have to give due attention to the shaping of human action by reason. Radicalism and instant Marxism doubtless have their place, but socialists who want to do anything constructive need more than that.

Social Justice

Coming to the formulation of educational objectives, socialists have to come to terms with some uncomfortable facts. First, the revolution has not happened yet, and even major socialist reform could be a long way off, and could take some time to carry out whatever the intention of the government in power. To design socialist education for a socialist society is one thing: but the more likely task is constructing, in a society at least partly capitalist, a system which will function adequately, deal with the worst defects, and can sustain the potential for the growth of a socialist system, when conditions suit. Which leads to the second awkward point, educational systems do not shape societies but reflect their needs and respond to their pressures. There was a time when reformers expected education to transform society by shaping future citizens in a more rational mould. Expecting comprehensive schools to destroy class barriers is a good example of this. There is little evidence that they have done anything of the kind(4), but on reflection this is just as well. This belief made it tempting to pass the buck to the schools, and expect them to take on the job of social reform unaided. But attitudes and opportunities are determined by many factors, such as housing, income, family circumstances, and a host of others. Most of them are quite beyond the school's control, however organised. It is a job for political and social action, in which education can, of course, play an important part; but it cannot do it alone. This is not a council of despair, rather a warning against expecting too much. If anything of value is to be achieved, realism is no less essential than idealism.

When we turn to immediate tasks in Scottish education, we are faced with the particular question of Scottish identity, and have to consider what account socialist policy should take of a distinctive Scottish system. For nationalists, the answer is clear enough, but socialists are bound to act on different criteria. Is not socialism more concerned with social justice than national tradition? Does it not take an international rather than a national view? Is it not more important to give education a nudge in the right direction than to bother about Scottish education and its peculiarities? Many socialists argue this way; but it is not necessary to wander into the byways of national mystique to make a case for the recognition of Scottish educational identity which will stand up on grounds of socialist principle.

Firstly, the opposition of national identity and membership of the wider community of mankind is false.(5) We are all many people, and identification at one level does not rule out any other. From our immediate families right up to mankind we recognise links which join us to others and make up part of our identity, for none is complete by himself. National identity is one of these, with a strong emotional content, which it would be foolish to ignore. Of course, this level of identity, like any other, has to be put in perspective, but this is not to deny its validity.

On the contrary: on all the evidence the Scots see themselves as an entity; in other words, being Scots is part of their being human. (This is true of any group). To expect us to become something else is to diminish us as humans by taking on another identity. No doubt it would be convenient if nationalities did not insist on being themselves; but they do. Socialists therefore have to accept this, respect it, work within its context, and appreciate the difference between national self-awareness and jingoism.

But there is also a practical point. If a small nation like Scotland (or Wales or Denmark or Albania) gives up its identity it has to assimilate to something else. In Scotland's case, this would mean being swallowed by England. But even if a good case could be made for this, assimilation does not happen instantly. Practices take time to filter from one system to another, to adapt and be put into effect. Meanwhile, things may have moved on. A good example is the erosion of the Scottish pattern of broader general education at school and university. It has not gone as far, yet, as in England, but the trend is that way, mainly through English influence. Recently, though, there have been second thoughts in England about the desirability of specialising quite so much quite so early: there is, therefore, a fair chance that Scotland could find itself perfecting a specialist system just as England moves away from it. Uncritical assimilation is a recipe for built-in obsolescence.

Contrariwise, constant pressure from a dominant neighbour can produce an equally unthinking rejection of any change. This has appeared recently in the form of defending the Edinburgh four-plus as part of the authentic Scottish tradition under attack from English cultural imperialism. Simple resistance is an understandable reaction, but surely no socialist would want to keep the bad features with the good just because they were distinctively Scottish (or, as in the above example, thought to be). Yet this kind of reaction—also a recipe for obsolescence—is what pressure to assimilate can produce.

More basically, maintaining—and developing—a distinctive Scottish system can be justified by the need for education to respond to the changing needs of society. Scottish society has needs and problems not identical with those of England, and is less likely to deal with them if education is planned in England; even the present system of providing special Scottish legislation assumes that what is needed is a **variant** of something already designed for English purposes. Naturally, there is no guarantee, but placing the control of Scottish education firmly in Scottish hands makes social responsibility more likely; and, as Scotland is a smaller country, the chances of devising more effective means of democratic control are rather better. Finally, it is worth considering the highly likely situation of a Tory government in Westminster and a Labour majority in Scotland; in such a situation, the government could block even minimal attempts to reform education, and could even reverse the process. It has happened before over the abolition of school milk and the reintroduction of powers to charge fees in local authority schools, both forced through against the opposition of most Scottish members.(6) Clearly, it could happen again while Westminster still has power to legislate on specifically Scottish matters.

It is also possible that the Scottish system has some characteristics and traditions that could be built on, since we have to start with what we have, anyway. The negative features have been mentioned already, and although some of them are international, others are more obviously Scots. The shadow of Knox's minatory fingure still falls over many schools, and plays no small part in making them grimmer than they need be. This is not to deny the need for order or application—those who imagine that lively teaching laced with sympathy will solve all problems can hardly have tried it in the ordinary schools; but many still go on the assumption that because learning is serious, it must also be grim.

But Knox, for all his finger-wagging, did establish some values that socialist policy could make use of. The idea that education is a social responsibility is still alive in the Scottish tradition, and any socialist would surely accept the idea of opening maximum educational opportunities to all "so that the Commonwealth may have some comfort by them."(7) The "lad o'pairts" tradition has always owed more to myth than to reality, and even as an ideal its limitations are obvious enough. But it had its points, notably in the refusal to set overtly class barriers in the way; and although Scottish society is far less classless than some Scots like to believe, most of the country is **relatively** free of the equation of educational attainment with social class that so bedevils the English system.

Much has been written on the Scottish tradition of generalism in education(8), and the extent of its survival is easy to exaggerate. Yet, in spite of erosion, something remains. The Scottish Certificate of Education is rather more broad-based in its application than the English G.C.E., and at university level the same idea can be seen in the survival of the "Ordinary" degree, and in the earlier stages of most Honours degrees as well.(9) The pressures towards specialisation are strong, but the basis is still there to be built on with rather less upheaval than would be required in England. Generalism is too complex an issue to go into here, but there are reasons why socialists should consider it favourably. The first is the humanist argument, the rejection of forcing people into roles where they must be incomplete. True, we no longer live in the world of the Renaissance "universal man"; the sheer growth of knowledge has seen to that. But that is no reason for cutting off most young people from most areas of human knowledge and experience. Broad-based **expertise** is hardly practicable, but the formal system is not much concerned with expertise until quite late in the process anyway. A broader range of **insight,** however, is surely more feasible to aim for. A person cut off from any appreciation of the modes of thought and processes of major fields is thereby diminished in his personal development, but understanding of the world, and his possible contribution to society.(10)

But the argument can be taken further than that, such is the pace of change that no school system, no curriculum can be expected to equip a young person for life, since we cannot know what his needs will be in even a couple of decades.(11) It is necessary to lay the basis of the capacity to learn (and, as needful, re-learn), and this will be even more than usually difficult if he is pushed into one line early on. "Learning to Learn" is no easy matter in any case, but at least a reasonable breadth and balance of **introduction** to ways of thinking avoids closing doors too soon. The argument has force for societies no less than individuals. The effect of the growing volume of knowledge is the need to co-operate with others in the formulation of policy, conduct of research, design of work programmes, or whatever; and this is not likely to be fruitful if people cannot even begin to communicate across specialist boundaries. Specialists there must be; but left to themselves, if they wield power or influence, they can become, quite literally, irresponsible. A wider awareness of what they are about can make the difference between total ineffectiveness, ill-informed meddling, and effective criticism and social responsibility.

Finally, it can be argued that socialist internationalism could be better served by keeping the Scottish system distinct. No educational aystem can stand still or look only to itself, for influences and contacts are bound to increase anyway. But, paradoxically perhaps, greater awareness of a Scottish pattern could make Scots more internationally aware. While Scotland is so closely tied to England, outside influences come overwhelmingly from one direction; but being distinct can make it possible to receive and use influences from many sources without feeling in danger of being swamped. As it happens, many of the educational importations from England have been of the elitist kind; but there are other models, and an autonomous Scottish system should be more receptive to them. Devolution is, of course, no guarantee against elitism, native or foreign, but at least it can provide a framework in which such trends can be identified and resisted.

A New Approach

What, then, can be done with Scottish education to move it further in the direction of further social justice? It must be recognised that whatever is done with the formal system will not be sufficient, given the limitations of the schools' ability to counteract social injustice, it is obvious educational reform has to be part of a much broader social effort. Some radical critics have gone much further than this, notably the "De-Schoolers" in the United States and elsewhere(12). Essentially, they argue that such is the power of dominant social classes to manipulate any kind of school system, formal schooling only serves to reinforce patterns of privilege and deprivation—worse, by adding apparent merit to distinctions that would otherwise be recognised as based on mere chance. There is some force in the analysis, less in the suggested remedies, which seem to come down to abolition of compulsory schooling and its replacement by a much more informal basis for acquiring skills and knowledge as the need arises. But there is little evidence, past or present, to suggest that this would improve matters. While the ability of schools to balance other social influences has been much overstated, it is not totally lacking; and it is not hard to guess who would benefit most from our system of informal learning—as long at any rate as society retains anything like its present structure.

While recognising the need to give much more attention to other means of learning, then, we are still left with the schools occupying a central position. The case for more pre-school education has been made often enough, even by Conservative governments, but less often acted upon. There is not much to be gained from providing even ideal conditions in schools if children entering them at five or so lack the skills to benefit from them. Nursery schools will not totally eliminate the grave disadvantages in language development, and many other areas, with which many children start school: but they can provide a much more stimulating and enriching environment than a great many homes can possibly do, and thus help even things up to some extent. At present, the demand for nursery school places greatly exceeds supply. Of course, it has its limitations but none as serious as the fact that a great many cannot hope to get it at all.

When we come to consider the primary and secondary schools, it becomes clear that there is little point in looking at them separately, for they are but different stages in the process of the general education of children. The reasons for their being separate are largely historical, and at a time when all have been going on to secondary schools of some sort, the justification of a clear cut at eleven or twelve has been two-fold—to select for different kind of secondary school, and to make a convenient division between learning the rudiments and, for some at least, pursuing more advanced study. With the constant filtering of "secondary" material, and specialist teaching, into the primary school, the second argument applies less and less: and if selection for secondary schools no longer is used, the same is true of the first. Thus the position of primary no less than secondary schooling hangs on the ever-green controversy of comprehensive reorganisation.

Whole books have been written on this issue, and doubtless there will be many more.(13) Most socialists are in any case, inclined to regard the matter as settled. Although it is not possible to argue the case here, it would be as well to note one or two points that must affect our attitude to the school system as a whole. Part of the trouble is that evidence is not conclusive, and is often replaced by assertion. For example, it is widely stated, especially on the Right, that comprehensive education is excellent in principle but "does not work"; we are told that clever children are "held back", that there has been a decline in standards of work and discipline, and that comprehensive schools are no guarantee of equality anyway. On the Left, the reaction has often been to shrug off such accusations, to deny their validity, or to assert that it is too early yet to make assessments of this kind. As usual, the situation is far from simple.

It is certainly true that final assessments are rather premature, given the shortage of time since many areas have been reorganised. What international evidence exists does not give much support to the contention that "the clever are held back"; like the slower children, they tend to show a slight improvement. One group does seem to do less well, namely the abler working-class children who would have gone into selective schools under the old system.(14) But the evidence is not conclusive in this country, mainly because there are not all that many fully comprehensive schools. This is obvious enough in parts of England where comprehensives have to compete with established grammar schools, and are thus likely to be, in effect, secondary modern schools with a small addition of the more academically-inclined. Scotland offers an extreme example of this in the case of Edinburgh's unusually large concentration of fee-paying selective schools, which results in a creaming-off of about a quarter of the city's children (more the higher one goes up the school), leaving the comprehensives with an unrepresentative intake.

As for the arguments about standards and discipline, we must be more careful than those who throw around sensational statements to back up a sweeping argument. The often-repeated assertion that illiteracy is on the increase seems to have derived from an N.F.E.R. study, in England, which suggested that literacy was not rising—disappointing, but not quite the same thing.(15) There has been more evidence of adult illiteracy, but comprehensive reschooling is too recent to be blamed for this. (Besides, a recent discovery does not prove that the thing discovered is itself recent.) Other criteria, such as the proportion of the age-group taking external examinations, could be taken as showing a rise in standards. As for behaviour, this can be looked at in two ways. There is much talk of school indiscipline, less evidence that it is all that new; any contemporary horror-tale can easily be capped by any old sweat from the junior secondary firing-line as far back as memory goes. Many teachers in formerly selective schools now have to face difficulties they are not used to, but again a recent discovery is not necessarily a new phenomenon. Whether "standards of behaviour" in general have declined we simply do not know, lacking firm evidence. If they have, this need not be laid at the door of the comprehensives. There are signs that young people (like their elders) are less prepared than formerly just to do what they are told, and possibly this spills over into anti-social behaviour more than it did. But, if this is so, it is a complex issue that a mere change of school structure can hardly explain; at any rate, selective schools have been making the same complaints. (They have been doing this for generations, of course. It might put things in perspective if it is remembered that in nineteenth century "public" schools in England, riot was commonplace; Rugby pupils on one occasion even blew down the door of the head's study with gunpowder .(16)

Interestingly, there has been little attempt recently to move the comprehensive argument over to the offensive, and put the onus on the defenders of selection. It would be possible to make a case for selection (after the lines, perhaps, of Plato's **Republic**), but to add that it "just wouldn't work". Nor does it—not, at any rate, without a substantial margin of error, using the best available predictive techniques, the error can still be as high as ten to twenty per cent either way; and it is greater the younger the child. This point could be made even if one accepted the principle of separating children into clear-cut categories (which even the classic theories of intelligence do not support, as they distribute intelligence in a continuum, not in distinct steps); but it is doubtful if selection really owes its origin to any coherent theory of intelligence at all.(17) It is notable that defenders of selection are less loud in their praises of schools for those who have **not** been selected; it is hardly surprising that junior secondaries have so few partisans, but if they were being consistent the entire selection lobby would take this position.

It must be admitted, though, that comprehensive schooling is no panacea, and socialists who insist that it is do little service in the long run. Quite apart from the effect of the independent and semi-independent schools (which might be dealt with some time), there remains the fact that neighbourhoods in either are rarely comprehensive, and even the most ingenious redrawing of boundaries can not always make them so. Even with good intentions, effective organisation, a reasonable supply and distribution of resources, and a little bit of luck (and there is no guarantee of any of these), **no** system of schooling can ensure a fair deal for **all** pupils while other factors, beyond the school's control, affect their chances one way or the other. It is as well to recognise these limitations and consider other ways of correcting inequalities.

Lifelong Learning

This shifts the discussion to what happens after compulsory schooling. One of the faults of the present system is that it closes doors on children as they go through the school, so that by the time they leave they have been processed into a role from which they have little chance of escaping. But if we can establish an open system which gives people the chance and encouragement to come back into the learning situation as the need arises at any point throughout life, one of the more objectionable features can be moderated at least. Some will continue to lag behind others, but at least the lag need not be fixed for life. It is not enough simply to extend further eudcation, adult classes, Open University courses and the like,admirable though these are; as it is, those already enjoying educational advantages tend to be the ones who make full use of these facilities. A more radical approach is needed, involving industry, the social services and community organisations as well as the formal education system. Sheer variety of provision would help, with full time and part time, long term and short term, general and specific courses; so would an active drive to find out the community's educational needs rather than simply offer courses and wait to see who turns up; so would greater flexibility and liaison between the various providing agencies to allow transfer from one type of programme to another, so that a course taken for a particular interest could become a bridge to a formal qualification should the need arise. The possibilities are enormous. The expansion of continuing education does not, of course, guarantee equality, but it does keep open the possibility for everyone of going as far as interest, need and capacity determine, a much more positive aim than thinking in terms of a fixed series of hurdles.

But there are other reasons why socialists in particular should pay close attention to the potential of lifelong learning. It fits the requirement of meeting social needs better than a closed system; since needs can hardly be predicted, a system of this kind is flexible enough to provide for them as they arise at any point in life. Further, it fits the humanist principle of considering the whole person rather than his economic role merely. The more opportunities there are to acquire new knowledge and skills, whether for vocational purposes, for the improvement of qualifications, or for fun, the more people can be free to explore their own potential, to their own and others' benefit. The notion that education is only something that happens to children in schools is basically as restrictive as the idea that its function is the favoured treatment of an elite.

When we turn from these general considerations to the actual structure of the school system, we need to spend a good deal of time and effort on practical details. There is no space for this here; what follows, therefore, is not intended as a blueprint but a sketch of a reformed system, an agenda for discussion. It is customary in most countries to base at least the earlier stages of education on some kind of age-range, and this is followed here. But only provisionally and with some misgivings; even in young children, chronological age is at best an extremely blunt instrument when is comes to predicting development. It may well be better to plan the process in terms of developmental stages rather than think in terms of age at all. Individual rates of development from one kind of thinking to the next, do differ, and it could be argued that letting learners proceed at their own pace, rather than impose an artificial one based on age, could do more than anything else to keep opportunities open. There is an extensive literature on this from the psychological point of view, but there is a need for more research in the practicability of basing school curricula and organisation on it.(18) Any ages given below, therefore, should be taken as very rough estimates indeed.

With that reservation, a sequence like this is worth considering:

1) **Pre-school.** Voluntary, but available to all who want it, full-day or part-day as required; age-range about 3-6. This is the stage before formal instruction is generally understood, where a vast amount of valuable learning takes place—language, number, space, colour, movement, social and other fundamental skills—through play and informal activity. The informality of the organisation could make it easier for parents who so wish to be directly involved, which could well have educational value for the parents as well as breaking down the barriers between school and the world in the child's eyes.

2) **Basic school.** Compulsory; age-range, say, 6-16. This is the stage for the basic "common core" of skills and knowledge, starting with the beginnings of formal learning and ending at the point of major differentiation. If this involves all children and young people, if the process is recognised as a continuous one, and if we reject the idea of selection for quite different types of school at age 12 or so, there are not really compelling educational arguments for splitting this stage into two distinct parts. (There may be considerations based on the availability of buildings, but these need not be long-term.) Given the degree of primary-secondary overlap that exists even now, institutional separation could be more of a nuisance than anything else in the future. Joining the stages that are now separate could provide for considerable flexibility in the progression from basic education in the rudiments of literacy and numeracy to the more discrete subject areas.(19)

It is not altogether appropriate to speak of "subjects", perhaps, since this has connotations of conveying bodies of information above all else. Some of this is necessary, of course; but if the idea of an open system of lifelong learning is taken seriously, the main concern of this stage must be "learning to learn". For this, there has to be a serious attempt to introduce pupils to methods of enquiry and ways of thinking characteristic of major areas of human experience; and at the same time pupils can be exposed to those areas that all citizens can be expected to have come in contact with, and in which more particular interests can build. Once again, discussion of such a curriculum needs far more space than exists here, but for the moment the following could be suggested: mother tongue, written and spoken(20); mathematics; understanding of the physical and social environment, through (among other things) understanding of fundamental concepts of physical and biological science, and social studies such as history, geography, and civic education; foreign language and culture; aesthetic studies such as literature, art, music, drama; physical and health education; and some familiarity with the processes and function of work skills.(21) Admittedly, this looks rather like a list of traditional subjects, but there is no reason why it need be taught like that. There **are** stages where it is more effective to handle them as distinct disciplines, but it is also important for our purpose that the connections be appreciated also; if rigidity is to be avoided, the subject divisions must be seen as a convenience rather than something absolute and impermeable.(22)

3. **Further school** (or perhaps junior college; some thought will be needed about the name). Post-compulsory; age—about 16 plus for some, though by that point age is not really relevant at all. This stage would fill the functions of the senior classes of the present secondary school and some of the courses in further education colleges. Those going straight on from basic school might take two years or so of further general education, still on a reasonably broad front, with the opportunity of taking a certificate equivalent to the present S.C.E., whether for entry to higher education or for some other purpose (examinations might not be the best way of doing this, and it might be worth thinking of some kind of 'educational profile' method: but this is a separate issue, not dependent on the institutional structure). Schools of this type could also be organised so as to provide opportunities for taking up study again after a period of work, or to offer part time or

day release courses, or to make it possible to pick up individual courses (whether for certification or not) as the students' need or wish directed. Another advantage would be more effective use of teachers and equipment. Few secondary schools can justify employing teachers of Arabic or Chinese or even Russian, or can make adequate use of computers or the more sophisticated kinds of laboratory equipment; but at least in urban areas schools of this type could, and if we can get away from the idea that a student must study in only one institution at a time, we could dramatically increase the range of available choice. It might be found convenient for some schools to go in for a degree of specialisation—more science or technical studies in this, more languages in that, more art and music in another; and if students can shop around, **they** need not be forced into a specialist mould.

Naturally, there would be problems. Objections could be expected from existing secondary schools, reluctant to lose the chance of more advanced teaching, and fearing a further division of their teaching profession. It could be further objected that this system would deprive older pupils of the opportunity to play a part in running the schools, and thus make the basic schools more juvenile and alienate the younger adolescents even further. There is some weight in these arguments, but there could be a solution in grouping basic schools and further schools in loose complexes, sharing staff and facilities: but admittedly this would not always be possible physically in many areas, at least until complete rebuilding could be undertaken. More seriously, this system would be hard to apply in small towns and rural areas though intelligent siting and imaginative use of transport, correspondence, radio, and television, and variations in the timing of courses (such as the use of intensive residential courses over shorter periods) would be worth considering as partial solutions.

4. **Higher Education:** (University or College). There is likely to be an overlap with the previous stage, particularly with vocational courses and adult courses of various kinds, but there are grounds for seeing this as a distinct entity. The institutions are there already, and it is easier to adapt them than try to unscramble the whole system. One prosaic but quite important difference between higher institutions and further schools would be size and number, but obviously there are differences in functions too. If we take universities as they are at the moment, they can be seen to perform a number of connected but distinct tasks; (1) Continuation of personal education at a more intensive level; (2) Higher professional training and qualification (their chief role in the present as in the past); (3) Original Research, individual or collective; (4) Conferring, acquiring, or confirming social status (often confused with the first two). The first three of these must be expected to play an important part in a socialist higher educational system, and since there are advantages in having them dealt with in the same institution by the same people (since teaching and research can often enrich each other), we can expect the universities to occupy a major position.(23)

But the other institutions of higher education must not be forgotten— the central institutions such as colleges of art and music, the higher technical colleges, the colleges of education, and, in some of their work, colleges of further education. At present (except for a few jointly organised courses such as the B.Ed. degree) these are quite separate from the universities legally, functionally and in general esteem. It needs to be asked whether this must be so. If they are held to be of a lower standard by enough people for long enough, there is always the danger that it becomes true, though in many cases it depends more on the status of the vocation for which these institutions provide. (The old chestnut about the colleges being vocational and the universities non-vocational still survives, in spite of the prominence of the university Faculties of Medicine and Law, but need not be taken too seriously.) Functionally, the main difference is that the colleges are, as a rule, more specifically concerned with one vocational area—they are, in spite of recent diversification, monotechnics. Legally, the distinction rests on the colleges' responsibility to the Secretary of State for Scotland, while the universities get their money from the Universities Grants Committee which is responsible to the Department of Education and Science in London. This arrangement, however, can be changed if need be.

If we are serious about lifelong learning, the rigidity of this barrier will have to be dealt with somehow. One way might be to squeeze the universities even more than at present, and go ahead with the development of other higher institutions more directly under public control. As well as being wasteful, this would be a mistake, losing a fruitful merging of general and professional teaching and research. Alternatively, the universities might be put under direct government control and merged with the colleges. This would have the attraction of tidiness and would more easily be made responsive to social needs, whether for the development of an open system or anything else. But this would also be a mistake; much of what the universities do is likely to be less effective with civil servants breathing down their necks. Another possibility would be to expand the role of the universities and work towards a complex of higher institutions under the university umbrella, taking in the present colleges as schools or faculties with a fair degree of autonomy. This need not involve total amalgamation—apart from anything else, there would be physical problems—but rather a federal structure with adequate provision for transfer and cross-validation of courses. From the standpoint of lifelong learning, there could be great value in this; eventually, it should be possible to provide a much wider range of choice of courses than are currently available to any individual, not just in subject-matter but in mode of study—full-time or part-time, long or intensive, general or professional, which could be taken for degrees, for professional retraining, or for personal interest, either in one continuous stage or by dropping out and coming back in again at any point during adult life as needs or wishes determine.(24)

So far, we have been looking at the structure of the formal system, but education is not just a matter os chools and colleges, however organised. Much more needs to be done to strengthen links with other educational activities and agencies in the whole community. There has been a good deal of loose thinking, and not a little nonsense, on the "remoteness" of schools, which are denounced as "artificial". Of course they are; and so are hospitals, factories or houses, so are unions, parties, laws and any form of social organisation short of main force. The charge of "irrelevance". is more to the point and deserves close attention, provided we are not carried away into the currently fashionable dismissal of any kind of learning not directly related to politics and work. The slogans of the instant revolutionaries about culture being "bourgeois" are essentially patronising and anti-humanist, since they seek to define people mainly by their roles. But workers are not just workers, and any attempt to make their education relevant to that function only makes them less completely human, and is thus anti-socialist. Apart from that, however, it must be admitted that many do see schools as remote from their needs and interests. Now, there is nothing wrong with institutions especially designed for learning, any more than for teaching or making things. But education is special in that it touches on so many facets of life; it may have a core, but it is blurred at the edges. This could be a strength, not a weakness; already there are many areas where learning takes place, and can be organised to supplement and enrich the learning of school pupils or adults—zoos, museums, theatres, libraries, botanical gardens and the like. This could be greatly extended to include factories, farms, printing offices, councils, courts, in effect the whole range of social activity. Conversely, schools could enter the life of the community more than they do, by involving people in the running of the schools, putting their facilities more readily at their disposal, paying more attention to their potential use for the education, entertainment and information of the community at large. The school can still play a distinctive role in society without being cut off from it.(25)

Space permits only a glance at the administration of the system, which will need careful working out in detail; but one or two general points may help to form it in accordance with the long term objectives:

1. The Scottish system must be autonomous. This means the whole system, including the universities, if they are to continue to play an important part. This does not mean rule by St Andrew's House or local politicians or whatever ministerial structure devolution may produce. The idea of "academic freedom" has often been used to justify, quite literally, irresponsibility, but that does not make it meaningless. When so much of the research and teaching in higher education takes place in the frontiers of knowledge, there is a case for some kind of cushioning mechanism between administration and academia, but two things need to be done to make this a positive step. One is greater democratisation of the institutions themselves, and the other is the extension of this principle into the whole field of higher education, not just the universities. Pending the development of the integration already proposed, some kind of Higher Education Council (which could take over the Scottish function of the CNAA (26) as well as the UGC) would be worth considering.

2. Whatever arrangements are made at local level (and some of the regions may well be thought too large) more must be done to make the running of education more responsive to the whole

community by involving parents and teachers directly in planning and organisation. At the level of the region (or whatever) this might be done through consultative committees of parents and teachers to work with the education committees, restructuring the law to require at least consultation. At the level of the individual school, a more definite shift of power is called for. As things stand, the school has a degree of autonomy in relation to the local authority, but it stops at the headmaster's office. Fortunately, the heads have more sense than to keep to themselves all the powers allowed by law, and in some schools power has been devolved to staff councils. But many do act the despot, whether benevolent or repressive or just plain mad. This often gives rise to discussions on the training or selection of headmasters, an important enough point but not the main one- it is more important to question whether any one man should have such power, even if he were a paragon of all the virtues. The running of a school is surely a matter for all concerned—teachers obviously, but to some extent parents and pupils too. Details of power and competence would have to be worked out, but recognition of the principle would be a first step. This question of participation is even more important at post-basic level, where the issues may be more complex and the need for flexibility crucial.

It is also imperative that the administration of the system does not resolve itself into yet another classical pyramid of authority, nor into the mixture of bureaucracy, muddle and ad-hockery that alternative structures are liable to. Dull business though it may be, definition of powers is necessary, since powers not allocated tend to be taken, and not necessarily by the right people. There also has to be an extensive network of consultation and feedback at all levels, involving parents' organisations, teachers' organisations, student unions, research institutions, cultural bodies of all sorts, and for that matter any other social organisations with an interest(27). Some of this goes on now, but simply making a commission available for the submission of evidence is not the same thing as having proposed reform aired and worked out by those who are going to have to operate it or will be affected by it. Of course it will mean more meetings and committees, and some will find it boring and frustrating and take no part. It can be hoped that active interest will grow if what is said and decided is seen to have some effect; few mind being bored if it leads somewhere. But some of it will remain boring and time-consuming. This is unfortunate, but democracy does mean harder work and a willingness to take on the dull as well as the exciting bits.

It would be ridiculous to pretend that any of the steps proposed will be easy. Some improvements, certainly, can at least in principle be solved with more money. But there is unlikely ever to be enough for that, and in any case our tasks are challenges to the imagination and the will no less than the purse. There will be failures, false starts, and decisions taken on evidence that later enquiry will call in doubt. Actions will often produce unforseen side-effects, and these will have to be dealt with in turn. Possibly, social developments and new knowledge will invalidate much of what has been suggested here. That is the way things happen, and we have to be ready for it. That is why it is vital for socialists to keep in view fundamental principles and immediate realities, not to expect miracles but not to despair either. Above all, in education as in other things, socialists have to remember what they are socialists for, the creation of a society fit for people to live in. By all means we should be concerned with catering for the needs of young people going to work, with industrial training and re-training; of course we have to educate for social living, to recognise the validity of everyone's culture, rather than convey the impression that learning is part of a middle-class package-deal. But in the end, socialist education has to be concerned with the full development of all sides of the individuals personal and social potential. These discussions are about the best way of achieving this, not about institutions and structures for their own sake. They will never be perfected—not the institutions, not the individual students, or teachers either, for the aim is to fill the gap between what people are and what they have in them to become.

1. Forbes Macgregor, **What is Education in Scotland?** (Akros, 1971).
2. Robert Bell and Nigel Grant, **A Mythology of British Education.** (Panther, 1974).
3. Nigel Grant, **Soviet Education** (Penguin 1972); **Society, Schools and Progress in Eastern**

Europe (Pergamon, 1969); Comparative education and the comprehensive schools, **Scottish Educational Studies** 1.1.1968, pp.16-23.

4. Julienne Ford, **Social Class and the Comprehensive School** (Routledge and Kegan Paul, 1969).

5. This point is more fully developed in N. Grant, Problems of cultural identity, **Comparative Education Society in Europe (British Section) Conference Report,** June 1974, pp.89-120.

6. The proportion was slightly reduced when certain Corporation schools were no longer permitted to charge fees, but the bulk of the fee-paying sector remained unaffected.

7. John Knox, **The First Book of Discipline** (1560).

8. George Davie, **The Democratic Intellect** (Edinburgh 1961).

9. For details, see: S.L. Hunter, **The Scottish Educational System** (Pergamon, 1972); R.E. Bell et al. (eds). **Education in Great Britain and Ireland** (Open University, 1973).

10. John Hajnal, **The Student Trap** (Penguin 1972).

11. E.g. George Parkyn, **Towards a Conceptual Model of Lifelong Learning** (Educational Studies and Documents No.12, UNESCO, Paris 197).

12. E.g. Ivan Illich, **De-Schooling Society** (Penguin 1973).

13. Most of the work on this is English; see Robin Pedley, **Comprehensive Education—A New Approach** (Gollancz 1956); C. Benn and B. Simon, **Half-Way There: Report on the British Comprehensive School Reform** (Penguin 1972); Robin Davis, **The Grammar School** (Penguin 1967); J. Ford **(op.cit.)** For an extremely thorough guide to the literature, see Dee Laurance, **Writings on Comprehensive Education** (CCE 1973), which contains 1500 references, indexed.

14. Torstein Husen, Productivity in comprehensive and selective educational systems. In: N.A. Matthysen and C.E. Vervoort (eds.), **Education in Europe: Sociological Research.** (Mouton, 1969).

15. National Foundation for Educational Research.

16. George M. Fraser, **Flashman** (Pan 1970). See also Bell and Grant **(op.cit.)**

17. P.E. Vernon, The Measurement of Abilities, Attitudes and Personality Traits. In: A.T. Welford (ed.), **Society, Problems and Methods of Study** (Routledge & Kegan Paul, 1962; rev. 1967). pp.62-68.

18. See R.D. Boyd, Analysis of the ego-stage development of school-age children. **Journal of Experimental Education** Vol.32, No.3, Spring 1964. Erikson Childhood and Society (New York 1950); Erikson, **Identity and the Life Cycle. Monograph Psychological Issues,** Vol.1, No.1, (N.Y. International Univ. Press, 1959). Jean Piaget, **The Psychology of Intelligence** (N.Y., Harcourt Brace 1950); Piaget, Principal factors determining intellectual evolution from childhood to adult life. In: E.L. and R.E. Hartley (eds). **Outside Readings in Psychology** (2nd ed.). (N.Y. Cromwell, 1959) pp.43-55. I am indebted to Tim Steward for valuable suggestions on this issue.

19. Eastern European and Scandinavian experience seems to bear this out.

20. For the vast majority, this would of course mean English; but there is need for due attention to the claims of Gaelic, both for native speakers and learners.

21. This idea has been extensively introduced in Soviet and Eastern European schools, under the name of 'polytechnical education', since the late 1950s. On the whole, it has not been a conspicuous success, and there has been some movement away from it, in most countries, since the late 1960s. But the defects seem to be in planning and practice rather than principle; the idea at least merits careful examination in the Scottish context. See Grant, **op.cit.,** and K. Smart, The polytechnical principle, in E.J. King (ed.) **Communist Education** (Methuen, 1965).

22. Obviously, there is a need for thorough examination of the basic curriculum. Some interesting suggestions are to be found in Raymond Williams, **The Long Revolution** (Penguin 1961).

23. For more extensive discussion, see R.E. Bell and A.J. Youngson (eds), **Present and Future in Higher Education** (Tavistock, 1973).

24. The Soviet Union and the Eastern European countries operate fairly effective systems of part-time study, with spells of paid leave for full-time attendance, and France has recently brought in a law providing for paid educational leave as a right.

25. See, e.g. Torstein Husen, **The Learning Society** (Methuen, 1974).

26. Council for National Academic Awards accredits degree courses in higher institutions other than universitites.

27. Widely used in the U.S.S.R. and Eastern Eruope, a redeeming feature of systems rather given to excessive centralisation and authoritarian methods of administration.